Information Management: Systems and Processes

Information Management:
Systems and Processes

Edited by Aiden Black

CLANRYE
INTERNATIONAL
www.clanryeinternational.com

Clanrye International,
750 Third Avenue, 9th Floor,
New York, NY 10017, USA

ISBN: 978-1-63240-705-4

Cataloging-in-Publication Data

Information management : systems and processes / edited by Aiden Black.
    p. cm.
Includes bibliographical references and index.
ISBN 978-1-63240-705-4
1. Information resources management. 2. Computer science. 3. Information science.
4. Information technology--Management. I. Black, Aiden.
T58.64 .I54 2018
658.403 8--dc23

For information on all Clanrye International publications
visit our website at www.clanryeinternational.com

Contents

Preface

Information is a valuable asset for all organizations. Its management involves planning, controlling, organizing, evaluating, of all information that flows in an organization. The interpretation and comprehension of data plays a crucial role in effective decision-making. The book traces the progress of the field of information management and highlights some of its key concepts and applications. It elucidates new techniques and their applications in a multidisciplinary approach. For someone with an interest and eye for detail, this book covers the most significant topics in the field of information management.

All of the data presented henceforth, was collaborated in the wake of recent advancements in the field. The aim of this book is to present the diversified developments from across the globe in a comprehensible manner. The opinions expressed in each chapter belong solely to the contributing authors. Their interpretations of the topics are the integral part of this book, which I have carefully compiled for a better understanding of the readers.

At the end, I would like to thank all those who dedicated their time and efforts for the successful completion of this book. I also wish to convey my gratitude towards my friends and family who supported me at every step.

Editor

The mediating effect of knowledge sharing between organisational culture and turnover intentions of professional nurses

Authors:
Everd J. Jacobs[1]
Gert Roodt[1]

Affiliations:
[1]Department of Industrial Psychology and People Management, University of Johannesburg, South Africa

Correspondence to:
Everd Jacobs

Email:
ejacobs@solplaatje.org.za

Postal address:
Private Bag X5030,
Kimberley 8300,
South Africa

Professional nurses routinely use highly developed domain knowledge in combination with experiential knowledge to deliver quality care. However, this knowledge is often lost to employers as the migration of professional nurses from the developing countries to the developed world has become a global problem. The objective of this study therefore was to determine the relationships between organisational culture, knowledge sharing and turnover intentions and thereafter to propose knowledge sharing as a mediating variable in this relationship in order to suggest a retention strategy. A cross-sectional field survey design with questionnaires was used on a sample of professional nurses ($N = 530$) in private and provincial hospitals in South Africa. The tri-variate procedure of Baron and Kenny for mediation testing was adopted. The results indicated that a positive correlation exists between organisational culture and knowledge sharing, but a significant negative correlation between organisational culture and turnover intentions, as well as between knowledge sharing and turnover intentions. Finally, the results indicated that knowledge sharing mediates the relationship between organisational culture and turnover intentions, although with a small effect size. The findings suggest that turnover intentions of nurses can be actively managed through contextual variables such as organisational culture and opportunities for knowledge sharing.

Introduction

South Africa's well trained professional nurses are a sought-after resource in high-paying industrial countries; this exodus will have a catastrophic effect on the delivery of health care over the next decade (Brits 2003; Ramadikela 2003). A few factors make the retention of professional nurses almost uncontrollable for nursing employers in South Africa (Kockott 2003):

- financial constraints to compete with remuneration offerings from international competitors
- current exchange rates to earn foreign money
- tax-free salaries.

However, it is suggested in this article that individuals do not become committed to an organisation by virtue of financial incentives only. Rather, individuals enter an organisation with certain needs, desires and skills and expect to find a work environment in which they can utilise their abilities and satisfy many of their needs, such as sharing and enhancing their knowledge (Lum, Kervin, Clark, Reid & Sirola 1998). The importance of knowledge management in a contextual setting is essential to this argument.

It is reported, although not yet empirically determined, that organisational culture in hospitals can contribute towards lower turnover (Coile 2001; Waldman, Smith & Hood 2003). It is also suggested in this article that knowledge sharing behaviour affect turnover intentions. There has been a growing acknowledgement that much organisational knowledge is tacit in nature, meaning it resides in the minds and experiences of people (Hislop 2003; Rowley 2003). Knowledge sharing occurs when an individual is willing to assist as well as learn from others in the development of new competencies (Rowley 2003). Very little research focused on knowledge sharing as a psychological need of people as well as the development of constructs to measure knowledge sharing and possible outcomes (Hislop 2003).

It is therefore postulated in this article that organisational culture will facilitate a positive attitude towards knowledge sharing and that the opportunities and challenges to fulfil the needs associated with knowledge sharing, will be so rewarding that people will be inclined to stay with the organisation. If this is true, employers will know which aspects of organisational culture predict lower intentions to quit and can embark on strategies around knowledge sharing activities to retain their talent.

A short literature overview of the three variables is discussed next. Special emphasis is placed on knowledge sharing as proposed mediating variable in this article and will therefore receive special attention in the theoretical overview and the development of a knowledge sharing construct.

Organisational culture

Organisational culture can be introduced as a set of values, beliefs and behaviour patterns that form the core identity of organisations and help in shaping the employees' behaviour (Van der Post, de Coning & Smit 1997). The study of organisational culture can be approached by identifying certain dimensions that shape behaviour and eventually can be regarded as the culture of the organisation. The dimensions include the following:

- conflict resolution
- culture management
- customer orientation
- disposition towards change
- employee participation
- goal clarity
- human resource orientation
- identification with the organisation
- locus of authority
- management style
- organisational focus
- organisational integration
- performance orientation
- reward orientation
- task structure.

Turnover intentions

Turnover intentions are seen as a mental decision intervening between an individual's attitude regarding a job and the stay or leave decision and that can be regarded as an immediate antecedent to stay or to leave (Fox & Fallon 2003). It has been successfully demonstrated in previous studies that behavioural intention to leave is consistently correlated with turnover and there is considerable support for the notion that intention to quit is probably the most important and immediate antecedent of turnover decisions (Fox & Fallon 2003).

Knowledge sharing

Hislop (2003), who reviewed a significant number of studies in knowledge management, reported that these studies have a limited empirical basis and the majority can typically be described as 'exploratory studies', which illustrates the lack of depth in contemporary understanding of how human and social factors affect knowledge management and sharing initiatives. To date, much of the research of knowledge sharing focused on economic benefits such as being competitive (Gupta, Lyer & Aronson 2000). Very little research focussed on knowledge sharing as a psychological need of people.

A common classification of organisational knowledge (Nonaka 1991) comprises explicit knowledge, which can be documented and shared and implicit or tacit knowledge, which resides in the minds, cultures and experiences within the organisation (Rowley 2003). Implicit or tacit knowledge includes the competence, experience and skills of employees. The management of tacit knowledge is primarily concerned with the management of the process of deriving value from knowledge. This is tightly coupled with processes such as training, learning, culture creation and knowledge sharing (Rowley 2003). Tacit knowledge is usually in the domain of subjective, cognitive and experiential learning. There has been a growing acknowledgement that much organisational knowledge is tacit in nature and for employers to benefit from their training and development programmes, there should be a willingness on the part of those workers who possess the necessary knowledge to share and communicate it (Hislop 2003).

In one of only a few quantitative empirical knowledge sharing studies reported in the literature, Ryu, Hee Ho and Han (2003) investigated knowledge sharing attitudes for physicians within hospitals. This study is of particular relevance as they operate in the same environment as professional nurses. Professional nurses routinely use highly developed domain knowledge in combination with experiential knowledge to deliver quality care. A limitation of this study was that it only measured physicians' readiness to share knowledge and did not focus on other contextual factors such as organisational culture.

Research Design
Research approach

The research question will be investigated (tested) by making use of a field survey to obtain primary data. A survey can be described as a study that is usually quantitative in nature and which aims to provide a broad overview of a representative sample of a large population (Mouton 2001). The study can be described as *ex-post facto* research, meaning that a researcher does not have full control over the variables (as the problem already occurred), but at least medium control can be obtained through applying inferential statistics (De la Rey 1978; Mouton 2001). The study is correlational in nature as it tests for mediation. According to Smit (1995) the correlational design can be seen as the best controlled and precise non-experimental design. Individuals will form the target dimension. The population is literate and will therefore have the ability to complete the questionnaires.

The strengths of this design are that the potential exists to generalise to large populations if appropriate sampling design has been implemented; high measurement reliability if proper questionnaire construction was implemented and high construct validity if proper controls have been implemented (Mouton 2001). Researchers using this design should be careful of sampling error, questionnaire error, high refusal and non-response, data capturing error and inappropriate selection of statistical techniques (Mouton 2001). These issues were addressed as will be discussed in the following sections.

Research sample

The target population can be described as registered professional nurses working in hospitals. Staff (or assistant) nurses were not included in the target population. Various important challenges and problems had to be addressed to determine the sampling frame and unit of analysis. According to figures by the South African Nursing Council (in 2004), there were approximately 93 000 registered professional nurses in South Africa (this figure must not be confused with the estimated 155 400 if staff nurses are also taken into consideration). Professional nurses are employed in different sectors (e.g. hospitals, municipalities, academic institutions and other industries); however, hospitals are the most important employers of professional nurses. It was therefore decided to only include professional hospital nurses.

The next step was to select which hospitals to include in the sampling frame. It was decided to include in the sampling frame five private hospitals and four provincial (government) hospitals in three different regions (provinces). The motivation for this was based on the assumption that different types of hospitals (private and government) in different regions and surroundings (urban and rural) will probably have different organisational cultures that will yield a sample with diverse characteristics.

The next step was to decide on the actual composition of the unit of analysis (more or less 1100 professional nurses work in the selected hospitals). Although the target population was determined to the set criteria as explained, it was decided to make use of a non-probability (convenience) census-based survey at each of the selected hospitals. A non-probability sample in this sense could be described as involving all respondents from a population (professional nurses) who were available to complete the questionnaire at a specific point in time (normally a two day period) in the hospital.

The respondents were not randomly selected, but all who met the criteria and were available were included. The limitations compared to systematic or stratified sampling methods are acknowledged. Their weakness can to some extent be mitigated by using knowledge, expertise and care in selecting samples, as was the case in this study. It seemed practically and ethically correct to utilise a convenience sample as employers were reluctant to allow time off to complete the questionnaires due to staff shortages and the complex shift system that determine working hours for registered professional nurses, as well as the research procedure to personally visit hospitals to ensure a high response rate of questionnaires.

The final sample consists of 530 respondents in the selected hospitals (more or less 50% of the population). This resulted in a sample with diverse characteristics regarding race, age, home language, number of dependents, level of seniority, qualifications, tenure in hospital and profession, working in different units and gender. The completion of the questionnaires was personally administered and anonymously handled.

Measuring instruments

Organisational culture: The *Organisational Culture Survey* (Van der Post *et al.* 1997) was applied in this study to measure organisational culture. This 97 item instrument measures fifteen dimensions of organisational culture (e.g. conflict resolution, culture management, customer orientation). The questionnaire was factor analysed according to a procedure suggested in order to determine the factor structure of the instrument. One of the advantages of this method is to minimise artefactors. This procedure includes first and second level factor analysis (Schepers 2004; Schepers 1992). The questionnaire yielded a Cronbach alpha of 0.989 indicating acceptable reliability.

Knowledge sharing: A literature study was conducted to compile a questionnaire as no suitable measure for *knowledge sharing* was found. Based on this conceptual model, a questionnaire consisting of 23 items was developed (see Annexure A). Each item has a 5-point intensity response scale anchored at extreme poles ranging from 'to no extent' or 'disagree' (low intensity) to 'a large extent' or 'agree' (high intensity). An example of a question is: 'to what extent do you share knowledge in this organisation to get recognition?'

The questionnaire consists of six sections representing different domains of knowledge sharing, namely:

- why knowledge is shared in the organisation (e.g. to get recognition; 5 questions)
- opportunities for knowledge sharing (e.g. to attend training courses; 3 questions)
- the contribution of knowledge sharing to the organisation (e.g. competitiveness; 3 questions)
- why others readily share knowledge (e.g. that trust exists; 6 questions)
- why one would not readily share knowledge (e.g. career would be in danger; 3 questions)
- why others do not readily share knowledge (e.g. colleagues do not want to do likewise; 3 questions).

Next, a factor analysis was conducted on the knowledge sharing questionnaire. The purpose of a factor analysis is to cluster the items that measure a specific concept and to reject those that do not contribute in measuring the concept. The knowledge sharing questionnaire was factor analysed according to the procedure suggested by Schepers (2004) in order to determine the factor structure of the instrument. One of the advantages of this method is to minimise artefactors. This procedure includes first and second level factor analysis.

The first level factor analysis was based on the intercorrelation matrix of all items. The eigenvalues of the unreduced item intercorrelation matrix were calculated and it was suggested that five factors be extracted based on the eigenvalues greater than unity (Kaiser, 1970). A Principal axis factoring yielded five factors explaining about 66% of the variance in the factor space. This result supported the theoretical foundation of the construction of the original questionnaire as factor 1 was described by items 18–23 (the two sections that determine reasons why nurses do not want to share knowledge). Factor 2 was described by items 12–17 (reasons why others share knowledge), whilst factor 3 (items 1–5) consists of the questions that measure reasons why one should share knowledge. Factor 4 (items 9–11) determined opinions to what outcomes knowledge sharing can contribute to (e.g. competitiveness), whilst factor 5 (items 6–8) determined opportunities for knowledge sharing.

For the second level factor analysis, the subscores of the five factors (referred to earlier) were intercorrelated. Again, eigenvalues were calculated and two factors were postulated. These two factors were extracted by means of principal axis factoring. Factor 1 explains about 44% and factor two about 20% of the variance in the factor space. Factor 1 consists of items 6–8 and 12–23. This factor can be renamed as 'opportunities and pre-requisites to share and/or not to share'. Factor 2 consists of items 1–5 and 9–11 and can be renamed as 'expected personal and organizational outcomes'. The result obtained from the iterative reliability analysis of the knowledge sharing questionnaire yielded a Cronbach alpha of 0.839 for factor one and 0.838 for factor two, indicating an acceptable reliability. No items were rejected in both the first and second level factor analysis.

Turnover intentions

Turnover intentions were measured by an unpublished 14 item questionnaire (Jacobs & Roodt 2004). The questionnaire was factor analysed and it yielded a Cronbach alpha of 0.839 indicating acceptable reliability.

Statistical analysis

The first objective was to determine the relationship between organisational culture, knowledge sharing and turnover intentions. This was tested by the Pearson product-moment correlation. The second objective was to test for mediation. Rather than only hypothesising a direct causal relationship between the independent variable and the dependent variable, a mediation model hypothesises that the independent variable causes the mediator variable, which in turn causes the dependent variable. The tri-variate approach for mediation testing of Baron and Kenny (1986) was applied to test for mediation. In general, a given variable may be said to function as a mediator to the extent that it accounts for the relation between the predictor and the criterion. To test for mediation one should estimate the following regression equations:

- regressing the mediator on the independent variable
- regressing the dependent variable on the independent variable
- regressing the dependent variable on both the independent variable and on the mediator.

Mediation holds if the combined regression of the independent variable (predictor) and mediator on the dependent variable (criterion) explain more variance than the predictor alone. Thereafter one should investigate the effect sizes of the partial Eta squared to provide an indication whether the mediation effect is small, medium or large. According to Baron and Kenny (1986), it is critical not only to examine the significance of the coefficients but also their absolute size.

Results

The Pearson moment coefficients indicated that a significant positive correlation exists between organisational culture and knowledge sharing ($r = 0.558$; $p < 0.01$), but a significant negative correlation between organisational culture and turnover intentions ($r = -0.521$; $p < 0,01$) and knowledge sharing and turnover intentions ($r = 0.418$; $p < 0.01$).

The first step in the mediation procedure is regressing the mediator (knowledge sharing) on the independent variable (organisational culture). Organisational culture explained 34% of the variance in knowledge sharing, thus supporting the first condition in the procedure to test mediation. The second step in testing for mediation is regressing the dependent variable (turnover intentions) on the independent variable (organisational culture). Organisational culture explained 27% of the variance in turnover intentions. The third step in testing for mediation is regressing the dependent variable on both the independent variable (organisational culture) and on the mediator (knowledge sharing). The independent variable (organisational culture) and mediator (knowledge sharing) explained almost 29% of the variance in turnover intentions. Since more variance is explained than by the independent variable alone (27%) mediation holds.

According to Baron and Kenny (1986), it is critical not only to examine the significance of the coefficients but also their absolute size. Mediation holds if the effect of the independent variable on the dependent variable is less in the third equation than in the second equation ($0.140 < 0.271$). Thus, knowledge sharing is a mediating variable albeit with a small effect size (0.027; Eta squared-rooted $= 0.164$). The following criteria were used to describe effect sizes:

- < 0.1 – no effect
- 0.1–0.3 – small effect
- 0.3–0.5 – medium effect
- 0.5 – large effect.

Discussion

This study contributed to a greater understanding of the importance of knowledge sharing in hospitals and amongst professional nurses by conducting a first and second level factor analysis as well as the tri-variate approach of Baron and Kenny to test for mediation. Firstly, the second level factor analysis clearly yielded the factor 'opportunities and pre-requisites to share and/or not to share'. This is a clear indication that knowledge sharing is the result of how nurses perceive their environment; it clearly indicates a huge responsibility on employers. Secondly, the second factor 'expected personal and organisational outcomes', indicates that nurses will share knowledge if they perceive desirable outcomes of their efforts. Furthermore, the significant negative relationship between knowledge sharing and turnover intentions clearly indicated that managers can indeed plan strategies and interventions to provide professional nurses with opportunities to share, including training courses, workshops and sharing in informal settings.

Knowledge sharing mediates the relationship between organisational culture and turnover intentions, although with a small effect size. However, it is clear that employers must create an organisational culture that is conducive to the pre-requisites necessary to ensure a willingness to share. The positive correlation between organisational culture and knowledge sharing clearly indicated the importance of organisational culture as a pre-requisite to share knowledge. It is recommended that nursing employers not only create opportunities to share, but also the incentives to learn and to study. The study provides evidence that in an 'electronic and computerised work environment' (explicit knowledge), the human being's 'perception towards knowledge sharing and capacity to share' (tacit knowledge) should not be neglected in order to understand knowledge management in its broader context.

Theoretically this study contributed to a better understanding of the importance of knowledge sharing behaviour in a contextual setting. It is recommended that knowledge sharing as theoretical and empirical concept needs further development and investigation, especially the development of knowledge sharing constructs should be a priority. The prerequisites (conditions) of knowledge sharing should also receive more attention. One possible line of thinking is to create experimental designs to measure direct cause-effect relationships of sharing behaviour and thereby control nuisance variables. It is furthermore suggested that if taken the consequences of the high turnover amongst nurses, more turnover models should be developed with different concepts such as organisational commitment, job satisfaction and organisational citizenship behaviours (OCB's) entered into the equation. The nursing population outside hospitals can also be involved in developing these models. Lastly, the importance of knowledge sharing as proposed in this study could be empirically tested in the health related environment for physicians, dentists, psychologists, medical rescue personnel, emergency services and laboratory technologists.

References

Baron, R.M. & Kenny, D.A., 1986, 'The moderator-mediator variable distinction in social psychological research: Conceptual, strategic, and statistical considerations', Journal of Personality and Social Psychology 51(6), 1173–1182. doi:10.1037/0022-3514.51.6.1173, PMid:3806354

Brits, E., 2003, 'Te veel verpleërs land-uit, sê RGN ('Too many nurses leave country, says HSRC'), Die Burger, 2 July, p. 7.

Coile, R.C., 2001, 'Magnet hospitals use culture, not wages, to solve nursing shortage', Journal of Healthcare Management 46(4), 224–228. PMid:11482240

De la Rey, R.P., 1978, Statistiese metodes in sielkundige navorsing, Universiteit van Pretoria, Pretoria, Suid-Afrika.

Fox, S.R. & Fallon, B.J., 2003., 'Modeling the effect of work/life balance on job satisfaction and turnover intentions', Paper presented at the 5th Australian Industrial and Organizational Psychology Conference, Melbourne, Australia, 2003.

Gupta, B., Lyer, L.S. & Aronson, J.E., 2000, 'Knowledge management: practices and challenges', Industrial Management & Data Systems 100(1), 17–21. doi:10.1108/02635570010273018

Hislop, D., 2003, 'Linking human resource management and knowledge management via commitment: A review and research agenda', Employee Relations 25(2),182–202. doi:10.1108/01425450310456479

Jacobs, E.J., & Roodt, G., 2005, 'The development of a predictive model for turnover intentions of professional nurses' unpublished doctoral thesis, Dept. of Human Resource Management, University of Johannesburg.

Kaiser, H.F., 1970, 'A second-generation Little Jiffy', Psychometrika 35, 401–415. doi:10.1007/BF02291817

Kockott, F., 2003, 'Government developing strategies to retain health professionals', Business Day, 21 January, p. 3.

Lum, L., Kervin, J., Clark, K., Reid, F. & Sirola, W., 1998, 'Explaining nursing turnover intent: Job satisfaction, Pay satisfaction, or Organizational commitment', Journal of Organizational Behaviour 19(3), 305–320. doi:10.1002/(SICI)1099-1379(199805)19:3<305::AID-JOB843>3.0.CO;2-N

Mouton, J., 2001, How to succeed in your master's and doctoral studies – A South-African guide and resource book, Van Schaik, Pretoria.

Nonaka, I., 1991, 'The knowledge creating company', Harvard Business Review 34(6), 96–114.

Ramadikela, N., 2003, 'Medical crisis looms in EC', Daily Dispatch, 24 September, p. 1.

Rowley, J., 2003, 'Knowledge management - the new librarianship? From custodians of history to gatekeepers to the future', Library Management 24(8), 433–440. doi:10.1108/01435120310501112

Ryu, S., Hee Ho, S. & Han, I., 2003, 'Knowledge sharing behaviour of physicians in hospitals', Expert Systems with applications 25(1), 113–122. doi:10.1016/S0957-4174(03)00011-3

Schepers, J.M., 2004, 'Overcoming the effects of differential skewness of test items in scale construction', SA Journal of Industrial Psychology 30(4), 27–43.

Schepers, J.M., 1992, Toetskonstruksie: Teorie en praktyk (Test construction: Theory and Practice). RAU Drukpers, Johannesburg.

Smit, G.J., 1995, Navorsingsmetodes in die Gedragswetenskappe. Opvoedkundige Uitgewers, Pretoria.

Van der Post, W.Z., de Coning, T.J. & Smit, E.V., 1997, 'An instrument to measure organizational culture', South African Journal of Business Management 28(4), 147–168.

Waldman, J.D., Smith, H.L. & Hood, J.N., 2003, 'Corporate Culture: The missing piece of the healthcare puzzle', Hospital topics 81(1), 5–16. doi:10.1080/00185860309598010, PMid:14513744

Annexure A: Knowledge Sharing Questionnaire. The following questionnaire measures your perceptions about knowledge sharing in your organization. You are requested to **cross (x) or circle (o) the number of your choice** which most accurately fits the extent to which you evaluate the organization in which you work. After you have read each question, please decide the degree to which your answer accurately describes your own situation and your feelings, using the following scale:

Example: To what extent do you share knowledge in this organisation ...	←———— Lower				Higher ————→	
Answer: 1. to get recognition?	To no extent	1	2	3	4	⑤	To a large extent
1. To what extent do you share knowledge in this organisation ...						
1.1. to get recognition?	To no extent	1	2	3	4	5	To a large extent
1.2. to be rewarded?	To no extent	1	2	3	4	5	To a large extent
1.3. to satisfy your self-fulfillment needs?	To no extent	1	2	3	4	5	To a large extent
1.4. to support management strategic objectives?	To no extent	1	2	3	4	5	To a large extent
1.5. to enhance your career?	To no extent	1	2	3	4	5	To a large extent

Annexure A CONTINUES: Knowledge Sharing Questionnaire. The following questionnaire measures your perceptions about knowledge sharing in your organization. You are requested to **cross (x) or circle (o) the number of your choice** which most accurately fits the extent to which you evaluate the organization in which you work. After you have read each question, please decide the degree to which your answer accurately describes your own situation and your feelings, using the following scale:

Example: To what extent do you share knowledge in this organisation ...	← Lower	1	2	3	4	Higher → 5	
Answer: 1. to get recognition?	To no extent	1	2	3	4	⑤	To a large extent
2. How often do you have the opportunity ...							
2.1. to attend training courses?	Never	1	2	3	4	5	Most of the times
2.2. to share your knowledge with colleagues?	Never	1	2	3	4	5	Most of the times
2.3. to attend informal gatherings where knowledge is shared?	Never	1	2	3	4	5	Most of the times
3. How much do you agree that knowledge sharing contributes to...							
3.1. the success of this organisation?	Disagree	1	2	3	4	5	Agree
3.2. the competitiveness of this organisation?	Disagree	1	2	3	4	5	Agree
3.3. the innovativeness of this organisation?	Disagree	1	2	3	4	5	Agree
4. To what extent do you experience that others share knowledge due to the following reasons...							
4.1. trust that exists in the organisation?	To no extent	1	2	3	4	5	To a large extent
4.2. the likelihood that colleagues will do likewise?	To no extent	1	2	3	4	5	To a large extent
4.3. it is highly valued by management?	To no extent	1	2	3	4	5	To a large extent
4.4. the organisational culture facilitates a learning environment?	To no extent	1	2	3	4	5	To a large extent
4.5. people who share knowledge are regarded as experts?	To no extent	1	2	3	4	5	To a large extent
4.6. it contributes to positive performance appraisals?	To no extent	1	2	3	4	5	To a large extent
5. To what extent you do not readily share knowledge due to the following reasons ...							
5.1. you are afraid your career would be in danger if you make mistakes?(-)	To no extent	1	2	3	4	5	To a large extent
5.2. not enough trust exists in this organisation? (-)	To no extent	1	2	3	4	5	To a large extent
5.3. others don't want to do likewise? (-)	To no extent	1	2	3	4	5	To a large extent
6. To what extent do you experience that others do not readily share knowledge due to the following reasons ...							
6.1. they are afraid their careers would be in danger if they make mistakes? (-)	To no extent	1	2	3	4	5	To a large extent
6.2. not enough trust exist in this organisation? (-)	To no extent	1	2	3	4	5	To a large extent
6.3. colleagues don't want to do likewise? (-)	To no extent	1	2	3	4	5	To a large extent

2

Knowledge management practices at an institution of higher learning

Authors:
Judith Mavodza[1]
Patrick Ngulube[2]

Affiliations:
[1]Zayed University Library,
Zayed University, Abu Dhabi

[2]Department of
Interdisciplinary Research,
College of Graduate Studies,
University of South Africa,
South Africa

Correspondence to:
Patrick Ngulube

Email:
ngulup@unisa.ac.za

Postal address:
PO Box 392, UNISA 0003,
South Africa

Background: This article underscores the fact that society is becoming more and more knowledge-based, and that the organisations that can identify, value, create and evolve their knowledge assets are likely to be more successful than those that do not. Knowledge management (KM) is about enhancing the use of organisational knowledge through sound practices of KM and organisational learning. KM practices encompass the capture and/or acquisition of knowledge, its retention and organisation, its dissemination and re-use, and lastly responsiveness to the new knowledge.

Objective: The focus of this study was on KM principles and practices that may be in place in the Metropolitan College of New York (MCNY). The argument is that KM and its survival principles and tools may help the College to improve performance. However, there is uncertainty about whether the use of KM principles and tools can partly solve the College's approach to improving the quality of education it provides.

Methods: A mixed methods research methodology encompassing a questionnaire, observation, interviews, and use of institutional documents was used in the investigation.

Results: The findings of the study indicate that KM concepts were not universally understood at MCNY.

Conclusion: There is a need to create a knowledge inventory at MCNY. This may help the College to develop appropriate institution-wide policies and practices for proper and well organised methods of integrating work processes, collaborating and sharing (including the efficient use of social media), and developing an enabling institutional culture.

Introduction

Society has become more and more knowledge-based. Therefore the organisations that can identify, value, create and evolve their knowledge assets are likely to be more successful than those that do not. Knowledge in a modern organisation is an essential resource especially because it is not readily replicated by rivals. Jain (2007) and Senge (1994) point out that some organisations are unable to function as knowledge-based organisations because they have learning disabilities. It is important for an organisation to have a clear understanding of what knowledge management (KM) means to its operations if it needs to consider using those KM practices that enhance efficiency and lend value to organisational knowledge. In this way knowledge becomes a strategic resource (Kok 2012).

These practices include knowledge generation, which encompasses activities that bring to light all the knowledge that is new to a group or to an individual. Knowledge generation comprises the exploitation of existing knowledge to create new knowledge, as well as finding new knowledge through interacting and collaborating with other individuals or systems (Nonaka 1991; Nonaka & Takeuchi 1995; Nonaka & Teece 2001). This process therefore involves the acquisition of knowledge if it is to be successful. The acquired knowledge is of limited value if it is not organised and stored for easy retrieval. Once it is available for retrieval, there is a need to have systems that enable its sharing and transfer. A process of knowledge retention results when an organisation is able to facilitate the capture and transfer of both formal and informal knowledge through knowledge networking, thereby using the available intellectual capital to its advantage.

As an academic institution, the Metropolitan College of New York (MCNY) operates in the new knowledge-based information environment that is characterised by radical and discontinuous changes. This carries a new mandate for knowledge creation and implementation in order to get benefits that are at the core of its education mission. Preparing students to meet the needs of today's society is one of the direct benefits of the use of KM practices. In this perspective, the main challenge for MCNY is to develop and implement KM processes in order to make its educational mission relevant to society. The challenge coincides with the concern raised by

Cohen (1989), the founder of the College, who expressed the sentiment that knowledge at the College was organised to encourage its practical application in human service practice and performance. This article aims to discuss the concepts, tools, processes and requirements of KM practices and their relevance to reaching the goal of quality education at MCNY.

Types of knowledge and knowledge management

As do many higher education environments, MCNY possesses explicit knowledge in the form of financial records necessary for meeting tax, payroll or accounting obligations, files of important historical documents, self-study documents, research articles, conference proceedings, and minutes of meetings. Photo albums and similar mementos of college activities and interests form part of the knowledge asset, as well as library databases. Townley (2001) points out that research and scholarship are the tangible assets of an academic institution. In addition to these tangible explicit knowledge assets there are the tacit or implied knowledge and human expertise of the people who work in the organisation, as well as everything that is contained in the intranets.

KM facilitates the utilisation and integration of tacit and explicit knowledge. It emphasises 'collaborative learning, the capture of tacit knowledge, and value-add obtained through best practices and data mining' (Gandhi 2004:373). Rowley (2003), Singh (2007), and Wen (2005) highlight the fact that KM encompasses both the management of people and of information. On the other hand, Barquin (2001) describes KM as a process with phases and components, embedded in time. There is more than one approach to this process; it has different structures and architectures, and there are expected outcomes and performance to be measured. Concurring with this view, Kok (2012) also points out the importance of identifying ownership and the source of knowledge, and providing mechanisms and incentives for sharing knowledge without possessiveness. The same point is expressed by Singh (2007:172) who is also of the view that KM 'implies the process of transforming information and intellectual assets into enduring value'. In practice this leads to a process of the interpreting and utilising of collective intelligence by a community of participants.

KM practices in higher education are actions aimed at improving the internal flow and use of information through knowledge acquisition and knowledge sharing for institutional effectiveness (Kidwell, Vander Linde & Johnson 2000; Williams *et al.* 2004). From the definitions given, it appears that KM is a process that enables an organisation to improve its performance by enabling learning and innovation whilst solving its problems, acknowledging and resolving gaps in its operations, and recognising knowledge (comprising people and information) as an organisational asset which has to be managed through enabling policies and institutional tools.

The knowledge management process and flow

Recognising knowledge as an asset and using it creatively does not always occur in an obvious manner. Nonaka and Takeuchi (1995) suggest that knowledge is transferred from one form to another because of a continuous process of interaction between tacit and explicit knowledge in an organisation. The result is the ability to create new knowledge which has economic worth and is essential for innovation. For this to take place, a space called *Ba* (Nonaka & Konno 1998), where knowledge is created and shared through social media, is needed. According to Nonaka and Konno (1998):

> *Ba* can be thought of as a shared space for emerging relationships. This space can be physical (e.g., office, dispersed business space), virtual (e.g., e-mail, teleconference), mental (e.g., shared experiences, ideas, ideals), or any combination of them. What differentiates *Ba* from ordinary human interaction is the concept of knowledge creation. *Ba* provides a platform for advancing individual and/or collective knowledge. It is from such a platform that a transcendental perspective integrates all information needed. *Ba* may also be thought of as the recognition of the self in all. According to the theory of existentialism, *Ba* is a context which harbors meaning. Thus, we consider *Ba* to be a shared space that serves as a foundation for knowledge creation. (p. 40)

This explanation suggests that spaces are *Ba* and each knowledge conversion mode is associated with its own *Ba*. Identifying and using the spaces as well as consciously operating in the knowledge conversion mode supports the evolving needs of a typical educational establishment to benefit from its knowledge capital. However, Chou and He (2004) point out that they do not find a comprehensive and feasible model that delineates the interrelationships between knowledge assets, and that knowledge creation processes are absent.

It may well be that the concern raised by Chou and He (2004) will be resolved by means of systematic and repeated studies of actual practice. The potential and environment to capture, create and use knowledge assets were present at MCNY.

Statement of the problem

Library support at MCNY is in the form of print and online resources, reference services and information literacy classes for all library users. The library currently suffers from an inability to provide every resource and service that the students and faculty require. This is confirmed by the MCNY Self-Study (2009:51) which states that there is consensus amongst students and staff that 'library resources and services are not adequate'. The reasons are financial as well as practical. Firstly, the library cannot survive in isolation and provide everything that the College library users need. The cost of books and other information resources has become too prohibitive to cope with, so networking with other librarians and libraries for interlibrary lending and discounts when purchasing material have become essential, but are still not sufficient. Secondly, if the money were available to buy every book and every update and new edition on the market, space limitations would be prohibitive. The floor and shelf space at the MCNY library cannot accommodate limitless numbers of books.

Thirdly, there are now so many resources provided online that the library has to find a balance between what is available in print and what is available online. Fourthly, with staff cuts that have taken place due to a shrinking budget, it is not possible to have a robust library staff complement to give sufficient attention to individual library users' needs. Fifthly, the library is a department within the larger institution and to a large extent operates within the managerial and organisational parameters of the institution. This means that decisions that may seem best suited for the library are not necessarily acceptable unless they give advantage and enhance relevance to the institution as a whole. In addition to these challenges, a new information environment has brought additional demands. Despite the given circumstances, the library is still expected to provide a consistently efficient and effective quality service.

Following the question raised by Creswell (2007:102), 'Why is this study needed?', and the suggestions of Hernon and Schwartz (2007:307) that the statement of the problem should 'withstand a reviewer raising the "so what" question', the problem statement in this case would be that the MCNY library is providing a service that needs quality improvement as it does not adequately address challenges posed by a fast-changing information environment. However, no documented study has investigated why this is so and what needs to be done to improve the situation.

There is uncertainty about whether the use of KM principles and tools can partly solve the library's approach to improving the quality of its service to its community in the modern information environment. KM has been implemented in commercial and business environments for the sake of operational advantages and financial gains. It may be possible that KM survival principles and tools would help the library to improve its performance and fulfil its mandate. Because librarians serve users who also consume the products of the retail, entertainment and mass media industries, their efforts have become more focussed towards creating library spaces that are inviting, dynamic and exciting for the library users. These entail, amongst other things, the implementation of Web 2.0 technologies. Web 2.0 is the second generation of web-based services and tools that emphasise online sharing and collaboration amongst users. They are not KM, but can be used as tools in KM practice.

The research problem is further addressed by looking at the research questions and possible sources of data. In the process of investigating the library-related problem KM practices that are relevant to the entire College are revealed.

Research questions

Research questions are used for obtaining both qualitative and quantitative data. Specific questions that informed this research are:

- What do librarians, faculty, and administrators understand KM to mean?
- What are the knowledge needs of the MCNY community?
- What knowledge retention policies, practices and gaps are in existence at MCNY?
- What modern technologies are in use at MCNY that enhance the environment for KM practice?
- What are the tools, methods and techniques used for knowledge retention, knowledge assessment, knowledge acquisition and knowledge transfer at the MCNY library?
- What are the recommendations regarding the implementation of KM practices that will enhance the value of the library service at MCNY?

Research methodology

Regarding the MCNY library this study adopted a case study approach. Whilst Creswell (2007) and Tellis (1997) see a case study as a research methodology, Stake (2005:438) views it as 'a choice of what is to be studied'. We tend to subscribe to the latter view. The research process for this case study was conducted through the use of a questionnaire, interviews, observation, and institutional documents. A sample drawn from the MCNY employee community was used for the quantitative phase.

Survey type sample size calculation was utilised, meaning that a sample error formula, rather than the power analysis formulae that are usually utilised in experimental research, was used. The decision in selecting the random sample was to have a confidence level of 95% and a 10% (0.10) sampling error. The result was a sample of 79 individuals, that is, 17.5% of the entire MCNY employee community. On the other hand, purposive sampling was used for qualitative data collection. All usable questionnaire responses were analysed using Microsoft Excel and the SurveyMonkey online survey software and questionnaire tool. Qualitative data analysis was achieved by identifying patterns and themes in the collected study data. To make sense of them, there was need for synthesis and summary.

Research results

A summary of the major findings was organised according to the themes raised by the research questions of the study. The results emanated from the entire College, and reflected questionnaire, interview, observation, and document review findings.

Research results indicate that there was a certain degree of understanding of KM concepts at MCNY. This was reflected by the fact that in the questionnaire, when asked if information and knowledge have the same meaning, 32 (78%) of the respondents disagreed with the notion that they mean the same thing, whilst 5 (12%) did not give an opinion, and only 4 (10%) agreed. The question of KM including information management had 33 (80%) respondents agreeing, 5 (12%) remaining ambivalent, and 3 (8%) disagreeing with it. Concerning whether KM is the same as information management, 31 (75%) disagreed, 6 (15%) gave a non-committal response, and 4 (10%) agreed. Amongst questionnaire respondents, 36 (88%) agreed that knowledge depends on information, 1 (2%) was ambivalent about giving an opinion, whilst 4 (10%) disagreed. These perceptions are reflected in Table 1.

Four interview participants expressed an understanding of what KM refers to whilst one was unsure. Twenty per cent of the observable events during the observation phase suggested that employees were involved with activities that could be classified as enabling to KM practice. These data suggest that being aware of KM or knowing what it means does not necessarily mean practicing it. In addition, there was no mention of KM in MCNY documents or archive. The implication of these results is that in practice this study was exploratory as the use of KM appeared to be a new concept to the way job responsibilities were fulfilled.

This study was also involved in identifying the knowledge needed to support the education goals of MCNY, establishing where knowledge is stored, and highlighting gaps. Questionnaire results indicate a certain appreciation of paper-based documents, computers in departments, personal computers and a central information system as sources and locations of knowledge. This is expressed by 19 (48%) questionnaire respondents agreeing that knowledge was found in paper-based documents, whilst 3 (8%) gave no opinion, and 17 (44%) did not agree; 17 (44%) disagreed that knowledge was in the heads of departmental members, whilst 16 (41%) chose not to give an opinion about that perception, and 6 (14%) agreed with it.

At the same time, 25 (64%) respondents were of the perception that the knowledge they needed to perform their job functions was on their personal computers or workstations whilst 9 (23%) gave a non-committal response and 5 (13%) disagreed. A significant number of 19 (48%) did not give an opinion about knowledge being kept in a central storage space, although 10 (26%) agreed and another 10 (26%) disagreed with that perception. It was interesting to note that 12 (31%) agreed, whilst 12 (31%) disagreed that knowledge storage was done on all computers in the departments they worked in, and 15 (38%) did not give an opinion. A non-committal response also seemed the most popular concerning the availability of knowledge in a central information system as indicated by 19 (48%) giving no opinion, whilst 10 (26%) agreed and 10 (26%) disagreed. These perceptions are reflected in Table 2. These data point towards a need for definite information and knowledge storage capabilities. All interview participants actually suggested the desirability of creating knowledge repositories for the improvement of capturing knowledge assets that include student projects, institutional records (archival and otherwise) and conference and symposium papers. Whilst the suggested repositories suggest a gap in knowledge storage, it also brings out the desire of study participants to determine what constitutes valuable information and knowledge worth retaining as the College's institutional memory.

Establishing its knowledge needs will affect the College's strategic planning. According to Stankosky (2005) and Mavodza and Ngulube (2011), it has an impact on an

TABLE 1: Understanding of knowledge management at Metropolitan College of New York.

Level of understanding	Agree		Neutral		Disagree	
	n	%	n	%	n	%
Information and knowledge mean the same thing	4	10	5	12	32	78
Knowledge depends on information	36	88	1	2	4	10
Knowledge management is the same as information management	4	10	6	15	31	75
Knowledge management includes information management	33	80	5	12	3	8

n, number of responses.

TABLE 2: Places where Metropolitan College of New York knowledge was stored.

Storage location	Agree		Neutral		Disagree	
	n	%	n	%	n	%
Paper-based documents	19	48	3	8	17	44
Heads of department members	6	14	16	41	17	44
Central information system	10	26	19	48	10	26
Personal computer or workstation	25	64	9	23	5	13
All computers in the department	12	31	15	38	12	31

n, number of responses.

organisation's ability to meet its goals and objectives, and its projection on how best to use its services and knowledge products for the future. Because these processes involve people in the organisation, there can be real barriers to their successful implementation. Some of these barriers are, for instance, the fact that KM may not necessarily be a way of doing daily business (as was the case at MCNY) and that a policy that can guide it therefore does not exist, fear of adopting new or different ways of doing things with its resulting human resistance, lack of appropriate organisational infrastructure to handle some KM practices, and the fact that KM may be deemed unsuitable for some settings.

Some respondents perceived organisational policy and/or directives as barriers that prevented them from storing information effectively: 11 (28%) agreed with this view, even if 18 (46%) gave no opinion and 10 (26%) disagreed. Having a majority of respondents give a non-committal response leaves an ambivalent interpretation, but all interview respondents were clear about the need for definite organisational directives if the MCNY working culture and environment were to change.

Whilst the MCNY use of an intranet, wikis and blogs falls into the category of KM tools, 21 (54%) questionnaire respondents felt that there were no proper organisational guidelines on sharing information. Four (10%) disagreed with that, but 14 (36%) gave no opinion. The view that the bureaucratic procedures involved in sharing were complicated was expressed by 15 (39%) who agreed with the statement. Seventeen (44%) gave a non-committal response whilst 7 (18%) disagreed with that perception. Perceptions on challenges in information storage are reflected in Table 3. This implied the importance of leadership at the MCNY to be cognisant of the advantages of KM practices, and to have its essentials incorporated into the organisation's strategic plan and strategic goals, as suggested by Stankosky (2005). This kind of executive support results in a KM policy that Jain (2007:379) refers to as the road map to answer questions about the 'what, why, how, and who' of KM, because this approach can result in systemic changes, not merely isolated changes in the operations of any single department.

This view partly concurs with the suggestion made by Singh and Kant (2008) that KM barriers include the lack of top management commitment, lack of technological infrastructure, lack of clearly defined methods or processes for KM practice, lack of an organisational structure that supports a KM strategy, lack of organisational culture, lack of motivation and rewards, staff retirement, lack of ownership of problems, and staff turnover. This reinforces the point made by Kok (2003) who writes that knowledge management practice is benchmarked by the use of enablers that include leadership, technology, culture and measurement. Despite these barriers, the modern information environment that includes a wide variety of information, information providers and platforms for doing so has made it necessary for organisations, including education institutions, to consider using KM tools and techniques to identify what tacit and explicit knowledge exists in the organisation, and what knowledge they might require in the future to enhance work processes.

The importance of capturing knowledge before it leaves the College, or institutional know-how, could be a priority if the need for its retention was realised. The implication of this statement is that besides the requirement to have guidelines or procedures on what knowledge to capture, it needs to be systematically organised. This is important because not all information is knowledge, and not all knowledge is valuable (Aswath & Gupta 2009). Acquired knowledge is of limited value if it is not organised and stored for easy retrieval, as was exemplified by the absence of an organised archive at MCNY. For example, observation results indicated that the MCNY archive needed proper organisation as retrieval depended more on the memory of individuals than on a finding aid. Broadbent (1998) suggests the 'purposeful management processes which capture often personal and contextual information that can be used for the organisation's benefit'. Valuable knowledge needs to be drawn out and retained so that there is continuity even when the creator leaves the organisation, and the retrieval of knowledge is not solely dependent on individuals' memory. Eventually, a knowledge bank (Branin 2003), repository (Bailey 2005) or portal may exist. The data captured from the study are suggestive of the fact that some knowledge was retained at the MCNY but clear policies and practices for doing through-out the college needed to be clear and in place.

In this study, it was essential to establish the College's KM capacity in key areas such as the ability to recognise experts within the College, leadership, institutional work culture, and technology. It was also important to find out whether using KM tools and techniques would help the College meet its goals. The study was therefore ultimately aimed at determining whether the College could use and was in fact using its knowledge assets effectively and efficiently. It was revealed that MCNY, as an institution of higher learning, had experts in various academic disciplines besides those in administrative and non-administrative positions. However,

KM was not part of its institutional work culture, a fact which was reflected and demonstrated in interviews as well as in the questionnaire results. Therefore it is important to identify and describe the knowledge needs of MCNY and enumerate the variables involved in the process of recognising experts.

Whilst the lack of a proper IT platform on which to share information was seen by 16 (41%) questionnaire respondents as a hindrance, 14 (36%) gave a non-committal response, but 9 (23%) disagreed with that notion (see Table 3). Kim and Abbas (2010) point to a lack of confidence on the part of potential contributors to a wiki, and sometimes a lack of clarity about how to make contributions. This was confirmed by 18 (46%) questionnaire respondents who gave no opinion about colleagues' failure to perceive that there was an urgent need to share information, 12 (31%) who agreed and 9 (23%) who disagreed with that perception. Furthermore, 17 (44%) gave no opinion about their own failure to realise an urgent need to share information, whilst 6 (15%) agreed, but 16 (41%) disagreed with that view; 15 (39%) gave a non-committal response about the lack of an open-minded sharing environment at MCNY, 15 (39%) agreed, but 9 (23%) disagreed; 12 (31%) gave no opinion about the lack of trust in other people's knowledge, 16 (41%) agreed with that perception, but 11 (28%) disagreed. Some respondents felt that their tasks did not require cross-departmental information sharing; this was confirmed by 13 (33%) who agreed, 17 (44%) who gave no opinion and 7 (18%) who disagreed. These data reflect the need and relevance of an institutional culture in information and knowledge sharing to facilitate knowledge acquisition. This view is also expressed by Kok (2012) who concludes that the use of internal and external knowledge and information can improve the process of decision making and enhance the development of innovative capacity, which will result in better effectiveness and efficiency. The discussed perceptions are demonstrated in Table 4.

TABLE 3: Challenges in storing information received more efficiently and effectively at Metropolitan College of New York.

Challenges experienced	Agree		Neutral		Disagree	
	n	%	n	%	n	%
No proper organisational guidelines on sharing	21	54	14	36	4	10
Bureaucratic procedures involved in sharing are complicated	15	39	17	44	7	18
No proper IT platform to share information	16	41	14	36	9	23
Organisational policy and/or directives	11	28	18	46	10	26

n, number of responses.

TABLE 4: Individual challenges faced in sharing information with people from other departments within the College.

Challenges faced	Agree		Neutral		Disagree	
	n	%	n	%	n	%
Colleagues do not seem to perceived that there is an urgent need to share	12	31	18	46	9	23
I do not see an urgent need to share information	6	15	17	44	16	41
Lack of open-minded information sharing	15	39	15	39	9	23
Lack of trust of other people's knowledge	16	41	12	31	11	28
My tasks do not require cross-department information sharing	13	33	9	23	17	44
I do not know about other people's knowledge needs	18	46	13	33	8	21

n, number of responses.

There may sometimes be a need to give incentives to employees to contribute to KM activities as this has been proved to be an effective way of encouraging them to be participative (Aharony 2011; Aswath & Gupta 2009; Barquin 2001; Weddell 2008). At MCNY the kinds of incentives used included the fact that attending courses, conferences or workshops was encouraged. This was expressed by 23 (59%) questionnaire respondents who agreed, whilst 10 (26%) were non-committal and 6 (15%) disagreed. With regard to the statement that time used for attending courses, conferences and workshops was taken from individual vacation days, 19 (49%) respondents disagreed with it, and 19 (49%) gave no opinion, whilst 1 (2%) agreed. According to Wen (2005):

> an organisational culture for sharing of knowledge and expertise should be established with appropriate rewards and incentives. Those staff members who share their tacit knowledge and experiences through writing, publishing, lecturing, tutoring, or mentoring should be appropriately recognised and rewarded. (n.p.)

Information flow was suggested in KM literature as the way knowledge could travel and grow within an organisation. Koenig (2003) credits the flow of formal and informal information up, down and across the enterprise as the source for improvements in operational productivity. Similarly, knowledge flow also requires a working environment that nurtures and accelerates the sharing of knowledge. Responding to the question of the impact of knowledge sharing on individuals, questionnaire respondents felt that it enabled their quick accomplishment of tasks as evidenced by 29 (71%) who agreed, whilst 5 (12%) gave no opinion, and 7 (17%) disagreed. They also felt that it improved their job performance as highlighted by 30 (73%) who agreed, whilst 6 (15%) were non-committal, and 5 (12%) disagreed. Amongst the respondents, 30 (73%) agreed that knowledge sharing was generally useful in their jobs, whilst 8 (20%) seemed ambivalent, and 3 (7%) disagreed with that perception. Table 5 demonstrates these perceptions.

Questionnaire responses indicated that knowledge sharing enabled individuals to react more quickly to change:

- 28 (68%) agreed with this statement
- 9 (22%) gave a non-committal response
- 4 (10%) disagreed.

All interview participants shared the view that information and knowledge sharing had the potential to turn individual knowledge into organisational knowledge for the College. Thus a curriculum-related symposium held at MCNY in 2009 and mentioned in interviews could be significant as a KM technique since it was intended to create an information transfer and sharing platform for faculty, the library and the rest of the college. These data suggest that knowledge sharing was viewed at MCNY as important in job performance, and imply that the potential to benefit from using KM tools and techniques that enabled retaining knowledge for subsequent re-use did exist.

The capability of individuals to operate in ways that enable KM practice is expressed by responses to the question whether knowledge sharing in the departmental environment

TABLE 5: Environment for sharing of knowledge and the individual in a department.

Employees' experience of knowledge sharing	Agree		Neutral		Disagree	
	n	%	n	%	n	%
Enables me to accomplish tasks quickly	29	71	5	12	7	17
Improves my job performance	30	73	6	15	5	12
Useful in my job overall performance	30	73	8	20	3	7
Enables me to react more quickly to change	28	68	9	22	4	10

n, number of responses.

was seen as facilitating knowledge storage. Twenty-one (51% respondents agreed, 14 (34%) gave a non-committal response, and 6 (15%) disagreed. The question whether knowledge sharing in the departmental environment facilitated knowledge retrieval had 27 (66%) agreeing, 9 (22%) giving no opinion, and 5 (12%) disagreeing; whilst the question whether knowledge sharing in that environment facilitated knowledge transfer had 31 (75%) agreeing, 6 (15%) giving no opinion, and 4 (10%) disagreeing. There was also the perception that it speeded up decision making: 28 (68%) agreed that it did, 8 (20%) gave a non-committal response, and 5 (12%) disagreed. The importance of knowledge sharing was corroborated by all interview participants. However, only 14% of observable events recorded could be categorised as knowledge sharing, suggesting that at MCNY, acknowledging that sharing was important may only have had a marginal relationship to actual sharing.

Knowledge Management-related issues and challenges at Metropolitan College New York

For Metropolitan College New York (MCNY) the main issues and challenges related to KM are:

- database and information systems need to be clearly organised
- except in classrooms, faculty have limited occasions for sharing knowledge
- a scientific approach to creating knowledge is needed
- it is important to encourage initiatives to use already created knowledge
- an awareness of the weaknesses of non-knowledge-based activities has to be created
- a proper organisational structure to create and transfer knowledge is necessary
- motivation programmes and encouragement to create and use knowledge need to be in place at MCNY.

The reasons for Knowledge Management initiatives in educational institutions

Educational institutions such as the MCNY are the best places for advancing KM initiatives for the following reasons:

- Students need to be aware of the benefits that are possible from a sound teaching–learning environment. That encourages them to market the College, enhancing student enrolment and retention in the process.
- Research knowledge and skills within different College departments can be shared systematically, which will enable creativity, particularly as it is likely that different

types of knowledge assets have differing influences on knowledge creation.

- The enhanced use of technology that is already in place can expedite the dissemination and sharing of knowledge.
- Networking activities within and outside the College can propagate healthy relations with the community and potential employers for its graduates.

Encouraging the implementation of Knowledge Management initiatives at Metropolitan College New York

The large number of part-time faculty and the slow hiring of new full-time faculty at MCNY can have an impact on the morale of those in the teaching area of the institution. It also makes it complicated to implement a system of regular measurement and accountability, and as a result teaching and research performance becomes difficult to measure. For this reason there are few incentives to perform. The following factors may encourage KM initiatives in the future:

- An open institutional culture is required with incentives to promote the integration of individual skills and experiences into institutional knowledge.
- It is important to recognise the many strengths of knowledge utilisation formally and informally.
- It is necessary to recognise that it is not only technology that supports KM activities. Social relations, networking and interaction are some of the main elements that arise from KM practices.
- There is a need to constantly bring new knowledge into the institution, and use it to enhance the MCNY experiential model of teaching and learning.
- Encouraging people to communicate with one another and share their ideas is essential.

Prerequisites to implement Knowledge Management initiatives at Metropolitan College New York

KM is a multidisciplinary and trans-disciplinary field and does not have prescriptive implementation methodologies. However, prior to implementing KM initiatives the following initial steps should be taken:

- To become aware of a KM strategy at MCNY, an assessment of the current situation needs to be carried out by highlighting existing KM activities and experience, outlining the benefits, explaining how these can be built upon, and exposing barriers to further progress. This will show how current KM practice (or lack of it) affects the ability of the staff in various departments to meet intended goals and will demonstrate the connection between faculty, staff, students and other institutions.
- It is essential to map the stock of knowledge at MCNY. Identifying expertise enables the College to push the sharing of best practices. This can be done by examining the performance results of faculty and staff. If best practices and styles are already in place, it is better to use them to enhance performance rather than attempting to invent new ways. Jain (2007:379) suggests a mapping knowledge or knowledge gap exercise: 'Knowledge mapping can identify organisational knowledge assets as well as knowledge gaps'. This exercise helps in the eventual measuring of the effectiveness and success of implementing KM tools and principles.

- The people who need knowledge at MCNY should be identified. It is very important to focus on mission-critical rather than just fashionable knowledge practices.
- It is important for institutional members to have easy access to knowledge. Manuals, instructions, catalogues, notices, computer facility and databases help in making knowledge visible so that it can be transferred easily around the MCNY and enable departments to use such knowledge for planning and making decisions.
- A policy to institutionalise KM initiatives should be developed. It is necessary to facilitate knowledge growth through institutional culture and incentives. Incentives can help to reinforce best practices, and at the same time to instil a shift in behaviour. Incentives can be based on an annual performance review on the basis of employee contribution to the institution's knowledge.

Summary and conclusions

The study established that motivation programmes to create and use knowledge was nonexistent at MCNY. Furthermore, research knowledge and skills within different College departments were not shared systematically, thereby enabling creativity and knowledge creation. In the KM-based society of the 21st century an organisation that fails to manage knowledge finds it difficult to sustain and grow its activities. It would benefit MCNY to move towards organisational efforts to create and share knowledge systemically and systematically. The plan to use KM practices implies the need to understand the context that different types of knowledge requires, as well as organising information (re-packaging it) in the manner most useful to the College community, particularly in an information environment that uses social networking functionalities extensively. It becomes possible to learn from previous experiences and situations, and be able to anticipate the specific requirements of MCNY.

At MCNY, establishing and maintaining a strong technological base focusing on the intended teaching–learning environment and promoting research activities, and creating and organising technology-based knowledge and knowledge-based networking are essential initiatives. Additionally KM practices need to be tapped from institutional skills and the already existing intellectual capital. A supportive institutional climate can therefore bring systemic transformation to the entire institution.

Acknowledgements
Competing interests

The authors declare that they have no financial or personal relationship(s) which may have inappropriately influenced them in writing this paper.

Authors' contributions

J.M. (Zayed University) and P.N. (University of South Africa) conceptualised the study together. J.M. (Zayed University) designed the study and collected some of the data that the study reports as part of her doctoral studies. P.N. (University of South Africa) converted the study into a publishable journal article and dealt with the comments of the reviewers and the editors.

References

Aharony, N., 2011, 'Librarians' attitudes towards knowledge management', *College & Research Libraries* 72(2), 111–126.

Aswath, L. & Gupta, S., 2009, 'Knowledge management tools and academic library services', *International Conference on Academic Libraries – vision and roles of the future academic libraries*, Delhi, India, October 05–08, 2009, pp. 187–192.

Bailey, C.W., 2005, 'The role of reference librarians in institutional repositories', *Reference Services Review* 33(3), 259–267. http://dx.doi.org/10.1108/00907320510611294

Barquin, R., 2001, 'What is knowledge management? Knowledge and innovation', *Journal of the KMCI* 1(2), 127–143.

Branin, J.J., 2003, 'Knowledge management in academic libraries: Building the knowledge bank at the Ohio State University', *Journal of Library Administration* 39(4), 41–56. http://dx.doi.org/10.1300/J111v39n04_05

Broadbent, M., 1998, 'The phenomenon of knowledge management: What does it mean to the information profession? Knowledge management: An emerging concern', viewed 24 January 2008, from http://www.sla.org/pubs/serial/io/1998/may98/broadben.html

Chou, S.W. & He, M.Y., 2004, 'Facilitating knowledge creation by knowledge assets', viewed 20 January 2008, from http://ieeexplore.ieee.org/xpl/articleDetails.jsp?arnumber=1265584. http://dx.doi.org/10.1109/HICSS.2004.1265584

Cohen, A., 1989, *The service society and a theory of learning linking education, work and life*, Audrey Cohen College, New York.

Creswell, J.W., 2007, *Qualitative inquiry and research design: Choosing among five approaches*, Sage, Thousand Oaks, CA.

Gandhi, S., 2004, 'Knowledge management and reference services', *The Journal of Academic Librarianship* 30(5), 368–381. http://dx.doi.org/10.1016/j.acalib.2004.06.003

Hernon, P. & Schwartz, C., 2007, 'What is a problem statement?', *Library & Information Science Research* 29, 307–309. http://dx.doi.org/10.1016/j.lisr.2007.06.001

Jain, P., 2007, 'An empirical study of knowledge management in academic libraries in East and Southern Africa', *Library Review* 56(5), 377–392. http://dx.doi.org/10.1108/00242530710750572

Kidwell, J.J, Vander Linde, K.M & Johnson, S.L., 2000, 'Applying corporate KM practices in higher education', *Educause Quarterly* 4, 28–33.

Kim, Y-M. & Abbas, J., 2010, 'Adoption of library 2.0 functionalities by academic libraries and users: A knowledge management perspective', *The Journal of Library and Information Studies*, 36(3), 211–218.

Koenig, M., 2003, 'Knowledge management, user education and librarianship', *Library Review* 52(1), 10–17. http://dx.doi.org/10.1108/00242530310456979

Kok, J.A., 2003, 'Role of leadership in the management of corporate knowledge', *South African Journal of Information Management* 5(3), viewed 19 July 2012, from http://www.sajim.co.za/index.php/SAJIM/article/view/363/353

Kok, J.A., 2012, 'Knowledge management @ DoTPW', paper presented to the International Knowledge Conference at the University of Stellenbosch Business School, Stellenbosch, 16–18 January, viewed 19 July 2012, from http://www.usb.ac.za/Common/Pdfs/KnowledgeManagementConference/JKok_Knowledge-Management_Department-of-Transport-and-Public-Works.pdf

Mavodza, J. & Ngulube, P., 2011, The use of knowledge management tools and techniques in library practices in an academic environment', *Mousaion* 29(2), 94–115.

MCNY Self-Study, 2009, *Self-study for Middle States Commission on Higher Education: Comprehensive accreditation review*, MCNY, New York.

Nonaka, I. & Konno, N., 1998, 'The concept of "*Ba*": Building a foundation for knowledge creation', *California Management Review* 40(3), 40–50.

Nonaka, I. & Takeuchi, H., 1995, *The knowledge-creating company: How Japanese companies create the dynamics of innovation*, Oxford University Press, New York, NY.

Nonaka, I. & Teece, D.J., 2001, 'Research directions for knowledge management', in I. Nonaka & D.J. Teece (eds.), *Managing industrial knowledge: creation, transfer and utilization*, pp. 330–335, Sage, London. http://dx.doi.org/10.4135/9781446217573.n17

Nonaka, I., 1991, 'The knowledge-creating company', *Harvard Business Review* 69(6), 96–104.

Rowley, J., 2003, 'Knowledge management – the new librarianship? From custodians of history to gatekeepers to the future', *Library Management* 24(8/9), 433–440. http://dx.doi.org/10.1108/01435120310501112

Senge, P.M., 1994, *The fifth discipline: The art and practice of the learning organization*, Doubleday, New York.

Singh, M.D. & Kant, R., 2008, 'Knowledge management barriers: an interpretive structural modelling approach', *International Journal of Management Science & Engineering Management* 3(2), 141–150.

Singh, S.P., 2007, 'What are we managing – knowledge or information?', *VINE: The Journal of Information & Knowledge Management Systems* 37(2), 169–179.

Stake, R.E., 2005, 'Qualitative case studies', in N.K. Denzin & Y.S. Lincoln (eds), *The Sage handbook of qualitative research,* pp. 121–135, Sage, Thousand Oaks, CA.

Stankosky, M.A., 2005, 'Advances in knowledge management: University research toward an academic discipline', in M. Stankosky (ed.), *Creating the discipline of knowledge management: The latest in university research*, pp. 1–14, Butterworth-Heinemann, Burlington, MA. http://dx.doi.org/10.1016/B978-0-7506-7878-0.50005-3

Tellis, W., 1997, 'Application of a case study methodology', *The Qualitative Report* 3(3), viewed 03 February 2008 from http://www.nova.edu/ssss/QR/QR3-3/tellis2.html

Townley, C.T., 2001, 'Knowledge management and academic libraries', *College & Research Libraries* 62(1), 44–55.

Weddell, S., 2008, 'Transforming reference into a proactive knowledge advisory service: A case study', *Reference Services Review* 36(2), 147–155. http://dx.doi.org/10.1108/00907320810873011

Wen, S., 2005, 'Implementing knowledge management in academic libraries: A pragmatic approach', *Chinese Librarianship: An International Electronic Journal* 19, viewed 04 December 2009, from http://www.white-clouds.com/iclc/cliej/cl19.htm

Williams, A., Giuse N., Koonce, T., Kou, Q. & Giuse, D., 2004, 'Using knowledge management practices to develop a state-of-the-art digital library', *MedInfo* 11(1), 99–103.

3

Knowledge management according to organisational size: A South African perspective

Authors:
Cornelius (Neels) Kruger[1]
Roy D. Johnson[1]

Affiliations:
[1]Department of Informatics, University of Pretoria, South Africa

Correspondence to:
Neels Kruger

Email:
neels.kruger@up.ac.za

Postal address:
IT Building, 5th Floor, Lynnwood Rd, Pretoria 0002, South Africa

Background: To date, few studies have focused on how embedded Knowledge Managment (KM) is found in the roots of an organisation. Specifically, not much is known whether employees and managers hold similar perceptions regarding KM or if organisational size plays a role in the establishment of KM maturity.

Objective: The objective of this article was to determine what role organisational size plays in the establishment of KM maturity and how different managerial levels viewed their organisations KM maturity.

Method: The authors gained insight into KM maturity in different industry groupings over a five-year period from a large urban South African University engaged in numerous collaboration programmes with industry. In total, 434 employees were interviewed over three grouping levels (operational, middle and senior management).

Results: The findings support arguments that irrespective of organisational size, knowledge-orientated issues are applicable to all organisations. However, with significant differences in scores recorded over all maturity sections in South Africa, the findings indicated that different sized organisations address knowledge-orientated issues differently.

Conclusion: Findings challenge the argument that the manner in which knowledge-orientated issues are addressed differ only slightly depending on organisational size. Smaller-sized organisations prefer a more personal approach, whilst larger-sized organisations prefer knowledge transfer via technology. Irrespective of organisational size, commitment holds the key to KM success. Commitment shown by middle management regarding KM is a differentiator.

Introduction

'Development of meaningful metrics for measuring the value, quality and quantity of knowledge is a key factor for long-term success and growth in KM Systems.' (Alavi & Leidner 1999)

From the time that Ikojiro Nonaka coined the term 'Knowledge Management' (KM) in a 1991 Harvard Business Review article, practically all organisations have started buying into the KM phenomenon. Many organisations, not realising that KM requires considerable planning and change management, failed in their endeavours dreadfully (Nasir 2003). At the time, studies conducted by Bain and Company (2001) indicated that about 35% of their world-wide sample of 451 companies were using KM and reported a satisfaction rating of about 3.5 on a 5-point scale. However, reservations regarding KM's value were shared by authors such as Alavi and Leidner (1999), Wilson (2002) and Kazimi, Dasgupta and Natarajan (2004). These authors argued that without substantial proof that KM adds value to organisations, the importance and sufficient commitment needed to embark on KM will be underplayed.

Kruger and Johnson (2011), building on the works of Jennex, Smolnik and Croasdel (2008), argued that discussions in various academic conferences and journals have revealed that there is still no consensus or framework for measuring KM's success. This strongly supports an argument made by Kim (2006) that there was still no standardised framework for measuring KM's success. Alavi (1999); Lee, Lee and Kang (2005); Salojarvi, Furu and Sveiby (2005); Kruger and Johnson (2011) concluded that companies still struggle to develop appropriate metrics to assess the effectiveness of KM initiatives because of limited mechanisms to track the cost and value of KM. According to Zaim, Tatoglu and Zaim (2007), this can be partially explained by the fact that KM was still in its early stages regarding the development of its theoretical base. In cautioning that little empirical work has been undertaken with only a small number of studies focusing on how embedded KM is within organisations, Kruger and Johnson (2011) warn that much work remains to be done both theoretically and empirically before KM can be regarded with the explanatory power that exceeds other frameworks. Beijerse (2000) also argues that for KM to reach any level of acceptance, more comprehensive studies in organisations of different sizes and types are needed.

Only a small number of studies from the year 2000 have focused on how embedded KM is in organisations and if organisational size plays a significant role in establishing KM maturity. Moffet and McAdam (2006:221) state that there is only, 'a paucity of study that empirically studies the effects of organisational size on the key factors of KM'. These authors contest that, 'the majority of studies, in common with other emergent business philosophies, are focused on larger organisations where, for example, readily available implementation resources are an underlying assumption (Moffet & McAdam 2006:221)'. Zanjani, Mehrasa and Modiri (2009:590) say that 'Despite the profusion of research about KM within large organisations, fewer studies tried to analyze KM in Small and Medium Enterprizes'. Sanghani (2008) states that not much is known regarding KM in small and medium-sized organisations. According to Sanghani (2008), this is primarily because new management philosophy and technology first being implemented in large organisations, and KM is no exception in this regard.

Much of the seminal work on KM features large multinational companies. Serenko, Bontis and Hardie (2007:610), in building on earlier works of Bontis (1999, 2001), argue that human capital is at the core of any knowledge-based enterprise and come to the conclusion that, 'Much of the extant KM/ICT literature is too general when it comes to describe the organisation in which these new efficiencies have a high probability of success'. These same authors caution, 'All organisations are not created equal. One of the biggest glaring differences is their size'. Sanghani (2008) as well as Zanjani, Mehrasa and Modiri (2009) stated that research on the topic of organisational size and KM maturity is insufficient and inundated with conflicting opinions and findings. Zanjani, Mehrasa and Modiri (2009) caution that:

> SMEs do not manage knowledge the same way as larger organisations. They normally do not have deep pockets to spend on resources such as land, labor and capital. SMEs must do more with less. (p. 592)

This is in contrast to literature with theory regarding best practice vis-à-vis KM processes and techniques (Garud & Kumaraswamy 2005) or the relationship between KM and Information and Communication Technologies (ICT) (Alavi & Leidner 2001; Becerra-Fernandez & Sabherwal 2001; Earl 2001; Davenport & Grover 2001; Ryu, Kim, Chaudhury & Roa 2005). There is only a paucity of research that empirically studies issues such as the following:

- What role does organisation size play in the establishment of KM maturity?
- Do the various managerial levels view their organisation's KM maturity differently?
- Irrespective of organisational size is KM applicable to all organisations?

Literature review

'Many questions arise in relation to Knowledge Management and organisational size.' (Moffett & McAdam 2006:222)

Organisations have to realise that a multitude of factors need to be taken into account before embarking on KM initiatives (Alavi & Leidner 2001; King, Kruger & Pretorius 2007). Strategy, leadership, culture, information technology, senior management support and structure are all critical factors to KM success (Davenport & Prusak 1998; Zack 1999; Grant 1991; Hasanali 2002; Snyman & Kruger, 2004; Xu et al. 2005). Of all these factors, it is leadership commitment (Martiny 1998) and the way we structure organisations that impact on most if not all the human dimensions of the organisation (McMillan 2002). According to Birkinshaw, Nobel and Ridderstrale (2002), the way knowledge is imbedded into a system is the extent to which knowledge is a function of the social and physical system in which it exists. Structure (the relationship between roles in an organisation and its different parts), is thus often seen as an invisible hand that brings organisations to life and gives life to organisations (Mabey, Salaman & Storey 2001). Davenport and Grover (2001) propose that the focus of KM, as primarily a human dimension, must be structurally based. Birkinshaw, Nobel and Ridderstrale (2002) argue that the strong association between the dimensions of knowledge and organisational structure indicates partial support for the 'fit' hypothesis in contingency theory. This promulgates a shift to all workers and not only those whose primary role is KM.

From the perspective of structural design, and especially in the context of KM, it is often cumbersome to treat the organisation as a unit of analysis. Doing so often disregards knowledge sharing practices within departments, business units or working groups, etcetra. For example, consider the structure of a large, multi-divisional organisation. The multi-divisional form of the organisation enables it to engage in completely different markets or products, without the need for much co-ordination (and knowledge sharing) between its divisions. Hence, whilst this might be classified as a large (or even very large) organisation, these are actually separate entities that just happen to have an organisational name in common (Kruger & Johnson 2010). The same applies to organisations which are really just shareholding collectives. KM investigations in such large organisational structures should be focused at the division or business unit and not at the organisation as a whole. According to Franken and Braganza (2006), the approach to organisational KM can thus not be an unqualified choice but must be closely aligned with the organisational form, structure and size. In debating KM issues, challenges and benefits, Alavi and Leidner (1999) argue that:

> there is consistency with the fact that KM systems can be accomplished with different technologies, the most effective of which likely depend upon an organisation's size and existing technical infrastructure. (p. 1)

Although the impact of organisational form, structure and size on group dynamics has been well explored in the social sience literature (Stoel 2002), authors such as Nor and Egbu (2010:234) contest that, 'the impact of size has received less attention in management'. With regards to KM, literature contains an implicit assumption that a standard approach with universal applicability to this process exists, regardless of organisational form, structure or size (Franken & Braganza 2006).

Moffett and McAdam (2006) question this proposition and ask if current KM models, frameworks and programmes can be applied across all organisations uniformly. Štrach and Everett (2006) stress that organisational size influences knowledge distribution, whilst Connelly and Kelloway (2003) argue that there is a negative relationship between organisational size and knowledge sharing. There seems to be some debate regarding the impact of organisational size and the successfull institutionilisation of KM (Nor & Egbu 2010). Unfortunately, with only a small numbers of cases reported, research often provides confusing results:

- As a result of changes in social interactions, there is a negative relationship between organisational size and knowledge sharing (Connelly & Kelloway 2003).
- As the size of an organisation unit increases, the effectiveness of internal knowledge flow dramatically diminishes whilst the degree of intra-organisational knowledge sharing decreases (Serenko, Bontis & Hardie 2007)
- The exact KM approach relies heavily on the type and size of the organisation (Davis, Watson & Man 2007; Zanjani, Mehrasa & Modiri 2009)

In contrast to this:

- Whilst many knowledge-orientated issues are applicable to all organisations, the manner in which they are addressed differ slightly depending on organisational size (Moffet & McAdam 2006).
- Organisational size does not have any effect on the initiation and use behavior of KM systems (Xu & Quaddus 2007).
- Senior general managers most commonly champion KM Systems (Alavi & Leidner 1999, 2001).

Observations of the South African business environment indicate a growing awareness and adoption of knowledge-based strategies and KM practices (Botha & Fouche 2002). The authors gained insight into KM in South African industry groupings over a five-year period from a large urban South African University engaged in numerous collaboration programmes with industry. Challenged to amalgamate Western cultures with African cultures, the South African environment portrays a model for businesses in a future full of continued change, diversity and even elements of silent intolerance and conflict (Finestone & Snyman 2005). Deep-rooted political and social requirements to integrate different cultures, not in a manner where one culture dominates whilst others become extinct over time (Prime 1999), make the South African environment unique in many aspects (King, Kruger & Pretorius 2007).

South Africa has been challenged to make the transition into the global economy whilst managing the vast diversity of its people (Prime 1999). South Africa has past political history that this article will not discuss in detail, except for a few factors believed to directly effect KM maturity. One of these factors is the policy of affirmative action. Affirmative action has the potential of empowering one group over the sanctioning of another which influences job security and

consequently leads to an unwillingness of people to share knowledge (Finestone & Snyman 2005).

Another barrier to KM in the South African context is the issue of language. People are reluctant to share knowledge if they cannot understand concepts or find it difficult to convey their message. Language problems in South Africa are heightened by nine ethnicities, each with its own communities, cultural languages and parlance (Prime 1999). Communication, which is a major element of knowledge-sharing and the vesting of KM maturity, is often severely hampered when having to deal with 11 official languages. Different communication styles are more prevalent in different cultures. White South Africans predominantly adhere to Western culture preferring an explicit style of communication such as written commitments (i.e. contracts) as the main indication of trust. In contrast, Black African cultures are more implicit in their manner of communication and prefer oral communication (King, Kruger & Pretorius 2007).

Strongly linked to communication, is the way South African organisations are managed. According to Prime (1999), in other multi-cultural countries, one culture typically dominates whilst others coexist. South Africa is differentiated by the influx of different cultural pressures that need to be integrated if businesses want to compete in the global economy. South Africa is unique because of its social, political and economic history. In contrast to other culturally diverse countries, South Africa aims to create a unified culture wherein European, African and Asian cultures are fused (Finestone & Snyman 2005).

Whilst the theoretical relevance of studying the link between organisational size and management might be well debated in literature, finding practical examples remains problematic. The intent of this article is to move past theoretical propositions and investigate KM maturity in different organisational groupings and sizes[1]. The contribution of this paper is to address the research questions that follow:

- What role does organisation size play in the establishment of KM maturity?
- How do the various managerial levels view their organisation's KM maturity?

Methodology and data collection

In this extremely diversified South African setting, the authors applied the questionnaire developed by Kruger and Snyman (2007) to a set of 86 organisations. The questionnaire appealed to the researchers primarily because it is built upon the proposition that for KM to be of value, it must progress (mature) to the point where knowledge is seen as a strategic resource with Information and Communication Technologies (ICT) and Information Management (IM) as enablers to KM. In this context, Kruger and Snyman (2007) support the argument made by Grey (1998) and define the difference between

---

1. Organisations selected represented a cadre of organisations servicing fairly homogenous markets/products. All organisations selected structures adhere to modern management theory that is organisational structures are mostly centralised, functionally specialised and hierarchical in nature.

knowledge and IM. The difference is that IM is concerned about working with objects (i.e. data or information) whereas KM is concerned about working with people. Emphasis was not placed on achieving total representation in determining a 'usable population' (population size that is applicable to both Secondary Data Analysis (performance assessment) and evaluative (KM Maturity assessment and performance assessment research), but rather on purposefully selecting a usable and obtainable population size for comparative purposes. Guided by the classification index supplied by the Johannesburg Stock Exchange (JSE) handbook of July–December 2005 (Profile's Stock Exchange Handbook 2005), organisations of similar size and similar operations were purposely selected and grouped together for the research to be undertaken. Considering that it would be difficult for personal knowledge sharing to flourish given issues such as language differences, time zones, geographical dispersion and cultural differences within the organisation, care was taken not to include large, global organisations or diversified organisations that engage in a number of different markets or products.

Preliminary research attempts showed an unwillingness of organisations to participate in the intended research because of organisational sensitivity and confidentiality plus availability of information. This problem was overcome by incorporating a research component into the curriculum of Master in Business Administration (MBA), Master in Information Technology (MIT) and Master in Commerce (MCom) students of a large urban university in South Africa. Because most of these students were active practitioners (97%) and considered 'senior' with regard to academic achievement as well as work experience, they became suitable surrogates to participate in the research project. (This research study involving human subjects was approved by an Ethics Committee of the same university).

After numerous lectures and discussions dealing with data, information, knowledge and KM, senior practitioners used the KM Maturity Assessment Questionnaire (KMMAQ) by Kruger and Snyman (2007) to critically evaluate the KM Maturity of their own organisation or one with which they were deeply familiar. To minimise bias caused by self reporting, subjects were instructed on the need for objectivity through group and one-on-one discussions as well as through individual debriefing when questions arose. Only volunteering practitioners (and organisations) were allowed to participate in the study. In total 178 senior practitioners from nine industry groupings participated in the research conducting three structured interviews per practitioner. In order to sample each of the managerial levels, practitioners were instructed to conduct structured interviews amongst operational personnel, middle management as well as strategic personnel in their respective organisations.

The study sample consisted of 434 employees from 86 South African based organisations. Considering the diversity of organisations participating in the study, the sample population included individuals from diverse backgrounds and cultures. The sample chosen was thus representative of the managerial levels present in organisations (operational personnel totalled 143, middle management 158 and senior management 133). Data collected by means of the structured KMMAQ was digitalised through keyboard entry and transferred to a rating system. In order to ensure a clean and error-free data set, the process of data capturing was closely monitored to ensure as few errors as possible. Newly imported data was checked for capturing errors via standard validation checks as applied by the university. Checks included frequencies, maximum, minimum, range and checks for missing values. All statistical calculations were verified by the Bureau for Statistical and Survey Methodology (Statomet). Statomet is a facility that focuses on the scientific design and management of research. Statomet provides statistical advice on all aspects of research design and management, and aims to improve the quality of research by rendering a multi-disciplinary service to public and private organisations.

After the verification process had been completed, all data collected was carefully prepared for tabular and graphic presentation, analysis and interpretation. The computer software used for analysis and modelling was SAS version 8.3 from the SAS Institute™. All graphs and figures were created using Microsoft Excel (2007). The analysis that follows consists of the descriptive statistics used for each question. Descriptive statistics involved arranging, summarising and presenting the data in such a way that the meaningful essentials of the data could be extracted and easily interpreted. Statistics used established the basic statistical measures of the response variable for every question covering aspects pertaining to ICT and IM. Unless specifically stated, in all instances, findings were elaborated upon from a positive affirmation 'yes, definitely' and 'yes, but not significantly'. Where the probability of exceeding the norm (p-value) was found to be less than 0.05, the decision rule was to reject the null hypothesis at a 5% level of significance. (Full details of all statistical analysis done, as well as a summary of all results obtained, are available on request from the authors).

Discussion, results and findings

Although the questionnaire by Kruger and Snyman (2007) addresses the total spectrum of KM maturity, this article only focuses on the role organisation size plays in the establishment of KM maturity and how the different managerial levels view their organisations KM maturity. We will explore this in the section below.

Knowledge management maturity by organisational size

In order to determine if organisational size plays a role in KM, it was decided to group participating organisations into four categories. Organisations with 100 and less employees were grouped into the 'small organisation' category. Organisations with between 101 and 2000 employees were grouped into 'medium-sized organisations', 2001–2005 employees into 'large organisations' and organisations of above 25 000 grouped into 'extra-large organisations'. The selection of organisational sizes led to a fairly even distribution of the total research population (Table 1).

Organisations selected represented a cadre of organisations servicing fairly homogenous markets or products. All organisations-selected structures adhere to modern management theory (i.e. organisational structures are mostly centralised, functionally specialised and hierarchical in nature).

Through a process of inductive reasoning, Kruger and Snyman (2007) have argued that certain issues, policies and strategies are crucial to effective and efficient KM. The main thrust of the argument was the proposition that when KM issues are institutionalised in chronological order, the institutionalising entity (i.e. organisation) becomes more strategically evolved. In essence, it was proposed that the process of institutionalisation of KM from within a managerial or strategic, rather than from within a technological perspective, aids in the transference of tacit knowledge into explicit knowledge, progressively enabling the exponential exploitation of the power of knowledge.

Kruger and Snyman (2007) propose that before any endeavour in KM commences, as a preliminary phase, a certain amount of ICT and information management (as enablers of effective KM) must be present in the organisation. The next phase, requires a realisation of the importance of KM as a formal function within the organisation, as well as associated drives to instil this realisation throughout the organisation. This phase in KM maturity is followed by conscious commitment, especially from business managers, to start embracing endeavours in KM. At this level of maturity, ICT and (IM) must already be geared towards supporting KM endeavours.

Phase 4 centres around the ability to consciously formulate a strategy (knowledge strategy) about knowledge as a strategic resource. Typically at this stage of maturity, ICT should by now also be geared to support the assimilation and distribution of knowledge in all spheres of the organisation. The next level of maturity deals with the ability to both exploit and explore the power vested in knowledge and KM (formulate KM strategies). The essence of this level of maturity is thus not only the ability to enhance strategy formulation intentionally, but also to streamline KM processes and procedures.

As soon as organisations are capable of enhancing strategy via KM, the final evolutionary step is the incorporation and utilisation of knowledge vested in the organisation's value chain and value chain partners. The primary requirement of this level of maturity is the ability to transcend the borders of the organisation. This is the ability not only to share data and information, but also knowledge and expertise with all stakeholders in the organisation's value chain.

In using the KMMAQ proposed by Kruger and Snyman (2007), an overall KM maturity score could be calculated for all participating organisations. The total score achieved was calculated by adding the scores in each maturity section together. These sections included 20 points for ICT as an Enabler of KM, 76 points for IM as an Enabler of KM, 88 points for the successful identification of KM Issues, Policies and Strategies, 94 points for Implementation of KM, 76 points for Ubiquitous Knowledge (extending KM beyond the borders of the organisation) and four points for Growth in KM (over the past five years). Different maturity sections contributed different weights to the overall maturity score achieved. The total score achieved per organisation, organisational grouping or organisational size was thus calculated by dividing the total score achieved by the total score achievable (358). The average KM maturity score obtained by all 86 participating organisations totalled 175.36 points, or 48.98%. With regard to growth in KM maturity, slightly more than twenty percent (20.28%) of interviewees indicated that their organisations experienced rapid growth in KM maturity over the past five years (2003–2007), 52.12% are of the opinion that although growth occurred it was not significant and 22.17% state that although no growth took place there will probably be growth within the next five years. Slightly more than five percent (5.43%) were of the opinion that a decline in KM growth occurred over the past five years (Table 2). Full details of all statistical analysis done as well as a summary of all results obtained are available from the authors on request.

In grouping organisations according to size, small organisations achieved an average KM maturity of 43.51% (155.76/358), whilst organisations with between 101 and 2000 employees (medium-sized organisations) averaged 50.03%. Large organisations (2001–25 000 employees) scored a bit lower than medium-sized organisations with a 48.87% average. Organisations with more than 25 000 employees (extra-large organisations) consistently outperformed all other organisations, scoring on average 53.75% (Table 3).

TABLE 1: Organisations per category.

Category	%
Small (1–100)	21
Medium (101–2000)	24
Large (2001–25 000)	21
Extra-large (25 001 +)	19

TABLE 2: Knowledge management maturity distribution of all questionnaires.

Variable	N	Mean (%)	Minimum	Maximum	Possible
Section 1 ICT Management	433	73.60	2	20	20
Section 2 Information Management	434	61.14	8	76	76
Section 3 KM Issues Policies and strategy	434	51.75	0	88	88
Section 4 Implementation of KM	433	46.50	9	90	94
Section 5 Ubiquitous knowledge	434	30.27	0	76	76
Section 6 KM growth over past five years	424	51.88	0	4	4
Total	434	-	47	311	358

N, number; ICT, information and communication technologies; KM, knowledge management.

This average could result from the resources available to extra-large organisations as discussed later.

An analysis of variance (ANOVA) with p-values < .0001, indicated that there is a significant difference between the mean scores achieved in different organisations based on size. Multiple comparisons (Least Squares Means) identified that the biggest differences occurred between small and all other organisational sizes. Medium-sized organisations achieved similar scores (< = 5%) to large and extra-large organisations, except for maturity Section 1 (ICT) and Section 5 (Ubiquitous Knowledge) where the mean scores of medium-sized organisations were significantly lower (> 5, than the scores of extra-large organisations. Scores of large organisations were similar (< = 5%) to other organisations' scores, except for Sections 1 (ICT) and 5 (Ubiquitous knowledge), where it was higher (> 5%), than small organisations' scores. Over all maturity sections, extra-large organisations scores' were higher (> 5%) than the scores achieved by small organisations. There was also a difference of more than 5% in scores achieved by extra-large organisations, compared to large organisations in Section 2 (IM) and between extra-large and medium-sized organisations in Section 5 (Ubiquitous knowledge). In essence small and extra-large organisations yielded different scores, with medium and large organisations forwarding similar scores.

Findings indicated that extra-large organisations are at an advantage when it comes to the institutionalisation of formal KM practice over all maturity sections. However, of interest is that although large organisations outperformed smaller organisations (small and medium-sized organisations) in Sections 1 (ICT) and 5 (Ubiquitous Knowledge) of the questionnaire, they were outperformed by medium-sized organisations when it comes to IM (Section 2) the formulation of KM Issues, Policy and Strategy (Section 3) and the institutionalisation of KM practice (Section 4).

As a rule, extra-large organisations do have access to considerably more resources than smaller sized organisations, possibly explaining why extra-large organisations (25 000+ employees) obtained higher scores for all maturity levels than all other organisational sizes. Extra-large organisations are also more likely to be mature with regard to implementing policies and strategies because of legal and mandatory requirements (Moffet & McAdam 2006). The lower scores achieved by large organisations compared to the scores achieved by medium-sized organisations (especially in maturity Section 2, Section 3 and Section 4) suggest that there could be a 'break-even point' between resources available and the successful institutionalisation of KM because of organisational size. This argument necessitated taking into account not only organisational size, but also the different managerial levels present within organisations. Specifically, analysis needed to include a study of the diffusion (point difference between managerial levels) of KM by organisational size and setting.

Knowledge management maturity as a function of managerial levels

In studying KM in such a multi-cultural environment as South Africa, King, Kruger and Pretorius (2007) found that most respondents who have three or fewer years of experience at an organisation are more likely to feel that the organisation has a corporate culture that encourages knowledge sharing. However, this feeling decreases with individuals who have four and seven years' experience in the organisation. According to King, Kruger and Pretorius (2007), the reason this value decreases could be the result of inexperience and/or competition for promotion. These authors argue that this contention is supported by the fact that individuals who have eight or more years of experience feel more secure in their jobs, agreeing to a greater extent that organisational culture is supportive of KM. King, Kruger and Pretorius (2007) proposed that experience is the biggest factor related to the frequency of respondents feeling they could benefit from a KM system. Specifically, they found that senior managers are the most likely to agree that the organisation would benefit from KM.

Figure 4 supports the findings of King, Kruger and Pretorius (2007) showing that senior managers scored their organisation's maturity at 53.48%; middle managers at 47.89% and operational personnel at 46.00%. This constitutes an overall difference in scores between senior management and operational personnel of 7.5%. Of interest is the difference between the scores where senior managers and middle managers (5.59%) is significantly higher than the difference in scores reported by middle managers and operational personnel (1.89%). Senior managers consistently rated the maturity of the different sections higher than middle and operational personnel. There is about a 10% discrepancy between the scores allocated by senior and middle managers to Section 3 of the questionnaire which deals with the formulation of KM issues, policies and strategies (Table 4)

Analysis of variances (ANOVA), with a p-value < .0001 indicated that there is indeed a statistical difference between the score recorded by the different managerial levels over maturity Section1 to Section 4. However, scores reported for maturity Section 5 and Section 6 were found not to differ significantly (0.07%) between the scores recorded by the different managerial levels. In order to determine where differences occurred, it was established that within Section 2 (IM), Section 3 (KM Issues, Policy and Strategy) and Section 4 (Implementation of KM) differences were found primarily between the values by operational and senior managers and middle and senior managers (The GLM procedure of Least Squares Means was used to determine where difference occurred). The values by operational personnel and middle managers were found not to be significantly different. These findings not only support the argument by King, Kruger and Pretorius (2007) that senior managers are more likely to agree that the organisation would benefit from KM, but also indicates at an over-estimation by some senior managers regarding, (1) the success of implementation

TABLE 3: Knowledge management maturity distribution organisational size.

Organisational size	Section						Total
	1	2	3	4	5	6	
Small	65.38	55.59	46.81	42.87	22.66	43.68	43.51
Medium	73.91	62.78	53.47	47.8	29.53	55.24	50.03
Large	76.01	59.75	50.38	45.5	33.39	51.78	48.87
Extra-large	79.1	66.71	56.58	50.04	36.29	56.25	53.75

TABLE 4: Knowledge management maturity as a function of different managerial levels.

Managerial level	Section						Total
	1	2	3	4	5	6	
Ops	69.79	57.8	47.1	44.38	28.62	47.69	46
Middle	72.15	60.32	49.59	45.94	29.65	53.22	47.89
Senior	79.46	65.72	59.33	49.46	32.79	54.88	53.48

of IM, (2) the efficiency and effectiveness of KM issues, policies and strategies and (3) sufficient support given to the institutionalisation of KM endeavours.

Knowledge management maturity as a function of managerial levels within organisational sizes

When differences in opinion with regard to KM maturity reported by the different managerial levels are viewed from the perspective of different organisational sizes, the picture changes dramatically (Table 5). As a point of departure, an Analysis of Variances (Two-way ANOVA) was done to determine if there is indeed a difference between the score achieved per organisational size and the scores recorded per managerial level. Again it was confirmed that the mean values recorded by the different managerial levels and organisational size are statistically different.

In comparing the totals by operational, middle and senior personnel to one another with a GLM Procedure (Least Square Means), it was confirmed that the scores of operational personnel and middle managers are similar in small, medium and large organisations. However, scores of operational personnel and middle managers in extra-large organisations were different. Also, within extra-large organisations, the scores of senior managers were found to be similar to the scores recorded by middle management.

Excluding small organisations, senior managers scored KM maturity fairly evenly over all maturity sections (Table 5). In contrast, middle managers within extra-large organisations scored maturity considerably higher than middle managers in other organisations. Of interest is that the decline in scores between senior and middle managers is the smallest within extra-large organisations and the largest within large organisations. In contrast, the difference in score between middle and operational personnel is the smallest within large and medium-sized organisations and the largest in extra-large organisations. These findings support Connelly and Kelloway (2003), plus Serenko, Bontis and Hardie (2007), that the size of the organisation does play a role in the diffusion of KM between the different managerial levels.

Within small organisations, operational personnel rated KM management maturity at 41.94%, middle management scored maturity basically the same at 42.27%, whilst senior managers forwarded a maturity score of 47.10%. The difference in score between top management and operational personnel (5.2%) is the lowest of all organisational sizes analysed. Of interest is that within small organisations there is a fairly even distribution between the overall scores attributed to senior, middle and operational personnel with regard to maturity in Section 2 (IM), Section 4 (Implementation of KM), Section 5 (Ubiquitous knowledge) and Section 6 (Growth in KM). However, in Section 3 (the identification and institutionalisation of KM Issues, Policies and Strategies), senior managers consistently recorded scores higher than those by interviewees from middle and operational personnel. This again hints at middle and operational personnel within small organisations viewing the formulation of KM issues, policies and strategies to be less successful than senior managers do.

In contrast to small organisations, scores attributed to senior managers in medium-sized organisations were consistently higher (54.83%) over all maturity sections than the scores recorded by middle and operational personnel totalling 48.34% and 47.55% respectively. Scores recorded by middle and operational personnel are nearly identical over all sections. Over all maturity sections there is a difference of about 7% between the scores recorded by senior managers, and middle and operational personnel. This strongly hints at a difference in perception regarding senior middle and operational opinions of KM maturity. Although senior managers in medium-sized organisations are starting to acknowledge the value of KM, it has possibly not evolved beyond the strategic level.

This quandary is supported by a senior manager in a medium-sized service delivery company stating that:

> 'We have experienced quite strong growth in terms of KM maturity over the last five years. This is indicated by the establishment of a number of initiatives including Organisational Education and Training and the establishment of a Research and Development department, a definite step towards active KM'. (Senior manager, delivery company)

This manager continues that, 'Despite the fact that the R&D department provides management and other verticals valuable information, they have yet to become actively

TABLE 5: Knowledge management maturity ratings as a function of different managerial levels within different organisational sizes.

Managerial level	Size				
	Small	Medium	Large	Extra-large	Average
Ops	41.94	47.55	45.18	49.45	46
Middle	42.27	48.34	46.08	55.62	47.89
Senior	47.1	54.83	55.67	56.26	53.48

involved in the formulation of strategies'. A senior manager at a South African water utility organisation shares a similar sentiment and argues that:

> 'Our organisation has realised the importance of KM as a strategic resource and has decided on KM principles. What is still outstanding is the formulation of organisational-wide knowledge policy that will enable the organisation to implement KM initiatives'. (Senior manager, South African water utility organisation)

A possible explanation for differences in scores could be that although there are clear-cut strategic initiatives driven by top managers, such strategy is not becoming policy resulting in managers and operational personnel not buying in and not becoming sensitive to KM initiatives.

In large companies, scores attributed to senior managers were considerably higher (55.67%) than the scores attributed to middle (46.08%) and operational personnel (45.18%) as seen in Table 5. Scores recorded by middle and operational personnel were again nearly identical over all maturity sections. The disparity of about 10% between the scores attributed to senior and middle management is mostly attributed to differences in scores in Section 2 (IM), Section 3 (Formulation of KM Issues, Policy and Strategy) and Section 4 (Implementation of KM) of the questionnaire. Comments made by middle managers working in a large pharmaceutical company manufacturing facility support the argument that senior management is overestimating KM maturity or supplying lip service to KM in stating that, 'the company does not have a clearly defined KM strategy and policy in place and staff members (especially management) are not evaluated on their ability to share knowledge'. This manager not only argues that perceptions surrounding KM differ greatly, but that there is also a 'perception that the ICT department is KM and not the enabler of KM'. He also expresses a strong opinion that, 'there is not a significant drive to get all employees involved in KM and expertise is held locally within functional departments, like IT, finance, production, etcetra.' This position was supported by the following quote from a senior manager working for a large financial institution:

> 'At the moment some members of the board are of the opinion that KM is part of IT management and should thus be incorporated into the IT department. This is creating confusion on who does what'. (Senior manager, employee, financial institution)

A senior manager at a large ICT company made a similar statement that:

> 'Our organisation has not yet reached a level whereby KM is able to seamlessly integrate with the eco-system of the enterprise. KM is still a separate entity although there is a great awareness, but its effectiveness is still yet to be realised'. (Senior manager, employee, ICT company)

At another large pharmaceutical company, managers indicated that various initiatives have been explored to effectively handle data and information. These managers are in agreement that there is an understanding of the importance of managing, securing and protecting knowledge as a strategic resource. However, according to one of the managers interviewed, 'Although our company realises the importance of KM policies and strategies, our implementations of KM as well as our level of ubiquitous knowledge are at lower maturity levels'.

Apart from Section 5, in extra-large organisations, scores attributed to senior (56.26%) and middle managers (55.62%) are significantly higher and smaller in difference than the scores recorded by operational personnel (49.45%). In some instances, scores recorded by middle managers were even slightly higher than the scores recorded by senior managers (Section 2 (IM) and Section 4 [implementation of KM]). This hints at differences in perception regarding the formulation of KM issues, policy and strategy, possibly being more the result of insufficient communication or the time delay associated with the diffusion of policy beyond the strategic domain, than unwillingness by management to implement KM. This argument is supported by a comment made by one of the executives interviewed in an extra-large organisation saying:

> 'The organisation has realised the importance of KM as a strategic resource and has decided on KM. What is still outstanding is the formulation of an organisational-wide knowledge policy that will enable the organisation to implement KM initiatives'. (Executive, extra-large organisation)

In the words of a senior manager from a major automotive parts manufacturer, 'Leadership and organisational culture are the two distinguishing inhibitors of levering existing knowledge to enhance performance and gain competitive advantage'. This manager also supplied an explanation for differences in scores by different managerial levels and argued that, 'While pockets of the company are advanced in knowledge creation and management, initiatives are not corporate-wide and therefore not sustainable'.

Conclusion

The South African scenario can be considered a benchmark for developing economies characterised by continued change, diversity and even elements of silent intolerance and conflict. The research results meet the demand for quantative research in providing an understanding within the particular South African context. In this article it is argued that the debate surrounding ICT, IM and KM is drawing attention away from the determining factor in KM's survival (i.e. acceptance and use). Current literature is largely neglecting this phenomenon. To date, not many studies are focusing on the amount of KM growth that is occurring in ordinary organisations, if organisation size plays a role in the establishment of KM maturity or if employees and managers hold similar opinion regarding KM.

In contrast, KM might be a fallacy not able to withstand the test of time as Wilson (2002) would contest with only

33.60% of South African organisations indicating that no growth or a decline in KM growth occurred over the period 2003–2006. South African industry can be considered a data point for Western industry with an environment characterised by continued change, diversity and even elements of silent intolerance and conflict. This finding is of extreme importance to KM practitioners, scholars and professionals. In moving past theoretical propositions and investigating KM as it relates to different organisational settings and managerial levels, it can be concluded that KM is taking on a new dimension. A dimension where KM is growing in stature and becoming a self-governing entity dependent upon, but separate from, ICT and IM.

To answer the question, 'What role does organisational size play in the establishment of KM maturity?', analysis of KM maturity revealed that there are significant statistical differences between small, medium, large and extra-large organisations. Findings support Moffet and McAdam's (2006) argument that irrespective of organisational size, knowledge-orientated issues are applicable to all organisations. This emphasises Moffet and McAdam's (2006) and Xu, Quaddus, Sankaran and Faranda's (2005) reservation that the manner in which knowledge-orientated issues are addressed differ only slightly depending on organisational size. The findings support that the concept of KM is applicable to all organisations and that there is basically no significant difference in KM between organisations of different sizes. These finding thus strongly support the arguments proposed by Xu *et al.* (2005). Of interest is that although KM elements are applicable to all organisations, it is the approach to implementation that seems to vary, as Moffet and McAdam (2006) rightfully contest. With significant differences in scores recorded over all maturity sections, findings strongly hint that different-sized organisations address knowledge-orientated issues differently. In support of findings by Moffet and McAdam (2006); Sadler-Smith, Sergeant and Dawson (1998); Corso, Martini, Paolucci and Pellegrini (2003), Xu, Quaddus, Sankaran and Faranda (2005), as well as Zanjani, Mehrasa & Modiri (2009), smaller-sized organisations prefer a more personal approach, whilst bigger-sized organisations prefer knowledge transfer via technology.

Findings revealed that although large organisations (NOT extra-large organisations) outperformed medium-sized organisations in Section 1 (ICT Management) and Section 5 (Ubiquitous Knowledge) of the questionnaire, they were often outperformed by medium-sized organisations with regard to the Management of Information (Section 2), the vesting of KM Issues, Policy and Strategy (Section 3) and the Institutionalisation of formal KM Endeavours (Section 4). As far as medium to large-sized companies are concerned, findings are thus supportive of Connelly and Kelloway's (2003) and Serenko, Bontis and Hardie's (2007) arguments that there could be a 'break-even point' between resources available (technology in support), the size of the organisation and the ability to share knowledge. However, in contrast to Connelly and Kelloway's (2003) and Serenko, Bontis and Hardie's (2007) findings that there is often a negative relationship between organisational size and knowledge sharing, extra-large organisations recorded the highest scores over most maturity levels. Of interest was that high scores were not only the result of consistency in achievement over all maturity levels, but also the result of higher than average scores recorded by middle management. This strongly indicates that diffusion of KM has a much larger impact on KM maturity than often anticipated. Hence, larger organisations are turning to collaborative systems where information flow is aided by personal contact, as proposed by McGovern and Norton (2002).

In answering the question, 'How do different managerial levels view their organisations KM maturity?', scores differ primarily between operational personnel and managers with regard to maturity in IM (Section 2), the identification of KM Issues, Policy and Strategy (Section 3) and the Implementation of KM (Section 4). An interesting observation is that there is about a 10% discrepancy between the scores allocated by senior and middle managers in Section 3 of the questionnaire, which deals with the formulation of KM Issues, Policy and Strategy. Middle and operational personnel do not share the same sentiment regarding the success of KM, as do senior management. Although this finding is not directly related to the argument proposed by King, Kruger and Pretorius (2007), the finding supports the notion that individuals with more than eight years experience are more likely to view organisational culture as supportive of KM. Excluding small organisations, senior managers scored KM maturity fairly evenly over all maturity sections. In contrast, middle managers within extra-large organisations scored KM maturity considerably higher than middle managers in other organisations. Of interest is that the decline in score between senior and middle managers is the smallest within extra-large organisations and the largest within large organisations. In contrast, the difference in score between middle and operational personnel is the smallest within large and medium-sized organisations and the largest in extra-large organisations.

Findings confirm that there is a symbiotic relationship between diffusion of KM between managerial levels and organisational size and that the two should not be studied in isolation. These findings thus support Connelly and Kelloway (2003) as well as Serenko, Bontis and Hardie (2007) that the size of the organisation does play a role in the diffusion of KM between the different managerial levels. However, there findings add a new dimension to the argument that there is a negative relationship between organisational size and knowledge sharing. As the size of an organisation unit increases, the effectiveness of internal knowledge flows dramatically diminishes, whilst the degree of intra-organisational knowledge sharing decreases. Findings hint that depending on the size of the organisation, the spread in diffusion between different managerial levels changes from large differences between all the lower levels of management (operational personnel and middle management) and senior management, to large differences between all managers (middle and senior management) and operational levels.

It becomes clear that although organisational size and the availability of resources are influencing the successful institutionalisation of KM, the establishment of sound KM practice and the sharing of knowledge might be more dependent on a deliberate, conscious and calculated managerial effort and support by top management (Xu *et al.* 2005). Irrespective of organisational size, commitment holds the key to KM success. This is in support of Connelly and Kelloway (2003) that management support for KM is a significant predictor of its success. Commitment by middle management will be a differentiator.

Limitations and applicability of the study

A limitation of the study was that it was based solely on South African industry. A second constraint is the level of aggregation, which could be overcome by closer examination of the component organisations. Replicating this study in other developing as well as developed countries would be most informative. In the same light, a longitudinal study might identify trends in different industries, regions and capital markets. The questionnaire used is intended to assess a company operating on free market principles and might be ineffective for use in assessing companies operating in an oligopolistic market.

The use of a 4-point Likert scale, used in the KM Maturity Questionnaire may not be sensitive enough. Expanding the number of possible responses might offer a more nuanced analysis of trends. Considering that the subjects of research have been drawn in as integral parts of the research design, manipulation caused by 'overly emotional or subjective involvement' could have occurred because of respondents serving their own, rather than the research needs. Another quandary to be further investigated is why middle management respondents in extra-large organisations are consistently closer to the scores reported by senior management than by operational personnel.

Whilst varying conceptions of KM exist amongst Eastern and Western theorists, this study provides valuable baseline data which can support further studies of both local and global significance. Such investigations can explore varying perceptions of technology, information and knowledge outside the scope of this study. However, this study does set the stage for investigating diversity in conceptions and implications for perceptions of management modes. The baseline data presented can thus inform other empirical studies that investigate differences regarding knowledge sharing in different sized organisations. Further studies can also probe the significance of cultural differences precipitated by race, age, ethnicity, gender, et cetera, in both further defining agreement on the meaning of these terms and also exploring the implications of such insights for usage and adoption of KM in all spheres of organisational diversification, including leveraging its potential for organisational innovation and advancement.

Acknowledgements
Competing interests

The authors declare that they have no financial or personal relationship(s) which may have inappropriately influenced them in writing this paper.

Authors' contributions

C.J.K. (University of Pretoria) was the project leader, responsible for the experimental and project design and for the drafting of the manuscript. R.D.J. (University of Pretoria) prepared the calculation and the tables, and revised and edited the manuscript.

References

Alavi, M. & Leidner, D.E., 1999, 'Knowledge management systems: Issues, challenges, and benefits', *Communications of the Association for Information Systems*, Vol. 1, Article 7.

Alavi, M. & Leidner, D.E., 2001, 'Review: Knowledge management and knowledge management systems: Conceptual foundations and research issues', *MIS Quarterly* 25(1), 107–136. http://dx.doi.org/10.2307/3250961

Becerra-Fernandez, I. & Sabherwal, R., 2001, 'Organisational knowledge management: A contingency perspective', *Journal of Management Information Systems* 18(1), 23–55.

Beijerse, R.P., 2000, 'Knowledge management in small and medium-Sized companies: Knowledge management for entrepreneurs', *Journal of Knowledge Management* 3(2), 94–110. http://dx.doi.org/10.1108/13673279910275512

Birkinshaw, J., Nobel, R. & Ridderstrale J., 2002, 'Knowledge as a contingency variable: Do the characteristics of knowledge predict organisational structure?', *Organisational Science* 13(3), 274–289. http://dx.doi.org/10.1287/orsc.13.3.274.2778

Bontis, N., (1999), 'Managing organisational knowledge by diagnosing intellectual capital: Framing and advancing the state of the field'. *International Journal of Technology Management* 18(5), 433–485. http://dx.doi.org/10.1504/IJTM.1999.002780

Bontis, N., 2001, 'Assessing knowledge assets: A review of the models used to measure intellectual capital', *International Journal of Management Reviews* 3(1), 41–60. http://dx.doi.org/10.1111/1468-2370.00053

Botha, D.F. & Fouché, B., 2002, 'Knowledge management practice in the South African business sector: Preliminary findings of a longitudinal study', *South African Journal of Business Management* 33(2), 13–19.

Bain and Company, 2001, *Management tools*, Boston, MA.

Connelly, C.E. & Kelloway, K., 2003, 'Predictions of employees perceptions of knowledge sharing cultures', *Leadership and Organisational Development Journal* 24(5), 294–301. http://dx.doi.org/10.1108/01437730310485815

Corso, M., Martini, A., Paolucci, E. & Pellegrini, L., 2003, 'Knowledge management configurations in Italian small-to-medium enterprises', *Integrated Manufacturing Systems* 14(1), 46–56. http://dx.doi.org/10.1108/09576060310453344

Davenport, T.H. & Prusak, L., 1998, *Working knowledge: How organisations manage what they know*, Harvard Business School Press, Boston, MA.

Davenport, T.H. & Grover, V., 2001, 'General perspectives on knowledge management: Fostering a research agenda, Guest editor's introduction Special Issue: Knowledge Management', *Journal of Management Information Systems* 18(1), 3–4.

Davis, R., Watson, P. & Man, C.L., 2007, 'Knowledge management for the quantity surveying profession, Strategic integration of surveying services', paper presented at the *FIG Working Week*, Hong Kong SAR, China 13–17 May.

Earl, M., 2001, 'KM strategies: Towards a taxonomy', *Journal of Management Information Systems* 18(1), 215–233.

Finestone, N. & Snyman, R., 2005, Corporate South Africa: making multicultural knowledge sharing work. *Journal of Knowledge Management* 9(3), 128–141. http://dx.doi.org/10.1108/13673270510602827

Franken, A. & Braganza, A., 2006, 'Organisational forms and knowledge management: One size fits all', *International Journal of Knowledge Management Studies* 1(1–2), 18–37. http://dx.doi.org/10.1504/IJKMS.2006.008843

Garud, R. & Kumaraswamy, A., 2005, Vicious and virtuous circles in the Management of knowledge: the case of infosys technologies. *Mis quarterly* 29(1), 9–33.

Gupta, A.K. & Govindarajan, V., 2000, 'Knowledge flows within multinational companies', *Strategic Management Journal* 21(4), 473–496. http://dx.doi.org/10.1002/(SICI)1097-0266(200004)21:4<473::AID-SMJ84>3.0.CO;2-I

Grant, R.M., 1991, 'The resource-based theory of competitive advantage: Implications for strategic formulation', *California Management Review*, 33(3), 14–135.

Grey, D., 1998, 'Knowledge management and information management: The differences', in *Smith Weaver Smith Inc.*, viewed 26 May 2008, from www.smithweaversmith.com/km-im.htm

Hasanali, F., 2002, 'The critical success factors of knowledge management', viewed 31 August 2005, from http://www.kmadvantage.com/docs/km

Jennex, M.E., Smolnik, S. & Croasdel, D., 2008, 'Towards measuring knowledge management success', in R. Sprague (ed.), *Proceedings of the 41st International Conference on System Science*, Waikoloa, Big Island, Hawaii, USA, IEEE Computer Society Press, Los Alamitos CA, Washington, Brussels, Tokyo, IEEE Computer Society, 2008.

Kazimi, J., Dasgupta, R.R. & Natarajan, G., 2004, 'The rise, fall and rise of knowledge management', viewed 12 August 2007, from http://www.zenzar.com/pdfs/km2.pdf

Kim, J.A., 2006, 'Measuring the impact of knowledge management', *IFLA Journal* 32(4), 362– 367. http://dx.doi.org/10.1177/0340035206074075

King, N., Kruger, C.J. & Pretorius, J., 2007, 'Knowledge management in a multicultural environment: A South African perspective', *Aslib Proceedings* 59(3), 285–299. http://dx.doi.org/10.1108/00012530710752061

Kruger, C.J. & Snyman, M.M.M., 2007, 'A guideline for assessing the knowledge management maturity of organisations', *South African Journal of Information Management* 9(3), viewed 15 October 2007, from http://www.sajim.co.za/index.php/SAJIM/article/view/34. http://dx.doi.org/10.4102/sajim.v9i3.34

Kruger C.J. & Johnson, R.D., 2010, 'Information Management as an enabler of knowledge management maturity: A South African perspective', *International Journal of Information Management* 30(1), 57–67. http://dx.doi.org/10.1016/j.ijinfomgt.2009.06.007

Kruger, C.J. & Johnson, R.D., 2011, 'Is there a correlation between knowledge management maturity and organisational performance?', *VINE - The Journal of Information and Knowledge Management Systems* 41(3), 265–295.

Lee, K.C., Lee, S. & Kang, I.W., 2005, 'KMPI: Measuring KM performance', *Information and Management* 42(1), 469–482.

Martiny, M., 1998, 'Knowledge management at HP consulting', *Organisational Dynamics*, August, pp. 71–78. http://dx.doi.org/10.1016/S0090-2616(98)90025-0

Mabey, C., Salaman, G.J. & Storey, J., 2001, 'Organisational structuring and restructuring', in G. Salaman (ed.), *Understanding Business Organisations*, Routledge, London.

McGovern, G. & Norton, R., 2002, 'Content critical: Gaining competitive advantage through high-quality web content', Pearson Education, London.

McMillan, E., 2002, 'Considering organisation structure and design from a complexity paradigm perspective' in G. Frizzelle & H. Richards (eds.), *Tackling industrial complexity: the ideas that make a difference*, pp. 123–136, Institute of Manufacturing, University of Cambridge.

Moffet, S. & McAdam, R., 2006, 'The effects of organisational size on knowledge management implementation: opportunities for small firms?', *Total Quality Management and Business Excellence* 17(2), 221–241. http://dx.doi.org/10.1080/14783360500450780

Nasir, J., 2003, *Impact of globalisation and knowledge management within a high tech manufacturing environment*, IBM Software Lab, Dublin.

Nor, F.M. & Egbu, C., 2010, 'The impact of organisation size on the implementation of knowledge sharing practice in quantity surveying firms in Malaysia', Papers and postgraduate papers from the special track held at the *CIB World Building Congress 2010*, 10–13 May 2010, pp. 234–244, The Lowry, Salford Quays, United Kingdom, viewed 12 June 2011, from http://cibworld.xs4all.nl/dl/publications/w102_pub349.pdf

Prime, N., 1999, 'Cross-cultural management in South Africa: Problems, obstacles, and solutions in companies', viewed 07 June 2011, from www.marketing.byu.edu/htmlpages/ccrs/proceedings99/prime.htm

Profile's Stock Exchange Handbook, July-December, 2005, Profile Media, Pietermaritzburg, Kwa-Zulu Natal.

Ryu, C., Kim, Y.J., Chaudhury, A. & Roa, H.R., 2005, 'Knowledge acquisition via three learning processes in enterprise enformation portals: Learning-by-investment, Learning by-doing, and Learning-from-others', *MIS Quarterly* 29(2), 245–278.

Sadler-Smith, E., Sargeant, A. & Dawson, A., 1998, 'Higher level training and SME's', *International Small business Studies* 30(2), 84–94.

Sanghani, P., 2008, 'Does organisation size matter for starting a knowledge management program?', *The Icfai University Journal of Knowledge Management* 6(1), 7–20.

Salojarvi, S., Furu, P. & Sveiby, K., 2005, 'Knowledge management and growth in Finnish SMEs, *Journal of Knowledge Management* 9(2), 103–122. http://dx.doi.org/10.1108/13673270510590254

Serenko, A., Bontis, N. & Hardie, T., 2007, 'Organisational size and knowledge flow: A proposed rheoretical link', *Journal of Intellectual Capital* 8(4), 610–627. http://dx.doi.org/10.1108/14691930710830783

Snyman, M.M.M. & Kruger, C.J., 2004, 'The interdependency between strategic management and strategic knowledge management', *Journal of Knowledge Management* 8(1), 5–19. http://dx.doi.org/10.1108/13673270410523871

Štrach, P. & Everett, A.M., 2006, 'Knowledge transfer within Japanese multinationals: Building a theory', *Journal of Knowledge Management* 10(1), 55–68. http://dx.doi.org/10.1108/13673270610650102

Stoel, L., 2002, 'Retail cooperatives: Group size, Group identification, communication frequency and relationship effectiveness', *International Journal of Retail and Distribution Management* 30(1), 51–60. http://dx.doi.org/10.1108/09590550210415257

Wilson, T.D., 2002, 'The nonsense of knowledge management', *Information Research,* 8(1), 144.

Xu, J. & Quaddus, M., 2007, 'Exploring the factors influencing end users' acceptance of knowledge management systems: Development of a research model of adoption and continued use', *Journal of Organisational and End User Computing* 19(4), 54–79. http://dx.doi.org/10.4018/joeuc.2007100104

Xu, J., Quaddus, M., Sankaran, S. & Faranda, B., 2005, 'Does size matter in knowledge management: A comparison between large Organisations and SMEs', in *Proceedings of the Fifth International Conference on Electronic Business*, Hong Kong, December, 05–09, pp. 556–561.

Zack, M.H., 1999, 'Developing a knowledge strategy', *California Management Review* 41(3), 125– 145. http://dx.doi.org/10.2307/41166000

Zaim, H., Tatoglu, E. & Zaim, S., 2007, 'Performance of knowledge management practice: A causal analysis', *Journal of Knowledge Management* 11(6), 54–67. http://dx.doi.org/10.1108/13673270710832163

Zanjani, M.S., Mehrasa, S. & Modiri, M., 2009, 'Organisational dimensions as determent factors of KM approaches in SMEs', *International Journal of Human Science* 4(8), 590–595.

4

Records management and risk management at Kenya Commercial Bank Limited, Nairobi

Authors:
Cleophas Ambira[1,2]
Henry Kemoni[2]

Affiliations:
[1]Kenya Commercial Bank Ltd, Kenya

[2]School of Information Sciences, Moi University, Kenya

Correspondence to:
Cleophas Ambira

Email:
cleophasambira@gmail.com

Postal address:
PO Box 1406-00502, Karen, Nairobi, Kenya

Background: This paper reported empirical research findings of an MPhil in Information Sciences (Records and Archives Management) study conducted at Moi University in Eldoret, Kenya between September 2007 and July 2009.

Objectives: The aim of the study was to investigate records management and risk management at Kenya Commercial Bank (KCB) Ltd, in the Nairobi area and propose recommendations to enhance the functions of records and risk management at KCB. The specific objectives of the study were to, (1) establish the nature and type of risks to which KCB is exposed, (2) conduct business process analysis and identify the records generated by KCB, (3) establish the extent to which records management is emphasised within KCB as a tool to managing risk, (4) identify which vital records of KCB need protection because of their nature and value to the bank and (5) make recommendations to enhance current records management practices to support the function of risk management in KCB.

Method: The study was qualitative. Data were collected through face-to-face interviews. The theoretical framework of the study involved triangulation of the records continuum model by Frank Upward (1980) and the integrated risk management model by the Government of Canada (2000).

Results: The key findings of the study were, (1) KCB is exposed to a wide range of risks by virtue of its business, (2) KCB generates a lot of records in the course of its business activities and (3) there are inadequate records management practices and systems, the lack of which undermines the risk management function.

Conclusion: The findings of this study have revealed the need to strengthen records management as a critical success factor in risk mitigation within KCB and, by extension, the Kenyan banking industry. A records management model was proposed to guide the management of records within an enterprise-wide risk management framework in the bank.

Records and records management

A record is defined by the International Standards Office (ISO) 15489–1:2001 standard as information created, received and maintained as evidence and information by an organisation or person in pursuance of legal obligations or in the transaction of business. This definition is shared by a number of authors, who contend that a record can be in any media, paper, electronic or microfilm (Ngulube 2001:155–173; Shepherd & Yeo 2003; Shepherd & Yeo 2006:9–12).

Records management is the activity responsible for the efficient and systematic control of the creation, receipt, maintenance, use and disposition of records, including processes for capturing and maintaining evidence of, and information about, business activities and transactions in the form of records (ISO 15489–1:2001). According to Ngulube (2001), records management is concerned with the creation, organisation, storage, retrieval, distribution, retirement and final disposal of records, irrespective of their form and media. From these definitions, we can therefore deduce that records management entails the application of professional approaches, including systems, standards, procedures and practices, in the care of records. Records management involves the systematic handling of every stage of records care from the time of creation to the records' disposal. The objectives of records management are (ISO 15489–1:2001):

- setting policies and procedures
- assigning responsibilities for records management at various level within the organisation
- setting best practice standards
- processing and maintaining records in safe and secure storage
- implementing access policies

- implementing a records retention and disposal policy
- integrating records management into business systems and processes
- assigning, implementing and administering specialised systems for managing records
- providing a range of services relating to the management and use of records.

Some of the benefits of setting up a good records management programme and practice in an organisation include (International Records Management Trust 2009:7–20; Roper & Millar 1999:5–20; Stephens 1995):

- Control of records creation and growth. An effective records management programme addresses both creation control (i.e. it limits the generation of records or copies not required to operate the business) and records retention (a system for destroying useless records or retiring inactive records), thus stabilising the growth of records in all formats.
- Improvement of efficiency and productivity. Time spent searching for missing or misfiled records is non-productive. A good records management programme can help any organisation upgrade its recordkeeping systems so that information retrieval is enhanced, with corresponding improvements in office efficiency and productivity.
- Ensuring regulatory compliance. The only way an organisation can be sure reasonably that it is in full compliance with laws and regulations is by operating a good records management programme which takes responsibility for regulatory compliance.
- Cost reduction. Professional records management helps organisations save on the costs of space and equipment, which are engaged to manage records that would otherwise have been disposed.
- Risk mitigation. Adequate records management protects organisations from risks resulting from insufficient or inadequate information such as weak management decision-making, a negative corporate image and the loss of client confidence.
- Assimilation of new records management technologies. A good records management programme provides an organisation with the capability to assimilate new technologies and take advantage of their many benefits.
- Knowledge sharing. A key perspective of organisational performance management is knowledge sharing. Proper records management ensures that critical knowledge is captured and preserved for sharing across the organisation to sustain competitive advantage and ensure continuity in service and product delivery.

Risk management

The Government of Canada's (2000) integrated risk management model (IRMM) defines risk as the uncertainty that surrounds future events and outcomes. It is the expression of the likelihood and impact of an event with the potential to influence the achievement of an organisation's objectives. Risks exist as operational, strategic, compliance or reputational risk (Central Bank of Kenya 2000; CBK 2005; Mwisho 2001:16–49). Operational risk, also called transaction risk, is the risk arising from fraud, error and the inability to deliver products or services, maintain a competitive position and manage information. Strategic risk is the risk arising from adverse business decisions or improper implementation of those decisions. Compliance risk is the risk arising from violations or non-conformance with laws, rules, regulations, prescribed practices, or ethical standards. Reputational risk is the risk to earnings or capital arising from negative public opinion (Buttle 1999; Chance 2004; Comptroller's Handbook 2008; Lore & Borodovsky 2002).

In the banking industry, risk management has become even more essential due to the nature of the business, which is essentially to safeguard people's money (Ioannis 2008:56–75). Banks deal with sensitive financial services that are equally marred by various risk issues that impact on their services to their clientele (Gup & Kolari 2005; Nyaoma 2005). With regard to risk management in the banking industry, records management is critical in minimising risk exposure within banks. Poor records management poses challenges to banks in their effort to manage risk. A number of scholars (Makhura 2008; Sampson 2003; University of Technology Sydney 2008; Williams 2007) contend that weak records management programmes, systems and practices have remained a problem and a major hindrance in developing watertight risk management strategies in the banking industry, as well as other financial institutions; hence, the challenge of managing risk in banks remains a complex matrix.

According to Gorrod (2004), commercial banks are exposed to risks such as frauds, system failures and failures to enforce compliance with existing regulatory framework. These risks are usually exacerbated by weak information and record management systems and practices. Gorrod's opinion is also shared by Borodzicz (2005) and Richard (2006), all of whom contend that effective records management is the foundation upon which institutions can demonstrate legal compliance, regulatory compliance, high standards of corporate governance and sustain operational efficiency. Records management may also deliver additional benefits to an institution through the reduction of overheads, the protection of assets and the streamlining of business processes.

Statement of the problem

In Kenya, it is a requirement by the Central Bank of Kenya (CBK) that all commercial banks must establish a risk management unit dedicated to risk management within the banks (CBK 2005). The CBK notes that risk-taking is an inherent element of banking and, indeed, profits are, in part, the reward for successful risk taking in business. Poorly managed risk can lead to losses and thus endanger the safety of a bank's deposits (CBK 2005; CBK 2006; Njuguna 2007).

This study was necessitated by the increasing neglect of records management at KCB, despite wide exposure to risks by the bank. The main research question was to establish the role of records management in risk mitigation at KCB. The nature of KCB's banking activities expose it to a variety of risks, including credit risk, liquidity risk, market risk, operational risks and interest rate risks. KCB has consequently, and pursuant to the CBK's requirements, established a risk management division, entirely dedicated to the function of risk management. This division has instituted a number of measures to mitigate risks in the bank. However, no decisive action has been taken by the division to improve records management in the bank as a risk management strategy. Consequently, records management in KCB remains low key, poorly administered and not a priority of the division in its risk management activities. Lack of enforcement of strong records management systems and practices continue to expose the bank to enormous risks accruing from weak records keeping regimes, ultimately undermining the entire function of risk management. There is no comprehensive records management policy and/or programme to guide the function of records management in KCB. In addition, KCB's strategic objectives do not mention anything to do with records or even information management. The management of records is decentralised, with every department or branch entirely responsible for its own records. There is no central control or supervision to ensure standardisation of records management practices across the bank. This is despite the fact that risk management at KCB enjoys central control from the risk management division located at its head office, which enforces uniformity across the KCB network. Consequently, existing records management systems and practices continue to undermine risk management efforts at KCB, especially for those risks accruing from inadequate records management.

The problem of weak records management at KCB therefore presented a potential research area that needed intensive and extensive investigations. This was necessary to establish the place and role of records management in mitigating risk in KCB and subsequently submit appropriate recommendations to improve the situation in KCB and, by extension, other commercial banks.

Aim of the study

The aim of the study was to investigate records management and risk management at Kenya Commercial Bank (KCB) Ltd, in the Nairobi area and propose recommendations to enhance the functions of records and risk management in KCB.

Specific objectives of the study

The specific objectives of the study were to:

- Establish the nature and type of risks to which KCB is exposed.
- Conduct business process analysis and identify the records generated by KCB and their roles in business activities.
- Establish the extent to which records management is emphasised within KCB as a tool to managing risk and its role in risk mitigation.
- Identify vital records of KCB that need protection because of their nature and value to the bank.

- Make recommendations to enhance current records management practices to support the function of risk management in KCB.

Research questions

The main concern for this study was to identify the role and place of records management in risk mitigation at KCB. This was addressed through the following research sub-questions:

- What are the main business activities of KCB and what records are generated out of these activities?
- What are the types of risks that KCB is exposed to in its activities?
- What is the nature of records management systems and practices at KCB?
- How adequately do existing records management practices support risk management?
- What framework informs the activities of vital records management and disaster management for records at KCB?

Significance of the study

The findings of the study are expected to help KCB strengthen risk management strategies by more specifically emphasising records management as a critical component in scaling up risk mitigation. The study will also enlighten the management and staff of KCB on the importance of records management in risk management. The study has revealed the impact of recordkeeping systems and processes on staff performance and their subsequent influence on risk management. The research contributes to the body of knowledge on records management and risk management and informs the development of policy, practice and theory of records management as an integral part of risk management in the banking industry. The study has also made appropriate recommendations useful for supporting risk management and has provided a records management model within the context of risk management that will foster risk management at KCB.

Methodology

The study population sample size constituted 36 respondents drawn from 5 KCB Nairobi branches (Moi Avenue, Jogoo Road, Kipande House, River Road and Sarit Centre) and 5 Head Office units. This population sample size included 19 non-management staff and 17 management staff, as indicated in Table 1.

The data collection instruments were face-to-face interviews complemented with observations. Qualitative approaches were used to analyse, present and interpret data. Data presentation is descriptive in nature and analysis has been done according to study objectives, primarily to focus on specific issues as defined by the objectives of the study.

This study utilised simple random sampling and purposive sampling. Simple random sampling was used in this study

TABLE 1: Study population sample size ($N = 36$).

Category	Population	Sample	%
Risk management managers	5	2	40.00
HR managers	2	2	100.00
IT manager, office automation	1	1	100.00
Branch managers	5	5	100.00
Branch operations managers	5	5	100.00
Manager, Central processing centre (CPC) archive	1	1	100.00
Manager, central archiving	1	1	100.00
Section heads	17	8	47.06
Clerical	53	11	20.75
Total	**90**	**36**	**40.00**

specifically in selecting the clerical and section head staff. The purposive sampling technique was extremely useful in this study for the selection of interviewees within the head office of KCB and its branches. It was also useful in identifying the branches within the Nairobi area from which the clerical and section head staff were selected randomly. The interviewees chosen were those with a direct strategic or operational role in both risk management and records management, such as branch managers, branch operations managers and risk management managers. The branches were purposely selected depending on their size and volume of activity, therefore a few large branches and a few small branches were selected.

Theoretical framework

The study was informed by Frank Upward's (1980) records continuum model (RCM) and the Government of Canada's (2000) IRMM. This was done through triangulation of the RCM and IRMM. Triangulation mixes theories, methods and multiple data sources to strengthen the credibility and applicability of findings (Hoque 2006).

The RCM was formulated in the 1990s by Australian archival theorist, Frank Upward (Xiaomi 2001). The Australian Records Management Standard AS4390 defines the RCM as a consistent and coherent regime of management processes from the time of the creation of records (and before creation, in the design of recordkeeping system) to the preservation and use of records as archives (Australian Standards Organisation AS4390 1996, Part 1: clause 4.22). The continuum concept captures the modern definition of records, that is, one which is inclusive of the key elements of content (the facts about the activity), context (information about the circumstances in which the record was created) and structure (relationship between the constituent parts). Flynn (2001:79–93) explains that the RCM is significant because it:

- Broadens the interpretation of records and recordkeeping systems offered by the lifecycle model. Such broadening is helpful, given the variety of contexts in which archivists and records managers operate and in which archives and records are used.
- Reminds us that records (including archives) are created and maintained for use as a result of business and administrative functions and processes, rather than as ends in themselves.

- Emphasises cooperation beyond the walls of repositories, especially between the closely related professions of archives administration and records management – a cooperation that is more important than ever in the contemporary climate of outsourcing and cross-sectoral working.

The IRMM was proposed by the Government of Canada in 2000, under its then new management framework entitled *Results for Canadians*. Integrated risk management is a continuous, proactive and systematic process to understand, manage and communicate risk from an organisation-wide perspective. It is about making strategic decisions that contribute to the achievement of an organisation's overall corporate objectives. The IRMM has four key elements for management of risk namely, (1) developing the corporate risk profile, (2) establishing an integrated risk management function, (3) practicing integrated risk management and (4) ensuring continuous risk management learning. As such, the IRMM provides a clearer and holistic step by step model for risk management. This model provides a clear pattern within which the function of records management can be evaluated as a tool for risk management. The model's presentation is such that it advocates for establishment of risk management frameworks across the organisation, right from the first step of developing a corporate risk profile. The IRMM does not focus only on the minimisation or mitigation of risks but also supports activities that foster innovation, so that the greatest returns can be achieved with acceptable results, costs and risks (Government of Canada 2000; Graham 2004).

Key findings at Kenya Commercial Bank
Business process analysis and records created

The bulk of business activities in KCB are direct financial activities. These include:

- local currency deposits
- credit facilities (loans, overdrafts, credit cards, short-term and medium-term loans, local bills discounts)
- guarantees (bid bonds, performance bonds, commercial guarantees)
- issuance of cheques
- safe custody
- foreign currency deposits
- international trade finance
- mortgage financing
- asset-based financing
- and community social responsibility.

Figure 1 indicates the distribution of financial and non-financial (control and support) activities at KCB, as reported by respondents.

Five (45.45%) of the eleven clerical staff interviewed were involved in teller activities, two (18.18%) in clearing activity at the central processing centre, two (18.18%) in back office operations at custody services and two (18.18%) in filing at the credit unit.

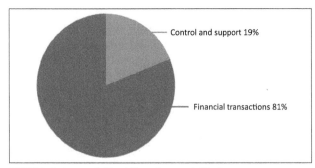

FIGURE 1: Business activities at Kenya Commercial Bank.

Branch managers are responsible for the day-to-day management of the respective branch. The branch operations managers report to the branch manager and are responsible for daily operational activities. A total of five branch operations managers were interviewed. Most of the core banking activities that relate to funds management, such as deposits, withdrawals, transfers and even loans, fall directly under the operations managers. Examples of records generated from these core financial activities include:

- transaction vouchers
- account statements
- customer files
- cheques
- daily ledger books
- investment reports
- loan performance reports
- fraud reports
- funds transfer reports
- forex statements
- circulars and daily correspondence relating to customers, staff and business issues.

Besides the financial activities, there are also support and control activities which include such activities such as HR management, auditing, clearing, financial management, information technology, and facilities and estate management. Examples of records generated from the non-financial support and control activities include:

- personnel records
- audit reports
- annual accounts and financial statements
- estate and facilities reports
- ICT deployment status reports and periodic financial turnover reports.

Risk management is a critical business activity within the banking industry. The findings indicated that the bulk of business activities in the bank are sensitive activities that relate to the core of the economy of the society – money. This implies that by the very nature of these business activities, the need for adequate risk management is high. Consequently, the need for records management in principle is also high, despite the inadequacies revealed in the study. From the findings of the study, it can be concluded that records management is a critical activity for KCB, given the need for strong risk management which records management underpins.

Nature and types of risks

The most prevalent type of risk in the banking industry is operational risk. The other risks include compliance, strategic and reputational risks, as indicated in Figure 2. Operational risks do not only include acts of fraud, management failures, weak systems and human error but also inadequate records management.

Of the 19 non-management respondents (clerks and section heads), 63.15% cited operational risk, whereas 70.00% of branch and operations managers cited operational risks as the most prevalent risks affecting their performance. All 10 (100%) branch managers and branch operations managers acknowledged exposure to risks (Table 2).

One of the two respondents (50.00%) from the risk management division noted that KCB is exposed to 'people risks, systems risks, process risks and threats from external events'. The other respondent (50.00%) reported that KCB is at the stage where risk culture sensitisation and embedment are taking place, which involves communicating on risk practice and culture, couching risk approaches in terms of value creation and preservation, identifying, analysing and evaluating the risks, and 'putting in place and implementing frameworks and policies for treating risks and monitoring and reviewing the risks'.

Both respondents from the HR division (100%) indicated that they are exposed to risks. Those risks cited included: 'risks of losing data through fire, computer crush and viruses', 'unauthorized access to records', 'frauds committed by staff who did not go through a thorough vetting process'. It can be concluded from these findings that there is a high risk exposure in KCB.

Records management status

The study revealed inadequacies in records management at KCB. There is no comprehensive professionally drawn

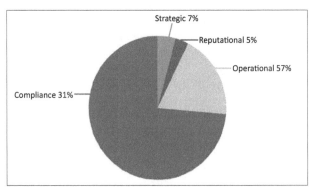

FIGURE 2: Risk profile at Kenya Commercial Bank.

TABLE 2: Types of risks cited by branch and operations managers (*n* = 10).

Type of risk	Times cited	%
Compliance risks	3	30.00
Operational risks	7	70.00
Reputational risks	1	10.00
Strategic risks	2	20.00

n, number.

records management programme (RMP) other than the operations manual, which is limited.

In relation to the availability of a formal RMP in their respective units or departments, 15 (78.95%) of the 19 clerks and section heads interviewed indicated that their departments do have a formal RMP. Two (10.52%) said they do not have such a programme and two (10.52%) said they did not know. However, when probed further, the respondents revealed that the RMP being referred to was the recordkeeping guidelines provided by KCB's operations manual and internal departmental or branch practices and not a formally and professionally drawn RMP for the bank. The scope of these guidelines was limited to retention and disposition of vouchers after an audit. In relation to satisfaction with existing records management practices and systems by the 19 non-management respondents, 1 (5.26%) respondent expressed satisfaction, 8 (42.11%) said they are entirely not satisfied, whilst 10 (52.63%) said they are partially satisfied.

Of the 10 branch managers and operations managers interviewed, 6 (60.00%) respondents said their branches or departments have an RMP in place, whilst 4 (40.00%) said they do not have a programme. Seven (70.00%) managers indicated that they have dedicated staff for records management, whereas three (30.00%) said they did not. Of the seven respondents with dedicated staff for records management, five (71.43%) indicated that these staff members have no formal training in this process, whereas two (28.57%) said that their staff members have just undergone on-the-job training. Eight (80.00%) of the ten respondents said their staff are well informed on the value of records management, whereas two (20.00%) said their staff lack the required knowledge. All 10 (100%) respondents acknowledged the inadequacy of existing systems in fostering efficiency and effectiveness within their branches.

The central archives did not have any form of documented guidelines on archiving records under their custody. The respondent reported to 'have all the information in the[ir] head' and nothing documented for reference. Indeed, even the KCB operations manual's provisions on records management do not cater for archiving and archiving management.

Both respondents (100%) from the HR division indicated that there is a formal policy for managing personnel records in KCB. On further probing the elements of the policy, the respondents indicated that the policy covers the following aspects: description of file – numerical description using staff numbers, components of personnel files, 'access controls to personnel information', 'access to HR registry' and retention of personnel files.

Feedback from the respondents of the risk management division was as follows: one respondent (50.00%) reported the absence of such a framework, whilst the other (50.00%) noted that each risk management discipline and each branch

provide detailed records management frameworks for their particular area of interest. Both (100%) respondents noted that proper recordkeeping is treated as a cornerstone of risk management by the risk management division. The two respondents cited concerns that the existing records management systems and practices in KCB do not adequately foster efficiency and effectiveness.

From these findings, it can be concluded that records management in KCB is inadequate and that it requires strengthening to sufficiently support risk management.

Records management as an integral part of risk management

The study findings revealed that there are enormous risks that arise as a result of inadequate records management in KCB. The respondents were asked which of the four categories of risks they thought was most affected by inadequate records management. Their responses are indicated in Figure 3.

Eighteen (94.74%) of the nineteen respondents indicated that they are exposed to risks arising from records management inadequacies, whilst one (5.26%) respondent reported a lack of exposure to any risk due to records management. These risks included:

- loss or misplacement of records
- long retrieval times affecting management decision-making
- inadequate information which affects quality of decisions
- dissatisfied customer due to delayed retrieval of customer records
- exposure to acts of fraud perpetrated through weak recordkeeping systems.

On whether existing records management systems sufficiently serve to mitigate risks, 7 (36.84%) observed that existing records management infrastructure does not mitigate risks at all, 6 (31.58%) said it partially mitigate risks and 6 (31.58%) said it sufficiently mitigate risks. When asked whether records management systems and practices impact their motivation in work, 17 (89.47%) respondents agreed, indicating that poor storage, misfiling and misplacement of files is frustrating to them and negatively impacts their work morale. Two (10.53%) respondents said their motivation is not affected by the existing systems.

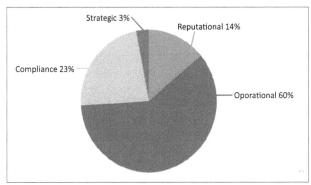

FIGURE 3: Risk categories most affected by inadequate records management systems.

Of the 10 branch managers and operations managers sampled, 3 (30.00%) said the existing records management practices in their branches sufficiently support risk mitigation, 2 (20.00%) said they offer no risk mitigation support and 5 (50.00%) said that these practices partially support risk mitigation. Regarding the prevalence of risk categories, 6 (60.00%) of the 10 branch managers and operation managers cited operational risks as the most prevalent, 1 (10.00%) cited reputational risks, 2 (20.00%) cited compliance risks and 1 (10.00%) cited strategic risks. Regarding the degree to which records management is valued as a risk management strategy, 7 (70.00%) respondents reported a high value, whereas 3 (30.00%) noted a very low value.

The respondent from CPC archiving reported there was a working relationship between the CPC archiving section and the risk management division. It was reported by the respondent that the risk division 'vets existing procedures at the CPC archiving section and flag risk areas that need mitigation.'

When asked whether the existing records management practices support the department in risk mitigation, one (50.00%) of the two respondents from the HR division said 'not fully', whereas the other respondent remarked 'no'.

It can be concluded from these findings that existing records management systems and practices at KCB do not adequately foster risk management and that they, in fact, contribute to risk exposure within KCB.

Management of vital records

The findings of the study revealed that KCB emphasises the management of vital records, given the investment made in storage equipment and authority controls for the handling of vital records. The bulk of vital records held in the bank are those belonging to clients who have deposited their important documents for safe custody. These include: title deeds, academic documents, wills, partnerships, agreements and investment certificates.

Thirteen (68.42%) of the nineteen clerks and section heads interviewed reported to have vital records in their units, whilst five (26.32%) said they do not hold vital records. One (5.26%) respondent reported to be unsure of whether their department has vital records or not. Those who reported to have vital records cited such records to include client security documents such as title deeds, company registration certificates in safe custody, academic certificates in safe custody and collateral documents such as car log books for clients afforded car loans. However, of the 13 who acknowledged the availability of vital records, only 8 (61.54%) reported to have a vital records management programme, whilst 4 (30.77%) said they have none. One (7.69%) respondent did not know.

Of the 10 branch managers and operations managers, 6 (60.00%) reported to have vital records and vital records management programmes in place, whilst 4 (40.00%) said they are not clear on the status of vital records in their units. Eight (80.00%) of the ten respondents expressed deep concern that the state of disaster management for records was only better for vital records in safe custody and very inadequate for the bulk of other records (i.e. those not in safe custody). Four (40.00%) respondents noted that some of the records storage areas had no access controls, meaning that anyone could access the rooms.

All (100%) the branch managers revealed that every KCB branch has a security safe – which is fireproof – to protect the vital documents. Registers to control access to the safes have also been prepared and are audited periodically. The emphasis on the vital records could be as a result of the direct financial implications of these records, given they are a source of business to the bank and therefore a core area on which to focus, as opposed to ordinary records, which are viewed to be of secondary concern.

It can be concluded from these findings that the bank has given priority to vital records management but not to the management of ordinary daily transactional records, which apparently tends to be the channel for most cases of fraud and the cause of most operational risks.

Respondents' recommendations

Recommendations from clerical staff and section heads

Amongst the recommendations made by the respondents were the following:

- 'computerisation of the records management processes'
- 'standardisation of arrangement and description of records and files'
- 'staff training in records management'
- 'establishment of a formal records management programme for KCB'
- 'centralisation of records management'
- 'improvement of records security and disaster management'
- 'appraisal of records to prevent accumulation of unnecessary records'
- 'designate specific staff to records management activities in all branches and departments'
- 'improve security of electronic records'
- 'establish methods to establish records authenticity'.

Recommendations from branch and operations managers

Recommendations by respondents under this category included:

- 'computerisation'
- 'training of staff on records management'
- 'centralisation of management of records'
- 'microfilming'
- 'improvement of disaster management for records'.

Recommendations from human resource managers

Recommendations by the HR managers were:

- 'more investment in electronic records which are easily stored, retrievable and accessed'
- 'increased training on records management'
- 'use of technology in records management'.

Recommendations by central processing centre archiving staff

The respondent from central processing centre (CPC) archiving suggested that, 'as a way forward, I feel we may need software that manages the system of the records archived'.

Recommendations from risk managers

The respondents from the risk management division made the following recommendations:

- 'digitising records and planning for comprehensive document management software'
- 'KCB should adapt modern records management practices, especially digitising critical records and instituting comprehensive records management systems with successive levels of offsite and secure electronic backup systems'.

Recommendations from central archives

The recommendations made by the respondent from central archives were:

- 'automation of the records management systems'
- 'invest in training of staff on importance and technical skills for records management'
- 'enforce internal controls and professional records management standards'.

Recommendations by Information Technology manager

The Information Technology (IT) manager made the following recommendations:

- 'There is need to control access to the e-records based on authorities within the various business units and branches that create and own the records.'
- 'A more comprehensive programme for managing e-records should be developed to match technology changes and business changes, instead of relying on the operations manual which may have aspects which are already obsolete'.
- 'Given increasing risk exposure, there is probably need to rethink the entire process of managing records and create better working relationship regarding records management between the IT, risk division and business units.'

Conclusion

This research endeavoured to study the role of records management in risk mitigation at KCB. A broader result of the study has been the recognition of the fact that records management has a strong impact on risk management. The study revealed that inadequate records management undermines risk management and it can be a breeding ground for more risks. The study also revealed that the nature of business at KCB exposes it to enormous risks that require comprehensive and integrated approaches to risk mitigation. Specifically, it revealed that KCB is faced with various risks associated with records management. The overall conclusion of the study is that existing records management systems and practices are inadequate and undermine the risk management function and that immediate attention by KCB management is required to review existing records management systems to ensure they sufficiently support risk management.

Recommendations

The study made the following recommendations that could be useful in strengthening records management as a critical success factor and integral part of risk management at the KCB head office and Nairobi area branches:

- Policy and procedures. There is need for the KCB operations division, which is responsible for developing all KCB operational procedures and standards, to develop a comprehensive enterprise-wide records management programme for KCB to control and standardise records management practices across the bank.
- Central control of records management. There should be a central office established within the operations division and a professionally trained records manager should be recruited to that office to control records management activities in the bank. An alternative to this, at minimum, should be a department to cater for records management under the risk management division.
- Training and sensitisation. The KCB training and development department should invest in staff training in records management, preferably for all the staff of the bank.
- Professional personnel for records management. The KCB retail, risk management and HR divisions should facilitate the establishment of positions of records officers in the departments and/or branches, or review the duties of filing clerks with a view to expanding them to cater for all day-to-day records management functions.
- Automation. There is need for the IT division, in conjunction with the operations division, to automate file tracking activities by the introduction of computerised file tracking systems. This will address concerns raised by the respondents of long retrieval periods due to misplacement and misfiling of records.
- Electronic records management. The KCB IT division, together with the operations division should also develop and implement a comprehensive electronic RMP.
- Quality assurance and systems audit. The risk management and auditing divisions should ensure enforcement of procedures to allow for consistent appraisal of records. This is paramount to avoid accumulation of records for unnecessarily long periods, compromising physical and intellectual control of the records and exposing KCB to risks.

- Integration. There is urgent need for the risk management division to integrate records management within the KCB's enterprise-wide risk management strategy.
- Vital records management. A comprehensive vital records management programme should be developed by the KCB operations division.
- Disaster management. A disaster management programme for records should be developed by KCB to establish standards for records protection. This programme should cover all aspects and types of disasters including artificial and natural.

Proposed records management model to support risk management

The study proposes a model that could be used to ensure adequate records management in KCB to support the function of risk management. The suggested model presents eight stages that KCB would have to go through to ensure there is adequate records management support for risk management. These stages and subordinate action points under each are shown in Figure 4. This model has been adapted from existing models on records management and risk management.

Step 1: Definition of associated risk profile for records management

Identify all risks associated with records management and relate records management to enterprise-wide risk management. Indicate how improved records management will assist in downscaling or eliminating these risks. Indicate the overall value of improved records management to the bank, with an emphasis on risk management benefits.

Step 2: Identification of human capital

Identify personnel requirements for the right people needed to drive the records management process. Identify what constitutes records management expertise, including professional qualifications, ICT skills and expected roles in the records management function. Identify other personnel who could be useful in the management of records, such as ICT staff, risk management experts and legal experts.

Step 3: Development of records management programme, policy and procedures

Draw up specific records management policy, programme and procedures manuals authorising and positioning the records management function within the company administrative hierarchy and defining its authorities of responsibilities.

Step 4: Prepare physical resource requirements

Establish storage areas for the records and necessary and appropriate storage equipment for all types of records – ordinary records, vital records and electronic records. Consider security, preservation and disaster management issues when allocating and preparing physical resources. Identify and set up locations for records centres and an

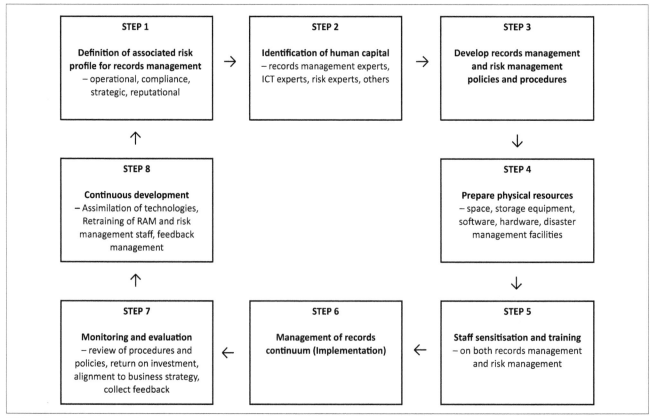

RAM, records and archives management.

FIGURE 4: The proposed records management model for Kenya Commercial Bank.

archival repository. Establish necessary ICT infrastructure for e-records and prepare disaster management and response tools and equipment.

Step 5: Staff sensitisation and training

Train all company staff on the value of records management in ensuring business growth, stability and risk management, clearly identifying the risks accruing from poor records management.

Step 6: Management of records in the continuum

This refers to the full day-to-day management of records in the organisation based on an established programme, policies and procedures, driven by physical resources and infrastructure and by the identified personnel and staff, from creation to disposition.

Step 7: Continuous development

This involves the continuous improvement of the records management systems to match the organisational changes, industry changes and paradigm shifts in records management and risk management practices.

Step 8: Monitoring and evaluation

The final step is to review the records management systems regularly to ensure they reflect the aspirations of the organisation and contribute to the overall success of the parent organisation.

Suggestions for further research

Records management and banking service delivery

There is need for further studies to reveal the current state of records management at KCB and its impact on service delivery. Research on the nexus between records management and service delivery would have a direct impact on risk mitigation because efficient service delivery systems contribute heavily towards risk mitigation.

Research in Kenya Commercial Bank branches outside the Nairobi area

This study limited itself to KCB branches in the Nairobi area, targeting the head office and five branches in Nairobi. There is need to conduct a similar study in other KCB Branches in Kenya and other countries where KCB operates to reveal the status of records management in these branches. This will be necessary to understand whether the findings of this study are indeed representative of the entire bank.

Research in other banks

There are approximately 50 commercial banks in Kenya. This study confined itself to KCB but it is suggested that a similar study could be conducted in other banks to reveal the status of records management and risk management across the Kenyan banking industry. This would be necessary to establish any similarities and differences amongst banks on records management practices and identify the factors contributing to these similarities or differences.

Electronic records management for banking

This study revealed that there is a significant use of electronic platforms to transact business in KCB. As a result, large numbers of electronic records are generated. Further research and development in the area of electronic records management in the banking industry would be useful to advise this industry on how it can deal comprehensively with electronic records management.

Acknowledgements

We thank all the respondents who participated in this study and provided us with useful data that formed the backbone of the study. We are deeply indebted to the Director of Human Resources at Kenya Commercial Bank, who approved the use of Kenya Commercial Bank as the case study for the research.

Author contributions

This article was written by Cleophas Ambira, with meaningful and concise contributions throughout the text by his supervisor, Prof. Henry Kemoni.

References

Australian Standards Organisation, 2004, 'Risk management standard (AS/NZS 4360:2004)', viewed 13 September 2008, from http://www.riskmanagemeent.com.au

Borodzicz, E., 2005, *Risk, crisis and security management*, John Wiley & Sons, New York.

Buttle, J., 1999, *Risk management in banking*, viewed 24 March 2008, from http://www.apra.gov.au/risk_management_banking.pdf

Central Bank of Kenya, 2006, *Prudential regulations for banking institutions*, CBK, Nairobi.

Central Bank of Kenya, 2005, *Risk management guidelines*, CBK, Nairobi.

Central Bank of Kenya, 2000, *Prudential guidelines for banking institutions*, CBK, Nairobi.

Chance, D.M., 2004, *An introduction to derivatives and risk management*, 6th edn., Thomson, Singapore.

Comptroller's Handbook, 2008, *Country risk management*, Comptroller of The Currency USA, Washington, DC.

Flynn, S.J.A., 2001, 'The records continuum model in context and its implications for archival practice', *Journal of the Society of Archivists* 22(1), 79–93. http://dx.doi.org/10.1080/00379810120037522

Glyn, H.A., 2004, 'Defining risk', *Financial Analysts Journal* 60(6), 19–25. http://dx.doi.org/10.2469/faj.v60.n6.2669

Gorrod, M., 2004, *Risk management system: Technology trends, finance and capital markets*, Palgrave Macmillan, Basingstoke.

Government of Canada, 2000, *Integrated risk management model*, viewed 20 September 2008, from http://www.tbs-sct.gc.ca

Graham, A., 2004, *Integrated risk management: Implementation guide*, viewed 02 October 2008, from http://post.queensu.ca/~grahama/

Gup, B. & Kolari, J., 2005, *Commercial banking: The management of risk*, 3rd edn., John Wiley & Sons, New York.

Hansson, S.O., 2007, 'Risk' in N.Z. Edward (ed.), *The stanford encyclopaedia of philosophy*, Stanford University, Stanford, viewed 20 September 2008, from http://plato.stanford.edu/entries/risk/

Hoque, Z., 2006, *Triangulation. What is it, when to use it and how to use it?*, viewed 25 September 2008, from http://72.14.205.104

International Records Management Trust, 2009, *Understanding the context of electronic records management*, pp. 7–20, IRMT, London.

International Standards Organisation, 2001, *ISO 15489-1:2001 Information and documentation: Records management standard*, ISO, Geneva.

Ioannis, V.K., 2008, 'Trust and risk communication in setting Internet banking security goals', *Risk Management Journal* 10(1), 56–75. http://dx.doi.org/10.1057/palgrave.rm.8250035

Kemoni, H., Ngulube, P. & Stilwell, C., 2007, 'Public records and archives as tools for good governance: Reflections within the recordkeeping scholarly and practitioner communities', *ESARBICA Journal* 26, 3–18.

Lore, M. & Borodovsky, L., (eds.), 2002, *The professional's handbook of financial risk management*, Butterworth-Heinemann, Oxford.

Makhura, M., 2008, 'The importance of records management in audit: South African experience', paper presented at the 16th ICA congress in Kuala Lumpur, 21–27th July.

Mwisho, A.M., 2001, 'Basic lending conditions and procedures in commercial banks', *The Accountant* 13(3), 16–49.

Nangomasha, C.T., 2009, 'Managing public sector records in Namibia: A proposed model', *Information Development* 25(2), 112–126. http://dx.doi.org/10.1177/0266666909104712

Ngulube, P., 2001, 'Guidelines and standards for records management education and training: A model for Anglophone Africa', *Records Management Journal* 11(3), 155–173. http://dx.doi.org/10.1108/EUM0000000007273

Njuguna, N., 2007, 'Implementation of Basel II risk management framework within banks and the prevention of financial crime', address by Prof. Njuguna, Governor, Central Bank of Kenya, Nairobi, 20 August.

Nyaoma, G.A., 2005, 'Risk management in banks', press statement issued on behalf of Central Bank of Kenya, Nairobi.

Richard, E., 2006, *Credit risk management policy & strategies: The case of a commercial bank in Tanzania*, BA Publications, Johannesburg.

Roper, M. & Millar, L. (eds.), 1999, *Managing public sector record*, pp. 5–20, IRMT, London.

Sampson, K.L., 2003, *Value added records management: Protecting corporate assets, reducing business risks*, 2 edn., Greenwood Publishing Group, Westport.

Shepherd, E. & Yeo, G., 2003, *Managing records: A handbook of principles and practices*, Facet Publishing, London. http://dx.doi.org/10.1108/09565690610654747

Shepherd, E. & Yeo, G., 2006, 'Why are records in the public sector organisational assets?', *Records Management Journal* 16(1), 9–12.

Stephens, R.B. (1995). 'Ten business reasons for records management in information and records management: Document based information systems', United States Environmental Protection Agency, viewed 20 December 2008, from http://www.epa.gov/records/what/quest1.htm

University of Technology Sydney, 2008, *Risk management programmes for records*, viewed 14 September 2008, from http://www.records.uts.edu.au

Upward, F., 2000, 'Modeling the continuum as a paradigm shift in recordkeeping and archiving processes and beyond – A personal reflection', *Records Management Journal* 10(3), 115–139. http://dx.doi.org/10.1108/EUM0000000007259

Williams, C., 2007, 'The research imperative and responsible recordkeeping professionals', *Records Management Journal* 17(3), 150–156. http://dx.doi.org/10.1108/09565690710833053

Xiaomi, A., 2001, 'A Chinese view of records continuum methodology and implications for managing electronic records', presentation at the International Symposium on OA System and Management of Archival Electronic Records: Theory and Practice, Handzhou, South East China, 11–13 November, viewed 20 August 2008, from http://www.caldeson.com/RIMOS/xannum.html

5

Towards a universal competitive intelligence process model

Authors:
Rene Pellissier[1]
Tshilidzi E. Nenzhelele[2]

Affiliations:
[1]School of Business Leadership, University of South Africa, Pretoria, South Africa

[2]Department of Business Management, University of South Africa, Pretoria, South Africa

Correspondence to:
Rene Pellissier

Email:
pellir@unisa.ac.za

Postal address:
PO Box 392, Pretoria 0003, South Africa

Background: Competitive intelligence (CI) provides actionable intelligence, which provides a competitive edge in enterprises. However, without proper process, it is difficult to develop actionable intelligence. There are disagreements about how the CI process should be structured. For CI professionals to focus on producing actionable intelligence, and to do so with simplicity, they need a common CI process model.

Objectives: The purpose of this research is to review the current literature on CI, to look at the aims of identifying and analysing CI process models, and finally to propose a universal CI process model.

Method: The study was qualitative in nature and content analysis was conducted on all identified sources establishing and analysing CI process models. To identify relevant literature, academic databases and search engines were used. Moreover, a review of references in related studies led to more relevant sources, the references of which were further reviewed and analysed. To ensure reliability, only peer-reviewed articles were used.

Results: The findings reveal that the majority of scholars view the CI process as a cycle of interrelated phases. The output of one phase is the input of the next phase.

Conclusion: The CI process is a cycle of interrelated phases. The output of one phase is the input of the next phase. These phases are influenced by the following factors: decision makers, process and structure, organisational awareness and culture, and feedback.

Introduction

In a highly competitive business environment, enterprises must be aware of what their competitors are doing (Weiss & Naylor 2010). Competitive intelligence (CI) has been described as a strategic tool that helps enterprises to be aware of their competitors' behaviours and plans (Haataja 2011). Competitive intelligence produces actionable intelligence that, in turn, helps enterprises in decision-making (Heppes & Du Toit 2009). Moreover, CI provides a competitive advantage to enterprises (Brody 2008). Competitive intelligence also helps enterprises to improve their performance (Shi 2011). Competitive intelligence evolved from economics, marketing, military theory, information science and strategic management (Muller 2006). It is a profession following a code of ethics developed by the Society of Strategic and Competitive Intelligence Professionals (SCIP). The code of ethics ensures that CI is conducted ethically and legally. Competitive intelligence is a process that consists of a number of steps.

Whilst the objectives of CI are clear, there is some confusion about how the CI process should be structured (Nasri 2011). Some scholars view CI process as a cycle, whilst others view it as a linear process (Bartes 2012; Cucui 2009). Some scholars outline many stages in the CI process, whilst others identify fewer stages (Nasri 2011). As Du Toit and Muller (2004), Venter and Tustin (2009), Nasri (2011) and Bartes (2012) caution, without a proper process and structure, it is difficult to develop CI. Hence, there is a need for a common understanding of the CI process.

Evolution of competitive intelligence

Competitive intelligence evolved from economics, marketing, military theory, information science and strategic management (Muller 2006). Competitive intelligence was characterised as being more focused on gathering information than on analysis (Cucui 2009). Moreover, there was very a weak connection between CI and the decision-making process. The focus was on developing information-gathering skills in CI professionals. According to Cucui (2009), analysis of the gathered information began in the 1980s. During this period, SCIP was established with the aim to ensure that CI is conducted in a professional manner. In the late 1980s, the connection between CI and decision-making was made. During this period, the competitive intelligence review was established (Cucui 2009). Since then, many universities offer courses in CI across the world.

Enterprises have CI units that analyse collected information professionally. According to Muller (2005), CI took root in South Africa in the mid-1990s and early 2000s. Competitive intelligence is evolving in complexity and importance to maintain pace with rapid business development (Heppes & Du Toit 2009). Since the end of the Cold War, CI – once widely used in the military environment – has rapidly infiltrated into business competition (Deng & Luo 2010).

Definition of competitive intelligence

There are many definitions of CI in the literature (Oubrich 2011; Weiss & Naylor 2010). Most of the definitions that have emerged over the years differ only in terms of semantics and emphasis (Fleisher & Wright 2009). Wright, Eid and Fleisher (2009) support this, stating that there has been tweaking of previous definitions, leaving out one word, adding another, but rarely anything more substantial. Brody (2008) concludes that, because CI is a process that is set in situations that are dynamic and in which the players are moving forward in a constantly changing business environment, the variety of definitions may be a reflection of that process of constant change. Fleisher and Wright (2009) argue that CI practitioners rarely have time for definitions, but are keen to understand how they can do their job better. For the purposes of this study, Brody's (2008) definition will be adopted because it is broad and simple. Brody (2008) defines CI as:

> the process by which enterprises gather actionable information about competitors and the competitive environment and, ideally, apply it to their planning processes and decision-making in order to improve their enterprise's performance. (n.p.)

Competitive intelligence objectives

The main objectives of competitive intelligence are to provide help in decision-making and to provide an enterprise with a competitive advantage. Competitive intelligence is a way to alert enterprises constantly of changes in the competitive environment (Muller 2005). Researchers have identified the following objectives of CI (Cucui 2009; Peltoniemi & Vuori 2008; Wright et al. 2009): enhancing the enterprise's competitiveness; predicting, with a high level of trust, the business environment's evolutions, competitors' actions, customers' requirements and even influences generated by political change; providing better support for the strategic decision-making process; revealing opportunities and threats by surveying weak signals and early warnings; processing and combining data and information to produce knowledge and insights about competitors; satisfying the information needs of decision-making and problem-solving, and decreasing reaction time; and devising marketing strategies.

Competitive intelligence process

Competitive intelligence is a process consisting of phases that are linked (Nasri 2011). The output of each phase is the input to the next phase (Bartes 2012). The overall output of the CI process is an input to the decision-making process (Wright et al. 2009). Most CI definitions clearly reveal that it is a process that produces actionable intelligence (Brody

2008). According to Du Toit and Muller (2004), without a proper intelligence process and structure, it is difficult to develop intelligence. Also, without the visible support of and utilisation of intelligence by top management, the process will be flawed (Nasri 2011). Put differently, the overriding influence on successful CI process is the existence of a management support, culture and structure that encourages and develops CI activities in companies (Nasri 2011). Therefore, management must plan, support and implement a CI process.

Given the confusion in the field of CI on how the CI process should be structured, some agreement within the CI field on this should be reached (Wright & Calof 2006). A study conducted by Carr (2003) discovered that CI experts describe the CI process as a cycle, as a linear process, using four-point models, as a scientific method and as a pyramid. Some scholars outline many phases in the CI process, whilst others identify fewer phases. Some scholars name the same phases differently, thereby adding to the confusion in the field of CI.

The following CI process models were established in the literature.

According to Calof (1998), the CI process is made up of obtaining a CI request, collecting information, analysing and synthesising information, communicating intelligence, and managing the CI process. This CI process model does not incorporate the capturing and storing of collected information.

Calof and Skinner (1998) view the CI process as a cycle made up of four phases: planning and direction, data collection, information analysis and intelligence dissemination. These two scholars term the information collection phase 'data collection' and omit information capturing and storing. Their CI process model does not incorporate influential factors such as decision-makers, feedback, organisational awareness and culture, and process and structure.

Kahaner (1998) also defines CI as a cycle process with four phases: planning and direction, data and information collection, analysis and dissemination of intelligence to those who will use it. This CI process model omits information capturing and storage and terms the information collection phase 'data and information collection' phase. Information consists of organised data. Therefore, in information there is data; there is no need to use both terms together in the name of this phase.

Melo and Medeiros (2007) add evaluation to Kahaner's (1998) CI process cycle to make it a five-phase cycle composed of planning, collection, analysis, dissemination and evaluation. These scholars also omitted information capturing and storage and the influential factors.

Cruywagen (2002) views the CI process as a cycle with a number of distinguishable phases, including planning and direction, collection, evaluation, analysis and dissemination.

Although Cruywagen (2002) incorporated feedback, the other influential factors such as decision-makers, organisational awareness and culture and process and structure are omitted. The information capturing and storage phase is also omitted.

Dishman and Calof (2002) establish six phases of the CI process: planning and focus, collection, analysis, communication, process or structure and organisational awareness and culture. Although this is an improved CI process model, it omits information capturing and storage and feedback. According to Viviers, Saayman and Muller (2005), the CI process is a cycle made up of planning and focus; collection; analysis; communication; and awareness, culture, process and structure. This CI process model also omits information capturing and storage and feedback.

Botha and Boon (2008) view the CI process as a cycle consisting of seven phases: intelligence needs and determining key intelligence topics; planning and direction; collection; information processing; analysis; dissemination; and intelligence users and decision-makers. This model incorporates influential factors as phases and omits feedback. However, unlike other scholars, they recognise the need to capture and store collected information.

Wright and Calof (2006) identify four phases of the CI process: planning or focus, collection, analysis and communication. They also indicate that process, structure, culture, awareness and attitude are undeniable influences of CI process success. Their CI process model omits information capturing and storage, decision-makers and feedback.

According to SCIP (2007), CI is a cycle with five phases: planning and direction, collection activities, analysis, dissemination and feedback. This CI process model omits information capturing and storage and other influential factors such as decision-makers, organisational awareness and culture, and process and structure.

Bose (2008) views the CI process as a cycle made up of planning and direction, collection, analysis, dissemination and feedback. This CI process model omits information capturing and storage and other influential factors such as decision-makers, organisational awareness and culture and process and structure.

According to Sawka and Hohhof (2008), the CI process is a cycle made up of the following interrelated phases: planning and direction, collection, analysis and production and dissemination. These scholars term the information analysis phase 'analysis and production'. This means that intelligence is produced in the analysing phase. Their CI process model omits information capturing and storage and all the influential factors previously mentioned.

According to Cucui (2009), CI is a process consisting of the following steps: monitoring business environment, gathering, analysing and filtering and disseminating intelligence. This

model differs from the rest of the scholars' models because of the phase names. The planning and direction phase is called 'monitoring business environment'. The information collection phase is called 'gathering' and the intelligence dissemination phase is called 'filtering and dissemination'. This CI process model also omits information capturing and storage and other influential factors mentioned.

Competitive intelligence, according to Shi, Mou and Wan (2009), is a cycle process made up of defining CI demand, gathering information, processing information and providing final services to meet the demand. Just like Cucui (2009), Shi et al. (2009) name their CI process phases differently. They omit information capturing and storage and all the influential factors.

According to Haddadi, Dousset and Berrada (2010), CI is a cycle process made up of understanding the need, researching and gathering information, processing information and disseminating information. These scholars use different phase names and omit information capturing and storage. They also omit all the influential factors and call the information analysis phase 'processing information'.

Muller (2002) identifies six phases in the CI process: planning and focus; collection; analysis; communication; process and structure and organisational awareness and culture. Strauss and Du Toit (2010) propose a seventh phase: 'skills development'. According to them, training clears up misconceptions regarding CI, improves communication, encourages easy transfer of expertise and skills and fosters a mindset of awareness within the enterprise. They conclude that the CI process is not complete without skills development. Their CI process model omits information capturing and storage and feedback.

The CI process, according to McGonagle and Vella (2012), is divided into five phases, each linked to the other by a feedback loop. These phases are: establishing the CI needs, collecting the raw data, evaluating and analysing the raw data, communicating the finished intelligence and taking action. Unlike most scholars, McGonagle and Vella's (2012) CI process model emphasises collection and analysis of data rather than information. Their model introduces the taking action phase, in which decision makers make decisions. They omit other influential factors such as organisational awareness and culture and process and structure.

Research results

From the CI process models discussed above, the following common and unique phases and characteristics were identified:

Cycle

The CI process is presented in a cycle of phases. The reason behind the use of a cycle is that the CI process never stops, but is continuous. Also, the cycle is used to indicate that the phases are interrelated. Therefore, the output of one phase is the input of the next phase. All scholars in this study represent the CI process as a cycle.

Establishing competitive intelligence needs

Some scholars identify this as the first phase of the CI process. Different names are given to this phase, such as 'obtaining CI request', 'intelligence needs and determine key intelligence topics', 'understanding the need', and 'defining CI demand'. According to Botha and Boon (2008), this phase involves identification of intelligence needs of decision-makers and narrowing these intelligence needs down to key intelligence topics (KITs). The KITs are those topics identified as being of greatest significance to an organisation's senior executives, providing purpose and direction for CI operations (Bose 2008). In this phase, the CI director identifies and prioritises both senior management and organisational key intelligence needs. Moreover, what the CI unit should research and to whom this intelligence should be delivered are determined in this phase (Strauss & Du Toit 2010).

Planning and direction

Some scholars call this phase 'planning and focus'. In some scholars' CI process models, this is the first phase, whilst it is the second in others. This phase defines the decision-makers' intelligence requirements. It requires knowledge of KITs. The KITs must be clear and not ambiguous. The intelligence requirements must be transformed into information requirements in order to determine if the required information already exists or not. The steps to acquire the required information must be clearly outlined (Nasri 2011).

Information collection

To some scholars, this is the second phase of the CI process, whilst it is the third phase in other models. This phase is referred to in different ways, such as 'data and information collection', 'collecting raw data', 'researching and gathering information', 'data collection', 'collection', 'gathering' and 'monitoring business environment'. The emphasis is on collection of publicly available information (Botha & Boon 2008). This is to ensure compliance with the code of ethics developed by SCIP. The information to be collected must be relevant to the KITs. Some common primary sources include government agencies, employees, suppliers, customers and conferences. Some common secondary sources include magazines, TV, radio, analyst reports and professional reports. Information can be collected through Internet searches, surveys, interviews, observation, media scanning and networking (Nasri 2011).

Information processing

This phase organises, systematises, implements and maintains a mechanism of capturing and storing information. Collected information is sorted and stored in a database. Information stored in electronic format is easy to analyse and disseminate (Nikolaos & Evangelia 2012).

Information analysis

Some scholars call this phase 'analysis' or 'analysis and production'. This is the core phase of the CI process (Viviers et al. 2005) and is the most challenging (Nikolaos & Evangelia 2012). Processed information must be interpreted and analysed to produce actionable intelligence. The analysis methods mostly used include PEST (political or legal, economical, socio-cultural and technological) analysis, scenario analysis, Porter's five forces model, SWOT (strengths, weaknesses, opportunities and threats) analysis and competitor profiling (Viviers et al. 2005).

Intelligence dissemination

Actionable intelligence is disseminated to decision-makers in this phase. Some scholars call this phase 'communication', 'intelligence dissemination', 'disseminating information', 'communicating the finished intelligence' and 'filtering and disseminating intelligence'. The finished product, which is actionable intelligence, is communicated back to the decision-makers in a format that is easily understood. The communication is in the form of a report, dashboard or meeting. Face-to-face, email and intranet communication are also used (Nasri 2011).

Taking action

This phase is also called 'intelligence users and decision-makers'. In this phase, the decision-makers use actionable intelligence to make decisions (McGonagle & Vella 2012). This phase leads to the identification of new intelligence needs by users of intelligence and decision-makers and the intelligence cycle or process is activated again (Botha & Boon 2008).

Skills development

In this phase, CI professionals are trained on how to conduct their different responsibilities. They get training on interpreting KITs, information collection, information analysis and intelligence dissemination.

Process and structure

Competitive intelligence requires appropriate policies and procedures, and a formal or informal infrastructure so that employees can contribute effectively to the CI system as well as gain benefits from the process. A CI code of ethics must also be incorporated in CI policies. The CI process depends on gathering people and resources from a range of internal units and encouraging employees to contribute to using and participating in the CI activities (Kahaner 1998).

Organisational awareness and culture

For CI to flourish in a company and for the discipline to be implemented and used optimally, there has to be an appropriate organisational awareness of CI and a culture of competitiveness. It is important to create the right environment for CI. It requires continuous staff training with emphasis on the importance of CI. Without proper awareness and attitudes that favour both intelligence and information sharing, it is difficult to develop intelligence within an organisation (Viviers *et al.* 2005).

Feedback

Feedback about the CI process is provided in this phase. This phase is also called 'evaluation'. This phase outlines the feedback from decision-makers and CI professionals (Frion 2009). Feedback and updates from CI professionals allow for midcourse adjustments and new issues to surface (Prescott 1999). The feedback provides opportunities for revisions of the original intelligence request as well as constructive feedback on the deliverable of previous requests facilitating a continuous improvement atmosphere (Nasri 2011). The CI process is improved through feedback (Oubrich 2011).

The frequencies of the phases and characteristics in CI process models are shown in Table 1 below. The table indicates that all scholars in this study view the CI process as a cycle made up of interrelated phases. Also, all scholars in this study have information collection and intelligence dissemination phases in their CI process models. The majority of the scholars have information analysis (89%) and planning and direction (78%) phases in their CI process models. A lesser percentage of the scholars (28%) have the following phases in their CI process models: establishing CI needs; process and structure; organisational awareness and culture and feedback. Only 17% of scholars had an 'information processing' phase in their CI process model. Also, only 11% of scholars had a 'taking action' phase, whereas only 6% of scholars had a skills development phase in their CI process model.

The extensive review of the literature and analysis of the above frequencies led to the formulation of a universal CI process model, as shown in Figure 1. The purposes of each phase of the CI process were thoroughly reviewed and analysed. This CI process model is a cycle because 100% of the scholars in the literature review consider the CI process to be a cycle. Phases that were called by different names, but which have the same purpose, were merged; for example, the planning and direction phase and the establishing CI needs phase were merged because they serve the same purpose. The phase is now called 'planning and direction' and defines the decision-makers' intelligence requirements.

TABLE 1: Characteristics and phases of competitive intelligence process models.

Characteristics	*f*	%
Cycle	18	100
Establishing CI needs	5	28
Planning and direction	14	78
Information collection	18	100
Information processing	3	17
Information analysis	16	89
Intelligence dissemination	18	100
Taking action	2	11
Skills development	1	6
Process and structure	5	28
Organisational awareness and culture	5	28
Feedback	5	28

f, frequency.

The proposed CI process model has an 'information collection' phase because all CI scholars in the above analysis deemed it necessary. During the information collection phase, information relevant to the KITs is collected legally and ethically from different sources. Most scholars made the assumption that collected information will automatically be sorted, captured and stored. As a result, only a few scholars had information processing as a phase in their CI process models. Although some indicated that information processing involves sorting, capturing and storing collected information, some mistook 'information processing' for 'information analysis'. Without information sorting, capturing and storing, there is a gap in the CI process. Therefore, the proposed CI process model has separated the information processing and information analysis phases. To clear up the confusion, the phase of information processing is called 'information sorting, capturing and sorting' in the proposed CI process model, and is self-explanatory.

Almost all the previous scholars had 'information analysis' as a phase in their CI process models. As a result, the proposed CI process model incorporates an information analysis phase. In this phase, stored information is analysed to produce actionable intelligence. Because all previous scholars incorporated intelligence dissemination in their CI process model, the proposed CI process model has a 'intelligence dissemination' phase. During this phase actionable intelligence is disseminated to decision-makers. Decision-makers use the actionable intelligence to make business decisions. Therefore, there is no need to have a separate 'taking action' phase.

'Skills development' is an inherent part of 'organisational awareness and culture', so the proposed CI process model does not have this as a separate phase. The proposed CI process model is a cycle with influential factors affecting it. Most scholars consider decision-makers; process and structure; organisational awareness and culture and feedback to influence the CI process. CI professionals must consider these factors throughout the CI process. Decision-makers must be contacted in case their inputs are required during the CI process. There must be feedback throughout the CI process phases. All organisational processes and structure that might affect the CI process must be considered throughout the CI process. There has to be an appropriate organisational awareness of CI and a culture of competitiveness. The smaller circle dips into the larger cycle to indicate that all phases are affected by the influential factors. The proposed CI process model is all encompassing, considering the extensive review of literature.

Discussion

There are many CI process models described in the literature. Most of these models differ from one another because scholars use different names for the same phases. Some scholars just add or subtract phases. This has led to a confused CI field.

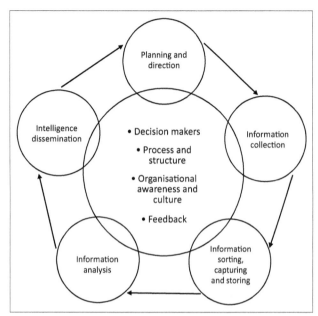

FIGURE 1: Competitive intelligence process model.

There was therefore a need to propose a universal CI process model.

The findings of this study reveal that all scholars view the CI process as a cycle of interrelated phases. This means that the output of one phase is the input of the next phase. Also, it means that the CI process is continuous and does not stop. All scholars have an information collection phase in their CI process models, as well as an intelligence dissemination phase. They realise that intelligence is used by decision-makers.

The findings reveal that the majority of scholars have information analysis in their CI process models. They acknowledge that information analysis is the core phase of the CI process. They realise that information is useless when it is not interpreted. However, there was some confusion between the information analysis and information processing phases. Those that had one of these phases did not necessarily have the other. Although some indicated that information processing involves the sorting, capturing and storing of collected information, some mistook information process for information analysis. Without information sorting, capturing and storing, there is a gap in the CI process.

Also, the majority of the scholars have a planning and direction phase in their CI process models. They realise that planning is important in a successful CI process. However, there was some confusion between the planning and direction phase and the establishing of CI needs phases. Those scholars who had a planning and direction phase indicated that establishing CI needs is done in this phase. Those who had the establishing CI needs phase indicated that this phase involves the establishment of CI needs and hardly mentioned anything about planning and direction.

The findings also reveal that fewer scholars incorporated process and structure, organisational awareness and culture and feedback into their CI process models. Perhaps this is because these are crucial influences on the CI process. Also, the findings show that feedback should be conducted throughout the CI process and not only at the end of the process. The findings also reveal that fewer scholars had taking action and skills development phases. Perhaps this is because there is an assumption that once the intelligence lands in the hands of decision-makers they will make decisions.

Conclusion

Without a proper process, it is difficult to develop CI (Du Toit & Muller 2004). There is disagreement in the CI field with regard to the CI process. Different names have been given to the phases in the CI process. There is also disagreement as to the number of phases in the various models. According to the model proposed here, establishing CI needs, planning and direction take place in the phase called 'planning and direction'. Influential factors, such as process and structure; organisational awareness and culture; feedback and decision-makers influence all the phases of the CI process. The proposed CI process model incorporates an information sorting, capturing and storing phase. Most scholars did not highlight the sorting, capturing and storing of information phase; an assumption was merely made that collected information would be sorted, captured and stored somehow. The suggested name for this phase, 'information sorting, capturing and storing', is intended to eliminate confusion between the information processing and the information analysis phases.

The proposed CI process model is a cycle, indicating that the process is continuous. It also indicates that the output of one phase is the input for the next stage. Decision-makers take actions after receiving actionable intelligence. Therefore, there is no need to have a separate phase called 'taking action'. Also, because skills development is a part of organisational awareness and culture, there is no need to have a separate 'skills development' item. The proposed CI process model above is comprehensive. This implies that implementing the proposed CI process model will simplify the CI process and ensure that all CI stakeholders will focus on what matters, namely producing actionable intelligence.

Acknowledgement

The authors would like to acknowledge the University of South Africa for the funding and support without which this research would not have been possible.

Competing interest

The authors declare that they have no financial or personal relationship(s) that may have inappropriately influenced them in writing this article.

Authors' contributions

T.E.N. (University of South Africa) initiated this research, conducted the literature review and wrote the analysis and conclusion. R.P. (University of South Africa) led and supervised this project, selected the journal and handled editorial matters.

References

Bartes, F., 2012, 'Increasing the competitiveness of company by competitive intelligence', paper presented at the 7th International Scientific Conference Business and Management, Vilnius, Lithuania, 10–11 May.

Bose, R., 2008, 'Competitive intelligence process and tools for intelligence analysis', Industrial Management & Data Systems 108(4), 510–528. http://dx.doi.org/10.1108/02635570810868362

Botha, D.F. & Boon, J.A., 2008, 'Competitive intelligence in support of strategic training and learning', South African Journal of Information Management 10(3), 1–6.

Brody, R., 2008, 'Issues in defining competitive intelligence: An exploration', Journal of Competitive Intelligence and Management 4(3), 3–16.

Calof, J., 1998, 'Increasing your CIQ – the competitive intelligence edge', The Economic Development Journal of Canada, viewed 13 January 2013, from www.ecdevjournal.com/pubs/1998/art022_98.htm

Calof, J.L. & Skinner, B., 1998, 'Competitive intelligence for government officers: a brave new world', Optimum 28(2), 38–42.

Dishman, P. & Calof, J.L., 2002, The intelligence process: front-end to strategic planning, University of Ottawa, Ottawa.

Carr, M.M., 2003, Super searchers on competitive intelligence, Reva Basch, New Jersey.

Cruywagen, A., 2002, 'Establishing the profile of a successful competitive intelligence practitioner', paper presented at the Competitive Intelligence World 2002 Conference, The Conference Park, Midrand, Johannesburg, South Africa, 20 November.

Cucui, A.P.G., 2009, 'A framework for enhancing competitive intelligence capabilities using decision support system based on web mining techniques', International Journal of Computers, Communications and Control 4(4), 326–334.

Deng, Z. & Luo, L., 2010, 'An exploratory discussion of new ways for competitive intelligence on Web2.0', International Federation for Information Processing 252(1), 597–604.

Du Toit, A. & Muller, M.L., 2004, 'Organizational structure of competitive intelligence activities: a South African case study', South African Journal of Information Management 6(3), Art. #308, 13 pages.

Fleisher, C.S. & Wright, S., 2009, 'Examining differences in competitive intelligence practice: China, Japan, and the West', Thunderbird International Business Review 51(3), 249–261. http://dx.doi.org/10.1002/tie.20263

Frion, P., 2009, 'What information behaviour can offer to competitive intelligence', paper presented at the International Symposium Models, Methods, Engineering of Competitive intelligence, Beaulieu-sur-Mer, France, 25–26 November.

Haataja, J., 2011, Social media as a source of competitive intelligence in a pharmaceutical corporation, published master's thesis, Degree Programme in Industrial Engineering and Management, School of Science, Aalto University, Helsinki.

Haddadi, A.E., Dousset, B. & Berrada, I., 2010, Xplor Every Where – The Competitive Intelligence System for Mobile, viewed 9 July 2013, from http://ieeexplore.ieee.org/stamp/stamp.jsp?tp=&arnumber=5945635

Heppes, D. & Du Toit, A., 2009, 'Level of maturity of the competitive intelligence function: Case study of a retail bank in South Africa', Aslib Proceedings: New Information Perspectives 61(1), 48–66.

Kahaner, L., 1998, Competitive intelligence: how to gather, analyze and use information to move your business to the top, Touchstone, New York.

McGonagle, J.J. & Vella, C.M., 2012, Proactive Intelligence, Springer-Verlag, London. http://dx.doi.org/10.1007/978-1-4471-2742-0

Melo, M.A.N & Medeiros, D.D., 2007, 'A model for analyzing the competitive strategy of health plan insurers using a system of competitive intelligence', The TQM Magazine 19(3), 206–216. http://dx.doi.org/10.1108/09544780710745630

Muller, M.L., 2002, Managing competitive intelligence, Knowres Publishing, Johannesburg.

Muller, M.L., 2005, 'Beyond competitive intelligence-innovation and competitive strategy', South African Journal of Information Management 7(1), Art. #244, 6 pages.

Muller, M.L., 2006, 'Parts of competitive intelligence: competitor intelligence', South African Journal of Information Management 8(1), Art. #209, 5 pages.

Nasri, W., 2011, 'Competitive intelligence in Tunisian companies', Journal of Enterprise Information Management 24(1), 53–67. http://dx.doi.org/10.1108/17410391111097429

Nikolaos, T. & Evangelia, F., 2012, 'Competitive intelligence: concept, context and a case of its application', Science Journal of Business Management 2012(2), 1–15.

Oubrich, M., 2011, 'Competitive Intelligence and Knowledge Creation – Outward insights from an empirical survey', Journal of Intelligence Studies in Business 1(1), 97–106.

Peltoniemi, M. & Vuori, E., 2008, 'Competitive intelligence as a driver of co-evolution within an enterprise population', Journal of Competitive Intelligence and Management 4(3), 50–62.

Prescott, J.E., 1999, 'The evolution of competitive intelligence: designing a process for action', APMP, 37–52.

Sawka, K. & Hohhof, B., 2008, Starting a competitive intelligent function, Competitive Intelligence Foundation, Alexandria.

Shi, Z., 2011, 'Foundations of intelligence science', International Journal of Intelligence Science 1(1), 8–16. http://dx.doi.org/10.4236/ijis.2011.11002

Shi, G., Mou, X. & Wan, X., 2009, 'Designing a network acquisition system of competitive intelligence', paper presented at the 8th IEEE International Conference on Dependable, Autonomic and Secure Computing, Chengdu, China, 12–14th December. http://dx.doi.org/10.1109/DASC.2009.61

Strauss, A.C. & Du Toit, A.S.A., 2010, 'Competitive intelligence skills needed to enhance South Africa's competitiveness', Aslib Proceedings: New Information Perspective 62(3), 302–320. http://dx.doi.org/10.1108/00012531011046925

Strategic and Competitive Intelligence Professionals (SCIP), Strategic and Competitive Intelligence Professionals, viewed 15 August 2012, from http://www.scip.org/

Venter, P. & Tustin, D., 2009, 'The availability and use of competitive and business intelligence in South African business organisations', Southern African Business Review 13(2), 88–117.

Viviers, W., Saayman, A. & Muller, M., 2005, 'Enhancing a competitive intelligence culture in South Africa', International Journal of Social Economics 32(7), 576–589. http://dx.doi.org/10.1108/03068290510601117

Weiss, A. & Naylor, E., 2010, 'Competitive Intelligence: How Independent Information Professionals', American Society for Information Science and Technology 37(1), 30–34. http://dx.doi.org/10.1002/bult.2010.1720370114

Wright, S. & Calof, J.L., 2006, 'The quest for competitive, business and marketing intelligence: a country comparison of current practices', European Journal of Marketing 40(5/6), 453–465. http://dx.doi.org/10.1108/03090560610657787

Wright, S., Eid, E.R. & Fleisher, C.S., 2009, 'Competitive intelligence in practice: empirical evidence from the UK retail banking sector', Journal of Marketing Management 25(9/10), 941–964. http://dx.doi.org/10.1362/026725709X479318

6

The impact of work experience of small and medium-sized enterprises owners or managers on their competitive intelligence awareness and practices

Authors:
Rene Pellissier[1]
Tshilidzi E. Nenzhelele[1]

Affiliations:
[1]Department of Business Management, University of South Africa, South Africa

Correspondence to:
Rene Pellissier

Email:
pellir@unisa.ac.za

Postal address:
PO Box 392, Pretoria 0003, South Africa

Background: Information technology has assisted in globalisation, which then assisted in making international trade easier. Consequently, businesses no longer compete with local competitors only but also with international ones, leading to intense competition in all business sectors. Businesses will hardly practice what they are not aware of and therefore needs to know about their competitive landscape. Competitive intelligence (CI) gathers information from both the internal and external business environments, and analyses these for use by decision makers. Whilst awareness of the importance of CI is wide, it is not practiced optimally, making the need for creating awareness of the benefits of CI important.

Objectives: The objective of this research was to establish the influence of owners' and managers' working experience of CI practice and awareness in the small and medium-sized enterprises (SMEs) environment.

Method: This research was quantitative in nature and a questionnaire was used to collect data from SMEs owners and managers in The City of Tshwane Metropolitan Municipality.

Results: This research indicates that SMEs in the study are aware of CI through education and training. Moreover, the study reveals that the working experience of owners and managers has a great influence on awareness and practice of CI and one should implement training programmes in this domain to assist with building competitive advantage.

Conclusion: Small and medium-sized enterprises owners or managers' years of working experience has a greater influence on awareness and practice of CI. Put differently, years of working experience is a great predictor of CI awareness and practice.

Introduction

Enterprises are faced with an increasingly competitive environment in which it is difficult to maintain a sustained competitive advantage (Shih, Liu & Hsu 2010). Guarda, Augusto and Silva (2012) state that competitive advantage can be understood as seeking unique opportunities that will give the enterprise a strong competitive position. According to Shih *et al.* (2010), in order to sustain a competitive position, managers should be prepared to respond promptly to changes in customer preferences, competitor strategies and technological advancements. For these reasons, many enterprises – whether public or private, and small or large – initiate their own competitive intelligence (CI) services to inform and prepare managers for changes in the external environment of the enterprise (Taleghani, Rad & Rahmati 2012; Bourret 2012). According to Deng and Luo (2010), CI plays an increasingly important role in the strategic management and decision-making of an enterprise. Muller (2007) indicates that the optimisation of CI by an enterprise requires an awareness and understanding of CI by the management of the enterprise.

The implementation and use of CI by SMEs has not been as well documented as in the case of larger enterprises (Tarraf & Molz, 2006). Smith, Wright and Pickton (2010) reveal that there is a dearth in the literature regarding CI awareness and practices in SMEs. Although CI research on SMEs has been undertaken in countries such as China, France, Turkey, United States of America, Belgium, Canada, Switzerland, Japan, Sweden, Australia and India, it is lacking in South Africa (Smith, Wright & Pickton 2010; Koseoglu *et al.* 2011). The purpose of this research is to establish the effect of the working experience of managers on CII awareness and practices in SMEs.

Small and medium-sized enterprises

The importance of SMEs in creating jobs and economic wealth is globally recognised (Olawale & Garwe 2010). SMEs employ more than 95% of the world's working population and are the main source of employment in developing countries (Abor & Quartey 2010). As a result, governments throughout the world focus on the development of the SME sector to promote economic growth (Olawale & Gware 2010). Olawale and Gware (2010) reveal that in South Africa, SMEs contribute 56% of the employment in the private sector and 36% of the gross domestic product (GDP). However, gaining a competitive advantage presents an enormous challenge for SMEs. Prior (2007) is of the opinion that SMEs have many competitors that offer similar products or services and operate in the same markets and locations. Moreover, SMEs have limited resources. Prior (2007) suggests that CI is the key to SMEs' competitiveness.

Definition of small and medium-sized enterprises

According to the *South African National Small Business Act 102 of 1996*, 'small business' means a separate and distinct business entity (including co-operative enterprises and non-government enterprises) managed by one owner or more which, including its branches or subsidiaries (if any), is predominantly carried on in any sector or subsector of the economy and which can be classified as a micro-enterprise, a very small enterprise, a small enterprise or a medium enterprise.

Classification of small and medium-sized enterprises

The most widely used framework for SMEs in South Africa is set out in the *South African National Small Business Act 102 of 1996*, which defines five categories of enterprises in South Africa. The definition is based on the number of employees (the most common definition) per enterprise size combined with the annual turnover categories and the gross assets (excluding fixed property). The five enterprise categories are as follows:

1. **Survivalist enterprise:** The income generated is less than the minimum income standard or the poverty line. This category is considered pre-entrepreneurial, and includes hawkers, vendors and subsistence farmers. (In practice, survivalist enterprises are often categorised as part of the micro-enterprise sector).
2. **Micro enterprise:** The turnover is less than the VAT registration limit (that is, R150 000 per year). These enterprises usually lack formality in terms of registration. They include, for example, *spaza* shops, minibus taxis and household industries. They employ no more than 5 people.
3. **Very small enterprise:** These are enterprises employing fewer than 10 paid employees, except mining, electricity, manufacturing and construction sectors, in which the figure is 20 employees. These enterprises operate in the formal market and have access to technology.
4. **Small enterprise:** The upper limit is 50 employees. Small enterprises are generally more established than very small enterprises and exhibit more complex business practices.
5. **Medium enterprise:** The maximum number of employees is 100, or 200 for the mining, electricity, manufacturing and construction sectors. These enterprises are often characterised by the decentralisation of power to an additional management layer. (Abor & Quartey 2010)

Competitive intelligence

To better understand CI, one has to know how it is formulated (Bourret 2012). Processed data produces information; processed information produces knowledge; and processed knowledge produces wisdom and intelligence (Bernstein 2011). Data consists of raw facts (Stair & Reynolds 2006). Information is a collection of facts organised in such a way that they have additional value beyond the value of the facts themselves (Stair & Reynolds 2006). Stair and Reynolds (2006) define knowledge as an awareness and understanding of a set of information and ways in which information can be made useful to support a specific task or reach a decision. According to Taleghani *et al.* (2012), knowledge exists in many different forms in organisations. Some of these are tangible, whilst others are more subtle and intangible by nature. Wisdom is the human ability to learn from experience and adapt to changing conditions (Post & Anderson 2003). Intelligence is a comprehensive ability to use one's existing knowledge or experience to adapt new situations or solve new problems (Shi 2011).

Evolution of competitive intelligence

Competitive intelligence is an amalgam of disciplines and evolved from economics, marketing, military theory, information science and strategic management (Juhari & Stephens 2006). According to Muller (2005), CI took root in South Africa in the mid-1990s and early 2000s. Whilst CI is a relatively new management tool, it is evolving in complexity and importance to maintain pace with rapid business development (Heppes & Du Toit 2009). Since the end of the Cold War, CI – once widely used in the military environment – has rapidly infiltrated into business environment (Deng & Luo 2010).

Definition of competitive intelligence

There are numerous definitions for CI in practice and literature, and no single definition is likely to be precise and universally accepted (Fleisher & Wright 2009). Brody (2008) argues that because CI is a process that is set in situations that are dynamic and in which the players are moving forward in a constantly changing business environment, the variety of definitions may be a reflection of the process of change. Brody's definition is adopted for the purpose of this study because it is broader and simpler than most CI definitions in the literature. Brody (2008) defines CI as:

> the process by which enterprises gather actionable information about competitors and the competitive environment and, ideally, apply it to their planning processes and decision-making in order to improve their enterprise's performance. (n.p.)

Competitive intelligence awareness

Competitive intelligence growth depends on the creation of awareness of its benefits and a change in the way that enterprises deal with and view information (Muller 2007). In terms of awareness, one has to address knowledge, understanding, perceptions, etcetera. Smith *et al.* (2010) there is a dearth in the literature regarding the awareness and use of CI in SMEs. According to Muller (2005), the need for creating awareness of the benefits of CI is important. Awareness creation has been done with success in other countries through the cooperation between media advocacy groups, workshops, training enterprises, academic courses, and full support of and participation in CI activities by the government.

Methodology

A survey was undertaken to collect data from SMEs in the City of Tshwane Metropolitan Municipality (CTMM) of Gauteng Province in South Africa. The CTMM is the largest municipality in South Africa. It is the capital city of South Africa. Data was collected from one hundred SMEs from nine locations in the CTMM using a quota sample. A quota sample was undertaken due to time and financial constraints. Locations were sampled in order to cover both urban and rural areas of the CTMM. The sample consisted of 74% urban and 26% rural SMEs in the CTMM. The locations included in the sample were Mabopane; Mamelodi; Soshanguve; Ga-Rankuwa; Eersterust; Atteridgeville; Winterveld; Silverton or Pretoria East; Pretoria CBD and Rosslyn. Data were collected using a questionnaire. Questionnaires were hand-delivered to enterprises that do not have access to e-mail. For the SMEs that had access to e-mail, the questionnaire was sent to them via e-mail. The questionnaire had two sections. The aim of the first section was to collect biography of SMEs. The aim of the second section was establish the awareness and practice of CI by SMEs.

One hundred and fifty questionnaires were distributed to the respondents hoping that at least one hundred would be returned by the cut-off date. Indeed, one hundred usable questionnaires were received by the cut-off date. E-mail and phone calls were used to follow up on distributed questionnaire. This ensured that the required one hundred questionnaires were returned. Therefore the response rate was 66.67%. The internal data reliability was calculated to be 0.806 (Cronbach' Alpha).

Results

Of these one hundred SMEs that participated in the survey, only one respondent (1%) was a sole proprietorship; fourteen respondents (14%) were partnerships; fifty five (55%) were close corporations; and thirty (30%) were companies. These forms of enterprises are defined by Nieman (2006) as follows: *proprietorship:* is an enterprise that has one owner and there is no distinction between the personal estate of the owner and the business estate. *Partnerships:* is an enterprise formed when a minimum of two and a maximum of 20 people conclude an agreement to do business as a partnership. *Close corporation:* is a separate legal entity and is regulated in terms of the *South African Close Corporation Act 69 of 1994.* The CC must be registered in term of this Act in order to attain separate legal entity status. A CC must have at least one member and not more than 10 members. *Companies:* is an association of

people incorporated in terms of the *Companies Act 61 of 1973.* A company can have share capital or can be incorporated not for gain, in which case it will not have share capital. Eleven business sectors or subsectors were identified from the literature. Only two additional industries were added by respondents as others and these are: cleaning industry (1%) and media and marketing (1%). The remainder of the respondents are spread as follows:

- finance and business services (8%)
- catering, accommodation and other trade (19%)
- retail and motor trade and repair services (23%)
- electricity, gas and water (2%)
- community, social and personal services (18%)
- wholesale trade, commercial agents and allied services (5%)
- construction (8%)
- manufacturing (12%).

Of the one hundred SMEs, fifteen (15%) had 21–50 employees, thirty (30%) had 11–20 employees, thirty six (36%) had 6–10 employees and nineteen (19%) had 1–5 employees. Concerning years of business operation, fifty (50%) were operating for 6 or more years, thirty nine (39%) were operating for 3–5 years and only eleven (11%) were in operation for 1–2 years. With regard to annual turnover, two (2%) SMEs were making a turnover between R6 million to R10 million, forty eight (48%) were making a turnover of between R1m and R5m and the rest (50%) were making less than R1m. Pertaining to owner or manager's educational qualification, five scales were identified, grade 8 to grade 10, grade 11 to grade 12, undergraduate diploma or degree, honours degree and masters or doctoral degree. Only five (5%) of the respondents had masters or doctoral degree, twenty one (21%) had honours degree, 47% had undergraduate diploma or degree and twenty seven (27%) had grade 11 or grade 12. Pertaining to owner or manager's years of working experience, only one (1%) of the respondents had less than one year of working experience, four (4%) had 1–2 years of working experience, fifty (50%) had 3–5 years of working experience and 45% had 6 or more years of working experience. Table 1 indicates owner or manager's years of working experience.

To establish SMEs' practice and awareness of CI, a five-point Likert scale ranging from 'strongly disagree' to 'strongly agree' was used. Numbers 1–5 we used with number 1 indicating 'strongly disagree' and number 5 indicating 'strongly agree'. Table 2 shows the different variables used to establish the awareness and practice of CI by SMEs. The aim of **variable 1** was to establish whether the respondents were aware of CI. The mean was calculated as 4.12 and the standard deviation was 0.671. The lower standard deviation indicates that there was less spread of responses to this question. The mean of

TABLE 1: Owner or manager's years of working experience.

Years of working experience	Number of respondents	% of respondents
3–5 years	50	50
6 or more years	45	45
1–2 years	4	4
Less than 1 year	1	1
Total	**100**	**100**

4.12 indicates that nearly all of the respondents indicated that they were aware of CI. **Variable 2** was intended to determine whether the respondents practiced CI in their businesses. The standard deviation of 0.687 reveals that there was less spread of responses to the question. Moreover, it indicates that more respondents concurred with the mean of 4.45. The mean reveals that the majority of the respondents agreed that they practice CI in their enterprises. **Variable 3** was designed to determine whether the respondents had a formalised CI function. The higher standard deviation of 1.143 indicates that there was more spread of responses to this variable. Also, it points out that fewer respondents concurred with the mean. The mean of 2.16 indicates that most of the respondents disagreed with the statement. This means that most of the respondents did not have a formalised CI function. The reason behind **variable 4** was to ascertain whether the respondents had a formalised CI process. The slightly higher standard deviation of 1.078 indicates that there was more spread of responses to this question. Moreover, it reveals that fewer respondents concurred with the mean. The mean of 2.01 indicates that most of the respondents disagreed with the statement, which means that they did not have a formalised CI process. The purpose of **variable 5** was to ascertain whether the respondents hired people or other businesses to collect information on their behalf. The mean and standard deviation were 3.10 and 1.202 respectively. The high standard deviation indicates that there was more spread of responses to this question. The mean of 3.10 signifies that more respondents hired people or other businesses to collect information on their behalf. **Variable 6** was intended to establish whether the respondents had a computerised CI system. The high standard deviation of 2.436 indicates that there was more spread of responses to this variable. The mean of 1.84 indicates that more respondents strongly disagreed with the statement. This means that most of the respondents did not have a computerised CI system.

The following strong positive linear correlations were established between variables in Table 3 and owners or managers years of working experience:

Pearson's coefficient of linear correlation (r) for variables 1 and owners or managers years of working experience was 0.746. Thus, there was a strong positive linear association between these two variables. The cross-tabulation (see Table 2) shows that all the respondents (100%) with less than 1 year, three out of four (75%) respondents with 1–2 years, 44 out of 50 (88%) respondents with 3–5 years, and 40 out of 45 (88.89%) respondents with 6 or more years of working experience were aware of CI. Thus, owners or managers with more years of working experience were to a larger extent aware of CI than those with fewer years of working experience.

Variable 2 and owners or managers years of working experience had a very strong positive linear association. Pearson's r for this variable was 0.953. The cross-tabulation (see Table 4 below) reveals that almost all the respondents with any number of years of working experience agree that they practiced CI. Thus, almost all the enterprises were

practicing CI regardless of the owner or manager's years of working experience.

Variable 4 had very strong positive linear association with owners or managers years of working experience. Pearson's r for this correlation was 0.926. The cross-tabulation (see Table 5 below) shows that all the respondent (100%) with less than 1 year, two out of four (50%) respondents with 1–2 years, 38 out of 50 (76%) respondents with 3–5 years and 33 out of 45 (73.33%) respondents with 6 or more years of working experience did not have a formalised CI process. Thus, most of the owners or managers with 3–5 years did not have a formalised CI process.

Pearson's r for variable 5 and owners or managers years of working experience was 0.803. Thus, there was a very strong positive linear association between these variables.

TABLE 2: Competitive intelligence awareness and practice variables.

Variable number	Variables for establishment of CI awareness and practice	M	SD
1	We are aware of competitive intelligence.	4.12	0.671
2	We practice competitive intelligence in our business.	4.45	0.687
3	Our business has a formalised competitive intelligence function.	2.16	1.143
4	We have a formalised competitive intelligence process.	2.01	1.078
5	We hire people or other businesses to collect information on our behalf.	3.10	1.202
6	We have a computerised competitive intelligence system.	1.84	2.436

CI, competitive intelligence; M, mean; SD, standard deviation.

TABLE 3: Correlation between awareness of competitive intelligence and owner or manager's years of working experience.

Variable 1	Owner or manager years of working experience				Total
	Less than 1 year	1–2 years	3–5 years	6 or more years	
Strongly disagree	0	0	1	0	1
Neutral	0	1	5	5	11
Agree	0	3	30	29	62
Strongly agree	1	0	14	11	26
Total	1	4	50	45	100

TABLE 4: Correlation between competitive intelligence practice and owner or manager's years of working experience.

Variable 2	Owner or manager years of working experience				Total
	Less than 1 year	1–2 years	3–5 years	6 or more years	
Strongly disagree	0	0	1	0	1
Disagree	0	0	0	1	1
Neutral	0	0	1	1	2
Agree	0	3	20	21	44
Strongly agree	1	1	28	22	52
Total	1	4	50	45	100

TABLE 5: Correlation between competitive intelligence process formalisation and owner or manager's years of working experience.

Variable 4	Owner or manager years of working experience				Total
	Less than 1 year	1–2 years	3–5 years	6 or more years	
Strongly disagree	1	0	22	17	40
Disagree	0	2	16	16	34
Neutral	0	1	7	5	13
Agree	0	1	4	6	11
Strongly agree	0	0	1	1	2
Total	1	4	50	45	100

The cross-tabulation (see Table 6 below) shows that all the respondent (100%) with less than 1 year, two out of four (50%) respondents with 1–2 years, 26 out of 50 (52%) respondents with 3–5 years, and 28 out of 45 (62.22%) respondents with 6 or more years of working experience agreed that they hired people or other businesses to collect information on their behalf. Thus, more respondents with 6 or more years of experience outsourced CI than those with fewer years of working experience.

There was a very strong positive linear association between variable 6 and owners or managers years of working experience. Pearson's r for this correlation was 0.913. The cross-tabulation (see Table 7 below) shows that all the respondent (100%) with less than 1 year, all the respondents (100%) with 1–2 years, 46 out of 50 (92%) respondents with 3–5 years and 28 out of 45 (62.22%) respondents with 6 or more years of working experience did not have computerised CI. Thus, most respondents with 3–5 years working experience did not have computerised CI.

Discussion

With most SMEs' owners or managers having a degree or diploma, they could use this formal knowledge to manage their enterprises. Additionally, the many years of working experience meant that the owners or managers were exposed to different business situations in their enterprises. With a diploma or degree and 3–5 years of working experience, it's no surprise that most of the SMEs have been in operation for 6 or more years. It is evident from the findings that SMEs contribute to job creation because majority of these SMEs employed 6–10 employees.

Although it is evident from the findings that these SMEs are aware of CI and practice it, they practice CI informally. Most of these SMEs did not have formalised CI process and function. Moreover, they do not have computerised CI system. Perhaps this could be because of the fact that SMEs

are small by nature and lack resources. Whilst the existing literature suggests that awareness of CI must be raised, the findings of this study reveal that the SMEs are aware of CI.

The findings reveal that SMEs' owners or managers with many years of working experience are more aware of CI than those with fewer years of working experience. Also, SMEs whose owners or managers have many years of working experience practice CI more than those with fewer years of working experience. Moreover, SMEs whose owners or managers have many years of working experience outsource CI than those with fewer years of working experience. This is because these managers or owners have been exposed to the turbulent business environment long enough to realise the strategic tools needed to survive. However, owners or managers with many years of working experience do not have formal CI processes and their CI is not computerised. Perhaps this is because of SMEs lack financial resources. Therefore, owners or managers' years of working experience has a greater influence on CI awareness and practice.

Conclusion

Although SMEs are a major contributor to a country's GDP, high competition makes it difficult for SMEs to survive. In order to survive and sustain their businesses, SMEs have to seek and obtain competitive advantage over their rivals. Competitive intelligence has been identified to provide enterprises with competitive advantage. This is because CI provides enterprise managers with information regarding their competitive environment and hence enables decision-making. Although there are pleas to raise awareness of CI amongst SMEs, the current study reveals that these SMEs are aware of CI. These SMEs are not only aware of CI but they also practice it. However, this study concurs with current literature in that SMEs practice CI informally (Muller 2005). This is evident in that these SMEs don't have formalised CI process and function. Moreover, these SMEs do not have computerised CI system. Also, just like larger enterprises, SMEs outsource CI to either individuals or other enterprises. We can therefore conclude that these SMEs are aware of CI and practice it informally.

The purpose of this research was to establish the influence of owner or manager's working experience on competitive intelligence practice and awareness of SMEs. Importantly, the study established that owners or managers with many years of working experience are more aware of CI and practice it than those with fewer years of working experience. Moreover, owners or managers with many years of working experience outsource CI more than those with fewer years of working experience. Therefore, SMEs owners or managers' years of working experience has a greater influence on awareness and practice of CI. Put differently, years of working experience is a great predictor of CI awareness and practice.

It was not the purpose of this research to establish what type of working experience influence the awareness and practice

TABLE 6: Correlation between competitive intelligence outsourcing and owner or manager's years of working experience.

Variable 5	Owner or manager years of working experience				Total
	Less than 1 year	1–2 years	3–5 years	6 or more years	
Strongly disagree	0	1	11	4	16
Disagree	0	1	9	7	17
Neutral	0	0	4	6	10
Agree	1	2	24	28	55
Strongly agree	0	0	2	0	2
Total	1	4	50	45	100

TABLE 7: Correlation between computerisation of competitive intelligence and owner or manager's years of working experience.

Variable 6	Owner or manager years of working experience				Total
	Less than 1 year	1–2 years	3–5 years	6 or more years	
Strongly disagree	1	2	26	21	50
Disagree	0	2	19	17	38
Neutral	0	0	4	7	11
Total	1	4	50	45	100

of CI. It was also not the purpose of this study to establish the kinds of qualification required to practice CI. Future study should be undertaken to establish the type of working experience that influence CI awareness and practice. Also, future study should be conducted to establish why SMEs do not formalise CI. A future study should be conducted to establish the influence of practicing CI informally on the success of SMEs.

Acknowledgement

The authors would like to acknowledge the University of South Africa (South Africa) for the funding and support without which this research would not have been possible.

Competing interest

The authors declare that they have no financial or personal relationship(s) which may have inappropriately influenced them in writing this article.

Authors' contributions

T.E.N. (University of South Africa) initiated this research; conduct literature review; analysis; and conclusion. R.P. (University of South Africa) led and supervises this project, selected the journal and handled editorial matters.

References

Abor, J. & Quartey, P., 2010, 'Issues in SME development in Ghana and South Africa', *International Research Journal of Finance and Economics* 1(39), 218–228.

Bernstein, J.H., 2011, *The Data-Information-Knowledge-Wisdom Hierarchy and its Antithesis*, viewed 14 May 2012, from https://journals.lib.washington.edu/index.php/nasko/article/viewFile/12806/11288

Bourret, C., 2012, 'Standards, evaluation, certification and implications for the study of competitive intelligence', *Journal of Intelligence Studies in Business* 2(1), 59–67.

Brody, R., 2008, 'Issues in defining competitive intelligence: An exploration', *Journal of Competitive Intelligence and Management* 4(3), 3–16.

Deng, Z. & Luo, L., 2010, 'An exploratory discussion of new ways for competitive intelligence on Web2.0', *International Federation for Information Processing* 252(1), 597–604.

Fleisher, C.S. & Wright, S., 2009, 'Examining differences in competitive intelligence practice: China, Japan, and the West', *Thunderbird International Business Review* 51(3), 249–261. http://dx.doi.org/10.1002/tie.20263

Guarda,T., Augusto, M. & Silva, C., 2012, 'Competitive advantage in e-commerce: the case of database marketing', *Advances in Intelligent and Soft Computing* 143(1), 123–130. http://dx.doi.org/10.1007/978-3-642-27966-9_18

Heppes, D. & Du Toit, A., 2009, 'Level of maturity of the competitive intelligence function: Case study of a retail bank in South Africa', *Aslib Proceedings: New Information Perspectives* 61(1), 48–66.

Juhari, A.S. & Stephens, D., 2006, 'Tracing the origins of competitive intelligence through history', *Journal of Competitive Intelligence and Management* 3(4), 61–82.

Koseoglu, M.A., Karayormuk, K., Parnell, J.A. & Menefee, M.L., 2011, 'Competitive intelligence: Evidence from Turkish SMEs', *International Journal of Entrepreneurship and Small Business* 13(3), 333–349. http://dx.doi.org/10.1504/IJESB.2011.041664

Muller, M.L., 2005, 'Beyond competitive intelligence-innovation and competitive strategy', *South African Journal of Information Management* 7(1).

Muller, M.L., 2007, 'Competitive intelligence in business: Latin America', *South African Journal of Information Management*, 9(2).

Nieman, G., 2006, *Small business management: A South African approach*, Van Schaik, Pretoria.

Olawale, F. & Garwe, D., 2010, 'Obstacles to the growth of new SMEs in South Africa: A principal component analysis approach', *African Journal of Business Management* 4(5), 729–738.

Post, G.V. & Anderson, D.L., 2003, *Management Information Systems: Solving Business Problems with Information Technology*, 3rd edn., McGraw-Hill/Irwin, Boston.

Prior, V., 2007, 'DYI detection: Competitive intelligence for SMEs', viewed 18 November 2010, from http://web.fumsi.com/go/article/manage/2483

Shi, Z., 2011, 'Foundations of Intelligence Science', *International Journal of Intelligence Science* 1(1), 8–16. http://dx.doi.org/10.4236/ijis.2011.11002

Shih, M., Liu, D.R. & Hsu, M., 2010, 'Discovering competitive intelligence by mining changes in patent trends', *Expert Systems with Application* 37(4), 2882–2890. http://dx.doi.org/10.1016/j.eswa.2009.09.001

Smith, J.R., Wright, S. & Pickton, D., 2010, 'Competitive intelligence programmes for SMEs in France: Evidence of changing attitudes', *Journal of Strategic Marketing* 18(7), 523–536. http://dx.doi.org/10.1080/0965254X.2010.529154

South African Government, *Close Corporation Act 69 of 1994*, viewed on 23 June 2012, from http://www.justice.gov.za/legislation/acts/1984-069-CCorp.pdf

South African Government, *National Small Business Act 102 of 1996*, viewed 18 November 2010, from http://www.info.gov.za/acts/1996/a102-96.pdf

Stair, R. & Reynolds, G., 2006, *Principles of information systems*, Thompson Course Technology, Boston.

Taleghani, M., Rad, S.K. & Rahmati, Y., 2012, 'The Role of Innovation in the Relationship between Knowledge Management and Competitive Advantage (An Empirical Study of Tourism Industry)', *Journal of Basic and Applied Scientific Research* 2(4), 3607–3614.

Tarraf, T. & Molz, R., 2006, 'Competitive intelligence at small enterprises', *SAM Advanced Management Journal* 71(4), 24–34.

7

Policy gaps and technological deficiencies in social networking environments: Implications for information sharing

Author:
Stephen M. Mutula[1]

Affiliation:
[1]Information Studies Programme, University of KwaZulu-Natal, South Africa

Correspondence to:
Stephen Mutula

Email:
mutulas@ukzn.ac.za

Postal address:
Private Bag X01 Scottsville 3209, Pietermaritzburg, South Africa

Background: With the growing adoption and acceptance of social networking, there are increased concerns about the violation of the users' legitimate rights such as privacy, confidentiality, trust, security, safety, content ownership, content accuracy, integrity, access and accessibility to computer and digital networks amongst others.

Objectives: The study sought to investigate the following research objectives to: (1) describe the types of social networks, (2) examine global penetration of the social networks, (3) outline the users' legitimate rights that must be protected in the social networking sites (SNS), (4) determine the methods employed by SNS to protect the users' legitimate rights and (5) identify the policy gaps and technological deficiencies in the protection of the users' legitimate rights in the SNS.

Method: A literature survey and content analysis of the SNS user policies were used to address objective four and objective five respectively.

Results: The most actively used sites were Facebook and Twitter. Asian markets were leading in participation and in creating content than any other region. Business, education, politics and governance sectors were actively using social networking sites. Social networking sites relied upon user trust and internet security features which however, were inefficient and inadequate.

Conclusion: Whilst SNS were impacting people of varying ages and of various professional persuasions, there were increased concerns about the violation and infringement of the users' legitimate rights. Reliance on user trust and technological security features SNS to protect the users' legitimate rights seemed ineffectual and inadequate.

Introduction

The social networking sites are impacting people of varying ages and of various professional persuasions, both in the developed and the non- developed world and have quickly gained acceptance and use in education, research, the corporate world, government, politics, professional practice, and in the general society. With the growing adoption and acceptance of social networking, there are increased concerns about the violation and infringement of the users' legitimate rights. The concept 'legitimate right' is used in this study to infer legal and moral rights – that is, valid claims by individuals on society to protect them from being denied the entitlement of human well-being on grounds of their utility through the force of law, or by education (Mill 1969). The legitimate rights discussed in this study include but are not limited to privacy, confidentiality, trust, security, safety, content ownership, content accuracy and integrity, access and accessibility. These rights are both legal and moral (Hart 1994), a fact emphasised by Wellman (1995) who avers that the core concept of a right is something common to the law and morality.

The purpose of this study was to investigate how the users' legitimate rights in the social networking environments were being protected. A social networking site refers to a public web-based space that allows individuals to create their profile, articulate a list of other users with whom they share a connection, view and traverse their list of connections in a reciprocal manner (Privacy Rights Clearing House 2012). The social networking sites are part of the wider social media – a group of internet based applications that build on the ideological and technological foundation of Web 2.0 and allow the creation and exchange of the user generated content (Kaplan & Haenlein 2010). The social media incorporates wikis, blogs, social bookmarking, internet forums, online communities, RSS feeds, tag-based folksonomies, podcasts, e-mail, virtual worlds, and instant messaging amongst others (Kaplan & Haenlein 2010). This study focused on the social networking sites particularly Facebook, Twitter, LinkedIn, Google+, Myspace, and YouTube because they are the market leaders in the industry (Lewis 2010).

This study was underpinned by the classical and the contemporary ethical traditions. From the classical traditional perspective, early scholarly engagement with regard to protecting legitimate rights of the users drew considerable insights from utilitarianism and deontology realms (Giles 2006; Boyd 2007). However, there is growing debate on whether the classical ethical traditions possess sufficient resources to illuminate the ethical implications of emerging information technologies such as the social networking or whether we need new ethical instruments. Kaplan and Haenlein (2010) therefore argue that the contemporary ethical traditions founded on computer ethics and philosophies of technology are needed to analyse how particular moral issues are embedded in the specific technologies. The contemporary ethical traditions include disclosive ethics; global information ethics; pragmatism (Van den Eede 2010); virtue ethics (Vallor 2010); feminist and care ethics (Hammington 2010) and intercultural information ethics (Capurro 2010). The contemporary ethical traditions largely define ethical standards in technological environments and consequently expand the scope and milieu of 'legitimate rights' beyond what is conventionally provided for by the classical traditions. The classical ethical traditions focus on privacy, confidentiality, contextual integrity, and freedom; whilst the contemporary ethical traditions add on this milieu access and accessibility, accuracy, security, trust, illegal surveillance, identity theft, intellectual property and copyright (World Summit on the Information Society [WSIS] 2005; Kaplan & Haenlein 2010; Mason 1986). This study focused on the legitimate rights proffered by both classical and contemporary traditions.

Research problem

There are several issues affecting the protection of the users' legitimate rights in the social networking environments. Evidence is growing that show the social networking service providers are neither keen nor able to protect the legitimate rights of the users. This behaviour may be attributed to the fact that the main marketing business model of the social networking service providers is based on the ownership of their customers' revealed information about themselves (Capurro 2010). For example, Facebook in September 2012 changed its user privacy policy, thus effectively depriving the users the right to vote on matters affecting them. The implications of Facebook policy change is that the users' content can be shared with third parties without their [users'] consent (Privacy Rights Clearinghouse 2012). Additionally, the affiliates or approved contacts of the SNS may copy and repost information without the users' permission (Privacy Rights Clearinghouse 2012). Nissenbaum (2004) in this regard points out that privacy is about context and the consequences of sharing the users' data without their consent is unethical and a violation of their privacy. The users' policies of the social networking sites invariably acknowledge that the content uploaded onto the sites is not necessarily guaranteed security because such content may be accessed by cookies. Zabala (2012) therefore points out that the more one enters social networking sites, the more one gets locked in – a closed silo of content, and one that does not give one full control over one's information in it. Similarly, Lovink (2011) asserts that in Facebook, individuals are not only tricked but also trick themselves into believing that they are free in creating and discovering their identity, when on the contrary they are prisoners of Facebook's – predefined choices, sentenced with the burden and illusion of endless – possibilities. Lovink (2011) concludes that we should no longer be naïve and trust commercial companies who deliver free services and take the responsibility of [*defining our lives*].

The issues about the users' legitimate rights in the SNS are weighty and require in-depth investigation to find the scope and extent of violations of such rights and how the situation can be ameliorated. It is for this reason that this study investigated the following research objectives.

Research objectives

This study sought to investigate how the legitimate rights of the users in social networking sites are being protected. The following objectives were addressed, to:

1. Describe the types of social networks.
2. Examine global penetration of the social networks.
3. Outline the users' legitimate rights that must be protected in the social networking sites.
4. Determine the methods employed by SNS to protect the users' legitimate rights.
5. Identify the policy gaps and technological deficiencies in the protection of the users' legitimate rights in the SNS.

Research design

A literature survey and content analysis were used to address the above research objectives. A literature review was used particularly to address objective one to objective three whilst content analysis of the social networking user policies was used to address objective four and objective five respectively. A literature survey was useful in providing the background information about the SNS with regard to global penetration and in unravelling the users' legitimate rights which must be protected. The content analysis of the user policies was helpful in identifying the policy gaps and technological deficiencies in the protection of the users' legitimate rights in the social networking environments. The user policies analysed were those of Facebook, Twitter, LinkedIn, Google+ and YouTube. These social networking sites were selected because they are the market leaders in the social networking industry. In reviewing the user policies, focus was placed on the user privacy guarantees, the methods of enforcing compliance with the policies, compensation when the users' rights are violated, the sanctions meted on errant users, verification of the credibility of information uploaded by the users, the role and responsibilities of the users, user training, intellectual property rights, and guarding servers against invasion.

The study was underpinned by both the classical and the contemporary ethical traditions. The classical tradition pervades early scholarly engagement with regard to protection of legitimate rights of the users and drew considerable insights from utilitarianism and deontological realms. The contemporary ethical traditions draw from computer ethics and philosophy of technology (Kaplan & Haenlein 2010; Giles 2006; Boyd 2007). The two ethical traditions define the milieu of 'legitimate rights' that must be protected in the social networking environments.

Results

The purpose of this study was to investigate how the legitimate rights of the users in the social networking sites are being protected. The study specifically sought to:

1. Describe the types of social networks.
2. Examine global penetration of the social networks.
3. Outline the users' legitimate rights that must be protected in the social networking sites.
4. Determine the methods employed by SNS to protect the user's legitimate rights.
5. Identify the policy gaps and technological deficiencies in the protection of the users' legitimate rights in the SNS.

The results based on each of the above research objectives are outlined in the sections that follow.

Types of the social networks

From the literature reviewed, five different types of the social networks (Privacy Rights Clearinghouse 2012) were identified namely - personal networks, status update networks, location networks, content sharing networks and shared interest networks. The *personal networks* allow the users to create detailed online profiles and connect with other users with emphasis on social relationships. The examples here include Facebook and MySpace. On the other hand, the *status-update networks* refer to social networks designed to allow the users to post short status updates in order to communicate with other users quickly. In this category, the example used is Twitter. In contrast, the *location networks* are founded on global positioning systems (GPS) technology and are designed to broadcast one's real-time location, either as public script or as an update viewable to authorised contact. The examples of the *location networks* include Google Latitude, Foursquare and Loopt. Besides, the *content sharing networks* are designed for sharing content including verbal and text-based exchanges, music, photographs and videos. In this category, YouTube and Flickr are the examples used amongst others. Finally, the *shared interest networks* are built around common interest of a specific group of people. These types of networks include amongst others LinkedIn. This study focused on the *personal networks*, the *status update networks*, the *content sharing networks* and the *shared interest networks*. The following social networking sites were therefore covered Facebook and Myspace, Twitter, YouTube and LinkedIn from the *personal networks*, the *status update networks*, the *content sharing networks*, and the *shared interest networks* categories respectively. The SNS from each of these categories are the most popular and widely used.

Global penetration of the social networks

The literature reviewed found that the social networking activity is growing phenomenally across the world with Facebook being the most widely used social networking site having exceeded a billion active accounts by October 2012 (Privacy Rights Clearing House 2012). Moreover, of the active Facebook users, 526 million used the site on daily basis (Backstrom, Dwork & Keinberg 2011). Globally, the Asian markets in general were found to be leading in terms of participation and in creating more content than any other region (Smith 2011). For example, in 2011, Philippines had a penetration of 83%, Hungary 80%, Poland 77%, and Mexico 76% with the growth areas worldwide being in the video clips (83%); the social networks (57%); the widget economy (the social network users with installed applications) (23%) and the blogging community (42 million bloggers) (Smith 2011). The results also indicated that Africa was not left behind and reached 48 million users in 2012 distributed as follows: 30 million users on Facebook, 6 million users on LinkedIn and 12 million users on Twitter (Mathen 2012). Most tweets (57%) in Africa were reportedly emanating from mobile devices (Onyango 2012). Furthermore, in 2012, the leading African countries on Facebook in terms of the user active accounts were Egypt (9.4 million), South Africa (4.8 million) and Nigeria (4.4 million) (Katlic 2012). Facebook was rated the most popular social networking site with an estimated between 550 million and 750 million monthly visitors in 2011 (eBizMBA 2011; Arico 2011). In addition, the largest demographic group on Facebook was those aged 35 to 54 years followed by those aged 18 to 24 years (Generation Y and Generation Z, respectively) (Corbet 2010). The fast growth of the social networking phenomenon globally may be attributed to the fact that traditional collaborative technologies such as the e-mail, and the telephone which are largely text and document-centred have become less efficient to drive innovation and productivity (Mathen 2012). Moreover, the rise of affordable handsets and the broadband connectivity was fuelling the spread of social networking activity. Farmington (2012), Chauke (2012) and Gosier (2008) are in agreement that the availability of cost-effective mobile and wireless solutions and the greater demand for connectivity has become the most important factors driving rapid growth of the social media.

The literature surveyed also found that the social networking sites were being applied to promote business as a new competitive tool with companies adopting the social software as a strategic part of their IT investment. In addition, companies have embraced the social software to bring about integration of disparate organisational units and workforce free of geographic constraints (Mathen 2012). In education, Rice (2011) pointed out that college students were using the social networking sites such as Facebook to communicate with each other about their coursework; writing status updates and posting pictures; and for social and educational purposes.

Users' legitimate rights that must be protected in the social networking sites

With regard to the users' legitimate rights, Buchanan (2012) identified anonymity, confidentiality of data, data integrity and data security as areas raising greatest ethical concern. Kaplan and Haenlein (2010) on the other hand, outlined several legitimate rights to which individuals are entitled which included privacy, ownership and access. They pointed out that adequate provision must be made to protect the privacy of subjects and maintain the confidentiality of any data that were collected. They also stated that a violation of privacy or breach of confidentiality presented a risk of serious harm to [*the users*] arising from exposure of personal or sensitive information, the divulgence of embarrassing or illegal conduct or the release of data protected under the law. Van den Eede (2010), Vallor (2010), Hammington (2010), Skog (2011), Light, McGrath and Griffiths (2008) from the classical utilitarianism and deontology perspectives identified privacy, confidentiality, contextual integrity and freedom as the most critical ethical concern. In contrast, WSIS (2005), Kaplan and Haenlein (2010) and Mason (1986:5) in the context of the new information technologies identified the following legitimate rights- access or accessibility, accuracy, security, trust, illegal surveillance, identity theft, intellectual property and copyright. Mason (1986) went further and posed the questions that must be addressed in an electronic age in order to protect the users' legitimate rights. The questions that must be asked include: What information about one's self or one's associations should a person reveal to others and under what conditions and safeguards? Who has the responsibility for the authenticity, fidelity and accuracy of information?

Who is to be held accountable for the errors in the information? How can the injured party be made whole? Who has the ownership of [*content*] and the channels through which the information is transmitted? How should access to this [*channels*] be allocated? What kinds of information can a person or an organisation have a right to or a privilege to obtain, under certain conditions and safeguards? Echoing the same view as Mason, WSIS Action Line 10 pronounces in generic terms human rights that must be protected in an information society environment. Such human rights include (WSIS 2005): universally held values, the common good, the fundamental values of freedom, equality, solidarity, tolerance, and shared responsibility.

Methods employed by the social networking sites to protect the users' legitimate rights

The content analysis of the user policies revealed that Facebook like other SNS rely heavily on client trust and good will to safeguard their [*clients'*] rights (Facebook 2012). The results also found that the social networking service providers particularly Facebook expected the users to adhere to some basic standards of ethical behaviour (Facebook 2012). For example, Facebook has a 'statement of rights and responsibilities' for governing behaviour of the users on its sites (Facebook 2012). This 'statement of rights and responsibilities' expects the users to grant Facebook exclusive, transferable, worldwide license to use their content.

Facebook user policy states that the service provider does not allow those under the age of 13 years or sex offenders convicts to use their services. Furthermore, Facebook policy states that if the users post content on its platform which infringes or violates someone else's rights, the accounts of those gullible will be disabled (Facebook 2012). In this regard, Facebook (2012) user policy stipulates that:

> If the client violates the letter or spirit of this Statement, or otherwise creates risk or possible legal exposure for us, we can stop providing all or part of Facebook to you. (n.p.)

In contrast, LinkedIn user policy states that the service provider does not provide personally identifiable information to the third parties without the user consent. Besides, the user policy states that LinkedIn provides the means to control viewing of customer contact information through the users' profile function. Like Facebook, LinkedIn policy states that the service provider does not accept abuse of LinkedIn service by the users who may wish to use it to spam, abuse, harass, or otherwise violate the User Agreement or Privacy Policy. Moreover, LinkedIn user policy states that it does not accept any information deemed to be injurious, violent, offensive, racist or xenophobic, or which may otherwise violate the purpose and spirit of LinkedIn and its community of users (LinkedIn 2012).

Google (2012) user policy dissuades illegal activities such as malicious products, hate speech, distributing personal and confidential information, account hijacking, distributing content that exploits children such as child pornography, unwanted promotional or commercial content, or unwanted or mass solicitation, sexually explicit material, violent or bullying behaviour. The YouTube Team (2012) in contrast states that every community features on its site involves a certain level of trust and every customer is therefore expected to comply with this requirement Furthermore, the YouTube policy asserts that the platform does not support pornography or sexually explicit content. The policy cautions the users to be aware that the YouTube Team works closely with law enforcement agencies and strives to report child exploitation. Furthermore, the policy states that it is against animal abuse, drug abuse, predatory behaviour, stalking, threats, harassment, invading privacy, hate speech, attacks, or humiliation. The policy says it respects copyright, free speech and defends everyone's right to express unpopular points of view.

Policy gaps in the social networking environments

The results from the content analysis exposed several gaps through which the users' legitimate rights are violated in the social networking sites. Steel and Vascellaro (2010) state that the social networking sites, particularly Facebook are confronted with an increasing scrutiny over their privacy practices from the consumers, the privacy advocates and the lawmakers. Various flaws are inherent in the user policies of the SNS. For example, largely all the SNS policies allow the advertising companies to harvest the users' information to meet their [*companies*'] commercial interests. In this regard, NSMNSS (2012) cautions the users that most of the social networking sites are commercially owned and for that matter are designed to generate revenue not simply for a social good but to encourage the users to navigate and participate in certain ways. Facebook has a new insertion in its data user policy that states:

> we may share information we receive with businesses that are legally part of the same group of companies that [*Facebook*] is part of or become part of the group [*the affiliates*]. (Facebook Site Governance 2012)

This policy change was preceded by Facebook's announcement on 22 November 2012 that it would no longer let the users have a say in its privacy policy formulation. Besides, Facebook asks the users to make their personal information public in addition to requiring them to use their actual names whilst registering.

The social networking user policies generally indemnify the service providers from liability in the event of any litigation arising out of a breach of rights of their users or third parties. For example, Facebook (2012) user policy states:

> If anyone brings a claim against us related to your [the user] actions and content, you will indemnify and hold us harmless from and against all damages, losses, and expenses of any kind (including reasonable legal fees and costs) related to such claim. (n.p.)

Twitter (2012) user policy in contrast states that it provides information to the law enforcement personnel seeking information about their users. Most of the Twitter profile information is public, so anyone can see it. The Twitter user policy like those of other major social networking sites only complies with the US law (Twitter 2012) and is not applicable in any other jurisdiction.

Technological deficiencies in the social networking sites

The technological gaps in the social networking environments are largely attributed to the security weaknesses of the internet technology. Danezis (2009) in this regard observes that the social networking sites have recently come under criticism for their poor privacy protection track record in part due to the internet's limited engineering features. The Privacy Rights Clearinghouse (2012) notes that identity thieves are a threat in the SNS as they obtain personal information based on the information a user posts online. The users on the SNS are vulnerable to online criminals who scam, harass and bully individuals. The criminals also use malware to infect content or computer programmes. Moreover, phishing attacks occur when e-mails, instant messages or other messages claiming to be from trusted sources ask for information. Additionally, hijacking of accounts occurs when a legitimate account is taken over by an identity thief for the purpose of fraud such as spamming or stealing private data.

Facebook like other SNS has no technological means of verifying the integrity, honesty, reliability, and accuracy of the information uploaded to their site by the users. Facebook acknowledges that there are no guarantees to ensure strict compliance with ethical provisions either through policy or technological interventions. In this respect, Facebook (2012) is explicit that:

> …We do our best to keep Facebook safe, but we cannot guarantee it especially, when the users access Facebook, using automated means such as harvesting bots, robots, spiders, or scrapers without our permission; or upload viruses; use someone else's login; bully, intimidate, or harass any user… [*In addition, Facebook does not guarantee that its platform is bug free, safe, and secure.*] (n.p.)

Similarly, LinkedIn acknowledges that whereas personal information the user provides will be secured in accordance with the industry standards and technology, the internet is not a 100% secure environment, consequently, there is no guarantee that the information may not be accessed, copied, disclosed, altered, or destroyed by the breach of any of the physical, technical, or managerial safeguards (LinkedIn 2012).

Twitter (2012) points out that it does not have explicit ways of e-mail verification or identity authentication of its users. Besides, some information stored by Twitter is automatically collected. Twitter acknowledges that the information they store from the users may not be accurate if the user has created a fake or anonymous profile. LinkedIn (2012) in contrast supports tracking customers' action online whenever such customers view and/or interact with LinkedIn pages, mobile applications, software IP address, and browser type operating system.

Discussion of results

The purpose of this study was to investigate how the legitimate rights of the users in social networking sites were being protected. The discussion of the results is based on each of the research objectives paraphrased into the sectional headings below.

Description of the different social networking sites

The first objective of the study sought to describe types of the social networks. The results found five different types of social networks namely:

1. personal networks
2. status update networks
3. location networks
4. content sharing networks
5. shared interest networks. (Privacy Rights Clearinghouse 2012)

The personal networks seem to be the most popular form of social networking sites as revealed by the highest penetration of Facebook worldwide. The high penetration of Facebook may be attributed to the fact that at its very foundation it was established to create detailed online profiles and facilitate connecting of the users with emphasis placed on the social relationships. Furthermore, the high penetration of Facebook may also be due to the fact that it emerged as a way to link a university cohort, many of whom are students with active accounts on the site, to one another to promote their scholarship. Facebook also connects people across the globe and is increasingly used for business profiles aimed at establishing links with customers. In contrast, MySpace which is in the same category as Facebook does not seem to attract comparable numbers of clients. This may be attributed to the fact that Facebook is an established brand and a market leader. MySpace was established for musicians to promote their brand and communicate with their fans and was not meant for all the public.

In the category of the status-update networks, the results indicated that Twitter was the most well- known but second to Facebook in global penetration. The popularity of Twitter may be attributed to its suitability in creating lines of communications between ordinary individuals and figures of public interest. For this reason, it serves effectively as a tool for political or civic mobilisation. Twitter is also suited for mobile gadgets which are portable and provide platform for broadcasting text quickly rather than images which may require high bandwidth. The location networks which are designed to broadcast one's real-time location, either as public or as an update viewable to authorised contact does not seem to have penetrated as fast as personal and status-update networks presumably because it requires specialised software. In addition, people may not be inclined to reveal their location for various personal reasons such as privacy. The content sharing networks such as YouTube and Flickr grew out of the need to share and exchange verbal, text, music, photographs and videos. However, their growth slackened in part because all types of the social networks can support the exchange and sharing of all forms of media. Finally, shared interest networks in which LinkedIn is the most well-known are built around common interest of a specific group of people. LinkedIn is therefore more specialised as it encourages social relations organised around professional lives (Kaplan & Haenlein 2010). This may perhaps explain why LinkedIn growth and penetration trails that of Facebook and Twitter. Weiss (2008) asserts that social networking activity in general has become a global phenomenon happening in all markets regardless of wider economic, social and cultural development and is now the number one online activity, accounting for 10% of all the users' time on the Internet (Lundsay 2010).

Status of social networking penetration

The second research objective of the study was to examine the global status of the social networks penetration. The results obtained from the literature reviewed found that the social networking was an online activity growing phenomenally across the world. Facebook was identified as the market leader in the industry and was the most widely used social networking site with over a billion active users in 2012 (Privacy Rights Clearing House 2012). Globally, the Asian

markets in general were leading in terms of participation and in creating more content than any other region (Smith 2011). Africa which has traditionally lagged behind other regions in technological innovations performed well reportedly because of the fast growth of mobile phones. It is instructive that the political revolution in North Africa that overthrew the regimes of Ben Ali of Tunisia, Hussein Mubarak of Egypt and Muammar Kaddafi of Libya were orchestrated through the social networks by young people using mainly Twitter and Facebook to mobilise the masses. The dramatic penetration of the social networking activity in Africa was made possible by the fact that 57% of tweets are emanating from mobile devices (Onyango 2012).

Users' legitimate rights in social networking sites

The third research objective of the study was to describe the users' legitimate rights that must be protected in the social networking environments. The results indicated that legitimate rights of individuals are underpinned by both the classical and the contemporary ethical traditions which collectively include pragmatism; virtue ethics; feminist and care ethics, intercultural information ethics, WSIS Action Line 10, Mason's ethical issues in electronic age, disclosive ethics; global information ethics; and intercultural information ethics (WSIS 2005; Kaplan & Haenlein 2010; Mason 1986; Van den Eede 2010; Vallor 2010; Hammington 2010 & Capurro 2010). The milieu of 'legitimate rights' gleaned from the two categories of ethical traditions were privacy, confidentiality, contextual integrity, access or accessibility, accuracy, security, trust, illegal surveillance, identity theft, intellectual property and copyright (WSIS 2005; Kaplan & Haenlein 2010).

Protection of the user's legitimate rights in social networking sites

The fourth research objective was to determine the methods employed by the SNS to protect the users' legitimate rights. The results obtained through content analysis revealed that the social networking service providers used largely policy and technological means in protecting the users' legitimate rights. From the policy perspective, most of the SNS relied on the clients trust to protect their legitimate rights; closing accounts of those gullible of violating the policy, dissuading the users from spamming, abusing, harassing or violating the user agreement policy or engaging in racist and xenophobic tendencies, predatory behaviour, stalking, hate speech, child pornography or account hijacking. Facebook, in addition, expects the users to adhere to some basic standards of ethical behaviour (Facebook 2012) that are stipulated in a 'statement of rights and responsibilities' and the 'user privacy policy' that govern their relationship with the users. The LinkedIn method of protecting the users' legitimate rights includes controlling the viewing of the customer contact information by other users through the use of profile function. Like Facebook, LinkedIn does not accept abuse of LinkedIn service by the users who could use it to spam, abuse, harass, or otherwise violate the 'user agreement' or 'privacy policy'. The results indicated that Google (2012) prohibits illegal activities including, hate speech, distributing personal and confidential information, account hijacking, child pornography, sexually explicit material, violent or bullying behaviour and so forth. The YouTube Team (2012) was found to rely on the users' trust to protect their [*the users*] legitimate rights.

Policy and technological gaps in SNS

The fifth research objective was to identify the policy gaps and technological deficiencies in protecting the users' legitimate rights in the SNS. This research objective like the fourth was addressed through content analysis of the SNS user policies. Moreover, this research objective has two perspectives: the policy gaps and the technological deficiencies. The policy gaps are discussed in this section whilst the technological deficiencies are covered in the next section. The results revealed that the protection mechanisms in the social networking environment were weak, leaving room for infringement of the users' legitimate rights. For example, Hacktivist Group Anonymous in late 2011 threatened an imminent attack to bring down Facebook saying 'everything you do on Facebook stays on Facebook, regardless of your privacy settings'. The results showed that the social networking user policies acknowledge that the service providers are unable to guarantee protection of the users ethical and moral rights. Lundsay (2010) for this reason says the social networking sites open the door to numerous risks including the breaching of confidentiality, conflicts of interest, and misuse of company resources.

Though Facebook user policy states that it does not allow those who are under the age of 13 or sex offenders convicts to use their services, the results did not find any explicit ways of ensuring that only the users who are over 13 years register to use their platform. The sanctions meted to those who violated other users' rights consisted merely disabling their accounts -an inadequate deterrent. The lack of adequate mechanisms for protecting the users' rights in the social networking environments was found to be exacerbated by the fact that no provision was made for compensation when the users' rights were violated. The results found that the user policies indemnified the service providers from litigation arising out of the users' action or inaction. The policy and technical loopholes with regard to protection of the users' legitimate rights opens doors for tremendous room for infringing on the users' legitimate rights. Steel and Vascellaro (2010) observe that the social networking sites can be misused in many ways including disclosure of confidential or other non-public information, fraud, privacy and damage to personal reputation. The results indicated that the users' policies allowed advertising companies to harvest the users' information (NSMNSS 2012) which was unacceptable and a breach of the users' rights.

Facebook's user policy change legitimising divulgence of the users' information without their consent (Facebook Site Governance 2012) in effect mean the users' rights can be violated with impunity. This is exacerbated by the fact that Facebook' pushes the users to make their personal information

public in registering on the site. For this reason, Capurro (2012) is concerned that personal data is being controlled and manipulated through surveillance in the SNS. The service provider has an obligation to present the users with clear and understandable explanations of the implications of the change of policy with regard to content that had already been posted and for whom it was meant. Though Facebook justified its change of policy action saying it was necessitated by the poor quality of comments it received from the users, education and training of the users should have preceded this decision. Skog (2011) in a study of the SNS in Scandinavia found that majority of the subscribers who are teenagers with an average of 18 years of age may not have a good grasp of the policies of the SNS to make adequately informed choices. Similarly, Kaplan and Haenlein (2010) are of the view that it remains unclear whether the users in online environments truly understand the implications of a breach to their privacy and whether they understand the privacy policies and terms of service.

Henderson, Hutton, and McNeilly (2012) found in a study using data obtained from Facebook that the 5 537 9405 potential users who were targeted by an advertisement on the site which appeared 220 859 times, only 38 users clicked on the advertisement. This result was revealing because prior to the recent Facebook policy change, it had a voting system which purported to give the users a voice in the policy making process. But it would seem that this approach was not an effective and inclusive way of soliciting the user participation. Moreover, on 01 June 2012 when the users were invited to endorse a governance policy that would see a change from voting system to feedback through regular engagements, only 342 632 of the close to one billion users participated accounting for only 0.04% (Facebook Site Governance 2012). Facebook at the time required 30% endorsement to effect a change on its user policy. Poor participation by the users could be attributed to the sheer size of Facebook making it difficult for the users to see the advert or simply the users' lack of interest because they do not understand the import of their privacy implications. Scarton (2010) noted in this respect that young people understand the internet very well, but may not understand the ethical boundary issues that surround it. Manders-Huits (2010) asserts that the SNS developers have a duty to protect and promote the interests of their users in autonomously constructing and managing their own moral and practical identities.

Technological weaknesses of the Internet

The results indicate that besides the policy gaps, there are several technical weaknesses inherent in the internet technology, which expose the users to abuse. Researchers at AT&T Labs and Worcester Polytechnic Institute in August 2012 found that 12 networking sites including Facebook, MySpace and Twitter had multiple ways that outside companies could access the user data. Kaplan and Haenlein (2010) consequently, decree technical failures to truly support privacy projections. Though the SNS provide the users with controls to manage settings to control who access their content, Danazis (2011) is of the view that simply providing fine grained controls for setting their preferences is not sufficient to support privacy as the users find the task of specifying who should access each new piece of content tiresome and cumbersome. Furthermore, the internet's technological weaknesses result in identity thefts, scamming, phishing attacks, account hijacking, spamming, and technical failures. The technical weaknesses of the internet make it difficult for the service providers to verify the integrity, honesty, reliability, and accuracy of the information uploaded by the users. In addition, automated mechanisms such as harvesting bots, robots, spiders, or scrapers easily track and access the users' information.

Conclusion and recommendations

The results of the study indicated that with the social networking impacting people of varying ages and professional persuasions both in the developed and the non-developed world and having quickly gained acceptance and use in education, research, the corporate world, government, politics, professional practice, and in the general society; there were increased concerns about the violation and infringement of the users' legitimate rights. The user trust and technological security features of the internet that the SNS used to protect the users' legitimate rights seemed ineffectual and inadequate.

The outcomes of this study have practical and policy ramifications. The results are expected to create awareness amongst the users through education and training about their obligations, responsibilities and vulnerabilities in the social networking environments with regard to their legitimate rights so that they can make informed choices. The SNS service providers are obliged to provide policy, legal and regulatory instruments to ensure full protection of the users' legitimate rights. Moreover, the users of the social networks should be educated about the policy provisions and the technical capabilities of the internet so that they can know what personal information to upload on the SNS, and be able to specify privacy settings which are sensitive to the social context in which their content can be shared with third parties.

This study relied largely on a literature survey and content analysis of the social network user policies to collect relevant information. The need for the users to give their experiences in the social networking environments in their own words could enrich the outcomes of this study. Besides, this study was only restricted to a handful of the most popular social networking sites but could be extended to cover all social networking sites. In addition, this study only concentrated on legitimate rights of the users in the social networking sites. Future research should be extended to other categories of the social media such as wikis, blogs, RSS and more.

The issue of protecting the users' legitimate rights in the social networking environments needs to find its way onto the annual agenda of WSIS Forum. The Forum monitors and evaluates the progress being made in the context of WSIS Plan of Action. This would enable relevant recommendations to be made for action by the UN member states with regard to protecting the users' legitimate rights in the social networking environments. Besides, governments, civil society and consumer protection agencies as stakeholders have more leverage than individual users to exert pressure on the social network service providers to improve their approaches to protecting the users' legitimate rights. These stakeholders should therefore become more involved in advocating for respect of the users' legitimate rights by the social networking service providers. The service providers who have received certification from accrediting agencies can be relied upon to provide a more trusted social networking environment. For example, LinkedIn has secured TRUSTe's Privacy Seal award signifying that its privacy policy and practices comply with transparency, accountability and choice with respect to the collection and use of the users' personal information. The users of the social networking sites should be encouraged to register with the social networking service providers that have received accreditation for compliance.

Acknowledgements
Competing interest

The author declares that he has no financial or personal relationship(s) that may have inappropriately influenced him in writing this paper.

References

Arico, J., 2011, 'Hackers threaten to take down Facebook', viewed 26 march 2012, from http://www.mobiledia.com/news/115338.html

Backstrom, L., Dwork, C. & Keinberg, J., 2007, 'Wherefore art thou R3579X?: Anonymous social networks, hidden patterns, and structural steganography', Paper presented at the International World Wide Web Conference, May 8–12, 2007, Banff, Alberta, Canada.

Boyd, D., 2007, 'Why youth (heart) social networking sites: The role of networked publics in teenage social life', in D. Buckingham (ed.), Youth, identity and social media', pp. 119–142. MIT Press, Cambridge, MA.

Buchanan, E.A., 2012, 'Internet research ethics (Stanford encyclopedia of philosophy)', Journal of International Commercial Law and Technology 4(40), 238–251.

Capurro, R., 2010, 'Global intercultural information ethics from an African perspective', Keynote address presented at the Second African Information Ethics Conference 2010, University of Botswana, Gaborone, 6–7 September.

Capurro, R., 2012, 'Ethical issues of social networks in Africa', Keynote address presented at the social networking sites conference, 2012, Kievets Groon Conference Centre, Pretoria, South Africa, 2–7 September.

Chauke, G., 2012, 'South Africa: The power of social networking sites in education', viewed 27 March 2012, from http://allafrica.com/stories/201203130926.html

Corbet, P., 2010, 'Facebook demographics and statistics report 2010: 145% growth in 1 year', viewed 3 April 2012, from http://www.istrategylabs.com/2010/01/facebook-demographicsand-statistics-report-2010-145-growth-in-1-year/

Danezis, G., 2009, 'Inferring privacy policies for social networking services', AISec 09, Chicago, IL. eBizMBA, 2011, Top 15 most popular social networking websites, viewed 3 April 2012, from http://www.ebizmba.com/articles/social-networking-websites

Facebook, 2012, Statement of rights and responsibilities, viewed 29 March 2012, from https://www.facebook.com/legal/terms

Facebook Site Governance, 2012, How can 1 bn users have their say in how their data is used?, viewed 23 November 2012, from http://www.siliconrepublic.com/new-media/item/30371-facebook-site-governance/

Farmington, C., 2012, Social networking sites boom and rise of affordable handsets to double mobile broadband market revenue in West and Central Africa by 2017, viewed 17 March 2012, from http://finance.yahoo.com/news/social-media-boom-rise-affordable-180000289.html

Google, 2012, User content and conduct policy, viewed 29 March 2012, from: http://www.google.com/intl/en/+/policy/content.html

Giles, D., 2006, 'Constructing identities in cyberspace: the case of eating disorders', British Journal of Social Psychology 45, 463–477. http://dx.doi.org/10.1348/014466605X53596, PMid:16984715

Gosier, J., 2012, *Social networking sites in Africa: Mobile innovations*, viewed 28 March 2012, from http://www.readwriteweb.com/

Harmington, M., 2010, 'Care ethics, friendship and Facebook', in D.E. Wittkower (ed.), *Facebook and Philosophy*, pp. 135–145, Open Court, Chicago.

Hart, H.L.A., 1994, The *concept of law*, 2nd edn., Clarendon Press, Oxford.

Henderson, T., Hutton, L. & McNeilly, S., 2012, *Ethics in online social network research, FRRIICT case study report*, viewed 23 November 2012, from http://torrii.responsible-innovation.org/case-studies/ethics-online-social-network-research.html

Kaplan, A. & Haenlein, M., 2010, 'Users of the world unite: The challenges and opportunities of social media', *Business Horizons* 53(1), 59-68. http://dx.doi.org/10.1016/j.bushor.2009.09.003

Katlic, T., 2012, *Facebook user growth rates in Africa*, viewed 27 November 2012, from http://www.oafrica.com/statistics/facebook-user-growth-rates-in-africa-june-2010-december-2011

Lewis, B.K., 2010, 'Social media and strategic communication: Attitudes and perceptions among college students', *Public Relations Journal* 4(3), Summer, 2010.

Light, B., McGrath, K. & Griffiths, M., 2008, 'More than just friends? Facebook, disclosive ethics and morality of Technology', Proceedings of the International Conference on Information Systems, Paris. *ICIS 2008 Proceedings*, paper 193, viewed 7 March 2013, from http://aisel.aiselnet.org/icis 2008/193

LinkedIn Corporation, 2012, *Privacy policy*, viewed 29 March 2012, from http://www.linkedin.com/static?key=privacy_policy

Lovink, G., 2011, Networks *without a cause: A critique of social networking sites*, Polity Press, Cambridge

Lundsay, J., 2010, 'Managing the workplace ethics of social networking sites', viewed 26 March 2012, from http://www.corporatecomplianceinsights.com/managing-the-workplace-ethics-of-social-media/

Manders-Huits, N., 2010, 'Practical versus moral identities in identity management, *Ethics and Information Technology* 12(91), 43–55. http://dx.doi.org/10.1007/s10676-010-9216-8

Mason, R.O., 1986, 'Four ethical issues of the information age', *Management Information Systems Quarterly* 10(1), 5–12. http://dx.doi.org/10.2307/248873

Mathen, M., 2012, 'Social networking sites: Enhancing customer experience', *Botswana Guardian*, 16 March 2012, p. 8.

Mill, J.S., 1969, 'Utilitarianism', in J. Robson (ed.), *The collected works of John Stuart Mill*, vol 10, p. 203, Routledge & Kegan Paul, London.

Nissenbaum, H.F., 2004, 'Privacy as contextual integrity', *Washington Law Review* 79(1), 119–157

NSMNSS, 2012, *Blurring the boundaries-new social media, new social science?*, viewed 23 November 2012, from http://nsmnss.blogspot.com

Onyango, E., 2012, 'Kenyans second top tweeters in Africa', *Daily Nation*, 26 January 2012, viewed 7 March 2013, from http://www.nation.co.ke/Tech/Kenyans-second-top-tweeters-in-Africa/-/1017288/1314162/-/ux3kf3/-/index.html

Privacy Rights Clearing House, 2012, *Social networking privacy: How to be safe, secure and social*, viewed 23 November 2012, from https://www.privacyrights.org/social-networking-privacy

Rice, A., 2011, 'Students push their Facebook use further into course work', viewed 26 March 2012, from http://chronicle.com/blogs/wiredcampus/students-push-their-facebook-use-further-into-academics/33947

Scarton, D., 2010, 'Google and Facebook raise new issues for therapists and their clients', viewed 23 November 2012, from http://www.washingtonpost.com/wp-dyn/content/article/2010/03/29/AR2010032902942.html

Smith, T., 2011, 'World map of global social networking sites usage', viewed 27 March 2012, from http://wearesocial.net/blog/2011/06/world-map-global-social-media-usage/

Skog, D., 2011, 'Ethical aspects of managing a social network site: A disclosive analysis', *International Review of Information Ethics* 16(12), 27–32.

Steel, E. & Vascellaro, J.E., 2010, 'Facebook, MySpace confront privacy loophole', viewed 23 November 2012, from http://online.wsj.com/article/SB10001424052748704513104575256701215465596.html

Twitter, 2012, *Guidelines for law enforcement*, viewed 29 March 2012, from http://support.twitter.com/entries/41949-guidelines-for-law-enforcement#

Vallor, S., 2010, 'Social networking technology and virtues', *Ethics and Information Technology* 12(92), 157–170. http://dx.doi.org/10.1007/s10676-009-9202-1

Van den Eede, Y., 2010, 'Conservatism of mankind or idle talk? A pragmatist approach to social networking sites', *Ethics and Information Technology* 12(2), 195–206.

Weiss, T., 2008, 'Social networking sites still on rise: Comparative global study', viewed 27 March 2012, from http://www.trendsspotting.com/blog/

Wellman, C., 1995, *Real rights*, Oxford University Press, New York.

World Summit on the Information Society (WSIS), 2005, *Plan of action*, viewed 28 March 2012, from http://www.itu.int/wsis/docs/geneva/official/poa.html#c10

YouTube Team, 2012, *YouTube community guidelines*, viewed 29 March 2012 from http://www.youtube.com/t/community_guidelines

Zabala, S., 2012, 'I'm wired, therefore, I exist. But your existence started to belong to others?', viewed 27 November 2012, from http://www.newstatesman.com/sci-tech/sci-tech/2012/07/im-wired-therefore-i-exist

8

Integrated Financial Management Information Systems: Guidelines for effective implementation by the public sector of South Africa

Author:
Christoffel J. Hendriks[1]

Affiliation:
[1]Department of Public Administration and Management, University of the Free State, South Africa

Correspondence to:
Chris Hendriks

Email:
hendrikscj@ufs.ac.za

Postal address:
PO Box 339, Bloemfontein 9300, South Africa

Background: Integrated Financial Management Information Systems (IFMIS) can improve public sector management by providing real-time financial information to managers in order to enhance their decision-making capabilities. The South African Public Service is currently busy with the implementation of an IFMIS. However, the implementation of such a project has proved to be a very demanding undertaking and has not been met with resounding success.

Objectives: The research was conducted in order to identify the challenges and risks that are involved in the implementation of the IFMIS in South Africa. After identification of the challenges and risks, solutions or guidelines were developed that may make the implementation more successful.

Method: The methodology that was used is that of a literature study where theories were explored and used to solve a research problem. Based on the theoretical research, solutions and guidelines were developed to solve challenges and risks experienced.

Results: The results indicated that there are a number of challenges involved with the implementation of an IFMIS. A set of best practice guidelines was developed that may make the implementation more successful.

Conclusion: The sheer size and complexity of an IFMIS poses significant challenges and a number of risks to the implementation process. There are, however, critical success factors or best practices that can be used for the project to succeed. It is recommended that these best practices be used by the South African Public Service.

Introduction

Governments in developing countries are increasingly exploring methods and systems to modernise and improve public financial management. For example, over the years, there has been an introduction of the Integrated Financial Management Information System (IFMIS) as one of the most common financial management reform practices, aimed at the promotion of efficiency, effectiveness, accountability, transparency, security of data management and comprehensive financial reporting. The scope and functionality of an IFMIS varies across countries, but normally it represents an enormous, complex, strategic reform process (Chêne 2009:3).

The sheer size and complexity of an IFMIS poses significant challenges and a number of risks to the implementation process that goes far beyond the mere technological risk of failure and deficient functionality. The introduction of an IFMIS can be regarded as an organisational reform which deeply affects work processes and institutional arrangements governing the management of public finance. Challenges and obstacles can have a devastating effect on the success of the implementation and management of the process and should not be underestimated (Rodin-Brown 2008:2; Hove & Wynne 2010:8).

Various factors determine the success of IFMIS development and implementation in developing countries. In this article the purpose is to identify some of the challenges and to present solutions that can serve as best practice guidelines in the implementation of an IFMIS. The research problem that this study aims to address is to identify the challenges relating to the implementation of an IFMIS and to present best practise guidelines that will facilitate a successful implementation of an IFMIS in the South African Public Sector. The methodology used is that of a literature study where theories are explored and used to solve a research problem. According to Cooper and Schindler (2006:719), theory is a set of systematically inter-related concepts, definitions and propositions that are advanced to explain or predict phenomena (facts). Good theories and models provide causal accounts of the world, allow one to make predictive claims under certain conditions, bring conceptual coherence to a domain of science and simplify our understanding of the world (Mouton 2001:177).

Definition of the concept

According to both Dorotinsky (2003:3) and Rozner (2008:1), an IFMIS is an information system that tracks financial events and summarises financial information. It supports adequate management reporting, policy decisions, fiduciary responsibilities and the preparation of auditable financial statements. In its basic form, an IFMIS is little more than an accounting system configured to operate according to the needs and specifications of the environment in which it is installed (Rodin-Brown 2008:2). In general terms, it refers to the automating of financial operations.

In the sphere of government operations, IFMIS refers to the computerisation of public financial management processes, from budget preparation and execution to accounting and reporting, with the help of an integrated system for the purpose of financial management (Lianzuala & Khawlhring 2008:1). Rodin-Brown (2008:2) identifies the following basic features that are necessary for integration:

- standard data classification for recording financial events
- internal controls over data entry, transaction processing and reporting
- common processes for similar transactions and a system design that eliminates unnecessary duplication of data entry.

According to the IFMIS Project Overview for South Africa (Van Deventer 2003:8), a corporate reference data (CRD) Management Module will provide for the features mentioned above.

Characteristics, objectives and advantages of an Integrated Financial Management Information System

According to Diamond and Khemani (2006:99) and Chêne (2009:2), a well-designed Integrated Financial Management Information System (IFMIS) contains the following characteristics: it is a management tool; it provides a wide range of non-financial and financial information; it is a system and it impacts on corruption.

Management tool

According to Hove and Wynne (2010:8), an IFMIS assists management in ensuring accountability for the deployment and use of public resources and in improving the effectiveness and efficiency of public expenditure programmes. By tracking financial events through an automated financial system, management is able to exercise improved control over expenditure and to improve transparency and accountability in the budget cycle as a whole. Diamond and Khemani (2006:99) argue further that, as a management tool, an IFMIS should support the management of change. As such, it should be viewed as part of the broader financial reforms of government, such as budget reforms.

As a management tool IFMIS also enables management to do the following (Barata & Cain 2001:248):

- Control aggregate spending and the deficit.
- Prioritise expenditure across policies, programmes and projects to achieve efficiency and equity in the allocation of resources.
- Make better use of budgeted resources, namely, to achieve outcomes and produce outputs at the lowest possible cost.

Provision of nonfinancial and financial information

An IFMIS provides decision-makers and public-sector managers with the information they need to perform their managerial functions. Rodin-Brown (2008:3) states that an IFMIS provides timely, accurate and consistent data for management and budget decision-making. By computerising the budget management and accounting system for a government, an IFMIS aims at improving the quality and availability of information necessary at various stages of public financial management, such as budgeting, treasury management, accounting and auditing (Dorotinsky & Matsuda 2001:3). An IFMIS allows users anywhere within the IFMIS network to access the system and extract the specific information they need. A variety of reports can be generated to address different budgeting, funding, treasury, cash flow, accounting, audit and day-to-day management concerns (Rozner 2008:1).

A system

The scope and functionality of an IFMIS can vary from a basic general ledger accounting application to a comprehensive system covering budgeting, accounts receivable or payable, cash management, commitment control, debt, assets and liability management, procurement and purchasing, revenue management, human resource management and payroll (Rozner 2008:1). Its role is to connect, accumulate, process and then provide information to all parties in the budget system on a continuous basis (Diamond & Khemani 2006:100). It is therefore imperative that the system should be able to provide the required information timely and accurately, because if it does not it will not be used and cease to fulfil its central function as a system.

An IFMIS can improve public financial management in a number of ways, but generally seeks to enhance confidence and credibility of the budget through greater comprehensiveness and transparency of information. The purpose of using an IFMIS is to improve budget planning and execution by providing timely and accurate data for budget management and decision-making (Chêne 2009:2). A more standardised and realistic budget formulation process is allowed for and improved control over budget execution is affected through the full integration of budget execution data.

Impact on corruption

One of the major benefits of an IFMIS is the impact that it can have on corruption, by increasing the risk of detection.

According to Chêne (2009:2), a well-designed IFMIS can provide a number of features that may help detect excessive payments, fraud and theft. These include, for example, automated identification of exceptions to normal operations, patterns of suspicious activities, automated cross-referencing of personal identification numbers for fraud, cross-referencing of asset inventories with equipment purchase to detect theft, automated cash disbursement rules and identification of ghost workers.

At the launch of the Human Resource (HR) module of the IFMIS in South Africa, the Minister of Public Service and Administration stated (Baloyi 2011):

> The implementation of the module is critical for supporting good governance. Corruption remains the biggest single threat to good governance in South Africa and in the public service and fighting it remains a major challenge. Through implementing the HR module, government departments will be in a better position to eliminate ghost workers and the abuse of leave. The module will enable management to manage the disciplinary process in the Public Service better and will also automate the declaration of financial interests by senior managers. (p. 1)

Background to the South African scenario

According to Nomvalo (2008:8), IFMIS in South Africa forms part of the broader financial management reforms of the South African government, which started in 1994 with the institutionalisation of democracy in South Africa. The reform process was executed in four phases. The first phase (1994–1998) entailed the introduction of Medium-Term Expenditure Frameworks and a new classification system compatible with Government Financial Statistics (GFS).

In the second phase (1999–2002), the Accounting Standards Board and improved economic classifications were introduced in aid of effectively managing increased government expenditures. During the third phase (2003–2006), the government introduced a framework for Public Private Partnerships (PPP) and additional frameworks and policies were provided in areas such as Supply Chain Management (SCM). In addition, a risk management framework was also developed, whilst the latest phase began in 2007 with the commencement of the project for an IFMIS (Nomvalo 2008:8)

The IFMIS implementation project in South Africa is a priority initiative led by the National Treasury to review and upgrade the government's transverse information technology (IT) systems. The objective of this project is to enhance the integrity and effectiveness of expenditure management and performance reporting in order to ensure effective service delivery (National Treasury 2009:3). Transverse systems are defined as the general administrative systems required by all national departments and the provincial departments of all nine provinces, which include:

- financial management
- human resource management

- integrated supply chain management (including asset and procurement management)
- related business intelligence, audit and decision systems.

The South African government currently owns and operates a large compendium of systems in the transverse systems arena such as:

- the Financial Management System (FMS)
- the Basic Accounting System which is cash accounting systems
- the Personnel and Salaries Management System (PERSAL), which can be described as a payroll system
- the Logistical Information System (LOGIS), which supports the asset management and supply chain functions
- Vulindlela, a business intelligence system
- the Police Financial Management System (POLFIN), which is a department specific cash management system for the South African Police Services (O'Sullivan 2008:9).

As a whole these systems present a number of problems, such as:

- functional duplication and technological proliferation that has a negative impact on the cost-effective spending of public funds
- difficulties in the implementation of uniform norms and standards across systems and operations
- poor inherent systems of inter-operability and aggregating of data that seriously compromise operational integrity and the generation of management information
- difficulty in synchronising the implementation of new legislation and regulations with the capabilities of multiple systems, each on its independent evolutionary path (Van Deventer 2003:5).

According to O' Sullivan (2008:9) the main reasons for the problems are the following:

- aging technologies are reaching the end of their life-span
- systems are fragmented and data integration is difficult
- economies of scale are not being realised
- new functional requirements arising from new legislation (such as the Public Finance Management Act or the Preferential Procurement Policy Framework Act) or new regulations (such as accrual accounting) are difficult to implement
- increasing support and maintenance costs of aging technologies
- inability to take advantage of new technologies such as web-services to extend the reach of service delivery
- inter-operability with other e-Government systems is difficult, if not impossible.

Thus, based on the above, one can assert that the longer this scenario continues, the more additional applications will be phased in and the more difficult it will become to rationalise government IT in South Africa.

In 2005, in order to give effect to the implementation of an IFMIS in South Africa, the South African cabinet approved a cabinet memo (resolution) that the transversal systems, namely, Supply Chain Management, Human Resources, Finance and Business Intelligence, should be replaced

(National Treasury 2009:3). Thus, the IFMIS aims to replace the different transversal systems currently in use with a single system.

In 2007, the National Treasury informed the Standing Committee on Public Accounts that the IFMIS would be fully implemented by 2011. Different phases would be launched and early releases could be expected by 2008/2009 (Maake 2007:7). The implementation of an IFMIS in South Africa took place according to a phased-in approach as opposed to a one-stage approach. Three distinctive implementation phases can be distinguished:

- **Phase 1: Master Systems Plan** - This phase culminated in a Master Systems Plan (MSP) detailing the project objectives and functional scope, which was presented to the Cabinet, which then authorised the project to proceed with Phase 2 in September 2005.
- **Phase 2: Capacity and architecture** - Phase 2 of the project focused on preparing the State Information Technology Agency (SITA) for its role as the Prime Systems Integrator (PSI). During this phase, a number of pressing user requirements was identified and the scope of Phase 2 was expanded to fast-track several Phase 3 deliverables. Two commercial, off-the-shelf (COTS) systems for Human Resource Management and Procurement Management were acquired and the development of an Asset Register was initiated. During Phase 2, SITA also acquired a suite of software to support an Integrated Development Environment (IDE) for the in-house development of the bespoke software components of the system, of which the Asset Register was the first.
- **Phase 3: Development and implementation** - Phase 3 entailed the development and procurement of the various systems components and their phased deployment. During this phase, detailed system specifications were developed for each functional requirement identified in the IFMIS Conceptual Architecture. Using these specifications, the IFMIS team built the software components and integrated them with the COTS software to provide a 'government off-the-shelf' system (colloquially called 'GOTS' by the team). The development of an IFMIS was done incrementally within a well-defined, modular framework. A risk-averse deployment strategy was developed whereby each piece of new functionality was implemented at a lead site to ensure that all functional requirements and end-user support structures were fully operational before the module was deployed nationally.

The team used Open Standards to guarantee inter-operability and made use of Free and Open Source Software (FOSS) wherever possible, unless proprietary software was shown to be significantly superior. This is in line with the Cabinet's policy on the use of Free and Open Source Software. It was expected to take approximately five to seven years to complete the development of an IFMIS (Maake 2007:5).

South Africa is currently implementing different modules of the IFMIS at lead sites in both the national and the provincial departments to ensure that all functional requirements are met (Govender 2012:1).

Challenges involved in the implementation of an Integrated Financial Management Information System

The sheer size and complexity of an Integrated Financial Management Information System (IFMIS) poses significant challenges and a number of risks to the implementation process that go far beyond the mere technological risk of failure and deficient functionality. Studies conducted in various countries such as Tanzania, Ghana, Uganda, Malawi, Kenya and Rwanda indicated that there are a number of challenges that may influence the successful implementation of an IFMIS (Diamond & Khemani 2006:110; Rodin-Brown 2008:2). Some of the most common challenges that may be faced by developing countries are discussed in the subsections that follow. It is necessary for these challenges to be discussed in order to develop guidelines for better implementation of an IFMIS.

Lack of capacity

The effective implementation, operation and maintenance of an IFMIS require staff with the necessary knowledge and skills. Lack of capacity is regarded as one of the main causes for the delay in the implementation process experienced by Ghana, whilst the emphasis that was put on capacity building through training in Tanzania was one of the main contributors to their success. (Diamond & Khemani 2006:112).

The lack of staff with IT knowledge and experience cannot be easily remedied by training and hiring. The salary structure and terms of employment in the public sector are usually not attractive enough to compete with the private sector and to incentivise candidates with the required IT-skills levels (Chêne 2009:4). Trained personnel also leave the government service, often for better job opportunities.

Brar (2010:55) argues that low capacity for system implementation at the sub-national level, such as provincial and regional governments, is one of the major challenges in the implementation of an IFMIS in developing countries. This aspect is especially relevant in the South African context with its nine provinces and the consequent demand that the duplication of efforts creates for skills and knowledge, of which a shortage already exists. Farelo and Morris (2006:11) contend that the human resource development issue within government needs prioritisation, the education system needs to be aligned with the information and communication technologies (ICT) demands of the country and scarce ICT skills need to be attracted and retained particularly within government.

Weak commitment to change

The implementation of an IFMIS is a complex, risky, resource-intensive process that requires major procedural changes and often involves high-level officials who lack incentives for reform (Chêne 2009:4). It demands a commitment to change:

change in technology; in processes and procedures; as well as changes in skills, responsibilities and behaviours (Rodin-Brown 2008:29). Considering the nature and complexity of the project it is essential for all participants to be fully aware of the magnitude of the undertaking. Decision-makers must be convinced that the benefits of an IFMIS exceed the risks, and participating departments must recognise the need for a new system (Chêne 2009:4). According to Peterson (1998:43), the commitment of senior managers is one of the most frequently cited factors deciding the success or failure of an information system. Chêne (2009:6), however, argues that the Ethiopian case study has proven that what matters most in the process is mid-level management's commitment to reform, as the changes ultimately have to be implemented at this level. Diamond and Khemani (2006:105) argue that project commitment at the highest levels of the political system, as well as bureaucracy, and continuous participation from the direct users of the system and other stakeholders in all phases of the project, is necessary for success. Case studies of more successful countries, such as Kosovo, the Slovak Republic, Tanzania and Ethiopia, indicate that the clear commitment of the relevant authorities is one of the main factors supporting successful implementation of an IFMIS (Chêne 2009:4).

Institutional challenges

The introduction of an IFMIS involves more than only the automation of public finance tasks and processes. Rodin-Brown (2008:7) identifies a number of institutional issues that should be anticipated and planned. These issues include, amongst other organisational arrangements, the legal framework and business functional processes.

Organisational arrangements

Chêne (2009:3) asserts that an IFMIS implies both efficiency reforms and reforms that change existing procedures. It involves organisational reform, which deeply affects work processes and institutional arrangements governing the management of public finance. Institutional reform is, however, not easily achieved and, according to the International Consortium of Governmental Financial Management (ICGFM) (2008:166), it takes time, commitment, champions and courage to achieve.

Indeje and Zheng (2010:6) contend that the introduction of a new information system fundamentally changes the way operations are carried out and therefore requires a carefully managed process. This process results in the creation of a new organisational culture, that is, change in the way the organisation operates. In Rwanda, for example, there were three teams responsible for the development of the IFMIS. Lack or little co-ordination between the teams resulted in the IFMIS being incompatible with the system developed for the Rwanda Revenue Authority (Hove & Wynne 2010:26).

Legal framework

An IFMIS must be underpinned by a coherent legal framework governing the overall public finance system (Chêne 2009:3). Amongst other things there should be clear legal guidance on the roles and responsibilities of all institutions in managing, controlling, and monitoring budget execution; the authorisation, commitment and release of funds; the basis of accounting (cash or accrual); reporting requirements; and, asset management, public investment and borrowing (Rozner 2008:2). According to Chêne (2009:5), the implementation of IFMIS in Tanzania was distinguished by revising and developing an enabling legislation which contributed to the success of the system.

Business processes re-engineering

An IFMIS generally implies fundamental changes in operating procedures and should be preceded by a detailed functional analysis of processes, procedures, user profiles and requirements that the system will support (Chêne 2009:3). Key high-level government goals will only be achieved if the IFMIS solution supports a wide range of business processes that transcend functional, business, organisational and geographic boundaries. IFMIS design should, therefore, be preceded by detailed functional analysis that underpins current functional processes, procedures, user profiles and requirements that the new system will support (Rozner 2008:2). In Ghana the design and development of IFMIS was not satisfying, because of problems with the reporting functionality. This was because of a lack of clear specifications on the reporting requirements and approval from government on the design of various reports (Diamond & Khemani 2006:130).

Business process re-engineering is a critical aspect of any IFMIS reform and requires a review of all systems, functional processes, methods, rules and regulations, legislation, banking arrangements and related processes (Rodin-Brown 2008:8). It will be necessary to establish new, standardised procedures throughout the government to formalise job descriptions and to improve arrangements and systems for internal and external control.

Technical challenges

Many IFMIS projects have failed because the basic system functionality was not clearly specified from the onset of the intervention. Chêne (2009:4) posits that an IFMIS must be carefully designed to meet the needs and functional requirements, including the accounting and financial management tasks the system should perform. Consideration must be given to the type of systems that will be implemented, for example, off-the-shelf (OTS) or custom-built systems that fit the requirements of the specific country. An analysis of the different systems used by developing countries indicates that they make use of both off-the shelf systems as well as custom-built systems. For example, Ghana and Uganda opted for a system designed and developed to fit their specific requirements, whilst Tanzania, Malawi and Kenya opted for off-the shelf systems. It is important to note that a determining factor in the success of the implementation is not in the type of system, (i.e. off-the-shelf or custom-built) but rather in the complexity of the system. One of the reasons for the success of Tanzania's project is, for example, their decision to purchase a less complex, mid-range commercial package (Diamond & Khemani 2006:112).

South African specific challenges

South Africa is at the moment busy with the implementation phase of its IFMIS and according to Maake (2012:2) the following are some of the challenges experienced:

- The IFMIS programme has proved to be more complex than what was originally envisaged.
- There was an initial lack of sufficient capacity in the State Information Technology Agency (SITA) as the Prime Systems Integrator (PSI) from the commencement of the project.
- The movement of some Phase 3 deliverables (acquisition and implementation of COTS products) to Phase 2 placed an additional burden on the IFMIS project.
- Misalignment between the HRM product procurement and the Payroll product development resulted in challenges relating to the duplicate capturing of data on IFMIS and PERSAL in the HRM lead sites.
- There was insufficient capacity at user departments to take on IFMIS modules, for example, inadequate ICT infrastructure, budgets and staff with sufficient functional capabilities.

Kotze (2012) argues that implementation of the IFMIS has the effect that existing knowledge and expertise that was created over a lengthy period of time no longer exists. Officials are not trained in the new systems, are uncertain regarding functional processes which may delay the implementation process and they make mistakes. The fear to make mistakes also leads to resistance towards IFMIS which may impact negatively on its successful implementation.

Furthermore, there are still challenges experienced related to the clarity of roles with the implementation of IFMIS in the provincial sphere where the Provincial Treasuries as important role players do not have clearly defined roles and responsibilities (Kotze 2012). The absence of detailed implementation plans at lower levels, where the IFMIS is actually implemented, also influences the implementation process negatively (Kotze 2012).

Guidelines for successful implementation of an Integrated Financial Management Information System

The requirements for the introduction of an Integrated Financial Management Information System (IFMIS) may differ from country to country, but there are critical success factors or best practices that are important for the project to succeed. The best practices include the following.

Change management

Change management can be described as the creation, maintaining and systematic evaluation of changes in an organisation (Barcan 2010:93). It aims at maximising an organisation's ability to achieve success through involved, educated and committed people. O'Sullivan (2008:40) asserts that change management includes a stakeholder management model, a communication strategy, a change-readiness assessment framework and certain design elements.

The management of the changes that accompany the implementation of an IFMIS can be regarded as one of the most critical, but also one of the most neglected aspects of IFMIS reforms. The success of IT reforms depends upon the capacity of the organisation to change, to manage the change and to survive whilst changing (Peterson 1998:38). Resistance to change may come from various stakeholders in the organisation, such as individuals with vested interests who benefited from previous methods, civil servants who see it as a threat to their jobs and people who resist change simply for fear of the unknown.

According to Rozner (2008:3), a change management strategy should be developed as soon as an IFMIS project is conceived, taking into consideration the change implications for diverse stakeholders, that is, from politicians and senior officials to heads of departments, civil servants and the IT personnel who will support the new systems. If this aspect is not addressed early in the project, the project will constantly be faced with resistance and obstacles from elected politicians, executive officials and personnel who will use the systems regularly.

The best way to overcome resistance to change will be through clear communication, education and training, as well as through 'quick wins' that demonstrate the benefits of the change (Rozner 2008:4). The communication can be done through a variety of media, workshops, seminars, training sessions, a website, conferences, or newsletters (Rodin-Brown 2008:24).

Ensuring project commitment

Various writers such as Peterson (1998:43), Chêne (2009:6) as well as Diamond and Khemani (2006:105) argue that the importance of commitment by politicians and management is vital to ensure success of the implementation of an IFMIS. Experience indicates that the best designed project will fail without firm commitment from all stakeholders involved, including politicians, as well as senior and middle management. Thus, Diamond and Khemani (2006:105) posit that ensuring project commitment at the highest levels of the political system and of management and continuous participation from the direct users of the system is necessary in all phases of the project.

In South Africa, political commitment was obtained through a cabinet resolution when Cabinet approved the IFMIS project in 2005. The President of the Republic of South Africa has also committed South Africa not only to participate, but also to compete internationally in the Information Society (Farelo & Morris 2006:7). For this purpose, the Presidential National

Commission on Information Society and Development (PNC on ISAD) was established in 2001 by the President of the Republic of South Africa to advise and to co-ordinate ICT initiatives broadly. The PNC on ISAD works closely together with the Minister of Communications on ICT strategies for the Information Society as a whole. Co-ordination of e-government, as well as the governance of ICTs within the government, is the responsibility of the Minister of Public Service and Administration, who is tasked with this process (Farelo & Morris 2006:7). Whilst political commitment may exist at the national political level, political commitment in the provincial sphere and commitment from officials at all levels involved must be ensured for success.

Creating a legal framework

It is important to have clear legal guidance on the roles and responsibilities of all institutions involved in the implementation of an IFMIS. According to Diamond and Khemani (2006:110), a legislative framework consists of the constitution, finance act and regulations, and needs to include:

- the roles and responsibilities of the treasury, and other departments responsible for the control and management of public finance
- the main form of government funds, receipt and custody of public funds, the annual process, submission and approval of estimates and the procedures for release of funds
- the basis of accounting and the form of annual accounts for audit and presentation to Parliament
- asset management and control, borrowing and investment.

Legal reforms, however, are seldom simple or swift, but this process need not obstruct IFMIS implementation (Rozner 2008:2).

In South Africa, the legislative framework for implementation of an IFMIS is enshrined in the Constitution of the Republic of South Africa (Republic of South Africa 1996) and the *Public Finance Management Act* (Republic of South Africa 1999). The Constitution confers extensive powers on the national government to determine the financial management framework over all organs of state, in all spheres of government. The National Government must, through national legislation, establish a national treasury and prescribe measures to ensure transparency and expenditure control in each sphere of government by introducing generally recognised accounting practices, uniform expenditure classifications, and uniform treasury norms and standards.

The *Public Finance Management Act* (Republic of South Africa 1999) which gives effect to the Constitution has the following key objectives:

- to modernise the system of financial management in the public sector
- to enable public sector managers to manage, but at the same time be held more accountable
- to ensure the timely provision of quality information
- to eliminate waste and corruption in the use of public assets.

The Act is part of a broader strategy on improving financial management in the public sector through various reform projects and strategies, such as budget and procurement reforms introduced by the first South African democratic government.

Solving technical challenges

IFMIS projects often fail because the basic system does not meet the requirements and tasks it should perform (Chêne 2009:4). The main aim of an IFMIS is to integrate all aspects of the government's budgetary cycle and provide suitable interfaces to other systems and entities. Barata and Cain (2001:247) posit that a technical appraisal of the IFMIS should identify the strengths and weaknesses of the system, taking into account the full picture of what the system is required to achieve.

In South Africa, this problem is dealt with by ensuring that the IFMIS Data Architecture is required to meet challenges posed by the sheer size and complexity of the system when considering the number of business domains included (finance, SCM, Human Resource Management and business intelligence). The mixture of COTS and bespoke developed subsystems interfaces with departmental core systems, with systems of business partners, with legacy systems during the lengthy phase-out period, and with constantly changing and diverging business requirements (O'Sullivan 2008:30).

Capacity building and training

Capacity building is a major factor affecting the success of IFMIS implementation, especially in developing countries (Chêne 2009:9). An IFMIS comprises more than only implementing a project; it also means planning for capacity building. A comprehensive training programme is therefore vital for the success of the project and should be compiled as early as possible. Training is essential to unlocking client readiness and is the best way to ensure sustainability of a system (Vickland & Nieuwenhuijs 2005:101).

According to Maake (2007:7), the challenges that South Africa faces include access to appropriate IT skills as well as appropriate functional skills by user departments. South Africa faces significant human capital development challenges in building the capacity required by an IFMIS. The shortage of skilled ICT people in the country is exacerbated by the emigration of highly skilled ICT personnel and other professionals to developed countries, and from the public to the private sector (Farelo & Morris 2006:6).

In order to build the necessary capacity, it is important to create a learning environment early in the project and to treat the whole process as a learning opportunity with training being part of an ongoing process. Training should be provided to senior managers, technical staff and end users, and should teach users how to use the new system and how it affects business processes. Diamond and Khemani (2006:108), however, argue that the training will not only include training in the use of the IFMIS for the respective operations and functions, but will also entail training in the new legal and regulatory framework, the new codes and classifications, and the new business procedures put in place.

A well-defined training programme will also assist in building capacity and help build confidence amongst users who, through the process, are reassured that there will be some constants amidst the change. Given the nature of institutions and organisations, capacity building is a never-ending process. It needs to be ongoing and permanent (Rodin-Brown 2008:24).

A phased approach to Integrated Financial Management Information System implementation

The implementation of an Integrated Financial Management Information System (IFMIS) is a comprehensive process that requires patience. The full project's life cycle, from the definition of objectives, to system specifications, to system procurement, configuration, testing, pilot installation and rollout, can take years to complete (Rozner 2008:4). According to Rodin-Brown (2008:1X), a phased approach offers the best chances for successful implementation of an IFMIS, as a project can be carefully monitored and reviewed regularly. There are high risks involved in implementing too many components of the system at once and to mitigate the risk it is recommended that a phased approach be followed that rolls out across government institutions in a gradual and flexible process.

Procurement specifications for an IFMIS are not as clearly definable as, for example, the specifications for a vehicle or stationery, which can be defined with clear specifications. An IFMIS seems to be definable, but in reality there are too many interdependent variables that need to be firmed up as the process of implementation evolves (Rodin-Brown 2008:14). By following a phased approach, the project can be separated into smaller manageable units that can allow for 'quick wins' that help sustain or renew commitment from all involved. As each phase is completed, stakeholders can carefully assess project progress and make the necessary adjustments.

South Africa, being in the fortunate position to benefit from recent experiences in other countries, followed a phased approach towards an IFMIS with Phase 1 being the development of a Master Systems Plan, Phase 2, Capacitating and Architecture, and Phase 3, Development and Implementation. At the moment, different modules are being tested for deployment at pilot departments, both nationally and provincially.

Project management and oversight

When implementing an IFMIS, strong project management is critical for the success of the initiative (Vickland & Nieuwenhuijs 2005:101). Project management entails more than managing the technical aspects of implementation. It also involves project planning methodologies to plan, implement and monitor the project, with project management responsibilities clearly identified.

An adequate project implementation team should therefore be established, ideally comprising a project manager, a public finance economist, a qualified accountant, a change management or training specialist, an IT-system specialist and a logistics specialist (Chêne 2009:8). At the same time, the programme manager must have the necessary managerial and leadership skills to direct and co-ordinate diverse activities executed by a wide range of specialists. The team should strive to adhere to the project implementation plan, but there should be flexibility to address inevitable changes, with approval through a programme governance structure.

In order to fulfil this role, the National Treasury in South Africa has set up a dedicated IFMIS project office composed of the following specialist functions: project management, systems engineering, domain specialists and information technology (Van Deventer 2003:12). The Programme Management Office (PMO) works with the IFMIS Programme Managers to monitor the execution of the project schedule and the budget. It is responsible for the development and implementation of policies and processes for the project. Project planning in the PMO is guided by the Project Management Body of Knowledge (PMBOK) framework and uses detailed project planning procedures derived from the Projects in Controlled Environments (PRINCE2) project management method. According to O'Sullivan (2008:11), the focus of this methodology is on the production of specific deliverables which ensure that planning and execution are based on measurable outputs that deliver strategic value.

Project implementation plan

The project implementation plan should cover immediate, medium-term and long-term IFMIS tasks and objectives, whilst a clear mission statement will help control the project direction, participant expectations and, ultimately, project costs. Rozner (2008:4) recommends that it should clearly define parameters, including the system objective and scope, the overall system conceptual design, expected impact and benefits, critical milestones and success factors, project implementation methodology, risk assessment or mitigation strategy, estimated costs and the financing arrangements.

Because the time span involving the implementation of an IFMIS is so long, it is inevitable that governmental changes, which often lead to structural changes, will occur. The project management implementation plan should therefore be revisited regularly to ensure that the situation has not changed substantially.

The South African IFMIS project implementation plan is derived directly from the IFMIS architecture effort. The principles adopted and the reference models developed from the MSP and the user-requirement specifications (URS) gave rise to the functional and technical architectures (O'Sullivan 2008:38).

Conclusion

IFMISs form part of the financial management reform practices of developing countries globally. It holds benefits such as effective control over public finances, contributes to the enhancement of transparency and accountability and serves as a deterrent to corruption and fraud.

The study has shown that difficulties can be experienced with the implementation of an IFMIS. It will thus not always achieve the desired functionality and impact on public financial management that was originally anticipated. Obstacles such as a lack of capacity, a lack of commitment, and institutional and technical challenges pose a risk to the successful implementation of an IFMIS.

It is thus important that best practice guidelines be followed when the public sector implement an IFMIS. Such a decision needs to be accompanied by a capacity-building programme, the obtaining of commitment of all role players, the creation of a legal framework, an agenda for effective change management, a strong project management team, a phased approach to implementation and a well-defined project implementation plan. South Africa had the benefit of learning from experiences in other developed as well as developing countries. An IFMIS is now being implemented and is in its testing phase and follow-up studies should be conducted at a later time to determine the benefits achieved.

Acknowledgements

Competing interests

The author declares that he has no financial or personal relationship(s) which may have inappropriately influenced him in writing this paper.

References

Baloyi, M.R., 2011, 'Address by the Minister for Public Service and Administration, Mr Masenyani Richard Baloyi, at the Integrated Financial Management System (IFMS) Human Resource (HR) go live celebration Pretoria Zoological Gardens', viewed 10 April 2011, from http://www.info.gov.za/speech/DynamicAction?pageid=461&sid=17409&tid=3100

Barata, K. & Cain, P., 2001, 'Information, not technology, is essential to accountability: Electronic records and public-sector financial management', *The Information Society* 17, 247–258. http://dx.doi.org/10.1080/019722401753330841

Barcan, L., 2010, 'New concepts in the change management within public organizations', *Young Economists Journal Revista Tinerilor Economisti* 8(14), 93–97.

Brar, P., 2010, *IFMIS in Africa: Some key issues*, viewed 11 April 2011, from http://www.eastafritac.org/images/uploads/documents_storage/IFMIS_Workshop_Day_1_Presentations.pdf

Chêne, M., 2009, *The Implementation of Integrated Financial Information Management Systems (IFMS)*, viewed 06 April 2011, from http://www.u4.no/helpdesk/helpdesk/query.cfm?id=196

Cooper, D.R. & Schindler, P.S., 2006, *Business Research Methods*, 9th edn., McGraw Hill, Boston.

Diamond, J. & Khemani, P., 2006, 'Introducing financial management information systems in developing countries', *OECD Journal on Budgeting* 5(3), 97–132. http://dx.doi.org/10.1787/budget-v5-art20-en

Dorotinsky, B., 2003, *Implementing financial management information system projects: The World Bank experience*, viewed 06 April 2011, from http://blog-pfm.imf/AIST2/Dorotinsky.ppt

Dorotinsky, W. & Matsuda, Y., 2001, *Financial management reform in Latin America: An institutional perspective*, viewed 06 April 2011, from http://www.gsdrc.org/docs/open/ PF32.pdf

Farelo, M. & Morris, C., 2006, *The Status of e-government in South Africa*, viewed 11 April 2011, from http://hdl.handle.net/10204/966

Govender, K., 2012, *Integrated financial management system and Persal projects: Departmental presentation*, viewed 26 July 2012, from http://www.pmg.org.za/report/

Hove, M. & Wynne, A., 2010, *The experience of medium term expenditure framework & integrated financial management information system reforms in sub-Saharan Africa: What is the balance sheet?*, viewed 07 April 2011 from http://www.acbf-pact.org/knowledge/documents/Occasional_ Paper 9.pdf

Indeje W.G. & Zheng Q., 2010, 'Organizational culture and information systems implementation: A structuration theory perspective', *Sprouts: Working Papers on Information Systems* 10(27), viewed 12 April 2012 from http://sprouts.aisnet.org/10-27.

International Consortium of Governmental Financial Management (ICGFM), 2008, 'Use of Financial Management Information Systems (FMIS) to improve financial management and accountability in the public sector', in *International Journal on Governmental Financial Management*, viewed 12 April 2012, from http://www.scribd.com/doc/10269078/Use-of-Financial-Management-Information-Systems-to-Improve-Financial-Management-and-Accountability-in-the-Public-Sector

Kotze, J.J., 2012, e-mail, 25 September, kobus@treasury.fs.gov.za

Lianzuala, A. & Khawlhring, E., 2008, *Mizoram IFMIS Project*, viewed 06 April 2012, from http://www.docstoc.com/docs/39661608/Mizoram-IFMIS-Project

Maake, B., 2007, *Presentation to National Treasury/Scopa Quarterly Meeting: Integrated Financial Management Systems (IFMS)*, viewed 09 April 2012 from http://www.pmg.org.za/docs/2007/ 070523ifms.ppt

Maake, B., 2012, *IFMS presentation to the CFO Forum*, viewed 20 September 2012, from http://oag.treasury.gov.za

Mouton, J., 2001, *How to succeed in your masters and doctoral studies: a South African guide and resource book*, van Schaik Publishers, Pretoria.

National Treasury, 2009, *e-Procurement in South Africa*, viewed 07 April 2012, from http://idbdocs.iadb.org/ wsdocs/getdocument.aspx?docnum=2258376

Nomvalo, F., 2008, *Case study PFM reforms, A South African perspective*, viewed 07 April 2011 from http://icgfm.blogspot.com/2008/12/case-study-pfm-reforms-south-african.html

O'Sullivan, G.S., 2008, *IFMS Architecture Executive Overview*, viewed 14 April 2012, from http://www.treasury.gov.za/ifms/secure/architecture.aspx

Peterson, S.B., 1998, 'Saints, demons, wizards and systems: why information technology reforms fail or underperform in public bureaucracies in Africa', *Public Administration and Development* 18, 37–60. http://dx.doi.org/10.1002/(SICI)1099-162X(199802)18:1<37::AID-PAD990>3.0.CO;2-V

Republic of South Africa, 1996, *Constitution of the Republic of South Africa, 1996 (No. 108 of 1996)*, Government Printer, Pretoria.

Republic of South Africa, 1999, *Public Finance Management Act, 1999 (No. 29 of 1999)*, Government Printer, Pretoria.

Rodin-Brown, E., 2008, *Integrated Financial Management Information Systems: A practical guide*, viewed 06 April 2011, from http://pdf.usaid.gov/pdf_docs/PNADK595.pdf

Rozner, S., 2008, *Best practices in fiscal reform and economic governance. Introducing integrated financial management information systems*, viewed 06 April 2011, from http://blog-pfm.imf.org/ pfmblog/files/ifmis_bpn_web1.pdf

Van Deventer, L., 2003, *Integrated Financial Management Systems (IFMS) Project Overview*, viewed 16 April 2011, from http://www.treasury.gov.za/ifms/secure/default.aspx

Vickland, S & Nieuwenhuijs, I., 2005, 'Critical success factors for modernising public financial management information systems in Bosnia and Herzegovina', *Public Administration and Development* 25, 95–103. http://dx.doi.org/10.1002/pad.354

9

Towards a universal definition of competitive intelligence

Authors:
Rene Pellissier[1]
Tshilidzi E. Nenzhelele[2]

Affiliations:
[1]School of Business Leadership, University of South Africa, Pretoria, South Africa

[2]Department of Business Management, University of South Africa, Pretoria, South Africa

Correspondence to:
Rene Pellissier

Email:
pellir@unisa.ac.za

Postal address:
PO Box 392, Pretoria 0003, South Africa

Background: Enterprises face intense competition caused by globalisation. Consequently, enterprises look for tools that provide a competitive advantage. Competitive intelligence (CI) provides a competitive advantage to enterprises of all sizes. There are many definitions of CI but no universally accepted one.

Objectives: The purpose of this research is to review the current literature on CI with the aim of identifying and analysing CI definitions to establish the commonalities and differences, to propose a universal and comprehensive definition of CI and to set the borders of CI for common understanding amongst CI stakeholders.

Method: The study was qualitative in nature and content analysis was conducted on all identified sources establishing and analysing CI definitions. To identify relevant literature, academic databases and search engines were used. A review of references in related studies led to more relevant sources, the references of which were further reviewed and analysed. Keywords 'competitive intelligence', 'marketing intelligence' and 'business intelligence' were used in search engines to find relevant sources. To ensure reliability, only peer-reviewed articles were used.

Results: The majority of scholars define CI as a process and acknowledge that CI is collected from the internal and external or competitive environment. They also outline the goals of CI, which are to help in decision-making and provide a competitive advantage.

Conclusion: The proposed definition outlines the process, purpose, source, deliverables, beneficiaries, benefit, ethicality and legality of CI, sets out the borders of CI and ensures a common understanding amongst CI stakeholders.

Introduction

Enterprises face intense competition caused by globalisation (Wright, Eid & Fleisher 2009). Consequently, enterprises look for tools that provide a competitive advantage (Weiss & Naylor 2010). Competitive intelligence (CI) is a tool that provides a competitive advantage to enterprises and help decision-makers (Fleisher & Wright 2009; Haataja 2011). CI evolved from economics, marketing, military theory, information science and strategic management (Muller 2006). As a profession, CI must follow a prescribed code of ethics (Roitner 2008). There are many definitions of CI in the literature. Although Brody (2008) explored the definitions of CI, he never attempted to come up with a universally accepted definition. This research aims to suggest a possible universal definition of CI.

Competitive intelligence process

Despite many researchers listing only five steps or stages of the CI process (Bose 2008), Botha and Boon (2008) identify seven steps, which are depicted in Figure 1 and briefly discussed thereafter.

Intelligence needs and determining key intelligence topics: Intelligence needs of decision-makers are ascertained and all intelligence leads are narrowed to key intelligence topics. *Planning and direction:* Plans and directions are formulated in order to fulfil the intelligence needs of decision-makers. *Collection:* Information is collected from the external environment in an ethical and legal manner. *Information processing:* Collected information gets captured and stored. *Analysis:* Stored information is analysed to produce actionable intelligence. *Dissemination:* Actionable intelligence is distributed to decision-makers. *Intelligence users and decision-makers:* New intelligence needs are identified.

Definitions of competitive intelligence

There are many definitions of CI in the literature (Weiss & Naylor 2010) and none has achieved worldwide acceptance (Roitner 2008). These definitions differ only by semantic changes in

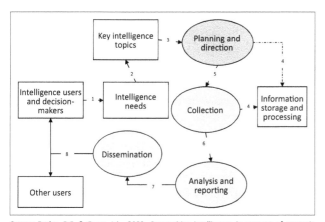

Source: Botha, D.F. & Boon, J.A., 2008, Competitive intelligence in support of strategic training and learning, *South African Journal of Information Management* 10(3), 1–6.

FIGURE 1: The competitive intelligence process.

language and emphasis (Brody 2008). Fleisher and Wright (2009) argue that CI practitioners rarely have time for definitions rather focus on doing their job better. Haddadi, Dousset and Berrada (2010) conclude that the lack of a universally accepted definition of CI makes it a field with unstable borders. CI is frequently confused with industrial espionage (Colakoglu 2011). Unlike CI, industrial espionage is considered unethical and illegal (Haddadi *et al.* 2010). According to Roitner (2008), CI is ethical and legal because it follows a code of ethics. Definitions of CI that exist in the literature are either process-oriented or product-oriented (Brody 2008). However, Roitner (2008) states that it is difficult to draw a line and to categorise CI as a process or a product as it comprises characteristics of both. There is therefore a need for a commonly agreed definition of CI (Roitner 2008). The literature shows that the definitions of CI have evolved over the years. The following definitions of CI were identified from the literature.

Some definitions outline the CI process, purpose and sources but overlook the deliverable, benefit, beneficiaries, ethicality and legality: CI is:

- A process of knowing what the competition is up to and staying one step ahead of them, by gathering information about competitors and, ideally, applying it to short- and long-term strategic planning (Dishman & Pearson 2003).
- The process of monitoring the competitive environment to help in making informed decisions about marketing, research and development and long-term strategies (Liu & Oppenheim 2006).
- A process of monitoring the competitive environment by pulling together data and information from a very large and strategic perspective, to predict or forecast what is going to happen in the competitive environment of an enterprise (Bose 2008).
- An ongoing, systematic evaluation of the external environment for opportunities, threats and developments that could have an impact on the enterprise and influence reactive decision-making (Strauss & Du Toit 2010).
- The process of collecting, analysing and applying information about products, clients and competitors to meet the enterprise's long-term and short-term planning needs (Othenin-Girard, Caron & Guillemette 2011).

Other definitions outline the CI process and purpose but neglect the sources, deliverable, benefit, beneficiaries, ethicality and legality: CI is:

- A process involving the gathering, analysing and communicating of environmental information to assist in strategic decision-making (Dishman & Calof 2007).
- The process of collection, treatment and diffusion of information that has an objective: the reduction of uncertainty in the making of all strategic decisions (Zeng *et al.* 2007).
- The process of taking large amounts of data, analysing that data and presenting a high-level set of reports that condense the essence of that data into the basis of business actions, enabling management to make fundamental daily business decisions (Stackowiak, Rayman & Greenwald 2007).

There are also definitions that acknowledge CI process, purpose, sources and deliverable but neglect the benefit, beneficiaries, ethicality and legality: CI is:

- A process that aims to monitor the external business environment of an organisation in order to identify relevant information for the decision-making process (Cheng, Chau & Zeng 2002).
- The transformation of raw information about the competitive external environment into intelligence to support business decisions (Hughes 2005).
- The conversion of data and information, gathered by an organisation from its external and internal environment, into intelligence that supports the organisational decision-making process (Santos & Correia 2010).

Other definitions acknowledge CI process, purpose, sources, benefit and deliverable, but neglect the benefits, beneficiaries, ethicality and legality: CI is:

- The process by which an enterprise collects useful information about its competitors and its competitive environment so that it can apply this information in its planning and decision-making processes to improve performance (Love 2007).
- The process by which organisations gather actionable information about competitors and the competitive environment and, ideally, apply it to their planning processes and decision-making in order to improve their enterprise's performance (Brody 2008).

Some definitions emphasise CI sources and ignore the process, purpose, deliverable, benefit, beneficiaries, ethicality and legality: CI is:

- The purposeful and coordinated monitoring of your competitors, wherever and whoever they may be, within a specific marketplace (Johnson 2005).
- Any type of activity aimed at monitoring competitors (potential and current) and gathering information of all types, including about human resource practices, sales and marketing, research and development and general strategy (Tarraf & Molz 2006).
- The collection of information from competitors, customers, suppliers, technologies, environments and potential business relationships (Calof & Wright 2008).

Some definitions outline the CI process, purpose and deliverable, but overlook the sources, benefit, beneficiaries, ethicality and legality: CI is:

- An activity of collecting, processing, storing and disseminating information that is used everywhere in the organisation in order to prepare better for the future and to avoid disasters (Rouach & Santi 2001).
- The process of transforming data and the transfer of this information to the knowledge used to support the business (decision-making) (Simoes, Coelho & Popovic 2009).

Other definitions emphasise the CI purpose and source but overlook the process, deliverable, benefit, beneficiaries, ethicality and legality: CI is:

- The action of gathering, analysing and applying information about products, domain constituents, customers, and competitors for the short-term and long-term planning needs of an organisation (Fleisher 2003).
- The purposeful and coordinated monitoring of competition within a specific marketplace and helps in decision-making (Agarwal 2006).

Still other definitions acknowledge the CI process and source but neglect the purpose, deliverable, benefit, beneficiaries, ethicality and legality: CI is:

- The process of monitoring the competitive environment (Hamblen 2000).
- A systematic process initiated by organisations in order to gather and analyse information about competitors and the general sociopolitical and economic environment of the firm (Colakoglu 2011).

Some definitions emphasise the CI process, purpose, source and benefit, but overlook the deliverable, beneficiaries, ethicality and legality: CI is:

- The process by which organisations actively gather information about competitors and the competitive environment and, ideally, apply it to their decision-making and planning processes in order to improve their business performance (Badr, Madden & Wright 2006).
- The process by which organisations gather information on competitors and the competitive environment, ideally using this in their decision-making and planning processes with the goal of adjusting activities to improve performance (Wright et al. 2009).

Some definitions emphasise the CI process, source and deliverable but overlook the purpose, benefit, beneficiaries, ethicality and legality: CI is:

- An actionable recommendation arising from a systematic process, involving planning, gathering, analysing and disseminating information on the external environment, for opportunities or developments that have the potential to affect a company or a country's competitive situation (Calof 2001).
- The information and study of the competitive environment, competitive opponents and competitive strategy, which is a procedure as well as a product (Changhuo & Xinzhou 2003).

The following definitions emphasise the CI process, purpose, beneficiaries and deliverable but ignore the source, benefit, ethicality and legality: CI is:

- A value-added product resulting from the collection, evaluation, analysis, integration and interpretation of all available information that pertains to one or more aspects of a decision-makers' needs, and that is immediately or potentially significant to decision-making (Fleisher & Benssousan 2003).
- A process that supplies employees at the management level of an organisation with relevant information in order to support tactical and strategic decision-making (Bucher, Gericke & Sigg 2009).

Other definitions acknowledge the CI purpose, deliverable and beneficiaries but ignore the process, source, benefit, ethicality and legality: CI is:

- A set of coordinated actions of research, treatment and distribution of useful information to stakeholders to enable their actions and decision-making (Haddadi et al. 2010).
- A set of procedures and data sources used by marketing managers to sift information from the environment that they can use in their decision making (Nasri & Charfeddine 2012).

Some definitions acknowledge the CI process, purpose, source, deliverable, ethics and beneficiaries but ignore the benefit and legality: CI is:

- A systematic, targeted, timely and ethical effort to collect, synthesise and analyse competition, markets and the external environment in order to produce actionable insights for decision-makers (Fleisher 2008).
- A systematic and planned process to ethically collect, analyse, synthesise and disseminate accurate, relevant, timely and actionable intelligence about customers, competitors, partners, markets and other environmental factors in order to asses and monitor external environment, provide early warning signals and support decision-makers in strategic and tactical decision-making (Haataja 2011).

One definition emphasises the sources and deliverable of CI but ignores the purpose, process, benefit, beneficiaries, ethicality and legality: CI is:

- Actionable information about the present and future behaviour of competitors, suppliers, customers, technologies, government, acquisitions, market and general business environment (Vedder & Guynes 2000).

This definition outlines the CI deliverable and purpose but neglects process, ethicality, legality, sources, benefit and beneficiaries: CI is:

- Information that is analysed and provides implications for strategic planning and decision-making (Groom & David 2001).

This definition acknowledges CI deliverable and benefit but overlooks the process, purpose, source, legality, ethicality and beneficiaries: CI is:

- Any actionable intelligence that could provide a competitive edge (Prescott & Miller 2001).

This definition emphasises the source, legality and ethicality of CI; it neglects the CI purpose, deliverable, benefit, beneficiaries and process: CI is:

- A legal and ethical collection of information about competitors' activities in the marketplace (Tan, Foo & Hui 2002).

This definition is very narrow; it refers to CI as data and overlooks the CI process, purpose, source, ethicality, legality, beneficiaries and benefit: CI is:

- The focusing, analysing and 'actioning' of data (Du Toit 2003).

This definition is broad and highlights CI process, ethicality, purpose, deliverable, source and benefit but ignores CI legality and beneficiaries: CI is:

- The systematic process by which organisations ethically gather and analyse actionable information about competitors and the competitive environment and, ideally, apply it to their decision-making and planning processes to improve their performance (Fleisher 2004).

This definition is broader and reveals CI process, source, deliverable, ethicality and legality but it overlooks CI purpose, benefit and beneficiaries: CI is:

- A continuously evolving process that involves discovering, analysing and using intelligence regarding competitors and the general business environment from publicly available, non-proprietary information sources and converting it into knowledge on a continuing basis (Blenkhorn & Fleisher 2005).

This definition outlines the CI process, benefit and source but neglects CI purpose, beneficiaries, deliverable, ethicality and legality: CI is:

- A process that increases marketplace competitiveness by analysing the capabilities and potential actions of individual competitors as well as the overall competitive situation of the firm in its industry and in the economy (Gray 2005).

This definition is very narrow and overlooks the CI purpose, deliverable, benefit, beneficiaries, ethicality, legality and source: CI is:

- The systematic collection, evaluation, and organisation of information (Hodges 2005).

This definition outlines the CI process, source, types of collected information and deliverable but it refers to CI as strategic knowledge and overlooks CI purpose, benefit, beneficiaries, ethicality and legality: CI is

- The analytical process that transforms disaggregated competitor information into relevant, accurate and useable strategic knowledge about competitor positions, performance, capabilities and intentions (Muller 2006).

This definition outlines the CI purpose, process, ethicality, legality, beneficiaries and deliverable. However, it ignores CI sources and benefit: CI is:

- A process that uses legal and ethical means to discover, develop and deliver the relevant intelligence needed by decision-makers in a timely manner (Pietersen 2006).

This definition outlines the CI process, deliverable, legality and source but it ignores CI purpose, benefit, beneficiaries, ethicality and legality: CI is:

- A process by which an organisation legally gathers, analyses and distributes the information about its competitive environment (Jin & Bouthillier 2008).

This definition reveals the CI process, purpose and beneficiaries but overlooks CI deliverable, source, benefit, ethicality and legality: CI is:

- The art of collecting, processing and sorting information to be made available to people at all levels of the firm to help to shape its future and protect it against current competitive threats (Zangoueinezhad & Moshabaki 2009).

This definition outlines the CI process and beneficiaries but it disregards CI purpose, source, benefit, deliverable, ethicality and legality: CI is:

- A process aimed to acquire information, filter and refine it to a suitable form and deliver it to the users within the organisation (Vuori & Väisänen 2009).

This definition acknowledges the CI process, purpose, source and ethicality, but overlooks CI deliverable, benefit, beneficiaries and legality: CI is:

- An ethical process for obtaining information on the competitive environment for use in organisational decision-making (Weiss & Naylor 2010).

This definition outlines CI deliverables, process, purpose, beneficiaries, source and type of information but ignores CI benefit, ethicality and legality: CI is:

- A combination of defining, gathering and analysing intelligence about products, customers, competitors and any aspect of the environment needed to support executives and managers in making strategic decisions for an organisation (Dey et al. 2011).

This definition outlines CI beneficiaries, purpose, source and types of information but pays no attention to the CI process, deliverable, benefit, ethicality and legality: CI is:

- An activity of the strategic management of information that aims to allow decision-makers to forestall the market trends and moves of competitors, identify and evaluate threats and opportunities that emerge in the business environment, and circumscribe actions of attack or defence that are more appropriate to the development strategy of the enterprise. (Magrinho, Franco & Silva 2011).

This definition points out CI purpose, benefits and beneficiaries but overlooks CI process, source, deliverable, ethicality and legality: CI is

- A management discipline that enables executives to make smarter, more successful decisions, thereby minimising risk, avoiding being blind-sighted, and getting it right the first time (Nikolaos 2012).

Research results

From the 50 definitions of CI outlined above, common and unique characteristics were identified. These characteristics are:

- *Process* indicates that CI is conducted step by step.
- *Product* indicates that CI is a deliverable of a completed process.
- *Practice/discipline* indicates that CI is a profession that follows a code of ethics.
- *Actionable* is used to indicate that CI leads to actions or decision-making.
- *Systematic* indicates that CI follows a planned procedure.
- *Ethical* indicates that CI follows an established code of ethics.
- *Legal* indicates that CI activities observe applicable laws in countries or regions where it is practised.
- *Purpose/goal* refers to the objectives of CI.
- *Information* refers to collection of facts or data.
- *Art* indicates that CI has its origin in the military.
- *Activity/method* refers to actions taken to complete the CI process.
- *External/competitive environment* indicates that information is collected from the external or competitive environment.

Figure 2 indicates CI definition characteristics and their frequency. Out of 50 definitions, 38 refer to CI as a process and four as a product. Thirty-five definitions declare that CI is collected from the external or competitive environment. Thirty-six definitions outline the purpose or goal of CI, which is to help in decision-making and provide a competitive advantage. Eight definitions indicate that CI is actionable. Only eight definitions outline that CI is ethical and five indicate that it is legally compliant. Six definitions refer to CI as information. Because of its military origin, three definitions refer to CI as an art. Seven definitions refer to CI as systematic. One definition refers to CI as an activity or method and another one refers to it as a practice or discipline. Figure 2 also highlights the percentage comparison amongst the CI characteristics.

The following comprehensive and universal definition is therefore proposed for CI: CI is:

> A process or practice that produces and disseminates actionable intelligence by planning, ethically and legally collecting, processing and analysing information from and about the internal and external or competitive environment in order to help decision-makers in decision-making and to provide a competitive advantage to the enterprise.

The extensive review of the literature and analysis of the above frequencies led to the formulation of the above CI definition. The proposed definition refers to CI as a process because the majority of the scholars acknowledge it as such. The definition also refers to CI as an ethical and legal practice because CI, like accounting, medicine and law, is a practice conducted by professionals. The definition indicates that CI produces and disseminates actionable intelligence (intelligence that leads to action). The proposed definition reveals that CI is collected from the external or competitive environment

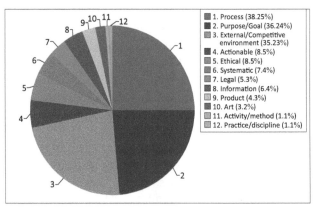

FIGURE 2: Characteristics of competitive intelligence definitions.

1. Process (38.25%)
2. Purpose/Goal (36.24%)
3. External/Competitive environment (35.23%)
4. Actionable (8.5%)
5. Ethical (8.5%)
6. Systematic (7.4%)
7. Legal (5.3%)
8. Information (6.4%)
9. Product (4.3%)
10. Art (3.2%)
11. Activity/method (1.1%)
12. Practice/discipline (1.1%)

because the majority of the scholars outline this in their definitions. Because information for CI is also collected from and about the internal environment, the proposed definition outlines this. The majority of scholars reveal that the purpose or goal of CI is to help decision-makers in decision-making and the proposed definition outlines this. The proposed definition also outlines the general added benefit of CI, which is to give enterprises competitive advantage. The proposed CI definition outlines the CI process, deliverable, ethicality, legality, source, purpose, benefit and beneficiaries. Therefore, this definition is comprehensive and clearly sets out the borders of CI for common understanding.

Discussion

The unwillingness of scholars to agree on and accept one definition of CI has led to endless definitions of CI and misunderstandings in the field. The notion that CI is both a process and a product has also led to several definitions: instead of finding ways to incorporate both process and product in one definition, scholars have opted to have separate definitions. The findings here reveal that the majority of these definitions refer to CI as a process. Most of these definitions highlight the purpose of CI, which is to help decision-makers in decision-making.

Whilst it is widely acknowledged that CI is ethical and legal, the majority of scholars fail to outline this in their definitions. The majority of scholars also fail to outline the CI deliverable in their definition. Some scholars refer to the CI deliverable as actionable information, recommendations, insight or knowledge instead of actionable intelligence. The Internet has led to information overload and referring to CI as information might render it useless.

Because of its military origins some scholars refer to CI as an art. Very few definitions refer to CI as an activity or method. Perhaps this is because most scholars value CI as a process rather than the components or steps that constitute the process. CI is a profession that follows a code of ethics, so some definitions refer to it as a practice or discipline. The majority of definitions reveal that CI is collected from the external or competitive environment. However, in practice, information for CI is also collected from within the enterprise. Although it is widely acknowledged that CI provides competitive advantage to enterprises, only a few scholars acknowledge this in their definitions. There is therefore no definition that is comprehensive. Most definitions focus only on certain aspects of CI, leaving out others.

Conclusion

Scholars have not agreed on one acceptable definition of CI. This has led to many definitions of CI that differ because one focuses on certain aspects of CI whilst leaving out other aspects. There is therefore no CI definition that is comprehensive. This means that the borders of the field of CI are not clearly outlined. Moreover, there is no common understanding amongst CI stakeholders. A universal definition of CI will ensure that CI stakeholders focus on implementing CI.

The purpose of this research was to review the current literature on CI with the aim of identifying and analysing CI definitions and finally to propose a universal CI definition. The proposed CI definition outlines what CI is, the deliverable of CI, the source of CI, how CI is produced, the purpose of its production, the beneficiaries of CI and its benefits. The proposed definition of CI incorporates most of the aspects that were lacking in most of the definitions of CI found. It also incorporates the aspects that were common in these CI definitions. The proposed definition of CI is therefore comprehensive and will ensure common understanding amongst CI stakeholders.

Acknowledgements

This work is based on the research supported by the National Research Foundation. The authors would also like to acknowledge the University of South Africa (South Africa) for the funding and support without which this research would not have been possible.

Competing interest

The authors declare that they have no financial or personal relationship(s) that may have inappropriately influenced them in writing this article.

Authors' contributions

T.E.N. (University of South Africa) initiated this research, conducted the literature review and analysis and wrote the conclusion. R.P. (University of South Africa) led and supervised this project, selected the journal and handled editorial matters.

References

Agarwal, K.N., 2006, 'Competitive intelligence in business decisions – An overview', Competition Forum 4(2), 309–314.

Badr, A., Madden, E. & Wright, S., 2006, 'The contribution of CI to the strategic decision making process: Empirical study of the European pharmaceutical industry', Journal of Competitive Intelligence and Management 3(4), 15–35.

Blenkhorn, D.L. & Fleisher, C.S., 2005, Competitive Intelligence and Global Business, Greenwood Publishing Group, Westport.

Bose, R., 2008, 'Competitive intelligence process and tools for intelligence analysis', Industrial Management & Data Systems 108(4), 510–528. http://dx.doi.org/10.1108/02635570810868362

Botha, D.F. & Boon, J.A., 2008, 'Competitive intelligence in support of strategic training and learning', South African Journal of Information Management 10(3), 1–6.

Brody, R., 2008, 'Issues in defining competitive intelligence: An exploration', Journal of Competitive Intelligence and Management 4(3), 3–16.

Bucher, T., Gericke, A. & Sigg, S., 2009, 'Process-centric business intelligence', Business Process Management Journal 15(3), 408–429. http://dx.doi.org/10.1108/14637150910960648

Calof, J., 2001, 'Competitive intelligence and the small firm—Requirements and barriers', in sbaer.uca.edu, viewed 13 November 2012, from http://sbaer.uca.edu/research/icsb/2001/paper16.pdf

Calof, J.L. & Wright, S., 2008, 'Competitive intelligence: A practitioner, academic and inter-disciplinary perspective', European Journal of Marketing 42(7/8), 717–730. http://dx.doi.org/10.1108/03090560810877114

Changhuo, B. & Xinzhou, X., 2003, Competitor analysis, Huaxia Press, Beijing.

Cheng, H., Chau, M. & Zeng, D., 2002, 'CI Spider: A tool for competitive intelligence on the Web', Decision Support Systems 34(1), 1–17. http://dx.doi.org/10.1016/S0167-9236(02)00002-7

Colakoglu, T., 2011, 'The problematic of competitive intelligence: How to evaluate and develop competitive intelligence', Procedia – Social and Behavioral Sciences 24(1), 1615–1623. http://dx.doi.org/10.1016/j.sbspro.2011.09.075

Dey, L., Haque, S.K.M., Khurdiya, A. & Shroff, G., 2011, 'Acquiring competitive intelligence from social media', in ACM Digital Library, viewed 17 January 2011, from http://dl.acm.org/citation.cfm?id=2034621&bnc=1

Dishman, P. & Calof J., 2007, 'Competitive intelligence: A multiphasic precedent to marketing strategy', European Journal of Marketing 42(7/8), 766–785. http://dx.doi.org/10.1108/03090560810877141

Dishman, P. & Pearson, T., 2003, 'Assessing intelligence as learning within an industrial marketing group: A pilot study', Industrial Marketing Management 32(7), 615–620. http://dx.doi.org/10.1016/S0019-8501(03)00030-0

Du Toit, A.S.A., 2003, 'Competitive intelligence in the knowledge economy: What is in it for South African manufacturing enterprises?', International Journal of Information Management 23(2), 111–120. http://dx.doi.org/10.1016/S0268-4012(02)00103-2

Fleisher, C.S., 2003, 'Should the field be called competitive intelligence or something else?', in Laurier, viewed 12 February 2013, from www.wlu.ca/documents/24243/CICI_Chapter_5_Fleisher.doc

Fleisher, C.S., 2004, 'Competitive intelligence education: Competencies, sources, and trends', Information Management Journal, March/April, 56–62. http://dx.doi.org/10.1108/03090560810877196

Fleisher, C.S., 2008, 'Using open source data in developing competitive and marketing intelligence', European Journal of Marketing 42(7/8), 852–866. http://dx.doi.org/10.1108/03090560810877196

Fleisher, C.S. & Benssousan, B.E., 2003, Business and competitive analysis, FT Press, Upper Saddle River.

Fleisher, C.S. & Wright, S., 2009, 'Examining differences in competitive intelligence practice: China, Japan, and the West', Thunderbird International Business Review 51(3), 249–261. http://dx.doi.org/10.1002/tie.20263

Gray, P., 2005, Competitive Intelligence, Business Intelligence Journal 15(4), 31–37.

Groom, J.R. & David, F.R., 2001, 'Competitive intelligence activity among small firms', SAM Advanced Management Journal, Winter, 12–20.

Haataja, J., 2011, 'Social media as a source of competitive intelligence in a pharmaceutical corporation', Master's thesis, School of Science, Aalto University.

Haddadi, A.E., Dousset, B. & Berrada, I. 2010, 'Xplor EveryWhere – The Competitive Intelligence System for Mobile', in IEEE Xplore®, viewed 13 April 2013, from http://ieeexplore.ieee.org/stamp/stamp.jsp?tp=&arnumber=5945635

Hamblen, M., 2000, 'Competitive Intelligence', Computerworld 34(5), 53.

Hodges, C., 2005, 'Competitive intelligence overview feeding the competitive analysis process', ASQ World Conference on Quality and Improvement Proceedings 59(1), 441–445.

Hughes, S., 2005, 'Competitive intelligence as competitive advantage', Journal of Competitive Intelligence and Management 3(3), 3–18.

Jin, T. & Bouthillier, F., 2008, 'Information behavior of competitive intelligence professionals: A convergence approach', Proceedings of the 36th annual conference of the Canadian Association for Information Science (CAIS), University of British Columbia, Vancouver, June 5–7, 2008.

Johnson, A., 2005, 'What is competitor intelligence?', in Aurora WDC, viewed 17 July 2011, from http://aurorawdc.com/whatisci.htm

Liu, C. & Oppenheim, C., 2006, 'Competitive intelligence and the development strategy of higher education in Tianjin, China', Information Development 22(1), 58–63. http://dx.doi.org/10.1177/0266666906060091

Love, A. 2007, 'Business intelligence: What is the right approach?', Chartered Accountants Journal 86(1), 18.

Magrinho, A., Franco, M. & Silva, J.R., 2011, 'Competitive intelligence system: A research model tested in Portuguese firms', Business Process Management Journal 17(2), 332–356. http://dx.doi.org/10.1108/14637151111122374

Muller, M.L., 2006, 'Parts of competitive intelligence: Competitor intelligence', *South African Journal of Information Management* 8(1), Art. #209, 5 pages.

Nasri, W. & Charfeddine, L., 2012, 'Motivating salespeople to contribute to marketing intelligence activities: An expectancy theory approach', *International Journal of Marketing Studies* 4(1), 168–175. http://dx.doi.org/10.5539/ijms.v4n1p168

Nikolaos, T., 2012, 'Competitive Intelligence: Concept, context and a case of its application', *Science Journal of Business Management* 2012(2), 1–15.

Othenin-Girard, C., Caron, C. & Guillemette, M.G., 2011, 'When competitive intelligence meets geospatial intelligence', *Proceedings of the 44th Hawaii International Conference on System Sciences*, Kauai, Hawaii, January 4–7, 2011.

Pietersen, M.A., 2006, 'Competitive intelligence at the Medical Research Council', Master's dissertation, Dept. of Information Science, University of Stellenbosch.

Prescott, J.E. & Miller, S.H., 2001, *Proven Strategies in Competitive Intelligence*, John Wiley & Sons, Inc., New York.

Roitner, A., 2008, 'Competitive intelligence in Austria: An empirical study', Master's dissertation, University of Vienna.

Rouach, D., & Santi, P., 2001, 'Competitive intelligence adds value: Five intelligence attitudes', *European Management Journal* 19(1), 552–559. http://dx.doi.org/10.1016/S0263-2373(01)00069-X

Santos, M. & Correia, A., 2010, 'Competitive intelligence as a source of competitive advantage: An exploratory study of the Portuguese biotechnology industry', paper presented at the 11th European Conference on Knowledge Management, Famalicão, Portugal, September 2–3, 2010.

Simoes, J.J, Coelho, P. & Popovic, A., 2009, 'Information quality improvement as a measure of business intelligence system benefits', *WSEAS Transactions on Business and Economics* 9(6).

Stackowiak, R., Rayman, J. & Greenwald, R. 2007, *Oracle Data Warehousing and Business Intelligence Solutions*, Wiley, Indianapolis.

Strauss, A.C. & Du Toit, A.S.A., 2010, 'Competitive intelligence skills needed to enhance South Africa's competitiveness', *Aslib Proceedings: New Information Perspective* 62(3), 302–320.

Tan, B., Foo, S. & Hui, S., 2002, 'Web information monitoring for competitive intelligence', *Cybernetics and Systems: an International Journal* 33(1), 225–251.

Tarraf, T. & Molz, R., 2006, 'Competitive intelligence at small enterprises', *SAM Advanced Management Journal* 71(4), 24–34.

Vedder, R.G. & Guynes, C.S., 2000, 'A study of competitive intelligence practices in organizations', *The Journal of Computer Information Systems* 41(2), 36–39.

Vuori, V. & Väisänen, J., 2009, 'The use of social media in gathering and sharing competitive intelligence', *9th International Conference on Electronic Business*, Macau, November 30–December 4, 2009.

Weiss, A. & Naylor, E., 2010, 'Competitive intelligence: How independent information professionals', *American Society for Information Science and Technology* 37(1), 30–34. http://dx.doi.org/10.1002/bult.2010.1720370114

Wright, S., Eid, E.R. & Fleisher, C.S., 2009, 'Competitive intelligence in practice: Empirical evidence from the UK retail banking sector', *Journal of Marketing Management* 25(9/10), 941–964. http://dx.doi.org/10.1362/026725709X479318

Zangoueinezhad, A. & Moshabaki, A., 2009, 'The role of structural capital on competitive intelligence', *Industrial Management & Data Systems* 109(2), 262–280. http://dx.doi.org/10.1108/02635570910930136

Zeng, L., Xu, L., Shi, Z., Wang, M. and Wu, W., 2007, 'Techniques, process, and enterprise solutions of business intelligence', *IEEE Conference on Systems, Man, and Cybernetics*, Taipei, Taiwan, October 8–11, 2007.

10

Barriers to tacit knowledge retention: An understanding of the perceptions of the knowledge management of people inside and outside the organisation

Authors:
Jacky Bessick[1]
Visvanathan Naicker[1,2]

Affiliations:
[1]Information Systems Department, University of the Western Cape, South Africa

[2]Graduate School of Business Leadership, University of South Africa, South Africa

Correspondence to:
Visvanathan Naicker

Email:
vnaicker@uwc.ac.za

Postal address:
Private Bag X17, Modderdam Road, Bellville, Cape Town 7535, South Africa

Background: Knowledge loss causes challenges for organisations that wish to remain competitive. These organisations must identify the risks that could lead to knowledge loss and become aware of issues that affect knowledge retention.

Objectives: The objective of this research was to identify tacit knowledge retention barriers that could cause knowledge loss in an organisation. The paper presents a framework for the assessment of the impact of these barriers and discusses the research findings in order to critique that framework.

Method: A quantitative strategy was used to interpret the findings. The target population is information technology (IT) professionals in a government organisation. Interviews were conducted in order to produce a more context-sensitive interpretation of the findings. A quantitative research approach was used to ensure the findings would precisely reflect the target population.

Results: The majority of respondents confirmed that career development requires professional development, training prospects and improves the employability of employees. The agreed result was that respondents seek autonomy, that is, the ability to make decisions. Job stress and burnout are experienced because of problems with in filling posts, and the competition between the private and public sectors for experienced IT employees.

Conclusion: Certain determinants were found that affect barriers in knowledge management: organisational commitment, job satisfaction, job characteristics and talent management. These need to be measured to prevent barriers from occurring. Implications are drawn from the study; these provide a focus for further research to bridge some gaps in information technology that currently limit the widespread use of knowledge management.

Introduction

As organisations evolve and render services, their employees gain experience and knowledge about their domain, the competitive environment and the client requirements. As this body of knowledge grows, it becomes more valuable, and develops the characteristics of an asset, which needs to be nurtured and utilised. Companies that value this asset tend to be more successful than those that have not yet recognised this fact. In a shrinking economy, this could mean the difference between the survival and failure of a business. The knowledge is typically gained by individuals who are not normally compelled to share or document it.

In environments where knowledge sharing is not the norm, staff can become the sole owners of domain knowledge, meaning that this knowledge is typically lost when the employee leaves an organisation. There will always be the risk that valuable knowledge is lost to an organisation that does not protect its information through a documented business process. Hence, this research seeks to investigate what the barriers are to tacit knowledge retention.

Knowledge management (KM) promotes classification, administration and sharing of an organisation's information assets. An information asset is organised information that is valuable and easily accessible to those who need it. Knowledge exists within the individual employees and is a key component for organisations that wish to be and remain competitive in the marketplace. It is therefore imperative for organisations to recognise it as a valuable resource (Bollinger & Smith 2001; Bender & Fish 2000).

According to Wiig (1997), management must focus on four areas in order to retain knowledge: initiating governance functions, focusing on staff functions, accepting the responsibility for operation functions to create, renew, organise and transfer knowledge assets, and leveraging knowledge assets, thereby ensuring knowledge is distributed and applied effectively through collaboration. Arif *et al.* (2009) present a retention model, which consists of a four-step process: socialisation, codification, knowledge construction and knowledge retrieval. Lee-Kelly, Blackman & Hurst (2007) state that the challenge in retaining knowledgeable workers is due to the relationships between a learning organisation, job satisfaction and the turnover of knowledge workers. The present exploratory fieldwork is intended to contribute to an understanding of the perceptions of KM by people both inside and outside the organisation.

Research problem

Most of existing research theory has revealed organisational commitment, which reflects the strength of the linkage between the employee and the organisation. Job satisfaction, which describes how comfortable the employees are in their jobs, and job characteristics, which describe the aspects specific to a job, constitute the main determinants that influence the retention of knowledge. Implementing strategies can ensure that the employees achieve the benefit they deserve. Hence, knowledge is retained, and barriers are overcome in the organisation. Coombs (2009), Lock (2003) and Van Dijk (2008) are of the view that an organisation should succeed if knowledge is retained by increasing the level of determinants, namely organisational commitment, job satisfaction, job characteristics and talent management.

Research questions

Valuable organisational knowledge is lost when experienced employees leave an organisation. Hence, the main research question is stated as: What are the barriers to tacit knowledge retention in a South African government organisation?

In addition, the following research sub-questions were also investigated:

- What is knowledge retention?
- What are the typical barriers to tacit knowledge retention?
- How do barriers impact knowledge retention in government organisations?

Literature review

This literature aims to understand the barriers to knowledge retention of information technology (IT) professionals in the public sector in South Africa. Rong and Grover (2009) articulate that knowledge is an important success factor for organisations; it influences performance and learning to uphold organisational competitiveness. Nonaka and Takeuchi (1995) separated knowledge into explicit and tacit knowledge bases. They claim that explicit knowledge can be transferred through KM mechanisms, such as document storage or electronic media, and that it is outside the human mind. Tacit knowledge, however, can only be transferred by the individual knowledge carrier; it cannot be captured, and is difficult to articulate explicitly. However, explicit knowledge can be expressed as a language, and may be conveyed amongst individuals (Bhardwaj & Monin 2006).

According to Kikoski, as cited by Alwis and Hartmann (2008), tacit knowledge is less known; it is an unusual form of knowledge, of which we are not really aware. Furthermore, it is not exchanged through language, but is acquired by sharing experiences and by observation (Alwis & Hartmann 2008). Therefore, tacit knowledge is considered more valuable, because it offers a context for people's thoughts, places and experiences. It normally requires considerable personal interaction and trust to share effectively (McAdam, Mason & McCrory 2007). Hence, a knowledge worker (KW) may be described as a person who wants to be valued for knowledge they own and who works with intangible resources. The desires and views of such people incorporate those of an expert or a thinker. Such people want to transform their knowledge, contribute to solving problems and effortlessly influence the organisation's decision making, strategic direction and priorities. Drucker (1959) states that there are three important stages organisations must go through in order for knowledge processes to be valued, captured and measured:

1. utilise creative knowledge
2. recognise that KWs add value to the organisation
3. introduce formalised education programmes to allow the knowledge workers to apply their knowledge, both theoretically and analytically. (n.p.)

Davenport and Prusak (as cited by Ramirez & Nembhard 2004) define a KW as a person who creates knowledge or uses knowledge in an influential way in the workplace: 'KWs [*are*] people with a high degree of education or expertise whose work primarily involves the creation, distribution or application of knowledge'.

Prusak (2001) affirms that KM is about people, the processes they apply to gather, share, transform, teach, learn and make use of information. According to Depres and Chauvel (1999), KM is an approach to improve efficiency, productivity, transparency and outward sharing of information that is used internally in decision making, thereby improving working relations and trust for workers in an organisation.

Knowledge sharing

Wang (2004) explains that knowledge sharing (KS) activities among the employees enable cooperation and are vitally important in shaping the organisation's investment. Hsu (cited by Jiacheng, Lu & Francesco 2010) describes KS as a form of individual behaviour that makes it possible to disseminate or transfer knowledge that has been created throughout the organisation. Reychav and Weisberg (2010) suggest that organisations have to acknowledge that knowledge represents a valuable intangible asset for creating and sustaining a competitive advantage. Knowledge sharing can occur when there is a relationship amongst employees – through trust and an open organisational structure – to facilitate transparent knowledge flows, and to provide an organisational culture of continuous learning (Riege 2005). Organisations face the challenge of losing knowledge from baby boomers (people born between 1945 and 1960). This could affect organisational performance negatively and would require the introduction of effective initiatives to transfer knowledge to the new generation of employees. This would mitigate the risk of any loss of productivity and profitability (Claes & Heymans 2008).

According to Riege (2005), the following KS barriers exist in some organisations:

1. Individual barriers, such as age and gender differences.
2. Differences in education levels.
3. Lack of trust and the failure to take ownership of intellectual property.
4. Organisational barriers, such as the lack of leadership and managerial direction.
5. The integration of KM strategy, and the sharing of initiatives in the company's goals.
6. Knowledge retention of highly skilled and experienced staff is not always a high priority; the lack of transparent rewards and recognition are both counterproductive.
7. Technological barriers, such as a lack of integration and the compatibility of IT systems and processes.
8. Reluctance to use IT systems.
9. Lack of technical support and lack of communication.
10. The lack of demonstration of all advantages of any new systems in preference to the existing ones. (n.p.)

Critical success factors for knowledge management

According to Girard and McIntyre (2010), KM initiative depends on many factors for success. These can be organised into five primary categories: leadership, culture, roles and responsibilities, information technology infrastructure and measurement.

Furthermore, managers should create a vision for KM, assist in directing the change effort, and develop strategies for achieving the vision. The chosen structure employed in a KM leadership group should model and teach employees and stakeholders the importance of KS and using a common vocabulary. Context-sensitive and user-friendly technology that guides the user to the information with ease could improve adoption rates, and training using best-practice examples would help when searching and sharing information quickly.

Measurement before, during and after the phased implementation of KM would make it possible to link KM efforts with some return on the initial investment. Figure 1 depicts the basic model presented by Joseph *et al.* (2007). This will be utilised in this research, as it defines the determinants: job satisfaction and organisational commitment.

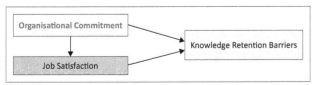

Source: Joseph, D., Ng, K.Y., Koh, C. & Ang, S., 2007, Turnover of information technology professionals: A narrative review, meta-analytic structural equation modelling and model development', *MIS Quarterly* 31(3), 547–577.

FIGURE 1: The old model.

A comprehensive review of the general KM literature revealed that there are a variety of dimensions to KM barriers (Lehner & Haas 2010). However, not all of these dimensions are equally important, nor are all of these relevant for the government sector. This study focuses on five dimensions that are cited most frequently in the KM literature; and these will now be discussed.

Organisational commitment: As defined by Coombs (2009), is the extent to which an employee experiences a 'sense of oneness' with their organisation and the employee's level of commitment to stay with an organisation. Associated factors, such as loyalty, trust, work-life policies, procedural justice and career development, have a potential influence that may cause a barrier to employees in an organisation. According to Greenhaus and Beutell (as cited by Bashir & Ramay 2008), work-life policies have an impact on work-life conflict, which they define as an incompatibility between responsibilities in the working environment and those to the family. Basher and Ramay (2008) indicate that a lack of work-life policies has a negative impact on organisational commitment. Wong, Tong and Mula (2009), Döckel, Basson and Coetzee (2006) and McKnight, Phillips and Hardgrave (2009) report that in order to develop employee trust in an organisation, management should steer clear of creating insincere promises that cannot be delivered on or commitments that cannot be achieved. IT professionals appreciate an open communication channel, in which management shares information regarding the business regularly and KS between colleagues can also occur.

Job satisfaction: This is an important organisational variable, and involves factors such as rewards, incentives, work exhaustion, competition and absenteeism. The word 'reward' is repeatedly discussed in the literature as an incentive that an organisation gives to employees in return for their involvement and performance; it can take the form of recognition, which is what employees most want (Allen *et al.* 2008, and Döckel *et al.* 2006). Lock (2003) states that a reward is a cash bonus or naming an employee 'employee of the month'. Potgieter and Pretorius (2009) affirm that incentives increase job satisfaction and deliver results that contribute to the organisation's goals.

It is evident from these employees that a lack of incentives worsens problems and produces poor results and the ballooning of costs in delivering systems. Extreme demands on time, such as being on call over weekends and vacations, can certainly lead to work exhaustion. Coombs (2009) and Lock (2003) both confirm that low morale, job stress and burnout experienced by public sector IT professionals are due to the problems that exist in filling posts. In addition, some factors that contribute to job satisfaction are competition between the private and public sector for experienced IT employees, the civil system that focuses on rules and regulations, control systems, the political situation and limited autonomy.

Job characteristics: As defined by Earle (2003), are those aspects that are specific to a job, for example knowledge and skills, mental and physical demands and working conditions that can be recognised, defined, and assessed. The IT professionals she surveyed in her study who earned a poor salary endeavoured to seek employment elsewhere. Allen *et al.* (2008) affirm that in order to retain or attract IT professionals, organisations should establish a positive relationship with employees and provide a pay enhancement programme. Coombs (2009) and Lacity, Iyer and Rudramuniyaiah (2008) believe that employees who seek autonomy demonstrate the ability to make decisions that are challenging and interesting and desire opportunities to apply these to their work activities. Coombs also states that employees want freedom and discretion in the arrangement of their work, and in determining work procedures; this has a positive influence on work performance. They also want responsibility for the outcome of their work and increased work motivation. According to McKnight *et al.* (2009), supervisor support is a developed relationship, characterised as being a partnership between a supervisor and his subordinates, and involves support, trust, information sharing, respect, career progress and valuing a mutual relationship. Lacity *et al.* (2008) state that a lack of supervisor support creates an undesirable attitude. This may contribute to poor work performance, lack of trust and poor support from subordinates.

Talent management: As argued by Joubert (cited by Van Dijk 2008), is a human resource process that produces an essential benefit for an organisation. Mentoring development (as described by Allen *et al.* 2008) is an informal training vehicle to improve the quality of human resource development. Glen (2007) indicates that mentoring development, employee competence and recruiting are factors associated with talent management. Van Dijk (2008) confirms that mentors play a vital role for IT professionals in providing opportunities for learning and career development and promoting the transfer of knowledge to ensure continuity of corporate knowledge. Mentoring development is a tangible approach to demonstrate that employees are valued and have a future in the organisation, and ensures that the organisation retains the best employees. Cunningham (2007) and Earle (2003) state that in order to recruit the best potential person for the job, the characteristics of the organisation must fit; the candidate's values and work attitude should be the focal point during a recruitment process, rather than just their specific skills and experience. Rectifying a wrong value fit choice is typically a very costly exercise.

Moreover, Allen *et al.* (2008) state that in the public sector there are various factors to consider:

- Lack of a reward system – IT professionals who are discouraged work defensively and not creatively; this can impact negatively on service delivery to the customers.
- Poor salaries influence IT professionals to find jobs elsewhere, which would prevent core knowledge from being retained within an organisation.
- Work exhaustion and burnout are the result of continued impractical work demands on the employee, which leads to a lack of innovative thinking and innovative services.
- The lack of time and the lack of mentor training and understanding prevent the transfer and sharing of knowledge; this results in continued poor skill outcomes, and can affect service delivery negatively. (n.p.)

According to Lockwood and Ansari (1999), knowledge retention includes all activities to protect knowledge in the organisation. Knowledge retention comprises three activities: acquisition, storage and retrieval. Further, Marshall (2005) affirms that knowledge retention is a division of KM, in which organisations use their combined intelligence to achieve their objectives by managing their cultural, social and technological environment.

Finally, the literature review reveals that barriers to knowledge retention do exist in IT organisations. Based on the literature, it is clear that organisations need to provide employees with incentives: financial or non-financial rewards, encouragement from management to share knowledge amongst employees, career development and mentoring programmes to retain knowledge. It is also clear that loyalty and trust contribute to employee behaviour, and need to be nurtured, as these qualities are of strategic importance to an organisation.

Other barriers are work-life policies, work-life conflict, poor salaries, relationships amongst colleagues and supervisory support. It is evident from the literature that the key success factor for a knowledge organisation is to grow, attract and retain talent.

Based on the above theoretical support, the researchers were interested to include two additional determinants: job characteristics and talent management, as these may be driving forces in knowledge retention barriers. The updated model is shown in Figure 2.

Research design and methodology

A quantitative method approach was used to collect the data. The choice was made to apply the quantitative research approach to ensure that the findings would precisely reflect the population, and in particular that population from which the sample was drawn (Vanderstoep & Johnston 2009). In this study, the target population was IT professionals in a government organisation. Simple random sampling was employed for this study.

According to Christensen, Johnson and Turner (2009), simple random sampling is the best sampling method to use to ensure an equal probability for all items in the population. Ten completed questionnaires were collected; these were used as a pilot study and were excluded from the main data collection process.

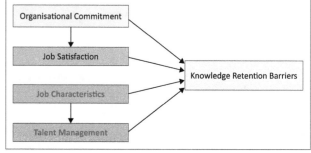

FIGURE 2: New model.

A total of 230 staff is employed by this branch, of which 60 individuals were asked to participate in the quantitative study. A closed-ended questionnaire was developed with brief answers based on a five-point Likert scale (see Table 3). The content of the questionnaire was developed after reviewing the literature on factors influencing the determinants' organisational commitment, job satisfaction and job characteristics.

The researchers held short interviews with the participants after completion of the questionnaire, to discuss whether, in their opinion, the questions were fair, whether any question offended them, and whether it was easy to complete. The results were used to make adjustments to the structure of two questions that the pilot group identified as making the questionnaire too long.

The questionnaire consisted of 30 questions, which were developed using the insight gained from the literature review. The literature review established a number of factors within each determinant that could be used to retain knowledge in the organisation. These factors were grouped under organisational commitment, job satisfaction, job characteristics and talent management. Statements were developed and presented in a questionnaire to determine whether the factors would introduce any barriers into the organisation.

Table 1 presents a summary of the statements, the supporting factors and the determinants.

TABLE 1: Statements and supporting factors.

Statement number	Factor	Determinant
7	Supervisor support	Job Characteristics
8	Poor salary	Job Characteristics
9	Work-life support	Job Characteristics
10	Autonomy	Job Characteristics
11	Training	Job Characteristics
12	Financial reward	Job Satisfaction
13	Non-financial reward	Job Satisfaction
14	Absenteeism (scheduled leave)	Job Satisfaction
15	Absenteeism	Job Satisfaction
16	Burnout and job stress	Job Satisfaction
17	Working environment	Job Satisfaction
18	Loyalty	Organisational Commitment
19	Procedural justice	Organisational Commitment
20	Trust	Organisational Commitment
21	Information sharing	Organisational Commitment
22	Career development	Organisational Commitment
23	Mentoring development	Talent Management
24	Recruiting	Talent Management
25	Employee competence	Talent Management

TABLE 2: Overall statements to measure determinants.

Determinant	Statement number
Job Characteristics	26
Job Satisfaction	27
Organisational Commitment	28
Retention Commitment	29
Talent Management	30
Overall Knowledge Retention	31

Overall statements that were developed in the questionnaire to measure the determinants are presented in Table 2, and they reaffirm the respondents' views. Furthermore, it was identified which determinants and factors appear to be negative and need management attention.

Statements 26, 27, 28 and 30 were used to measure whether a determinant was negative or positive. The factors that were sorted into each determinant in statements 7–25 were measured to determine whether a barrier or a gap was highlighted as negative (-) or positive (+) in the model. These results determined whether a determinant was a barrier or a gap. Statement 29 was used to measure the respondents' retention commitment. Statement 31 was used to measure the respondents' knowledge retention.

60 participants were targeted; 56 questionnaires were returned. These were checked for accuracy and completeness. Two participants telephonically contacted the researcher after the data had been captured and their questionnaires were therefore not included; two individuals did not complete the questionnaire at all. A return rate of 94% was reached. The categories of data were compiled for an ordinal dataset. The data analysis was completed using Microsoft Excel. This meant that the data capturing time was reduced to a minimum, which facilitated ease of analysis.

Tables and percentages were used to present and interpret the numerical data. The purpose of analysing the data in table format, categorised and displayed in textual and numerical form, allowed for fast viewing.

Demographic data

Section A of the questionnaire contained the demographic data items, statements 1–6. Of the 56 respondents whose questionnaires were analysed, 41% had worked for the organisation for 11 years or more and 29% had the designation of being middle management. The majority (80%) of the respondents were male, 57% indicated that their first language was English, 39% were between the ages of 31 and 40, and 64% indicated that they had a diploma or a degree.

Research questionnaire and results

The research was conducted in Cape Town, at an Information Communication Technology company. The responses from statements 7–31 obtained from the respondents are summarised as percentages in Table 3.

Discussion

Only statements that displayed significant changes have been discussed, due to space constraints. Statement 7 was obtained from the literature, and confirms that career development requires opportunities for professional development, training prospects and career advancement opportunities and improves the employability of the employees to the organisation. According to McKnight et al. (2009), supervisor support requires a developed relationship,

TABLE 3: Summary of responses.

Statement number	Response	Strongly disagree (%)	Disagree (%)	Uncertain (%)	Agree (%)	Strongly agree (%)
Job Characteristics						
7	I receive constant support from my supervisor on my career development.	13	12	14	45	7
8	I am paid enough for the work I do.	13	38	11	34	4
9	My organisation subscribes to a work-life support programme.	13	14	27	41	5
10	I have the freedom to make decisions.	5	29	22	39	5
11	My supervisor arranges training pertaining to my job.	5	25	4	52	14
Job Satisfaction						
12	I receive a financial reward for my job.	13	32	21	30	4
13	I receive a non-financial reward for my job.	20	44	16	15	5
14	I am off work for voluntary reasons.	10	19	13	37	21
15	I am off work for involuntary reasons.	23	43	15	17	2
16	I experience a lot of stress and burnout in my job.	2	25	11	42	20
17	I am comfortable in my working environment.	17	20	11	59	5
Organisational Commitment						
18	I continuously provide my services to the organisation.	0	0	2	60	38
19	Our rules and procedures are fairly applied to all employees.	27	20	23	28	2
20	Overall, we have very capable and proficient senior management.	14	29	32	23	2
21	In my group, information is shared freely.	7	31	13	44	5
22	My organisation offers career development.	13	21	20	46	0
Talent Management						
23	I have a mentor to support me in my current job.	15	42	13	28	2
24	My organisation recruits the best person for the job.	18	39	27	16	0
25	We have competent employees in the organisation.	7	23	25	45	0
Job Characteristics						
26	I am satisfied with the benefits my organisation offers.	6	25	22	45	2
Job Satisfaction						
27	I am satisfied with my job.	4	12	9	73	2
Organisational Commitment						
28	I have a strong commitment to continue my services in this organisation.	4	5	22	55	14
Retention Commitment						
29	I will be with this organisation five years from now.	2	9	43	39	7
Talent Management						
30	My organisation subscribes to an individual development plan.	24	40	12	24	0
Overall Knowledge Retention						
31	Overall, I believe the organisation does retain the knowledge of its knowledge workers.	22	29	25	24	0

a partnership between a supervisor and a subordinate; this involves support, trust, information sharing, respect, career progress and expressing a mutual relationship. The uncertain results for statement 9 indicate that it might be possible the respondents have not been with the organisation long, do not understand the benefit of the work-life support programmes, have not been introduced to or made aware of these programmes or that they have utilised the programme, but it did not meet their needs.

The agreed result in statement 10 was supported by the literature, according to Coombs (2009) and Lacity *et al.* (2008). It applies to employees who seek autonomy, have the ability to make decisions, seek challenges and opportunities to apply their working skills. These authors further state that many employees want the freedom and discretion to arrange their own work, and to determine work procedures that have a positive influence on their performance and that increase their motivation.

For statement 16, the literature confirms that job stress and burnout are experienced by public sector IT professionals, due to problems that exist in filling posts, and competition

between the private and public sectors for experienced IT employees (Coombs 2009; Lock 2003). In addition, continuous pressure, expectations and deadlines make employees vulnerable to work exhaustion and burnout (Lacity *et al.* 2009; Allen et al. 2008).

The disagreement and uncertain percentage for statement 20 is very high in comparison with the developmental statement 22, which is about the responsibility of management. Wong *et al.* (2009) and Döckel *et al.* (2006) argue that in order to develop employee trust, management should steer clear of making dubious promises that cannot be delivered on, or commitments that cannot be achieved. The research findings establish that knowledge loss challenges derive from various factors which have an influence on the determinants and may cause barriers. The determinants are presented in Figure 3, categorised as organisational commitment, job satisfaction, job characteristics and talent management. The research findings indicate that the rules and procedures are not fairly applied to all employees, which was confirmed by Bashir and Ramay (2008). Bashir and Ramay (2008) further contend that, although the outcome may be unfavourable to all employees, fair and acceptable processes should be followed.

The results of the investigation presented in Table 2 show a number of noticeable gaps and barriers at the organisation. It is clear from the findings that talent management and job satisfaction are barriers within the organisation. Issues of trust, procedural justice and poor salary reflect negatively and may impose barriers for the organisation. Figure 4 presents the barriers and gaps of the findings. On the issue of trust, it was found that respondents do not have trust in their managers. This is further compounded by insincere promises made by employers, as found by a number of researchers (Wong *et al.* 2009; Döckel *et al.* 2006; McKnight 2009). Emerging from the findings was communication, especially as it relates to trust. Managers should be open and honest with their communication; and the expectations of employees to management must be clearly communicated (Wong *et al.* 2009; Döckel *et al.* 2006; McKnight 2009).

The findings confirm that respondents experience lots of stress and burnout in their jobs. Lacity *et al.* (2008) and Allen *et al.* (2008) claim that continuous work pressure, deadlines and impractical expectations can make employees particularly vulnerable to work exhaustion and burnout. Coombs (2009) and Lock (2003) confirm that burnout and job stress are experienced by public sector IT professionals due to the problems experienced in filling posts, competition between the private and public sectors for experienced IT employees, civil system rules and regulation focuses, control systems and political undercurrents. The findings confirm that the respondents do not receive adequate rewards for the job they do. As stated by Allen *et al.* (2008) and Döckel *et al.* (2009), a reward is 'an incentive given to employees in return for their job involvement, performance and recognition, which is most wanted by employees'. Lockwood and Ansari (1999) contend that an attractive base salary, with the inclusion of a bonus and stock options, is important to IT professionals. They further point out that, for the most part, government salary classification systems are restrictive when compared with those offered by the private sector.

The findings indicate that the respondents do not have a mentor to support them in their current jobs. The literature also found that mentors play a vital role in providing learning and career development opportunities for IT professionals (Van Dijk 2008). This augurs well for the continuous transfer of knowledge and contributes to easy introduction of new IT professionals into the work environment.

Recommendations for further investigation

Due to limited time, only one IT organisation was used in this study. Since the study was undertaken in the Western Cape province of South Africa, further studies of this nature could be conducted in other Information Communication Technology departments in the eight remaining provinces. These could be used to develop a roadmap of how to tackle knowledge retention challenges. It can be stated that this study has unearthed sufficient evidence to assist the organisation in its knowledge retention endeavours.

Conclusion

Knowledge retention, as identified in the literature, is important to protect the knowledge in organisations. It involves three activities: acquisition, storage and retrieval. It presents a vehicle to cut down on errors and re-inventions, and to reduce costs associated with knowledge loss. In addition, knowledge retention can be classified as an action that makes knowledge available to contribute to organisational operations and allow these operations to be sustainable through efficiency and effectiveness.

Determinants of barriers to knowledge retention were identified, such as organisational commitment, job satisfaction, job characteristics and talent management. Factors were identified and need to be measured to prevent such barriers from occurring in an organisation. Poor salaries influence IT professionals to find jobs elsewhere, which prevents core knowledge from being retained within an organisation. Furthermore, work exhaustion and burnout can occur as a result of continuous impractical work demands by the employer, which can lead to a lack of innovative thinking and services. The lack of time and the lack of mentor training

---

Determinant **Organisational Commitment**	Determinant **Job Satisfaction**
Factors - Procedural Justice - Trust + Career Development	Factors - Burnout - Reward Practices - Job Stress
Determinant **Job Characteristics**	Determinant **Talent Management**
Factors - Poor Salary + Training Opportunities + Autonomy + Supervisor Support + Work-life Support + Training	Factors - Mentoring Development - Recruiting + Employee competence

Note: More negative than positive factors in a determinant = Barrier. More positive factors than negative factors in a determinant = Gap.

FIGURE 3: The determinants. Less than 45% (minus -), more than 49% (plus +).

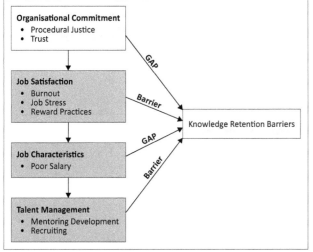

FIGURE 4: Barriers to tacit knowledge retention.

and understanding also prevents the transfer and sharing of knowledge, which results in continuous poor skill outcomes. Finally, a lack of trust can leads to poor decision making and to poor service delivery.

This study highlights the barriers and gaps that exist in a government organisation and places renewed focus on the potential knowledge retention barriers in the context of South African government organisations.

Acknowledgements

Competing interest

The authors declare that they have no financial or personal relationship(s) that may have inappropriately influenced them in writing this article.

Authors' contributions

Both authors, J.B. (University of the Western Cape) and V.N. (University of the Western Cape and University of South Africa) contributed equally to the research and the writing of this article.

References

Allen, M.W., Armstrong, D., Reid, M.F. & Riemenschneider, C.K., 2008, 'Factors impacting the perceived organisational support of IT employees', *Information & Management* 45, 556–563. http://dx.doi.org/10.1016/j.im.2008.09.003

Alwis, R.S. & Hartmann, E., 2008, 'The use of tacit knowledge within innovative companies: Knowledge management in innovative enterprises', *Journal of Knowledge Management* 12(1), 133–147. http://dx.doi.org/10.1108/13673270810852449

Bashir, S. & Ramay, M.I., 2008, 'Determinants of organisational commitment: A study of information technology professionals in Pakistan', *Journal Behavioural & Applied Management* 9(2), 226–238.

Bender, S. & Fish, A., 2000, 'The transfer of knowledge and the retention of expertise: The continuing need for global assignments', *Journal of Knowledge Management* 5(2), 125–137. http://dx.doi.org/10.1108/13673270010372251

Bhardwaj, M. & Monin, J., 2007, 'Tacit to explicit: An interplay shaping organisation knowledge', *Journal of Knowledge Management* 10(3), 72–85. http://dx.doi.org/10.1108/13673270610670867

Bollinger, A.S. & Smith, R.D., 2001, 'Managing organisational knowledge as a strategic asset', *Journal of Knowledge Management* 5(1), 8–18. http://dx.doi.org/10.1108/13673270110384365

Christensen, L.B., Johnson, R.B. & Turner, L.A., 2007, *Research Methods, Design, and Analysis*, 11th edn., Pearson Higher Education, Boston.

Claes, R. & Heymans, M., 2008, 'HR professionals' views on work motivation and retention of older workers: A focus group study', *Career Development International* 13(2), 95–111. http://dx.doi.org/10.1108/13620430810860521

Coombs, C.R., 2009, 'Improving retention strategies for IT professionals working in the public sector', *Information & Management* 46, 233–240. http://dx.doi.org/10.1016/j.im.2009.02.004

Cunningham, I., 2007, 'Talent management: Making it real', *Development and Learning in Organisations* 21(2), 4–6. http://dx.doi.org/10.1108/14777280710727307

Depres, C. & Chauvel, D., 1999, 'Knowledge management(s)', *Journal of Knowledge Management* 3(2), 110–120. http://dx.doi.org/10.1108/13673279910275567

Döckel, A., Basson, J.S. & Coetzee, M., 2006, 'The effect of retention factors on organisational commitment: An investigation of high technology employees', *SA Journal of Human Resource Management* 4(2), 20–28. http://dx.doi.org/10.4102/sajhrm.v4i2.91

Drucker, P., 1959, *Landmarks of Tomorrow*, Harper and Row Publishers, New York.

Earle, H.A., 2003, 'Building a workplace of choice: Using the work environment to attract and retain top talent', *Journal of Facilities Management* 2(3), 244–257. http://dx.doi.org/10.1108/14725960410808230

Girard, J.P. & McIntyre, S., 2010, 'Knowledge management modelling in public sector organisations: A case study', *International Journal of Public Sector Management* 23(1), 71–77. http://dx.doi.org/10.1108/09513551011012330

Glen, C., 2007, 'Fostering talent opportunity: Getting past first-base', *Strategic Direction* 23(10), 3–5. http://dx.doi.org/10.1108/02580540710824220

Jiacheng, W., Lu, L. & Francesco, C.A., 2010, 'A cognitive model of intra-organisational knowledge-sharing motivations in the view of cross-culture', *International Journal of Information Management* 30, 220–230. http://dx.doi.org/10.1016/j.ijinfomgt.2009.08.007

Joseph, D., Ng, K.Y., Koh, C. & Ang, S., 2007, Turnover of information technology professionals: A narrative review, meta-analytic structural equation modelling and model development', *MIS Quarterly* 31(3), 547–577.

Lacity, M.C., Iyer, V.V. & Rudramuniyaiah, P.S., 2008, 'Turnover intentions of Indian IS professionals', *Information Systems Frontiers* 10(2), 225–241. http://dx.doi.org/10.1007/s10796-007-9062-3

Lehner, F. & Haas, N., 2010, Knowledge-Management success factors – Proposal of an empirical research', *Electronic Journal of Knowledge Management* 8(1), 79–90.

Lock, G.E., 2003, '"Living, valuing and sharing" – A case study of retaining IT professionals in the British Columbia public service', *Career Development International* 8(3), 152–158. http://dx.doi.org/10.1108/13620430310471069

Lockwood, D. & Ansari, A., 1999, 'Recruiting and retaining scarce information technology talent: A focus group study', *Industrial Management & Data Systems* 99(6), 251–256. http://dx.doi.org/10.1108/02635579910253805

Marshall, R., 2005, 'Reinvest, recruit and rebuild to protect the future of IT', *Human Resource Management International Digest* 13(6), 3–5. http://dx.doi.org/10.1108/09670730510619240

McAdam, R., Mason, B. & McCrory, J., 2007, 'Exploring the dichotomies within the tacit knowledge literature: Towards a process of tacit knowing in organisations', *Journal of Knowledge Management* 11(2), 43–58. http://dx.doi.org/10.1108/13673270710738906

McKnight, D.H., Phillips, B. & Hardgrave, B.C., 2009, 'Which reduces IT turnover intention the most: Workplace characteristics or job characteristics?', *Information & Management* 46, 167–174. http://dx.doi.org/10.1016/j.im.2009.01.002

Nonaka, I. & Takeuchi, H., 1995, *The Knowledge-Creating Company*, Oxford University Press, New York.

Potgieter, D. & Pretorius, L., 2009, 'Retention of technical professionals – A reminder for engineering and technology organisations', *South African Institution of Civil Engineering* 17(4), 37–42.

Prusak, L., 2001, 'Where did knowledge management come from?', *IBM Systems Journal* 40(4), 1002–1007. http://dx.doi.org/10.1147/sj.404.01002

Ramirez, Y.W. & Nembhard, D.A., 2004, 'Measuring knowledge-worker productivity: A taxonomy', *Journal of Intellectual Capital* 5(4), 602–628. http://dx.doi.org/10.1108/14691930410567040

Reychav, I. & Weisberg, J., 2010, 'Bridging intention and behaviour of knowledge sharing', *Journal of Knowledge Management* 14(2), 285–300. http://dx.doi.org/10.1108/13673271011032418

Riege, A., 2005, 'Three-dozen knowledge-sharing barriers managers must consider', *Journal of Knowledge Management* 9(3), 18–35. http://dx.doi.org/10.1108/13673270510602746

Rong, G. & Grover, V., 2009, 'Keeping up-to-date with information technology: Testing a model of technological knowledge renewal effectiveness for IT professionals', *Information & Management* 46, 376–387. http://dx.doi.org/10.1016/j.im.2009.07.002

Van Dijk, H.G., 2008, 'The talent management approach to human resource management: Attracting and retaining the right people', *Journal of Public Administration* 43(3.1), 385–395.

Vanderstoep, S.W. & Johnston, D.D., 2009, *Research methods for everyday life, blending qualitative and quantitative approaches*, Jossey-Bass, San Francisco.

Wang, P.J., 2004, 'An exploratory study of the effect of national culture on knowledge management factors, expectations and practices: A cross-cultural analysis of Taiwanese and U.S. perceptions', Unpublished doctoral dissertation, George Washington University, Washington, DC.

Wiig, K.M., 1997, 'Knowledge management: Where did it come from and where will it go?', *Expert Systems with Applications* 13(1), 1–14. http://dx.doi.org/10.1016/S0957-4174(97)00018-3

Wong, A., Tong, C. & Mula, J.M., 2009, 'Knowledge-sharing acts as a significant antecedent to organisational commitment in a Confucian culture: A quantitative study of employees in the Hong Kong ICT industry', *20th Australasian Conference on Information Systems*, pp. 691–701.

11

Integrating knowledge seeking into knowledge management models and frameworks

Authors:
Francois Lottering[1]
Archie L. Dick[1]

Affiliations:
[1]Department of Information Science, University of Pretoria, South Africa

Correspondence to:
Francois Lottering

Email:
frankie.lottering@partner.bmw.co.za

Postal address:
Private Bag X20 Hatfield, Pretoria 0028, South Africa

Background: A striking feature of the knowledge management (KM) literature is that the standard list of KM processes either subsumes or overlooks the process of knowledge seeking. Knowledge seeking is manifestly under-theorised, making the need to address this gap in KM theory and practice clear and urgent.

Objectives: This article investigates the theoretical status of the knowledge-seeking process in extant KM models and frameworks. It also statistically describes knowledge seeking and knowledge sharing practices in a sample of South African companies. Using this data, it proposes a KM model based on knowledge seeking.

Method: Knowledge seeking is traced in a number of KM models and frameworks with a specific focus on Han Lai and Margaret Graham's adapted KM cycle model, which separates knowledge seeking from knowledge sharing. This empirical investigation used a questionnaire to examine knowledge seeking and knowledge sharing practices in a sample of South African companies.

Results: This article critiqued and elaborated on the adapted KM cycle model of Lai and Graham. It identified some of the key features of knowledge seeking practices in the workplace. It showed that knowledge seeking and sharing are human-centric actions and that seeking knowledge uses trust and loyalty as its basis. It also showed that one cannot separate knowledge seeking from knowledge sharing.

Conclusion: The knowledge seeking-based KM model elaborates on Lai and Graham's model. It provides insight into how and where people seek and share knowledge in the workplace. The article concludes that it is necessary to cement the place of knowledge seeking in KM models as well as frameworks and suggests that organisations should apply its findings to improving their knowledge management strategies.

Introduction

For some companies, knowledge management (KM) starts with specific information technology (IT) applications. Other companies leave KM to their human resources or marketing departments. However, 'intelligent' companies formulate knowledge management strategies (KMSs) to guide the development of their knowledge management capabilities (Seeley 1999).

Being the best in a highly competitive business world is no longer good enough. It is necessary to be better than the best. This means that companies can never stop improving. There are many tools and techniques businesses use to gain a competitive edge. Many of these are fads that come and go or that quickly fall away to be replaced by the next big promise to give companies the edge over their competitors. However, there is consensus that a more enduring and reliable success factor is knowledge, or as Prusak (2001:11) puts it: 'In the emerging economy, a firm's only advantage is its ability to leverage and utilise its knowledge.'

KM is not entirely new. For hundreds of years we 'knowledgeable' human beings have been doing KM, although not in the strict theoretical sense of the term. As humans, we have been telling stories around campfires and in other locales for centuries. In this sense, there has always been knowledge sharing. In the agricultural and industrial ages, fathers and mothers handed down the secrets and knowledge of their trades to their sons and daughters.

This is much the same in today's information or post-industrial age. In companies and organisations, team leaders or mentors explain the 'ins and outs' of their jobs to new employees. Cruywagen, Swart & Gevers (2008) explain that knowledge about discoveries made thousands of years ago, and passed on to succeeding generations through storytelling, apprenticeships and in written form, has helped to promote the rise of modern industries. Sharing expertise and exchanging ideas has led to the creation of new knowledge and applying this new knowledge to common problems has resulted in countless innovations (Cruywagen *et al.* 2008:101).

KM has indeed become a strategy for increasing competitiveness (Bell & Jackson 2001). Despite this, there is still speculation that KM is a fad and possibly a fading endeavour (Cruywagen *et al.* 2008). This speculation includes concerns that models, frameworks and strategies drive KM and that they fail to consider factors like the behaviour and perspectives of those who use the knowledge, the historical and cultural contexts of companies and the size of the companies. This tension between 'promoting competitiveness' and 'a passing fad' makes further investigation compelling.

Most KM models and frameworks present KM best practices but fail to address the contextual differences between organisations. As a result, KM initiatives often fail 'and fuel the fear that KM is simply just another passing fad' (Cruywagen *et al.* 2008:101). To account for these contextual differences, they emphasise that KM models and frameworks need to shift their focus from best practice to best-fit approaches. The two approaches use KM models and frameworks with different outlooks as their bases. The implication is that KMS strategies change according to the KM models or frameworks that companies adopt.

A significant contextual concern that best-fit approaches to KM models, frameworks and strategies raise is that they fail to recognise sufficiently *all aspects* of the knowledge behaviour of users. What is more striking in the KM literature is that standard lists of KM processes either subsume or overlook the processes of knowledge seeking. In other words, the processes of knowledge seeking are manifestly under-theorised in the KM literature (King, Chung & Haney 2008; Lai & Graham 2009). Therefore, it is necessary to address this gap in KM theory and practice clearly and urgently.

In order to address this gap, this study investigates the need to consolidate the status of the knowledge-seeking processes in KM models and frameworks. It also statistically describes knowledge seeking and knowledge sharing practices in a sample of companies. Taken together, the two components can integrate the knowledge seeking processes into a KM model that will enable companies to design KMSs that leverage the actual knowledge seeking practices of employees and improve best-fit approaches.

Theoretical status of knowledge seeking

The literature has already identified more than 160 KM models and frameworks around the world. In an analysis of these models and frameworks, Heisig (2009) called for the harmonisation of the wide range of diffuse KM terms and concepts in order to standardise and consolidate them.

He discovered six KM processes that KM models and frameworks use most frequently. They are 'create', 'identify', 'share', 'acquire', 'use' and 'store'. Heisig (2009) did not explicitly identify knowledge seeking or searching as a category or as a term. However, terms like 'searching', 'locating', 'gathering' and 'sourcing' in the six main KM categories come closest to the idea of knowledge seeking.

Therefore, there is little more than a hint of knowledge seeking in Heisig's comprehensive review. This shows that it still receives inadequate attention as a process or activity or in relation to other processes like knowledge sharing.

Even the well-known and established models and frameworks do not refer to knowledge seeking. The socialisation, externalisation, combination and internalisation (SECI) model of Nonaka and Takeuchi (1995) does not deal with why, how and where users would seek and share knowledge. The emphasis in the SECI model, in the current analysis, falls too heavily on knowledge creation and does not mention knowledge seeking. Furthermore, in the Cynefin model of Snowden (2002), which adapts the SECI model, there is no sustained focus on knowledge seeking behaviour. However, recent theoretical work has begun to examine the need to integrate knowledge seeking with KM models and frameworks.

Sanjeev and Gee-Woo (2005) investigated the attitudes and intentions that influence people's knowledge seeking behaviour in electronic knowledge repositories. They found that knowledge seeking is as an aspect of knowledge sharing in the same way that knowledge contribution is an aspect of knowledge sharing. Hsieh (2009) conducted research on 'human centric knowledge seeking strategies', in which he identified knowledge stakeholders as external customers, internal support staffs and co-workers as bearers of tacit knowledge. Hsieh identified methods that knowledge seekers use to obtain knowledge from knowledge stakeholders. He believes that knowing who the knowledge stakeholders are and leveraging their knowledge is crucial for firms' benefit.

The work of Han Lai and Margaret Graham (2009) contains the most convincing argument for the importance of knowledge seeking in KM. They draw on the cycle model of King, Chung, and Haney (2008) to present an adapted KM cycle model that emphasises knowledge seeking. They distinguish between information seeking and knowledge seeking, as well as the differences between the knowledge seeker and the knower. After reviewing several KM models and frameworks, they introduce knowledge seeking as a new concept in KM and propose an adapted KM cycle to represent their ideas.

Lai and Graham argue that knowledge seeking is essentially a learning process and a crucial part of KM. Knowledge seeking is about people in the workplace who construct knowledge through problem solving and experiential learning.

They reviewed several ways of knowing and selected the constructivist approach as the most appropriate for knowledge seeking. Knowledge seekers construct knowledge for, and by, themselves. This happens when people encounter problems in the workplace that trigger the learning process. Learning occurs from trying to solve the problems and from experience.

This conception has closer connections with a practice-based perspective of knowledge, located within a constructivist discourse (Hislop 2009:10, 33). In this view, knowledge is embedded in human activity or work practices and emphasises sharing and acquisition through social interaction and through watching and doing. One can conclude that knowledge seeking in the workplace is an experiential learning process that improves the seekers' knowledge structure to solve problems or achieve goals.

Using these ideas, Lai and Graham group the KM processes of creation, acquisition and utilisation under knowledge seeking. They group transfer, sharing, storage and refinement with information management. Their model splits into two blocks: knowledge seeking and information management (see Figure 1).

In this model:

- refinement is an activity that selects, codifies or reduces knowledge to information
- storage is actually a database, a book or an object that stores this information
- transfer is actually information transfer.

However, utilisation is committed by people who have received helpful information and constructed it into their own knowledge structure by a learning process that is an act of knowing (Lai & Graham 2009:471). Creation and acquisition, taken from the King, Chung and Haney cycle model, are added to utilisation in the knowledge-seeking block.

Lai and Graham admit that their model is illustrative and not definitive. It is still evolving and undergoing tests in the field. However, it does provide a way forward to understanding the important processes of knowledge seeking and its effect on organisational performance. They locate organisational performance in the knowledge-seeking block but fail to expand on this. Significantly, knowledge sharing is located in the information management block as a process that is not the essence of real knowledge management. These are provocative claims that Lai and Graham make. However, this study cannot assess them fully.

The KM literature reveals that scholars have not yet addressed knowledge seeking adequately. References to knowledge

seeking are either absent or veiled, or they are unsatisfactory in the standard KM models and frameworks. Lai and Graham have done the most significant work to integrate knowledge seeking with KM models and frameworks and their adapted KM cycle model deserves more attention.

The empirical component of this article will describe some of the features of knowledge seeking in practice in order to critique and elaborate on Lai and Graham's adapted KM cycle model. Their separation of knowledge seeking from knowledge sharing (in the information management block) suggests that sharing is only about externalised or explicit knowledge. This raises the question of whether one can separate the two processes so sharply from each other and whether both processes cannot or do not occur together in practice.

Evaluations of their views of knowledge seeking as learning and empirical tests of their model are necessary. These assessments will require further research that this study cannot undertake here. Nevertheless, it can make a modest contribution to their model through an empirical examination of some of the features of knowledge seeking.

Research design

The research methodology combines quantitative and qualitative approaches and draws on secondary and primary sources. The target group was three South African companies.

Company A is a small business intelligence consultancy that focuses on high-end market products. Its projects involve planning, implementing and maintaining various business intelligence products and systems. Most projects are long-term, but there are several ad hoc short-term projects.

Company B is an IT department located within a larger company. The employees of the department are responsible for the IT infrastructure of the organisation. Their tasks range from physically installing machines to setting up users on the system and resolving IT related issues. The department requires knowledge about systems and procedures to be stored and easily communicated or shared with new employees for faster induction into the department.

Company C is an insurance company that deals with claims and calculates insurance rates and fees. The company is countrywide and consists of offices spread across the country. However, this study included only the Johannesburg-based branch.

Purposeful sampling is ideal for this study because it looks at the people who seek and share knowledge in the workplace. This is true of the companies the researchers selected and, because all of them engage in these processes, the researchers decided to include all employees in the target groups instead of selecting samples from each. Therefore, this is a population study of the target groups because all their employees are information-rich participants.

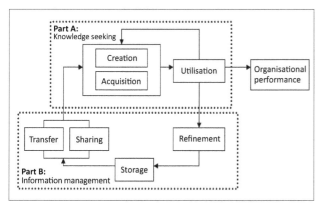

Source: Adapted from Lai, H. & Graham, M., 2009, 'Knowledge Seeking in KM – Towards an Adapted KM Cycle', *The 10th European Conference on Knowledge Management*, Proceedings of ECKM 2009, Vicenza, Italy, 03–04 September.

FIGURE 1: Lai and Graham's (2009) adapted knowledge management cycle model.

The researchers collected their data from questionnaires. The questionnaires consisted of 25 closed and open-ended questions that probed the features of knowledge seeking and sharing. The questions were in four sections. Section A is about the demographic details of the participants, Section B asks questions about knowledge seeking, Section C asks questions about knowledge sharing and Section D tries to identify the knowledge-management tools that employees prefer to use. The researchers mailed the questionnaires electronically to company managers who distributed them to the participants. The managers collected and returned them to the researchers.

Reliability, validity and integrity of the data

In order to ensure the reliability, validity and integrity of the data, the researchers:

- pretested the content and format of the questionnaire with a sample
- made the questionnaire as comprehensible and explicit as possible
- protected the identity of participants to persuade them to answer freely
- triangulated the KM literature, the empirical data and the responses to the open-ended questions to assure validity
- submitted the questionnaire to the University of Pretoria's Research Ethics Committee for approval before administering it.

Response rates

The various response rates were:

- for company A, the researchers distributed 20 questionnaires and respondents returned 13, yielding a response rate of 65%
- for company B, the researchers distributed 15 questionnaires and respondents returned 11, yielding a response rate of 73%
- for company C, the researchers distributed 33 questionnaires and respondents returned 19, yielding a response rate of 57.5%.

The overall response was 43 of 68 questionnaires for the three companies, a rate of 63%.

The researchers used descriptive statistics to organise, summarise and visualise the data and to describe features of knowledge seeking and searching. They analysed the open-ended questions by categorising words and meanings.

Results

The researchers consolidated the data from the questionnaires into a single data set instead of separate data sets for the different companies because the focus was on the processes of knowledge seeking and knowledge sharing instead of comparing them between companies. The data therefore represents knowledge seeking and sharing for all the companies instead of each individual company.

Profile of respondents

Only 14% of the respondents were women. Therefore, the data on knowledge seeking and sharing is skewed towards men. It may be useful in a future study to discover whether there are any gender differences in knowledge seeking and sharing in the workplace. Most respondents were between 21 and 40, with almost half that number in their twenties. As with gender, the differences in knowledge seeking and sharing according to age would permit further study. About half (22) of the respondents have been at their companies for more than six years. This means that there is a balanced representation of more experienced and less experienced seekers and sharers of knowledge.

Knowledge seeking

Almost all respondents said they use the Internet and/or consult colleagues when they seek knowledge to solve problems in the workplace. Sixty per cent consult knowledge repositories and books, whilst 23% use other sources. Colleagues are the greatest sources of knowledge. The high preference for consulting colleagues confirms the human-centric quality of trust relationships when seeking knowledge. People construct knowledge in their conversations about problems with their trusted colleagues. The near-rival source of the Internet suggests that employees prefer it to the KM system of data and knowledge repositories. Some respondents identified training courses, forums and subscription services as other sources of knowledge.

Sixty per cent of the respondents 'often' find the knowledge they are looking for to solve a problem or perform some or other function in their work. When the researchers correlated this data with those of previous questions, they found that colleagues successfully supply the answers employees need to solve problems in the workplace. This reinforces the continued use of colleagues as a first choice and the importance of trust when seeking knowledge. None of the respondents 'never' succeeded to find the knowledge they sought. This could indicate that knowledge seeking persists until employees find answers to their problems and confirms the 'pull' of knowledge seeking.

When the researchers asked the respondents where they seek knowledge when time is limited, the respondents' answers follow.

Table 1 shows that it is quicker to consult colleagues when seeking knowledge under the pressure of time. It also shows that knowledge seekers with time constraints or in urgent situations rely on trusted and human-centric sources. The high score for the Internet challenges consulting with colleagues and the social dimension of knowledge seeking because it is always quick and easy to use. One expects a low figure for books and knowledge repositories because they can be time consuming to sift through without the handy 'search' function.

When the researchers asked respondents why they answered as they did to the previous question, their answers follow.

Most respondents prefer to ask colleagues when time was short. This is understandable because a colleague who already has the knowledge to answer a question or solve a problem would be able to communicate the knowledge much faster than if respondents had to search for the knowledge themselves.

This confirms Snowden's (2008) often-quoted statement that one always knows more than one says and always says more than one can write down. The data were much the same in the three companies. Each company had a higher percentage of knowledge seekers who chose to ask colleagues.

The Internet was not far behind because most people are very quick to use Google when seeking knowledge to solve workplace problems. One can describe the knowledge-searching era as the 'Google era'. However, its obvious limitation is the sheer volume of information on the Internet. It can result in more time spent searching for what one needs because of the abundance of useless information it contains. Few knowledge seekers said they would search in a knowledge repository when in a hurry because this can be time-consuming especially if it is not well-maintained or if an employee is unskilled in search techniques.

The researchers asked the respondents where they would seek knowledge in an ideal situation. Their answers follow.

Table 2 supports previous statements about the 'Google era', as 86% of employees preferred the Internet as a search tool. Even though most users previously relied on colleagues for knowledge when pressed for time, the slight drop in number may be because respondents do not want to seem ignorant or because they are too shy to ask. However, asking colleagues is part of everyday learning in the workplace and is a learning process that is '...an integral and inseparable aspect of social practice' (Lai & Graham 2009:469).

The high number of respondents who would prefer to use knowledge repositories shows how important it is to maintain them properly. They are beneficial for knowledge seekers because they are useful for contributing, retaining and reusing knowledge.

The small number of respondents who prefer books as sources of information is not surprising because of their cumbersome nature. Seminars and conferences emerged as other sources of knowledge.

TABLE 1: Seeking knowledge with limited time.

Knowledge seeker	Source of knowledge retrieval				
	Internet	Colleague	Data or knowledge repository	Book	Other
Respondent total	35	37	12	3	3

Note: $N = 43$

TABLE 2: Seeking knowledge in ideal situations.

Knowledge seeker	Source of knowledge retrieval				
	Internet	Colleague	Data or knowledge repository	Book	Other
Respondent total	37	24	28	9	9

Note: $N = 43$

The data corroborates the constructivist approach to learning that Lai and Graham (2009:469) advocated. They stated that 'individuals construct knowledge through an interpretive interaction with the social world they experience'. This happens at several levels and uses several sources.

When the researchers asked respondents to explain their answers to the previous question, they indicated the main reason for the high level of confidence in the Internet is that it is fast, convenient and contains a wealth of knowledge. There was also a high response rate for knowledge repositories because it is better to have knowledge in central repositories and avoid reinventing the wheel. In addition, it is specific to the field in which they are seeking knowledge and solutions to problems. The practical implication of this is to establish these systems if they do not already exist. Colleagues, once again, are valuable sources, but respondents indicated that it depends on whether one knows who to ask for the knowledge.

Seeking knowledge from within organisations

The researchers asked respondents how often they seek knowledge from within their organisations. This is a good indication of the need to create opportunities for employees to seek, share and acquire knowledge because 35% of respondents seek knowledge a 'couple' of times a month and 25% of respondents seek knowledge once a week within their companies. Table 2 shows that 2% never seek knowledge from within their companies. Even though this figure seems negligible, it may indicate a lack of trust.

Seeking knowledge from outside organisations

The researchers also asked the respondents to indicate how often they seek knowledge from outside their organisations. The data shows that up to 33% of respondents look outside their companies for knowledge.

One can explain the reason that knowledge seekers tend to look outside for knowledge by the 'pull' force in knowledge construction that Lai and Graham described. Knowledge seekers are determined to construct their own knowledge and solve workplace problems even if it requires 'pulling' knowledge from external sources. Simply 'pushing' knowledge onto knowledge seekers, according to Lai and Graham (2009:470), 'does not necessarily lead to enhanced knowledge creation'. However, this means that it is necessary to introduce internal systems and infrastructure to make it easy to find knowledge and to provide opportunities for employees to share and seek knowledge internally.

Knowledge sharing

Sixty per cent of the respondents 'always' share knowledge with colleagues, whilst none 'never' did. This shows that most have a mindset of sharing and distributing knowledge throughout their organisations. This interesting feature of organisational culture reflects forward thinking. The biggest issue with previous mindsets have been the age-old saying

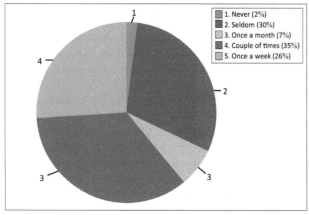

Note: *N* = 43

FIGURE 2: Seeking knowledge from within organisations.

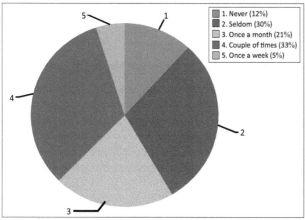

Note: *N* = 43

FIGURE 3: Seeking knowledge from outside organisations.

that 'knowledge is power'. This saying applies mostly in the context of 'if I have the knowledge then I have the power and I am indispensable'. This is counter-productive to organisational learning and knowledge growth. The strength of the 'pull' of knowledge seekers increases the knowledge available to organisations.

The researchers asked respondents to indicate why they share knowledge with colleagues. Several respondents indicated that they shared knowledge for the benefit of their companies and goals. Some respondents also said that they share their knowledge because it is a requirement of their jobs. A few respondents also indicated that they shared their knowledge with colleagues to avoid re-inventing the wheel. When one compares the number that was willing to share knowledge to the number of knowledge seekers, it is clear that knowledge seekers are usually also knowledge sharers. This links the two KM process closely.

Email and face-to-face are the preferred methods of sharing knowledge. This is mainly because of the ease of face-to-face sharing, as well as social interaction and trust between colleagues. If colleagues are in the same office or have easy access to others, as in open-plan designs, it is usually easier to explain concepts and share ideas person-to-person. There is often a loss of meaning and misinterpretation with emails,

but they are quick and easy forms of contact and sharing. A noteworthy point is that 65% of respondents indicated that they preferred to look for knowledge in knowledge repositories. However, here only 19% shared knowledge with colleagues through knowledge repositories. This could mean that the companies do not use repositories. Alternatively, it could mean that the seekers are happy to seek knowledge in repositories but that the companies have not yet instilled the processes, of recording and sharing knowledge, into employees.

The researchers also asked respondents to indicate how they would prefer to share knowledge in an ideal situation. Most respondents indicated face-to-face as the ideal method of transferring and sharing knowledge in the workplace. This feature of knowledge sharing corroborates the social and trust-based nature of knowledge seeking and sharing.

However, knowledge repositories scored high in Company C. This suggests that they are useful in industries where there are standardised knowledge solutions to problems. Emails also featured prominently because of their ease of use as well as their recording and archiving properties.

Experiential methods featured in the category of 'other'. These respondents explained that they preferred sharing knowledge by showing colleagues how to solve problems or letting them gain experience by doing a task themselves with some supervision. This range of ideal methods for sharing knowledge supports the constructivist learning approach that Lai and Graham advocated. It involves seeking information, making sense and learning by doing, through experiences or problem solving.

Knowledge repositories

Ninety-three per cent of the respondents indicated that they would use knowledge repositories to seek knowledge to get solutions to workplace problems. This does not negate consultation with colleagues. However, it does indicate its usefulness as another source of knowledge and as an alternative learning strategy in companies.

It also corroborates data the article has already reported, where 46% of respondents indicated that they share their knowledge because their companies will benefit. The codification for retention of this knowledge is where repositories become significant. Repositories are especially useful for inducting new employees who often seek knowledge to complete tasks. Repositories also prevent the loss of many years of knowledge and experience. Therefore, they are useful for knowledge seeking and sharing.

When the researchers asked respondents why they would use knowledge repositories, most confirmed them as central points for knowledge seekers and sharers; that they bind the two processes as sources for answers to problems and as places to deposit solutions to problems for future knowledge seekers.

All the companies understood the need to retain, share and create knowledge and respondents shared similar reasons for using knowledge repositories. They act as central points of organisational learning. The few who mentioned that repositories were not useful indicated that they could be cumbersome and time-consuming.

Discussion

The data make it possible to describe some of the main features of knowledge seeking and its relation to knowledge sharing. They also reveal some of the benefits and limitations of the Lai and Graham model.

Knowledge seekers prefer human-centric contact and social interaction because most approached colleagues when trying to solve problems. This emphasises the importance of the quality of trust in acquaintances instead of strangers and it shows a preference for personal contact over KM system facilities.

Thirty-three per cent said that they seek knowledge outside their companies. This shows a stronger sense of loyalty to internal colleagues and a reluctance to seek knowledge outside their companies. It also emphasises trust, collegiality and, importantly, the strength of the demand or pull factor in knowledge seeking that will drive people to look more widely to solve problems as well as their willingness to use other learning methods.

Most knowledge seekers share their knowledge face-to-face with colleagues. Therefore, the two processes are closely related and hard to separate in practice. They interact and overlap so that, in the course of seeking knowledge, people will also share it. One can regard this as a mutual learning situation in which both parties benefit as they seek and share knowledge. In other words, the demand or pull factor in knowledge seeking, and the supply or push factor in knowledge sharing, are deeply social in nature. This feature reveals a benefit and a shortcoming in the Lai and Graham model.

The benefit is that Lai and Graham see knowledge seeking as a different kind of process in a KM model and framework than is knowledge creation or knowledge acquisition. They assign a broader or more comprehensive scope for knowledge seeking in their model. Knowledge seeking, if it is a process, step or phase, seems to be more generic in character and can interact with all the other KM processes in special ways. However, we know too little about knowledge seeking in KM at this point to say much more than this.

The shortcoming of the Lai and Graham model is that it separates knowledge seeking from knowledge sharing. As the questionnaire data show, one cannot separate them as easily in practice. In addition, problem solving and learning is more social than situated learning theory, but they emphasise the individual as a learner and a knowledge seeker in their preferred experiential learning model.

Most respondents indicated that they would ideally use knowledge repositories to seek knowledge to find solutions to workplace problems. This indicates their usefulness as other sources of knowledge and as alternative learning strategies. Repositories are especially useful for inducting new employees who seek knowledge to complete tasks. Repositories also prevent the loss of many years of knowledge and experience and they are useful for both knowledge seeking and knowledge sharing.

Lai and Graham adopt the cognitive approach to knowledge construction and they review several approaches to learning in the workplace that favour the individual knowledge seeker. A limitation of their approach is that there are several learning theories and learning styles. In addition, there is more than one approach to knowledge construction, like cognitive constructivism and social constructivism.

Even though the argument for their choice is convincing, other approaches may be equally applicable despite their own shortcomings. In other words, there should be room for more theoretical approaches to the study of knowledge seeking in KM. Another limitation is the model's focus on people as 'knowers' or knowledge seekers. KM implies that entities, like organisations and companies, can also 'know' in the sense that people do. Therefore, companies can also seek knowledge, solve problems and learn. Future studies should investigate the most suitable approaches for collective or group learning, problem solving and 'knowing'. Therefore, the Lai and Graham model is too individualistic.

Based on these observations about the features of knowledge seeking and the benefits and limitations of the Lai and Graham model, the researchers can propose a modified knowledge seeking knowledge-based KM model.

Knowledge seeking

This is the core of the model. Although it is generic in character and, unlike knowledge creation, knowledge acquisition, knowledge seeking is a theoretical element that one can no longer overlook or assume in KM models and frameworks. One can understand knowledge seeking using the concepts of knowledge construction, learning theories,

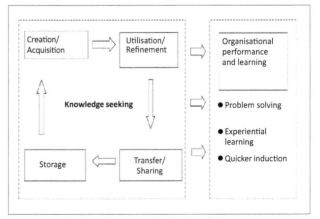

FIGURE 4: Knowledge seeking model based on knowledge management.

learning styles and problem solving. Knowledge seeking is a generic and special kind of process that interacts with other KM processes in ways that still have to be investigated.

Creation and acquisition

Most knowledge seekers acquire knowledge from colleagues to solve problems. This shows that knowledge seeking is closely interrelated with knowledge creation and acquisition, and that learning from colleagues involves human-centric and trust relationships as important qualities in workplace problem solving. The practical implication of the connections is that it would be useful to establish working environments that promote social contact with colleagues and that are conducive to building trust relationships.

Utilisation and refinement

The demand or pull factor to solve problems will drive knowledge seekers to look for and use sources outside their companies. Learning continues through the utilisation and refinement processes when knowledge seekers select and use information sources outside their companies and refine them into useful knowledge to make sense of, and solve, problems. In doing so, knowledge seekers undergo experiential learning and they can share these experiences with colleagues.

Transfer and sharing

Most knowledge seekers share their knowledge socially with colleagues. The two processes are closely integrated and hard to separate in practice. When people seek knowledge, they will also share it. The practical implication is that organisations can successfully build repositories using the knowledge that knowledge seekers acquire.

Storage

Organisations need to store knowledge for reuse because they cannot afford to lose already created and acquired knowledge. One needs to look at storage from the point of view of the knowledge seeker. In other words, employees should be skilled in search techniques. They should also adopt positive attitudes to seeking the knowledge that repositories store.

Organisational performance and learning

Integrating knowledge seeking as a KM process in a KM model or framework will improve organisational performance and organisational learning in a number of ways:

- organisations will resolve problems more effectively because of special provisions in their workplaces to construct environments that accommodate alternative individual learning methods, like the oral, printed and visual styles
- recognising experiential and other learning methods as ways of solving problems will improve personal and company growth
- practical arrangements to accommodate the interrelatedness of knowledge seeking and knowledge sharing will ensure

quicker induction of new personnel and smooth transitions into companies; this will reduce the time lag for new personnel to become productive.

Just as Lai and Graham's model builds on that of King, Chung and Haney (which drew from other well-known models), this proposed model advances that of Lai and Graham. Further research is necessary to flesh out this model's components in order to cement the place of the knowledge seeking process in KM models and frameworks.

Conclusion

Most KM models and frameworks overlook the knowledge seeking process. Despite this, knowledge seeking can enrich an understanding of KM and improve the chances of successfully implementing KM strategies in businesses. Studies of knowledge-seeking behaviour will improve decision-making in the workplace through a deeper understanding of how people solve problems and how they learn through experience.

Knowledge seeking occurs in companies, regardless of whether they have strategies, frameworks or designs, because people always seek knowledge to solve problems. They usually share this knowledge with colleagues. However, a deeper understanding of the process of knowledge seeking can add value to the design of a 'best-fit' KM strategy, although future studies need to investigate this.

Such a KMS will promote organisational goals better because it uses an understanding of how employees seek and share knowledge in the workplace as its basis. This understanding will improve organisational methods, tools and procedures. In a recursive approach, in which ongoing investigations produce updated insights about how knowledge seekers solve problems and apply a range of learning styles, KM and KMS will become more effective.

Acknowledgements
Competing interests

The authors declare that they have no financial or personal relationship(s) that may have inappropriately influenced them when they wrote this paper.

Authors' contributions

F.B.L. (University of Pretoria) and A.L.D. (University of Pretoria) were responsible for all efforts in writing the manuscript.

References

Bell, D. & Jackson, L., 2001, 'Knowledge management: understanding theory and developing strategy', *Competitiveness Review* 11(1), 1–11.

Cruywagen, M., Swart, J. & Gevers, W., 2008, 'One Size Does Not Fit All – Towards a Typology of Knowledge-Centric Organisations', *The Electronic Journal of Knowledge Management* 6(2), 101–110.

Heisig, P., 2009, 'Harmonisation of knowledge management – comparing 160 KM frameworks around the globe', *Journal of Knowledge Management* 13(4), 13–41.

Hislop, D., 2009, *Knowledge Management in Organisations: a critical introduction*, Oxford University Press, New York.

Hsieh, M., 2009, 'Human centric knowledge seeking strategies: a stakeholder perspective', *Journal of Knowledge Management* 13(4), 115–133. http://dx.doi.org/10.1108/13673270910971879

King, W., Chung, T. & Haney, M., 2008, 'Knowledge Management and Organizational Learning', *The International Journal of Information Science* 8(2), 19–35.

Lai, H. & Graham, M., 2009, 'Knowledge Seeking in KM – Towards an Adapted KM Cycle', *The 10th European Conference on Knowledge Management*, Proceedings of ECKM 2009, Vicenza, Italy, 03–04 September.

Nonaka, I. & Takeuchi, H., 1995, *The knowledge creating company: how Japanese companies create the dynamics of innovation*, Oxford University Press, New York.

Prusak, L., 2001, 'Where did knowledge management come from?', *IBM Systems Journal* 40(4), 1002–1007. http://dx.doi.org/10.1147/sj.404.01002

Sanjeev, S. & Gee-Woo, B., 2005, 'Factors Influencing individual's knowledge seeking behaviour in electronic knowledge repository', *The 13th European Conference on Information Systems, Information System in a Rapidly Changing Economy*, Proceedings of ECIS 2005, Regensburg, Germany, 26–28 May.

Seeley, C., 1999, 'Crafting a Knowledge Management Strategy. Part One – Balancing Corporate Dreams with Cultural Reality', *Knowledge Management Review* 11, 18–21.

Snowden, D., 2002, 'Complex acts of knowing: Paradox and Descriptive Self-awareness', *Journal of Knowledge Management* 6(2), 100–111. http://dx.doi.org/10.1108/13673270210424639

Snowden, D., 2008, 'Redefining knowledge', *The Cognitive Edge Network*, viewed 14 March 2010, from http://cognitive-edge.com/blog/entry/5576/rendering-knowledge

12

Using the cloud to provide telemedicine services in a developing country

Author:
Liezel Cilliers[1]

Affiliation:
[1]Information Systems Department, University of Fort Hare, South Africa

Correspondence to:
Liezel Cilliers

Email:
lcilliers@ufh.ac.za

Postal address:
50 Church Street, East London 5201, South Africa

Background: According to the World Health Organisation (WHO) 'Telemedicine is the use of medical information exchanged from one site to another via communications to improve a patient's health'. Despite the documented advantages of telemedicine, especially in developing countries, the implementation of this technology has been slow, with most projects not succeeding past the pilot phase.

Objectives: The aim of the article is to provide critical success factors (CSF) that will enable the deployment of telemedicine in the cloud in order to improve health care services in developing countries.

Methods: A thorough literature review was performed of peer reviewed articles in order to identify possible barriers for telemedicine to be deployed in the cloud. Furthermore, the Technology Organization Environmental Model was used in order to group the barriers according to the various factors and, from this process, critical success factors were formulated for consideration.

Conclusion: Five critical success factors were formulated in order to implement telemedicine making use of the cloud in developing countries. These include having a national integrated plan for telemedicine; promoting best practices within a legislation framework; involving the end user; providing education to improve levels of telemedicine awareness amongst staff and patients, and addressing technological issues.

Introduction

The average doctor to patient ratio in South Africa is estimated to be 1:1300, whilst in some rural areas this ratio can reach up to 1:100 000 (IRIN 2008; Jacobs 2007). The accessibility and quality of health care services in rural and urban areas can be improved by making use of Information and Communication Technologies (ICT). In particular health information systems, and especially telemedicine, have been identified by the World Health Organisation (WHO) as possible tools in this process (Fichman *et al.* 2011; WHO 2011). Telemedicine provides access to specialised health care in rural areas (WHO 2011). This means that patients need not travel far, to urban hospitals, for treatment by a specialist, thus, this reduces waiting times and transportation costs. In addition, health care workers in the rural areas also benefit from telemedicine as they receive support and education from their urban colleagues (WHO 2011; Wootton *et al.* 2009).

Despite the advantages mentioned in the previous paragraph, the uptake of telemedicine in South Africa has been slow (Van Dyk, Fortuin & Schutte 2012). Motsoaledi (2010) reported that only 34% of existing telemedicine sites in South Africa were operational. Some of the reasons provided for this poor result include the unreliable electricity supply which results in the unreliability of the technology, poor connectivity and low Internet bandwidth (Mars 2012; Jack & Mars 2008).

Other factors that have been reported in literature include a lack of sustainable finance to implement telemedicine infrastructure, and also a lack of skill to maintain the technology (Cilliers & Flowerday 2013). The aim of this article is to investigate cloud computing as a possible solution to some of the technological problems mentioned above. In order to accomplish this goal, a thorough literature search was conducted on the most popular academic databases: Pubmed, EBSCO, ProQuest and JSTOR. The purpose of the search was to identify relevant high quality studies that documented the barriers to the implementation of telemedicine in developing countries. For this reason, databases that were likely to yield original research in this area were targeted.

The rest of the article is structured as follows: The next section provides an overview of cloud computing, including the advantages, services provided and different deployment types available. This is followed by the barriers that have been reported to the successful implementation of cloud computing in various fields, whilst the section after that provides examples of various types of telemedicine projects that have been introduced in health care. From this the barriers are integrated with the Technology Organization Environmental (TOE) Framework with specific reference to telemedicine. Finally, the last section will identify and discuss the critical success factors (CSF) that must be considered if cloud computing is used to provide telemedicine services.

Cloud computing

Ragent and Leach (2010) define cloud computing as '...an Internet based computing model which enables convenient, on-demand network access to shared resources, software and information which is provided to computers and other devices.'

The main advantage of cloud computing is that it increases productivity and decreases the cost of Information Technology (IT), which was expensive prior to the invention of the cloud (ISACA 2009). Koch and Brakel (2012) identified various key benefits about why health organisations should make use of the cloud instead of traditional Information and Communication Technologies (ICTs). Some of these benefits of the cloud are listed below (Koch & Brakel 2012):

1. It reduces IT costs. Health care organisations can reduce the cost of IT infrastructure investments and on-going maintenance expenditures by paying only for the services they need.

2. It reduces implementation risks. Cloud computing can be deployed rapidly as the purchasing of hardware, licenses and software is not needed.

3. Flexibility is increased. The cloud provides more flexibility in the response and speed of health staff as they can access information and applications at any time, and from anywhere.

4. Health staff are enabled to focus on core areas – health staff can focus on patient care as the technology is maintained and provided by a third-party.

5. It improves scalability. Health care organisations only pay for the telemedicine services that they need. For telemedicine that could mean bandwidth, tailored telemedicine software programs or storage space.

The next section will introduce the various cloud computing services that are on offer.

Types of cloud computing services offered

Cloud computing can provide various types of services. The three main types of services are illustrated in Figure 1 and briefly discussed below.

- **Software as a Service (SaaS):** Amrhein and Anderson (2009) define SaaS as a model in which 'the consumer uses an application, but does not control the operating system, hardware or network infrastructure on which it is running'.

- **Platform as a Service (PaaS):** In this model 'the consumer does not manage or control the underlying cloud infrastructure, network, servers, operating systems, or storage; but the consumer has control over the deployed applications and possibly the application hosting environment configurations' (Baize 2011).

- **Infrastructure as a Service (IaaS):** The IaaS model of cloud computing offers the user the capability to rent computing, storage, networks and other computing resources with the added capability 'to deploy and run arbitrary software, which can include operating systems and applications' (Baize 2011).

The SaaS service will be more beneficial to departments with little skill or capacity, whilst more mature departments may prefer the PaaS or IaaS service structures. The next section will investigate the deployment models associated with cloud computing.

Deployment models of the cloud

According to Cisco (2009), a cloud deployment model defines where the physical servers are deployed and who manages them. There are four recognised deployment models that are used in cloud computing: Private, Community, Public, and Hybrid clouds.

The public cloud is also referred to as the external cloud where the 'infrastructure is made available to the general public' through web browsers, but offers limited customer control (Truong *et al*. 2012). In contrast, the private cloud systems emulate public cloud service offerings within an organisation's boundaries to make services accessible for one designated organisation. Private cloud computing systems make use of virtualisation solutions and focus on consolidating distributed IT services often within data centres belonging to the company (Gonçalves & Ballon 2011). The community cloud infrastructure is shared by numerous organisations. The community cloud is a more expensive option as compared to the public cloud, as the operational costs are spread over fewer user organisations than the public cloud. However, this type of cloud provides the benefit of

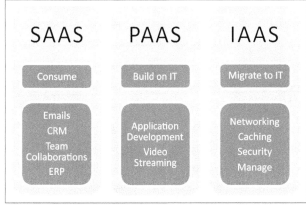

Source: Amrhein, D. & Anderson, P., 2009, 'Cloud computing use cases white paper: Version 2.0', viewed 04 September 2014, from http://www.cloudusecases.org/Cloud_Computing_Use_Cases_Whitepaper-4_0.odt

FIGURE 1: Types of Services offered by cloud computing.

offering a higher level of privacy, security and compliance. This is the type of cloud computing in which organisations are compelled to invest more trust, and adopt because of its safety features, especially for organisations that deal with critical or fragile information (Baize 2011). The last cloud computing type is called the Hybrid cloud and:

> is a composition of two or more clouds (private, community or public) that remains unique entities, but is bound together by standardised or proprietary technology that enables data and application portability. (Baize 2011)

In order to integrate telemedicine beyond the borders of South Africa, a community cloud may be considered. Alternatively, a public or private cloud type can be used according to the budget and security considerations of the particular telemedicine project.

Barriers to cloud computing

A study conducted by Boss *et al.* (2007) notes that with any new technology there are potential barriers that can be expected. According to Low, Chen and Wu (2011), a barrier is defined as a substance or obstacle which prevents a human being from attaining a particular goal. The barriers listed below are adopted from a literature study conducted by Duhaime (2011).

According to Schwab (2010), fear of vendor lock-in is a situation whereby a person using the cloud services cannot easily change to other technologies. Reliability concerns are one of the main reasons new users are reluctant to trust third-party cloud providers to store or process sensitive or personal information (Comninos 2011). This is especially important in the health context where patient data will be transmitted and stored by making use of telemedicine.

Source: Adapted from Duhaime, D., 2011, 'The pros and cons of cloud computing', ExpectFocus® III, Summer.

FIGURE 2: Generic barriers to the implementation of cloud computing.

Comninos (2011) further posits that reliability issues are closely related to connectivity issues, because the features of cloud computing makes use of the Internet as the main transporting device. This was previously also a concern for health providers, but with the increased network coverage in South Africa, it has now been addressed (Jack & Mars 2008). Performance concern is an additional challenge concerning cloud adoption in health care settings. The performance concerns of cloud computing for telemedicine are wide-ranging and include the availability of cloud related services in South Africa, awareness of the cloud, dispersal of the cloud, and the width and depth of cloud adoption (Malhotra 2010). Malhotra (2010) mentions some of the key challenges for performance improvement. These include the following:

- storage services
- scaling
- network services
- scheduling
- service level agreement templates
- optimal location of data centres and software components
- efficient SQL query processing
- architecture and process improvement.

Cloud computing is seen as inherently insecure. This is because security in the cloud is often intangible and less visible than many other forms of computing, and contributes to the perceived lack of control on the users' part. Despite these challenges, there are examples of successful telemedicine deployment in both developed and developing countries. The next section will provide a discussion about such examples.

Telemedicine and the cloud

Telemedicine in the cloud is not confined to providing health care service, but can also be developed for specific instruments. This section provides an overview of a variety of these projects both in developed and developing countries:

- In Brazil a proposal was developed by the Federal University of Santa Catarina to employ wireless sensor networks which are used to monitor patients. The information obtained is made available in the cloud to medical staff and can be processed by relevant expert systems whilst stored there (Rolim *et al.* 2010).
- Melvin and Pranesh (2013) have designed an Immediate Medical Care Unit (IMCU) that is able to provide basic health care services to the rural areas in India. The IMCU is an interactive machine that collects data from the patient, such as blood tests and blood pressure readings. It also integrates this information with the existing patient's record, making continuous care possible. In order to perform these activities cloud computing is used to interconnect the different databases.
- Germany has introduced a health smart card for all insured patients. The smart card contains administrative information, electronic health records and medical data such as prescriptions and emergency information. A smart card can be used by patients who must consult with different health professionals in order to keep their

medical information up to date. This would be useful in telemedicine as both the treating and referring health professionals will have access to this information via the cloud (Lohr, Sadeghi & Winandy 2010). In order to do this the information must be stored in the cloud. Whilst the International Organisation for Standardization has provided security and privacy guidelines for this process, the current challenge is the interoperability of the various systems that do exist (ISO 2013).

- Hsieh and Hsu (2012) developed a cloud computing based telemedicine application which makes use of a 12–lead ECG telemedicine service that greatly improved the current accuracy of reports in telecardiology. The readings can be viewed on both mobile and fixed devices connected to the cloud network, and have been reported to be convenient, efficient and inexpensive for clinicians in rural areas to use.

- Cloud computing enables researchers from different countries to collaborate as vast amounts of information can be stored and made available in this environment. The information can be analysed by researchers to provide guidelines for better decision-making, and new developments in treatment and medicine (Arphitha 2013).

- The Picture Archiving and Communication System (PACS), used for medical images in many hospitals, is experiencing scalability and maintenance issues resulting from the high volume of images that are taken daily. Cloud computing is considered to be a possible solution to this problem as images can be stored at lower cost, it provides high scalability and availability of images, and is recoverable in a disaster situation. Cloud computing can also be used in telemedicine as it provides the same advantages with the added benefit of specialist reporting in a short time period for the patient. This can be crucial in an emergency situation in the rural areas where no radiologist is available (Teng et al. 2010).

The next section will discuss the TOE framework as it relates to telemedicine and the cloud.

Technology Organization Environment framework

The TOE framework has been chosen for this research study because of its use in an analytical framework that is appropriate for studying the adoption and assimilation of different types of IT innovation. The framework was developed from a theoretical basis and is supported by consistent empirical evidence (Oliveira & Martins 2011). The TOE framework makes use of technological, environmental and organisational contexts for implementing cloud computing, to deploy telemedicine services in a developing country. The barriers that have been identified in the previous section are now considered in relation to telemedicine and are aligned accordingly into the three different contexts of the TOE framework.

Technology

Telemedicine initiatives in Africa are often announced with much excitement, but few survive beyond the pilot phase (Mars 2013). Telemedicine has become an integral part of the Department of Health's E-health plan in South Africa, but this means that the ICT infrastructure must be in place to support telemedicine. One of the inhibitors to telemedicine in rural areas is a stable electricity supply and the high cost of connectivity in South Africa. In addition, ICT must be maintained and supported by qualified staff (Mars 2013).

Reliability of cloud technology is important as it will be used in the health care domain. If connectivity and bandwidth are a problem, the asynchronous mode of telemedicine can be used, whereby a message is sent to a specialist to review an issue at a later stage or at their convenience. For this approach all that is needed is a basic computer with Internet connectivity and a camera (Singh 2009).

The cost of making use of cloud computing can be a concern as the technology must be integrated into existing IT infrastructure. However, once this has been implemented, the cost of maintaining the cloud is not a concern for the user. Similarly, the user only pays for the telemedicine services he or she requires and, thereby, saves money (Duhaime 2011).

Organisation

One of the factors that have been identified as a possible obstacle for the successful implementation of telemedicine is user acceptance (Nwabueze et al. 2009). Change management, and making use of communication and education is, therefore, necessary to reduce the resistance to the introduction of telemedicine in the initial stages of implementation (Cilliers & Flowerday 2013). This is equally important when cloud computing is used to deploy telemedicine services, as privacy concerns and a lack of control can contribute to the low acceptance rate of the technology.

Users of the cloud often mention that they perceive themselves to have less control over the services that the cloud offers, and the measures in place to protect their information than over other services. Mauch, Kunze, and Hillenbrand (2012) state that multi-tenancy is a key element to cloud computing and, thus, a 'one size fits all' approach is not suitable. They further acknowledge that architecture must be designed in such a way to allow for customisation for a specific user according to their needs, otherwise telemedicine will simply add steps to the clinical workflow and increase the workload of already overburdened health staff (Mars 2013).

Environment

The South African Minister of Health, Dr. Motsoaledi (2010), suggested that legislation regarding telemedicine must be prioritised in future. In response, The Health Professions Council of South Africa has worked on the *'Guidelines for the Practice of Telemedicine'* for the past seven years. Criticism of their definition of telemedicine is that it is too broad and it omits the important keywords: 'information', 'communication' and 'technology' (Mars 2013).

Issues such as liability, accountability, licensure, jurisdiction, confidentiality, data security and the use of telemedicine in health technology across borders must be addressed as a matter of urgency. This is important as the patient is not in a face-to-face contact situation with the health care worker treating them, and they may never have any communication with the specialist responsible for the diagnosis or treatment plan (Cilliers & Flowerday 2010). Accepted practices include that the specialist provides a second opinion whilst the referring doctor will remain responsible for the patient. Where telemedicine is practiced across borders, this raises the question of licensure for the specialist (Motsoaledi 2010).

Similarly, there are privacy and security concerns surrounding cloud computing. Rosado *et al.* (2012) state that because cloud computing is a relatively new computing model, there are concerns about security at all levels (e.g. network, host, application and data levels). There are new challenges arising in cloud computing, some of which are principally exacerbated by the cloud models. Thus, the risk is directly dependent on the cloud service and cloud deployment model (Mauch *et al.* 2012).

Madhavaiah, Bashir and Shafi (2012) identify that cloud computing, as an emerging IT model, has only had an arguably short period to be developed into a fully formed paradigm. The availability and, therefore, choice and agility, of the technology remains limited. In the next section the CSFs that will address the identified problems will be discussed.

Critical success factors

In the previous section the barriers for making use of the cloud to provide telemedicine services in developing countries were discussed and aligned to the TOE framework. In summary, the following critical areas were identified:

- technology: vendor lock-in; reliability; scale and cost
- organisation: change management; lack of control
- environment: security; accountability, licensure and agility.

CSFs are defined as the critical areas in which an organisation or the individual must succeed, in order to achieve their mission. CSFs also involve examining and categorising the impact of those critical areas (Salaheldin 2009). The following five CSFs are used to address the critical areas that will allow telemedicine services to be deployed, by making use of cloud computing in developing countries.

CSF 1: National integrated plan for telemedicine

Telemedicine has become an integral part of the Department of Health's E-health plan in South Africa and the Department must take responsibility for the implementation of telemedicine. If the Department of Health provides a national integrated plan for the implementation of telemedicine in all provinces, it will address the problem of vendor lock-in as the entire system must make use of one system. The telemedicine system will also be integrated across all provinces, making the coordination of health services in the country much easier. If the cloud is used as the deployment strategy for telemedicine

services in the country, it will also limit cost as the Department of Health will only pay for the service and not infrastructure or IT maintenance. With the use of a national integrated plan, security concerns are also addressed as the minimum security standards will be provided for the entire system.

CSF 2: Best practices within a legislation framework

With the advent of telemedicine, the provision of health care services has changed. Health care can now be provided across borders and without the patient ever knowing who is responsible for their diagnoses. This raises privacy and ethical concerns that must be addressed within a legal framework. If a proper legal framework is in place, it will also provide for more control than at present for the user, as they are aware of their rights and responsibilities within the system. The security concerns within cloud computing must also be addressed via legislation. These concerns are especially important where patient information is transmitted or stored making use of the cloud as it raises serious privacy concerns if the information was to be breached.

CSF 3: Involve the end user

The end user refers to both the health care worker and patient. This factor speaks to the change management problem that was identified in the previous section. If the end user is aware of the technology, legislation and best practices surrounding making use of the cloud to provide telemedicine services, there will be less resistance than might otherwise occur. This is especially important in a developing country where computer literacy and awareness of technology is low. This factor also links to CSF 4.

CSF 4: Provide education to improve levels of awareness

The end users, both patients and health care workers, must be educated about the advantages and potential risks of telemedicine and cloud computing. With this knowledge, it will increase the user acceptance of the technology.

CSF 5: Address technology issues

Cloud computing continues to be a relatively new paradigm with many challenges. Despite this, if attention is given to the specific technology problems within the context of telemedicine, it will not only increase the utilisation of telemedicine in the cloud, but also contribute to the wider context of cloud computing. Specific technology factors that must be introduced include the reliability, cost and availability of the technology. These are important as telemedicine services must be consistently reliable if they are to be of any use. The cost of deploying telemedicine services that make use of the cloud will decrease as more deployment options become available. The cost of bandwidth, which is very expensive in South Africa, must also be decreased in order to make this a viable technology. In developing countries, especially where IT infrastructure is poorly developed, cloud computing makes use of existing Internet connections to deploy telemedicine, without requiring more infrastructure or financial investments than are already in place.

TABLE 1: Critical success factors (CSFs) and the Technology Organization Environmental (TOE) framework.

Critical success factors	Technology Organization Environmental framework
CSF 1: National integrated plan for telemedicine	Technology; Environment
CSF 2: Best practices within a legislation framework	Organisation; Environment
CSF 3: Involve the end user	Organisation
CSF 4: Provide education to improve levels of awareness	Organisation; Technology
CSF 5: Address technology issues	Technology; Environment

The CSFs presented in this section attempt to address the barriers that were identified by Duhaime (2011) to make use of cloud computing in order to deploy telemedicine services in South Africa. Table 1 shows how the CSFs can be mapped to the three contexts of the TOE framework.

Conclusion

This article provided CSFs that must be considered when deploying telemedicine services in a developing country making use of cloud computing. The benefits of telemedicine have been documented in literature, but despite this, only a third of the telemedicine sites in South Africa are functional. In order to address some of the problems that have been cited as the reason for this poor result, cloud computing was introduced as a possible solution. Telemedicine services can be hosted in the cloud and the Department of Health can buy only those services that are needed. This is cost effective as the infrastructure and maintenance cost is deferred to a third party. The barriers that can prevent this technology being used to deploy telemedicine services were identified and CSFs were formulated to address these. Future research should focus on how each of these CSFs influence the implementation of telemedicine in more detail than is presently available. In addition, there is currently no effective measure to determine the cost of investment in telemedicine as it is very difficult to measure the impact the technology has on the health environment. This prohibits further investment and infrastructure development.

Acknowledgements

Competing interests

The author declares that she has no financial or personal relationship(s) that may have inappropriately influenced her in writing this article.

References

Amrhein, D. & Anderson, P., 2009, 'Cloud computing use cases white paper: Version 2.0', viewed 04 September 2014, from http://www.cloudusecases.org/Cloud_Computing_Use_Cases_Whitepaper-4_0.odt

Arphitha, S., 2013, 'Cloud computing: A boon to healthcare', Policy 6, 12-15.

Baize, B., 2011, 'In Cloud We Trust', Cloud Computing 16, 21–30.

Boss, G., Malladi, P., Quan, D., Legregni, L. & Hall, H., 2007, Cloud computing, IBM White Paper, Armonk.

Cilliers, L. & Flowerday, S., 2010, Critical success factors for Telemedicine Centres in African countries, University of Fort Hare, Alice.

Cilliers, L. & Flowerday, S., 2013, 'Health information systems to improve health care: A telemedicine case study', SA Journal of Information Management 15(1), 1–11. http://dx.doi.org/10.4102/sajim.v15i1.541

Cisco, 2009, 'Cloud computing in higher education: A guide to evaluation and adoption', Cisco White Paper, SanJose.

Comninos, A., 2011, 'Southern African Internet Governance Forum Issue Papers', SANGONeT for the Southern African Internet Governance Forum, 1–3 September 2011, Johannesburg, South Africa.

Duhaime, D., 2011, 'The pros and cons of cloud computing', ExpectFocus® III, Summer.

Fichman, R.G., Kohli, R., Krishnan R. & Kane, K.C., 2011, 'Editorial overview-the role of information systems in healthcare: Current research and future trends', Information Systems Research 22(3), 419–428. http://dx.doi.org/10.1287/isre.1110.0382

Gonçalves, V. & Ballon, P., 2011, 'Adding value to the network: Mobile operators' experiments with software-as-a-service and platform-as-a-service models', Telematics and Informatics 28, 12–21. http://dx.doi.org/10.1016/j.tele.2010.05.005

Hsieh, J.C. & Hsu, M.W., 2012, 'A cloud computing based 12–lead ECG telemedicine service', BMC Medical Informatics and Decision Making 12(1), 77–89. http://dx.doi.org/10.1186/1472-6947-12-77

IRIN, 2008, 'South Africa wanted – 4,000 doctors', viewed 05 January 2013, from http://www.plusnews.org/Report/79241/SOUTH-AFRICA-WANTED-4-000-doctors

ISACA, 2009, 'Cloud Computing: Business Benefits With Security, Governance and Assurance Perspectives', An ISACA Emerging Technology White Paper, Rolling Meadows.

ISO, 2013, 'Technical Committee 215: Health informatics', viewed 05 January 2014, from http://www.iso.org/iso/iso_technical_committee?commid=54960

Jack, C. & Mars, M., 2008, 'Telemedicine a need for ethical and legal guidelines in South Africa', South African Family Practice 50, 60–61. http://dx.doi.org/10.1080/20786204.2008.10873698

Jacobs, F., 2007, '185 – The patients per doctor map of the world', viewed 05 January 2013, from http://bigthink.com/strange-maps/185-the-patients-per-doctor-map-of-the-world

Koch, A. & Van Brakel, P., 2012, 'Why health organizations should make use of the Cloud instead of traditional Information and Communication Technologies (ICTs)', Proceedings of the 14th annual conference on World Wide Web Applications, 7–9 November, Cape Town, South Africa.

Lohr, H., Sadeghi, A.R. & Winandy, M., 2010, 'Securing the e-health cloud', Proceedings of the 1st ACM International Health Informatics Symposium, 11–12 November, Arlington, United States of America, pp. 220–229.

Low, C., Chen, Y. & Wu, M., 2011, 'Understanding the determinants of cloud computing adoption', Industrial Management & Data Systems 111(7), 1006–1023. http://dx.doi.org/10.1108/02635571111161262

Madhavaiah, C., Bashir, I. & Shafi, S.I., 2012, 'Defining cloud computing in business perspective: A review of Research', SAGE 163–173. http://dx.doi.org/10.1177/0972262912460153

Malhotra, N.K., 2010, 'Review of cloud research marketing', in N. K. Malhotra (ed.), Review of cloud research marketing, vol. 7, pp. 85–96, Emerald Group Publishing Limited, Bingley.

Mars, M., 2012, 'Telepsychiatry in Africa – a way forward?', African Journal of Psychiatry 15, 215–217. http://dx.doi.org/10.4314/ajpsy.v15i4.27

Mars, M., 2013, 'Telemedicine and advances in urban and rural healthcare delivery in Africa', Progress in cardiovascular diseases 56(3), 326–335. http://dx.doi.org/10.1016/j.pcad.2013.10.006

Mauch, V., Kunze, M. & Hillenbrand, M., 2012, 'High performance cloud computing', Future Generation Computing Systems 59(6), 1408–1416.

Melvin, F. & Pranesh, R., 2013, 'Independent medical care unit for rrual health care development', International Journal of New Trends in Electronics and Communication 1(1), 15–18.

Motsoaledi, M., 2010, 'Speaking notes for Dr. A.P Motsoaledi', 1st Southern African Telemedicine Conference Keynote address, viewed 22 February 2013, from http://www.doh.gov.za/show.php?id=2104

Nwabueze, S.N., Meso, N.P., Kifle, N., Okoli, C. & Chustz, M., 2009, 'The effects of culture of adoption of Telemedicine in medically underserved communities', in Proceedings of the 42nd Hawaii International Conference on System Sciences, Hawaii, United States of America, pp. 1–10.

Oliveira, T. & Martins, M.F., 2011, 'Literature review of information technology adoption models at firm level', The Electronic Journal Information Systems Evaluation 14(1), 110–121.

Ragent, F. & Leach, C., 2010, 'Can you trust the cloud?', A Practical Guide to the Opportunities and Challenges Involved in Cloud Computing, Cloud Computing, viewed 04 September 2014, from http://www.xerox.com/thoughtleadership

Rolim, C., Koch, F., Westphall, C., Werner, J., Fracalossi, A. & Salvador, G.A., 2010, 'Cloud computing solutions for patient's data collection in health care institutions', 2nd International Conference on Health, Telemedicine, and Social Medicine, pp. 95–99.

Rosado, D.G., Gomez, R., Mellado, D. & Fernandez-Medina, E., 2012, 'Security analysis in the migration to cloud environments', Future Internet 4(2), 469–487.

Salaheldin, S.I., 2009, 'Critical success factors for TQM implementation and their impact on performance of SMEs', International Journal of Productivity and Performance Management 58(3), 215–237. http://dx.doi.org/10.1108/17410400910938832

Schwab, K., 2010, 'The Global Competitiveness Report', World Economic Forum, Geneva, Switzerland.

Singh, V., 2009, 'Telemedicine and mobile telemedicine system', viewed 02 February 2013, from http://www.works.bepress.com/vikas_singh

Teng, CC., Mitchell, J., Walker, C., Swan, A., Davila, C. *et al.*, 2010, 'A medical image archive solution in the cloud', in Software Engineering and Service Sciences (ICSESS), 2010 IEEE International Conference.

Truong, H.L., Pham, V.T., Thoai, N. & Dustdar, S., 2012, 'Cloud computing for education and research in developing countries', in L. Chao (ed.), *Cloud computing for teaching and learning: Strategies for design and implementation*, pp. 64–80, Information Science Reference, Hershey.

Van Dyk, L., Fortuin, J. & Schutte, C., 2012, 'Maturity model for telemedicine implementation', *Proceedings of the eTELEMED 2012: The Fourth International Conference on eHealth, Telemedicine, and Social Medicine*, 30 January – 04 February, Valencia, Spain, pp. 69–71.

WHO, 2011 *'What is eHealth: The World Health Organisation (WHO) definition'*, viewed 06 January, 2013 from http://www.ehealthexpert.org/defehealth

Wootton, R., Patil, N.G., Scott, R.E. & Ho, K., 2009, *'Telemedicine offers solutions for Telehealth in the Developing World'*, Royal Society of Medicine Press, London.

13

Strategies for information management in education: Some international experience

Authors:
Andy Bytheway[1]
Isabella M. Venter[1]

Affiliations:
[1]Department of Computer Science, University of the Western Cape, South Africa

Correspondence to:
Andy Bytheway

Email:
andy.bytheway@gmail.com

Postal address:
Private Bag X17, Bellville 7535, South Africa

Background: Recent analysis of the management of information and communications technologies in South African education suggests strongly that there is only limited strategic thinking that might guide policy-makers, school principals, teachers, learners and suppliers of educational technologies. It is clear that here in South Africa, as elsewhere, the actual practice of technology-mediated education is driven more by the available technologies than by actual learner needs, good management principles and the wider national imperative. There might be lessons to be learned from experience elsewhere.

Objectives: This article reports and analyses conversation with eight international educators in Europe, Canada, the United States, New Zealand and Australia. All are managing the impact of technology in different ways (reactive and pro-active), at different levels (pre-primary through to senior citizen), in different roles (teachers, administrators and senior managers) and in different contexts (schools and universities).

Method: Open-ended conversations with educators and educational administrators in developed countries were recorded, transcribed and analysed. The qualitative analysis of the content was done in the style of 'open coding' and 'selective coding' using a qualitative content analysis tool.

Results: Whilst technology is still seen to drive much thinking, it is found that that success is not derived from the technology, but from a full and proper understanding of the needs and aspirations of those who are directly involved in educational processes, and by means of a managerial focus that properly recognises the context within which an institution exists.

Conclusion: Whilst this result might be expected, the detailed analysis of the findings further reveals the need to manage investments in educational technologies at different levels and in different ways.

Introduction

Education is rapidly becoming digitised at all levels, including the production, dissemination and transfer of knowledge. Despite the clear need for educators and learners to share knowledge, it is interesting that the initial impetus for introducing information technology (IT) into education often comes from the technology itself rather than from educational need. This can be seen as 'technology push', as opposed to the 'educational pull' that arises from a proper articulation of the needs of different educational activities and subjects (Anderson *et al.* 2002; Baker-Eveleth *et al.* 2007; Barron *et al.* 2003). The technology push-pull arguments have prevailed for decades in business and the public sector, but it is now widely recognised and agreed that information and communications technology (ICT) investments should be justified on the basis of the benefits that will be gained (Ward & Daniel 2005). It follows that the benefits of ICT investments must be effectively managed in education, as they are elsewhere; as Ward and Daniel argue: in education (as in any kind of enterprise) the 'pull' is more important than the 'push'; managing *information* promises more benefit than managing *information technology*.

But, what exactly is it that sits between the achievement of the benefits of good information management and the technology that underpins it? And what is meant by 'information management'?

These are questions that all managers must ask, even in education. It is therefore surprising to find a lack of specific research into the management of ICT in education, despite the fact that these are times of great technology-induced change (Botha 2009; Motala 2009; Bytheway 2013). Change is happening fundamentally at the level of social behaviour (Angell 2000; Shirky 2008), and in education and knowledge management in South Africa and elsewhere (Moloi 2007; Omona, Van der Weide & Lubega 2010). In reading educational research, the word 'management' is not often found: a review of more than 700 articles published over the last 20 years found very few that specifically addressed the management of information technology and information systems in education; some are old and many are from developed regions of the world (Michael 1998); some point clearly to practice in regular management in business in order to find answers (Uys 2007:239), others argue for the use of systems analysis methods (Hardman & Paucar-Caceres 2010:168) or they verge on speculation (Bhusry & Ranjan 2012:315). When management is mentioned, it is often to decry the problems created by 'management', as if managers were separate from the real world of educational practice.

Of course, the degree of 'push' and 'pull' and the nature of the needed benefits depend on the context. In different countries significantly different levels of achievement might be found. For example, in Singapore it is now more than 25 years since the introduction of a system through which parents could check, each day, what their children had learned at school, using their television set linked up to the local education management systems – and that was before the general availability of the world wide web (Maslin 1990). At the other end of the scale, education in South Africa, a developing country, is reported to be in a precarious condition (Jansen 2012). In spite of many experts' belief that the introduction of ICTs into education will solve problems, experience with educational ICT initiatives in South Africa is variable, according to local research undertaken at different levels (Brown 2010; Bytheway 2004, Bytheway *et al.* 2010; Davids 2009; Koch 2006; Madiba 2009; Republic of South Africa 2004). A special problem is the induction of disadvantaged students with only a rural background, where cultural issues can present special challenges and where a free association with technology is found to be helpful to those students (Rahimi 2010). The educational 'pull' in a vibrant and successful context such as Singapore will have little in common with the needs of impoverished rural regions of Africa, where there might be no electricity and no data communications services.

In much of the expert analysis that is available, there is little that specifically addresses the *management* of information at a strategic level, or even at a systems level. The focus is commonly on pedagogy, didactics, specific technologies or contextual and social issues. The question arises: do we need to widen our viewpoint, and examine the educational processes and information resources that can be improved by better *information management*, rather than the generalities of *context* or the specifics of *information technology*? Hence, the central problem addressed here is that *the benefits of technology investments in education are not realised in South Africa.*

The problems in South Africa, and the evident belief that information technology offers solutions to some of our problems but has not really delivered them, partly because of the dependency on teacher attitudes (Chigona *et al.* 2011), led to the idea of a review of international experience with and attitudes to the management of digitised information and of information technology in education, by means of conversations with educators and administrators working

in international education. This article explores how information technology is typically managed in selected countries, by an analysis of eight international conversations with educators and administrators that set out to explore the extent to which information and information technology are managed strategically in education, with what benefits to stakeholders.

Firstly, the article reviews the strategic management of information technology from a general perspective, drawing on theories from business management; a generic framework for the analysis of strategic alignment is introduced and then used to organise an open coding of the qualitative data derived from the eight conversations. A further selective coding and stakeholder analysis then examines the benefits of ICTs in education according to the different stakeholder groups, the benefits that they seek and the extent to which strategic planning might help.

The question at the heart of this work is: *does strategic planning help to deliver the benefits of information management in education?* As will become evident, 'information management' is considered to include a range of management activity, from technology through to strategy.

Strategic management of ICTs

There is extensive literature on strategic planning; in progressive businesses it is routine to undertake periodic analysis of internal and external challenges and opportunities, especially those relating to ICTs. The challenges and opportunities arising from information technology are a feature of much of that literature, but all organisations still find it difficult to achieve the anticipated results. Even in developed countries, in the public sector, huge amounts of money have been wasted in fruitless information technology projects (The London Independent 2010).

Difficulty prevails

Delivering benefits from any ICT investment is difficult, and it is all too easy to sweep failure under the 'carpet' of blame-games, shifting circumstances and general obfuscation about what is really needed. This is unfortunate, especially when there is such a long history of research and thought leadership about strategic information systems management. For at least 30 years this has been one of the hottest topics in the business research domain and its development can be traced over time (Zachman 1987; Baets 1992; Henderson & Venkatraman 1993; Edwards & Peppard 1997; Bytheway 1998; Luftman 2000; Kearns & Lederer 2000; Ward & Peppard 2002; Venkatesh *et al.* 2003; Ward & Daniel 2005) Over time the scope of research has broadened, for example to deal with other contextual issues that constrain success, such as human factors and organisational politics, something that the typical IT manager seems to find very difficult (Knights & Murray 1994; Chatham & Patching 2000)

Strategic management of ICTs in education

Strategic management is sometimes crudely reduced to a question with three parts: *where are we now, where do we want to be* and *how shall we get there?* The first real question, of course, is *where do we want to be?* This is where we debate and decide our objectives, the risks that are involved, the allocation of resources to strategic initiatives and so on. This then all depends on what people (those with influence) think about an organisation's strategic objectives and whether they perceive benefits that will accrue to their advantage. These influential people are the *stakeholders*, and these are the people we need to understand.

The remainder of this article presents an established framework for information management that joins issues of technology with issues of strategy and uses it to analyse the content of eight conversations with educators and educational administrators that illustrate how role-players in different countries are dealing with the management of ICTs in education. This provides some evidence with which to address the three questions above.

A framework for information management

During the 1990s, business managers and academics strove to find answers to critical questions about managing information in organisations. An early, extensive, review of literature concerning information systems 'success' was well received, is widely cited and has since been updated (DeLone & McLean 1992, 2003). More recently (as noted) there has been increasing attention to the management of benefits rather than actual or perceived success, but huge problems are still evident even in developed, supposedly capable countries (Chatterji 2007; The London Independent 2010; Ward & Daniel 2005). In the face of all this, how can the complexities of managing information in organisations be addressed?

Frameworks emerge

In the history of these matters, Zachman (1987) stands as a seminal source, but his frequently cited framework (a six-by-six matrix) was too complex for many managers to work with, having six layers of technology management down one side and six different perspectives on the business across the top: 36 different points of concern (the intersection of the six rows and six columns of the matrix) were just too many for many busy managers to handle.

Others have sought simpler views of the problem, and another frequently cited example is the Henderson and Venkatraman (1993) framework. It relates business and IT issues at the internal and external levels using a two-by-two matrix. This model is attractively simple at first sight, but it leads to a range of unanswered questions and lacks the elegance and symmetry that makes these things memorable. It implies dependencies and relationships between its conceptual components, but these are not immediately evident on a first reading, and as these authors admit in the original presentation of the idea, one has to go elsewhere to get the detail that is needed to operationalise the framework.

The information management body of knowledge

When these and other models are analysed and combined in order to understand what we need to be able to do well, a pattern emerges:

*   **Information technology:** which comprises the requisite infrastructure for systems.
*   **Information systems**: which support an organisation's operational processes.
*   **Organisational processes:** which deliver benefits through improved performance.
*   **Organisational benefits:** that are sought by stakeholders.
*   **Organisational strategy:** that is realised by the delivery of required benefits (Bytheway 2004).

This arrangement of ideas has been developed, refined and tested. It is familiarly known as the 'IMBOK' (Information management body of knowledge). Recently it has been used to assess the perceived information management competencies of a large South African bank, and there is an archive of data from other sources that stands as a resource for future research (Bytheway 2011).

However, here we will use it in its simplest form, to provide a structure for the analysis of the international conversations. Figure 1 provides a simple overview.

As can be seen, the IMBOK framework divides the management domain into five (shaded) areas: technology, systems, processes, benefits and strategy. At the four intersections (the arrows) are the components of 'value' transfer and delivery: projects, process change, operations and performance; also, the imperatives: strategic imperatives, operational targets, user requirements and systems requirements.

So, to understand ways to maximise the benefits of investments in educational ICTs, we can now ask:

*   What technologies are used in education?
*   What systems assist education activities?
*   What educational processes prevail and how are they changed by ICTs?
*   What are the benefits and how are they measured?
*   What strategies guide the use of ICTs in education?

Method of working

In a trip around the world, seven open-ended conversations with educators and educational administrators in developed countries were recorded (with permission) and have since

FIGURE 1: The information management body of knowledge (IMBOK).

been transcribed and analysed; one later conversation with an education assessment consultant in the United Kingdom makes up the eight (see Table 1).

The general approach adopted for the analysis of the content was in the style of 'open coding' and 'selective coding' (Strauss & Corbin 1998). Space precludes a detailed discussion of this qualitative approach to research, but the paragraphs below make it clear: they first present the open coding, by way of summary, and then the selective coding, based upon the domains of the IMBOK as described above.

Open coding

The first reading of the interview transcripts led to 26 a *posteriori* categories, as shown in Figure 2. On review, these categories were grouped into sets relating to:

- Activities of different kinds within education (principally administrative or educational).
- Contextual issues at the level of education, change and society at large
- The domains of the IMBOK.
- Issues open to further investigation.
- Resources of different kinds at different levels.
- Stakeholder references, indicating who is involved.

There was also a catch-all category of 'Others' that accommodated some of the academic references to theories of education and technology management.

The chart in Figure 2 tabulates the number of instances of coding of each category, across all of the interviews. Of course, to just count the frequency of occurrence of categories is a simple approach to analysis, but it provides a first view of the nature and content of the conversations and the focus of the respondents' interests.

As can be seen, a range of categories emerged from the open coding analysis, the most frequently occurring being *information technology* and the least frequent *basic resources*. Here we are principally concerned with those categories that map to the five layers of the IMBOK, as indicated by the 'IMBOK' prefix in the chart. Note therefore that the evidence presented here will be very selective because of the focus on the IMBOK as an analytical framework (and because of space constraints); the analysis does not represent the full richness of the 1139 actual instances of categorisation, and the 26 768 words that comprise the substance of the eight conversations.

Interesting findings from the open coding include the following observations:

- Information technology drove much of the conversation, overriding issues of strategy, process, systems and (most worryingly?) *benefits*.
- There were many more *problems* than benefits articulated by the respondents.

TABLE 1: The eight conversations.

Person	Organisation	Location
Engineer	Senior citizens club	California, USA
Technology teacher	High school	New Zealand
Learning management system manager	Business faculty	New Zealand
Senior academic	University	Ohio, USA
Teacher	Primary school	Minnesota, USA
Teacher	Kindergarten	Australia
Learning chair	Business school	Canada
Consultant	Education consultancy	York, UK

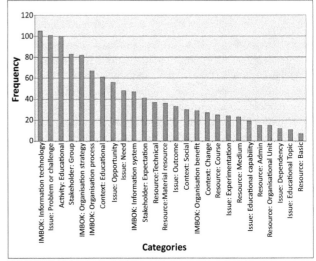

FIGURE 2: Open coding, 26 categories.

- As is often found in these kinds of conversation, discussion of technologies and problems were in the context of the educational *processes and activities* wherein they are found, rather than the deeper issues of benefits, experimentation and capability.
- *Opportunities*, *needs*, *expectations* and *resources* were all represented in the middle range of frequencies.

Hence, we find that there is a range of issues that extends from technology to strategic benefits, but the bias towards technology 'push' is strong.

The selective coding drives the analysis down into the issues of alignment, where we can see more clearly how information is managed, what benefits there are and whether there is any real strategic context within which management takes place.

Selective coding

From the 26 categories that emerged in the open coding, there are five relating directly to the five domains of the IMBOK:

- technology
- systems
- processes
- benefits
- strategies.

These five domains provide a useful framework with which to examine strategic management issues, and the principal portion of the analysis that follows is based on these five domains. It is useful to start by presenting the selected domains and their frequencies in the coding, this time in the same sequence in which the IMBOK presents them (see Figure 3). This allows us to see the extent to which the conversations dwelt upon these five principal domains. We can see these as five *specific* discourses within the general discourse about education and the way that information is managed therein.

In summary:

- As already noted, the most frequently occurring discourse concerned *information technology*. This (it can be argued) is inevitable, when conversation is predicated on the emergence of ICTs in education, but it cautions us that much conversation might be grounded in the availability and enticing capabilities of information technology rather than simple educational need – we come back yet again to issues of technology 'push' and 'pull'.
- *Information systems* did not figure greatly in the conversations; the very concept of an 'information system' or 'application' was almost completely absent. This contrasts with business and public sector working, when we frequently see references to the 'Payroll', 'ERP (enterprise resource planning)', 'CRM (customer relations management)' and other typical 'applications' that are to be found therein. When information systems *are* referred to in the conversations, the references are generally rather weak except (in just one case) when referring to the 'learning management system' (LMS).
- *Organisational processes* were discussed more often, partly because in conversations there is usually a bias towards 'what I do and how', rather than 'why'; there is some interesting evidence within this process discourse about how ICTs are affecting and changing what happens in education.
- The *benefits of ICTs* were infrequently referenced and were often tangential, being implied rather than being explicitly articulated. This helps us to understand a major part of the problem, because if the organisation at large does not perceive or understand (and then manage) the benefits, then all the benefits are as good as lost. A strong discourse on the intended benefits of an ICT investment is essential if managers are going to have clear targets to aim for.
- The *strategy* discourse emerged weakly, in different ways and from different perspectives, and once again strategic issues were mostly implied rather than clearly articulated. However, this indicates that the seeds of strategic thinking are there, and in fairness to all in education we already know that change can take a long time and is never easy.

The paragraphs that follow present selected evidence that exemplifies some of the stronger evidence that is to be found in the conversations.

Who are the stakeholders?

These eight wide-ranging conversations were not structured in any particular way, and it is inevitable that the evidence turns around the role of teachers, learners and management.

However, there is evidence of other critical stakeholders, and at the end of the day we have to remind ourselves that success comes from a balancing of all stakeholder expectations and an investment in resources and processes that will serve those expectations in a balanced way.

In the analysis of the conversations, there is evidence of 13 stakeholder groups, as indicated in Figure 4; of course, the frequencies of reference are not high enough, nor is the sample of respondents necessarily wide enough, to put a high level of significance on this result. Nevertheless, the analysis in the figure provides a clue as to which stakeholder groups might be the most important to consider, in the opinion of the respondents. And these stakeholder groups are not confined to teachers and learners, or students and professors; it is found that managers, communities, parents, administrators, other schools, suppliers and government are all factors in managing for success. A further investigation, in more detail, might reveal an even wider range of 'interested parties' and a better understanding of their relative importance, but we must assume that anyone, in any one of these stakeholder groups, could impact adversely on education in one or many educational institutions. When it comes to the adoption and integration of information technologies, it has been strongly argued that success will only emerge when the needs and expectations of all stakeholders are accommodated in the planning and implementation (Edwards & Peppard 1997).

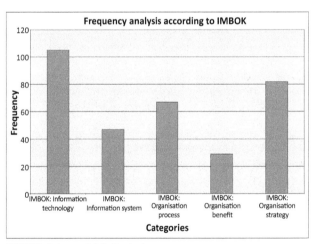

FIGURE 3: Category distribution by frequency.

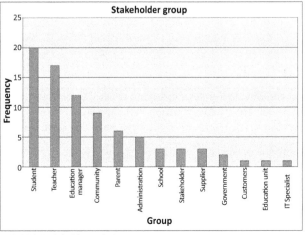

FIGURE 4: Stakeholder analysis.

Thus, these are the stakeholder groups that need to be understood, whose expectations will set the criteria of success or failure and who might in their own way impact on the efforts of educators and educational managers to deliver the best results. Their expectations are not only defined in terms of the benefits that they recognise, but also defined by the benefits that they seek.

Discussion

Insights into the way that information management can affect the outcome of our investments in educational technology and our efforts to improve and advance our educational processes, and deliver strategic educational benefits, all come from a more detailed inspection of what was said by this diverse group of educators and administrators. The paragraphs that follow present selected evidence from the conversations, within the five domains of the IMBOK.

Technology

As we have seen, there is a range of technology that was talked about, but the educational benefits that technology brings were often more implied than expressed. Computers dominated the conversations and even concern about the variety of brands in use was evident. The systems within a brand (and the 'trendiness' of the systems) were also evident in terms of obsolescence and the preference for new rather than upgraded technologies:

> 'We've just introduced the iPads - we have six iPads, three of them are the new iPad 2, they came today … at this time we use the 'blackboard' app where they can write their words or their sentences as if it with chalk, rather than have a traditional slate in front of them'. [Teacher, Kindergarten, Australia]

The replacement of the low-cost chalkboard with a very expensive continuously evolving tablet technology might not be the first choice of a developing country. The 'electronic' or 'interactive' whiteboard is one example that is becoming more common and does seem to bring benefits, although there is still some learning to be done in terms of how it might best be used and how it might be fully integrated into educational practice:

> 'We have been networked, we have connected classrooms, which means that I can sit in the library with the interactive white board on, and have the television screen on, and talk to a class in [a different place altogether and] say [to our learners] "here is another school, what would you like to say to them?"' [Teacher, Kindergarten, Australia]

Apparently, today's learners are so attuned to looking at (and learning from) a screen that it really appeals to them – even 'special needs' children – and there might be clear benefits from building a relationship with a distant peer group, as hinted here. But it is not always easy for teaching staff to learn new technologies and applications at the same rate as their learners – sometimes there is simple resistance, even in higher education:

> 'Faculties [teaching staff] are the biggest resistance - the students' biggest complaint is that faculty won't use it enough: "we want to use the technology and you won't". The faculty will say they don't have time'. [Learning Chair, University, Canada]

Sometimes it all seems much too challenging:

> 'Faculty need to be able to shift their way of thinking about the learning experience. So that's one part of that shift from the teaching paradigm - deliver information - to the learning paradigm … so I see it as the duty of faculty to bring all these tools into the learning experience because it's like an apprenticeship process'. [Senior academic, University, USA]

Increasingly, students at higher education institutions choose (or are expected) to work with their laptops and not with pen and paper. One consequence is a whole additional layer of technology that requires a laboratory to be 'locked down' for an examination:

> 'We do some massive online testing. 220 students yesterday doing essay online in a lock-down exam, at the same time, in five labs … we do a lot of lock-down, we actually use software to lock down the lab computers or even the student's own computers so they only have access to Blackboard, Turn-it-in. Some faculty adopt it, some don't'. [Learning Chair, Business school, Canada]

The complications of choosing to use technology accumulate as we do so. But at the institutional level some technologies are so basic that they are a 'must-have', otherwise students would simply choose to go to another institution with better facilities. Of course, understanding exactly which technologies qualify as 'important' is a strategic issue, not a technological issue. And between the technology and the achievement of strategic objectives come the information systems (or 'applications') that technology enables, and the processes that are enhanced by the systems.

Information systems

The more information-intensive areas of education showed very clearly how information systems are helping educators deal with large numbers of students and massive numbers of documents:

> 'Next term we will have nearly 2000 students in Business 101 and 102, and these are all being taught in collaborative manner. So there are 20 tables of 6 students each, every hour, dealing with business problems - the students submit one paper and review six within three days, and that involves 12 000 virtual copies of these papers going around and none getting lost'. [Learning management system manager, Business faculty, New Zealand]

Are there benefits from systems that handle such large numbers of students in this way? Probably, but detailed evidence of information systems that assist in education activities was actually limited. The balance of investment between administration and academic systems is a point of concern, and there is a tendency to invest in administrative systems first, although the connections with academic activity might be clear in specific cases:

> 'I actually did an administrative systems strategy for [the university] and they implemented most of it … the area that we spent a lot of time on is academic support, administration of course management systems, and content'. [Learning Chair, Business school, Canada]

Assessment of learning figured strongly in the conversations. Traditional modes of teaching, learning and assessment are changed by the use of technology. For example, traditional assessment by means of tests and examinations can be substituted by the use of 'discussion boards', another example of an information system:

'I teach a class on business and 15% of the evaluation is based on the discussion board. I post a topic every week and I rate them on the number of posts, the quality of posts. I also rate them on helping one another, and it's got to be timely'. [Learning Chair, Business school, Canada]

Of course, systems merely augment the propensities of their users: if people like to live with chaos then they can create even greater chaos; if they like to be organised, then they can be even more organised. If they like to keep things and not throw them away, they can keep more things for longer:

'I was asked on the ferry this morning 'Sir, are you the "father" of [the learning management system]?' and I said 'Well, one of them!' and he said 'I just came back to the university, I've been away five years and when I logged in everything is still there! All the classes were there that I took before, all my notes, all my stuff, that's an amazing system!' I said "that's the way we designed it"'. [Learning management system manager, Business faculty, New Zealand]

For a university that wants to distinguish itself, and stand out as a great place to work as well as to learn, this is the sort of thing that we are looking for. But, it's a pity when systems fail, in this case one that was not developed in-house but by 'experts':

'The [bought-in] system was absolutely airtight up until recently, however the output [from the new version] is not time-stamped and depending on the vagaries of the local network and so on you could get an enrolment before a deletion, or a deletion before enrolment, or the system could wind up just deleting the people out of the course and nobody knew where they went ... This was a $20M investment, hundreds of people involved, some of them making more than $100k per year, and it looks like we have to write our own middleware!'. [Learning management system manager, Business faculty, New Zealand]

The conversations highlighted the reality that fundamental systems-related changes are at hand. In discussing plagiarism, and what to do about it, Google and Wikipedia quickly come up in conversation, but do they count as 'systems'? Are 'Google docs' (an example of 'software-as-a-service') to be seen as 'systems'? We are reminded that we do not have to do everything for ourselves any more. Web-based services, combined with the myriads of 'apps' for iPads and Android tablets, guarantee that we will increasingly reach outside our boundaries in order to find the systems and services that we need, in open markets and at very low cost. But not all 'open' applications are small, and the tension between commercially available and open source systems is palpable:

'In 2009 we completed the transition [to Sakai] ... I think it was a wise investment. But that's an example where you have to convince people in leadership positions that you are doing the right thing. For the longest time they said, "you're gonna use open source? What are you gonna do when it breaks?" My answer is: "look at these other schools, we are in a community"'. [Senior academic, University, USA]

The use of learning management systems was a recurring feature of the conversations, but what about other important educational activity, such as research? The substance and mode of research working is changing rapidly. Where a doctoral thesis might once have had a few photographs or drawings pasted in on blank pages, or bound in at the end, today we expect the all-singing all-dancing presentation of everything (that we made move, or sing or dance) in our research to be immediately available in the digital archive. Taken overall, the effort involved in achieving technology-induced change is keenly felt:

'So in a sense, by divesting some technology we take on new responsibility to guide and control the process and train people. And so we still need to look at all the assets that we have to make this happen, but to me I think it's a renaissance period for us, it's massive change, but it's so fun! It's like being on one of those roller coasters, you know? With the economic drag we felt like we were down here, but now we are going up again! It's really exciting, and a little scary'. [Senior academic, University, USA]

Clearly, this respondent is an optimist and an enthusiast. When it comes to changing the processes of education (dare we say 're-engineering' the processes?) things are not all that simple.

Process

Prevailing conventional education paradigms show signs of the impact of a developing technological world. Thus, knowing what goes on in a particular context is an important pre-requisite to understanding where an investment in technology might help. Tragically, the conversations reveal that learners are running ahead of many of the teachers, and teachers' control of teaching and learning processes is thereby threatened. Certainly the pace of change is a challenge that is more easily met by the learners (who have no 'baggage' to carry) than by the teachers, who are sometimes hidebound by their baggage. But when teachers choose to rise to the challenge there are rewards: 'It's amazing that the teachers create the content. It's the teachers that teach it so they are the ones to know what they want and what's good to learn' [Teacher, Kindergarten, Australia].

Not true of all, no doubt, but the liberation that comes from developing one's own material, as distinct from being told to teach from the 'standard' book that is chosen by some kind of educational authority, is a worthwhile reward for all positively oriented teachers, provided that they have the competency to deal with the pedagogical challenges that arise in designing and developing education programmes of different kinds.

New educational designs were evident in the high school in New Zealand:

'We've got a different setup in our school because we have what they call an open forum. There is no classroom. You teach in what we call a learning commons. What happens is, in a commons you can have four classes running at the same time. A common would be ... about the same size as this house. A class would be this size, so you would be here, and there next door (points to the kitchen) there would be another one. You can see them, hear them'. [Technology teacher, High school, New Zealand]

This was backed up by innovative use of cloud services, which are now an essential feature of learning at this school:

'I said to them, you are going to go into groups of five, the group leader is going to set up a Google doc and give you all editor rights, including me. The group leader is going to assign each person two sections and you are going to answer all the questions in your section. It worked quite well - you get a few stupid comments ... [but] one of the better students was a group leader and he basically blocked out two of the students in his group'. [Technology teacher, High school, New Zealand]

The use of Google Docs™ has since become more prevalent and the benefits (and other consequences) are becoming clearer. It is part of a move to make much more use of the social web in education. Close analysis of the evidence suggests a growing divergence between the formal and social aspects of educational processes; we must be aware of all the issues, and we must manage the change that will ensue in order to assure the benefits.

Benefits

We need to understand and communicate the benefits that are within our grasp, because it is the benefits that engage stakeholders when change is needed. Business models are changing dramatically and education is no different. But the whole question of strategic management in education, so important to the successful achievement of change, still seems to lie under the surface. Education is not immune to change, and has to be able to manage it. The conversations indicate that there is evidence of planning, but there is equal evidence of happenchance and improvisation. The following anecdote illustrates the need for strategic thinking based on understanding the benefits:

'One of the reasons we [switched to Sakai] is that there is an open source community of users that support the use of Sakai. Like other schools we seriously questioned whether Blackboard is the right choice at this point because it costs an awful lot of money and that was killing us; we asked how do we get support from Blackboard? Well it turns out that Blackboard had created a community of users that you could share your problems with, they get back to you and help. But I'm, like, 'Isn't that open source? That's open source isn't it? But we're paying someone to do this?' We don't want to do that, so we switched [to Sakai] in 2007'. [Senior academic, University, USA]

There are long-term operational and financial implications in decisions like these. But change is not just operational, it is fundamental; how we see knowledge and our perceptions of managing knowledge are changing, in very interesting ways:

'If something is classed as research, then one would assume that it is done in a rigorous manner and accepted by a body of scholars who are all agreed, and so if I presented a hypermedia [work] of, say, the structure of knowledge, it could be a taxonomy, some

kind of graphical representation of the linkages of concepts and so on. If I found that these were accepted and integrated into the minds and work of other scholars, then the fact that I had rendered this representation of knowledge ... should be an even more compelling argument that I am a member of the research community ... and so this might be a shorthand way of avoiding writing thousands of pages'. [Learning management system manager, Business faculty, University, New Zealand]

This short monologue has profound implications. At one level we see people happily playing with, or even working with, 'mind maps'. But a mind map is just one example of how technology and systems allow us to deal with what we know in new and quite different ways. As the world still struggles to normalise and standardise the relatively simple thing that is metadata (such as the descriptive data about academic papers and books: author names, journal titles, publishers and so on) we have little prospect of normalising and standardising what knowledge is; but we are already a long, long way from the Dewey decimal classification system, and with these portentous issues in mind we have to agree that this all becomes highly strategic.

In summary, there is useful evidence of the potential benefits of information technology and information management here, but grasping them requires strategies that might redefine what education actually is.

Strategy

The stimulus that comes from new technologies drives much strategic change, in organisations of all kinds. Business, government and civil society all benefit from new ways of working and communicating. The answer, we are told, is to align our technology and organisational strategies:

[Luftman] is an American academic, former consultant. He did some quite interesting work on alignment ... [but] he has found 'the least aligned industry is education'! The reason is that there are multiple stakeholders with frequently conflicting goals, whereas in other businesses there are not. [In education] it's administration versus academics, academics versus students, and students versus administration. [Learning Chair, University, Canada]

Here is interesting evidence (Luftman 2003) that education really is late in understanding and adopting strategic management, but is strategic alignment 'doable' in education? Academic management is not universally known for its ability to manage everything well, and academics allow themselves the luxury (or is it a privilege?) to do what they want to do, much of the time. We have found that there are significant benefits to be gained, but tightening up the management of the many dependencies between technology acquisition and strategic success is what is needed, and this is indeed challenging.

At the heart of the confusion involved in aligning technology and strategy is the proper management of information, and of the information-enabled processes that we undertake to deliver educational value.

Results

The selected evidence presented here is from eight conversations and is therefore hardly definitive, but it helps us to adjust our thinking and achieve a balance. There is evidence of a range of stakeholders, and the ways in which they can help or hinder. There is evidence of a range of benefits that are sought, and we begin to see different kinds of benefit for the different stakeholders. Finally, even in these developed countries we see only passing signs of true strategic planning, but some evidence that planning does lead to better outcomes.

We are left with the most important question: *does strategic planning help to deliver the benefits of information management in education?*

It seems to depend on circumstances. Despite a concern for the ability of educational institutions to manage their technologies well, there is evidence that when educational organisations do get their strategic act together there are real benefits: for the teachers, for the learners and for other stakeholders. However, it is clear that the circumstances of the institution determine the nature of the strategy or strategies adopted.

Strategies for innovation, radical change and operational excellence

A closer examination of the specific evidence about strategies reveals thinking at three difference levels:

- A desire to innovate and discover new opportunities.
- A commitment to undertake radical organisational change.
- A simple ambition to work efficiently and effectively.

The high school in New Zealand is a good example of innovation. It is a new school with no baggage from its history that it has to deal with: it has new buildings, new ideas and new resources. Most importantly, its management meets regularly and drives the further development and refinement of the ideas by managing 're-invention':

> One of the good things about the school is that it is totally new … it's quite revolutionary! In the average school if something doesn't work people turn around and say 'these new ideas, new systems do not work …' and go back to the old way … Whereas in our case we have a strong tendency to say 'OK, it doesn't work, we have to re-invent ourselves'. The old way is not physically available, so you have to say 'right, let's re-invent ourselves'. [Technology teacher, High school, New Zealand]

This is real innovation, untrammelled by the baggage of a history.

The university in Auckland reveals quite a long history of careful and progressive management of its information technology, and although there are some signs of traditionalist thinking, the business school that contributed to these conversations has magnificent buildings and luxurious facilities within them. They seem to have close associations with business that keep their feet on the ground, and the management imperative probably rubs off when they meet and talk to their business friends. They are certainly making strategic use of the latest technologies:

> There is a thing called 'infopath' which is building what appears to be a document but is actually a series of attributes that can be queried and mailed - this goes as input to Sharepoint and so basically common stuff – course description, course reports – all that kind of thing now sits in a repository in Sharepoint and it's versioned, and we can look at and across all of the documentation that used to be hard copy, and start to understand what it is that we can do with it. And [*yet*] we don't have integrated systems. Or the systems we have are not integrated enough. [Learning management system manager, Business faculty, University, New Zealand]

This looks like a strategically capable university that has a long history of proactively managing radical change (in relation to traditional university practice).

The university in the United States adopts a very traditional stance, but is highly aware of trends and has active programmes in place to consider its options and maintain its competitive standing (and, make no mistake, it is in a *very* competitive situation):

> I think the challenge may be the senior leadership are always having to face those [*competitive*] issues and prioritise … especially at a time of economic strain. Recently we did two successive rounds of cuts so, you see we are not a public institution and yet we are constrained by financial changes in the market. We rely on an endowment for certain spending. [Senior academic, University, USA]

Almost all of the strategic management effort in this institution is directed at operational efficiency, and maintaining the critical services that good students expect.

And so we find evidence of 'innovative', 'radical' and 'operational' strategies.

In the evidence, there are 82 instances of conversation that were coded as having a direct link to strategy; these are subdivided into the three subdivisions of strategy (see Figure 5). It is found that the majority of the instances reveal an operational approach to strategy (efficiency and effectiveness), rather than being truly strategic (grasping opportunities and managing them proactively) or innovative (making new opportunities through experimentation and invention)

One might conclude that any educational institution that is willing and able to *innovate* will easily stand out from the crowd and ease itself much more successfully into the future, provided it can manage the innovation (and the consequential changes) well. Those that cannot innovate must focus on what is possible: being *distinguished* by doing some things very well and in different ways, or being *economical* by means of excellent administration and low-cost

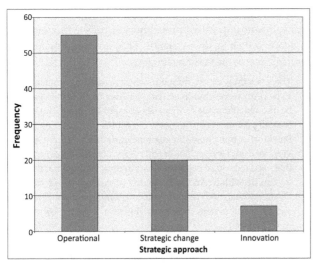

FIGURE 5: Analysis of management.

educational services. Technology can contribute to any of these, but doing more than one at the same time is confusing for staff and for students.

Implications of the work

This work began with the observation that education in South Africa is in a poor condition, and that there has been substantial investment in information technology that was intended to improve the quality of education, with variable results. Rather than looking at the problem from the 'bottom up', as often happens when looking at the impact of technology on pedagogy and didactics, it was decided to look at it from the 'top down', with a management perspective, and borrowing ideas from the domain of regular business management, and looking at information management broadly, not only as technology and systems:

- International experience confirms the importance of stakeholders, and the need to understand their roles and their expectations. Different stakeholder groups are looking for different benefits, and these differences need to be managed. South Africa presents special challenges relative to international experience, because of issues of language, ethnicity and context, thus making a strategic approach to information management doubly important.

- A further important issue, related to stakeholder expectations, is that the derived benefits of information management can be simple (leading to improved efficiency), complex (requiring institutional change in the cause of effectiveness) or innovative (new kinds of teaching and learning through evolutionary thinking). These different kinds of benefit cannot be achieved in parallel, they are conflicting. It is necessary to manage strategically by admitting and negotiating the benefits that are most appropriate to a situation. In most cases (from the conversations), the expected benefits were operational; in South Africa that might not be enough and more radical ideas might be needed.

- Perhaps most important to South Africa is that boundaries are dissolving, and education is becoming an international phenomenon. That might be of little interest

to rural South African learners who are stuck in the traditional educational paradigm, but it is exacerbating the divide between the 'haves' and the 'have-nots'.

Conclusion

What can be seen from this analysis of international conversations, perhaps predictably, is that technology is both a threat and an opportunity. But there is evidence that education is – through the introduction of technology – becoming a very international business. This challenges every country to take stock of what it needs to do, where its educational capability and resources might come from and how they might be managed.

So will strategic planning help to deliver the benefits of information technology investments through good information management? We do not know; it is not yet clear that this is the case, despite the evidence found here. As we proceed further into the digital age, we need to be conscious that:

- ICT itself is, first and foremost, a *cost driver* not a *benefit driver*: benefits come from improved processes that deliver improved organisational performance. But education is increasingly recognised as an incremental process that is driven by the individual learner, not by the institution.
- It is necessary to be certain about (and committed to) the delivery of *benefits to all stakeholders*, not just teachers and learners, but the tensions between stakeholders are real and impede a simple agreement about what the benefits actually are, as argued by Luftman (2000, 2003). Truly strategic thinking sets targets, manages demand and supply and ensures that all our investments in ICTs are directed at real benefits, for real stakeholders.
- Education systems are a part of a global ecology that is rapidly *eliminating geographical and cultural boundaries*, with real consequences for the prospects of our young populations. Even the best strategy managers struggle to deal with the huge gulf of understanding that can arise when cultures clash.

Life in education is full of surprises and so not everything can be planned. Improvisation is the stuff of innovation, and so teaching practice must not be constrained. But the *balance* between planning and improvisation must be understood and managed. What cannot be tolerated in countries and regions where education is desperately needed is the chaotic and anarchistic behaviour that might result if the adoption of ICTs in education is not well managed, in ways to deliver real benefits to the most important stakeholder: the learner.

Acknowledgements
Competing interests

The authors declare that they have no financial or personal relationship(s) that may have inappropriately influenced them in writing this article.

Authors' contributions

A.B. (University of the Western Cape) undertook research design and data collection, and drafted the article. I.M.V. (University of the Western Cape) mentored and contributed significantly to the finalisation of the article.

References

Anderson, J., Van Weert, T., Buettner, Y., Duchâteau, C. & Fulford, C., 2002, *Information and communication technology: A curriculum for schools and programme of teacher development*, UNESCO, France.

Angell, I., 2000, *The new barbarian manifesto: How to survive the information age*, Kogan Page, London, England.

Baets, W., 1992, 'Aligning information systems with business strategy', *The Journal of Strategic Information Systems* 1(4), 205–213. http://dx.doi.org/10.1016/0963-8687(92)90036-V

Baker-Eveleth, L., Eveleth, D.M., O'Neill, M. & Stone, R.W., 2007, 'Enabling laptop exams using secure software: Applying the technology acceptance model', *Journal of Information Systems Education* 78, 413–420.

Barron, A.E., Kemker, K., Harmes, C. & Kalaydijian, K., 2003, Large-scale research study on technology in K- 12 school: Technology integration as it relates to national technology standards', *Journal of Research on Technology in Education* 35, 489–508. http://dx.doi.org/10.1080/15391523.2003.10782398

Bhusry, M. & Ranjan, J., 2012, 'Enhancing the teaching-learning process: A knowledge management approach', *International Journal of Educational Management* 26(3), 313–329. http://dx.doi.org/10.1108/09513541211213372

Botha, N., 2009, 'Analysis and summary of the research themes of the concept papers received in response to the two national calls from the NRF, National Research Foundation', viewed 14 August 2010, from http://www.nrf.ac.za/files/Document%203-Summary%20research%20themes%20national%20research%20agenda%20June%2009%20_2_.pdf

Brown, C., 2010, 'Excavating the meaning of information and communication technology use amongst South African university students: A critical discourse analysis', doctoral thesis, Dept. of Information Systems, University of Cape Town.

Bytheway, A., 1998, 'Academic CS/IS Infrastructure in South Africa: An exploratory stakeholder perspective, *Proceedings of SAICSIT* November 1998', Cape Town, South Africa.

Bytheway, A., 2004, *ICT in Higher Education research project*, University of the Western Cape, Bellville.

Bytheway, A., 2004, 'Information management body of knowledge (IMBOK)', Cape Technikon, Cape Town.

Bytheway, A., Sadeck, O., Dumas, C., Chigona, W., Chigona, A., Mooketsi, B. & Fanni, F., 2010, 'Integrating ICTs into the classroom: Assisting teachers in disadvantaged primary schools', *Proc 2010 eSkills Summit*, Cape Town, South Africa.

Bytheway, A., 2011, 'Assessing Information Management Competencies in Organisations', *Electronic Journal of Information Systems Evaluation* 14(2), 179–192.

Bytheway, A., 2013, 'Qualitative Research without money: Experiences with a home-grown Qualitative Content Analysis tool', *The Journal of Community Informatics* 9(4).

Chatham, R. & Patching, K., 2000, *Corporate politics for IT managers: How to get streetwise*, Butterworth-Heinemann, Newton.

Chatterji, S., 2007, 'Bridging business and IT strategies with enterprise architecture: Realising the real value of business-IT alignment', *Information Systems Control Journal* 3, 1–2.

Chigona, W., Bladergroen, M., Cox, S., Dumas, C. & Van Zyl, I., 2011, 'Educator discourses on ICT in Education', in *E-Skilling for Equitable Prosperity and Global Competiveness*, South African Department of Communications, East London, South Africa.

Davids, Z., 2009, 'The educators' perspective on the factors that influence the success of ICT school initiatives within the Western Cape', master's thesis, University of Cape Town, South Africa.

DeLone, W.H. & McLean, E.R., 1992, Information systems success: The quest for the dependent variable', *Information Systems Research* 3(1), 60–95. http://dx.doi.org/10.1287/isre.3.1.60

DeLone, W.H. & McLean, E.R., 2003, 'The DeLone and McLean model of information systems success: A ten-year update', *Journal of Management Information Systems* 19(4), 9–30.

Edwards, C. & Peppard, J., 1997, 'Operationalizing strategy through process', *Long Range Planning* 30(5), 753–767. http://dx.doi.org/10.1016/S0024-6301(97)00056-3

Hardman, J. & Paucar-Caceres, A., 2010, A soft systems methodology (SSM) based framework for evaluating managed learning environments', *Systemic Practice and Action Research* 24(2), 165–185. http://dx.doi.org/10.1007/s11213-010-9182-4

Henderson, J.C. & Venkatraman, N., 1993, Strategic alignment: Leveraging information technology for transforming organizations', *IBM Systems Journal* 32(1), 4–16. http://dx.doi.org/10.1147/sj.382.0472

Jansen, J., 2012, 'Seven costly mistakes', *Times Live*, viewed n.d., from http://www.timeslive.co.za/opinion/columnists/2012/04/05/seven-costly-mistakes

Kearns, G.S. & Lederer, A.L., 2000, 'The effect of strategic alignment on the use of IS-based resources for competitive advantage', *The Journal of Strategic Information Systems* 9(4), 265–293. http://dx.doi.org/10.1016/S0963-8687(00)00049-4

Knights, D. & Murray, F., 1994, *Managers divided*, John Wiley, Chichester.

Koch, A., 2006, 'A conceptual model for a Co-operative Education Management system for tertiary institutions in South Africa', doctoral thesis, Cape Peninsula University of Technology, Cape Town, South Africa.

'Labour's computer blunders cost £26,326 bn', The London Independent, viewed 24 August 2010, from http://www.independent.co.uk

Luftman, J., 2000, 'Assessing business-IT alignment maturity', *Communications of the Association for Information Systems* 4, 1–51.

Luftman, J., 2003, 'Assessing IT/business alignment', *Information Systems Management* 20(4), 9–15. http://dx.doi.org/10.1201/1078/43647.20.4.20030901/77287.2

Madiba, M., 2009, 'Investigating design issues in e-learning', doctoral thesis, Dept. of Information Systems, University of the Western Cape, Bellville, South Africa.

Maslin, N., 1990, *The intelligent island*, television broadcast, BBC, London.

Mason, R.O. & Mitroff, I.I., 1973, 'A program for research on management information systems', *Management Science* 19(5), 475–487. http://dx.doi.org/10.1287/mnsc.19.5.475

McFarlan, F.W., 1984, 'Information technology changes the way you compete', *Harvard Business Review* 62(3), 98–103.

Michael, S.O., 1998, 'Best practices in information technology (IT) management: insights from K-12 schools' technology audits', *International Journal of Educational Management* 12(6), 277–288. http://dx.doi.org/10.1108/09513549810238020

Moloi, K., 2007, 'An overview of education management in South Africa', *South African Journal of Education* 27(3), 463–476.

Motala, E., 2009, *Guidelines informing the NRF's choices and priorities for Education Research Funding: A report prepared pursuant to the NRF's regional workshops held during October and November 2009*, NRF, Pretoria.

Omona, W., Van der Weide, T. & Lubega, J., 2010, 'Using ICT to enhance knowledge management in higher education: A conceptual framework and research agenda', *International Journal of Education and Development Using ICT* 6(4), 83–101.

Rahimi, F., 2010, 'The role of information and communication technology (ICT) in a higher education institution: With specific reference to disadvantaged students, cultural aspects and motivation', doctoral thesis, University of Pretoria, South Africa.

Republic of South Africa, 2004, *White paper on education*, Government Printers, Pretoria, South Africa.

Shirky, C., 2008, *Here comes everybody: the power of organizing without organizations*, Penguin, New York.

Strauss, A.L. & Corbin, J.M., 1998, *Basics of qualitative research: Techniques and procedures for developing grounded theory*, Sage Publications, Thousand Oaks.

Uys, P., 2007, 'Enterprise-wide technological transformation in higher education: The LASO model', *International Journal of Educational Management* 21(3), 238–253. http://dx.doi.org/10.1108/09513540710738683

Venkatesh, V., Morris, M.G., Davis, G.B. & Davis, F., 2003, 'User acceptance of information technology: Toward a unified view', *MIS Quarterly* 27, 425–478.

Ward, J. & Daniel, E., 2005, *Benefits management: Delivering value from IS and IT investments*, Wiley, Chichester.

Ward, J. & Peppard, J., 2002, *Strategic planning for information systems*, 3rd edn., Wiley, Chichester.

Zachman, J.A., 1987, 'A framework for information systems architecture', *IBM Systems Journal* 26(3), 590–616. http://dx.doi.org/10.1147/sj.263.0276

14

Aligning Web content and organisational strategy: Towards increasing funding

Authors:
Khutso Maahlo[1]
Molefe Ratsoana[1]
Martie A. Mearns[2]

Affiliations:
[1]Centre for Information and Knowledge Management, University of Johannesburg, South Africa

[2]Department of Information and Knowledge Management, University of Johannesburg, South Africa

Correspondence to:
Martie Mearns

Email:
mearnsm@uj.ac.za

Postal address:
PO Box 524, Auckland Park 2006, South Africa

Background: The effectiveness with which the Aurum Institute manages to communicate its organisational strategic objectives through its website was investigated. Despite its ground breaking research and programs which have made a positive impact on the community, the major problem that it faces is funding its core.

Objectives: An investigation of the website's content was carried out to determine the extent to which the organisational strategy is reflected to potential funders visiting the site. Requirements for aligning the content with the organisational strategy were identified.

Method: Content analysis was used where secondary data, such as website content and organisational strategic objectives, was analysed. An interview was also conducted with Aurum's knowledge manager to gain an in-depth understanding of the organisation's strategic objectives and to validate the initial findings.

Results: The results show that the website content was not effectively representative of Aurum's strategic objectives, and that the website structure did not effectively share the information that supports the decision-making process of potential investors. Recommendations were presented to the organisation in the form of a prototype website which reflects the desired website content that is representative of Aurum's strategic objectives.

Conclusion: Further research is required in determining the effect that a strategically driven website could possibly exert on the funding potential of the organisation. The theoretical approach used in this study can be used as a scoping exercise in organisations of a similar business nature.

Introduction

Website content that is effectively integrated with the strategic objectives of an organisation uncovers opportunities of increasing its audience base, specifically in the case where the website is geared towards drawing the attention of potential investors or funding opportunities. According to Akakandelwa (2011:421), websites act as connection and communication points for information users with electronic information. As a result, most corporations, organisations or institutions are making efforts to launch themselves into the virtual world of the World Wide Web. Rocha (2012:374) explains online perspective of organisations today, that they: '(I)nvest time and money to develop and maintain their website's quality. These websites should establish an effective information and communication channel between organisations and their clients'.

Panopoulou, Tambouris and Tarabanis (2008) note the following:

> Literature suggests that the sophistication of websites is related to a number of characteristics and features regarding interface and aesthetics, navigation, consistency and patterns, content relevancy and accuracy, accessibility, security and currency of information. (p. 518)

However, these characteristics and features need to 'be reviewed regularly to determine whether they are fulfilling the reasons for which they were developed' (Chiou, Lin & Perng 2011:1463).

It has been identified that, despite the recognised importance of having a website, most organisations do not plan properly for it. Nacar and Burnaz (2011:276) and Liao, Proctor and Salvendy (2008:44) highlight that 'content preparation could be handled from two main perspectives: the information content to be provided and the structure of how this information is to be presented'. The information content and structure need to be addressed in the website strategy of the organisation. Organisations also make use of website strategies to communicate and collaborate with stakeholders and inform them of the products and services that the organisation must provide (Chiou, Lin & Perng 2010:286). The website strategy development process ensures that an organisation addresses the strategic objectives that the website should achieve, one of which should be to effectively communicate its vision, mission and objectives, together with evidence that supports these aims, to its users.

It has become increasingly important that an organisation operates from a business strategy that ensures the efficient allocation of resources to relevant tasks. This is even more important for non-profit organisations (NPOs) because their funding comes from external sources. The same principle applies to their website strategies. NPOs are required to effectively communicate their mission and vision to the users of their website by certifying that their strategic objectives are well communicated. It is the purpose of this article to report on research conducted at the Aurum Institute. The Aurum Institute is an NPO based in South Africa whose aim is to improve on the health of the community through innovation in Tuberculosis and HIV and AIDS research (Aurum Institute 2012:3). Prof Gavin Churchyard, CEO of the Aurum Institute stated in the annual report of 2010 that 'one of the major problems that face us is funding our core' (Aurum Institute 2010:45). Aurum owns a website on which interested parties and potential funders can access information about the institute and its research initiatives. In addressing the above-mentioned funding issue, Aurum's website content was assessed to establish if it is effectively aligned to the strategic objectives of the organisation.

An organisation can make use of a website as a medium which will be accessed to transfer information and knowledge, and facilitate positive outcomes of the decision-making process made by the investors (Bou-Llusar & Segarra-Cipres 2006:106). The website designers need to analyse the content using relevant analysis tools to ensure that it is of sound quality, relevant, timely and that it facilitates decision-making. The organisation needs to identify the content it wishes to present on the website which will appeal to the targeted audience. Bill Gates (1996) also emphasised the power of persuasion that content possesses. He states that the quality and presentation of the content has the power to lure or push the audience away. In this context it is argued that *a conscious inclusion of organisational strategy into website content is required to enhance Aurum Institute's credibility, strengthen its organisational relations and increase its competitive advantage for better funding opportunities.*

This argument is based on the findings generated through the investigation that addressed the following main research question:

How effective is the Aurum Institute's website content in portraying their strategic objectives towards potentially attracting external funding or sponsorships?
In order to have addressed this research question the study was guided by the following sub-questions:

- What is the content quality and condition of the current website of the Aurum Institution?
- What are the organisational goals, objectives, values and strategy of the Aurum Institution and how are they currently represented by the website?

- What needs to be carried out to ensure that the Aurum Institute's content is aligned with its objectives?
- Using the findings from the above sub-questions, what website content will be suitable for the implementation of a website that will represent organisational goals and attract investments?

A qualitative approach was followed to collecting and analysing data, collecting and analysing secondary data as well as to conducting an in-depth interview. The secondary data comprised of Aurum's knowledge audit that was completed a year prior to the commencement of this study, and the inclusion of the current website content and the organisation's strategic objectives. A structured interview took place with the knowledge manager of Aurum Institute to fill the data gaps identified. All results were analysed and recommendations derived and integrated in the new prototype website.

Literature review

Dias and Reinhard (2004:5) maintain that organisations can add value to the business processes and activities by understanding the importance of Internet technologies and their platforms. Bailey (2010) mentions Gates (1996) who claimed that organisations could facilitate the management of information and the creation of quality website content, which will result in added value to the processes, procedures, communication and collaboration channels of those organisations. Chiou *et al.* (2010:286) stated that implementing a website strategy within the organisation can increase communication and collaboration with its stakeholders and customers. Moustakis, Tsironis and Litos (2006:60) identified the important factors that characterise websites of good quality; these include the following:

- content
- navigation
- structure and design
- look and feel
- multimedia used.

Huizingh (2000:124) emphasised the importance of the structure and quality of content as a result of the vital role they play in persuading stakeholders and customers.

The nature of Aurum's business necessitates that the organisation attracts potential investors to ensure that projects are well resourced and are effectively executed. De Troyer (1998:2) identified that users experience problems with organisations' websites; these include, amongst others, unclear mission statements of the organisation, no clearly defined target market and poor management of content. An organisation can increase the satisfaction levels of its stakeholders and increase revenue through effective information and knowledge sharing with them (Mpindiwa 2010:4). According to Hernandez, Jimenez and Martin (2009:362) a large number of studies in the 1990s placed much emphasis on website design (the content, use and objective of the website) but failed to identify the factors that improve the organisation's website strategy. It is imperative that the organisation understands the website strategy as well as its purpose in the organisation's communication plan before it is integrated.

Website strategy

According to Hernandez *et al.* (2009:364) organisations engaged in electronic commerce aided by an effective website strategy have the potential of being exposed to a larger market than organisations that do not effectively incorporate website strategy. Schmidt, Cantallops and Dos Santos (2008:504) stated that the implementation of the website strategy in the organisation enhances communication with stakeholders, and improves marketing mix and business practices. The website strategy is utilised by individuals or organisations to inform their audiences about the services and products offered by the organisation (Chiou *et al.* 2010:282). As part of their website strategy it is important that organisations identify the characteristics that enhance the interaction and relationship of the organisation with its stakeholders and customers (Baloglu & Pekcan 2006:174). Hernandez *et al.* (2009:364) identified these characteristics as the factors that are inherent in the Web Index Assessment (WIA) which facilitate effective and efficient access to the organisation's information through the website. Below is a brief summary of the factors that improve the quality of a website:

- **Accessibility**: this term refers to the ability of potential and current users to identify and access the website and its content. The volume of traffic that reaches the website influences the accessibility of the content on the website. There are two indicators that measure accessibility to the website; these are the position of the website on the search engine results and the popularity of the website. Search Engine Optimisation (SEO) and Search Engine Marketing (SEM) are tools that are used to measure the accessibility of the website. The SEO tool works to improve the traffic of the website using the search engines by submitting targeted keywords. The SEM tool works to obtain free search listings from the search engines by purchasing the search listings. It aims at increasing the traffic by improving the website's visibility on the search engines.

- **Speed**: this factor plays a vital role in the satisfaction levels of users and facilitates effective transactional processes on the virtual space. Website designers need to ensure that the loading time of the website is fast, and failure to do so will lead to a potential loss of users searching for information to other websites. Websites with a slow loading time increases the possibility of pushing potential customers away. Hernandez *et al.* (2009:364) stated that if a website takes more than 10 seconds to load, the website has a high chance of losing the user.

- **Navigability:** website designers need to put in place applications that will ensure ease of use and ability to find the content on the website. Poorly designed websites may result in inaccessibility to valuable information which could have the potential of dissuading stakeholders or customers to invest in or purchase into the organisation. Hernandez *et al.* (2009:364) further identifies the factors that website designers should consider in the design of the website which will enable users to successfully navigate through the website. Firstly, the content should be classified and organised according to a relevant topic and headings; secondly, the information should be labeled; thirdly, the navigation system should be designed in such a way that it will guide the user through the content and fourthly, the users must be guided to the information they need in order to make decisions.

- **Content quality:** the basic goal of implementing a website strategy is to provide information that is relevant to the organisation. There are two functions, or roles, that content plays on the website. (1) It informs the audience about the organisation's background, the products and services it offers, and the vision of the organisation. The information should be regularly updated and relevant. It should also be precise to ensure that a user has a full understanding of the organisation without being subjected to information overload. (2) It facilitates communication and interaction between the organisation and the customers. Website designers need to create a communication medium that will be used to share content with the customers and also interact with them (Hernandez *et al.* 2009:364).

By identifying the above characteristics an organisation can determine the website features that are important to incorporate into its website strategy.

Grigoroudis *et al.* (2008:1346) explain the following about quality and communication: Organisations invest time and money to develop and maintain their website's quality. These websites should establish an effective information and communication channel between organisations and their clients.

Hussainey and Mouselli (2010:6) maintain that stakeholders need to be well informed in order to make good decisions regarding purchases or investments in the organisation. Stakeholders are persuaded by the aesthetics and the manner in which the content is displayed on the website when they decide about investing in the organisation (Hussaney & Mouseli 2010:6). Huizingh (2000:124) claims that the engagement of stakeholders with the organisation is dependent on the information shared by the organisation, together with its ability to communicate the potential growth and return on investment of the organisation. Organisations that are non-profit in nature depend on financial assistance to successfully implement their projects. It is therefore of the utmost importance that the information they share with their stakeholders, through their website, communicates their plans for growth and the potential return on investment.

Porter (2001:64) recognises the importance of considering corporate strategies when designing the website strategy. He identifies principles that organisations could use as guidelines when positioning the website strategy in the organisation to ensure that it complements the corporate strategies. Gakhar (2012:74) states that an effective alignment of the website strategy to the organisational strategies increases investment opportunities for the organisation and potential customers. The alignment plays a vital role in the decision-making process of the potential investor and determines the outcome of the decision-making process.

Investment criteria used by investors and funders

According to Kollman and Kuckertz (2010:5) there are investors who raise money and then look for an organisation that has the potential to yield a high return on their investment. The investors engage in investment processes where the deal origination is determined. The deal is screened, evaluated and the structure of the investment is analysed to identify whether or not the structure will support the execution of the project at hand (Kollman & Kuckertz 2010:9). Once the investment decision has been made, the investor will monitor the performance of the organisation to ensure that the goals and objectives that were set are being executed effectively. The organisation is constantly monitored to determine whether it is producing the desired results or not. There is an additional set of investment criteria which will be discussed in the ensuing section.

When investing in organisations, an investment criterion is used to evaluate the potential of the organisations that seek investment opportunities. Kollman and Kuchertz (2010:27) have identified the factors that investors consider before investing in an organisation or providing funds that will facilitate for completion of the organisation's projects. Below is a discussion of these factors:

- *Personalities of the entrepreneurs:* the skills, capabilities and competencies of the leaders of the organisation are assessed based on the achievements of the organisation under their leadership. Leaders play influential roles in the behaviours and attitudes of employees by setting the culture that filters throughout the organisation. The business practices that are employed by the leaders are assessed to see whether or not they are ethical and whether they are efficient in achieving the goals and objectives or not. The reputation of leaders is also assessed to reduce risks of losing returns as a result of the leader reputation-factor.
- *Experiences of entrepreneurs:* investors assess the organisation's growth and the development that has taken place over a certain period of time by looking at its track record. There are activities and business practices that require organisations to be accredited or qualified for practice. The investor evaluates the business qualifications and the technical qualifications of the organisation and its staff to ensure they have the relevant experience.

- *Products or services:* the needs of customers continuously evolve and require organisations to be flexible, innovative and responsive to those needs. Investors assess products and services and identify how the organisation adds value to the final product. The organisation claims its competitive advantage from its unique selling point, core competencies and capabilities which are assessed to identify whether or not they will be able to sustain the innovation rate.
- *Market characteristics:* the potential risks and threats that reside in the market of the target investment are identified and assigned weights to calculate the potential impact of a threat. The potential growth of the market is also assessed by measuring how the market accepts new products and services. The market players and external factors that influence the operation of the organisation are also identified and assessed.
- *Financial characteristics:* the investor assesses the potential return on investment when considering an investment in the specific organisation. The financial characteristics of the organisation determine whether or not the investor will invest in the organisation or will seek other investment opportunities (Kollman & Kuchertz 2010:27).

The above-mentioned investment criteria are factors that were considered when the strategic objective measurement indicators were developed to assess Aurum's website.

There are different types of investors, which include, firstly, international investors who are located in a different country from where they invest. Secondly, the other type of investor is the domestic investor who resides within the same country in which the investment lies (Kollman & Kuchertz 2010:15). International and local investors who seek investment opportunities often make use of Internet technologies to access different websites of organisations that seek investment opportunities. The content quality, the accessibility, navigability and the downloading speed of the website will determine whether the investor is more likely or not to invest in the organisation. Organisations make use of websites as a medium that can transfer information and knowledge which can facilitate positive outcomes for the decision-making process followed by the investors (Bou-Llusar & Segarra-Cipres 2006:102).

Methodology

The Aurum Institute was used as a case study to examine the factors that determine the quality of a website's content and how information and knowledge is shared by the organisation with its customers and stakeholders. Secondary data was analysed which included the outcome of Aurum's knowledge audit (which was performed one year prior to this study by Aurum's knowledge manager), Aurum's website content as well as their organisational strategy document. Liebowitz *et al.* (2000:3) defines a knowledge audit as a tool appropriate to evaluate how the organisation would need to be changed to better facilitate for the flow and sharing of information and knowledge. The website content and the strategy document were compared to identify any discrepancies that existed between the two data components.

Data was collected using an observation schedule to assess the characteristics of Aurum's website and to evaluate the content. As a result of the dynamic nature of the website, where regular changes are made, the content was captured, for a period of one week, for website observation. This approach is in line with the principles of 'one–way–mirror' research to allow the analysis of website content and secondary data without any alterations of the content (Healy & Perry 2000:119). This approach allowed the authors to provide a description of what was experienced and measure that which was observed (Krauss 2005:760).

A qualitative approach to collecting and analysing data was employed to produce the findings for the research problems identified. The qualitative method of collecting data provided the authors with descriptive data, which facilitated processing and the unearthing of findings that are in-depth and descriptive. This type of research is empirical, according to Wacker (2008:10), because the study's expected results or findings are used as inputs into the designing processes of the prototype website, which will represent the desired website strategy. Secondary data were collected for analysis, which included Aurum's organisational strategy document as well as their website content. The website was analysed and compared to the organisational strategies to identify the gaps. After the analysis of the secondary data, an interview with the knowledge manager was conducted. This was to allow for the validation, triangulation and clarification of the data findings and insight regarding the assessment of the website content against the organisational strategy. The interview also clarified matters for the development of a prototype website. The nature of the data prescribed the descriptive analysis techniques for the analysis of secondary data.

Coding was used to analyse the secondary data qualitatively. This analysis was applied to identify the associations between the different aspects of the data or codes using a relationship analysis technique, as identified by Saldaña (2009:3). The collection and analysis of data were performed with the aim of creating a website prototype that will successfully compliment the organisational strategic objectives of Aurum, and potentially increase investment opportunities. The organisational strategic objectives were translated into measurement indicators, and used as benchmarks to measure how each webpage on the website represented each of the identified objectives.

Ethical practices were considered in the collection and analysis of data. The Aurum Institute's strategic objectives that were used in the secondary data analysis, are confidential and have strategic value to the organisation. Disclosing this information may jeopardise the success of the organisation and its projects and therefore the data analysis used undisclosed codes. In the interview session the information of the participant remained confidential, and permission was requested from the organisation to conduct the research. The highest technical skills and methodologies were employed in handling the data to avoid fabrication of the data.

Limitations that were encountered included the fact that Aurum's website content was subject to change at any given moment. The results of the content analysis only apply to a specific period of time as the website content has since been updated, edited or removed. However, the lessons learnt from the findings remain applicable from a holistic perspective regardless of editorial and maintenance updates.

Findings: Website content representative of organisational goals

Descriptive analytical tools were used to identify the patterns and the relationships between the organisational website and the corporate strategic objectives from the identified sources of secondary data.

The results, from the analysis, were used as inputs in the designing and development of the website prototype. The

TABLE 1: Representation of organisational strategic objectives by each webpage.

Webpage visited	Objective						Total objectives per page
	1	2	3	4	5	6	
Home page	3	2	1	3	3	3	15
Management team	1	1	1	3	1	3	10
Aurum in the news	3	1	1	3	1	1	10
Aurum events	3	3	1	3	3	3	16
Aurum staff awards	1	1	1	1	1	1	6
Career opportunities	1	1	1	1	1	3	8
Aurum training	3	2	1	3	1	3	13
Scholarships	1	1	1	3	1	3	10
Publications	1	3	1	1	1	3	10
Funders	1	1	1	3	1	1	8
Collaborators	1	1	1	3	3	1	10
Contact us	1	1	1	2	1	1	7
Total representativeness of website	-	-	-	-	-	-	**123/213**

Keys: 1 = Hidden; 2 = Obscure; 3 = Visible

first prototype presentation was based on a gap analysis that resided between the website and the organisational strategic objectives.

The strategic objectives were translated into measuring indicators against the website to identify how each webpage represents the strategic objectives. Table 1 illustrates how each objective was represented by each of the webpages.

After the development of the first prototype, an interview was conducted with Aurum's knowledge manager and aligned to the knowledge audit that was conducted prior to this study. This interview also triangulated the requirements necessary to successfully represent the organisational strategic objectives. The feedback received from the interview was incorporated into the re-designing stage of the prototype which was then used as recommendations to the organisation.

Table 1 illustrates the analysis of Aurum's website content against the organisational strategic objectives that were used as the measuring indicators. The webpages were individually assigned weights using a three–point scale which determined whether or not the strategic objectives were (1) not effectively represented or hidden, (2) obscure or ambiguous, or (3) visible and clear. The highest total that a webpage could score was 18. The maximum possible weight of 213 was calculated by multiplying the six objectives with the highest possible weight (3 – visible) that the webpage could score per objective. Each webpage was given a total weight out of a possible maximum of 18 (webpage weight is the sum of all the points attained from each objective per webpage). The results derived from the analysis of the findings presented in Table 1 are subsequently discussed:

- **Home page:** This page was allocated a score of 15 out of 18, meaning it is 83% representative of Aurum's strategic objectives. This webpage achieved this weighting score by including information regarding disease management with specific focus on prevention, treatment and care of the communities. The programs that the institute engaged in were also covered and included on the home page. The home page is the information users' first point of contact with the organisation's content, therefore a score of 83% indicates that it is more representative of Aurum's strategic objectives. This high representativeness enables the information user to obtain a clear understanding of the organisational strategic objectives and gives funders an idea of projects they could potentially sponsor.
- **Management team:** This page was allocated a score of 10 out of 18, meaning it is 56% representative of Aurum's strategic objectives. This was achieved by including information about the staff responsible for leading Aurum. Information on their professional qualifications was also made available. This information enables the potential funder to gain insight in the credibility of the management team that leads the organisation.

- **Aurum in the news:** This page was allocated a score of 10 out of 18, meaning it is 56% representative of Aurum's strategic objectives. This was achieved by the page's inclusion of the various news articles and information on community work carried out around the country. This information is vital as it could assist potential investors to assess the publicity and reputation of Aurum.
- **Aurum events:** This page was allocated a score of 16 out of 18, which indicates that it is 89% representative of Aurum's strategic objectives. This representation was achieved by the page's inclusion of information about the events that Aurum has hosted and projects it undertook. This information is relevant for potential investors as they are able to see the outcomes of investments made by other funders. This thus gives them an idea of how their funding would be spent should they decide to invest in Aurum.
- **Aurum staff awards:** This page was allocated a score of 6 out of 18; this shows that it is 33% representative of Aurum's strategic objectives. This was achieved through the page's inclusion of information on the awards that were given to Aurum's staff who performed exceptionally well. Although this information adds value, and could be useful for potential investors by enabling them to identify the skills and abilities of the Aurum staff, this page should be on the institute's intranet and not the website. This is because it is more focused on internal staff affairs and internal recognition of performance.
- **Career opportunities:** This page was allocated a score of 8 out of 18, meaning it is 44% representative of Aurum's strategic objectives. This was evident in the page's inclusion of information on the vacancies that are currently available at the Aurum Institute, together with a description of the vacant positions. The 44% is understandably low, resulting from the nature of the page.
- **Aurum training:** This page was allocated a score of 13 out of 18, meaning it is 72% representative of Aurum's strategic objectives. This was accomplished by the page's inclusion of information on the clinical training, counselling training courses, seminars, bookings for training, downloads and past programs. This information is very important for potential investors as it provides insight into the quality of the curriculum offered by the Aurum Institute.
- **Scholarships:** This page was allocated a score of 10 out of 18, meaning it is 56% representative of Aurum's strategic objectives. This was achieved by including information on the scholarships provided by the organisation, which demonstrates a corporate social responsibility on Aurum's part, through provision of education or skills development programs. This attempt by Aurum to empower the community (corporate social responsibility) is likely to attract potential investors.
- **Publications:** This page was allocated a score of 10 out of 18, meaning it is 56% representative of Aurum's strategic objectives. It included information on topics of interest

including the prevention, treatment and control of the HIV and TB pandemic. This page's representativeness percentage should be higher given that Aurum is a health research institute. Together with the research available, information should be provided on how this research will help Aurum in eradicating the scourge of TB and HIV and AIDS.

- **Funders:** This page was allocated a score of 8 out of 18, meaning it is 44% representative of Aurum's strategic objectives. It contained information on the funders who have worked with the organisation. This representativeness percentage should be higher as this information should give potential investors the confidence and security to dedicate resources to the Aurum Institute.

- **Collaborators:** This page was allocated a score of 10 out of 18, meaning it is 56% representative of Aurum's strategic objectives. This was achieved through the inclusion of information on those organisations, both international and domestic, that the Aurum institute works with to successfully improve the welfare of communities. This page's representativeness should also be higher, given that it is one of the pages that are most likely to be visited by potential investors.

- **Contact us:** This page was allocated a score of 7 out of 18, meaning it is 39% representative of Aurum's strategic objectives. It included Aurum's contact details at head office as well as the addresses of the different branches. The nature of this page allows it to score in this percentage as it is generally not a content heavy page.

Based on the results presented above, it is now known that Aurum's website content, as a whole, is 57.7% representative of the institute's strategic objectives. The percentage was calculated by dividing the sum total of all the webpages (123) with the maximum total that the webpage could score (213). From the measurement indicators used on the individual webpages, it was illustrated how the website achieved this percentage. A result of 57.7% indicates that Aurum's website content does not successfully communicate the organisational strategic objectives. The analysis of the results above also offers a clear indication of the webpages on which the organisation's objectives should have or have been displayed.

Conclusion

The significance of this study was to establish the extent to which Aurum's website content is aligned to the organisation's strategic objectives. Based on the research findings it is evident that Aurum's website content is not effectively representative of these strategic objectives. The reason for this could be attributed to information overload, insufficiency in relevant information and the presentation of content. These issues could be negatively affecting the funding, causing the difficulties that Aurum currently faces. It has been noted, however, that some of the webpages are not meant to contain too much information and, thus,

contributed to the low percentage that Aurum scored in its overall representativeness of the strategic objectives.

The theoretical approach that was taken can be utilised to assess the websites of other organisations that aim to achieve similar results. The results from this study are appropriate for application to other NPOs, as well as for–profit organisations, to analyse their website content. During the literature review phase of this study a shortage of academic research, on the importance of website content alignment to the strategic objectives of an organisation, was realised. Further research must be conducted on this topic, particularly for non-profit organisations, as this has an impact on the potential funding that they could attract. Additional research will need to be conducted on the measurement of the funding that the Aurum Institute would attract, once their website content has been aligned to the strategic objectives of the organisation. In other words, two types of website should be measured and compared for how effective each is at attracting funding or sponsorships, one which has website content that is aligned to its organisational strategic objectives, in comparison to one that is not thus aligned. This would require a longitudinal research approach.

The processes of website planning and defining the purpose of the website content should be largely influenced by the organisational strategic goals of the Aurum Institute, to ensure that relevant content is placed on the website. Aligning Aurum's website content with the strategic objectives of Aurum will enable the organisation to effectively communicate information that is relevant to the target audience (potential investors), and will successfully facilitate quick and positive decision-making by the potential investor. The factors that constitute a successful website strategy include the loading speed, navigability, ease of access, and available content. These factors are most likely to influence the decision-making processes of stakeholders and potential investors. Further research opportunities exist to identify a model that will evaluate the information needs of investors.

This study provides Aurum with insight, on the specific aspects of their website that are currently lacking, for improved communication of its organisational objectives. The analysis shows the webpages where the organisation's objectives are visible, and where they are not, but should be visible. Furthermore, the website can now be developed into an effective platform that effectively reflects the essence of the organisation, in order to specifically gain the attention of potential funders who would need to know whether or not their funding intent is directed at the correct funding recipient.

It can be concluded that when a website's content is aligned to the strategic objectives of the organisation, and does so on a website structure that is easy to navigate and presents the information in an easily consumable manner, the website could be effective in drawing the attention of the user, which could ultimately translate into increased and improved funding.

Acknowledgements

Competing interests

The authors declare that they have no financial or personal relationship(s) that may have inappropriately influenced them in writing this article.

Authors' contributions

K.M. (University of Johannesburg) and M.R. (University of Johannesburg) conducted the research as postgraduate students under the supervision of M.M. (University of Johannesburg). M.M. conceptualised the project and K.M. and M.R. collected and analysed the relevant data with supervision support from M.M.

References

Akakandelwa, A., 2011, 'An exploratory survey of the SADC e-government website', *Library Review* 60(5), 421–431. http://dx.doi.org/10.1108/00242531111135317

Aurum Institute, 2010, 'Annual Report 2010', viewed 18 August 2012, from http://www.auruminstitute.org/phocadownload/annual_report_2010.pdf

Aurum Institute, 2012, 'Company profile', viewed 04 August 2012, from http://www.auruminstitute.org/publications.php

Bailey, C., 2010, 'Content is king by Bill Gates', viewed 12 September 2012, from http://www.craigbailey.net/content-is-king-by-bill-gates.html

Baloglu, S. & Pekcan, Y.A., 2006, 'The website design and internet site marketing practices of upscale and luxury hotels in Turkey', *Tourism Management* 27, 171–176. http://dx.doi.org/10.1016/j.tourman.2004.07.003

Bou-Llusar, J.C. & Segarra-Cipres, M., 2006, 'Strategic knowledge transfer and its implications for competitive advantage: an integrative conceptual framework', *Journal of Knowledge Management* 10(4), 100–112. http://dx.doi.org/10.1108/13673270610679390

Chiou, C.W., Lin, C. & Perng, C., 2010, 'A strategic framework for website evaluation based on the review of the literature from 1995–2006', *Information and Management* 47, 282–290. http://dx.doi.org/10.1016/j.im.2010.06.002

Chiou, C.W., Lin, C. & Perng, C., 2011, 'A strategic website evaluation of online travel agencies', *Tourism Management* 32(6), 1463–1473. http://dx.doi.org/10.1016/j.tourman.2010.12.007

De Troyer, O., 1998, *Designing well-structured websites: Lessons to be learned from database schema methodology*, Tilburg University, Tilburg.

Dias, I. & Reinhard, N., 2004, 'Methodology for web presence strategy formulation: A case study', Proceedings *17th Bled e-Commerce Conference*, Slovenia, 21–23 June, Brazil.

Gakhar, D.V., 2012, 'Perception of stakeholders on web-based corporate reporting practices', *Journal of Advances in Management Research* 9(1), 64–76.

Gates, B., 1996, 'Content is king', Wordpress, San Francisco.

Grigoroudis, E., Litos, C., Moustakis, V., Politis, Y. & Tsironis, L., 2008, 'The assessment of user-perceived web quality: application of a satisfaction benchmarking approach', *European Journal of Operational Research* 187(3), 1346–1357. http://dx.doi.org/10.1016/j.ejor.2006.09.017

Healy, M. & Perry, C., 2000, 'Comprehensive criteria to judge validity and reliability of qualitative research within the realism paradigm', *Qualitative Market Research – An International Journal* 3(3), 118–126. http://dx.doi.org/10.1108/13522750010333861

Hernandez, B., Jimenez, J. & Martin, M.J., 2009, 'Key website factors in e-business strategy' *International Journal of Information Management* 29, 362–371. http://dx.doi.org/10.1016/j.ijinfomgt.2008.12.006

Huizingh, E., 2000, 'The content and design of websites: an empirical study', *Information & Management* 37, 123–134. http://dx.doi.org/10.1016/S0378-7206(99)00044-0

Hussainey, K. & Mouselli, S., 2010, 'Disclosure quality and stock returns in the UK', *Journal of Applied Accounting Research* 11(2), 154–174. http://dx.doi.org/10.1108/09675421011069513

Kollman, T. & Kuckertz, A., 2010, 'Evaluation uncertainty of venture capitalists' investment criteria', *Journal of Business Research* 63, 741–747. http://dx.doi.org/10.1016/j.jbusres.2009.06.004

Krauss, S.E., 2005, 'Research paradigms and meaning: A primer', *The Qualitative Report* 10(4), 758–770.

Liao, H., Proctor, R. W. & Salvendy, G., 2008, 'Content preparation for cross-cultural e-commerce: a review and a model', *Behaviour and Information Technology* 27(1), 43–61. http://dx.doi.org/10.1080/01449290601088424

Liebowitz, J., Rubenstein-Montano, B., McCaw, D., Buchwalter, J. & Browning, C., 2000, 'The knowledge audit', *Knowledge and process management* 7(1), 3–10. http://dx.doi.org/10.1002/(SICI)1099-1441(200001/03)7:1%3C3::AID-KPM72%3E3.0.CO;2-0

Nacar, R. & Burnaz, S., 2011, 'A cultural content analysis of multinational companies' websites', *Qualitative market research: An international Journal* 14(3), 274–288. http://dx.doi.org/10.1108/13522751111137505

Moustakis, V., Tsironis, L. & Litos, C., 2006, 'A model of website quality assessment', *The Quality Management Journal* 13(2), 22–37.

Mpindiwa, L., 2010, 'Impact of intranet as a knowledge sharing tool: experiences of ZIMRA', *World Library and Infromation Congress: 76th IFLA General Conference and Assembly*, Gothernburg, Sweden.

Panopoulou, E., Tambouris, E. & Tarabanis, K., 2008, 'A framework for evaluating websites of public authorities', *Aslib Proceedings* 60(5), 517–546. http://dx.doi.org/10.1108/00012530810908229

Porter, M., 2001, 'Strategy and the internet', *Harvard Business Review*, March, 1–20.

Rocha, A., 2012, 'Framework for a global quality evaluation of a website', *Online Information Review* 36(3), 374–382. http://dx.doi.org/10.1108/14684521211241404

Saldaña, J., 2009, *The coding manual for qualitative researchers*, Sage, London.

Schmidt, S., Cantallops, A.S. & Dos Santos, C.P., 2008, 'The characteristics of hotel websites and their implications for website effectiveness', *International Journal of Hospitality Management* 27, 2008, 504–516. http://dx.doi.org/10.1016/j.ijhm.2007.08.002

Wacker, J.G., 2008, 'Tragic conceptual flaws of theory – building empirical research', *Decision Line*, October, 10–13.

15

Preserving traditional medical knowledge through modes of transmission: A post-positivist enquiry

Authors:
Janet Adekannbi[1]
Wole M. Olatokun[1]
Isola Ajiferuke[2]

Affiliations:
[1]Africa Regional Centre
for Information Science,
University of Ibadan Nigeria

[2]Faculty of Information and
Media Studies, University of
Western Ontario, Canada

Correspondence to:
Janet Adekannbi

Email:
janet.adekannbi@gmail.com

Postal address:
PO Box 9936, U.I. Post Office,
Ibadan, Oyo State, Nigeria

Background: In Nigeria, most rural communities lack access to orthodox medical facilities despite an expansion of orthodox health care facilities and an increase in the number of orthodox health care providers. Over 90% of Nigerians in rural areas thus depend wholly or partly on traditional medicine. This situation has led to a call for the utilisation of Traditional medical practitioners in primary-healthcare delivery. Hence, the persistence of the knowledge of traditional medicine, especially in the rural communities where it is the only means of primary health care, has been a concern to information professionals.

Objectives: This study investigated the role which the mode of transmission plays in the preservation of traditional medical knowledge.

Method: A post-positivist methodology was adopted. A purposive sampling technique was used to select three communities from each of the six states in South-Western Nigeria. The snowball technique was used in selecting 228 traditional medical practitioners, whilst convenience sampling was adopted in selecting 529 apprentices and 120 children who were not learning the profession. A questionnaire with a five-point Likert scale, key-informant interviews and focus-group discussions were used to collect data. The quantitative data was analysed using descriptive statistics whilst qualitative data was analysed thematically.

Results: The dominant mode of knowledge transmission was found to be oblique (66.5%) whilst vertical transmission (29.3%) and horizontal transmission (4.2%) occurred much less.

Conclusion: Traditional medical knowledge is at risk of being lost in the study area because most of the apprentices were children from other parents, whereas most traditional medical practitioners preferred to transmit knowledge only to their children.

Introduction

Traditional medical knowledge (TMK), an aspect of indigenous knowledge (IK), is mostly tacit in nature and is passed on from one person to another (Osemene, Elujoba & Ilori 2011). Elders are considered to be the legitimate custodians of this knowledge which was handed down to them by their ancestors, and they are in turn expected to pass it on to others (Owuor 2007). The persistence of IK is basically a function of its transmission. According to Cavalli-Sforza and Feldman (1981), this transmission can take three modes, namely vertical, horizontal and oblique. Vertical transmission takes place from parents to their children, horizontal transmission between individuals of the same generation and oblique transmission from individuals of one generation to unrelated individuals of the next generation (Hewlett & Cavalli-Sforza 1986).

Hewlett and Cavalli-Sforza (1986) examined transmission of bush skills and cultural knowledge amongst the Aka Pygmies of the tropical forest region of Central Africa. The study revealed that vertical transmission (parent to child) was by far the most important mechanism for IK transmission, accounting for 80% of the cases studied. A related study by Ohmagari and Berkes (1997) reported that parents were primarily responsible for their children's education although other members of extended families were readily available to take over these responsibilities whenever needed. Lozada, Ladio and Weigandt (2006) also analysed medicinal and edible plant utilisation in Cuyin Manzano, a small rural population located near the Andean forests of Argentina. Interviews were carried out in 16 families in order to examine the present use of wild plants. The study reported that the transmission of wild-plant knowledge was mostly vertical through family dissemination. Similar patterns of plant use were found in young and old people alike, and learning was as a result of family tradition. In a recent study, Demps *et al.* (2012) reported that, amongst the Jenu Kuruba, a tribal community in South India, children tend to acquire the local knowledge required for collecting wild honey from their parents.

However, studies on cultural transmission have reported that horizontal and oblique transmission are more important during adulthood than during childhood as individuals gain exposure to a greater variety of social models as they grow older (Aunger 2000; Demps *et al.* 2012; Hewlett & Cavalli-Sforza 1986). Hence, they have opportunities to update what they had learned from parents or to seek specialised knowledge (Henrich & Broesch 2011; Henrich & Henrich 2010).

For example, some studies have shown the dominance of the horizontal mode of transmission of IK (Aunger 2000; Eyssartier, Ladio & Lozada 2008), especially considering the fact that the amount of time children spend with parents decreases with age (Aunger 2000). Usually, children spend large portions of time with siblings and age peers which give them the opportunity to share knowledge. Reporting this pattern, Rogoff (1981) suggested that direct interaction of Kenyan children with adults declines significantly as they grow older as they engage more with other children in the same age and sex cohort. Moreover, later in life, young adults turn to age peers rather than to parents for information, most probably due to similarity in their social positions (Reyes-García *et al.* 2009). New information provided by age peers might allow a person to update the information previously acquired from parents (Aunger 2000).

Aunger (2000) reported that, in a community of horticulturalists and foragers in the Democratic Republic of Congo, the degree of non-parental transmission was insignificant in the belief system, at least during the early years of life when most knowledge about which food to avoid was acquired. The study however noted that, as individuals grew older and were influenced by people from outside of their close family, they continued to learn about their culture, obliterating to some degree the traces of knowledge acquired earlier from parents. This observation was also reported by Eyssartier *et al.* (2008) amongst the Pilcaniyeu and Cuyin Manzano communities in North-Western Patagonia, Argentina, where the transmission of traditional plant knowledge begins at an early age, as a family custom. However, horticultural learning continued into adulthood during which time locals interchange knowledge and practices, probably relearning and changing their previously acquired information. This knowledge may or may not agree with what they have learnt as a family tradition.

The influence of the horizontal mode of transmission is especially evident in the absence of a parental generation. This observation was made by Setalaphruk and Price (2007), noting the contribution of other social contacts and interaction channels. In a study carried out in a rural community in Northeast Thailand, it was observed that some children primarily acquired their knowledge of wild food resources through peers as their parents were away and as they have not engaged in gathering with their grandparents. Such children had an opportunity to learn the practical knowledge about wild food resources with friends during their play and interactions in the fields.

Oblique transmission takes place from individuals of one generation to unrelated individuals of the next generation (Hewlett & Cavalli-Sforza 1986). This can take the form of one-to-one, one-to-many (when one person, for example a teacher, transmits knowledge to many people of a younger generation) or many-to-one (when an individual learns from older adults other than the parents) (Cavalli-Sforza & Feldman 1981). Very few studies have reported on the oblique form of transmission. Hewlett and Cavalli-Sforza (1986) reported transmission by others, probably the whole social group (many-to-one), as important for sharing and dancing. This form of transmission was reported by Reyes-García *et al.* (2009) as important during adulthood in the transmission of ethno-botanical knowledge and skills amongst the Tsimane adults in the Bolivian Amazon. Henrich and Henrich (2010) found that about one third of Fijian women interviewed learned specific food taboos from older, knowledgeable women who were not their kin.

In Nigeria, there is no evidence of literature that extensively investigate modes of transmission amongst traditional medical practitioners (TMPs). Traditional medical practice was chosen as the form of IK to study because, in Nigeria, most rural communities lack access to orthodox medical facilities. There has been an expansion of orthodox health care facilities and an increase in the number of orthodox health care providers, but these are not accessible to the majority of people living in rural communities as over 90% of Nigerians in rural areas depend wholly or partly on traditional medicine (Oladele & Adewunmi 2008), a situation that will most probably not change in the near future. This situation has led to a call for the utilisation of TMPs in primary-healthcare delivery (Alves & Rosa 2007; Elujoba, Odeleye & Ogunyemi 2005; Olatokun 2010; World Health Organisation [WHO] 2001). Hence, the persistence of the knowledge of traditional medicine, especially in the rural communities where it is the only means of primary health care for the rural poor, has been a concern to information professionals, especially in developing countries.

This study was carried out to examine the modes of TMK transmission amongst TMPs in selected communities in South-Western Nigeria with the aim of answering the following questions:

1. What are the modes of traditional medical knowledge transmission evident amongst TMPs in South-Western Nigeria?
2. What are the reasons for the observed trend?
3. What does the observed trend portend for the preservation of TMK?

The remainder of this paper is organised as follows: The details of the study's research methodology are presented in the next section, followed by the findings and discussion. The article ends with conclusions from the study and suggestions for further study.

Research methodology

The study adopted a post-positivist methodology using both quantitative and qualitative approaches. The quantitative approach requires that the research is objective, whilst the qualitative approach recognises subjectivity in research, relying on opinions, feelings and emotions of respondents (Ratner 2002). The South-West geo-political zone of Nigeria was the study area. South-West was purposively selected because, according to previous studies (Ajaiyeoba *et al.* 2004; Akinyemi *et al.* 2005; Mafimisebi & Oguntade 2010; Ogbole, Gbolade & Ajaijeoba 2010; Oladele & Adewunmi 2008; Olatokun 2010; Soewu & Adekanola 2011; Soewu & Ayodele 2009), there is a high proliferation of TMPs in the region, and the Yoruba people have a strong link with African traditional medicine. According to Soewu and Ayodele (2009), Yorubic medicine, a traditional medical system which is widely practised on the African continent, is based on the culture and mythological beliefs of the Yoruba people.

The people of South-Western Nigeria are mainly of the Yoruba ethnic group and distributed over six states, namely Oyo, Ogun, Ondo, Osun, Ekiti and Lagos. South-West is the second-most populous region in Nigeria with a population of over 27 million according to the 2006 census figures (Olagunju 2012). The natural vegetation is composed of coastal and swampy forest, high forest, rainforest and derived savannah towards the north. The people living in the rural areas make up about 70% of the total population, and their main occupations include farming, fishing, blacksmithing, pottery making and indigenous medical practices (Olagunju 2012).

The study population included TMPs, apprentices and children of TMPs who were neither learning nor practicing the occupation. The choice of the TMPs from amongst other major occupational groups was based on their relevance in primary-healthcare delivery in developing countries, including Nigeria, as reported in the literature. The technique of purposive sampling was used to select three communities from each of the six states in South-Western Nigeria. Each state was divided into three, based on senatorial districts. One local government was purposively selected from each senatorial district, and a community was selected from the local government. The choice of local government and rural communities was based on the recommendation of the head of traditional medical practitioners in each state, and this recommendation was based on the concentration of TMPs in the selected areas. The snowball technique was applied in selecting TMPs. Using the technique, each TMP introduced the researcher to other TMPs. Neis *et al.* (1999) reported using a snowball sampling technique to select local experts in a study conducted amongst fishermen living along the northeast coast of Newfoundland, Canada. Jesajas and Packham (2003) and Ngunyulu and Mulaudzi (2009) also adopted the technique in their studies. Convenience sampling was however used in selecting the apprentices and children of the TMPs who were not learning nor practicing the profession. In all, a total of 228 TMPs, 529 apprentices and 120 children of TMPs, who were not learning nor practicing the profession, participated in the study.

Data collection and analysis

Focus-group discussions (FGDs) and interviews were used in collecting qualitative data whilst questionnaires were adopted in collecting quantitative data.

Eighteen in-depth interviews were held with key informants who were leaders of the associations of TMPs in each locality. This interview preceded the FGDs. The interview provided additional information on knowledge transmission amongst the TMPs, especially information that could not be revealed during FGDs. This information proved useful as additional guide in data collection when carrying out the FGDs. Interviews were also held with the TMP's children, aged 21–47, who were not in the occupation. Interviews were conducted with them in order to understand why they are not engaged in the occupation. Two FGDs were held in each state with seven to nine participants in each group. The groups were heterogeneously based on the demographic characteristics of respondents. The FGD provided information on the group's opinions, beliefs and attitude towards knowledge transmission. A five-point Likert questionnaire was used to collect quantitative data from the TMPs and apprentices after the FGDs were conducted with the TMPs. A total of 757 copies of questionnaire (Ekiti – TMPs 37, apprentices 101; Lagos – TMPs 39, apprentices 90; Ogun – TMPs 40, apprentices 85; Ondo – TMPs 39, apprentices 83; Osun – TMPs 35, apprentices 91; Oyo – TMPs 38, apprentices 79) were administered, and a 100% return rate was achieved because they were researcher-administered. Data collection took place over a period of six months.

Both the FGD guide and the interview schedule included questions on the TMPs' view of transmission of their knowledge to their children and others. The questionnaire was divided into two sections. Section-A contained questions on demographic attributes of the TMPs and other pieces of information that were required for the study, including age, sex, marital status, educational level, religion, number of children and number of children in their occupation. Section-B, which was completed by the apprentices, contained questions on demographic attributes and other information such as the amount of knowledge acquired. For data collected with the questionnaire, frequency distribution was used for analysis. Data collected through the FGD and in-depth interview was analysed thematically. The data was transcribed into text, and the transcribed text was searched to identify recurrent themes conveying similar meanings. Such recurrent themes were illustrated with some quotations from the original text in order better to communicate their meanings.

Findings and discussion

This section presents the findings from the study. Findings from quantitative and qualitative data are presented separately. These findings are also discussed.

Findings from quantitative data
Demographic characteristics of TMPs

Of the 228 TMPs, 138 (60.5%) were men. The percentage of male TMPs varied from 54% to 68% in the six states. The mean age of the respondents was 54 years. The respondents' ages ranged from 31 to 80 years. About 40% of the respondents were between the ages of 41 and 50, and this group was followed by those between the ages of 51 and 60 (31.1%). Respondents between the ages of 71 and 80 constituted only 8.3% of the sample. An overall examination of the age category showed that the sample had more middle-aged respondents. However, a deviation from the general trend was observed in the Ekiti and Lagos States where respondents between the ages of 51 and 60 made up the largest proportion of respondents (Table 1).

The frequency distribution of the TMPs' religion showed that 101 (44.3%) were Muslims, 92 (40.4%) belonged to traditional religion and 35 (15.4%) were Christians. Generally, Muslims were dominant amongst the respondents. However, this was only the case for the Ekiti, Osun and Oyo States whilst respondents who belonged to traditional religion were dominant in Lagos, Ogun and Ondo. The highest level of education amongst members of TMPs was secondary education (43.4%). In the same group, 38.2% had only primary education whilst 18.4% had no formal education. A breakdown of this category showed that, whilst most of the respondents in Ogun, Ondo and Osun attained secondary education, a large proportion of respondents in Ekiti, Lagos and Oyo concluded their education at the primary level. It was interesting to observe that all the respondents in Ondo had either primary or secondary education; none were without formal education.

Only 29.4% of the TMPs transmitted all their knowledge of traditional medicine. Whilst 68.9% transmitted just more than half of their knowledge, less than two per cent transmitted only half of their knowledge. The study observed that, generally, TMPs have a positive attitude towards the transmission of their knowledge.

Demographic characteristics of apprentices

Results revealed that 292 (55.2%) apprentices that participated in the study were men whilst 237 (44.8%) were women. Male apprentices that participated in the study were more than the females in all the states with the exception of Lagos

where 54.4% of the apprentices who participated in the study were women (Table 2). The mean age of the respondents was 27 years. The minimum age of the respondents was 16 years whilst the maximum was 45 years. About 70% of the respondents were between the ages of 21 and 30. This general trend was observed in each state except in Ogun where 57.6% of respondents were aged between 26 and 35 years.

Overall, 58.6% of apprentices were Muslims, and 25.5% belonged to a traditional religion whilst 15.9% were Christians. A similar trend was noted in all six states as between 50% and 65% of apprentices in each state were Muslims. The highest level of education attained by apprentices was the secondary level (85.1%) with only 1.3% having received no formal education. A similar pattern was observed in all the states. Ondo had the highest proportion of apprentices (96.4%) with secondary education whereas Ekiti had the lowest (76.2%). In Lagos and Ogun, the apprentices were educated at least at the primary level.

More than 90% of the apprentices had spent one to five years learning the occupation. The expected length of training was one to five years for 73.7% of the apprentices, with six to 10 years the expected length of training for about 25% of the apprentices. Only 7.2% had spent six to 10 years acquiring the knowledge of traditional medicine. Of the 1074 children of the TMPs, only 291 (27.1%) were either learning or practicing the occupation. In addition, only 29.3% of apprentices who participated in the study acquired their knowledge through the vertical mode whereas 67% obtained knowledge through the oblique mode of acquisition. About 60% of the apprentices acquired more than half of their knowledge of traditional medicine from their TMPs. Only 9.1% acquired all the knowledge they possess from the TMPs whereas 23.4% acquired half of their knowledge from TMPs.

Demographic characteristics of children (non-TMPs)

A total of 120 respondents, who were children of TMPs, but not learning nor practising as TMPs, participated in the study. The average age of the respondents was 31 years. Of

TABLE 1: Demographic distribution of TMP's by state.

Measure	Sub-measure	States (%)					
		Ekiti	Lagos	Ogun	Ondo	Osun	Oyo
Sex	Male	59.5	59	67.5	64.1	54.3	57.9
	Female	40.5	41	32.5	35.9	45.7	42.1
Age	31–40	16.2	12.8	5	7.7	5.8	7.9
	41-50	18.9	23.1	45	59	51.4	39.5
	51–60	35.1	25.6	25	33.3	17.1	31.6
	61–70	16.2	23.1	12.5	0	20	18.4
	71–80	13.6	15.4	12.5	0	5.7	2.6
Religion	Christianity	13.5	23.1	15	12.8	11.4	15.8
	Islam	54.1	33.3	40	41	51.4	47.4
	Traditional	32.4	43.6	45	46.2	37.2	36.8
Educational Level	None	21.6	23.1	20	0	22.9	23.7
	Primary	51.4	41	35	23.1	31.4	47.4
	Secondary	27	35.9	45	76.9	45.7	28.9

TABLE 2: Demographic distribution of apprentices by state.

Measure	Sub-measure	States (%)					
		Ekiti	Lagos	Ogun	Ondo	Osun	Oyo
Sex	Male	51.5	45.6	55.3	69.9	51.6	59.5
	Female	48.5	54.4	44.7	30.1	48.4	40.5
Age	16-20	9.9	2.2	3.5	15.7	9.9	16.5
	21-25	25.7	30	23.5	42.2	33	36.7
	26-30	36.7	40	29.4	34.9	37.4	36.7
	31-35	20.8	23.3	28.2	7.2	18.6	10.1
	36-40	6.9	4.4	14.1	0	1.1	0
	41-45	0	0	1.3	0	0	0
Religion	Christianity	20.8	18.9	15.3	4.8	12.1	22.8
	Islam	60.4	53.3	64.7	50.6	63.7	58.2
	Traditional	18.8	27.8	20	44.6	24.2	19
Educational Level	None	3	0	0	1.2	1.1	2.5
	Primary	20.8	10	15.3	2.4	14.3	17.8
	Secondary	76.2	90	84.7	96.4	84.6	79.7

TABLE 3: Profile of respondents - children (non-TMPs (*n* = 120).

Measure	Item	*f*	%
Sex	Male	63	52.5
	Female	57	47.5
Age	21-25	13	10.8
	26-30	41	34.3
	31-35	51	42.5
	36-40	13	10.8
	41-45	1	0.8
	46-50	1	0.8
Religion	Christianity	54	45
	Islam	54	45
	Traditional	12	10
Education level	Secondary	111	92.5
	Tertiary	9	7.5
Education aspiration	None	5	4.2
	NCE	8	6.7
	OND/Technical college	2	1.7
	HND	30	25
	Bachelor degree	68	56.6
	Masters	7	5.8

f, frequency; NCE, National College of Education; OND, Ordinary National Diploma; HND, Higher National Diploma.

all the children, 52.5% were men whilst 47.5% were women. Muslim and Christian respondents were equally represented at 45% each whilst respondents that belonged to a traditional religion were only 10%. All the respondents had some formal education with the minimum being secondary school (92.5%) whilst 7.5% of respondents had attained a tertiary level of education. About 82% of the respondents aspired to have either a Higher National Diploma (HND) or a bachelor's degree, and about 6% of respondents looked forward to having their master's degree (Table 3).

Modes of knowledge transmission amongst TMPs in South-Western Nigeria

The three modes of transmission, namely vertical, horizontal and oblique, were observed in all the communities. The oblique mode of transmission was the most common. About 70% of the apprentices were not children of the TMPs but rather children of other people. Only about 30% of the apprentices were children of the TMPs. This result is in sharp contrast with what was observed regarding the mode of knowledge acquisition by the TMPs (Figure 1). This is not surprising as further results showed that, of the 1074 children of the 228 TMPs, only 291 (27.1%) were either learning to become or had already become TMPs. This was the trend in all six states. Overall, about 67% of the apprentices were not children of the TMPs.

Findings from qualitative data

The findings from FGDs and in-depth interviews showed that TMPs are very interested in transmitting their knowledge to their children as shown in some of their responses.

'You see, whether traditional medical practitioners or Imams or Christians, a person who fails to transmit his knowledge to his child, that 'my child come and learn this thing', when he dies, he dies in vain'. (Camp Community)

'We inherited it, we must also leave it for some people ... If I want to cut a leaf, I will take my child there, 'I am going to cut so-and-so leaf, let us go'. When I cut the leaf, he will see it and next time when I say 'go and cut so-and-so leaf' he will recognize it since I had cut it in his presence earlier'. (Olode Community)

Responses by some of the participants however showed that vertical transmission was not automatic but depended on the attitude of the child:

When we were young, our fathers will study the attitude of their children. A child who is cool-headed and not a trouble maker, our fathers will ponder: 'If I transmit my knowledge to this child, I hope he will not bring my name or the family name to disrepute, I hope he will follow it and use it as specified.' If they realized that the child is a trouble maker who will bring the family name into disrepute, they will rather die with their knowledge'. (Igbonla Community)

Many of the participants also expressed their views on transmitting their knowledge of traditional medicine to others who were not their children: 'Anybody is my child. Whoever wants to acquire this knowledge is my child' (Eporo Community); 'Whoever wants to learn this work from me, I'll teach willingly because I don't want this work to perish' (Butubutu Community); 'It is compulsory we give it to another person's child as long as it is not a very powerful medicinal knowledge' (Kajola Community).

Further:

'Not just your child alone. There are others who are not your children but when you are comfortable with their attitude you might transmit your knowledge and that child will praise you forever just as I always praise the *baba* who taught me'. (Igbonla Community)

'About what we know, me must teach our children … another person's child too who comes to us we teach, because what we also know is not only what our fathers taught us. Other fathers also taught us, that is why we must also teach children of other parents'. (Olode Community)

Participants expressed their minds on the limitations of the oblique mode of knowledge transmission specifically in relation to incomplete transmission of knowledge and lack of trust in apprentices: 'My master did not teach me everything. My master did not transmit all his wisdom to me because you don't have everything. You can't take everything from your master' (Labaile Community).

Further:

'Another person's child is difficult to teach. You might teach him and thereafter he will use the power against you. One must be careful with teaching a child who was not born into traditional medicine'. (Fakale Community)

'If a person says he wants to learn it, we can teach him, but only our children inherit all our knowledge, it is our children, they inherit our knowledge. So that when it becomes obvious that we are dying, we will call our child who knows how to read and write and instruct the child to write everything. We will not hide anything from him. He will write everything completely'. (Olode Community)

'You see this knowledge you are talking about, transmitting it to another person's child is difficult, it is difficult, this is the reason, o [long emphasis]; you see the work of traditional medicine is powerful you see, when I wanted to learn this work from baba, the baba was not my father, he was not my father's brother, he was not my mother's brother … when I got to him, he first watched me for about 4 years, he used that period to study me, whether he will reveal the knowledge to me or not. But when he realised that I had an open mind to what I came for, he then revealed the knowledge to me … so I will study the person first just as baba studied me … because somebody might be sent to spy out your power … It is more important to transmit the knowledge to one's child … one's child is different from an outsider'. (Labaile Community)

Whilst vertical transmission was without cost, horizontal and oblique modes were not free. Many of the TMPs reported that they received money before transmitting their knowledge:

'When an outsider comes and says, 'Please I heard about something you have, please give me', we will say, 'Well then, go and bring so and so amount'. Once he brings it, we will teach him well and he will know it'. (Olode Community)

The TMPs were asked why they receive money from children of other parents and generally their responses are reflected in those of two TMPs as the following:

'We cannot give it free because when we wanted to receive it from our fathers in those days, you might have to work in his farm for five days. Then, you will keep going to his house every day, and they will tell you that baba has gone to the farm. You will go to him at his farm, and you will work for him so much

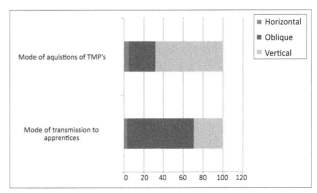

FIGURE 1: A stacked bar graph showing modes of acquisition by TMPs and modes of transmission to apprentices.

until he is satisfied and he sees that 'yes, this child is in fact a good child, I will give him this knowledge', and he will give him'. (Ago-Ayo Community)

'We suffered before we learnt this work o [long emphasis]. You make a living with your secular education. We suffered. We carried loads, we cleared bushes, we cut trees, we washed clothes before they gave us knowledge of traditional medicine'. (Camp Community)

Reasons for the observed modes of transmission

The TMPs reported that most of their children were not interested in acquiring TMK. Reasons for this lack of interest included a preference for formal education even by their parents, laziness, lack of patience and interest in quick money-making businesses. Others who showed some interest did so for wrong reasons as reflected in some of their responses:

'It is not that they can't teach others but who will want his child to learn traditional medicine. Even you sitting down, you cannot allow your child to do so, you will rather send him to school. If your child lives with me, can I tell him to go to the bush and cut some leaves for me? It is not possible'. (Oke-Ojumo Community)

'No youth can acquire traditional medical knowledge because most of them are interested in quick wealth'. (Labaile Community)

'They prefer to be 419s (fraudsters), they are not interested in practising traditional medicine. Once they have some knowledge of traditional medicine, they become 419s, defrauding people everywhere, and this can lead to their death'. (Eporo Community)

They are rather interested in daily work that will bring quick money such as breaking gravel and loading sand, that is most common among them. (Fakale Community)

A lack of interest by children of TMPs as reported by their parents was corroborated by the children who were not in the profession. Few of them were comfortable with their parents' occupation, as indicated by the following quotes: 'It is God's gift for those who have the knowledge. It is a good job'; 'They should just continue with their work of healing as long as they are happy with it'; 'As long as he is happy, what is my problem about how he gets his source of livelihood?'

However, some children expressed negative feelings about their parents' profession – traditional medicine –

when they were asked about their views on their parents' occupation. Some of them were not supportive of their parents' occupation because they believed that traditional medicine as a job is dirty: 'It is a very stressful and dirty work'; 'It is dirty, orthodox medicine is more prestigious'.

Some believed that traditional medicine is shrouded in secrecy: 'My parent's work is good but I don't have interest because it has some secret power'; 'It is an ungodly work which I do not have interest in. It is about being in the secret cult'.

Strong religious sentiments were the basis for the negative views of some of the children. Some specific responses along this line were: 'God does not support such work. You will worship idols'; 'Islam does not support idols. I have chosen Islam'; 'I pray she changes and know Jesus as I do now. The work will not take her anywhere'; 'I would not be happy to see my father perish in hell but what can I do?'; 'It is an ungodly work. I do not support bowing down or relying on idols for power'.

The reason for the observed lack of interest of children of TMPs can be viewed from two perspectives. The first is related to their educational aspirations. Most of them aspired to acquire degrees in tertiary institutions and did not perceive TMK as valuable for their future needs. Tsuji (1996) and Grenier (1998) identified educational systems as one of the means by which IK is being lost. Subsequent studies have shown that educational systems caused bias in the attitude of the younger generation towards IK (Akullo *et al.* 2007; Dube & Musi 2002).

Another source of bias is associated with the religious beliefs of children of TMPs. Many of them believed that traditional medicine should exclusively be practiced by the adherents of traditional religion whilst the adherents of Christianity and Islam should not be involved in traditional medicine. In view of this, they condemned and resisted their parents' efforts to impart the knowledge to them. Such religious bias has been traced to the days of African colonial rule when traditional medicine was perceived to be a threat to the spread of colonial power and Western religious belief systems. African traditional medicine was labelled as 'witchcraft', and this has continued to influence modern perceptions of African traditional medicine (King *et al.* 2009).

Findings from this study concerning a lack of interest by youths in acquiring TMK agree with reports from other studies (Ragupathy *et al.* 2008; Srithi *et al.* 2009; Voeks 2007; Voeks & Nyawa 2001). A lack of interest in traditional values amongst the younger generation has been worsened by exposure to modern education (Giday *et al.* 2003). Srithi *et al* (2009) studied the transfer of TMK amongst the Mien in Northern Thailand and reported that some elderly Miens who were custodians of this knowledge complained that 'it is difficult to find younger people with an interest in learning skills concerning local healthcare'. Amongst the Chepang

communities of the Mahabharat hills of the central part of Nepal, Rijal (2008) listed Western education as one of the factors responsible for the limited knowledge of plant that the younger generation has. In a similar study by Voeks (2007) amongst communities in the Eastern Bahia State, North-East Brazil, there was little interest on the part of the young ones in the communities to sustain the medicinal knowledge of their communities. For example, young boys between the ages of 13 and 17 clearly stated that 'they knew very little about the medicinal properties of the plants and that they were distinctly uninterested in learning them' (Voeks 2007:13).

In South-Western Nigeria, Oladele, Alade and Omobuwajo (2011) reported that the younger generations are not active in the practice of traditional medicine. In their study on the conservation and cultivation of medicinal plants by TMPs in the Aiyedaade Local Government area of Osun State, the authors noted that more than half of the practitioners had no apprentices at the time of the study. This was attributed to the decision of the younger ones to prefer formal education and other activities, leaving them no time to acquire TMK. A similar observation was made in a more recent study by Salako and Sholeye (2012) where all the traditional healers who participated in their study were middle aged and elderly.

Implication for the preservation of TMK

The discussion on the implications of the findings from this study can begin with the age of the apprentices. The study observed that apprentices of TMK were mostly between the ages of 21 and 30 years. Fewer than 10% of apprentices were between the ages of 16 and 20, and the youngest apprentice was 16 years. This tends to suggest that most young ones in the region begin to show interest in acquiring TMK only after their secondary school education. Very young children were not seen as active apprentices of TMK in the region. It can be inferred that the young ones in this region perhaps decide to learn traditional medicine because they have nothing else to do. Thus, given any other opportunity, they would likely abandon acquisition of TMK.

Concerning the mode of transmission, findings show that most of the apprentices were not children of the TMPs. However, most apprentices that have a vertical relationship with the TMPs are in the group of apprentices who have acquired at least more than half of the knowledge of traditional medicine whereas, for apprentices in the oblique mode, they are mostly in the group of apprentices that have acquired at most half of their TMPs knowledge. An explanation for this is that children of TMPs spend more time with their parents compared to those who have a horizontal or oblique form of relationship with the TMP. Apprentices in the latter categories return to their homes each day and do not have the opportunity to learn at informal settings. However, the situation of the group with horizontal relationships is reminiscent of the teaching approach encouraged in ancient

Israel where parents could take advantage of walking with their children on the road, eating with them at home, lying with them in bed and being in other informal settings to teach them. Hence, apprentices with vertical relationships have opportunities to learn more than those with other forms of relationships. Added to this is the observation by Akintilo (2000:250) that traditional medical practice in South-Western Nigeria is shrouded in secrecy because most of the TMPs make covenants with their ancestors not to disclose 'the secrets of the practice to strangers'.

Another explanation for the finding in the previous paragraph can be deduced from some of the responses from focus-group discussions and in-depth interviews held with TMPs. Whilst all TMPs are comfortable transmitting their knowledge to apprentices irrespective of their relationship, children of TMPs who are learning about traditional medicine tend to be at an advantage compared to apprentices who have horizontal or oblique relationships with the TMPs. According to the participants, they are more comfortable transmitting all their knowledge to their children. Other apprentices will also benefit from receiving this knowledge from the TMPs but the acquisition of everything they know about traditional medicine is believed to be the exclusive right of their children.

The findings of this study contradict the opinion that the transmission of TMK is mainly through family inheritance (Christian 2009). From the discussions held with TMPs, they are very comfortable transmitting their knowledge irrespective of their relationship with the learner, but most would not transmit all their knowledge to those who are not their children. Most of the TMPs do not see anything wrong with this. It was inferred that TMPs who acquired their knowledge through others who are not their parents are aware that they themselves did not acquire all the required knowledge of traditional medicine. The implication of this is that, in this situation where we have more apprentices in oblique relationship with the practitioners, TMK risks being incompletely transmitted, and eventually, vital aspects of the knowledge might be lost. No matter how good the attitude of an apprentice is and no matter how long he or she stays with the TMP, as long as he or she is not related to the custodian, that particular knowledge might not be transmitted.

Conclusion

The place of TMK in the nation's healthcare, especially at the rural level, justifies the need to show more than passive interest in the transmission of the knowledge. The study has shown that, whilst the oblique mode is the dominant way of acquiring the knowledge, the vertical mode has shown to be the best way of ensuring complete transmission and acquisition of TMK. Generally, TMPs freely transmitted their knowledge irrespective of their relationship with apprentices, but due to issues of trust, they are more comfortable transmitting all their knowledge to their children. Hence, TMK in this region risks being lost because of the preference of most TMPs to

transmit all their knowledge only to their children. Future studies could be carried out in other regions of Nigeria in order to provide a comparison as well as a complete picture of modes of knowledge transmission amongst TMPs in the country.

Acknowledgements

Competing interests

The authors declare that they have no financial or personal relationship(s) that may have inappropriately influenced them when they wrote this article.

Authors' contributions

J.A. (University of Ibadan) was the lead researcher; W.M.O. (University of Ibadan) and I.A. (University of Western Ontario) supervised the project and made vital contributions to the research design and analysis.

References

Ajaiyeoba, E.O., Falade, C.O., Fawole, O.I., Akinboye, D.O., Gbotosho, G.O. & Bolaji, O.M., 2004, 'Efficacy of herbal remedies used by herbalists in Oyo State Nigeria for treatment of plasmodium falciparum infections: A survey and an observation', African Journal of Medicine and Medical Sciences 33(2), 115–119.

Akintilo, A.A.A., 2000, 'Information and communication patterns in traditional medical practice in South-Western Nigeria and interface with National Health Information System', PhD thesis, Africa Regional Centre for Information Science, University of Ibadan.

Akinyemi, K.O., Oladapo, O., Okwara, C.E., Ibe, C.C. & Fasure, K.A., 2005, 'Screening of crude extracts of six medicinal plants used in South-West Nigerian unorthodox medicine for anti-methicillin resistant Staphylococcus aureus activity', BioMed Central Complementary and Alternative Medicine 5(6).

Akullo, D., Kanzikwera, R., Birungi, P., Alum, W., Aliguma, L. & Barwogeza, M., 2007, 'Indigenous knowledge in agriculture: A case study of the challenges in sharing knowledge of past generations in a globalized context in Uganda', paper presented at the World Library and Information Congress: 73rd International Federation and Library Associations and Institutions General Conference and Council, Durban, South Africa, 19–23rd August.

Alves, R.R.N. & Rosa, I.M.L., 2007, 'Biodiversity, traditional medicine and public health: Where do they meet?', Journal of Ethnobiology and Ethnomedicine 3(1), 14. http://dx.doi.org/10.1186/1746-4269-3-14

Aunger, R., 2000, 'The life history of culture learning in a face-to-face society', Ethos 28(3), 445–481. http://dx.doi.org/10.1525/eth.2000.28.3.445

Cavalli-Sforza, L.L. & Feldman, M.W., 1981, Cultural transmission and evolution: A quantitative approach, Princeton University Press, N.J., Princeton.

Christian, G.E., 2009, 'Digitization, intellectual property rights and access to traditional medicine knowledge in developing countries: The Nigerian experience', paper prepared for the International Development Research Centre, viewed 18 February 2011, from http://idl-bnc.idrc.ca/dspace/bitstream/10625/41341/1/129184.pdf

Demps, K., Zorondo-Rodríguez, F., García, C. & Reyes-García, V., 2012, 'Social learning across the life cycle: Cultural knowledge acquisition for honey collection among the Jenu Kuruba, India', Evolution and Human Behavior, 33, 460–470. http://dx.doi.org/10.1016/j.evolhumbehav.2011.12.008

Dube, M.A. & Musi, P.J., 2002, 'Analysis of indigenous knowledge in Swaziland: Implications for sustainable agricultural development', African Technology Policy Studies Working Paper Series, no. 34, viewed 11 February 2011, from http://www.atpsnet.org/content/files/documents/working%20paper%20series%2034.pdf

Elujoba, A.A., Odeleye, O.M. & Ogunyemi, C.M., 2005, 'Traditional medicine development for medical and dental primary health care delivery system in Africa', African Journal of Traditional, Complementary and Alternative Medicines 2(1), 46–61.

Eyssartier, C., Ladio, A.H. & Lozada, M., 2008, 'Cultural transmission of traditional knowledge in two populations of North-Western Patagonia', Journal of Ethnobiology and Ethnomedicine 4(25), 1, viewed 10 July 2012, from http://www.ethnobiomed.com/content/pdf/1746-4269-4-25.pdf

Giday, M., Asfaw, Z., Elmqvist, T. & Woldu, Z., 2003, 'An ethnobotanical study of medicinal plants used by the Zay people in Ethiopia', Journal of Ethnopharmacology 85, 43–52. http://dx.doi.org/10.1016/S0378-8741(02)00359-8

Grenier, L., 1998, 'Working with indigenous knowledge: A guide for researchers', paper prepared for the International Development Research Centre, viewed 17 May 17 2012, from http://www.idrc.ca/openebooks/847-3/

Henrich, J. & Broesch, J., 2011, 'On the nature of cultural transmission networks: Evidence from Fijian villages for adaptive learning biases', *Philosophical Transactions of the Royal Society B* 366, 1139–1148. http://dx.doi.org/10.1098/rstb.2010.0323

Henrich, J. & Henrich, N., 2010, 'The evolution of cultural adaptations: Fijian food taboos protect against dangerous marine toxins', *Proceedings of the Royal Society B* 277, 3715–3724. http://dx.doi.org/10.1098/rspb.2010.1191

Hewlett, B.S. & Cavalli-Sforza, L.L., 1986, 'Cultural transmission among Aka pygmies', *American Anthropologist* 88(4), 922–934. http://dx.doi.org/10.1525/aa.1986.88.4.02a00100

Jesajas, H. & Packham, R., 2003, 'Combining indigenous knowledge and agricultural science knowledge: A case study from Kisar Island, Indonesia', in A. Cristovao & L.O. Zorini (eds.), *Farming and rural systems research and extension: Local identities and globalization*, 5th European International Farming System Association Symposium proceedings, Florence, Italy, April 8–11, 2002, pp. 777–786, viewed 22 January 2012, from http://ifsa.boku.ac.at/cms/fileadmin/Proceeding2002/2002_WS05_28_Jesajus.pdf

King, R., Balaba, D., Kaboru, B., Kabatesi, D., Pharris, A. & Homsy, J., 2009, 'The role of traditional healers in comprehensive HIV/AIDS prevention and care in Africa: Untapped opportunities', in R.G. Marlink & S.T. Teitelman (eds.), *From the ground up: Building comprehensive HIV/AIDS care programs in resource-limited settings*, viewed 24 June 2012, from http://ftguonline.org/ftgu-232/index.php/ftgu/article/view/2047/4090

Lozada, M., Ladio, A.H. & Weigandt, M., 2006, 'Cultural transmission of ethnobotanical knowledge in a rural community of NorthWestern Patagonia, Argentina', *Economic Botany* 60(4), 374–385. http://dx.doi.org/10.1663/0013-0001(2006)60[374:CTOEKI]2.0.CO;2

Mafimisebi, T.E. & Oguntade, A.E., 2010, 'Preparation and use of plant medicines for farmers' health in Southwest Nigeria: Sociocultural, magico-religious and economic aspects', *Journal of Ethnobiology and Ethnomedicine* 6(1), 1. http://dx.doi.org/10.1186/1746-4269-6-1

Neis, B., Felt, L.F., Haedrich, R.L. & Schneider, D.C., 1999, 'An interdisciplinary method for collecting and integrating fishers' ecological knowledge into resource management', in D. Newell & R.E. Ommer (eds.), *Fishing places, fishing people: Traditions and issues in Canadian small-scale fisheries*, pp. 217–238, University of Toronto Press, Toronto.

Ngunyulu, R.N. & Mulaudzi, F.M., 2009, 'Indigenous practices regarding postnatal care at Sikhunyani village in the Limpopo province of South Africa', *Africa Journal of Nursing and Midwifery* 11(1), 48–64.

Ogbole, O.O., Gbolade, A.A. & Ajaiyeoba, E.O., 2010, 'Ethnobotanical survey of plants used in treatment of inflammatory diseases in Ogun State of Nigeria', *European Journal of Scientific Research* 43(2), 183–191.

Ohmagari, K. & Berkes, F., 1997, 'Transmission of indigenous knowledge and bush skills among the Western James Bay Cree women of Subarctic Canada', *Human Ecology* 25(2), 197–222. http://dx.doi.org/10.1023/A:1021922105740

Oladele, A.T. & Adewunmi, C.O., 2008, 'Medicinal plants used in the management of malaria among the traditional medicine practitioners (TMPs) in South-Western Nigeria', *African Journal of Infectious Diseases* 2(1), 51–59.

Oladele, A.T., Alade, G.O. & Omobuwajo, O.R., 2011, 'Medicinal plants conservation and cultivation by traditional medicine practitioners (TMPs) in Aiyedaade Local Government Area of Osun State, Nigeria', *Agriculture and Biology Journal of North America* 2(3), 476–487. http://dx.doi.org/10.5251/abjna.2011.2.3.476.487

Olagunju, O.S., 2012. 'The traditional healing systems among the Yoruba', *Archaeological Science Journal* 1(2), 6–14.

Olatokun, W.M., 2010, 'Indigenous knowledge of traditional medical practitioners in the treatment of sickle cell anaemia', *Indian Journal of Traditional Knowledge* 9(1), 119–125.

Osemene, K.P., Elujoba, A.A. & Ilori, M.O., 2011, 'An overview of herbal medicine research and development in Nigeria', *Research Journal of Medical Sciences* 5(4), 228–232. http://dx.doi.org/10.3923/rjmsci.2011.228.232

Owuor, J.A., 2007, 'Integrating African indigenous knowledge in Kenya's formal education system: The potential for sustainable development', *Journal of Contemporary Issues in Education* 2(2), 21–37.

Ragupathy, S., Steven, N.G., Marutfhakkutti, M., Velusamy, B. & Ul-Huda, M.M., 2008, 'Consensus of the "Malasars" traditional aboriginal knowledge of medicinal plants in the Velliangiri holy hills, India', *Journal of Ethnobiology and Ethnomedicine* 4(1), 8. http://dx.doi.org/10.1186/1746-4269-4-8

Ratner, C., 2002, 'Subjectivity and objectivity in qualitative methodology', *Forum Qualitative Sozialforschung /Forum: Qualitative Social Research*, 3(3), Art. 16, viewed 18 January 2013, from http://nbn-resolving.de/urn:nbn:de:0114-fqs0203160

Reyes-García, V., Broesch, J., Calvet-Mir, L., Fuentes-Peláez, N., McDade, T. & Parsa, S., 2009, 'Cultural transmission of ethnobotanical knowledge and skills: An empirical analysis from an Amerindian society', *Evolution and Human Behavior* 30(4), 274–285. http://dx.doi.org/10.1016/j.evolhumbehav.2009.02.001

Rijal, A., 2008, 'A quantitative assessment of indigenous plant uses among two Chepang communities in the central Mid-Hills of Nepal', *Ethnobotanical Research and Application* 6, 395–404.

Rogoff, B., 1981, 'Adults and peers as agents of socialization: A highland Guatemalan profile', *Ethos* 9, 18–36. http://dx.doi.org/10.1525/eth.1981.9.1.02a00030

Salako, A.A. & Sholeye, O.O., 2012, 'The perception and beliefs on tuberculosis among traditional healers in Remo North Local Government Area, Ogun State, SouthWestern Nigeria', *Journal of Public Health and Epidemiology* 4(6), 184–188.

Setalaphruk, C. & Price, L.L., 2007, 'Children's traditional ecological knowledge of wild food resources: A case study in a rural village, Northeast of Thailand', *Journal of Ethnobiology and Ethnomedicine* 3, 33. http://dx.doi.org/10.1186/1746-4269-3-33

Soewu, D.A. & Adekanola, T.A., 2011, 'Traditional medical knowledge and perception of Pangolins (Manis sps) among the Awori people, SouthWestern Nigeria', *Journal of Ethnobiology and Ethnomedicine* 7(1), 1–11. http://dx.doi.org/10.1186/1746-4269-7-25

Soewu, D.A. & Ayodele, I.A., 2009, 'Utilisation of Pangolin (Manis sps) in traditional Yorubic medicine in Ijebu province, Ogun State, Nigeria', *Journal of Ethnobiology and Ethnomedicine* 5, 39. http://dx.doi.org/10.1186/1746-4269-5-39

Srithi, K., Balslev, H., Wangpakapattanawong, P., Srisanga, P. & Trisonthi, C., 2009, 'Medicinal plant knowledge and its erosion among the Mien (Yao) in Northern Thailand', *Journal of Ethnopharmacology* 123(2), 335–342. http://dx.doi.org/10.1016/j.jep.2009.02.035

Tsuji J.S.L., 1996, 'Loss of traditional ecological knowledge in the Western James Bay region of Northern Ontario, Canada: A case study of the sharp-tailed grouse, *Tympanuchus phasianellus phasianellus*', *The Canadian Journal of Native Studies* 16(2), 283–292.

Voeks, R.A., 2007, 'Are women reservoirs of traditional plant knowledge?: Gender, ethnobotany and globalization in Northeast Brazil', *Singapore Journal of Tropical Geography* 28, 7–20. http://dx.doi.org/10.1111/j.1467-9493.2006.00273

Voeks, R.A. & Nyawa, S., 2001, 'Healing flora of the Brunei Dusun', *Borneo Research Bulletin* 32, 178–195.

World Health Organisation, 2001, *Legal status of traditional medicine and complementary/alternative medicine: A worldwide review*, viewed 20 October 2011, from http://apps.who.int/medicinedocs/pdf/h2943e/h2943e.pdf

16

An empirical study on website usability elements and how they affect search engine optimisation

Authors:
Eugene B. Visser[1]
Melius Weideman[1]

Affiliations:
[1]Faculty of Informatics and Design, Cape Peninsula University of Technology, South Africa

Correspondence to:
Melius Weideman

Email:
weidemanm@cput.ac.za

Postal address:
PO Box 652, Cape Town 8000, South Africa

The primary objective of this research project was to identify and investigate the website usability attributes which are in contradiction with search engine optimisation elements. The secondary objective was to determine if these usability attributes affect conversion. Although the literature review identifies the contradictions, experts disagree about their existence.

An experiment was conducted, whereby the conversion and/or traffic ratio results of an existing control website were compared to a usability-designed version of the control website, namely the experimental website. All optimisation elements were ignored, thus implementing only usability.

The results clearly show that inclusion of the usability attributes positively affect conversion, indicating that usability is a prerequisite for effective website design. Search engine optimisation is also a prerequisite for the very reason that if a website does not rank on the first page of the search engine result page for a given keyword, then that website might as well not exist.

According to this empirical work, usability is in contradiction to search engine optimisation best practices. Therefore the two need to be weighed up in terms of importance towards search engines and visitors.

Introduction

Search Engine Optimisation (SEO) is the process of designing or making alterations to a website in such a way that the search engines can find and index the given website with greater ease, resulting in improved rankings (Weideman 2009:14). Website usability (WU) refers to the 'feeling' of how easy a website is to use, as experienced by a human user (Nielsen & Loranger 2006:xvi). Both of these website attributes are important for different reasons and both require a concerted effort to implement on a website. SEO is needed to please one specific audience, namely search engine crawlers, whilst WU is aimed at the human user audience. These two audiences are highly dependent on each other, but sometimes operate in a way where one disregards the other.

Johnson (2008) associates the development of civilised societies with WU and usefulness. The same author stated that neither the development of civilised societies nor WU is considered to be consistent. With the launch of the first graphical web browser (i.e. Mosaic) in 1993, enthusiasts with no experience in usability and/or design started creating a variety of websites. Almost two decades later, websites are often still not developed with WU or usefulness in mind as a primary objective (Johnson 2008; Nielsen 2007).

According to James (2002) WU is of major importance to attract and retain visitors. Nielsen (2003) agrees with this author, stating that website usability is crucial for survival. One reason for this phenomenon is stated as being that if a visitor's needs are not satisfied on a particular website the visitor will simply leave and visit a website that will do so (Kritzinger & Weideman 2008).

Because WU is of crucial importance, it was deemed necessary to define usability from various perspectives. Bruno and Al-Qaimari (2004:1–2) accumulated multiple definitions for usability compiled by different authors, indicating how those definitions evolved over time.

Shackel (1981): '[a system's] capability in human functional terms to be used easily and effectively by the specific range of users, given specified training and support, to fulfil a specific range of tasks, within a specific range of environmental scenarios'.

Neilson and Shneiderman (1993): 'ease of learning (learnability), speed of performance (efficiency), low error rate, retention over time (memorability), and user attitude (subject satisfaction)'.

Preece (1994): 'a measure of the ease with which a system can be learned or used, its safety, effectiveness and efficiency, and the attitude of its users towards it'.

Preece (1997) International Standard Organisation (ISO/ DIS 9241–11.2): 'the extent to which a product can be used by specified users to achieve specific goals with effectiveness and satisfaction in a specified context of use'.

Krug (2000): 'making sure that something works well: that a person of average (or even below average) ability and experience can use the thing – whether it's a website, a fighter jet, or a revolving door – for its intended purpose without getting hopelessly frustrated'.

Although these practical examples differ in some ways, they all appear to agree that 'targeted users', 'complexity of tasks', 'type of technology' and 'the environment' affect usability and interaction in some way. However, it is not surprising to see that Krug (2000) as well as Nielsen and Loranger (2006) were the only ones that referred to a website within their definitions of usability. This is a result of the fact that these definitions were created after the 1990s, during which period the Internet was born.

Eisenberg, Quarto-vonTivadar, Davis and Crosby defined WU more recently as follows:

> Usability addresses the ways a site effectively implements the body of knowledge concerning a visitor's ability to interact successfully in an online environment. The goal of usability is to remove any obstacles impeding the experience and process of online interaction.

> (Eisenberg, Quarto-vonTivadar, Davis and Crosby 2008:158)

This definition identifies the mechanical usability problems and not persuasive usability problems. It is evident that the definitions constructed prior to 2000 were predominantly based on software engineering (human interface design). Although the definitions after 2000 considered websites within the usability definition, there are clear differences between website usability and software usability (human interface design). In an attempt to clearly show this difference, the two concepts are defined in the following section.

Website usability

Consider for a moment that a user intends to purchase a product and/or service on the Internet. The user is browsing the Internet in search of the appropriate product at the right price and eventually lands on a website where the product and price is satisfactory. If the user encounters an error during the checkout procedure (or during browsing), no obligation exists that will force the user to return to the same website to attempt the buying (browsing) process again. In fact, it makes better sense to search for a competitor website as it is simply easier to do so than to find out how to fix the error, if possible at all.

Software usability (human interface design)

Once a software product has been purchased for use within an office or home environment, the product must sustain its usefulness, over and above its actual purpose, by means of usability. Usability in this instance refers more to error handling and the understanding of how the software operates. If a critical error occurs during the use of a software package, a user must be able to recover from the error with minimal effort and not be hampered in the process due to loss of data. This is important because it is impractical for the user to buy another product in the hope that a similar error will not occur again.

Previous work

No SEO or WU contradictions other than identified by Nielsen and Loranger (2006:166) (keywords) have been identified during the review. Ironically, when considering WU experts' opinions regarding SEO best practice in terms of concept and application, the contradictions start to surface. The website usability attributes listed in this section have been identified by the current authors to be in contradiction to SEO, based on the website usability definition of Eisenberg *et al.* (2008:158).

Trust and credibility as a website usability attribute

Barnard and Wesson (2003:258–259) have identified the WU attribute trust as being a critical success factor. According to the same authors, Internet users have serious concerns regarding their privacy on the Internet. Ease-of-use, credibility of information on a website and security all form part of the WU trust attribute (Barnard & Wesson 2003:259). Although many different ways exist to address trust, Nielsen and Tahir (2001:10–13, 201) suggest emphasising the following information on a website as part of WU:

- privacy policy
- about us
- company overview webpage (company values, management team, etc.)
- feedback
- testimonials
- contact information.

Eisenberg *et al.* (2008:32, 192, 195, 196, 240) agrees with Nielsen and Tahir (2001) on the WU sub-attributes and add that the WU attributes of credibility and trust are interwoven. In addition, Nielsen (2005) states that an author photo (company owner) can offer a more personable impression, which in turn enhances credibility and thus also trust. In addition, the photo can also connect the virtual and physical world, making it easier for the visitor to relate to the owner.

Single page view, content and frames as website usability attributes

Bevan (2005) compared the draft International Organisation for Standardisation and/or Draft International Standard

(ISO/DIS 9241–151:2005) design and usability guidelines (International Standard for user-centred design of web user interface) and the Health and Human Service (HHS) design and usability guidelines (US Department of Health and Human Service). The HHS guidelines suggest that the content, page lengths, number of words and sentences should be limited on a website in the interest of WU. The ISO guidelines concur with the HHS guidelines and adds that content on a webpage should fit on the expected size of a display area. In addition, the HHS guidelines suggest the use of frames in certain circumstances whereby the ISO 9241–151 guidelines indicate that frames should be used with care. The HHS guidelines also suggest placing important items to the top of all webpages, indicating that less emphasis should be applied to content when considering the WU attributes trust and credibility.

Johnson (2007:169) states that too much text is 'bad writing' and is something that frequently occurs on websites. The author suggests as a guideline that text on each page should be halved. The remaining text should then be halved again. Nielsen and Loranger (2006:30–35) interpreted content from a slightly different perspective and estimate that visitors often view a webpage for 45–60 seconds. The same authors estimate that a visitor could read a maximum of 200 words during that time period. This indicates that the amount of text placed on a webpage is only important and considered from a visitor's perspective and not from a search engine's perspective. It is thus the message that is conveyed (webpage objective) in the 200 words of text that is read by the visitor during the time constraint of 60 seconds. In summary, the ideal length in terms of number of words should be found – enough to allow search engines a rich harvest of keywords, but not too many to frighten off human readers.

Keywords as a website usability attribute

Weideman (2009:55) claims that keyword usage, including density, on webpages ranks two out of 17 factors in importance in SEO implementation. However, according to Nielsen and Loranger (2006:166), keyword density is the one SEO element that is in direct contradiction to WU. The same authors state that SEO consultants often overload content with the same targeted keywords reducing readability. It is thus suggested to use multi-word phrase targeting. Johnson (2007:153) conversely, states that using different terms for the same concept is one of the best ways to confuse users. According to Johnson (2007), users will spend all their time attempting to figure out how the terms relate as opposed to spending time achieving the user's objective. Thus, keyword density as well as keyword inclusion are factors to be avoided from a WU perspective. In research currently underway the authors attempt to investigate the crossover point between keyword rich body text and spamdexing (Zuze and Weideman 2010).

Images as a website usability attribute

According to Ngindana and Weideman (2004), visitors often prefer graphic-based webpages as opposed to text-based webpages. The same authors have found that Flash and/ or graphic images are aesthetically pleasing to visitors, especially when using graphics as part of a websites' navigation. It is thus clear that graphical aids allow for easy visitor navigation. George (2005:171,178) agrees and found that visitors first notice colours and images before browsing from left to right and top to bottom, indicating that visitors first and foremost focus their attention on images.

Nielsen and Loranger (2006:247) believe that large blocks of text in images (text images) should be used in moderation. The use of text images is not recommended for a number of reasons. However, snippets of text such as found in navigation buttons are appropriate.

Eisenberg *et al.* (2008:168–169) agrees with Ngindana and Weideman (2004) and explains that powerful images placed 'above the page fold' can draw a lot of attention and could thus be used to emphasise what a business wants the visitor to focus on.

In summary, WU attributes focus primarily on what makes the website visitor respond. WU experts tend to consider search engines where possible. However, search engines are not considered as a priority. This is confirmed by some website usability experts who state that search engines do not carry credit cards (Eisenberg *et al.* 2008:223). Although this statement is true, the irony is that search engines could potentially drive a large number of visitors (with credit cards) to a website.

Search engine optimisation contradictions

Conceptually the single most important SEO element (namely content) is negatively affected by:

- trust and credibility (i.e. privacy policy, about us, company overview, feedback, testimonials and contact form)
- single page view
- minimising content
- frames
- keywords
- images.

Search engines depend on content to fully understand the purpose of any given website. Trust and credibility are both built by the use of generic content which does not assist the search engine in identifying the purpose of the particular website. The lack of keywords along with minimising content will limit the search engines' ability to be more successful at an interpretation of the websites' purpose.

Murphy and Kielgast (2008:90) state that more than 85% of all purchases that occur on the Internet started with a search. Further research demonstrates that there are three major search engines (i.e. Google, Yahoo! and MSN/Live/ Bing) that dominate the search engine market with Google being by far the biggest (Sullivan 2004; Sullivan 2006). Recent figures released indicated that Bing has taken over the second

TABLE 1: Search engine market share (Sullivan 2004; Sullivan 2006; Searchenginewatch 2009).

Search engine market share	2004 Web Side Story (Sullivan 2004)[†]	2006 Nielsen/NetRatings (Sullivan 2006)[‡]	2009 Nielsen (Searchenginewatch 2009)[§]
Google	40.90%	49.20%	64.60%
Yahoo!	27.40%	23.80%	16.00%
MSN/Live/Bing	19.60%	9.60%	10.70%
Other Search Engines	12.10%	17.40%	8.70%

[†], Sullivan, D, 2004, Google tops, but Yahoo switch success so far, viewed 04 May 2010, from http://searchenginewatch.com/3334881; [‡], Sullivan, D., 2006, Nielsen NetRatings Search Engine Ratings, viewed 01 May 2010, from http://searchenginewatch.com/2156451; [§], Searchenginewatch, 2009, Top search providers for August 2009, viewed 01 May 2010, from http://searchenginewatch.com/3634991

position after Yahoo!. Over the past five years Google was the only search engine that demonstrated continuous growth in search engine market share as opposed to the other search engines (Sullivan 2004; Sullivan 2006; Searchenginewatch 2009). Table 1 illustrates each of the three major search engines with their respective search engine market share.

Search engines make use of artificial intelligence programs called website crawlers or spiders that 'crawl' the Internet and index websites. Indexing a website is when search engine crawlers create a duplicate of each webpage, saving the replica in a data repository (index) as search engines associate a webpage to a particular Uniform Resource Locator (URL). When a user does a search, the Search Engine Result Page (SERP) listings returned to the visitor are extracted from the search engine repository and not from the Internet (Weideman 2009:24). The link in each listing is thus a pointer to the appropriate website (Searchenginewatch 2007; Visser 2007:24–36).

Search engines make use of crawlers for indexing, with interpretation limitations; this indicates that the content used on a website is the one primary SEO element that provides fundamental information to search engines about a particular website. This fact is confirmed by each of the three major search engines in their respective 'guidelines for best practices':

1. **Google:**
   - 'Create a useful, information-rich site, and write pages that clearly and accurately describe your content' (Google 2010c).
   - 'One of the most important steps in improving your site's ranking in Google search results is to ensure that it contains plenty of rich information that includes relevant keywords, used appropriately, that indicate the subject matter of your content' (Google 2010b).
   - 'If fancy features such as JavaScript, cookies, session IDs, frames, DHTML, or Flash keep you from seeing all of your site in a text browser, then search engine spiders may have trouble crawling your site' (Google 2010c).
   - 'Frames can cause problems for search engines because they don't correspond to the conceptual model of the web. In this model, one page displays only one URL' (Google 2010a).

2. **MSN/Live/Bing:**
   - 'In the visible webpage text, include words users might choose as search query terms to find the information on your website' (Live 2010).
   - 'Don't put the text that you want indexed within images' (Live 2010).

3. **Yahoo!:**
   - 'Original and unique content of genuine value' (Yahoo 2010).

Considering the content recommendations by Google, Yahoo! and MSN/Live/Bing, many authors have also discovered and emphasised that sufficient content is an essential SEO element (Visser 2007:118; Weideman and Chambers 2005; Kritzinger and Weideman 2008; Eisenberg *et al.* 2008:222; Weideman 2009:59–60). As noted earlier, sufficient text content will ensure both a yield of enough keywords for a visiting crawler and content of value for the human visitor.

Trust and credibility

Search engine optimisation contradiction: Some authors emphasise that the WU attributes of trust and credibility (privacy policy, about us, company overview, feedback, testimonials and contact form) should be prioritised on all websites. This WU attribute is in contradiction with SEO as the content utilised in the sub-attributes have no direct association with what visitors search for (product or visitors needs) as described above in search engine guidelines for best practices.

Single page view, content and frames

Search engine optimisation contradiction: Single page views and content limitations (as suggested by WU experts) prevent search engines from eliciting a better interpretation of any given websites' purpose. The more content a website has the more weight-carrying key phrases the website could potentially rank for. Search engines reward qualitative and quantitative websites (featuring solid, informative and useful content) with good rankings for specific search terms or phrases.

Frames can be described as separate rectangular blocks all present on a single webpage. Each frame contains its own content, which functions independently from any other frame on the same webpage. Frames thus prevent search engines from associating an entire webpage to a particular URL, implying that the content utilised on a frame based website is in fact invisible to search engines. As a result, frames are often listed as an undesirable website design element – their absence is claimed to improve website visibility (Weideman 2009:114).

Keywords

Search engine optimisation contradiction: Keyword variations, frequency and density are essential for SEO. This forms part of a technology named 'theme-ing', used to emphasise products or business elements (keywords) to search engines. WU authors believe that increasing the keyword frequency and density could reduce readability (Nielsen & Loranger 2006:166).

Images

Search engine optimisation contradiction: Visitors often prefer graphic-based webpages as opposed to text-based webpages. Search engines are unable to read or interpret any text placed within an image. If text (especially keywords) is placed within images, that text is invisible to search engine crawlers. Text within images can therefore not assist search engines to be more successful at interpretation of any given websites' purpose. In summary, if any webpage content on any website cannot be indexed or interpreted correctly, then those webpages cannot possibly rank for targeted keywords.

Methodology

The following website usability attributes, which are in conflict with SEO elements, were examined in a pre-test post-test, quantitative methodological design:

- Trust and credibility: Essential for WU, but adds no value to SEO as the non related content could dilute emphasis for ranking purposes.
- Single page view and content: Essential for WU, but search engines rely on content to better interpret a website's

content and keyword emphasis for ranking purposes.
- Keywords: Avoiding keyword overload is essential for WU. However, search engines depend on keyword density and inclusion for emphasis purposes in terms of ranking.
- Images: Essential for WU in terms of being aesthetically pleasing to visitors. Unfortunately, search engines are unable to make an accurate interpretation of images and can thus reduce content and keyword emphasis in terms of ranking.

The primary experiment includes the use of an existing website (created by a non-technical designer with minimal knowledge of WU and SEO), which was used as the *control website* (CW: www.copywriters.co.za). A new website was developed by implementing the above WU attributes and ignoring all contradictory SEO elements, termed the *experimental website* (EW: www.copywriters.co.za/ppc/). The EW was placed in a subdirectory of the CW (/ppc/), allowing the EW to function independently from the CW. In order to ensure integrity of the experiment, a *robots.txt* file was placed in the root of the www.copywriters.co.za website, explicitly instructing the search engine crawlers not to index the EW (/ppc/). In addition, no links of any kind were created from the CW to the EW and vice versa. The EW is thus accessible only via the URL (i.e. via a direct link to the EW).

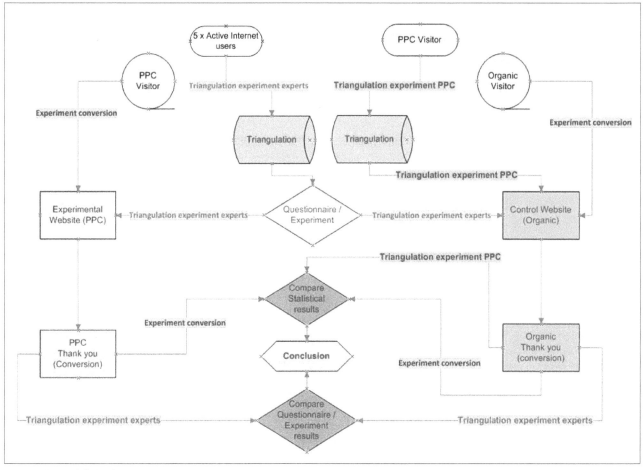

FIGURE 1: Research design diagram.

Control website

Search engine traffic consists of two types: organic (unpaid search result listings) and Pay Per Click, also known as PPC (paid search result listings). The traffic sources for the CW are search engines (organic) traffic, as well as direct and referrer traffic. *Direct traffic* is when a visitor visits the CW directly (by typing in the URL directly into the browser or by means of bookmarks and/or favourites), without making use of a search engine. *Referrer traffic* is when a visitor visits the CW via a link from another website, also without making use of a search engine (Google 2009).

Organic results occupy the primary real estate (left and centre) of the SERPs. These organic search results are governed by search engine algorithms, which are kept secret to avoid abuse. The better a particular website satisfies the search engine algorithm according to a keyword search, the better that particular website will rank organically (Neethling 2008:3). Good organic search results do not guarantee financial success. However, theoretically the better a particular website ranks, the more traffic that website should receive due to the fact that on average 67% of search engine users do not look beyond the first SERP (Weideman 2009:32).

Experimental website

The traffic source for the EW is purely PPC. PPC results occupy the right side and in some instances the top of a typical SERP. The use of an organic search engine algorithm does not apply to PPC results at all. However, an algorithm does exist to determine the priority ranking of PPC results by means a basic formula:

PPC ranking = quality score x bid price.

The bid price is determined by the user, whilst the PPC search engine algorithm uses a number of factors to determine the quality score.

Both the CW and the EW sell the exact same products. However, the way in which the two websites draw visitors differ, which indicates that the website traffic source alone cannot be utilised as a performance measuring tool. Thus performance measurements were made by considering the number of conversions obtained from the amount of website traffic obtained (conversion or traffic ratio) of each website over the same period of time, which were then compared (keeping the traffic source in mind). Additional factors, such as time spent on site, page views and Return On Investment (ROI) were also considered as measuring tools.

For triangulation purposes, an interview was conducted with five active Internet users as part of the experiment. A number of questions were created with the purpose of obtaining fundamental information as to the actual impact of each WU attribute. The interview results combined with the statistical results provided a clear indication as to whether WU attributes affect 'on page' conversion. Lastly, on completion

of the first experiment, the experimental traffic source (PPC) was redirected to the CW for the same period of time. The objective was to test the PPC traffic source (as a 'trusted' traffic source), by exposing similar visitors to the CW as exposed to the EW for comparison purposes (Figure1).

The research design diagram (Figure 1) can be divided into four vertical parts (conceptually). Each vertical part represents a portion of the experiment:

- PPC visitors on the far left – primary experiment
- 5 x Active Internet users just to the left of the centre line – triangulation
- PPC visitors just to the right of the centre line – triangulation
- Organic Visitors on the far right – primary experiment.

Results

The CW has been active on the Internet since 2006, obtaining visitor traffic from a variety of sources. Website traffic statistics for the CW was obtained over the same period as the EW. The EW was launched in December 2009, obtaining visitor traffic from PPC only. The EW PPC campaign (targeting only Google) was created on the same day the EW was launched, with a budget of R5257.17 for the duration of 49 days. The PPC campaign towards the EW was terminated on the 31st of January 2010.

During the 49 days the CW and the EW combined received 8020 visitor traffic from all traffic sources ('All visitors'; see Figure 2 for the graphical presentation of these results). Of the 8020 visitors, 5544 were non search engine visitors ('NON SE T'; see Figure 2), indicating that 5544 visitors landing on the CW only from referrer websites and/or direct traffic. The remaining 2476 visitors was search engine traffic ('SE T'; see Figure 2), which included PPC traffic. This indicates that both the CW and the EW received a combined volume of search engine traffic of 2476 visitors. The 2476 search engine traffic visitors were then categorised into organic (true search engine traffic) and PPC (paid search engine traffic). The analysis indicated that the total organic search engine traffic was 782 visitors ('SE Organic T'; see Figure 2) and the total

FIGURE 2: Snapshot breakdown and analysis of website traffic.

PPC search engine traffic was 1694 visitors ('SE PPC T'; see Figure 2).

The analysis indicated that a grand total of 1694 visitors landed only on the EW over a period of 49 days ('SE PPC T'; see Figure 2). Subtracting 1694 PPC visitors from 8020 all visitors or adding 5544 non search engine traffic visitors to 782 organic search engine traffic visitors produces a grand total of 6326 visitors, which landed only on the CW only over a period of 49 days ('Tot Non PPC T'; see Figure 2).

Control website (www.copywriters.co.za)

The CW received 6326 visitors (from various sources) over a period of 49 days. These 6326 visitors viewed on average 1.5 webpages per visit. Each visitor spent on average 55 seconds on the website. Considering the number of visitors that landed on the CW and webpages viewed and time spent on the website over a period of 49 days; 21 unique visitors submitted the contact form successfully (converted into a lead). Of these 21 conversions, two visitors actually purchased the service to the total value of R2071.48.

Experimental website
(www.copywriters.co.za/ppc/)

The EW received 1694 visitors (from PPC only) over a period of 49 days. The 1694 visitors viewed on average 1.1 webpages per visit. Each visitor spent on average 17 seconds on the website. Considering the number of visitors that landed on the EW and webpages viewed and time spent on the website over a period of 49 days; 59 unique visitors submitted the contact form successfully (converted into a lead). Of the 59 conversions, four visitors actually purchased the service to the total value of R5128.85 (Table 2).

Statistical analysis

A statistical analysis was done on the results of the primary experiment to determine whether or not there is a statistically significant difference in the measured variables between the CW and the EW. The test initially intended for this experiment was the Student's T-test. However, due to the

population values not following a normal distribution, it was decided to use a non-parametric method to compare distributions. The statistical analysis was thus based on the Mann-Whitney U test. The summary the statistics for each variable, which includes the p-value and identifies whether the p-value is significant or not (Table 3).

This analysis indicates that Visitors, Average Page Views per Visits and conversions are all significantly different when comparing the CW values to the EW values. Average time on site per Visitor was not considered as being significantly different. This was due to four extremely large values obtained on the EW, which resulted in an increased mean. The ROI was also not considered as being significantly different. The reason being that, out of 77 conversions, only six conversions actual resulted into sales. Comparing four sales for the EW to two sales from the CW is not statistically sound, due to the difference in sample size.

Triangulation

It was deemed prudent to use the opinions of active Internet users to confirm or reject the WU attributes analysed in the primary experiment. The secondary objective for the interview was to identify any additional WU attributes that may have been overlooked, which would encourage users to complete the online process as per the primary experiment. It was considered necessary because WU can best be interpreted by actual website users.

An interview was arranged with five randomly selected participants with a minimum of 10 years of Internet exposure and activity. The interviews were done face to face allowing the participant to browse through each website before and during the interview. The participants were also instructed to make an enquiry on each website prior to the interview. The interview questions were predominantly closed and set on the WU attributes identified and applied in the primary experiment. Three of the interview questions were open ended, providing each participant the opportunity to make any additional WU comments and/or recommendations in terms of enticing the visitor to convert on each (CW & EW) website.

TABLE 2: Analysis of the control website (CW) traffic versus the experimental website (EW) traffic (primary experiment).

Combined number of visitors 8020	Visits	Average		Conversions	ROI
		Page views per visitor	Time On Site (in seconds)		
Control website	6326	1.5	55	21	R2071.48
Experimental website	1694	1.1	17	56	R5128.85

ROI, Return On Investement.

TABLE 3: Summarised statistics for each variable.

Variables	Mann-Whitney U Test	p-Value	Conclusion
Visitors	2208	< 0.001	Significant Difference
Average Page Views per Visit	1664	< 0.001	Significant Difference
Average Time on site per Visit	1343	> 0.05	No Significant Difference
Conversion	780	< 0.006	Significant Difference
Return on Investement (ROI)	1053	> 0.05	No Significant Difference

p, probability value.

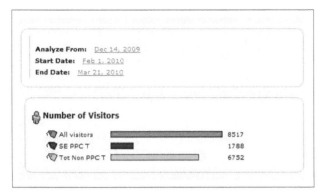

FIGURE 3: Triangulations – Snapshot breakdown of traffic sources.

The accumulated results obtained from the interviews leaned towards the importance of security, minimising content and making the contact form as easy as possible to complete. The only additional attribute that was mentioned was the design factor. Although identified by an interviewee, the design factor was not considered due to the subjective nature of such an attribute.

As part of triangulation, PPC traffic was redirected from the EW to the CW for 49 days after the primary experiment had ended. Therefore EW was made dormant, allowing the CW to receive all forms of traffic. The objective of the triangulation experiment was to test PPC as a traffic source in order to determine the quality of PPC traffic visitors in terms of conversions.

During the 49 days, the CW received 8517 visitors from all traffic sources, including PPC traffic ('All visitors'; see Figure 3). Of the 8517 visitors, 6752 visitors were non PPC visitors ('Tot Non PPC T'; see Figure 3). The remaining 1788 visitors were PPC visitors ('SE PPC T'; see Figure 3).

Table 4 provides the comparison between the triangulation experiment and the primary experiment. The triangulation experiment obtained PPC traffic along with all other forms of traffic (search engine, direct and refer traffic). The EW (from the primary experiment) obtained PPC traffic only.

Table 4 indicates that during the triangulation experiment, the CW drew 8517 visitors (all forms of traffic), of which only 29 visitors converted. The EW (in the primary experiment) conversely received 1694 visitors from PPC only, whereby 56 visitors converted.

The fact remains that the triangulation experiment obtained five times more traffic (including PPC traffic) than the EW (primary experiment). However, the EW obtained approximately 50% more conversions as opposed to the

number of conversion obtained during the triangulation experiment.

Although it is generally perceived that PPC is a 'trusted' traffic source, the PPC traffic in this instance did not radically increase conversions. When considering Table 4 in terms of conversions obtained, it is clear that the traffic source as such is thus not a variable to consider that may have an impact on conversions in this instance. In addition, it is generally accepted that the more traffic a website receives, the more visitors should convert. This indicates that WU is the real impact factor in terms of conversion during the primary experiment.

Conclusion

The primary objective of this research project was to determine the WU attributes which are in contradiction with SEO elements. Although some experts in both fields do not acknowledge that any contradiction exists, the literature review clearly identifies those contradictions. WU experts specify that certain WU attributes will affect 'on page' conversions, which are in contradiction to the SEO elements, whereby some of these SEO elements are specified by the major search engines in their best practice guidelines.

The secondary objective of this research project was to determine whether or not WU attributes identified do in fact have an effect on conversions. The primary experiment provides evidence that WU attributes do have an effect on conversion. Depending on the purpose of any particular website, whether it is to entice a visitor to buy, sign up for a newsletter, create an account, request a quote or anything that requires the visitor to interact with any website form, suggests that WU is not a luxury, but a prerequisite for that particular type of websites' success.

The results from the primary experiment (Table 2) indicate that the CW obtained three and a half times more traffic than the EW. However, the EW obtained almost three times the amount of conversions obtained by the CW. Although the ROI was not considered as being significantly different in terms of the p-value, it still provides some indication as to the value of the applied WU attributes.

As part of the project, an interview was conducted for triangulation purposes. The objective of the interview was to get active Internet users to confirm or reject the WU attributes analysed in the primary experiment. The secondary objective for the interview was to identify any additional WU attributes that may have been overlooked which would encourage users to complete the online process as per the

TABLE 4: Summary and comparison of the triangulation experiment and the experimental website (primary experiment).

Website	Visits	Average		Conversions	ROI
		Page views per visitor	Time On Site (in seconds)		
Control Triangulation	8517	1.4	21	29	R1497.00
Experimental	1694	1.1	17	56	R5128.85

ROI, Return on investment.

primary experiment. The results obtained merely confirmed the importance of the WU attributes already identified.

Lastly, a triangulation experiment was conducted in order to test PPC as a traffic source in terms of conversion. PPC visitors can be considered to be more serious about making a purchase. The triangulation experiment provided evidence that the traffic source is not really a variable to consider in this instance.

The limitations of this research project include that it was decided to use a non-parametric method to compare distributions. It was done due to the population values not following a normal distribution (which made direct comparison difficult). Furthermore, the research was conducted over a relatively short period of time (49 days). Finally the fact that two different sized samples were used made statistical comparison harder.

The next logical step would be to test the SEO elements and ignore all contradicting WU attributes. A second experimental website (EW2) could be created, whereby the rankings of the CW can be compared to the rankings of the EW2. Conversion and/or traffic ratio of each website (CW & EW2) can also be measured over the same period of time (49 days), which can then be compared not only to one another, but also the results obtained in the EW. The results obtained will further indicate the impact of the SEO and WU contradictions. This might also be a good opportunity to investigate the possible 'theme-ing' technology and its effectiveness.

References

Barnard, L. & Wesson, J.L. 2003, 'Usability issues for E-commerce in South Africa: An empirical investigation', *Proceedings of the Annual Conference of the South African Institute of Computer Scientists and Information Technologists (SAICSIT)*, Pretoria, 2003, September 17–19, pp. 258–267.

Bevan, N., 2005, 'Guidelines and Standards for Web Usability', *Proceedings of the 11th International Conference on Human-Computer Interaction*, Las Vegas, 2005, July 22–27, pp. 1–10.

Bruno, V. & Al-Qaimari, G. 2004, 'Usability Attributes: An Initial Step Toward Effective User-Centred Development', *Proceedings of the Annual Conference of the Australian Computer-Human Interaction Special Interest Group (CHISIG)*, Wollongong, 2004, November 22–24, pp. 1–4.

Eisenberg, B., Quarto-vonTivadar, J., Davis, L.T. & Crosby, B., 2008, *Always be testing: The complete guide to Google website optimizer*, Sybex, Indianapolis.

George, C.A., 2005, 'Usability testing and design of a library website: An interactive approach', *OCLC System & Services* 21(3), 167–180. doi:10.1108/10650750510612371, PMCid:2431148

Google, 2009, *Back to Basics: Direct, referral or organic – definitions straight from the source*, viewed 02 May 2010, from http://analytics.blogspot.com/2009/08/back-to-basics-direct-referral-or.html

Google, 2010a, *Frames*, viewed 29 April 2010, from http://www.google.com/support/webmasters/bin/answer.py?hl=en&answer=34445

Google, 2010b, *Little or no original content*, viewed 01 May 2010, from https://www.google.com/support/webmasters/bin/answer.py?hl=en&answer=66361

Google, 2010c, *Webmaster guidelines*, viewed 27 April 2010, from http://www.google.com/support/webmasters/bin/answer.py?hl=en&answer=35769

James, J.P., 2002, 'Usability and usefulness of ergonomics web sites: a preliminary investigation', *South African Journal of Information Management* 4(1), viewed 02 May 2010, from http://www.sajim.co.za

Johnson, J., 2007, *GUI Bloopers 2.0, Second Edition: Common User Interface Design Dont's and Dos*. Morgan Kaufmann, San Francisco.

Johnson, J., 2008, *Web Usability in 2008: Mediocre*, viewed 01 May 2010, from http://www.uiwizards.com/WebUsability2008.pdf

Kritzinger, W.T. & Weideman, M., 2008, 'Finding the synergy: search engine optimization vs. website usability', *Proceedings of the 10th Annual Conference on World Wide Web Applications*, Cape town, 2008, September 3–5, viewed 04 May 2010, from http://www.zaw3.co.za

Live, 2010, *Guidelines for successful indexing*, viewed 01 May 2010, from http://help.live.com/help.aspx?mkt=en-US&project=wl_webmasters

Murphy, H.C. & Kielgast, C.D., 2008, 'Do small and medium-sized hotels exploit search engine marketing?', *International Journal of Contemporary Hospitality Management* 20(1), 90–97. doi:10.1108/09596110810848604

Neethling, R., 2008, 'Search engine optimisation or paid placement system-user preference' unpublished MTech thesis, Dept. of Information Technology, Cape Peninsula University of Technology, Cape Town.

Ngindana, M.W. & Weideman, M., 2004, 'Visibility to search engines: A comparison between text-based and graphic-based hyperlinks on e-Commerce websites', *Proceedings of the 6th Annual Conference on World Wide Web Applications*, Johannesburg, 2004, September 1–3, Johannesburg, viewed 01 May 2010, from http://www.zaw3.co.za

Nielsen, J. & Tahir, M., 2001, *Homepage usability: 50 websites deconstructed*, New Riders Press, United States of America.

Nielsen, J. & Loranger, H., 2006, *Prioritizing web usability*, New Riders Press, Berkeley.

Nielsen, J., 2003, *Usability 101: Introduction to usability*, viewed 02 May 2010, from http://www.useit.com/alertbox/20030825.html

Nielsen, J., 2005, *Web usability: The top ten design mistakes*, viewed 04 May 2010, from http://www.useit.com/alertbox/weblogs.html

Nielsen, J., 2007, *Top ten mistakes in web design*, viewed 01 May 2010, from http://www.useit.com/alertbox/9605.html

Searchenginewatch, 2007, *How search engines work*, viewed 02 May 2010, http://searchenginewatch.com/2168031

Searchenginewatch, 2009, *Top search providers for August 2009*, viewed 01 May 2010, from http://searchenginewatch.com/3634991

Sullivan, D, 2004, *Google tops, but Yahoo switch success so far*, viewed 04 May 2010, from http://searchenginewatch.com/3334881

Sullivan, D., 2006, *Nielsen NetRatings Search Engine Ratings*, viewed 01 May 2010, from http://searchenginewatch.com/2156451

Visser, E.B., 2007, 'Search engine optimisation elements' effect on website visibility: The Western Cape real estate SMME sector', unpublished MTech thesis, Dept. of Information Technology, Cape Peninsula University of Technology, Cape Town.

Weideman, M. & Chambers, R., 2005, 'Application of best practice towards improving Web site visibility to search engines: A pilot study', *South African Journal of Information Management*, 7(4), viewed 30 April 2010, from http://www.sajim.co.za

Weideman, M., 2009, *Website Visibility: The Theory and Practice of Improving Rankings*, Chandos Publishers, Oxford. Yahoo, 2010, *Yahoo! Search content quality guidelines*, viewed 01 May 2010, from http://help.yahoo.com/l/us/yahoo/search/basics/basics-18.html

Zuze, H. & Weideman, M., 2010, 'Keyword density in website body text – search engine spamdexing? Poster presentation', *Proceedings of the 12th World Wide Web conference* (ZAW3-10), Durban, 2010, September 21–23.

17

Innovation in a complex environment

Author:
René Pellissier[1]

Affiliation:
[1]Department of Business Management, University of South Africa, South Africa

Correspondence to:
René Pellissier

Email:
pellir@unisa.ac.za

Postal address:
PO Box 392, UNISA 0003, South Africa

Background: As our world becomes more global and competitive yet less predictable, the focus seems to be increasingly on looking to innovation activities to remain competitive. Although there is little doubt that a nation's competitiveness is embedded in its innovativeness, the complex environment should not be ignored. Complexity is not accounted for in balance sheets or reported in reports; it becomes entrenched in every activity in the organisation. Innovation takes many forms and comes in different shapes.

Objectives: The study objectives were, firstly, to establish the determinants for complexity and how these can be addressed from a design point of view in order to ensure innovation success and, secondly, to determine how this changes innovation forms and applications.

Method: Two approaches were offered to deal with a complex environment – one allowing for complexity for organisational innovation and the other introducing reductionism to minimise complexity. These approaches were examined in a qualitative study involving case studies, open-ended interviews and content analysis between seven developing economy (South African) organisations and seven developed economy (US) organisations.

Results: This study presented a proposed framework for (organisational) innovation in a complex environment versus a framework that minimises complexity. The comparative organisational analysis demonstrated the importance of initiating organisational innovation to address internal and external complexity, with the focus being on the leadership actions, their selected operating models and resultant organisational innovations designs, rather than on technological innovations.

Conclusion: This study cautioned the preference for technological innovation within organisations and suggested alternative innovation forms (such as organisational and management innovation) be used to remain competitive in a complex environment.

Introduction

A complex environment

The modern world has been inundated by catastrophic events that change the business and social environment and break society's confidence in stability. In addition, there seems to be new challenges for the 21st century. Meieran's (2012) lists of 20th century innovation issues include: water supplies, the automobile, electricity and air transportation. In contrast, he believes innovation issues for the 21st century include food and water production, resource protection and energy conservation. The Center for Strategic and International Studies (2012) identify seven revolutions for the 21st century, (1) population (growth, aging, migration and urbanisation), (2) resource management (food, water, energy and climate), (3) technology (computation, robotics, biotechnology and nanotechnology), (4) information (data growth, access or privacy, education), (5) economics (global integration, new players, debt, poverty and inequality), (6) security (new security dynamics, health and cyber security) and (7) governance (civil society and non-profit organisations, multilaterals and the future outlook).

The on-going worldwide financial crisis highlights the sensitivity and interrelatedness of businesses. It also hints at developing economies being more inclined to accept change in crises (even to live in uncertainty and instability) than developed economies because of their inherent capacity to deal with ongoing discontinuous change. Developing economies, especially, are more prone to the implementation of non-linear solutions because of the nature of the variables, the changes and interplays between the variables, the significant human foci and the consequent organic nature of competitiveness. These variables introduce an unavoidable element of unpredictability or randomness into any science that can be accommodated by a complex solution. Complexity management allows for pattern recognition which requires focusing on competencies, activities, technologies or resources signalling patterns that will have a positive or negative impact on strategy or operations.

A complex theory possibly provides the only platform for stability in an otherwise unruly and dynamic world. Complexity principles could replace the mechanistic ones based on a well-behaved universe. This article explores the effect of complexity (external and internal to the organisation) on organisational innovation and design. In this regard, three determinant questions should be asked:

1. 'What are the determinants for complexity in the business environment?'
2. 'How can these be addressed from a design point of view to ensure innovation success?'
3. 'How will that change innovation forms and applications?'

The research design is qualitative as the research focuses on emergent phenomena; that is, the emergence of complexity science in the innovation domain. Interviews were conducted with a selection of chief executive officers (CEOs) in developed and developing economies to determine the extent of organisational innovation in each.

Business as a complex system requires the acknowledgement that we cannot control organisations to the degree that a mechanistic perspective will. Moreover, as the system's environment changes, so does the behaviour of its agents. Thus, the behaviour of the system as a whole can change. Linear strategies and technologies become irrelevant with a shift to patterns and relationships between entities.

Reasons for organisational innovation in a complex environment

Taylorism

Existing management theory is embedded in the four primary functions: planning, organising, leading and controlling. It presupposes a linear approach where inputs and outputs are related and productivity occurs when outputs are bigger than inputs, in line with Newton's three laws of motion. In 1911, Scientific Management entered the scene with Taylor's four principles (in Fayol 1987), namely, (1) replacing rule-of-thumb work methods with methods based on a scientific study of the different tasks to be done, (2) scientifically selecting, training and developing each employee rather than passively leaving them to train themselves, (3) providing detailed instruction and supervision of each worker in the performance of that worker's discrete task and (4) dividing work equally between managers and workers, so that the managers apply scientific management principles to planning the work and the workers actually perform the tasks. Taylor insisted that it is only through, (1) *enforced* standardisation of methods, (2) *enforced* adoption of the best implements and working conditions and (3) *enforced* cooperation that this faster work can be assured. He felt that the duty of enforcing the adoption of standards and enforcing this cooperation rests with management alone (Fayol 1987). From this definitive management paradigm more 'scientific' control became the norm enabling the mass-production revolution to benefit mainly the new elite (e.g. black Ford motor cars around 1920).

Technology change and a new science

Technology is changing at an unprecedented rate and we often find ourselves adrift amidst resultant discontinuous change. There is no luxury of anticipating and planning for change; rather, as Stephen Hawking (in Porter-O'Grady & Malloch 2003:36), states, 'change is'. Instead of being guided by a set of concrete principles, management in the 21st century must be fluid and adaptable to keep pace with changing conditions (Porter-O'Grady & Malloch 2003). In the 20th century, organisations focused on finding and performing the right processes; whereas, in the 21st century, the focus is on delivering the desired outcomes (Porter-O'Grady & Malloch 2003). The process (or work) itself does not guarantee that the intended outcome will be achieved. Our understanding of the future changes on a daily basis and some would argue that the future is, in fact, unknowable (Stacey, Griffin & Shaw 2000). In 21st century organisations, relationships between people inside organisations are the domain and work of leadership, rather than movement toward some preselected organisational goal or benchmark. In order to thrive amidst the unknown, leadership must embrace new ways of being and interacting (Hamalainen & Saarinen 2006). These new ways of being, need to be consistent with the change in the nature of our workplaces. That is, leadership should be such that it assists to end attachments to old structures or roles and create new contexts for work (Porter-O'Grady & Malloch 2003).

Wheatley (1999) laid the groundwork for deeper investigation into the utility of the new sciences as a way of conceptualising and understanding leadership in the 21st century. She focused on, (1) order out of chaos, (2) information forming and informing us, (3) relationships that enrich and allow for diversity and (4) a vision as an invisible field that can enable us to recreate our workplaces and our world. Although Wheatley's ideas have been viewed by some as more metaphor than science (Stacey *et al.* 2000:143), she made ideas that had previously been the domain of physicists accessible and compelling to a much wider audience. Wheatley reflected on Weick's (1979:122) observation on the dilemma organisations face: 'The environment that the organisation worries about is put there by the organisation'. Axelrod and Cohen (2000:59) also provided a comprehensive description of complexity as applied to organisations, as these authors saw the complexity science approach as having rich possibilities for bridging the gap between 'hard science' and 'humanism'. Works such as Axelrod and Cohen, and Wheatley represent a definite move away from the mechanistic 20th-century paradigm of leadership. However, as we start to move away from old ways of thinking, there seem to be some ideas that are more difficult to let go of than others.

The living present and a changing conception of time

From a transformative point of view, the future is under perpetual construction, rather than predetermined as in rational causality. This means that human interaction that takes place in the living present perpetually modifies and shapes the future. The concept of time plays a central role in understanding organisations as complex responses processes (CRPs) and warrants further discussion. We agree with Fonseca's (2002) definition of an organisation as a temporary stabilisation of themes or habits that serve to organise the experience of being together that takes place locally and in the living present.

CRPs represent another decisive step away from the mechanistic leadership models of the previous century. Stacey *et al.* (2000) felt this terminology (i.e. CRPs) was needed to differentiate their view of complex relational human organisations from the more commonly used terminology of complex adaptive systems that leads us to think of human organisations as objectified systems. The theory of CRPs is, in essence, a theory of the process of human interaction (Stacey *et al.* 2000). A key concept that is essential in understanding organisations as CRPs, is the idea that human communication and the act of relating occurs in the living present (here and now). The living present provides a starting point for conceptualising causality in a new way. Rather than thinking of causality in a traditional rational way (moving toward a mature state or pre-selected goal), focusing on the living present allows us to conceptualise causality in a transformative way.

Choice and intentionality arise in, and influence, the micro-time structure of the living present. This brings us to the nature of novelty or change. In transformative causality, the future is under perpetual construction and is changed by our movement toward the future: 'The future is unknowable but yet recognizable' (Stacey *et al.* 2000:52). From a CRP stance, human interaction is understood as paradoxical and dialectical (Fonseca 2002; Stacey *et al.* 2000) and our movement toward the future is movement toward an unfinished whole rather than a finished state.

Non-causality and systems thinking

One concept we seem reluctant to let go of is the rational view of causality. Rationalism frames the organisation as progressing toward predetermined or preselected goals (the rise and popularity of strategic planning in the 20th century is a manifestation of rationalist causality). The rationalist view of causality is that organisations are moving toward a future that is preselected by the organisation or toward some other finished state (Stacey *et al.* 2000).

Another lingering organisational lens that is used extensively is systems thinking. Early on, systems were viewed as machines and, later, we came to use systems thinking as a way to see organisations as living systems. Either way, systems thinking has been criticised for having an objectifying bias (Hamalainen & Saarinen 2006:17); that is, the person looking at the system necessarily views himself or herself as external to that system. The 'detached observer' is an easy and comfortable position for most people, as it has been used in many of the organisational leadership tools developed in the 20th century. However, organisational life in the 21st century is highly complex and relational and third-person,

detached views of organisational life fail to address the crux of leadership today. A new way of seeing and conceptualising organisations is needed.

Informationology

Modern management has changed with the advent of an information-based economy. Information has changed interactions – with each other, with business and between businesses and entities. With information, there are a plethora of new meanings and decisions, there is a change in relationships and there is a change in the very way we conduct ourselves as individuals, as leaders and managers and as organisational entities (Pellissier 2001). Some of these are, (1) relationships and communication, (2) the elasticity of knowledge, (3) an over-reliance on experts, (4) the trade-off between richness and reach, (5) a tendency to control and (6) speed and innovation.

There are many roles of information, some of which may even overlap (Anderson 1995; Shenk 2009), including:

1. as a complexity (the more information required specifying a system, the more complex it is)
2. as memory (information is a record of accumulated knowledge)
3. as communication (information is a means of social interaction)
4. as intellectual property (information with legally defined ownership interests)
5. as market enabler (information that permits efficient markets to function)
6. as context (information regarding the location, time or environment where the action takes place (Google, in itself, presents a self-organising system organising around and following questions asked)
7. as enabler for social interaction (hits are highly visible in the rapidly growing social networks such as Facebook, Google+ and Twitter, by establishing links and building relationships as a 're-tribalisation' of humanity, as expressed by Shenk [2009:932] when he talks about strict censorship of Internet connections in repressive governments).

Growing complexities of resource allocation and the need for different planning models

The process of planning has to articulate the strategy and the management of that strategy. From planning comes the vital means of connecting the mission of the present to the vision of the future. Part of addressing goals, objectives and strategy implementation, involves the allocation of resources within budgetary constraints. This handicaps flexibility by its focus on cost cutting and efficiencies. Mostly, the budget defines the plan that defines the strategy.

Peterson (1999) addressed an essential ingredient of strategic planning – the organisational and environmental interface. Institutional planning must include a comprehensive process of monitoring and adjusting for realities of the external environment (Taylor, De Lourdes Machado & Peterson 2008). Complexity encourages a segmentation of the environment. This allows for the impact of the environmental factors on resources and resource flows to be examined, which helps determine resource predictability and the environmental locus of control with regards to resource flows. The strategic management and competitive advantage processes become linear and sequential rather than being seen as one set of activities, related and linked as one. This kind of planning relates more to operations than to strategy. Furthermore, resource allocation is not a linear process and cannot directly lead to strategy selection and implementation as is required in a linear model. This planning style does not relate to the need for adaptability with regards to the environment. The main goal of the strategic planning and implementation should focus on growth and maturity and not on internal processes and resources.

Innovation

Generally speaking, innovation is knowledge used in a unique and different way. Innovation is new thinking. That thinking can be radical, disruptive or incrementally different. But it is not more of the same – it is renewal and renovation. Innovation is generally the result of cumulative dynamic interaction and learning processes involving many stakeholders. Here innovation is seen as a social, spatially embedded, interactive learning process that cannot be understood independently of its institutional and cultural context (Cooke, Heidenreich & Braczyk 2004; Fornaciari & Dean 1998; Lundvall 1992). Because Roberts's (1999) definition (of innovation) maintains that an innovation can only be seen as innovation if it is has implementation and commercial value, it is important to measure the impact of innovation. Ravichandran (2000:263) believe that measuring the impact of innovation activities will depend on:

1. the typology
2. the degree of departure from the preceding product or service or process
3. the extent of usefulness of the innovation
4. the volume of profitability generated.

Smith (2010) identifies four types of innovation based on the work conducted by Henderson and Clark (1990):

- incremental (refining and improving the existing design within an established architecture)
- modular (use is made of new technology and components, within an existing system)
- architectural (an established system links existing components in a new way)
- radical (involving a completely new design using new components).

In the last case, the innovation can be disruptive. Henderson and Clark's (1990) framework shows that systems and components in innovation are inextricably linked, for instance, architectural innovation reconfigures an established system to link existing components in a new way. We like to define innovation as a continuum of activities incorporating

the above notions: innovation as renovation is the outcome of a series of interrelated activities on a continuum, starting with creative discovery, then entrepreneurship and, finally, commercial exploitation. In this, leadership is redefined, processes, systems and culture may be redesigned and organisations search for and find new meaning. This definition allows for technological (product or process) innovation but also includes organisational or management innovation activities.

Innovation within the framework of a knowledge-based economy goes far beyond the linear or chain linkage models that have long been used in innovation theory to explain innovation processes in high-tech knowledge industries. Strambach (2002) suggests that the interdisciplinary view of innovation systems is concerned with understanding the general context of the generation, diffusion, adaptation and evaluation of new knowledge, which determines innovativeness. It follows that the focus is on non-technical forms of innovation as defined above. Common characteristics of the different approaches to innovation, as identified by Edquist (1997), include, (1) innovation and learning at the centre, (2) a holistic and evolutionary perspective and (3) an emphasis on the role of institutions. The increasing interdependence of technological and organisational change is a significant feature of systems of innovation, which means that technological innovation and organisational innovation have become increasingly important. These are combined with more diverse knowledge requirements, which include not only technical know-how, but also economic, organisational and sociological knowledge and competencies. The second reason for the increased interest in non-technical innovations is associated with the connection between the organisational innovation and the corresponding learning capacity. The acceleration of change that is part of the globalisation process means that organisational learning processes are becoming increasingly important for creating and maintaining competitiveness.

Some innovation theorists (such as Smith 2010) believe innovation is meaningless without technology. Technology is a great platform for innovation achievement, but it is certainly not the only one. Technology is a good enabler for certain types of innovation. But real innovation comes from the inner self and individual contributions and thoughts need to be given a place in organisations and in society to breed. We know that innovation takes place in the domains of product, process and/or service. However, there is more: innovation also takes place in leadership, culture, processes and systems, design, products and technology. Innovation is a thinking skill more than a doing skill. It transforms our views of current reality and focuses on renewal and regeneration. Zohar (1990) believes that:

> Most transformation programs satisfy themselves with shifting the same old furniture about in the same old room. Some seek to throw some of the furniture away. But real transformation requires that we design the room itself. Perhaps even blow up the old room. It requires that we change the thinking behind our thinking – literally that we learn to rewire our corporate brains. (p. 114)

However, Zohar's 'real transformation' is really innovation.

Technological innovation is not enough

Technological innovation comprises implementing technologically new products and processes and significant technological improvements in products and processes. The product or process should be new from the point of view of the firm that introduces it. In statistical and innovation research based on the Oslo Methodology (Organisation for Economic Co-operation and Development 2005), innovation covers all possible grades of novelty: from products and processes new globally (known as absolute innovations), through products and processes new on a market or in a country, where a given firm is operating, to products and processes new only to a given firm, but implemented in other firms, domains of activity or countries (so-called imitation innovations). Technological innovation is, in itself, undergoing change with the shifts in industrial revolution. This is the result of the evolution of technology. We summarise this as occurring in three industrial revolutions Firstly, there was the birth of the factory (e.g. tasks completed by hand in weavers' cottages are now completed in single cotton mill, leading to the mechanisation of textile industry), which developed around the late-18th century in Britain. Secondly, were the moving assembly line and mass production fostered by Henry Ford in the early 20th century. Both these revolutions led to enormous wealth and urbanisation. The third industrial revolution, on the other hand, is the result of digital manufacturing and technology convergence – clever software, new materials, dexterous robots, new printing (e.g. three-dimensional printing) and Web-based services. This has resulted in mass customisation and, as a revolution, has several consequences:

1. customers are happy because of faster lead times and better products
2. governments providing subsidies favour the previous products and services in order to protect their investments
3. the lines between manufacturing and services are becoming blurred.

Technological innovation is created as a result of innovation activity comprising scientific research, technical, organisational, financial and market activities in order to improve a product, process or system. Technical or esthetical modifications that do not influence the performance, property, costs, et cetera, are not considered technological innovations. Generally, we are concerned with process innovations – 'performing an activity in a radically different way' (Davenport 1993:10), service innovations – 'a new way of providing a service, often with a novel and very different business model … even an entirely new service' (Smith 2010:23) and product innovations – 'a core design concept that performs a well-defined function' (Abernathy & Clark 1985). Product, process or service innovations thus comprise both systems and components, calling for an integrative model for innovation beyond the instrumentalism versus radicalism approach of the past.

Organisational innovation encompasses all of these, whilst highlighting the way businesses operate (Birkinshaw, Hamel & Mol 2004). These authors maintain that organisational and management innovation is difficult, as it questions existing practices and processes and our assumptions on the nature of the way things are and therefore places an enormous responsibility on leadership acknowledging complexity in order to innovate. In this article, we will focus more on the latter.

Whilst innovation concerns the processes of implementation, relying mainly on organisational communication and power in the domains of production, adoption, implementation, diffusion, or commercialisation of creations (Spence 1994), creativity remains exclusive to the relation established between the creator and his product, where not even originality and usefulness are important, but only the notion of 'trying to do better'. The latter is connected to cognitive and emotional processes taking place at the individual level (Sousa, Monteiro & Pellissier 2008; Sousa, Pellissier & Monteiro 2009a, 2009b). If we relate creativity to problem definition, and innovation to decision implementation, this last step requires a series of problem definitions, in order to carry out a decision or an idea, thereby making it difficult to separate these concepts at an organisational level. In fact, when we move from the individual level to the team and organisational levels, creativity and innovation become increasingly difficult to separate, so that we must agree with Basadur (1997), when he says there is no difference between organisational creativity and innovation. Therefore, the moment we move to other levels besides the individual, we will use these terms (creativity and innovation) as synonyms, referring to organisational creativity as a system devoted to enhance creativity in organisations and thus using the definition proposed by Basadur (1997).

As to the several approaches to identify types of innovation, either by separating the adoption of products and processes from its development (Cebon, Newton & Noble 1999) or, in a more classical way, product and process innovation (Adams 2006), most authors agree that innovativeness, or organisational (and management) innovation, is a separate type of innovation, which represents the potential of the workforce to promote changes to benefit of the organisation. As Huhtala and Parzefall (2007:299) mention, 'to remain competitive in the global market, organisations must continuously develop innovative and high quality products and services, and renew their way of operating', and they also maintain that companies increasingly rely on the employees' continuous ability to innovate. Also, even though innovation may take place through the adoption or development of an existing product or service, through investments in research and development (R&D) or in technology acquisition, it is only through developing and sustaining a creative workforce that the organisation will succeed in maintaining the necessary potential to overcome difficult problems and situations that cannot be solved through investments only (Cebon et al. 1999). To this end, technological innovation is seen as a result of an innovation activity comprising research (scientific), technical, organisational, financial and market activities. Technological innovation means objective improvement of the properties of a product or a process or a system of delivery relatively to the already existing products and processes. Less significant, technical or aesthetical modification of products and processes which do not influence the performance, property, costs or materials consumption, energy consumption and components consumption are not considered technological innovations. As Desrochers (2001) puts it, technological innovation can manifest in any business activity, for example in a basic activity, as well as in secondary and other activity (as defined in the system of national accounts), and in the auxiliary activity of sales department, accounting department, IT department et cetera (e.g. the computerisation of a sales department or a finance department of the enterprise can be considered a technological innovation).

The creative workforce potential is both the ability to retain creative managers and employees (Macadam 2006) and to provide an environment where each one will feels free and willing to contribute to organisational success. Aspects such as raising job complexity, employee empowerment and time demands, together with low organisational controls (decision-making, information flow and reward systems), are said to raise employee creativity (Adams 2006). However, more elements are necessary in order to make people willing and able to contribute to organisational effectiveness. For instance, supportive leadership, knowledge acquisition and team work procedures favouring creativity (Unsworth 2005) can add to success. Creative people (either managers or employees) are committed to their work and organisation and so they may bring in important issues, provided that top management values their work and ideas. In fact, according to a *Gallup Management Journal* survey (Hartel, Schmidt & Keyes 2003), engaged employees are more likely to 'think outside of the box' and produce creative ideas than disengaged people; they also are more receptive to new ideas. The research concludes that engaged people tend to find and suggest new ways to improve their work and business processes, which may lead to the assumption that creative people have a deeper understanding of the organisational processes, by being in a privileged position to identify, define and find organisational problems.

To a certain extent, most of these can be achieved by the implementation of complex systems and the concept of resilience engineering to the business fundamentals. This is attained by elevating the importance of creativity and entrepreneurship and providing a system through which current goals are realised by new ideas and can flourish. What is required is the freedom to create, the content and process skills to be able to create and a supportive human environment (peers and team leader). The issues surrounding the potential of an organisation to innovate are still in its beginnings, although McLean (2005), Puccio *et al.* (2006) and, especially, Basadur (1987, 1994, 1997), have all engaged in empirical research in this regard. The major challenges are

to define criteria to evaluate the impact of organisational innovation on process and product innovation (Wolfe 1994).

In organisational innovation, the unit for innovation is the organisation itself (Wolfe 1994). Although the outcome of the innovation may be process, product or service, the innovation needs to be undertaken through the creative inputs of the individuals and/or management. As to measures of innovation, Dalal (2008) mentions the qualitative measure of emotional and psychological impact the innovation produces on the users (the 'aha!' moments), the quantitative measures of the total population of end users using the new innovation (and even helping co-create it) and the net new revenue generated for the company that can be attributed to the new innovation.

Complexity-based emergent management theory

Complexity allows a two-tiered focus in business, (1) its performance system, which is responsible for the performance of current goals and tasks for immediate survival and (2) its adaptation system, which is responsible for the long-term sustainability through the generation of new ideas, operations and behaviours. It generates possible futures for the total systems. Successful resilient organisations should be robust in terms of both subsystems but tend to concentrate on only one (Robb 2000). The term 'complexity' has two distinct applications (Standish 2008), namely, (1) as a quality (i.e. complexity deals with our ability to understand a system or object) and (2) as a quantity (i.e. complexity deals with something being more than complicated). Complexity as a *quality* is what makes the systems complex and complexity as a quantity describes, for example, human beings being more complex than a nematode worm. Thus, complex systems constitute a class of systems that are more difficult to deal with than traditional analytical systems. For this reason, complex and simple systems form a continuum, characterised by the chosen complexity measure. The two applications of complexity are inherently observer or context dependent, leading to a disparate collection of formalisations of the term. Thus, being able to establish easy to measure proxies for complexity is often important and most proposals for complexity are of this nature (Standish 2008:10). Complexity as a *quantity* can normally be decomposed in a linear way and can be directly compared (e.g. 5 cm can be broken into five equal parts and directly compared). Complex systems, on the other hand, cannot be divided and the individual segments compared. This is because of the interrelations between the subsystems that can quickly lead to combinatorial explosions. This leads to three definitions of complexity (Standish 2008). Firstly, there is the number of parts definition (e.g. a car is more complex than a bicycle because it has more parts, but a pile of sand is not as complex because each grain of sand is conceptually the same and the order of the grains is not important). Secondly, there is the definition relating to the number of distinct parts (e.g. both a shopping list and a Shakespearean play consists of the same 26 letters of the alphabet, this is not a good measure of complexity). Lastly, there is a context-dependent definition of complexity.

When we relate business to complex adaptive systems (CAS) – also called learning systems (Robb 2000) – we look for ways to successfully adapt to changing environmental conditions. Complexity science focuses on relationships between individuals, teams or between organisations and businesses. Accepting business as being a complex system requires that we acknowledge that we cannot control organisations to the degree that a mechanistic perspective will imply, but only that we can influence where the organisation is going and how it will evolve. From this view, organisations are CAS nested in larger CAS (for instance, the economy or the country in which it is based, or the industry in which it operates). Lastly, complexity science allows an organic view of organisations and its resources. Resilient organisational structures, in focusing on the skills, culture and architecture, address this matter and will be discussed in a separate section.

Simon (1996) defines a complex system as one made up of a large number of parts that have many interactions. Complex systems change inputs to outputs in a non-linear way because the components interact with each other through a web of feedback loops (Anderson 1999a:217). Thompson and MacMillan (2010:6) describe a complex organisation as a set of interdependent parts which, together, make up a whole that is interdependent with some larger environment. In organisation theory, complexity is treated as a structural variable that characterises both organisations and their environments. In terms of the first mentioned, Daft (1992:15) equates complexity with the number of activities or subsystems within the organisation. This, he maintains, can be measured along three dimensions, namely, (1) vertical complexity (the number of levels in the organisational hierarchy), (2) horizontal complexity (the number of job titles or departments across the organisation and (3) spatial complexity (the number of geographical locations. With regards to the environment, complexity is equated with the number of different items or elements that must be dealt with simultaneously (Scott *et al.* 1998:230). Galbraith (1982) proposes that organisational design should try to match the complexity in structure to complexity in environment. Casti (1994) points out that, in non-linear systems, interventions to make a change to one or two parameters can drastically change the behaviour of the whole system. Moreover, the whole can be very different from the sum of the parts.

CAS consists of agents that interact with each other and, in doing so, generate new behaviours for the systems as a whole (Lewin & Regine 1999). These lead to the following caveats:

- Patterns of behaviour in these systems are not constant.
- As the system's environment changes, so does the behaviour of its agents. Thus, the behaviour of the system as a whole can change.
- Complexity science focuses on relationships between individuals, teams or between organisations and businesses.
- Business as a complex system requires acknowledgement that we cannot control organisations to the degree that a mechanistic perspective will.

- CAS allow for an organic perspective and the ability to deal with the human element in process design.

Complex designs are formulated to attend to the tensions of paradoxical strategies which may emanate from inconsistencies or contradictions in the products, services, marketplace, processes, rewards and/or competencies associated with different strategies (Smith 2010). Considerable attention has been given to agent-based models of organic systems (McKelvey 1999). In modelling complex systems, we should note that agent-based models need to avoid adoption of social concepts that assume away many of the phenomena of interest. In fact, McKelvey (1999) argues, if at least some social phenomena, which are typically assumed to arise through rational behaviour, arise instead because of complex dynamics that are little influenced by conscious intent, then we need to allow for this in the foundation assumptions incorporated into the model design. In artificial intelligence, for instance, attempts to accommodate rational order have involved incorporating simplified rule sets or incorporation into agent design.

Linking complexity and innovation

What do these two phenomena have to do with each other? Complexity science is the scientific study of complex systems. These systems have many parts that interact to produce patterns of behaviour that cannot readily be explained by the behaviour of its individual elements. Therefore complexity in business helps us better understand the importance of relationships and the interactions of innovations. Complexity science is used in modern business applications because of its ability to explain change and stability and the underlying dynamics produced by patterns in systems and, most importantly, self-organisation and emergence. This means that individual agents in a system cannot control the behaviour or the outcomes of the system because these agents are the consequences of interactions within the system and with other systems. Consequently, complex systems are, by nature, unpredictable and can lead to renewal and change (radical or otherwise). This makes complexity science invaluable to innovation. From an innovation point of view, this means that the best way to understand the dynamics of change and innovation is to employ complexity science.

Yet, complexity science does more than that – it allows for diversity, relationships and cooperation. Complexity science changes how management works. The inherent self-organisation and unpredictability mean that there is less control. Leadership thus requires change as there is less control and more focus on small actions to influence patterns of interaction. Smaller organisations are, of course, more flexible and thus more able to be innovative. Thus, the size of the organisation counts because it is easier to develop relationships and creativity in a smaller group and there may be a greater willingness to release control. Larger organisations seem to become inflexible and rule-bound. Their flexibility is normally embedded in specific units, but overall, there is a notion that adaptive and resilient systems are characterised by order or disorder, or stability or flexibility. In a complex environment, there is no 'either/or'.

To apply complexity to innovation, one needs certain principles. Zimmerman, Lindberg and Plsek (2012) suggest the following:

- The provision of opportunities for a diverse group of people to interact creatively.
- The design of processes to develop creativity, for example, appreciative enquiry, open space, conversation cafes.
- The adoption of a shorter-term perspective stimulating experimentation and sense-making of the ideas, instead of developing a grand plan or long-term blue print.
- The management of innovation should be centralised (to develop an innovation culture organisation-wide) and decentralised (encouraging experimentation at the local level). This is the principle of non-linearity, where the strategy allows small changes effecting large-scale change.
- Leadership should have the ability to listen to promising developments, create network opportunities and communications across the organisation and allow for pattern recognition and new innovations to unfold.

Complexity science requires a change in leadership to support the innovation. This new leadership should:

- Create a culture of innovation. Leadership cannot make innovation happen, but they foster innovation by providing the time and space for creativity, communication and interaction.
- Listen and learn to determine what is emerging in the organisation or in its environment.
- Learn by taking risks and allowing experimentation in the form of ideas or processes.

Two frameworks in this regard are proposed below. Framework 1 employs complexity and CAS in innovation, whilst framework 2 uses a reductionist approach seeing complexity as something negative to the organisation.

Framework 1: Using complex adaptive systems

Rosen (1991) founded the school of thought which believes that complex systems cannot be described by a single best model, as reductionists promote. Instead, a whole collection of models exist that, in the limit, collectively describe the system. Standish (2008:9) mentions that in all cases of recognised emergence, the observer has defined at least one semantic and one syntactic model of the system; these models are 'fundamentally incommensurate'. Moreover, emergence in this sense can be called complex. Models that have a finite specification can never be complex, because the specification contains all there is to know about the system – the more complex the system, the less knowable the organisation is (Perrow 1967); however, it is not so easy with non-linear systems. Obviously, causal models are inadequate because of their interconnectedness and feedback loops, even when the relationships between the independent and dependent variables are denoted by some logarithmic or exponential function. There are six important aspects to be considered in modelling complex systems (Anderson 1999b; Kaufman 1993):

- Many dynamic systems do not reach either a fixed-point or a cyclical equilibrium.
- Processes that appear to be random may be chaotic, revolving around identifiable attractors deterministically and rarely return to the same state.
- The behaviour of complex processes can be quite sensitive to small differences in initial conditions, so that two entities with similar initial states can follow radically different paths over time.
- Complex systems resist simple reductionist analyses because their interconnectedness and feedback loops preclude holding some system constant in order to study others in isolation. Because descriptions at multiple scales are necessary to identify how emergent properties are produced, reductionism and holism are complementary strategies in analysing such systems.
- Complex patterns can arise from the interaction of agents that follow relatively simple rules; that is, emergent patterns can appear at every level in a hierarchy.
- Complex systems tend to exhibit self-organising behaviour; that is, from starting in a random state, they usually evolve toward order instead of disorder.

There are many forms of dynamic systems, for example, general systems theory, cybernetics, chaos theory or catastrophe theory – all of which address systems where a set of equations determine how a system moves through its state space over time. Another modelling technique examines regularity that emerges from the interaction of individuals connected in CAS. The presiding feature is that at any level of analysis, order is an emergent property of individual interactions at a lower level of aggregation. Anderson (1999b), in his study of complex organisations, found that these organisations exhibit non-linear behaviours. He found that these organisations characterise four key elements that are prevalent in organisation design, namely:

1. agents with schemata
2. self-organising networks sustained by importing energy
3. co-evolution to the edge of chaos
4. system evolution based on recombination.

It follows that organisational designs for complexity will require incorporation of these elements. Specifically, complex organisations establish and modify environments within which effective, improvised self-organised solutions can evolve and managers influence strategic behaviour by altering the fitness and landscape for local agents and reconfiguring the organisational architecture within which the agents adapt. Lewin and Regine (1999) identify five principles in CAS:

- Agents interact and mutually affect each other in a system – this focuses on relationships between and amongst people, teams and companies.
- Agents' behaviours in a system are governed by a few simple rules – in business, rules become practices and these practices are guided by shared values and beliefs.
- Small changes can lead to large effects, taking the system to a new attractor – multiple experimentation on a small scale is the most productive way to lead change rather

than to attempt to leap too quickly to a perceived desired goal on a large scale.

- Emergence is certain, but there is no certainty as to what it will be – create conditions for constructive emergence rather than trying to plan a strategic goal in detail. This includes nurturing the formation of teams and creativity within teams and evolving solutions to problems (not designing them). Hierarchical and central control should give way to distributed influence and a flat organisational structure.
- The greater the diversity of agents in a system, the richer the emergent patterns – seek diversity of people in terms of culture, expertise, age, personalities and gender, so that people interact in teams (thus creativity has the potential to be enhanced).

A substantive element of complexity in organisational designs is made up of organisational resilience. Robb (2000) defines a resilient organisation as one able to sustain competitive advantage through its capability to deliver excellent performance against current goals, whilst effectively innovating and adapting to rapid, turbulent changes in the environment. The first requires consistency, efficiency, elimination of waste and maximising short-term results, whilst the second requires foresight, innovation, experimentation and improvisation, with an eye on long-term benefits (Johnson-Lenz 2009). The two modes require different skills sets and organisational designs (e.g. the move from 'just-in-time' production to 'just-in-case' resilience). These organisations exhibit particular characteristics in the sense that they, (1) can create structure and dissolve it, (2) provide safety in the face of change (although this is not necessarily security or stability), (3) manage the emotional consequences of continuous transformation, change, anxiety and grief and (4) learn, develop and grow. The resilience community agrees that resilience architecting (also called resilience engineering) occurs over the three phases of a disruption. In the pre-disruption phase, the system should take steps to anticipate the disruption and avoid the disruption, if possible. In the survival phase, the system should absorb the disruption so that it can recover in the recovery phase. In the recovery phase, the system resumes some degree of its original goals, including the survival of the humans in it. Disruptions are the initiating event that may lead to a catastrophic event. Disruptions may be either external, such as terrorist attacks or natural disasters, or internal, such as human or software errors.

Resilience has four primary attributes: capacity, flexibility, tolerance, and inter-element collaboration. Capacity requires that the system be sized to handle the maximum and most likely events, such as terrorist attacks and natural disasters. However, a system cannot depend on capacity alone; the other attributes must be present to handle unpredicted events. Capacity includes functional redundancy. Flexibility requires the system to be able to reorganise. For example, plans must be in place to allow the command and control to shift upwards in the event of a serious disruption, such as a terrorist attack. Tolerance allows the system to degrade

gracefully in the face of an attack; that is, all resources would not become inoperative after the first strike.

One of the most important resilience attributes is inter-element collaboration. This attribute allows all elements of the system to interact and cooperate with each other as in collaborative innovation systems. There are numerous activities relating to resilient organisations, these are (Pellissier 2011:156):

- **Resilient organisations actively attend to their environments:** Monitoring internal and external indicators of change is a means of identifying disruptions in advance. Resilient organisations seek out potentially disturbing information and test it against current assumptions and mental models. They work to detect the unexpected so they can respond quickly enough to exploit opportunity or prevent irreversible damage. In short, they anticipate being prepared.
- **Resilient organisations prepare themselves and their employees for disruptions:** Attentive preparations build a team that imagines possibilities and displays inventiveness in solving problems. Managers know how and when to allow employees to manage them for focused productivity as well as adaptive innovation. Resilient organisations cross-train employees in multiple skills and functions. They know that when people are under pressure, they tend to revert to their most habitual ways of responding.
- **Resilient organisations build in flexibility:** Even whilst executing for lean and mean performance, resilient organisations build in cushions against disruptions. The most obvious approach is the development of redundant systems – backup capacity, larger inventories, higher staffing levels, financial reserves, and the like. But those are costly and not always efficient. Flexibility is a better approach.
- **Resilient organisations engage suppliers and their networks in devising makeshift solutions to temporary disruptions, thereby using flexible strategies:** They implement policies that encourage flexibility in when and where work is undertaken. Employees who are used to telework and virtual workspaces adapt more quickly and are more productive following a crisis. In addition, research shows that flexible work practices contribute to greater employee resilience, productivity, commitment and to lower levels of stress.
- **Resilient organisations strengthen and extend their communications networks – internally and externally:** A robust and redundant communications infrastructure holds up in a crisis. Social networks amongst employees at resilient organisations are rich, varied and visible. People who have trust relationships and personal support systems at work and with friends and family are much more able to cope with stress and change. Good connections and communications also apply to external relationships with suppliers and customers. A key is to recognise what is important to meet organisational goals and to listen to those with needed expertise and ideas wherever they are in the value web. Resilient organisations use networked communications to distribute decision-making. As much

as possible, they push decisions down to where they can be made most effectively and thus quickly. This, in turn, requires good access to information at all levels of the organisation.

- **Resilient organisations encourage innovation and experimentation:** In times of great uncertainty and unpredictability, the success and failure of small-scale experiments can help map a path to the future. Resilient organisations engage in market research, product development, and ongoing operations and service improvements. They invest in small experiments and product trials that carry low costs of failure.
- **Resilient organisations foster a culture of continuous innovation and ingenuity to solve problems and adapt to challenges:** A side benefit is that employees who believe they can influence events that affect their work and lives are more likely to be engaged, committed, and act in positive ways associated with resilience. Some organisations also have internal idea markets to surface new ideas and innovations. Others use 'crowdsourcing' to engage people externally in solving a given problem.
- **Resilient organisations cultivate a culture with clearly shared purpose and values:** When an organisation's sense of purpose is shared by its employees, suppliers and customers, those networks can provide flexibility to help it through a disruption. Engaged employees will seek out opportunities to try new approaches, find creative solutions and achieve great results.

Framework 2: Complexity reduction

The second framework tries to reduce complexity and sees complexity as negative towards the organisation. It is not easy to compress non-linear systems into a parsimonious description. Simon (1996:1) believes that the central task of the natural sciences is to show that complexity is but a mask for simplicity. In the Social and Management Sciences, the tendency seems to be to reduce complex systems to simpler ones by abstracting out what is unnecessary or not important. Most organisational scientists, who view organisations as natural systems, point out that rules often do not govern actions and that rules can change without behavioural consequences and behaviour can change without modifications to rule systems (Scott 1992).

Normally, competitive advantage is about new product development and the introduction of distinctive offerings. In fact, technological innovation seems to be the most prevalent form of innovation. There is a school of scientists that believe that the longer an organisation has been in existence, the less likely it will allow for radical innovation (Anderson 1999a).

The literature abounds with case studies about innovators and entrepreneurs who make things happen. However, there is a point where the innovation leads to a decrease in profitability because of the complexity that it incurs. The continued launch of new products and services or changes in design or movement styles lead to complexity. This is supported by a survey conducted by Bain Consulting (2012),

which found that excessive complexity increases costs and slows growth because of the way complexity gets embedded in the supply chain. The corporate response seems to be to launch an intervention (such as lean manufacturing or six sigma). This, however, does not simplify complexity; it merely reduces it in certain areas. There are numerous reasons for the spread of complexity: bad economic data, overly optimistic sales expectations, entrenched managerial assumptions and, in developing economies: globalisation, labour problems, customisation versus market size one, new technologies, political instability, lack of infrastructure, resources and capacity, and lack of planning. Bain Consulting (2012) believes that downturns reveal organisational weaknesses and that a nimble, focused organisation could become 'sluggish and ineffectual' in a period of downturn. They see a major cause of this sluggishness as complexity-product complexity, organisational complexity and process complexity. The costs of complexity are usually hidden, so CEOs are often unaware of the magnitude of the problem. When the downturn hits, CEOs may feel unsure how to tackle it or fail to identify the short-term actions that can reduce costs and create flexibility so the company can adjust to the new market conditions. They may also neglect the longer-term steps necessary to balance complexity reduction with innovation as the company pulls out of the downturn and begins to grow consequently – there needs to be a balance between innovation and complexity. Consider manufacturing, which is a strong American economic enabler. From a strategic point of view, the addition of new products increases growth. From an operational point of view, this addition adds complexity and thus decreases profitability. Moreover, increased customisation results in unexpected demand peaks that can easily lead to a drop in quality. The traditional financial systems are unable to account for the relationship between product proliferation and complexity costs, as the costs are embedded in the way the organisation undertakes its business. There seems to be an optimum point for innovation, unless there is a management of the resultant complexity (Gottfredson & Aspinall 2006).

Some protagonists believe in reduction to diffuse complexity. For instance, Gottfredson and Aspinall (2006) proposed a 'Finding the model T Ford' approach. The approach is based on determining the innovation 'fulcrum'; that is, determining the right balance between innovation and complexity. The following practices are required:

1. Raise the bar: requiring a higher rate of return on new products not only makes it more difficult to arbitrarily add variations, it also boosts internal innovation discipline.
2. Postpone complexity: the farther down the value chain complexity is introduced, the less it costs.
3. Institutionalise simplicity in decision-making: executives must pinpoint responsibility for innovation decisions.
4. Stay balanced: a company's innovation fulcrum can shift. Sometimes customers value cost and quality more than having choices.

Technology, postponing complexity to later in the value chain and changing customer tastes can all affect where the right fulcrum point is located.

A comparison between developed and developing organisations

In a study of 14 mid-sized organisations from either a developed or a developing economy, the respective CEOs were interviewed. The purpose of the study was not to generalise but functioned as a pilot study to determine issues of complexity and organisational innovation between the two economic entities. Seven middle-sized South African companies were selected as the developing economy partner and seven middle-sized US companies were selected as the developed economy partner. The CEOs of each were asked to describe their understanding and deployment of organisational innovation and complexity. They were also given a set of complexity and organisational design issues and asked to comment about the extent to which their companies were exposed to these and how they perceived the solutions. The interviews focused on the extent of their organisational innovation and their understanding and implementation of complexity to achieve the innovation. Below is a sample of responses from four of the companies involved in the study.

Company A

This is a medium-sized US firm specialising in health and education research and operating out of several cities in the USA. According to the CEO, larger, more nimble firms had better systems to enable them success, whilst, in Company A, there was an over-focusing on quality and accreditation of research outputs rather than on market position and competition. Two primary problems existed: an over-emphasis on research quality and an under-emphasis on efficiencies, both of which lead to budget constraints. Operational problems included inefficiencies and lack of structure. This company's strategy seems to rely on a re-engineering approach in terms of the following elements:

1. appointment of senior research specialists
2. building teams
3. creation of management systems and accountability
4. change in culture
5. becoming client-focused
6. specialising on something specific.

Their strategy is certainly linear – in the CEO's own words, it is aimed at 'putting the firm on a straight path and staying on that path'. He also maintains that:

> 'A linear strategy was required because of the competitive nature and scale of the environment and a required change in one direction. We are not in a tumultuous environment and had to adapt to the new path and merely be able to stay on that path.' (CEO, Company A)

Evaluation of Company A's strategy

The CEO did acknowledge that there were two conflicting objectives – making money and being efficient – which may have required a complex solution, but, he felt that, as long as they stayed in the new path, they should be successful. The CEO did not understand the role or value of adaption, resilience or agility.

Company B

This is a medium-sized bank in the USA. When the current president of the bank took over, there was little wrong with the strategic direction; however, there was no vision, only the mission. The new president decided not to select objectives but identified three key priorities that inform their strategy and remain constant, (1) fiscal soundness, (2) focus on customers and (3) focus on the community. Believing that management has changed substantially over the last 20 years, the president practices the following with regards to strategy, which includes the following principles:

1. strategy is about common sense
2. strategy is a journey not a destination, with the journey indicating the general direction
3. it is important to track who you are
4. you need to communicate that you are a real person.

Further to this last point, the bank president states, 'Don't sit up there, go down to the people and ask them what they would do if they were president.' The elements of Company B's strategy were, (1) a flat organisational structure, (2) the use of teambuilding exercises and (3) a collaborative approach to management.

Evaluation of Company B's strategy

Employees felt confident enough to discuss issues inside the discussion room and not amongst themselves in the corridors, rather than resorting to complaints outside the discussion room. Company B featured a smaller management team and was subject to less interference from the Board. Although its structure was now flexible, some employees did not agree with the new approach and left the bank, thereby providing a natural exit for employees in disagreement with the general flow of the strategy and its implementation. Thus, there is stability within the unstable environment.

Company C

This is a medium-sized risk management venture in South Africa. The CEO, who, at the time of this survey, had been appointed for one year, sees his role as 'never lonely, participative and directive, experiential and experienced participative'. Their strategy consists of the following elements:

1. strategic management is very important, although flexible
2. strategy is monitored as a journey as often as twice a week
3. there are no 'analogue activities', only 'acting and thinking digitally'
4. engaging in strategic planning is a continuous process using the concept of a sense-making loop from uncertainty to a shared understanding
5. their intent is to manage future risks before they take place
6. the execution of their strategy employs action learning, experiential learning and serious play are the methodology framework for the planning sessions
7. a talent analysis, learning and communication styles linking assignments to a group of various competencies.

Teams change depending on the task.

Evaluation of Company C's strategy

Strategy in Company C happens as continuous loops, rather than as a planned exercise. This strategy is very flexible and teams are formed based on a specific need. There is a feeling of openness and conviviality amongst the employees and the CEO is seen as friend and not as executive.

Company D

This is a medium-sized (family-owned) manufacturing organisation in South Africa, which also exports to other countries. In regards to how he views his role within the organisation, their CEO writes:

> 'At times I play the classic 'lonely' CEO, off by myself thinking and dreaming of what could/should be within the organisation. Creative inspiration or concrete decision may come at any time including during the wee hours, driving my daughters to school or while having lunch. I am participative during many "blue sky" meetings, where my role is decisive in theory but I am just another voice for the most part.' (CEO, Company D)

Strategy and innovation are seen to be linked and to provide the overarching framework for their daily actions, but putting too much emphasis on the process can choke the organics out of running an organisation. The CEO does believe in non-linearity and will:

> 'Literally talk to everyone and anyone in the organisation on an hourly basis. I never assume that I have all the answers and many times the best ideas and concepts will arise from a chance encounter with a staff person. So I don't leave those encounters to "chance" – I create them often.' (CEO, Company D)

They are constantly re-evaluating their vision, mission, values and strategy using a process that includes regular meetings with top and middle management and by carefully listening to line-level employees and customers every day. Their main goals are to achieve a strong position in the industry-related marketplace, maintain a very high level of product quality and make their business a fun and interesting place to work and to turn a profit in doing so.

Evaluation of Company D's strategy

Company D's strategy is linear, with traces of non-linearity. Their strategies include marketplace analysis, competitive analysis and informal SWOT (strengths, weaknesses, opportunities and threats) analysis. Their strategy has changed from a 'shoot from the hip' organisation to one more analytical, reviewing numbers carefully.

Discussion

There can be no generalisation because of the small, non-probabilistic sampling. However, some degree of relative comparison can be made and the pilot study sets the stage for a more robust study across the two economies to follow. From the interviews, a number of points came to light, including that more South African organisations were, by nature, complex, whilst more US organisations were, by design, linear, despite being inherently complex. The US companies were not comfortable with the CAS model and endeavoured to use some form of reductionism to achieve

results when faced with complexity. Also, the US companies were more involved in experimental products, strategic alliances, meetings, communication with customers, communication within projects, but less so in teambuilding, exploitation (refining and extending existing technologies) and exploration (searching and experimenting with new technologies). In fact, it seems that South African companies are managed using complexity techniques and all innovation forms by nature, whilst the US ones favoured a reductionist approach focusing on technological innovation and trying to simplify structures and processes.

Technology was favoured by both groups as the factor most considered in a complex environment. As was expected, the US companies did not experience the developing economy indicators (problems with labour, productivity, clashing cultures, training and development, understanding and implementing new technologies, geographical dispersion, communication or quality). The South African companies had problems with: value and supply chains, new innovations, inadequate knowledge management and business intelligence, low capacity utilisation, no link between people and process, performance criteria and badly articulated connections between business units. On the other hand, the South African companies were more involved in exploiting and exploring opportunities and thus could be classified as engaging in the complexity suggested in Framework 1. Although this is not conclusive evidence, there seems to be adversity (even rigidity) in the US companies to explore forms of complexity and innovation other than, at most, technological innovation, and a feeling of comfort in reducing complexity, as per the proposed Framework 2.

Conclusion

Complexity is neither complicatedness nor over-determination. Complexity is a cross-disciplinary field with its own approach to knowledge-creation that includes a set of methodological approaches. As such, it offers distinct and innovative perspectives on the evolution of systems and the behaviours of the actors within them. And, it should be noted that complexity, in itself, is not an 'either/or' to traditional management models. Instead, it expands and augments these models. Complexity theory is particularly relevant for organisations facing rates of external change that exceed their internal change (McKelvey 1999). Unlike systems with a fixed-point or cyclical equilibrium, the instability in the global environment has a more dynamic equilibrium in which actions can lead to small, medium or large cascades of adjustment.

Brown and Eisenhardt (1998) suggest that single business units achieve rapid evolutionary progress through improvisational moves based upon a few simple rules, responsibilities, goals and measures. These authors offer a new strategic paradigm for navigating the tumultuous markets:

> the key strategic challenge facing managers in many contemporary businesses is managing this change. The challenge is to react quickly, anticipate when possible, and lead change

where appropriate. A manager's dilemma is how to do this, not just once or every now and then, but consistently. (p. 23)

Synergy amongst units follows when units have distinct roles participating in the larger focus. Collaboration is focused on a few key areas. Evolution is preferred over the radical revolution preached and implemented by the re-engineers of the 1990s.

We agree that a nation's competitiveness lies in its innovativeness. Innovation is a dangerous beast that bodes evil and destruction when used inconsiderately because of the changes and possible aggravated complexity it incurs. This makes innovation management critical. It also requires a deep understanding of the nature and forms of innovation and a willingness to create opportunities for creativity. Technological innovation is not necessarily the best innovation. However, with an increasingly complex environment and complexity within the organisation following on innovations, organisational innovation seems required. In this research, a comparison was made between developed and developing economies with regards to how companies handle their innovations whilst coping with complexity. There is reason to believe that developing economies are more able to handle the extent of complexity than their developed counterparts.

This research is by no means final or complete. The pilot study should be extended to a bigger sample from both economies. Questions that need to be addressed include, (1) the extent to which complexity hinders or support innovation, (2) new typologies for innovation within a complex environment and (3) a point of convergence between developed and developing economies – when and why?

Acknowledgements

Competing interests

The author declares that she has no financial or personal relationships which may have inappropriately influenced her in writing this paper.

References

Abernathy, W.J., & Clark, K.B., 1985, *Resilience maps*, viewed 02 February 2010, from http://www.provenmodels.com/571/transilience-maps/k.b.-clark--w.j.-abernathy

Adams, R., 2006, 'Innovation measurement: A review', *International Journal of Management Reviews* 8(1), 21–47. http://dx.doi.org/10.1111/j.1468-2370.2006.00119.x

Anderson, J.A., 1995, *An introduction to neural networks*, MIT Press, Cambridge.

Anderson, P., 1999a, 'Seven levers for guiding the evolving enterprise', in J. Clippinger (ed.), *The biology of business: Decoding the natural laws of enterprise*, p. 315, Jossey-Bass, San Francisco. http://dx.doi.org/10.1287/orsc.10.3.216

Anderson, P., 1999b, 'Complexity theory and organisation science', *Organisation Science* 10(3), 216–232.

Axelrod, R. & Cohen, M.D., 2000, *Harnessing complexity: Organisational implications of a scientific frontier*, Basic Books, New York.

Bain Consulting, 2012, *An exploration of the world economy*, viewed 12 June 2012, from http://www.bain.com/publications/articles/

Basadur, M., 1987, 'Needed research in creativity for business and industrial applications', in S.G. Isaksen (ed.), *Frontiers of creativity research: Beyond the basics*, p. 298, Bearly Limited, Buffalo.

Basadur, M., 1994, *Simplex: A flight to creativity*, The Creative Education Foundation, Buffalo.

Basadur, M.S., 1997, 'Organisational development interventions for enhancing creativity in the workplace', *The Journal of Creative Behavior* 31(1), 59–73. http://dx.doi.org/10.1002/j.2162-6057.1997.tb00781.x

Birkinshaw, J., Hamel, G. & Mol, M.J., 2008, 'Management innovation', *The Academy of Management Review* 33(4), 825–845.

Brown, S.L. & Eisenhardt, K.M., 1998, *Competing on the edge: Strategy as structured chaos*, Harvard Business School Press, Boston.

Casti, J., 1994, *Complexification: Explaining a paradoxical world through the science of surprise*, HarperCollins, New York.

Cebon, P., Newton, P. & Noble, P., 1999, 'Innovation in organisations: Towards a framework for indicator development', Melbourne Business School Working Paper #99–9, Melbourne Business School, Melbourne.

Center for Strategic and International Studies, 2012, *Seven revolutions*, viewed 21 June 2012, from http://csis.org/program/seven-revolutions

Cooke, P., Heidenreich, M. & Braczyk, H.J., 2004, *Regional innovation systems*, Routledge, London.

Daft, R.L., 1992, *Organisation theory and design*, 4th edn., West Publishing, St Paul.

Dalal, S., 2008, *The innovation boot camp*, The Institute for Effective Innovation, Orange.

Davenport, T.H., 1993, *Process innovation: Reengineering work through information technology*, Harvard Business School Press, Boston.

Desrochers, P., 2001, 'Local diversity, human creativity and technological innovation', *Growth and Change* 32, Summer, 369–394.

Edquist, C., 1997, *Systems of innovation: Technologies, institutions and organisations*, Pinter, London.

Fayol, H., 1987, *General and industrial management: Henri Fayol's classic*, Rev. Irwin Gray, David S. Lake Publishers, Belmont.

Fonseca, J., 2002, *Complexity and innovation organizations*, Routledge, London.

Fornaciari, C.J & Dean, K.L., 2001, 'Making the quantum leap: Lessons from physics on studying spirituality and religion in organizations', *Journal of Organizational Change Management*, 14(4), 335–351.

Galbraith, J.R., 1982, *Designing complex organisations*, Addison-Wesley, Reading.

Gottfredson, M. & Aspinall, K., 2006, 'Innovation versus complexity: What is too much of a good thing?' *Harvard Business Review* November, 1–9.

Hamalainen, R.P. & Saarinen, E., 2006, 'Systems intelligence: A key competence for organisational life', *Reflections* 7(4), 17–28.

Hartel, J., Schmidt, F. & Keyes, L., 2003, *Well-being in the workplace and its relationship with business outcomes: A review of the Gallup studies*, American Psychological Association, Washington, DC.

Henderson, R.M. & Clark, K.B., 1990, 'Architectural innovation: Reconfiguration of existing product technologies and the failure of established firms', *Administrative Science Quarterly* 35, 9–30. http://dx.doi.org/10.2307/2393549

Huhtala, H. & Parzefall, M-R., 2007, 'A review of employee well-being and innovativeness: An opportunity for a mutual benefit', *Creativity and Innovation Management* 16(3), 299–306. http://dx.doi.org/10.1111/j.1467-8691.2007.00442.x

Johnson-Lenz, P. & Johnson-Lenz, T., 2009, *Six habits of highly resilient organizations*, viewed 02 February 2010, from http://www.peopleandplace.net/perspectives/2009/2/2/six_habits_of_highly_resilient_organizations

Kaufman, S., 1993, *The origins of order*, Oxford University Press, New York.

Lewin, R. & Regine, B., 1999, *The soul at work: Unleashing the power of complexity science for business success*, Orion Business Books, London.

Lundvall, B.A., 1992, *National systems of innovation: Towards a theory of innovation and interactive learning*, Palgrave-MacMillan, London.

Macadam, C., 1996, 'Addressing the barriers of managing change', *Management Development Review* 9(3), 38–40.

McKelvey, B., 1999, 'Complexity theory in organisation science: Seizing the promise or becoming a fad?', *Emergence* 1(1), 5–32. http://dx.doi.org/10.1207/s15327000em0101_2

McLean, L.D., 2005, 'Organizational culture's influence on creativity and innovation: A review of the literature and implications for human resource development', *Advances in Developing Human Resources* 7, 226–246.

Meieran, G.S., 2012, *21st century innovations*, viewed 28 June 2012, from http://www.engineeringchallenges.org/cms/7126/8275.aspx

Organisation for Economic Co-operation and Development, 2005, *Oslo Manual: Guidelines for collecting and interpreting innovation data*, OECD, Paris, viewed n.d., from http://www.oecd.org/science/innovationinsciencetechnologyandindustry/2367580.pdf

Pellissier, R., 2001, *Searching for the quantum organisation: The IT circle of excellence*, Juta, Cape Town.

Pellissier, R., 2011, 'The implementation of resilience engineering to enhance organisational innovation in a complex environment', *International Journal of Business and Management* 6(1), 145–164.

Perrow, C., 1967, 'A framework for the comparative analysis of organizations', *American Sociological Review* 26, 854–866. http://dx.doi.org/10.2307/2090570

Peterson, M.W., 1999, 'Using contextual planning to transform institutions', in M. Peterson (ed.), *ASHE reader on planning and institutional research*, pp. 224, Pearson Custom Publishing, Needham Heights.

Porter-O'Grady, T. & Malloch, K., 2003, *Quantum leadership: A textbook of new leadership*, Jones and Bartlett, Sudbury.

Puccio, G.J., Firestien, R.L., Coyle, C. & Masucci, C., 2006, 'A review of the effectiveness of CPS training: A focus on workplace issues', *Creativity and Innovation Management* 15(1), 19–33. http://dx.doi.org/10.1111/j.1467-8691.2006.00366.x

Ravichandran, T. & Rai, A., 2000, 'Quality management in systems development: An organizational system perspective', *MIS Quarterly* 24(3), 381–415.

Robb, D., 2000, 'Building resilient organizations', *Organization Design Practitioner* 32(3), 27–32.

Roberts, E., 1999, 'Managing invention and innovation', *IEEE Engineering Management Review* 17, 3–13.

Rosen, R, 1991, Life Itself: A Comprehensive Inquiry into the Nature, Origin, and Fabrication of Life (Complexity in Ecological Systems), Columbia University Press, New York.

Scott, W.R., 1992, *Organisations: Rational, natural and open systems*, Prentice-Hall, Englewood Cliffs.

Scott, M., Gaylard, H., Wallace, S. & Edmonds, B., 1998, 'SDML: A multi-agent language for organisational modeling', *Computational & Mathematical Organization Theory* 4(I), 43–70.

Shenk, D., 2009, *Data smog: Surviving the information glut*, Harper Collins e-Books.

Simon, H.A., 1996, *The sciences of the artificial*, 3rd edn., MIT Press, Cambridge.

Smith, D., 2010, *Exploring Innovation*, 2nd edn., McGraw-Hill Education, Berkshire.

Sousa, F., Monteiro, I. & Pellissier, R., 2008, 'Creativity and problem solving in the development of organisational innovation', in Legardeur, J. & De Sousa J.P. (eds.), *Towards new challenges for innovative management practices, ERIMA '08 proceedings* 2(1), Barcelona, Spain, 06–07 November, pp. 5–11.

Sousa, F., Pellissier, R. & Monteiro, I., 2009a, 'Creativity and problem solving in the development of organisational innovation', *Discussion Papers No. 1: Spatial and Organisational Dynamics*, Research Centre for Spatial and Organization Dynamics and University of Algarve, Algarve.

Sousa, F., Pellissier, R. & Monteiro, I., 2009b, 'Measures of effectiveness of creative problem solving in developing team creativity', in De Boeck Supérieur (ed.), *Projectics/Proyéctica/Projectique*, PROJECTICS '09 proceedings 2009(3), Bidart-San Sebastian, France, 26–27 November, pp. 41–52.

Spence, W.R., 1994, *Innovation: The communication of change in ideas, practices and products*, Chapman & Hall, London.

Stacey, R.D., Griffin, D. & Shaw, P., 2000, *Complexity and management: Fad or radical challenge to systems thinking*, Routledge, London.

Standish, R.K., 2008, *Concept and definition of complexity*, viewed n.d., from http://arxiv.org/pdf/0805.0685.pdf

Strambach, S., 2002, 'Change in the innovation process: New knowledge production and competitive cities – The case of Stuttgart', *European Planning Studies* 10(2), 215–231.

Taylor, J.S., De Lourdes Machado, M. & Peterson, M.W., 2008, Leadership and strategic management: Keys to institutional priorities and planning', *European Journal of Education* 43(3), 369–386. http://dx.doi.org/10.1111/j.1465-3435.2008.00363.x

Thompson J.D. & MacMillan, C., 2010, 'Business models: Creating new markets and societal wealth', *Long Range Planning* 43(2–3), 291–307. http://dx.doi.org/10.1016/j.lrp.2009.11.002

Unsworth, K.L., 2005, 'Creative requirement: A neglected construct in the study of employee creativity?', *Group Organisation Management* 30, 541–560. http://dx.doi.org/10.1177/1059601104267607

Weick, K., 1979, *The social psychology of organisation*, Random House, New York.

Wheatley, M.J., 1999, *Leadership and the new science: Discovering order in a chaotic world*, Berrett–Koehler, San Francisco.

Wolfe, R.A., 1994, 'Organisational innovation: Review, critique and suggested research directions', *Journal of Management Studies* 31, 405–431. http://dx.doi.org/10.1111/j.1467-6486.1994.tb00624.x

Zimmerman, B., Lindberg, C. & Plsek, P., 2012, *Edgeware: Lessons from complexity science for health care leaders*, VHA Inc., Dallas.

Zohar, D., 1990, *The quantum self: Human nature and consciousness defined by the new physics*, William Morrow, New York.

18

Record management practices in labour organisations in Botswana

Authors:
Trywell Kalusopa[1]
Patrick Ngulube[2]

Affiliations:
[1]Department of Library and Information Studies, University of Botswana, Botswana

[2]Department of Interdisciplinary Research of the College of Graduate Studies, University of South Africa, South Africa

Correspondence to:
Patrick Ngulube

Email:
ngulup@unisa.ac.za

Postal address:
PO Box 392, UNISA 0003, South Africa

Background: This article is part of a doctoral research study that, amongst others, assessed e-records readiness and examined the current records management practices in labour organisations in Botswana.

Objective: The main objective of the study was to examine records management practices in labour organisations in Botswana

Methods: A quantitative paradigm largely guided this study. The researchers used a survey research strategy. Methodological triangulation of both quantitative and qualitative data collection methods complemented the strategy. The researchers surveyed all of the 50 registered labour organisations in Botswana. Of these, 45 responded. This is a response rate of 90%. The researchers obtained their data through structured questionnaires, semi-structured interviews, document reviews and observations.

Results: The study showed that labour organisations in Botswana had some form of records management function. However, the management of both paper-based and electronic records was not satisfactory and fell short of the best-recognised records management standards and practices.

Conclusion: Although the researchers limited the study to labour organisations, it sheds light on the challenges of managing records that most organisations in Botswana face. Its results provide useful strategic recommendations to promote effective records management in labour organisations in Botswana and elsewhere in Africa.

Introduction

All organisations create records to support, and provide evidence of, their transactions. Consequently, records, regardless of their formats, are important sources of information and knowledge. They ensure effective transparency and accountability in decision-making and contribute to national development (International Records Management Trust [IRMT] 2003; Kemoni 2007). Therefore, sound management of records, whether electronic or paper, has become a topical issue globally.

The World Bank (2006) and the IRMT (2003) concur that records are essential for the effective and productive functioning of private and public organisations. They assert that records register the decisions and activities of governments and other organisations and serve as benchmarks against which they can measure their future activities and decisions. Without records, there can be no rule of law and no accountability (IRMT 2003; World Bank 2006). In addition, without good records, organisations make ad hoc decisions without the benefit of institutional memories.

Kalusopa (2011) observes that, for labour organisations to participate meaningfully in the national development process, they must develop the capacity to manage records and information. The reason is that the challenges of conceiving, initiating, implementing, monitoring and evaluating activities will always require reliable, pertinent and timely records as well as information (Kalusopa 2011).

Therefore, this article records empirical findings about the extent to which labour organisations in Botswana manage their records in the context of good records management practices.

Contextual setting – labour organisations in Botswana

Labour organisations, or trade unions, are member-based and comprise workers who have come together to achieve common goals in areas like wages, working hours and conditions (Rainsberger 1998:1). Many labour organisations exist to advance the cause of workers by engaging with social and economic orders. They could accept an order and, within it, achieve a 'favourable set of economic terms and employment conditions, or they may seek to overthrow the existing economic system and replace it with another' (Rainsberger 1998:1).

Labour organisations in Botswana are not very distinctive. However, one can divide them into two broad categories: public and private sector organisations.

Public sector labour organisations are largely those in the public service, local government and education sectors whilst the private ones are those that operate in the industrial and commercial sectors of the economy.

Available statistics show that there are 50 registered labour organisations in Botswana (Registrar of Trade Unions 2011). The main national labour federation is the Botswana Federation of Trade Unions (BFTU). It is a federation of 29 labour organisations, or affiliates, and represents about 58% of the legally registered trade unions in the country. The other 42% operate legally, but outside the structure of the BFTU (Kalusopa 2011). A splinter federation, the Botswana Federation of Public Service Unions (BOFEPUSU), formed recently. At the time of writing this article, this federation did not have legal registration.

A literature review showed that, from the early 1970s, labour organisations in Botswana tended to undergo structural, legislative and ideological transformations. The most recent and significant changes to labour legislation, in 2004, allowed freedom of association. It led to a proliferation of labour organisations in Botswana. It also led to labour organisations becoming actively involved in the national development process.

At the level of organisations, unions provide workers with a collective voice. At national level, they work with government and other stakeholders to provide harmonious labour relations. Therefore, one can say that labour organisations in Botswana are a cornerstone of socioeconomic development because they are part of a system of industrial relations and productivity that tries to balance the need for enterprises to remain competitive with the aspiration of workers for higher wages and better working conditions (Friedrich Ebert Stiftung [FES] 2008; Kalusopa 2011). Therefore, like elsewhere in the world, the roles of labour organisations in Botswana go far beyond workplace trade unionism (FES 2008). Labour organisations strive to ensure the transformation of development needs so that they no longer serve only the narrow interests of government or global capital and, instead, focus also on advancing the interests of workers and the people (Kanyenze, Kondo & Martens 2006). Consequently, the role of labour organisations is to monitor and measure progress with inclusive participatory national economic processes and good corporate ethics that the principles of openness, integrity and accountability underpin (Kanyenze, Kondo & Martens 2006).

However, as several studies have pointed out, for labour organisations to perform their role meaningfully in organisations and at national level in Botswana, they need to develop their capacity to manage records and information effectively (FES 2008; Kalusopa 2009; Kalusopa 2010; Kalusopa 2011).

Methodology

The main purpose of the study was to examine records management practices in labour organisations in Botswana. A quantitative paradigm largely guided the study. The researchers used a survey research strategy. Methodological triangulation of the quantitative and qualitative data collection methods complemented it.

The researchers surveyed the 50 registered labour organisations in Botswana. Of these, 45 responded. This is a response rate of 90%. They obtained their data from structured questionnaires, semi-structured interviews, document reviews and observations. They analysed the quantitative data to produce a set of descriptive results and analysed the qualitative data for a set of thematic results. They compared the two sets of results to produce a single interpretation and drew conclusions.

Findings and discussion

In discussing the findings of the study, it is prudent to emphasise that records management theory and practice underline the need to develop a records and information framework or environment that complies with international records management standards. In particular, the ISO 15489 (International Standards Organisation, Records and Documentation – Records Management), referred to as ISO 15489-1 (2001), is a useful guide.

The International Standards Organisation used the Australian Standard AS 4390 as its basis to develop ISO 15489 (Information and Documentation-Records Management – Part 1: General) in response to consensus amongst some ISO member countries to standardise international best practices in records management. It applies to records, irrespective of their formats or media, which public or private organisations create or receive during the course of their activities (ISO 2001a:4). The findings and discussions are its tenets of best records management.

The researchers present and discuss them under the themes that follow:

- legislative and regulatory framework
- creating and capturing records
- uses of records
- formats of records
- organising and classifying record collections
- accessing and retrieving records
- appraising, retaining and disposing of records
- storing and preserving records
- staffing and training
- managing vital records and disasters
- managing mail
- managing emails
- managing e-records.

Legislative and regulatory framework

Record management best practice means that organisations should provide adequate evidence of their compliance with the regulatory environment in the record of their activities. These are usually statutes, mandatory standard practices, codes of best practice and codes of conduct and ethics. The nature of the organisations and sectors determine the regulatory elements (ISO 15489–1: Section 5).

The survey revealed that there was some guidance about the requirements for managing records in the relevant acts, instructions and instruments. However, there was no detailed guidance, which labour organisations need to manage their records, about relevant policies and practices.

It confirms the findings of several studies that reveal the challenges that relate to effective legislative and regulatory frameworks for managing records, regardless of their formats, in countries in the East and Southern Africa Regional Branch of the International Council on Archives (ESARBICA) (IRMT 2008; Keakopa 2006; Nengomasha 2009).

The findings also show that the Botswana National Archives and Records Services (BNARS) Act of 1978 was amended in 2007 in order to strengthen work on current or active records, including electronic records. However, further analysis shows that the BNARS act has a strong emphasis on managing records in the public service. In effect, BNARS has undertaken to play an advisory role to government on managing records and does not extend this to other organisations, like labour organisations. BNARS confirmed in interviews that their major problem was insufficient professionally skilled personnel (Kalusopa 2011).

Creating and capturing records

Scholars of records management theory and practice agree that, in principle, organisations should create and capture records for every activity that involves more than one party and that they should identify and record every process that generates records (Bearman 1994:300; Reed 1997:222; Shepherd & Yeo 2003:102).

Therefore, records must be authentic, complete and usable. For example, even information communication technology (ICT) systems must be able to generate or capture the 'metadata' that record the contents, contexts and structures of records within the business processes that produce them (IRMT 2008:30). According to Shepherd and Yeo (2003:102),

when assessing the need to create and capture records, it is essential to consider:

- the requirements of the organisations or particular business units that need records to provide evidence and information for operational use
- the requirements of the organisations, particular business units or external stakeholders that need evidence to ensure accountability
- the cost of creating, capturing and maintaining the records that organisations require and the risk to them if they do not have these records.

A policy for creating records is also necessary. It should stipulate the requirements for capturing, registering, classifying, retaining, storing, tracking, accessing and disposing of records (ISO 15489-1 2001:7).

Therefore, the survey sought to ascertain the types of records labour organisations create, which functions create the most records, and if they had recordkeeping systems.

The researchers asked labour organisations to state the extent to which each main activity created records. They used a Likert scale to measure the levels of agreement or disagreement about which activity generated records. Most of them (38, or 84%) cited internal and external communication. Other responses follow:

- 37 (82%) agreed that it was union administration
- 34 (75.6%) agreed that it was services to members
- 34 (75.6%) agreed that it was collective bargaining
- 32 (71.1%) agreed that organising and mobilisation produced most records
- 30 (66.7%) agreed that it was education and training activities
- 27 (60%) agreed that it was sending solidarity information
- 27 (60%) agreed that it was correspondence to, and discussions with, international trade union bodies (see Table 1).

Observations and interviews revealed that most of the labour organisations had some forms of recordkeeping systems that administrative staff, mostly receptionists and secretaries who had some office practice qualifications or experience, usually managed.

Interviews and observations also revealed that some limited administrative procedures or instructions guided the creation of records. They included conventions or codes

TABLE 1: Activities that produce records in labour organisations (N = 45).

Activities that produce records	Strongly agree	Agree	Neutral	Disagree	Strongly disagree	No response	Total
Collective bargaining	16 (35.6%)	18 (40%)	3 (6.7%)	1 (2.2%)	-	7 (15.6%)	**45 (100%)**
Organising	15 (33.3%)	17 (37.8%)	5 (11.1%)	3 (6.7%)	-	5 (11.1%)	**45 (100%)**
Internal and external communication	15 (33.3%)	23 (51.1%)	2 (4.4%)	-	-	5 (11.1%)	**45 (100%)**
Services to members	12 (26.7%)	22 (48.9%)	6 (13.3%)	1 (2.2%)	-	4 (8.9%)	**45 (100%)**
Education and training	13 (28.9%)	17 (37.8%)	9 (20%)	3 (6.7%)	-	3 (6.7%)	**45 (100%)**
Sending solidarity information	7 (15.6%)	20 (44.4%)	8 (17.8%)	2 (4.4%)	-	8 (17.8%)	**45 (100%)**
Discussions with international bodies	8 (17.8%)	19 (42.2%)	3 (6.7%)	4 (8.9%)	1 (2.2%)	10 (22.2%)	**45 (100%)**
Union administration	18 (40%)	19 (42.2%)	2 (4.4%)	1 (2.2%)	-	5 (11.1%)	**45 (100%)**

about creating records like letters, memos and reports. The codes contained titles, greetings and reference numbers that organisations should use. However, there were no well-defined or clear procedures or policies to guide the creation of records in most of the labour organisations.

The absence of record creation guidelines and policies is not new in the ESARBICA region. Kemoni (2007) focused on records management for public service delivery in Kenya. Kemoni (2007:290) found that 88 (56%) records management units did not have a policy for creating records, whilst 107 (68%) admitted they 'did not have a list of activities which constituted the basis for record creation'. Kemoni (2007:291) bemoaned the negative effects of not creating 'authentic, reliable, complete, unaltered' records. The situation in labour organisations will probably be similar. Therefore, the absence of a creation policy could have severe implications for labour organisations. Most of these trade unions handle members' cases, disputes, financial obligations within and outside the organisations that require evidence. It would be in their interest to ensure that there is confidence about the authenticity of the records they create or capture for current and future use.

Uses of records

Organisations create and keep records so that designated users, mostly from within the organisations and occasionally from outside them, can use them when they need to. Any records management system that captures records must have systems that allow users to use the records systematically (Shepherd & Yeo 2003:216). Therefore, organisations create records for a purpose.

The study revealed that most labour organisations keep records that assist them in their work. The researchers asked respondents to state, using a multi-response list, the main users of most of these records. The study revealed that the executive leaders (41, or 37.3%), followed by union staff (28, or 25.5%), used the records most. See Table 2.

It was surprising to note that only 21 (19.1%) organisations indicated that the general members were the main users of the records, given that labour organisations are supposed to be member-driven. The implication is that, despite the claims that shared beliefs, which members drive, underline trade union values, the evidence suggests that the organisational culture of labour organisations reflects a mixture of 'power' and 'role' where there is centralised power around a few people that some level of bureaucrats identified.

The interviews revealed two salient points that one can attribute to this state of affairs. One is that most of members were not actively engaged in seeking information but relied on leaders for it. The other is the effect of the organisational culture on records management.

One can define organisational culture as the values, attitudes, beliefs and behaviours that characterise the working environments, objectives and visions of organisations (Hofstede 1980:1). Shepherd and Yeo (2003:45) posit that organisational

culture affects the different approaches or strategies to managing records. Using Handy's (1993) conceptualisation, Shepherd and Yeo (2003:45) present organisational cultures as power (with a strong sense of power at the centre), role (built on bureaucracy), task or achievement (focused on projects or outcomes) and cluster or support (without a definite structure and a tendency to be fluid).

Shepherd and Yeo (2003) argue that a role culture relies on regulation whilst a power culture relies on the day-to-day supervision of lower levels by the powerful. In this regard, they argue that managing records thrives on regulation 'and is best suited to organisations with role culture'. They argue further that the issue of external and internal accountability is central to a role and power culture and that:

> record management based on the need for external accountability may be marketable in role culture rather than power culture... [while] internal accountability is an important issue in both role and power culture. (p. 45)

Although Shepherd and Yeo (2003:42) assert that trade unions have power cultures, a close analysis of the organisational culture of most labour organisations in the present study showed that most of them had a mixture of power and role cultures.

Therefore, most labour organisations in Botswana have centralised power around a few 'elected' people with semblances of formal bureaucratic organisational structures. A power culture tends to control information from the centre – the elected executive at the expense of the general members.

Perhaps other findings in the study will confirm this. It used a multi-response list that indicated that the labour organisations actually used most of the records for administration (41 responses, or 20.3% of the responses) and trade union finance (40 responses, or 19.8%) rather than for collective bargaining (32 responses, or 15.8%) or organisation and recruitment (34 responses, or 16.8%) that would actively involve members. See Table 3.

Formats of records

In addition to recording the policies and procedures for creating records in labour organisations, it is equally important for ISO-compliant records management programmes to record the types and formats of records that organisations create and maintain.

The format is particularly critical in the electronic environment, where the lifespan of a particular format limits its accessibility. The survey revealed that the paper format still dominated most of the records. Based on a multi-response list, the labour organisations indicated that the types of paper format were largely lever arch files (36 responses, or 20%) and loose papers in folders (30 responses, or 17%). See Figure 1.

Figure 2 shows that semi-structured (emails), with 29 responses (21%), unstructured (the Microsoft software package – Word, Excel and PowerPoint), with 28 responses (20%) and structured (databases), with 14 responses (10%)

TABLE 2: Users of records in labour organisations (N = 45).

Users	Frequency	
	Total	%
Union staff	28	25.5
Executive leaders	41	37.3
Members	21	19.1
Not very sure	20	18.2
Total	**110**	**100**

TABLE 3: Purposes for which labour organisations use records (N = 45).

Purposes	Frequency	
	Total	%
Non-trade union matters	1	0.5
Trade union personnel	25	12.4
Trade union policy	29	14.4
Collective bargaining	32	15.8
Organising and recruitment	34	16.8
Trade union finance	40	19.8
Trade union administration	41	20.3
Total	**202**	**100**

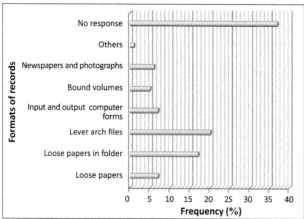

Source: Authors' own data

FIGURE 1: Format of records in labour organisations (paper).

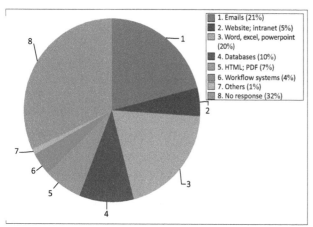

Source: Authors' own data

FIGURE 2: Format of records in labour organisations (electronic).

were the most common electronic formats for records in most labour organisations.

The dominance of paper and unstructured e-records (basic word processing) is similar to the findings of Moloi (2006:58)

and Keakopa (2006:218) for the public sector in Botswana. Keakopa (2006:218) confirmed that, in all government agencies, there were records in both paper and electronic formats with 'the bulk of the records usually in paper format'. Keakopa (2006:218) states that although 'paper [was] a common medium of transmission and storage of information, electronic records [were] slowly becoming more common'.

Furthermore, the current study established, through interviews, that information about current record types and formats in most labour organisations was largely incomplete. This was because there were no systematic records surveys or inventories to capture the many records the organisations had created.

A records survey captures information about the records organisations hold, amongst others. Records surveys help to 'identify what records exist, which records need to be captured into recordkeeping systems, how long they need to be kept and where they should be located' (Northern Territory National Archives Services 2006:2). The information:

> must be gathered on existing records to assess how adequately the recordkeeping requirements of the organisation are being met and whether improvements are required particularly when developing systems and controls for capturing and maintaining' records. (p. 2)

A records inventory is usually a product of a records survey and can be useful for:

> planning a range of records management activities including disposal scheduling and procedures, secondary storage services, vital records protection, and rationalisation of the storage and management of active records future records. (Northern Territory Archives Services 2006:2)

Other researchers have focused on the issues of records surveys in the context of appraisal, retention and disposal. However, they have also emphasised the need for regular records surveys (Kemoni 2007:317; Ramokate & Moatlhodi 2010:80). Labour organisations could also note and follow this advice.

Organising and classifying record collections

The timely and accurate retrieval of records depends largely on how well organised and classified the records are. Therefore, records classification systems should reflect the business activities of organisations. Organisations need to determine the degree of classification control they require for their business purposes (ISO 15489-1: Section 9.5).

Shepherd and Yeo (2003) also pointed out that:

> classification schemes are based on an analysis of functions processes and activities... [and] document the structure of a records management system and the relationship between records and the activities that generate them. (p. 73)

Other researchers and authorities emphasise that any effective records management programme requires classification (Kemoni 2007; Reed 2005). Vocabulary control tools usually support classification systems. They give organisation-specific definitions and explain the usage of terms.

The interviews and observations revealed that most labour organisations were not aware of the procedures for filing paper and electronic records, although most had developed some form of classification. Therefore, in the absence of well-defined, organisation-wide classification structures, most of the localised systems in labour organisations rely on the initiative and memory of union staff members, like secretaries and administrative staff, about how to classify records. Furthermore, when the researchers asked them to state how they organised their records, 16 (18.8%) indicated that they classified their records alphabetically and another 16 (18.8%) that they did so chronologically (Figure 3).

The researchers also observed that, because of the shortcomings that arise from not having file plans, most labour organisations had designed a number of homegrown record classification systems for hard copy and electronic records. They could improve efficiency for some labour organisations in the short term. However, in the long term, creating ad hoc and non-standard systems could undermine the objectives of integrating and sharing information resources.

Although they focused on the public sector, the earlier studies of Kemoni (2007) in Kenya and Nengomasha (2009) in Namibia also revealed the lack of updated classification systems. For example, Nengomasha (2009:212) found that two of the eleven institutions (18%) did not have classification systems. However, even when they did have classification systems, most were outdated or not in use. Kemoni (2007:296) also found that, despite the claim of written classifications, observations showed the contrary. The study revealed that 'in the majority of the ministries, the classification schemes available were handwritten and some were in a state of deterioration, that is, they were faded, worn out and torn'.

The situation seems to be the same in the public sector in Botswana. Ramokate and Moatlhodi (2010:74) conducted a micro-appraisal of public records. It showed that most records in state departments were 'chaotic and un-co-ordinated' and 'among the other problems... [there was]...poor classification of records, as records were created and captured haphazardly without being informed by analysis of business process or functions'. In another study at the Gaborone City Council (GCC), Tshotlo and Mnjama (2010:23) revealed that, although it maintained a register or index in the Records Management Unit, in terms of 'physical arrangement, 8 (66.6%) indicated their records [were] not arranged in any logical manner' and that they were 'in the process of developing a comprehensive file classification system'.

Therefore, it is clear that the problems of organisation and classification the labour organisations face still prevail in the central and local governments of Botswana. Nevertheless, these organisations boast about a professional and technical records management cadre from the BNARS.

Accessing and retrieving records

Effective retrieval systems that reflect the different levels of aggregation and formats are necessary. In paper systems, access is to a specific item in the file (or to the whole file). In the electronic environment, users require metadata at all levels (Shepherd & Yeo 2003:217). Electronic records systems should include and apply controls for access to ensure that the integrity of records remains uncompromised. They should provide and maintain audit trails or other methods to show that they protect records effectively from unauthorised use, alteration or destruction (ISO 15489-1 2001: Section 8.3.6).

ISO 15489 also requires that organisations record the movement of records to ensure that users can locate the records whenever they need them. Tracking mechanisms can record the item identifier, the title, the person or unit that has an item and the time or date of the movement. The system should track the issue, transfer between persons and the return of records to their 'home' location or storage, as well as their disposal or transfer to any other authorised external organisation, including an archives authority (ISO 15489-1 2001: Section 9.8.3).

This study revealed that, when it comes to retrieving paper records, 24 (53.3%) of the labour organisations indicated that they took minutes to retrieve information when they needed it, whilst 14 (31.1%) of them indicated that they took hours to locate information (see Table 4).

This situation was the same in the electronic environment.

With regard to access, 23 of the labour organisations (21.7%) indicated that the main problem they encountered was the shortage of staff trained to manage records. Another notable problem was the lack of, or poor, layout of records management (RMU) units (17.9%), as Table 5 shows.

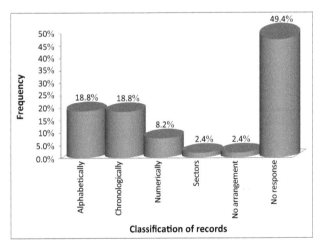

Source: Authors' own data

FIGURE 3: Classification of records in labour organisations.

TABLE 4: Length of time required to retrieve information in a paper-based environment (N = 45).

Length of time	Frequency	
	Total	%
Minutes	24	53.3
Hours	14	31.1
Days	1	2.2
Weeks	1	2.2
Months	1	2.2
Never located in some cases	2	4.4
No response	2	4.4
Total	**45**	**100**

When the researchers asked the labour organisations to state whether there were any systems for tracking paper records, 24 (53.3%) indicated that they did not have any tracking systems whilst 21 (46.7%) indicated that they had. In general, 31 (68.9%) of the labour organisations said they did not have detailed procedures for tracking records, regardless of their format, whilst 13 (28.9%) indicated that they had.

The interviews and observations established that there were no file movement cards, for example. Therefore, when the researchers asked the labour organisations to state, using a multi-response list, the tools they used to track manual records, 26 (39.4%) said they checked files on shelves physically to track the use of records. Only seven (10.6%) used file tracking cards, five (7.6%) used subject indexes and four (6%) used computerised systems (see Table 6).

In a study in the public sector in Kenya, Kemoni (2007:179) also found that, for paper records, 127 (80.9%) respondents indicated that they did not have procedures for tracking files. However, 120 (76.4%) respondents indicated that file tracking registers were tools that they used widely to track records, whilst the remaining 37 (23.6%) indicated that they used file-tracking registers and checked files physically.

The trend was similar in Botswana. Tshotlo and Mnjama (2010:24) confirmed that, although six (50%) of the respondents at the GCC cited movement as a method they used to track their physical files, officers did not monitor the movement from one office to another. With regard to labour organisations, Tshotlo and Mnjama (2010:24) confirmed the poor record management practice of using human memory for tracking files. Three (25%) respondents indicated this. They indicated that the retrieval time ranged from 'a few minutes to sometimes' at the GCC.

TABLE 5: Problems that labour organisations face when providing access to records (*N* = 45).

Problems faced	Frequency	
	Total	%
Staff do not understand user needs	6	5.7
Files torn and dusty	7	6.6
Files bulky	10	9.4
Action officers retaining files	12	11.3
Users know little about the records the trade union holds	13	12.3
Active and inactive files mixed up	16	15.1
Lack of or poor RMU layout	19	17.9
Staff lack training in managing records	23	21.7
Total	**106**	**100**

TABLE 6: Tools labour organisations use to track the use of records (*N* = 45).

Tools	Frequency	
	Total	%
Computerised system	4	6
Subject index	5	7.6
File tracking card	7	10.6
Human memory	9	13.6
File-tracking register	15	22.7
Physical checking of files on shelves	26	39.4
Total	**66**	**100**

Appraising, retaining and disposing of records

Organisations cannot retain files, irrespective of their format (paper or digital), indefinitely. The reason for this is the cost of storage and maintenance as well as slower and difficult access because of the high volumes.

Records management does, in theory and in practice, emphasise that it is necessary to use appraisal techniques to support decisions about retention, that is 'which records can be destroyed at an early stage, and which merit longer-term or indefinite retention' (Shepherd & Yeo 2003:217). In terms of Section 8.3 of ISO 15489-1, records systems should be able to facilitate and implement decisions about retaining or disposing of records.

Therefore, the effective management of records requires that there are procedures for the timely disposal of records that organisations no longer need to support current business or those that they do not need to retain for legacy purposes.

Consequently, the survey tried to establish whether labour organisations have developed tools and procedures for disposing of its records. Surprisingly, most labour organisations (35, or 77.8% of the 45) indicated that they had some form of retention and disposal programme whilst 10 (22.2%) indicated that they did not.

However, follow-up interviews showed that most labour organisations did not have a clear grasp of what such a programme entailed. In general, there was considerable confusion about retention requirements and the need to retain records for accountability purposes. Some respondents thought that 'indefinite' retention was necessary whilst others felt that they could dispose of records as soon as they had served their immediate purposes.

The reality was that, whilst legislation should provide for some basic retention requirement for financial records, for example, there were no clear policies or procedures for retaining or disposing of records in most labour organisations. In some respects, most labour organisations had no retention schedules, but relied on standing instructions (like financial regulations for keeping records for seven years) or standard trade union administrative instructions.

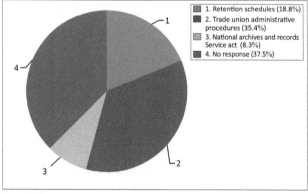

Source: Authors' own data

FIGURE 4: Instruments that guide disposal in labour organisations.

Figure 4 shows that 17 (35%) indicated that trade union administrative procedures were common instruments that guided records disposal in most labour organisations. The National Archives and Record Services Act was the least used instrument in labour organisations – only four (8.3%) used this instrument.

This survey also showed that, just as with paper records, currently there are no clear rules and procedures that authorise the retention and disposal of the data the ICT systems hold. The implication of this is that the creators and users of records are able to capture, manipulate and delete data at their own discretion without any regard for the evidential value of the records.

In addition, of the 45 labour organisations, 28 (62.2%) did not destroy records that they had not appraised, 15 (33.3%) indicated they did destroy records after appraising them and two (4.5%) did not respond. As a result, most of the labour organisations were clogging their recordkeeping systems.

Table 7 shows that most of the labour organisations tended to keep records permanently because they had no retention schedules. Therefore, it seems that most labour organisations require technical records management knowledge to deal with this problem and find an appropriate method to assess.

The IRMT (2003:5) showed that, amongst other challenges, there were no records retention and disposal policies in the ESARBICA region. Another study by Ngulube and Tafor (2006:62) confirmed this trend in Kenya, Namibia, South Africa, Tanzania and Zimbabwe. Other studies that Mutiti (2001), Ngulube (2004), Wato (2006), Wamukoya and Mutula (2005) conducted in the ESARBICA, that Kemoni (2007:317) conducted in Kenya and that Nengomasha (2009) conducted in Namibia, all confirm the absence of records retention and disposal policies.

In Botswana, Moloi (2006:58), Ramokate and Moatlhodi (2010:75) as well as Tshotlo and Mnjama (2010:23) confirm this. For example, Ramokate and Moatlhodi (2010:75) argued that policies for retaining and disposing of records in the public sector were non-existent, most of them 'date back to 1981' and were outdated. Tshotlo and Mnjama (2010:26) also note that, although some records at the GCC had moved to BNARS, 'it was not clear how the officers reached the decision to transfer the records', given that there were no retention and disposal schedules. This suggests that labour organisations in Botswana were in the same position as public sector organisations were and faced similar challenges.

However, Ramokate and Moatlhodi (2010:81) were optimistic about the public sector. They believed that, with the on-going computerisation of the BNARS project, called the National Archives and Records Management System (NARMS), records retention and disposal would be part of the automated system. They envisaged that the system would have 'mandatory functions' that would 'apply retention periods for records and provide a trigger for their implementation'. It would be the responsibility of the departments concerned to 'review and approve disposal action on the highlighted records'.

Storing and preserving records

Storage is essential for managing records because it ensures that records are secure, intact and accessible for as long as users need them (Shepherd & Yeo 2003:173). Storage refers to physical space and to using dependable media. Section 9.6 of ISO 15489-1 (2001) states that records require storage conditions and handling processes that take into account their physical and chemical properties. Records, irrespective of their formats, require high quality storage and handling. Organisations should also store records in media that ensure their usability, reliability, authenticity and preservation for as long as users need them.

The survey revealed that each trade union centralised its storage of records at its secretariat whilst some officials kept records in their offices. There were no well-resourced and fully-fledged records management units, but many had some form of functional recordkeeping system.

Table 8 shows that 28 (36.4%) of the labour organisations used steel cabinets for storing current records whilst 20 (26%) used cupboards. The rest used adjustable shelves (11.7%), wooden racks (11.7%), non-adjustable shelves (10.4%) and the floor (3.9%).

In addition, with regard to the adequacy of the equipment the labour organisations used, 32 (71.1%) of the 45 reported that they used equipment that did not sufficiently cater for records storage whilst only 13 (28.9%) indicated that it was sufficient.

Some of these findings concur with those of Kemoni (2007:309), who found that the most common storage equipment in the

TABLE 7: Retaining records in labour organisations (N = 45).

Type of trade union records	Retention periods of records in labour organisations							
	0–5 years	6–10 years	11–15 years	16–20 years	20–25 years	Permanent preservation	No response	Total
Financial	10 (22.2%)	4 (8.9%)	-	-	1 (2.2%)	27 (6%)	3 (6.7%)	45 (100%)
Human resources	4 (8.9%)	6 (13.3%)	-	-	1 (2.2%)	30 (66.7%)	4 (8.9%)	45 (100%)
General administration	3 (6.7%)	4 (8.9%)	1 (2.2%)	1 (2.2%)	2 (4.4%)	32 (71.1%)	2 (4.4%)	45 (100%)
Union policy	3 (6.7%)	2 (4.4%)	1 (2.2%)	1 (2.2%)	-	34 (75.6%)	4 (8.9%)	45 (100%)
Membership	3 (6.7%)	4 (8.9%)	-	1 (2.2%)	2 (4.4%)	32 (71.1%)	3 (6.7%)	45 (100%)
Organising and recruitment	7 (15.6%)	4 (8.9%)	1 (2.2%)	1 (2.2%)	2 (4.4%)	25 (55.6%)	5 (11.1%)	45 (100%)
Collective bargaining	4 (8.9%)	4 (8.9%)	-	-	4 (8.9%)	27 (6%)	6 (13.3%)	45 (100%)

public sector in Kenya was steel cabinets and that there were problems with the inadequacy of storage equipment. Other studies, like those of Wamukoya and Mutula (2005:75) in the ESARBICA and Nengomasha (2009:209) in Namibia, confirm the pattern.

In addition, 18 (16.7%) labour organisations also indicated that they encountered problems of lost files and torn and dusty records whilst 17 (15.7%) faced the problem of unauthorised access (see Table 9).

Nengomasha (2009:167) also found that 78% of the respondents in the public sector in Namibia had experienced a case, or cases, of lost records because of misfiling by registry staff, wrong reference numbers that action officers used and sending mail directly to action officers. In the public sector in Botswana, Moloi (2006:58) revealed that most respondents indicated that they encountered recordkeeping problems, amongst them being 'lost or missing files'.

With regard to the preservation strategies and practices for paper-based and digital resources, the study revealed that most labour organisations faced major problems. They include poor storage of electronic versions of documents or records, poor strategies for moving to newer hardware and software technologies, poor management of access control and using defective storage media.

The problems of digital preservation are also not new in Botswana. Kalusopa and Zulu (2009) surveyed 35 public and private institutions that they identified as having the actual ability or potential to manage digital materials in the country. These included institutions that operated in library services, archives and records management, museums, geological surveys, health, legal, education, research, revenue collection authorities, the financial services sector and media organisations (radio, television and newspapers). The study also revealed, amongst others:

- the absence of coordinated national initiatives and programmes on digitisation
- gaps in the necessary human resource requirements in terms of knowledge, skills and abilities to drive digital preservation
- the absence of standards for digital material preservation in terms of hardware, software, media and metadata storage.

Staffing and training

According to international records management practice (ISO 15489-1 2001: Section 11), organisations should establish ongoing programmes for training in managing records. Organisations can design or set up this training together with external bodies.

The survey established that most of the people who manage records and information in most labour organisations (35, or 77.8%) had not received any education and training in managing records and only 10 (22.2%) indicated that they had. The multi-response list showed that 10 (22.2%) indicated that they had received certificates as their highest levels of professional education or training in records or information management, whilst six (13.3%) had received diplomas in records or information management.

In addition, 36 labour organisations (41.9%) regarded seminars and workshops as the most useful for meeting the training needs in records management. Only seven (8.1%) of the labour organisations regarded on-the-job training as useful (see Table 11).

Studies that the IRMT (2003:5) conducted in the ESARBICA region showed a lack of core competencies in managing records and archives. Nengomasha (2009:178) also cited the lack of training as one of the factors that led to poor recordkeeping in the public service in Namibia, where only

TABLE 8: Storage of current records in labour organisations ($N = 45$).

Place of storage	Frequency	
	Total	%
Floor	3	3.9
Non-adjustable shelves	8	10.4
Wooden racks	9	11.7
Adjustable shelves	9	11.7
Cupboards	20	26.0
Steel cabinets	28	36.4
Total	**77**	**100**

TABLE 9: Problems labour organisations face when storing records ($N = 45$).

Problems faced	Frequency	
	Total	%
Lost file folios	8	7.4
Torn file covers	13	12.0
Unauthorised access	17	15.7
Torn and dusty files	18	16.7
Lost files	18	16.7
No response	34	31.5
Total	**108**	**100**

TABLE 10: Highest levels of education or training in records or information management ($N = 45$).

Level of education	Frequency	
	Total	%
Advanced diploma	-	-
Other	-	-
Diploma	6	13.3
None	7	15.6
Certificate	10	22.2
No response	22	48.9
Total	**45**	**100**

TABLE 11: Most useful ways of meeting the training needs in records management ($N = 45$).

Ways of meeting training needs	Frequency	
	Total	%
On-the-job training	7	8.1
Internships	9	10.5
Using consultants	12	14
Training in records schools	22	25.6
Seminars and workshops	36	41.9
Total	**86**	**100**

two (20%) of the ten heads of the recordkeeping functions reported that they had attended some records management training or awareness course.

On the other hand, according to Keakopa (2006:178), Botswana had done quite well in training a records management cadre although a challenge remained in terms of training in electronic records and generally inadequate staffing in the public sector. Moloi (2006:52) confirmed that, of 14 state departments, 13 (93%) had a well-trained cadre in records management. Two (14.3%) had master's degrees, two (14.3%) had bachelor degrees and five (35.7%) had diplomas. Only one (7.1%) reported no training at all. This suggests that, unlike the labour organisations, the public sector in Botswana has benefited from the government's robust long-term human resource development strategy. However, more training in records management is still necessary, particularly for managing e-records.

Managing vital records and disasters

Vital records are those that labour organisations cannot operate without and which they need to sustain their operations during, or after, a disaster or calamity. Examples include legal and financial records. Therefore, managing vital records and disasters requires that organisations protect their records in order to maintain business continuity (ISO 15489-1 2001: Section 4.2.5.2).

Good records management practice means identifying vital records and information and then developing a records security policy. Managing vital records and disasters refers to mitigation and recovery because it relates to emergency preparedness. Usually contingency planning is essential. NARA (2011) lists as issues:

- determining the most critical activities that organisations must perform in a disaster
- identifying which records support those critical activities and the resumption of normal operations
- identifying which records series or electronic information systems contain information organisations need to protect their legal and financial rights, and the people that their actions affect directly, and preserving copies of these records
- establishing and implementing a plan to recover records (regardless of the medium of recording) that are damaged in an emergency or disaster.

The survey sought to determine whether labour organisations appreciated and valued the need to identify and manage their most valuable records, that is, those without which they could not function. The survey showed that most labour organisations were aware of the need for managing vital records and the implications of a disaster.

Table 12 summarises the labour organisations' admission that they need to protect their vital records in the event of disasters. Thirty (23.4%) said they identified vital records, 24 (18.8%) developed records protection measures, 22

(17.2%) identified potential disasters, 20 (15.6%) developed appropriate facilities for storing vital records, 18 (14.1%) said they assigned responsibilities for this purpose whilst 14 (11%) said that they conducted audit and test programmes in anticipation of disasters.

Of those that indicated the need for a vital records management programme and for disaster preparedness, 23 (18.1%) of the respondents stated that the disasters that were likely to affect records in labour organisations were computer system failures, followed by unauthorised intrusions (22 organisations, or 17.3%) and leaking roofs (see Table 13).

These results confirm the findings of other studies, like those of Kemoni (2007:320), who found that 40 (89.2%) of the respondents in the Kenya public sector survey 'confessed that they neither had criteria for evaluating potential hazards nor disaster management plan'.

In Botswana, the Hlabaangani and Mnjama (2008:63) empirical study of disaster preparedness confirmed that information centres in Botswana were badly prepared for disasters, lacked disaster preparedness plans, had inadequate policies and procedures, staff that were ill-equipped for managing disasters and that there was an absence of conservation and restoration facilities.

With regard to identifying vital records, the study revealed that none of the information centres had identified and listed their vital information materials. Tshotlo and Mnjama (2010:29) confirmed that nine (75%) of the respondents at the GCC in Botswana believed that the organisation did not have a disaster plan, although they emphasised securing 'confidential records...housed and managed by the secretary in the Town Clerk's office'. The town clerk is the chief

TABLE 12: Indication of the need for vital records programmes in labour organisations (N = 45).

Needs	Frequency	
	Total	%
Audit and test programme procedures	14	11.0
Assign responsibilities	18	14.1
Develop appropriate facilities for storing vital records	20	15.6
Identify potential hazards	22	17.2
Develop measures to protect records	24	18.8
Identify vital records	30	23.4
Total	**128**	**100**

TABLE 13: Disasters likely to affect records in labour organisations (N = 45).

Disasters	Frequency	
	Total	%
Bomb threats	3	2.4
Explosions	5	3.9
Floods	10	7.9
Food and drink in storage area	11	8.7
Pest infestations	17	13.4
Leaking roofs	18	14.2
Sabotage	18	14.2
Unauthorised intrusions	22	17.3
Computer system failures	23	18.1
Total	**127**	**100**

executive officer of the city council. In all, the study reported that there were no clear guidelines to deal with disasters.

The government of Botswana formulated a National Policy on Disaster Management that the Presidential Directive No. CAB 27/96 approved in 1996. In addition, the National Disaster Management Office (NDMO), a unit that falls under the Development Division in the Office of the President, was established (Hlabaangani & Mnjama 2008:64) in 1998. The national policy for disaster management recognises that Botswana is prone to a number of disasters like drought, floods, severe weather (hail and lightning strikes), veld fires, epidemics, pest infestations, industrial accidents and chemical spills (Hlabaangani & Mnjama 2008). However, the policy does not deal with disasters that affect individual organisations but with emergencies in communities. Therefore, the national policy encourages government and non-governmental organisations to develop their own internal disaster plans because of the dangers these disasters pose. Labour organisations will do well to embark on designing their own sectoral disaster plans.

Managing mail

Managing mail is a critical component of managing records in organisations. Operational and service effectiveness demands that organisations handle mail in timely and cost-effective ways.

The researchers asked respondents, using a multi-response list, to state the key mail management functions that the labour organisations performed. The results showed that receiving mail had the highest score of 36 (16.2%), then opening mail, with 29 responses (13.1%) and delivering mail to action offices, with 26 responses (11.7%). They were the leading activities that constituted the mail management programme in labour organisations. Respondents did not rate filing mail (9.9%), sorting mail (9.5%), classifying mail (6.8%) and controlling mail movement (5.9%) highly, yet they are key to managing mail effectively.

Most respondents indicated, in interviews, that they had received criticism for their delayed or perceived lack of response to official communications. Observations also showed that there were inconsistent application file reference numbers on outgoing correspondence, thereby undermining the maintenance of a complete record of correspondence.

Table 14 shows that, of the labour organisations that responded, 30 (66.7%) did not use any tools for circulating mail. Only four (8.9%) used file movement cards, whilst one (2.2%) used systematic searches.

TABLE 14: Tools labour organisations use to control the movement of mail (N = 45).

Tools	Frequency	
	Total	%
Systematic searches	1	2.2
File movement cards	4	8.9
Daily lists of wanted files	5	11.1
No tools for circulating mail	30	66.7
No response	5	11.1
Total	45	100

There were no clear guidelines for the types of correspondence that organisations should track. This leads to delays in processing in-coming and out-going correspondence that the organisations receive.

Other studies in the public sector in the ESARBICA indicated that there were attempts to introduce some elaborate mail management programmes, although they mentioned some challenges in managing mail. For example, Kemoni (2007:295) reported that, in the Kenya public service, all had a mail management programme and that 129 (82.2%) respondents cited receiving, sorting, opening, classifying, filing and delivering mail to action officers as their mail management activities.

In Botswana, Tshotlo and Mnjama (2010:26) indicated that there was a mail management programme at the GCC, although they mentioned that there were some delays in circulating mail. However, unlike public organisations, labour organisations did not report having a well-established mail management programme. This suggests that labour organisations need to re-examine all business processes for receiving, distributing, tracking and managing correspondence. They should attend specifically to redundant processes and bottlenecks. Labour organisations could also learn from other organisations that have modernised their systems and use technology to process, distribute and manage mail more efficiently.

Managing emails

Although most labour organisations reported they had, as per organisational policy, not adopted emails as official ways of communicating, 25 (55.6%) of the organisations said that they used it 'very often' and 10 (22.2%) said they used it 'often'. This yields a combined score of 35 (77.8%). Furthermore, follow-up interviews revealed that labour organisations thought that they had some cases where the admissibility and authenticity of email communication had been questioned as evidence of transactions in executing their work. They believed that, whilst email may be as good a record as any other, many were still apprehensive about the authenticity of emails. Sixteen (35.6%) respondents indicated that they used the Internet very often. However, only three (6.7%) labour organisations indicated they used it at times or very often in their work. The rest were not at all sure (see Table 15).

Labour organisations also indicated that the challenges of authenticity and admissibility were key reasons that had led to the slow adoption of ICTs. This seems to suggest that email poses huge challenges for most labour organisations. One of the major reasons was that there were no policies or procedures about using and managing emails. For example, in most of the labour organisations, the users created and disposed of emails and attachments mainly at their own discretion without referring to institutional standards or controls. Some users said they 'archived' messages, whilst others printed and filed messages they thought were official and important.

TABLE 15: Extent of use of ICTs in labour organisation functions (N = 45).

Communication tool	Neverused	Rarely used	Used at times	Used often	Used very often	No response	Total
Fax	1 (2.2%)	4 (8.9%)	7 (15.6%)	8 (17.8%)	21 (46.7%)	4 (8.9%)	45 (100%)
Telephone	1 (2.2%)	1 (2.2%)	2 (4.4%)	7 (15.6%)	31 (68.9%)	3 (6.7%)	45 (100%)
Cellphone	2 (4.4%)	2 (4.4%)	1 (2.2%)	8 (17.8%)	29 (64.4%)	3 (6.7%)	45 (100%)
Internet	8 (17.8%)	-	4 (8.9%)	7 (15.6%)	16 (35.6%)	10 (22.2%)	45 (100%)
Email	4 (8.9%)	-	1 (2.2%)	10 (22.7%)	25 (55.6%)	5 (11.1%)	45 (100%)
Website	17 (37.8%)	1 (2.2%)	3 (6.7%)	2 (4.4%)	3 (6.7%)	19 (42.6%)	45 (100%)
Web 2.0 (Facebook)	19 (42.2%)	2 (4.4%)	1 (2.2%)	1 (2.2%)	-	22 (48.9%)	45 (100%)
Web 2.0 (YouTube)	21 (46.7%)	1 (2.2%)	-	-	-	23 (51.1%)	45 (100%)
Web 2.0 (Twitter)	21 (46.7%)	-	-	1 (2.2%)	-	23 (51.1%)	45 (100%)

ICT, communication technology.

These challenges are not unique to labour organisations. In Botswana, several scholars have alluded to these challenges. Keakopa (2008:80) confirmed that most organisational policies tended to concentrate on regulating usage rather than managing the resulting records. Keakopa (2008:80) revealed that there were no clear policies for creating, using, storing, retaining or disposal of email in Botswana. Similar studies in Botswana, by Moloi (2006), Tshotlo and Mnjama (2010), Nengomasha (2009) in Namibia and Sejane (2005) in Lesotho, all refer to the absence of clear policies about managing emails. Tshotlo and Mnjama (2010) recently revealed that, at the GCC in Botswana:

> basically, respondents use[d] computers for e-mail… typing of documents and sending of correspondence, but whatever information is sent or received via e-mail remain[ed] with individuals who [were] at [liberty] to delete or save the e-mail… (p. 30)

Managing e-records

With regard to managing e-records, it was clear from the survey that most labour organisations were likely to conduct their operations and business using ICTs although they would continue to create, receive, maintain and use paper records in the foreseeable future. The current study concurs with the earlier study of the IRMT (2003:5). It showed that there were various barriers to managing e-records in developing countries. In fact, the most prevalent challenges labour organisations experienced with managing electronic records were that there were insufficient staff members with expertise in managing records (24.5%), lack of relevant training (21.7%) and low awareness of ICT issues (17%). See Table 16.

TABLE 16: Challenges of managing electronic records in labour organisations (N = 45).

Challenges	Frequency	
	Total	%
Insufficient staff with expertise in managing records	26	24.5
Inadequate funding to buy enough computers and accessories	21	19.8
Lack of relevant training	23	21.7
Poor communication between users and information technology (IT) officers	4	3.8
Security	7	6.6
Technology obsolescence	7	6.6
Low awareness of ICT issues	18	17
Total	106	100

Studies in Botswana that Keakopa (2006), Moloi (2006), Tshotlo and Mnjama (2010) carried out in the public sector and local government confirm these findings. For example, Keakopa (2006:135–136) revealed that, in Botswana, there were challenges about managing paper and electronic systems, back-up procedures, the long-term preservation of electronic records, issues of access and coping with change from manual to computerised systems. Moloi (2006:105–107) also mentioned lack of procedures, the absence of policy and legislative frameworks as well as a lack of skills, amongst others, as challenges that the public sector faces.

Tshotlo and Mnjama (2010:30–32) conducted a records management audit in a local government and the GCC. They revealed several challenges, like the absence of records management policies to guide the creation, storage, access, retention and disposal of records.

Recommendations and strategies

Labour organisations in Botswana should consider the recommendations and strategies that follow to improve their records management practices.

Legislative and policy framework

The study found that the legislative framework was weak. Although there was some guidance about the requirements for records management in the relevant acts, instructions and instruments, there was no detailed guidance about the policies and practices that labour organisations need to manage records.

Therefore, for labour organisations to become aware of, and comply with, any legislative requirements that relate to records and information, they will need to develop and introduce a range of internal policies, standards and procedures to enable them to fulfil the statutory obligations and to improve their operational efficiency. They could use other countries, like the United Kingdom (UK), Australia, the United States of America (USA) and South Africa as models for benchmarking these policies. The models from these countries focus on responsibilities and obligations and specify monitoring and compliance mechanisms. The best of these models also recognise the interdependence between paper and digital records and the need to integrate and co-ordinate the management of records in all media.

Creating and capturing records

From the survey, it is clear that most labour organisations lacked policies and procedures for creating records. There were no recognised procedures and standards for titling, indexing, classifying and describing records so that organisations could organise them systematically and retrieve them easily.

Therefore, the researchers recommend that labour organisations develop policies for creating records that stipulate the requirements for capturing, registering, classifying, retaining, storing, tracking, accessing records and disposing of them (ISO 15489-1 2001:7). Organisations need these policies, standards and procedures to manage records throughout their life cycles based on records continuum principles. For example, the mechanisms of best practice behind the records continuum model emphasises that, in an electronic environment, there is a need for:

> identifying records of organisation activities that need to be retained, then implementing business systems designed with built-in recordkeeping capability [that] ensures capturing records of evidential quality as they are created. (Xiaomi 2003:27)

Organising and classifying

The researchers established that there were no well-defined classification schemes to guide the organisation of records in most labour organisations. Therefore, the researchers recommend policies, standards and procedures for organising, numbering and describing or indexing records. Developing a classification and filing system should use the functions the labour organisations perform as their basis (Shepherd & Yeo 2003; ISO 25489 2001). Once in place, organisations should make the file classification systems available to all staff members to increase acceptance and ownership.

Tracking and accessing files

The researchers established that tracking files was problematic and this made access cumbersome. They recommend that labour organisations design and implement effective systems for tracking files and actions in paper-based and digital recordkeeping systems and ensure that they build adequate audit trails into all systems so that they can maintain a history of access to, and use of, records. Organisations can, and should, link the monitoring and use of records to track workflow and actions because they will increase efficiency. This is particularly effective for the electronic environment (ISO 15489-1 2001: Section 8.3.6).

Appraisal, retention and disposal

Labour organisations should examine all the legislation that affects the retention and disposal of records and determine their own business needs before continuing to retain all categories of available records. A comprehensive record survey of existing records should support this.

Labour organisations should develop comprehensive schedules for retaining and disposing of records that they

keep up to date and implement as a matter of routine. They should determine their retention requirements for all the main categories of their records by assessing their value for supporting administrative, financial, legal, historical, research or information needs. Labour organisations should also develop efficient mechanisms for disposing of, or destroying, the records they no longer need, whether they are hard copy or digital. The processes should be secure, complete and carefully recorded.

Labour organisations should develop policies and standards to support the protection and security of records throughout their life cycles until they can safely destroy or delete them. These could include email policies, policies for using records outside offices, policies for managing the records of staff who leave the organisations and policies for applying retention rules for all electronic data and information.

Storing and preserving records

The survey revealed that storage and preservation records are weak. Labour organisations should establish functional record-keeping management units. This would also lead to the rationalisation of their storage requirements and improve the accessibility of semi-current records that are bundled together with current files on shelves. Implementing retention schedules could create a balance between creating and disposing of records (as the organisations create new records, so they destroy older ones that are no longer useful). This will save storage space and time that staff would otherwise spend looking for records.

The study also established that, in terms of preservation strategies and practices between paper-based and digital documents, most labour organisations faced similar problems. They include poor storage of electronic versions of documents or records, poor migration strategies to newer hardware and software technologies, poor control of access as well as using defective storage media.

The researchers recommend that labour organisations develop programmes for preserving digital materials. Detailed studies on needs and the reorganisation of analog systems for identifying, selecting and classifying materials for digitisation should precede them.

Access and retrieval

Introducing retention and disposal schedules could help labour organisations to control the destruction of records that are no longer useful. Labour organisations should also improve their retrieval procedures. Retention schedules would also ensure easy retrieval as there would be fewer current records to search. The retention schedules should apply to both paper and electronic records. Another possibility is to use intern students of record management from the University of Botswana during their winter break or on a part-time basis to assist with appraising and decongesting the records that are blocking their recordkeeping systems.

Managing vital records and disasters

The study shows that there is no policy or programme for identifying, managing and protecting vital records in the event of a disaster in most labour organisations. Therefore, it is necessary to identify vital records and information and then develop policies for managing disasters that could work together with the ICT security policies for protecting records and information. Labour organisations should design and implement well-orchestrated disaster management plans and review them regularly.

Managing mail

The study also found that there was dissatisfaction with the current procedures for handling both incoming and outgoing mail in labour organisations, and which respondents said were very inefficient.

Labour organisations will need to re-examine all their business processes for receiving, distributing, tracking and managing correspondence or mail. They should pay specific attention to redundant processes and bottlenecks. They could learn from other organisations in the public and business sectors that have modernised their systems and use a variety of mail management technologies to make processing, distributing and managing mail more efficient.

Staffing for, and training in, managing records

The researchers recommend that labour organisations employ qualified personnel to run the record and information management functions. They could also work hand in hand with institutions like the University of Botswana (UB) to develop short-term winter programmes to improve their skills bases. Other organisations in the public sector, like BNARS, the Botswana National Library Services (BNLS) and NGOs like the Botswana Council of Non-Governmental Organisations (BOCONGO) have benefited from similar arrangements in the past.

In addition, labour organisations should have comprehensive programmes to orientate their staff members about the central role of records in their organisations and the need to manage them properly. They could achieve this through continuous refresher courses. Labour organisations should design programmes that sensitise staff to managing records and good recordkeeping practices and conduct them regularly. Training and awareness modules that incorporate trade union (business) knowledge and understanding could complement them.

Managing e-records

It is necessary to incorporate records management components into both electronic business and office systems so that they can capture records seamlessly and protect the integrity of records over time. Labour organisations need policies and procedures that allow them to manage paper and digital records as integrated wholes. The policies and procedures should also apply to managing emails.

Conclusion

This article has attempted to record the state of the current records management practices in labour organisations in Botswana. The findings show that, although some records management functions do exist, they fall below envisaged records management standards in all labour organisations. Problems include:

- creating and capturing records
- organising and classifying records
- access and security
- storing records
- appraising, retaining and disposing of records
- human resource capacity
- managing vital records and disasters
- managing mail, including integrating e-records.

The researchers recommend that labour organisations adopt and implement best records management practices in order to promote successful and effective records management. It would help them to achieve their goals.

Acknowledgements

The researchers thank two anonymous reviewers for their comments.

Competing interests

The authors declare that they have no financial or personal relationship(s) that may have inappropriately influenced them when they wrote this paper.

Authors' contributions

The authors conceptualised the study together. T.K. (University of Botswana) designed the study and collected some of the data that the study reports as part of his doctoral studies. P.N. (University of South Africa) converted the study into a publishable journal article and dealt with the comments of the reviewers and the editors.

References

Akotia, P., 2002, *Financial records management project: Phase three*, paper submitted to the Government of Uganda, DFID Kampala, 17–28 January.

Bearman, D., 1994, *Electronic evidence strategies for managing records in contemporary Organisations*, Archives and Museums Informatics, Pittsburgh.

Friedrich Ebert Stiftung (FES), 2008, *Trade unions in Botswana*, FES, Gaborone.

Handy, C.B., 1993, *Understanding organisations*, 4th edn., Penguin, London.

Hlabaangani, K. & Mnjama, N., 2008, 'Disaster preparedness in information centres in Gaborone, Botswana', *African Journal of Library, Archives and Information Science* 18(1), 630–74.

Hofstede, G., 1980, '*Culture's consequences, international differences in work-related values*', Sage Publications, Beverly Hills.

International Records Management Trust (IRMT), 2003, *Evidence-based government in the electronic age: case summaries*, viewed 20 May 2008, from http://ww.irmt.org/evidence/index.html

International Records Management Trust (IRMT), 2008, *Integrating records management in ICT system: good practice indicator*, IRMT, London.

International Organisation for Standardisation (ISO), 2001, *ISO 15489-1 Information and documentation-records management-part 1 general*. ISO, Geneva.

Kalusopa, T., 2011, 'Developing an e-records readiness framework for labour organisations in Botswana', PhD Thesis, University of South Africa, Pretoria.

Kalusopa, T., 2010, 'E-records readiness – can we build a contextual and conceptual framework for labour organisation in Botswana?' *ESARBICA Journal* 29, 124–146.

Kalusopa, T., 2009, 'Challenges of information and knowledge management in trade union in Botswana within the context of millennium development goals', *Journal of African Studies and Development* 1(1), 1–7. http://dx.doi.org/10.1108/01604950910971125

Kalusopa, T. & Zulu, S., 2009, 'Digital heritage material preservation in Botswana: problems and prospects', *Collection Building* 28(3), 98–107.

Kanyenze, G., Kondo, K. & Martens, J., 2006, *The search for sustainable human development in Southern Africa*, ANSA, Harare.

Katuu, S., 2004, *Report on an investigation of electronic records in the Commonwealth*, Unpublished manuscript, Johannesburg.

Keakopa, S., 2006, 'Management of electronic records in Botswana, Namibia and South Africa: Opportunities and Challenges', unpublished PhD Thesis, University College, London.

Keakopa, S.M, 2008, 'Management of electronic mail: a challenge for archivist and records managers in Botswana, Namibia and South Africa', *ESARBICA Journal* 27, 73–83.

Keakopa, S.M., 2010, 'Overview of archival and records management developments in the ESARBICA region', *The Journal of the Australian Society of Archivists* 38(1), 51–77.

Kemoni, H.N., 2007, 'Records management practices and public service delivery in Kenya', PhD Thesis, University of KwaZulu-Natal, Pietermaritzburg, South Africa.

Moloi, J., 2006, 'An investigation of e-records management in government: case study of Botswana', unpublished MA Thesis, University of Botswana.

Mutiti, N., 2001, 'The challenges of managing electronic records in the ESARBICA region', *ESARBICA Journal*, 20(3), 57–61

Mutula, S.M. & Brakel, P., 2006, 'E-readiness of SMEs in the ICT sector in Botswana with respect to information access', *The Electronic Library,* 24(3), 402–417. http://dx.doi.org/10.1108/02640470610671240

Mutula, S.M. & Wamukoya, J., 2007, 'E-government readiness in east and southern Africa', *Encyclopedia of Digital Government* 2, 571–579.

National Archives and Records Administration (NARA), 2011, *Vital Records And Records Disaster Mitigation And Recovery: An Instructions Guide,* viewed 20 May 2011, from http://www.archives.gov/recordsrecordsmanagement/policyand_guidance/prod3rev.htm

Nengomasha, 2009, 'A study of electronic records management in the Namibian public service in the context of e-government', PhD thesis, University of Namibia.

Ngulube, P., 2004, 'Implications of technological advances for access to the cultural heritage of selected countries in sub-Saharan Africa', *Government Information Quarterly* 21, 143–155. http://dx.doi.org/10.1016/j.giq.2004.01.003

Ngulube, P. & Tafor, V., 2006, 'An overview of the management of public records and archives in the member countries of the East and Southern Africa regional branch of the international council on archives (ESARBICA)', *Journal of the Society of Archivists* 27(1), 57–83. http://dx.doi.org/10.1080/00039810600691288

Northern Territory National Archives Services, 2006, *Guidelines for Conducting a Records Survey*, viewed 05 May 2011, from http://www.nt.gov/nreta/nta/records/pdf/conducting_survey.pdf

Rainsberger, P.K., 1998, Collective bargaining historical models of collective bargaining in the *U.S. Steward Notes* 1(2).

Ramokate, K. & Moatlhodi, T., 2010, 'Battling the appraisal backlog: a challenging professional obligation for Botswana National Archives and Records Services' *ESARBICA Journal* 29, 67–86.

Registrar of Trade Unions, 2011, *Trade union registration statistics*, Office of the Registrar of Trade Unions, Gaborone

Reed, B., 1997, 'Electronic records management in Australia', *Records Management Journal* 7(3), 1–13.

Reed, B., 2005, 'Records' in S. McKemmish, M. Piggott, B. Reed & F. Upward (eds.), *Archives: recordkeeping in society*, pp. 101–130, Centre for Information Studies, Wagg, NSW. http://dx.doi.org/10.1108/eb027111

Sejane, L., 2005, 'An investigation into the management of electronic records in the public service in Lesotho', MA thesis, University of KwaZulu-Natal.

Shepherd, E. & Yeo, G., 2003, *Managing records: a handbook for principles and practices*, Facet Publishing, London.

Tafor, V.F., 2003, 'Digital technology–understanding the problems posed by information technology in generating and managing records from a Third World perspective', *ESARBICA Journal* 22(1), 72–76.

Tshotlo, K. & Mnjama, N., 2010, 'Records management audit: the case of Gaborone City Council', *ESARBICA Journal* 29, 5–35.

Wamukoya, J. & Mutula, S., 2005, 'Capacity-building requirements for e-records management: the case in east and Southern Africa', *Record Management Journal* 15(2), 71–79. http://dx.doi.org/10.1108/09565690510614210

Wamukoya, J. & Mnjama, N., 2007, 'E-government and records management: an assessment tool for e-records readiness in government', *The Electronic Library* 25(3), 274–284. http://dx.doi.org/10.1108/02640470710754797

Wato, R., 2006, 'E-records readiness in the ESARBICA Region: challenges and the way forward', *ESARBICA Journal* 25, 69–83.

World Bank, 2006, *Why records management? Records management as a key support for development effectiveness*, viewed 20 January 2008, from http://web.worldbank.org/WBSITE/ EXTERNAL/EXTABOUTUS/EXTARCHIVES/

Xiaomi, A., 2003, 'An integrated approach to records management', *Information Management Journal*, July/August, 24–30.

19

Integrating eHealth in HIV/AIDS intervention programmes in South Africa

Authors:
Babasile D. Osunyomi[1]
Sara (Saartjie) S. Grobbelaar[1]

Affiliations:
[1]Department of Engineering and Technology Management, Graduate School of Technology Management, University of Pretoria, South Africa

Correspondence to:
Sara Grobbelaar

Email:
s.grobbelaar@gmail.com

Postal address:
Graduate School of Technology Management, Lynnwood Drive, Pretoria 0001, South Africa

Background: With an estimated 12.2% of its population infected in 2012, South Africa has the highest percentage of people living with the human immunodeficiency virus and acquired immunodeficiency syndrome (HIV/AIDS) in the world. Although the mortality rate of the epidemic is decreasing, it has adverse impacts on the socio-economic development status and human capital of South Africa.

Objective: The key aim of this article is to explore the status quo of the implementation of information and communication technologies (ICTs) in selected intervention programmes in the South African HIV/AIDS care delivery value chain. The contribution of this article is the mapping of key intervention activities along an HIV care value chain and to suggest a roadmap towards the integration of ICTs in service delivery programmes.

Method: 20 managers of HIV/AIDS intervention programmes were surveyed, followed by semi-structured in-depth interviews with these respondents. A further five in-depth interviews were conducted with experts in the ICT area for exploring the uses of and barriers to integrating ICTs in the HIV/AIDS care delivery value chain.

Results: The researchers mapped the barriers to implementation and ICT tools utilised within the HIV/AIDS care delivery value chain, which proves to be a useful tool to explore the status quo of technology in such service delivery programmes. The researchers then considered the wider policy environment and provided a roadmap based on the analysis and the South Africa eHealth strategy for driving development in this sector.

Conclusion: The authors found that South Africa's eHealth environment is still nascent and that the South African eHealth strategy does not place enough emphasis on systems integration and stakeholder engagement or the planning and process of uptake of ICTs by target audiences.

Introduction and problem statement

The prevalence of the human immunodeficiency virus and acquired immunodeficiency syndrome (HIV/AIDS) epidemic in South Africa (SA) is at 12.2% of the population, which accounts to 6.4 million individuals living with the virus (Shisana *et al.* 2014). The devastating effect of the HIV/AIDS epidemic is not only evident in the reduced life expectancy of South Africans (52.6 years) but also negatively affects the country's economy and the development of human capital (Bollinger & Stover 1999; Kaiser Family Foundation 2012; UNDP 2010).

In the South African context, various historical and contextual factors affect the extent to which the country is able to effectively respond to the epidemic:

- From the political context: 'Denialism' of the gravity and impact of the HIV/AIDS pandemic in the 1990s, the resultant undermining of antiretroviral (ARV) rollout and inequalities in power and authority led to poor management of the disease at the governmental level (Knight 2006; Marais 2005).
- From the socio-economic context: This is characterised by a high unemployment rate and endemic poverty, poor service delivery in municipalities outside large centres coupled with insufficient funding made available to combat the disease (Ntuli *et al.* 2003; Venter 2013). HIV/AIDS is also highly stigmatised which makes reaching affected people more difficult (Eba 2007; Ntuli *et al.* 2003). The South African healthcare context is furthermore characterised by limited and geographical inequalities in access to healthcare services and skills (Department of Health [DOH] 2011; Health Charter 2005; Lawn & Kinney 2009; Ntuli *et al.* 2003).
- Technologically, although South Africa has the most advanced ICT platform in Africa there is a digital divide between urban and rural settings and between the rich and poor

(Akinsola, Herselman & Jacobs 2005; Sikhakhane & Lubbe 2005; World Economic Forum 2012). There are also different levels of eHealth maturity across and within provinces with a wide range of legacy information systems, which leads to little or no interoperability and communication between these systems (DOH 2012a, 2012b).

Thus far, research has shown that education alone is not adequate to effect the desired behavioural change amongst most individuals (Rachel 1999). ICTs have the potential to accelerate the development and implementation of productive HIV prevention programmes and interventions, by building a capable health system, thereby reducing barriers in accessing quality services (Scheibe, Brown & Bekker 2012).

The key aim of this article is to explore the range of barriers to integrating eHealth applications in selected South African HIV/AIDS service delivery programmes. To this end the authors developed an HIV/AIDS care delivery value chain framework and explored how service delivery can be strengthened through ICTs. Following this, the focus of the analysis was on the programme level and the review entailed uncovering issues in utilising ICTs faced by practitioners in a range of HIV/AIDS service delivery programmes.

By mapping suggestions that have been made by HIV/AIDS intervention programme staff as well as ICT specialists, the authors draw some conclusions on how activities along the HIV/AIDS care delivery value chain can be strengthened through ICTs. The aim is to draw conclusions from this analysis for the eHealth policy environment and develop an implementation roadmap.

Literature review
Introducing the HIV/AIDS care delivery value chain framework

With the specific focus of this article on the status quo of the services and applications component, the article draws on the integrated product and services management system model by Weeks (2012). The authors mapped the various categories of the HIV/AIDS value chain framework and populated the activities column. Table 1 forms the basis of the framework against which the analysis of intervention programmes and the status quo of ICT support mechanisms on South African HIV/AIDS service delivery programmes will be mapped (Porter 2010:26).

The role of ICTs in supporting healthcare delivery

The roles and benefits of supporting activities in the health sector with technological mechanisms have been acknowledged in the literature (Geers & Page 2007). De Tolly and Alexander (2009) state that there exist significant opportunities in South Africa for adopting ICTs and in particular mobile technologies to aid initiatives in the HIV/AIDS sector.

With the focus on ICTs as an enabler of health service delivery, Table 2 provides a breakdown of various eHealth tools available to support health programme delivery.

Table 2 outlines identified information system tools which include discussion forums, blogs, social networking sites, collaborative websites and virtual networks. These tools could be useful in the wide dissemination of useful health information by providers to patients and the wider

TABLE 1: The HIV/AIDS value chain for service delivery and care.

Value chain component	Goals to be achieved in this category	Activities towards achieving goal
Advocacy, prevention and screening	Permanently prevent the transmission of the HIV/AIDS virus from an infected individual to an uninfected individual.	Identify high-risk individuals Conduct HIV tests Promote risk reduction strategies Modify behavioural risk factors Connect patients with primary care systems Create medical records
Diagnosis and staging	Detailed result of the individual's HIV/AIDS status: the stage of the infection is determined. The aim of this stage is to device a treatment management plan for the individual.	Formal diagnosis and staging Determine transmission method Identify others at risk Create a management plan Formulate a treatment plan
Medical management	Develop an adequate medical intervention management plan that reduces the progression of the disease, through nutritional interventions and a rapid prevention and intervention of opportunistic infections.	Initiate therapies to delay onset Treat co-morbidities that affect progression Improve patient awareness Connect patient to care team
Intervening measures	Promote early intervention plans for the infected individual, by improving adherence to first-line drug therapy and to slow the emergence of drug resistance.	Initiate ARV therapy Prepare patients for disease progression and side effects of treatment Manage secondary infections and associated illnesses
Disease management	Continuous plans and support for patient's adherence to medications, need for social assistance, nutritional support, patient's clinical status and monitoring of the risk of transmitting the virus to an uninfected person.	Manage the effects of associated illnesses Manage the side effects of ARV therapy Determine additional nutritional needs Prepare patient for end-of-life management Primary care and health maintenance
Managing complications	Provides required care to facilitate recovery from deteriorations in the patient's clinical status and to provide additional support.	Initiate drug therapies Manage acute illness Manage infection Manage side effects Provide additional support

Source: Adapted from Porter, M.E., 2010, 'Value based global health care delivery', Princeton global health colloquium, 24 September 2010, viewed 23 July 2013, from http://www.isc.hbs.edu/pdf/20100924_Princeton%20GHD.pdf

TABLE 2: Information system for health care providers and consumers.

Providers	Patients and wider public
Individual electronic health information	
Discussion forums	Media platforms (radio and television)
Blogs	Online social support programmes
Social networking sites	Discussion forums
Collaborative websites	Blogs
Virtual worlds	Social networking sites
	Collaborative websites
	Virtual worlds
Information systems for disease management	
Electronic health records	Directories of health care professionals and institutions
Patient information systems	Health information (either a spectrum of searchable information or
Hospital information systems	more narrowly defined content)
General practitioner information systems	Personal health records or health care information system
National electronic registries	Patient Web portal
National drug registries	
General information systems	
ARTIS	
Health management information systems	
Distance learning and electronic resources	

TABLE 3: Disease management delivery tools and support tools for policymakers.

Providers	Patients and wider public
Remote diagnosis, point-of-care technology	Patient Web portal
Transaction processing	Telemonitoring
Clinical decision support system	Home monitoring and messaging system
Care plan management	Smartphone applications
Appointment booking and management	Email and SMS
Service delivery	Pagers
Supply chain planning and collaboration	**Policymakers and health programme management**
Order tracking and delivery coordination	Risk analysis
Telehealth, mHealth	Compliance monitoring and reporting
E-prescription (prescription and test ordering support)	Performance monitoring of servive providers and programmes
Electronic referrals and specialist letters	Skills evaluation
Electronic health events summariss, prescriptions and test ordering	Healthcare operations management
Medications management	Clinical practice improvement
Alerts monitoring and management	Health programme design and optimisation
Chronic disease management	Health policy development
Clinical decision support	Clinical research
Adverse event monitoring	Rapid access to information for disease surveillance and modelling

public at a reasonable cost and also support learning, communication and dissemination of information between service providers.

Information systems (also shown in Table 2) may ensure effective disease management and provide the means to monitor, control and evaluate the geographical spread of the disease. It also could be used to track the timely distribution of life-saving resources to patients and also to monitor, evaluate and ensure the constant availability of resources. The tools identified in this section include patient information systems, hospital information systems, general practitioner information systems, national electronic registries, national drug registries, general information systems, antiretroviral information systems, health management information systems, distance learning and electronic resources.

As far as disease management delivery tools are concerned (Table 3), these ICTs may be employed to ensure effective

delivery of services. Again a series of tools can be identified that apply to service providers, patients and the wider public as well as policymakers.

The tools highlighted in Table 3 can be useful in ensuring proper diagnosis of diseases irrespective of the patient's location, provide service providers with effective decision-making tools, create an adequate strategy and plan in managing the disease, monitor resources, ensure proper prescriptions of drugs and provide productive service delivery to target recipients.

Also, the benefits of integrating supply chain management capacity through ICT infrastructure are to facilitate effective transaction processing, to promote supply chain planning and collaboration and to coordinate order tracking and delivery (Aurumo, Inkilainen & Kauremaa 2005). Through such mechanisms, ICT infrastructure could support constant availability of ARVs and other vital resources, providing an effective means of estimating the quantities of resources to be ordered and to monitor factors that could hinder the operations of the programs (Chandani 2006).

On the policy side, design and support for HIV intervention programmes deployed should be directed through detailed understanding and mapping of the epidemiology of HIV for designing an appropriate mix of prevention programmes. As discussed, ICTs can be employed as enabling mechanisms in monitoring and tracking healthcare service delivery and the overall performance of the health system (DOH 2012a). The next step is now to proceed to introduce an overarching policy framework for eHealth and the implications that may have on the development of a strategy and implementation thereof in South Africa.

A policy framework and review of services and applications for eHealth systems

The World Health Organisation (WHO) and International Telecommunication Union (ITU) have developed a toolkit for providing guidance to the development of a national eHealth strategy (WHO 2012). This to a large extent has informed the South African eHealth strategy, which will support the development of an eHealth system over the medium term.

Drawing on the WHO's document as well as a review of the South African eHealth policy's compliance to these guidelines, the authors outline the key components for such a strategy (Foster 2012). The purpose of this is to provide a larger policy framework within which to place the primary research findings for this study and to highlight the barriers to using ICTs at present on a practical level. See Figure 1.

A range of coordination related components have been identified that need to be included in the capacity development of supporting and eHealth environment (WHO 2012) (see Figure 1):

- The *leadership and governance* component includes activities to coordinate the initiative, engage with stakeholders, manage operations and monitor and evaluate outcomes of programmes.

- The *strategy and investment* component includes strategic planning for the creation of an enabling environment considering financing and funding mechanisms and investment support aligned with national priorities.
- The *legislation, policy and compliance* component includes the aspects of the policy environment to legislate and regulate the use of and access to data and the development of the eHealth environment and to regulate standards compliance.
- The *standards and interoperability* component refers to the range of standards that will need to be adopted to ensure interoperability of various systems and enable the exchange of information between them.

Human resource capacity development aspects identified in the toolkit are:

- *Workforce*: This ensures that the necessary eHealth knowledge and skills are available through internal expertise, technical cooperation or partnership with the private sector and also the development of effective eHealth education and training programmes to build an adequate health workforce.
- *Consumer literacy*: Although not included as a separate component in the WHO toolkit, given the SA environment and developing country context, the authors include electronic literacy and user-friendliness as a crucial aspect of the development of a system (WHO 2012).

ICT environment components identified in the toolkit are:

- *Infrastructure*, which refers to the physical infrastructure that is required to support exchange of information across geographical and health sector boundaries.
- *Services and applications*, which includes the actual implementation of ICT tools for eHealth and the software applications through which they are delivered.

The South African eHealth strategy places much emphasis on eHealth maturity of the South African health system. Various stages of readiness for a health system are considered, mostly based on the readiness of the system to transition to an eHealth environment looking at data flow and collection, data utilisation and integration, resource capacity and scope and scale. The objectives of the South African eHealth strategy covers improvements on existing ICT platforms, development of a novel platform and a plan for further research and development in the utilisation of ICT infrastructure (DOH 2012a, 2012b).

Scrutinising the range of challenges that have been outlined in the strategy for the South African environment (DOH 2012a, 2012b), it is clear that they are mostly centred along a need to coordinate and to develop partnerships and alliances. This is required to overcome disparities in systems such as different levels of eHealth maturity, disparate information systems in provinces with no interoperability and various silos of information (DOH 2012a, 2012b).

There are also low levels of cooperation and collaboration across sectors and stakeholder groups. Furthermore, a

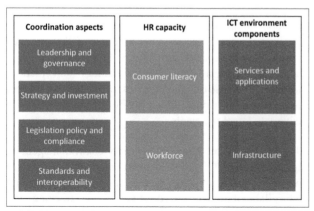

FIGURE 1: Summary of components of an eHealth strategy.

Source: Adapted from World Health Organization (WHO), 2012, *National eHealth strategy toolkit*, viewed 10 February 2014, from https://extranet.who.int/iris/restricted/handle/10665/75211

wide range of different structures exist for ICT support in the various provinces. As a key enabler towards operability the strategy highlights the need for ensuring standards is in place. Issues around inequality are also raised such as inequity of expenditure and access to healthcare and broadband connectivity (DOH 2012a, 2012b).

Foster (2012) found that, in general, the South African eHealth strategy complies with the guidelines as outlined by the WHO (2012). Foster however found that the stakeholder management and engagement aspect in developing the study has not been dealt with effectively in the document.

Research method and design

The methodology used for the study is a mixed method approach. Semi-structured in-depth interviews were conducted with practitioners in HIV management organisations and specialists in the ICT and healthcare technology management fields.

The interview participants were chosen from various HIV intervention programmes all across South Africa and fell into two categories:

- Category A: Semi-structured interviews were conducted with health care practitioners and professionals from 20 HIV management organisations. The aim of these interviews was to achieve an in-depth view of the status quo of utilising ICTs in selected intervention programmes in South Africa. Topics covered during this discussion included the level of utilisation, benefits from utilisation, challenges experienced and the perceived effectiveness of the employment of ICT tools in delivery programmes.
- Category B: Semi-structured interviews were conducted with five experts in the ICT and health technology management field. These interviews provided us with a view of the potential improvements and requirements for the expansion of the utilisation of ICTs to support HIV/AIDS intervention programmes.

During the course of the research study, the authors also completed an extensive review of each participating organisation's website to know more about their programmes and the activities covered and how the activities fit into the HIV/AIDS care delivery value chain framework.

As explained in the literature review, the objective of the devised HIV care value chain framework is to guide the analysis against an established framework in order to ensure that services can be designed and shortcomings of the system in supporting the implementation of ICTs in programmes can be analysed (Rhatigan et al. 2009; UNAIDS 2011).

In terms of the spread of organisations that were interviewed, it was ensured that the geographical representation included projects running on the city or town level (11 interviews),

TABLE 4: Sample description.

Location	N	ICTs used	No ICTs used
Rural	9	1	8
Urban	11	11	0
Total	20	12	8

ICTs, information and communication technologies

TABLE 5: Distribution of intervention programmes' activities around HIV/AIDS.

Row labels	Rural	Urban	Total
Prevention and screening	5	9	14
Counselling	5	6	11
Diagnosis and staging	6	6	12
Medical management	1	5	6
Intervening measures	2	5	7
Disease management	5	5	10
Managing complications	5	4	9
Advocacy	0	5	5
Science of HIV	0	4	4

district level (three interviews), provincial level (three interviews) and national level (three interviews). This is important as it was expected that the types of activities as well as nature of challenges to utilise ICTs may differ across these projects.

Results and discussion

As shown in Table 4, the research interviews revealed that 12 out of the 20 participating programmes employ ICT tools in enhancing their intervention programmes, whilst eight indicated that they do not utilise any ICT tools. Nine of the 20 participating programmes serve rural communities, whilst the remaining 11 serve urban settings. Important to note is that eight of the nine HIV care programmes in rural programmes do not utilise ICTs in their delivery programmes whereas the programmes surveyed that operate in urban areas all utilise ICTs.

Table 5 shows the range of activities covered by the participating programmes along the stages of the HIV/AIDS care delivery value chain (as discussed in the literature review). We have segmented the responses according to rural and urban target areas. The value chain areas covered by each of the interventions may be explained by the various focus areas of the programmes.

It can be concluded from inspecting the distribution of responses in Table 5 that the urban interventions contained in the sample tend to be more comprehensive programmes as many of them provide services along the HIV/AIDS care delivery value chain. A good number of them are also programmes that have provincial or national reach, which then implies that it is also common for these programmes to be better resourced and have access to crucial infrastructure and skills.

As shown in Figure 2, the eight organisations that do not employ ICT tools indicated that the rural location of their organisation, inadequate access to funding, inadequate access to required ICT infrastructure, a lack of ICT knowledge and

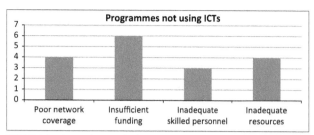

FIGURE 2: Barriers to the use of information and communication technologies in HIV/AIDS management programmes ($N = 20$).

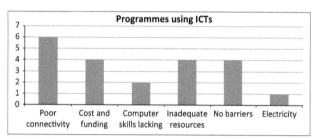

FIGURE 3: Barriers to the use of information and communication technologies in HIV/AIDS management programmes ($N = 20$).

insufficient human capital are the key barriers encountered within their organisation's ICT implementation strategy. This finding is in line with reports in the literature on the digital divide between urban and rural areas; this may however furthermore also be due to the nature of the programmes, which are usually smaller, localised programmes with limited resources.

The in-depth interviews with ICT experts also highlighted a range of barriers to the implementation of the ICT-based intervention programmes, many of which were to do with the creation of an enabling environment through ensuring privacy and confidentiality of patient information, support for adhering to current legal, clinical and ethical guidelines and obtaining informed consent from patients prior to the implementation of ICT tools. Furthermore, they highlighted financial implications, inadequate ICT supporting infrastructure and insufficient access to skilled ICT professionals.

As reflected in Figure 3, organisations that do use ICT tools to enhance their programmes identified barriers to implementation including poor connectivity, the varying levels of maturity of infrastructure, capabilities and systems across South Africa, lack of computer knowledge and skills and inadequate resources, whilst four organisations indicated that their organisation is not experiencing any barriers with utilising ICT tools and technologies.

The benefits identified by the ICT experts interviewed included improved adherence to ARV therapy, adequate and unified information databases, improved reach of coverage, global connectedness to information and expertise, easy access to useful information and facilities, effective drug dispensing and distribution, improved data gathering capacity and improved awareness in target populations about the epidemic (see Figure 4).

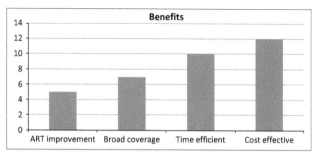

FIGURE 4: Benefits of employing information and communication technology tools in HIV/AIDS management programmes ($N = 12$).

We therefore progress to map the various ICTs that were indicated by the respondents during the interview process; these tools are mapped and compared along the range of activities in the HIV/AIDS care delivery value chain.

When considering inputs gained from ICT experts as well as comparing the ICT tools used by the HIV management organisations with the potential ICT tools suggested by the ICT and health care technology management experts in Figure 4, it was confirmed that for the programmes studied, the implementation of ICTs is still nascent. Applications such as mobile applications for HIV/AIDS, pharmaceutical information systems and a national HIV/AIDS database for monitoring, controlling and managing the epidemic are yet to be employed on a large scale in the programmes reviewed.

Limitations of the study

The key limitation of this study is that due to time and resource constraints the researchers could only conduct in-depth interviews with 20 HIV intervention programme managers. The findings were however supplemented through interviews with five ICT and health care experts in order to ensure that the finding from the interviews may be tested against their expert knowledge and linked to a larger policy framework.

Although the authors believe that the value chain mapping is a useful approach, future studies should aim to do a more comprehensive mapping of the various barriers and facilitators of uptake of ICTs in HIV/AIDS intervention programmes.

Conclusion

The researchers found that although the South African government has identified eHealth as a priority and developed an eHealth strategy that does address the range of components as suggested by best practice, implementation is lagging. The primary data gathering and analysis process revealed that the implementation of ICTs to support HIV/AIDS programmes and their interventions are still in a nascent phase. Issues to be addressed for the large-scale roll-out of an eHealth system are typical of those of a country that is in the *developing and building up phase* of an eHealth system (WHO 2012).

Although South Africa has a well-developed ICT environment and sectors such as banking and e-commerce are well developed, eHealth implementation is lagging due to a range of issues and practical problems more specifically related to coordination and governance. Furthermore, major constraints identified revolve around privacy issues, the massive cost implications of the implementation of a countrywide ICT platform, inadequate ICT infrastructure and resources and lack of required knowledge and skills.

A key finding (in line with the South African eHealth strategy) is that a major priority remains the integration of existing systems on a provincial and national level. This also needs to be mindful of the large disparities between systems on the provincial level, availability of funding and varying maturity levels of eHealth systems across the country. Key enablers towards this end uncovered in the research include:

- There remains a lack of standards and a coordinated approach to ICT or eHealth tool development, evaluation and dissemination.
- The key concern around privacy, security and confidentiality needs to be addressed to develop public trust in these tools.
- Monitoring and evaluation of the systems need to be ensured for learning and ongoing quality assurance of services.

We therefore conclude that an effective ICT governance structure is needed to assume responsibility for establishing and ensuring the consistent application of nationwide standards, legislation, policies and processes that need to be adhered to in order to ensure systems compatibility on a regional, national and international level.

We however also offer a number of additional considerations for the effective implementation of eHealth systems in South Africa, which have been found to not be effectively addressed in the South African eHealth strategy:

- Various stakeholder groups such as different groups of consumers, health care providers, policymakers and government departments need to be consulted more effectively. This must be done to ensure their value propositions are addressed and that systems adequately address their needs.
- Specific planning and support need to be put in place to consider an uptake plan for ICT application. Barriers to adoption have been identified in this article to include on the supply side but also demand side. For instance, in order for ICTs to be rolled out on a large scale, consideration must be given to ICT and eHealth literacy of the target populations of these interventions, which is not specifically addressed in the eHealth strategy.
- Much work also still remains to develop sustainable business models for ICT and eHealth tools for a thriving

eHealth industry where the private sector can take the lead to develop solutions.

In conclusion, it must be stressed that the temporal element of the implementation of the eHealth strategy needs to be taken into consideration. To the end of outlining priorities and the sequence of implementation, the authors propose a phased approach for the range of suggested priority areas for a medium-term planning framework. We outlined factors around coordination, capacity development and the ICT environment (see Figure 5).

Phase 1: An enabling environment and migration to a single platform: As the first and the currently ongoing phase towards the implementation of eHealth, the process of characterising the policy context and the nature of government support going forward should be prioritised. As has been shown in the analysis and review of the South African eHealth strategy, standardisation, interoperability, privacy and data protection have been identified as high priority areas to address.

Furthermore, infrastructure development, the role of government procurement in stimulating the demand side, the development of appropriate business models and human resources capacity development need to be carefully conceptualised during the initial phase of implementing the eHealth strategy.

Phase 2: Driving uptake and upscaling: Following the development of an enabling environment, the implementation of standards and incentive systems should be prioritised to ensure support for the wide-scale uptake of eHealth technologies. Here, issues such as the development of ICT infrastructure and increasing access to such resources should assist in the process.

Specific planning and support need to be put in place to consider an uptake plan for eHealth. Here, barriers to adoption have been identified considering issues on the supply side but also on the demand side. For instance, on the demand side, ICT and eHealth literacy need to be addressed along with government procurement planning to create a market and to stimulate technology development.

Phase 3: Focus on stimulating demand and mainstreaming eHealth: A final phase for the large-scale roll-out and adoption of ICTs in eHealth programmes will entail the integration into mainstream health services and a drive towards infrastructure maturity. ICT infrastructure could be leveraged to create rich databases for planning support and service delivery monitoring.

Finally, during this phase, the eventual success and sustainable continued existence of the additional services and benefits for ICT support on health programmes is reliant on the successful entry of private sector players through the implementation of sustainable business models.

Stage	Activities	Possible ICT Delivery Tools as outlined by literature and experts		ICT Delivery Tools used intervention programmes in SA	
		Providers	**Patients and wider public**	**Providers**	**Patients and wider public**
Advocacy, prevention and screening	Identifying high risk individuals; Conducting HIV test; Promoting risk reduction strategies; Modifying behavioural risk factors; Connecting patients with primary care systems, Creating medical records	National HIV/AIDS database system; Health promotion activities through SMS, and mobile applications social media networks; mHealth; Traditional media platforms (radio and television)	SMS, mobile applications; Internet, E-mail and social media networks; Electronic billboard; Personal health records	SMS and phone calls; Internet, E-mail and social media network; Radio and television broadcast; Skype; Whatsapp	SMS and phone calls; Internet, E-mail and social media network; Radio and television broadcast; Skype; Whatsapp
Diagnosis and staging	Formal diagnosis and staging; Determine transmission method; Identify others at risk; Create management plan; Formulate a treatment plan	Remote diagnosis, Point of Care Technologies, Patient database; Risk analysis and profiling, clinical decision support, National HIV/AIDS database system; E-Health, e-prescription, medications management, care plan management	SMS, mobile applications; Internet, E-mail and social media networks; Personal health records	SMS and phone calls; Internet, E-mail and social media network; Coretalk application	SMS and phone calls; Internet, E-mail and social media network
Medical management	Initiate therapies delay onset; Treat co-morbidities that affects progression; Improve patient awareness; Connect patient to care team	National HIV/AIDS database system; e-Health (i.e. EHR and m-Health); Clinical decision support system, appointment booking and management	SMS, mobile applications; Internet, E-mail and social media network, Electronic billboard; Personal health records; Patient web portal; Health information	SMS and phone calls; Internet, E-mail and social media network, Skype; Whatsapp, Microsoft Excel; TherapyEdge	SMS and phone calls; Internet, E-mail and social media network, Skype; Whatsapp; Microsoft Excel
Intervening measures	Initiate ART; Prepare patients for disease progression and side effects of treatment; Manage secondary infections and associated illnesses	e-Health (i.e. EHR and m-Health); Pharmaceutical database record; Hospital information systems,. e-prescription, care plan management, medications management, chronic disease management	SMS, mobile applications; Internet, E-mail and social media network, Personal health records; Patient web portal; Patient monitoring	SMS; TherapyEdge	SMS
Disease management	Manage the effects of associated illnesses, Manage the side effects of ART; Determine additional nutritional needs; Preparing patient for end-of-life management; Primary care and health maintenance	e-Health (i.e. EHR and m-Health); Pharmaceutical database record, chronic disease management, alerts monitoring and management	SMS, mobile applications; Internet, E-mail and social media network; Personal health records; Patient monitoring, Home monitoring and messaging	SMS and phone calls; social media network; Whatsapp; Datafax; SAS data capturing software; TherapyEdge	SMS and phone calls; social media network; Whatsapp
Managing complications	Initiate drug therapies; Manage acute illness; Manage infection; Managing side effects; Provide additional support	National HIV/AIDS database system; E-Health (i.e. EHR and m-Health), Hospital information systems,. Pharmaceutical database record, adverse events monitoring, alerts monitoring and management, medications management	SMS, mobile applications; Internet, E-mail and social media network; Patient monitoring, Home monitoring and messaging, adverse event monitoring	SMS and phone calls; social media network; Whatsapp; TherapyEdge	SMS and phone calls; social media network; Whatsapp

FIGURE 5: A typology for employing information and communication technologies in the HIV/AIDS value chain (Activities adapted from Porter, M.E., 2010, 'Value based global health care delivery', Princeton global health colloquium, 24 September 2010, viewed 23 July 2013, from http://www.isc.hbs.edu/pdf/20100924_Princeton%20GHD.pdf; ICT tools populated from the literature by the author).

Developing and building (2014 to 2016)	Growth (2017 to 2018)	Maturity (2019 onwards)
• *Focus on establishing enabling environment and migration to single platforms nationally*	• *Uptake and up-scaling*	• *Focus on stimulating demand and mainstreaming e-Health*
Coordination • Established policy context and support from Government • Long term government support for investment in and adoption of e-Health • Standardisation and interoperability • Address barriers to adoption such as data protection and privacy (compliance with legislative issues) • Migration of traditional provincial systems to new platforms	• Adoption of standards by health ICT vendors and continued standards development • Provincial ICT plans aligned with national strategy • Incentives for e-Health systems integration in basic service delivery • Infrastructure growth and access	• Infrastructure maturity • Integration of e-Health into core health services • Respond to expectations of citizens for more efficient, effective and personalised services • Leverage emerging health information data sources to support public health planning, management and monitoring • Undertake evaluation and monitoring to ensure that e-Health delivers according to health priorities
Capacity and ICT environment • Infrastructure development planning • e-Health demonstration programmes • Stakeholder engagement in order to drive development of appropriate systems • Development of HR capacity to develop ICT system • Appropriate business models developed in close cooperation with private sector • Advocacy of benefits • Government procurement planning – benefit assessment	• Planning for capacity building and training in audiences and stakeholders • Partnerships leveraged for continued training of workforce • Continues learning through implementation monitoring and continued engagement with wider stakeholder groups • Developed government procurement planning and systems for e-Health solutions	• Policies geared towards stimulating demand and large scale roll-out of e-Health • Government procurement effectively leveraged for establishing vibrant e-Health industry • Private sector participation effectively managed and leveraged through sustainable business models

FIGURE 6: eHealth development roadmap.

Acknowledgements

Competing interests

The authors declare that they have no financial or personal relationship(s) that may have inappropriately influenced them in writing this article.

Author's contributions

The primary research in this article was completed as part of B.D.O.'s (University of Pretoria) master's thesis, as supervised by S.S.G. (University of Pretoria). Both authors contributed to the article conceptually and in the write-up.

References

Akinsola, O.S., Herselman, M.E. & Jacobs, S.J., 2005, 'ICT provision to disadvantaged urban communities: A study in South Africa and Nigeria', *International Journal of Education and Development using Information and Communication Technology (IJEDICT)* 1(3), 19–41.

Aurumo, J., Inkilainen, A. & Kauremaa, J., 2005, 'The role of information technology in supply chain management', viewed 24 March 2013, from http://legacy-tuta.hut.fi/logistics/publications/NOFOMA_2005_IT_in_SCM.pdf

Bollinger, L. & Stover, J., 1999, 'The economic impact of AIDS in South Africa', the POLICY project, Futures Group International, viewed n.d., from http://www.heart-intl.net/HEART/030106/TheEconomicImpact.pdf

Chandani, Y., 2006, 'Inventory management: Distribution, ICS, LMIS', viewed 23 April 2013, from www.who.int/entity/hiv/amds/(2.8)InvMgmtChallengesfinal.ppt

De Tolly, K. & Alexander, H., 2009, 'Innovative use of cellphone technology for HIV/AIDS behaviour change communications: 3 pilot projects', viewed 27 January 27 2015, from http://www.w3.org/2008/10/MW4D_WS/papers/kdetolly.pdf

Department of Health (DOH), 2011, 'Human resources for health South Africa 2030: Draft HR strategy for the health sector 2012/13 – 2016/17: Consultation document V5', viewed 06 June 2013, from http://www.info.gov.za/view/DownloadFileAction?id=152426

DOH, 2012a, 'Development of eHealth strategy for South Africa', report delivered at WHO–ITU meeting National eHealth strategy development: Country experience and next steps, Geneva, Switzerland, 24–26 July 2012.

DOH, 2012b, 'eHealth Strategy South Africa 20122016', viewed 23 October 2013, from http://www.lib.uct.ac.za/governmentpublications/govpub-news/ehealth-strategy-south-africa-2012-2016/

Eba, P.M., 2007, 'Stigma[ta]: Re-exploring HIV-related stigma. AIDS Review 2007', Centre for study of AIDS, University of Pretoria, Pretoria, South Africa.

Foster, R., 2012, 'The development of the South African eHealth Strategy assessed against the recommendations of the WHO / ITU eHealth strategy toolkit', *Journal of the International Society for Telemedicine and eHealth* 1(2), 2013.

Geers, B. & Page, S., 2007, 'ICT for mitigating HIV/AIDS in Southern Africa', report, 2nd edn., Swedish Program for ICT in Developing Regions (SPIDER), Stockholm, Sweden.

Health Charter, 2005, 'CHARTER: The charter of the public and private health sectors of the Republic of South Africa', viewed 06 June 2013, from http://www.capetown.gov.za/en/CityHealth/Documents/Legislation/Health%20Charter%20of%20South%20Africa.pdf

Kaiser Family Foundation, 2012, 'The global HIV/AIDS Epidemic: Fact sheet', viewed 12 March 2013, from http://www.kff.org/hivaids/upload/3030-17.pdf

Knight, R., 2006, 'South Africa 2006: Population and HIV/AIDS', South Africa delegation briefing paper, viewed 18 September 2014, from http://richardknight.homestead.com/files/SouthAfrica2006-PopulationanandHIV-AIDS.pdf

Lawn, J.E. & Kinney M.V., 2009, 'The Lancet: Health in South Africa: An executive summary for The Lancet series', viewed 05 June 2013, from http://download.thelancet.com/flatcontentassets/series/sa/sa_execsum.pdf

Marais, H., 2005, 'Buckling: The impact of AIDS in South Africa 2005', Centre for study of AIDS, University of Pretoria, viewed 18 September 2014, from http://www.sarpn.org/documents/d0001789/

Ntuli, A., Ijumba, P., McCoy, D., Padarath, A. & Berthiaume, L., 2003, 'HIV/AIDS and health sector responses in South Africa. Treatment access and equity: Balancing the act', Regional Network for Equity in Health in Southern Africa (EQUINET) discussion paper number 7, September 2003.

Porter, M.E., 2010, 'Value based global health care delivery', Princeton global health colloquium, 24 September 2010, viewed 23 July 2013, from http://www.isc.hbs.edu/pdf/20100924_Princeton%20GHD.pdf

Rachel, K., 1999, 'Sexual behavioural change for HIV: Where have theories taken us?', UNAIDS, viewed 05 March 2013, from http://www.unaids.org/en/media/unaids/contentassets/dataimport/publications/irc-pub04/jc159-behavchange_en.pdf

Rhatigan, J., Jain, S., Mukherjee, S.J. & Porter, M.E., 2009, 'Applying the care delivery value chain: HIV/AIDS care in resource poor settings', Harvard Business School working paper 09-093, viewed 23 July 2013, from http://www.hbs.edu/faculty/Publication%20Files/09-093.pdf

Scheibe, A., Brown, B. & Bekker, L.G., 2012, 'ICT & HIV prevention: Experiences from a biomedical HIV prevention trial among men who have sex with men (MSM) in Cape Town, South Africa', viewed 12 March 2013, from http://www.digitalcultureandeducation.com/volume-4/thehive_3004_html/

Shisana, O., Rehle, T., Simbayi, L.C., Zuma, K., Jooste, S., Zungu, N., *et al.*, 2014, *South African National HIV prevalence, incidence and behaviour survey, 2012*, HSRC Press, Cape Town, South Africa.

Sikhakhane, B. & Lubbe, S., 2005, 'Preliminaries into problems to access information – the digital divide and rural communities', *South African Journal of Information Management* 7(3), 12 pages.

UNAIDS, 2011, *Global HIV/AIDS response. Epidemic update and health sector progress towards universal access. Progress report*, viewed 12 March 2013, from http://www.unaids.org/en/media/unaids/contentassets/documents/unaidspublication/2011/20111130_ua_report_en.pdf]

UNDP, 2010, *Millennium development goals: Country report 2010*, viewed 12 March 2013, from http://www.za.undp.org/content/dam/south_africa/docs/Reports/The_Report/MDG_October-2013.pdf

Venter, F., 2013, *HIV Treatment in South Africa: The challenges of an increasingly successful antiretroviral programme. South African health review 2012 – 2013*, viewed 10 September 2014, from http://www.hst.org.za/publications/south-african-health-review-2012/13

Weeks, R.V., 2012, 'A technology perspective of healthcare services management', *Acta Commercii 2012*, 173–185.

World Health Organization (WHO), 2012, *National eHealth strategy toolkit*, viewed 10 February 2014, from https://extranet.who.int/iris/restricted/handle/10665/75211

20

Knowledge sharing through social media: Investigating trends and technologies in a global marketing and advertising research company

Authors:
Dina Adamovic[1]
Andrea Potgieter[1]
Martie Mearns[1]

Affiliations:
[1]Department of
Information and Knowledge
Management, University of
Johannesburg, South Africa

Correspondence to:
Andrea Potgieter

Email:
apotgieter@uj.ac.za

Postal address:
PO Box 524, Auckland Park
2006, South Africa

Background: The purpose of this study was to investigate social media technology trends in Nielsen – a global information and measurement company – and to establish how these technologies can help the company to create a knowledge-sharing culture.

Objective: The objective of this study was to investigate trends in knowledge-sharing technologies in Nielsen.

Method: The researchers distributed semi-structured questionnaires to a sample of employees in Nielsen's Television Audience Measurement Department. They also conducted interviews with specific employees in this department to gain a better understanding of employees' attitudes toward, and perceptions of, the use of social media tools for creating a knowledge-sharing culture at Nielsen. The researchers validated the data to see whether it could support the research and used triangulation to create a holistic view of the data they received from the questionnaires.

Results: The findings of the study revealed that respondents had a positive attitude to sharing knowledge with one another through using social media tools. However, some respondents thought that technology, in general, was 'the tree of good and evil'. The survey findings showed that Nielsen did have social media tools. However, not all employees were aware of these tools or were willing to use the tools to share knowledge. This study highlighted the possible advantages of the social media for sharing knowledge and how Nielsen could use the tools more widely.

Conclusion: In order for a knowledge sharing culture to thrive at Nielsen, its employees need to engage more with social media tools in their business practices.

Introduction

Nielsen – a global information and measurement company – provides clients with an understanding of consumer needs that it bases on consumer behaviour. Nielsen delivers critical media and marketing information, analytics and industry expertise about what consumers watch (consumer interaction with television, online and mobile devices) and what consumers locally and globally. In companies like Nielsen, sharing knowledge between employees is vital.

In practice, knowledge sharing is evident when employees share their tacit knowledge with one another. If communal sharing of knowledge is commonplace within a company, a knowledge-sharing culture will manifest and this culture allows employees to exchange valuable information with each another. Social media technologies can assist the process of sharing knowledge in organisations because it allows easy and instant communication. The unique features of social media technologies, which are digital in nature, enable companies like Nielsen to determine the best strategy to increase knowledge sharing with other companies. However, this research aimed to establish the degree to which Nielsen employees have embraced social media technologies in order to share knowledge within the organisation.

Foss, Husted and Michailova (2010) mention several reasons for focusing on sharing knowledge in organisations:

- 'knowledge sharing is designed to transform individual knowledge into organisational knowledge'
- modern organisational culture is synonymous with knowledge sharing processes
- organisations that share knowledge 'may lead to improved innovation capacity, ... and therefore, to sustained competitive advantage'.

Social media is a dynamic field that Nielsen can use to manage its knowledge sharing. '[Social Media] is used as a communication tool where employees within the organisation will be able to engage in knowledge sharing' (Jones, Temperley & Lima 2009).

The researchers conducted this study on a team of employees in the Nielsen Television Audience Measurement Department. They analysed gaps and trends in the organisation in order to evaluate knowledge sharing within Nielsen. They conducted qualitative research to perform an in-depth analysis of what employees' thoughts are about social media tools and sharing knowledge.

Nielsen's attempt to use the social media specifically for sharing knowledge between employees makes sense. Gaffoor and Cloete (2010) support the idea that technology aids knowledge sharing:

> The age of technology where knowledge and information serve as key strategic tools in the organisational context, creates the opportunity for organisations to adopt the role of knowledge-based organisations that thrive on the competence of knowledge workers. (n.p.)

Whilst Nielsen aims to create a knowledge-sharing environment through using social media tools, for its employees to share knowledge optimally it is important for the company to facilitate and cultivate engagement between employees – no matter how. Employees are important assets in an organisation as their intellectual capital (IC) is a resource that is embedded in their actions and capabilities (Longo & Mura 2011). What employees do with their IC is extremely important because 'every employee has a sphere of influence along with their individual knowledge, and this is where a knowledge sharing culture can begin' (Gurteen 1999).

For example, there are company wikis and discussion forums at Nielsen. However, not all employees are aware that these tools exist and, therefore, they do not contribute through these channels. This means that they miss finding solutions to problems and possibly supplying solutions to the problems that other employees have. This level of ignorance about social media tools is a barrier to sharing knowledge and improving business performance.

Nielsen must embrace the use of social media tools in their effort to create a knowledge-sharing culture. However, there also has to be buy-in from all the employees that the company expects to use these tools to share their knowledge:

> In a highly competitive business environment, a firm's ability to develop new products, services and processes better than its competitors depends on how effective knowledge sharing practices are established and spread among employees. (Almahamid, Awwas & McAdams 2010:n.p.)

The crux of a knowledge-sharing culture lies with the employees, who need to interact and communicate with one another in order to share their tacit knowledge. Kang, Chen, Ko and Fang (2010) state that 'driven by a knowledge economy, many organisations have recognised knowledge as a valuable intangible resource that holds the key to competitive advantage'.

This article aimed to highlight social media trends in the effective sharing of knowledge between the employees of the Television Audience Measurement Department of the Nielsen Company.

Research methodology

The purpose of this study was to investigate social media technology trends in the Nielsen Company and to establish how these technologies can help it to create a knowledge-sharing culture. The article will highlight which social media technologies the Nielsen's Television Measurement Department is currently using and will make suggestions about which tools it could incorporate to cultivate a knowledge-sharing culture in the company.

The researchers used evaluative research. Therefore, the research design was empirical, numeric and used textual data. Based on this, one can argue that the researchers drew the results from hybrid data with medium control: 'The preparation of such a design facilitates research to be as efficient as possible yielding maximal information' (Kumar 2008:14).

The choice of a qualitative methodological research design meant that the researchers could increase validity through triangulation. Triangulation increased their chances to control and assess certain threats that could have influenced the results. The research question and the field participants were the reasons for the decision to use triangulation in the research. The researchers used a qualitative design 'to test the conjecture; and when the phenomenon was measured, further qualitative descriptions were developed from the numerical results' (Morse, Niehaus, Wolfe & Wilkins 2006).

Questionnaires are part of qualitative research methods. They allow:

> the correct choice of appropriate methods and theories, the recognition and analysis of different perspectives, the reflections on the research as part of the process of knowledge production; and the variety of approaches and methods. (Flick 2009:n.p.)

Therefore, the researchers used semi-structured questionnaires that included both closed and open-ended questions as the data collection instruments. They included descriptive questions because the aim was to gather in-depth *descriptions* of, and *perceptions* about, social media tools as useful media for creating a knowledge-sharing culture at Nielsen.

The researchers completed the data analysis process, through which they derived the research findings, after collecting the completed questionnaires. They gathered additional data and insight on certain topics as engagement with groups of employees emerged whilst they were completing the questionnaires.

The Nielsen Television Audience Measurement Department consists of approximately 50 people. The researchers received 32 completed questionnaires from the 40 that they handed out. The 32 completed questionnaires were sufficient to represent the entire department as the researchers calculated the response rate (n) as 80%.

The sampling method that the researchers used in this study was purposive sampling. This enabled the researchers to:

- investigate which social media technologies Nielsen's Television Audience Measurement Department was using at the time of the study
- identify other forms of knowledge sharing that Nielsen was practising
- determine which social media technologies Nielsen was using to facilitate knowledge sharing.

The purposive sampling method allowed the researchers to answer the research problem, which was to establish the extent of the use of social media technologies to enable or improve knowledge sharing in Nielsen.

Research results

The researchers conducted statistical and descriptive analyses because they kept their data analysis techniques in mind before developing the questionnaires. It is for these reasons that they asked closed as well as open-ended questions throughout the questionnaire.

A discussion of the results will follow the answers the respondents gave to the questions in the questionnaire that follow:

- What types of Social Media tools were used by Nielsen?
- What medium of communication did employees prefer (whether it is face-to-face or electronic communication)?
- Whether employees were willing to share their knowledge with others.
- What employees preferred as communication medium when they had a problem or question that needed to be answered.
- Did colleagues help one another in problem solving?
- Whether the employees within Nielsen believed that Social Media could create a knowledge-sharing culture.

The types of social media tools Nielsen employees used

Figure 1 presents the social media tools that Nielsen employees used. Skype was by far the most common tool they used. Employees used Skype to communicate with employees at the South African branch, where the researchers conducted the study, as well as to communicate with employees who worked in international branches. It was clear that Nielsen regarded Skype as an important business tool because Nielsen used it for different purposes, including daily interaction with international colleagues.

Managers used Skype for international conference calls. It allowed them to communicate with employees around the

world on a daily basis. This was a textbook example of the 'new' way of doing business: 'Blogs, microblogs (e.g. Twitter) and instant messaging tools (e.g. Skype) have provided new communication tools to interact more effectively with others in opened communities' (Razmerita, Kirchner & Sudzina 2009).

Communicating regularly is crucial for Nielsen, as it is for many other companies, because Nielsen deals with many data that need to be up-to-date and available on demand. Employees also used 'Office Communicator' every day because it is an easy tool for employees to use to communicate and collaborate with each another, especially if they work in different departments or in other globally positioned locations. Office Communicator is similar to Skype because it allows people to chat using instant messaging (IM), make personal computer (PC)-to-PC phone and video calls, share files and manage information other colleagues can see.

The interesting aspect of Figure 1 is that Nielsen had many of the common social media tools, like blogs, wikis and collaboration sites. However, employees were not using these tools to their maximum capability and potential. For example, if Nielsen connected and grouped their blogs to their international branches, they could create a knowledge-sharing culture between employees and managers. This would reduce the re-creation of knowledge and employees could record valuable information for current and future use. Respondents stated that they either did not know that the social media tools existed at Nielsen or that they knew about the social media tools but they did not see them as tools that would help them in their day-to-day activities.

Other ways of sharing information or knowledge that the researchers identified through the survey were email, the Nielsen intranet (local area network), face-to-face meetings or discussions, telephone conversations, training, communication boards and 'Windows Live Messenger'. Ninety per cent of the respondents indicated that email was their preferred method of sharing knowledge, other than the social media tools.

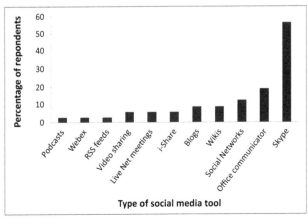

Source: Authors' own data

FIGURE 1: Social media tools that Nielsen employees used.

These results emphasise that technology plays a major role in the communication processes that occur daily at Nielsen. It is clear that Nielsen employees use technology every day and that a concerted effort to encourage the optimal use of social media tools could benefit the company even more.

The preferred modes of communication

Figure 2 shows whether employees preferred electronic or face-to-face communication. Most respondents (66%) preferred electronic communication to face-to-face communication because they said that electronic communication was faster, more convenient and employees could store the information for use at a later stage. Skype is one example of a social media tool that can store information after conversations. Employees can also have live meetings or conference calls and are able to see each other with the use of webcams.

Through Skype, employees can talk 'face-to-face' with international colleagues and they can use usual chat – where employees type conversations in an IM way – if they desire. Employees can view the information that contacts shared via Skype over a period of three months and they can record this information for future use if they need to.

The reasons that employees preferred electronic communication to face-to-face communication were:

- that Nielsen is a global company and face-to-face communication is not always possible
- electronic communication makes it easier and faster to communicate with international employees and to get the information that employees need faster
- employees can record electronic communication for future use and can keep information that they have sent
- electronic communication allows geographically dispersed groups to communicate interactively and simultaneously through text, sound and video
- conference calls are cost-effective
- electronic tools are easy to use and communication is transferred and received no matter where the person may be
- electronic communication is more convenient.

The positive attitude about electronic communication is also evident in these direct quotes from the questionnaires:

- 'It lets you combine numerous texts into a single message.'
- 'I can do so in my office with other reports and processes running.'
- 'You get to see the people you are communicating with and it is easier.'
- 'I can save what has been discussed or shared'.

With regard to face-to-face communication, 31% of the respondents stated that it is easier to grasp or understand something when communicating with the person *in* person. They saw electronic communication as impersonal and 'it can easily be misunderstood'. This is true because people do not get to see the emotions and reactions of others when they communicate using electronic tools and they may not

resolve issues that may arise because misunderstandings could occur.

Although only 31% of the respondents regarded face-face communication as important, it remains an important means of communication because employees are able to walk to another's office in seconds to find a solution to their problems. However, when this type of close contact is not possible, it is crucial for employees to acknowledge the advantages of technology for quick interaction and that they can use it wherever possible because it is easier to record this communication and the resulting information and knowledge if they do so in an electronic format.

Electronic communication is revolutionising business communication. Organisations can transform passive employees into active participants because they can contribute to content, add or change content and share content. Wasko and Faraj (2005) state, 'In electronic networks, individuals contribute knowledge and help others despite the lack of a personal, face-to-face relationship'. Nielsen provides these communication tools. However, the problem is that employees resist using these tools or are unaware that the tools are available.

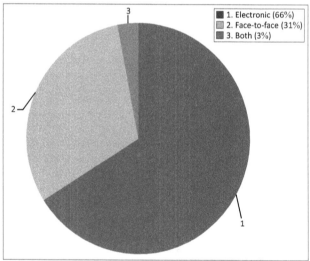

Source: Authors' own data

FIGURE 2: Preferred mode of communication.

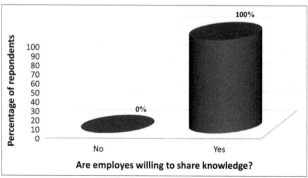

Source: Authors' own data

FIGURE 3: Employees' willingness to share knowledge.

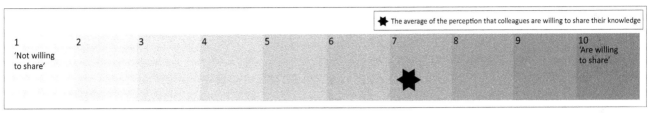

Source: Authors' own data

FIGURE 4: To what extent are your colleagues willing to share their knowledge?

The willingness of employees to share their knowledge

Nielsen managers do not have a problem with employees who do not want to share their knowledge because 100% of respondents stated that they were willing to share their knowledge with colleagues. Therefore, the problem is not that Nielsen employees are unwilling to share their knowledge. Instead, they are just not aware of the electronic tools available to them or they are unconvinced that these tools could help them to share their knowledge effectively. Figure 3 shows whether employees were willing to share their knowledge or if knowledge sharing was absent at Nielsen. All respondents stated that they were willing to share their knowledge and that they observed the same from their colleagues.

Employees at Nielsen are willing to share their organisational knowledge because their culture is open and vibrant and employees believe in helping one another. The researchers observed the employees in the Television Audience Measurement Department throughout the day of the interviews and employees needed to confirm certain processes from time to time. When these needs arose, employees would walk to a manager's office and resolve whatever was causing them uncertainty.

Managers were always willing to help and the environment was friendly. This encouraged employees to communicate with one another as well as with their managers. The department was organised so that two to three employees worked in a spacious cubicle where they were close to each another. This made it easier to communicate and assist one another.

The Television and Audience Measurement Department offices had an arrangement so that employees could walk to another's office or cubicle if they had a problem. Sometimes this was not possible. An example is if the person they needed to answer a question was out of the office. In these cases, the employees who wanted to ask the question would use email or Skype to contact the other person.

The researchers posed the question that follows to the respondents: 'In your experience, to what extent are colleagues willing to freely share their knowledge and information with others?'. The researcher recorded the responses using a Likert scale where 1 denoted 'not willing to share' and 10 denoted 'are willing to share'.

The results averaged 7 on the Likert scale. This showed that not all employees were willing to share their knowledge, but that most employees were willing to share their knowledge and experiences with other people (see Figure 4).

Preferred modes of communication when asking questions

One should note that only 31 of the 32 respondents answered this particular question. Figure 5 below gives the statistics of the medium of communication employees preferred to use when they had a problem or question to which they needed an answer.

Respondents preferred walking to another's office when they had a question or problem, with 45% of the respondents indicating this as the preferred method of communication in such a case. The second most preferred method of communication when posing a question was a blog, wiki or Skype, as 32% of the respondents preferred this medium. The researchers established that employees regarded blogs, wikis or Skype as the most time conserving options because they could post the question and continue to work whilst waiting for a reply. 'The question can be addressed in real time, but without having to walk to the person's office'.

The 23% of respondents who preferred to email their questions did so because the information they received from the email would be in writing as 'proof' in case future disputes arose.

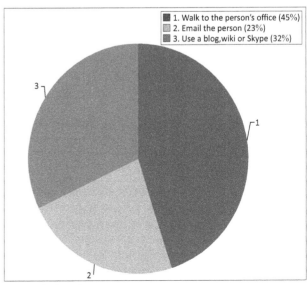

Source: Authors' own data

FIGURE 5: Employees' preferred medium when they have a question or problem.

Other reasons for preferring email, as an option, was that it was fast and saved time.

The willingness of colleagues to help each another to solve problems

Figure 6 below illustrates that colleagues were indeed willing to assist each another to solve problems, with 72% of respondents indicating that colleagues do help each another. None of the respondents indicated that they were *not* willing to assist colleagues to solve problems. The 28% of respondents who indicated that they are only 'sometimes' willing to help colleagues stated that this was because they did not have answers and had to refer colleagues to someone else for help.

It was clear that Nielsen's employees were open to communication and willing to assist each another wherever they could. This is extremely important for establishing a knowledge-sharing culture because 'most researchers and practitioners agree that a major part of knowledge in an organisation is in tacit form' (Suppiah & Sandhu 2011). Knowledge resides in the minds of employees and they can only share it in writing or through face-to-face or electronic interaction. From engaged discussions, the researchers established that most Nielsen employees were open with one another about their tacit knowledge and that they would assist others wherever possible.

Employee perceptions of the contribution of the social media towards building a knowledge-sharing culture

In its conclusion, the questionnaire asked respondents whether they thought that creating a knowledge-sharing culture, by using social media tools, would benefit Nielsen. Figure 7 gives the results.

Most respondents (94%) answered 'yes' to this question. This confirms that most employees thought that incorporating social media tools would improve Nielsen's knowledge-sharing culture. Therefore, its managers should encourage and participate in social media technologies because it is clear that there will be buy-in from employees. One expects this positive response towards the social media because, according to Dawson (2009):

> [Social Media] is deeply changing the expectations of knowledge workers as to how they can build their own personal brand within a corporation, not just find knowledge they need or socialize. (n.p.)

The 6% of the respondents who answered 'no' to this question were the employees who do not agree that the social media would help to create a knowledge-sharing culture because they still believe that face-to-face communication is the most effective mode of communication and that technology should not change the 'old ways' that worked well. The organisation could persuade those who do not agree that technology could encourage sharing knowledge at least to try

these technologies for themselves if the managers provided incentives to the people who contribute through social media tools.

Conclusion

This article investigated social media technology trends within the Nielsen Company and established how these technologies could help the company create a knowledge-sharing culture.

The study established that the Nielsen Company has incorporated specific social media tools and technologies. However, employees do not necessarily use them optimally. Nielsen does have elements of a knowledge-sharing culture because employees are willing to share their knowledge with others by using various modes of communication. Therefore, there is knowledge sharing at Nielsen and social media tools are available to employees, but Nielsen has not yet fully realised the potential for sharing knowledge using social media tools. In order to fill this gap, integrating social media tools into the daily work processes and tasks of employees will help to solve the problem because employees will collaborate and communicate by regularly using these tools. This will lead to the habitual sharing of knowledge through social media tools.

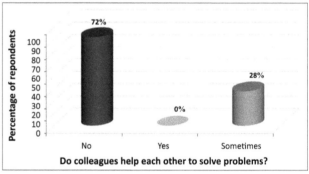

Source: Authors' own data

FIGURE 6: Colleagues who help each another to solve problems.

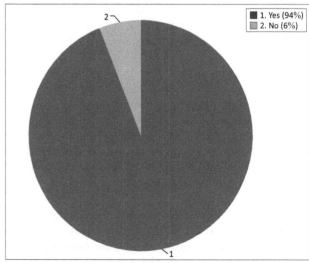

Source: Authors' own data

FIGURE 7: Perceived possibility of whether the social media can create a knowledge-sharing culture.

This study focused on only one department at Nielsen. Therefore, the researchers do not know whether the willingness to share knowledge prevails throughout the organisation. It is an area for further research.

Further investigation into the most effective social media tools that Nielsen could use in the rest of the organisation is possible. Researchers could compare the data from follow-up studies with the data from this study and they could draw further conclusions and make suggestions. Such research could help other organisations who are hoping to establish knowledge-sharing cultures through using social media tools: 'From a managerial perspective, it is timely for research on knowledge sharing to pay more attention to the link between knowledge sharing and organisational performance' (Foss, Husted & Michailova 2010).

Sharing knowledge is a crucial business objective. Therefore, it is important for Nielsen to tap into the intellectual capital of its employees to create competitive advantage through creativity and unique ideas.

International research concludes that companies that have embraced the social media continue to report that they are receiving measurable business benefits. Ninety per cent of these companies report at least one benefit to their business. 'These benefits ranged from more effective marketing to faster access to knowledge' (Bughin & Chui 2011).

Acknowledgements

Competing interests

The authors declare that they have no financial or personal relationship(s) that may have inappropriately influenced them when they wrote this paper.

Authors' contributions

D.A. (University of Johannesburg) completed this research as part of the Information Management Honours degree module of 'Research Methodology'. M.M. (University of Johannesburg) was the Research Methodology lecturer and provided guidance for the research design and execution of the empirical process. A.P. (University of Johannesburg) compiled the final article for this publication.

References

Almahamid, S., Awwad, A. & McAdams, A.C., 2010, 'Effects of Organisational Agility and Knowledge Sharing on Competitive Advantage: An Empirical Study in Jordan', International Journal of Management 27(3), 387–388.

Bughin, J. & Chui, M., 2011, 'McKinsey on business technology: the rise of the networked enterprise; Web 2.0 finds its payday', McKinsey quarterly, Spring 2011, viewed 06 September 2011, from www.mckinseyquarterly.com

Dawson, R., 2009, Implementing Enterprise 2.0: A practical guide to creating business value inside organisations with web technologies, Advanced Human Technologies, London.

Flick, U., 2009, An introduction to qualitative research, SAGE Publications, London.

Foss, N.J., Husted, K. & Michailova, S., 2010, 'Governing knowledge sharing in organizations: levels of analysis, governance mechanisms and research directions', Journal of Management Studies 47(3), 455–482. http://dx.doi.org/10.1111/j.1467-6486.2009.00870.x

Gaffoor, S. & Cloete, F., 2010, 'Knowledge Management in local Government: the case of Stellenbosch Municipality', South African Journal of Information Management 12(1), 1–2.

Gurteen, D., 1999, 'Creating a Knowledge Sharing Culture', Knowledge Management Magazine 2(5), 1–2.

Herrick, A., 2011, Insights 2012: How Digital Innovation Impacts Your Business, viewed 06 September 2011, from http://www.sapient.com/assets/Imagedownloader/1061/Insights2012.pdf

Jones, B., Temperley, J. & Lima, A., 2009, 'Corporate reputation in the era of Web 2.0: the case of Primark', Journal of Marketing Management 25(9), 936. http://dx.doi.org/10.1362/026725709X479309

Kang, Y.C., Chen, G.L., Ko, C.T. & Fang, C.H., 2010, 'The exploratory study of online Knowledge Sharing by applying wiki collaboration system', Scientific Research 2(1), 243–244.

Kumar, R., 2008, Research Methodology, APH Publishing Corporation, New Delhi.

Longo, M. & Mura, M., 2011, 'The effect of intellectual capital on employees satisfaction and retention', Information & Management 48(2011), 278–287. http://dx.doi.org/10.1016/j.im.2011.06.005

Morse, J.M., Niehaus, L., Wolfe, R.L. & Wilkins, S., 2006, 'The role of the theoretical drive in maintaining validity in mixed-method research', Qualitative Research in Psychology, 3(4), 290–291.

Punch, K.F., 2005, Introduction to social research: qualitative and quantitative approaches, SAGE Publication, London.

Razmerita, L., Kirchner, K. & Sudzina, R., 2009, 'The role of Web 2.0 tools for managing knowledge at individual and organisational levels', Online Information Review 33(6), 1022–1023. http://dx.doi.org/10.1108/14684520911010981

Suppiah, V. & Sandhu, M.S., 2011, 'Organisational cultures influence on tacit knowledge – sharing behaviour', Journal of Knowledge Management 15(3), 464.

Wasko, M.M. & Faraj, S., 2005, 'Why should I share?', MIS Quarterly 29(1), 35–57.

21

Knowledge-creation in student software-development teams

Author:
Mzwandile M. Shongwe[1]

Affiliation:
[1]Department of Information Studies, University of Zululand, South Africa

Correspondence to:
Mzwandile Shongwe

Email:
shongwem@unizulu.ac.za

Postal address:
Private Bag X1001,
Kwadlangezwa 3886,
South Africa

Background: Knowledge-creation is a field of study that has gained popularity in recent times. Knowledge-creation is the creation of new ideas or new innovations. In computing, software-development is regarded as knowledge-creation. This is because software-development involves the creation of a new innovation (software). Knowledge-creation studies in this field tend to focus mainly on knowledge-creation activities in business organisations. They use experienced, professional software-development teams as subjects, largely ignoring novice student development teams. This has denied the field of computing valuable knowledge about how novice teams create knowledge.

Objectives: The study addressed this gap in the literature by investigating knowledge-creation in student software teams.

Method: An ethnographic study was conducted on six student teams developing software in a management-information systems (MIS) course. They were conducting a systems-development project at a university during a term of study. Data were collected over a period of four months through participant observation and interviews.

Results: The results reveal knowledge-creation activities such as problem definition, brainstorming, programming and system documentation. Students use the Internet, books, class notes, class presentations, senior students and professional software developers as sources of information. Mobile phones and BlackBerry devices facilitate knowledge-creation. Challenges to knowledge-creation are the lack of material and financial resources, a lack of technical skills, a lack of time, students staying off-campus and ambivalent team members.

Conclusion: The conclusion drawn from this study is that student teams are capable of creating knowledge (a working system) just like professional teams, but the knowledge-creation process is slightly different.

Introduction

Knowledge-creation is a field of study that has gained popularity in recent times (Mitchell & Boyle 2010). Knowledge-creation is the creation of new ideas or new innovations, for example, a new product, service or process. In computing, software-development is regarded as knowledge-creation (Bailin 1997). Software-development is a process of expressing someone's intensions of how a machine should work (Bailin 1997). Bailin further states that knowledge is generated by building, operating and maintaining the system during the software-development process. This knowledge includes lessons learned during the development of the system, experience gained over time when using the system and broader knowledge acquired over time by the development and customer organisations. Dorairaj, Noble and Malik (2012:1) give a knowledge-management perspective of software-development as '... a series of knowledge-intensive activities that encompasses gathering requirements, analysing problems, designing, coding, testing, and ensuring the software remains up-to-date and bug-free'. Software-development is regarded as knowledge-creation because it is an innovative process which leads to the generation of new ideas and the creation of new software products.

Studies have been conducted in the field of computing to investigate the phenomenon of knowledge-creation. For example, Linden and Cybulski (2009), Wan *et al.* (2010) and Arent and Norbjerg (2000) to name but a few investigated knowledge-creation processes in pattern mining, requirement-elicitation process (REP) and software-process improvement (SPI) respectively. The conclusion of these studies was that all these activities are knowledge-creation activities. The problem with these studies is that they tend to focus mainly on knowledge-creation in business organisations. They also tend to use experienced, professional software-development teams as subjects, largely ignoring public institutions such as higher education institutions and thus ignoring the development teams amongst novice students. This has denied the field of computing valuable knowledge about how novice teams create knowledge. In fact, these novices are future developers, and yet, they are largely ignored by researchers. For example, we do not know what the knowledge-creation activities in software-development teams amongst students entail. What channels of communication facilitate knowledge-creation in student teams? What information sources do students use to create knowledge? And what challenges do student teams face when they create knowledge? A lot has been written about professional, experienced teams. For example, we know what the knowledge-creation activities in professional teams entail (Poh & Erwee 2004). We also know that professional teams use technology and networks of peers (communities of practice) to facilitate knowledge-creation and transfer (Alavi & Leidner 2001; Kimmerle, Cress & Held 2010; Wasko & Faraj 2000; Wenger 1998). We are also aware that rising costs, limited time to complete projects and abandoned projects are some of the challenges concerning knowledge-creation faced by professional development teams (Heeks 2002; Lindvall, Rus & Sinha 2002; Lyytinen & Robey 1999). However, we do not know what is happening in student teams. The study set out to answer these questions in the context of software-development as knowledge-creation.

This article is structured as follows: The following section presents the theoretical foundations on knowledge-creation. That is followed by the methodology and then the results and discussions. Lastly, I present conclusions and recommendations for further research.

Theoretical foundations

This section will briefly highlight the theoretical foundations of knowledge-creation. Firstly, I shall discuss the distinction between data, information and knowledge, and then I shall discuss knowledge-creation.

Data, information and knowledge

The concepts of knowledge, data and information may seem similar, but their meaning may not be uniformly understood. Data is unprocessed information (Hey 2004). It could be bits and numbers with no meaning (Rumizen 2002). Information is data that has been processed for a useful purpose and can be used for decision-making. Chaffey and Wood (2005) describe information as data with value to the understanding of a subject and in a context. Knowledge is '… information possessed in the mind of individuals: it is personal information related to facts, procedures, concepts, interpretations, ideas, observation and judgment' (Alavi & Leidner 2001:109). Knowledge could take several perspectives or forms: a state of mind, an object, a process, a condition of having access to information or a capability (Alavi & Leidner 2001). In software-development, knowledge could be seen from the perspective of either the process or the object. The object is the output or end-product (the software). The process

perspective entails the software-development process, for example, generating new ideas, refining them and applying them in the development process. Knowledge could be tacit or explicit (Nonaka & Takeuchi 1995; Polanyi 1962). Tacit knowledge is what the knower knows, knowledge that is derived from experience and that embodies beliefs and values (Nonaka & Takeuchi 1995). It is personal and difficult to formalise, making it difficult to communicate and share with others (Elfving & Funk 2006; Gladstone 2000; Li & Gao 2003). Explicit knowledge is knowledge that has been articulated and, more often than not, captured in the form of text, tables, diagrams and product specifications (Nickols 2000). In software-development, tacit knowledge resides in the developer's mind. It is the hidden knowledge in the form of the experiences of the developer. Explicit knowledge is the end product (the system) and the documentation.

Knowledge-creation

Knowledge-creation is a series of processes and activities that add value to produce an outcome or output such as a product, service or process (Mitchell & Boyle 2010). Holsapple and Singh (2001:84) define knowledge-creation as '… an activity that produces knowledge by discovering it or deriving it from existing knowledge'. It is the coming into existence of new knowledge (Phan & Peridis 2000). It involves the definition of a problem and makes use of complex and discontinuous events to solve the problem (Parent et al. 2000; Styhre, Roth & Ingelgard 2002). Knowledge-creation involves the monitoring, production and transfer of knowledge resources within and outside of the organisation (Holsapple & Singh 2001). When defined as a process, knowledge-creation refers to the generation of new ideas that reflect a significant enrichment of existing knowledge. It is defined as an outcome or output when activities and initiatives are undertaken to generate new ideas or objects. It means that new knowledge is diffused, adopted and embedded as new products, services and systems (Mitchell & Boyle 2010). Knowledge-creation takes place at individual, group, organisational and inter-organisational levels (Nonaka & Takeuchi 1995). It is widely agreed that knowledge-creation takes place first at individual level and then amplified at group, organisational and inter-organisational levels (Nonaka & Takeuchi 1995). In fact, it is believed that organisations only offer a space or context in which the knowledge created by individuals is amplified and applied in organisational routines and processes. The organisation could be what Nonaka, Toyama and Konno (1998) refer to as 'ba' – a shared context where knowledge is created.

Knowledge-creation activities

According to Nonaka and Takeuchi (1995), knowledge is created in five steps: sharing tacit knowledge, creating concepts, justifying concepts, building a prototype and cross-levelling knowledge. At the sharing stage of tacit knowledge, individuals share emotions, feelings and mental models through face-to-face interactions. Creating concepts involves the sharing of both tacit and explicit knowledge. After sharing tacit knowledge, organisational members then articulate the tacit knowledge into explicit knowledge through written concepts. Justifying concepts is a phase whereby created concepts are determined whether they are useful or not in the organisation. The justified concepts are then converted into a tangible or concrete product or model called an archetype. After knowledge has been created, it is levelled across the organisation. This could be inter-organisational or intra-organisational (Nonaka 1994; Nonaka & Takeuchi 1995). This notion is also shared by Wan *et al.* (2010). Examples of knowledge-creation activities in software-development are the following: constructing a software routine, brainstorming, discovering a pattern, solving a problem or achieving a creative insight (Holsapple & Singh 2001).

Knowledge-creation theories

A number of theories are used to study knowledge-creation in organisations. Widely used theories include, amongst others, the organisational learning theory (Argyris & Schon 1978), the learning-organisation (Senge *et al.* 1994) , the theory of organisational knowledge-creation or SECI (Nonaka & Takeuchi 1995), the knowledge-integration theory (Grant 1996) and the communities of practice theory (Wenger 1998). Argyris and Schon's organisational learning theory explains how knowledge is created by the learning of individuals and groups in organisations which facilitate learning at organisational level. Senge's learning-organisation theory defines the principles of a learning organisation. These principles are personal mastery, systems thinking, team learning, mental models and building a shared vision. These principles are believed to facilitate learning in departments and sections of the organisation, which leads to the whole organisation learning and becoming a learning organisation. Nonaka and Takeuchi's theory of organisational knowledge-creation explains how individuals, teams and entire organisations create knowledge by the conversion of tacit and explicit knowledge through four processes: socialisation, externalisation, combination and internalisation. Grant (1996) focuses on knowledge-integration and innovation within a firm. Grant explores the coordinating mechanisms of how individuals in a firm integrate knowledge to foster innovation. Wenger's theory explains how small, informal teams in organisations share and create knowledge from each other through social interactions. Lee and Cole's (2003) community-based model of knowledge-creation explain how knowledge is created by a software community of practice operating outside of formal organisational boundaries.

These theories focus mainly on how knowledge is created in organisations (except Lee and Cole's [2003] model). They explain that knowledge is created, firstly, at individual level and at group level before it becomes organisational knowledge. They also present different scenarios under which knowledge is created. The main limitation of these theories and knowledge-creation literature in general is that the focus is mostly on knowledge-creation by professionals in business organisations. Little has been done to investigate amateur, student teams despite the fact that they are the

future innovators. The current study tries to fill this gap in the literature by focusing on students' knowledge-creation activities.

Knowledge-creation in software-development

Software-development is regarded as knowledge-creation (Bailin 1997). It is a knowledge-intensive task, which involves a process of discovery and invention, accumulation, analysis, cognition and integration (Bailin 1997; Dingsoyr 2002; Mitchell & Nicholas 2006). This means that software-development processes (systems analysis, coding, documentation, testing, etc.) are knowledge-creation processes. During these activities, individuals and teams acquire knowledge from different sources; apply their previously acquired knowledge; store acquired knowledge in databases, routines, and procedures and share their knowledge with others to produce a knowledge output (the software product).

A number of studies have been conducted to investigate the knowledge-creation phenomenon in computing. A few examples can suffice. Arent and Norbjerg (2000) investigated software-process improvement (SPI) and concluded that they are knowledge-creation activities. Kess and Haapasalo (2002) investigated knowledge-creation through a software-project review process, and they constructed a tool to improve the software-development process. Klint and Verhoef (2002) investigated how the principles of knowledge-management could be applied in knowledge-creation. Linden and Cybulski (2009) investigated knowledge-creation in pattern mining. This led to the enrichment of the knowledge-creation framework proposed by Wickramasinghe and Lichtenstein. Morner and Von Krogh (2009) explored the conditions under which successful knowledge-creation takes place. They proposed three conditions (perceptibility, systemic memory and modularity) under which the knowledge-creation process could be stabilised. Wan *et al.* (2010) investigated knowledge-creation in requirement-elicitation process (REP) and concluded that it is a knowledge-creation process. Neves *et al.* (2011) conducted a systematic review of knowledge-creation in agile software-development teams and found two knowledge-creation activities, comprehensive software documentation and responding to change as knowledge-creation activities. Spohrer *et al.* (2013) also investigated knowledge-creation activities in peer programming teams working on information-systems development in a large software organisation. They found that knowledge is created by exchanging opinions, solutions, and code, and developers who are observing their peers thus learn from their actions. They found that knowledge is created at individual and team level. If we look at the literature, we can conclude that student teams in software-development are rarely studied. In the list of studies mentioned above, none have used students as subjects, hence the importance of this study.

Methodology

An interpretive, qualitative study was conducted on student software-development teams. Interpretive studies assume that people create their own subjective meanings as they interact with the world around them (Lee 1991; Olikowski & Baroudi 1991). Ethnography was chosen as a research method. Myers (1999) defines ethnography as a study where the researchers immerse themselves in the lives of the people being studied. Ethnographers aim to place the phenomena being studied in the social and cultural context of the people studied. Myers (1999) further states that the ethnographer has to spend a considerable amount of time in the field and to collect data not only through interviews and documents but also through participant observation. In this study, a class of six software-development project teams (24 students) was studied. The groups were supposed to develop an e-commerce interactive website for a client. The researcher joined the class at the beginning of the semester before the project started. He was briefed about the project just like the students and given all necessary documentation. He attended all lectures, presentations and meetings that the teams had. These activities took place in the students' computer laboratory, lecture halls and the library. The aim was to be part of the teams as if the researcher was one of them. Lectures were held once a week for the whole semester. Presentations were held based on need such as when there was a milestone deliverable (e.g. project plan). The teams also had meetings almost daily to discuss and develop the system. During these activities (lectures, presentations and team meetings), the researcher observed and interviewed teams. During observation, detailed notes were taken on how the students developed the system. The researcher observed how, where and what ideas team members shared and the impact of these ideas on the completion of the project. Group interviews were conducted to supplement observation data. They were used to seek further clarification on certain development processes such as the information sources and communication channels used by teams in their projects. The study was conducted for the whole semester, which was four months long. Qualitative content analysis was then used to analyse the responses. Qualitative content analysis is a method for the subjective interpretation of text data through coding and themes or category identification (Hsieh & Shannon 2005). In this study, data were coded and classified into categories. Ethnography has been used before by Suchman (1995) and Myers and Young (1997), amongst others, to study information-systems development.

Results and discussions

This section responds to the research questions posed in the study.

Knowledge-creation activities

This section answers the following question: What knowledge-creation activities do student teams undertake? The results reveal a number of activities which are undertaken at individual and team level.

Individual knowledge-creation activities

The results indicate that individual team members performed a number of activities during the knowledge-creation process. Major individual activities were coding, documentation, preparing slides for presentations, designing the user interface, research and information gathering, sourcing finance and other relevant activities assigned to the individual. One respondent stated: 'I was mainly the website designer, but I also did documentation such as project plan, feasibility study and other activities'. Another reported that '... as an individual, I created forms in the prototype'. Others reported on other minor activities that they did such as writing minutes and arranging future meetings. The importance of individual knowledge activities was emphasised by all group members. One member stated:

> 'The contribution of each member was great. For every task we had to break it down to individual activities. In so doing we shared ideas which enabled us to finish the project quicker'.

These results are consistent with the knowledge-creation literature which highlights the importance of the individual in knowledge-creation, for example Grant (1996). Simon (as cited in Grant 1996:112) shares the same sentiments. Nonaka and Takeuchi (1995) present an excellent account of how individuals create knowledge which is then infused into the whole organisation. In this particular case, individuals used their creative abilities to build the different parts of the system. They used their own existing and newly acquired knowledge to carry out the tasks at hand. These individual activities contributed immensely to the completion of the project. The completed individual tasks would then be taken to the next level of discussion and further refinement. That was at the team level. The team's knowledge-creation activities are discussed in the following section.

Knowledge-creation activities of the team

The tasks given to individuals were then consolidated and adopted at group level. Each individual would bring their tasks to the team for further discussions. The team would reject or adopt the task as team knowledge. Tasks such as coding, preparing documentation and presentations and others were discussed at team level. In fact, all individual tasks were further discussed by the teams before they were accepted to be project knowledge. One such important task that was discussed at team level was problem definition, that is, what the project entailed. At first, students had no idea about what to do. One student lamented: 'I had no idea what I was supposed to do'. These sentiments were echoed by other students who reported that, '... we did not have a clue on what to do'. The teams then converged, discussed the problem and sought assistance from the lecturer and senior students. That was when they understood what they were supposed to do. They reported: 'It was after we met as groups that we shared ideas and came to understand what we had to do'. Morne and von Krogh (2009) also state that, in knowledge-creation, the first step usually lies in a single software problem with which a programmer is confronted. Nonaka and Takeuchi (1995) refer to such a state as intentional creative chaos. According to Nonaka and Takeuchi (1995), 'intentional creative chaos' is a situation whereby management creates a sense of crisis in the organisation by proposing challenging goals. Organisational members respond by defining the problem and finding solutions to the problem. In student teams, the lecturer evokes a crisis by giving students a huge real-life problem, which they have never come across before and which they have to deliver to a real customer within a short space of time. It is after they have met as a team that they properly defined the problem, understood it and planned how to solve it.

Knowledge-creation in teams is also emphasised by a number of knowledge-creation theories. These theories (Hedlund 1994; Nonaka & Takeuchi 1995; Senge *et al.* 1994; Wenger 1998) agree that teams play a crucial part in knowledge-creation. It is at team level where rough ideas are refined and developed into knowledge.

Information sources for knowledge-creation

A number of information sources were used by student teams during the knowledge-creation process. Information sources such as class presentations, the lecturer and lecture notes, text books, the Internet and external sources (senior students and professional software developers) were used.

Class presentations were a good source of information. After a major milestone, for example system analysis, budgeting, prototyping and documentation, the group would present the deliverable to the whole class and lecturer. Other teams and the lecturer would then interrogate the presenting group by asking questions and commenting about the deliverable. Presenters were criticised, praised and advised on how to do the project better. One student stated that '... presentations helped us to know what we did right, where to correct and how to improve the project'. Another one concurred that '... presentations helped us to get clarity as to what is really required from us'. All the groups agreed that the presentations helped them to gain new knowledge about the project in one way or the other. Teams stated that they gained knowledge from the presentations from other teams. They learned communication and presentation skills and to work under pressure. It boosted their morale when they realised that they were making progress. On an individual note, team members indicated that class presentations helped them to gain knowledge from others.

The lecturer also played a crucial role in the knowledge-creation process. Apart from giving them the problem to solve, the lecturer was also involved in helping the teams solve the problem. Apart from teaching, the lecturer played the role of advisor and mentor. At times, classes would be conducted to teach students how to carry out certain activities of the project. Before the start of each major deliverable (e.g. systems analysis), the lecturer would conduct a lecture on the next activity. This helped students understand what was required of them and how to tackle the problem at hand. The lecturer also played a crucial role during the presentations. He would criticise the students' work, offer advice on how the work should be done and give credit to teams that did well. Students would also consult the lecturer for advice whenever they had problems with their projects. This was

confirmed by a respondent who stated that '... the lecturer gave us motivation to finish the project'. Another one concurred that '... the lecturer helped by explaining what [*was*] expected'. Another one stated that '... the lecturer made us to attend classes, and provided us with technical skills'. Not all students were happy with the lecturer's role though. Some indicated that the lecturer did not play any role in their knowledge-creation process. They stated: 'The lecturer did not play any role in the successful completion of the project. We struggled while he was present'. Others stated that '... the lecturer had little impact on the project'.

Students also regularly used the Internet for information. The teams indicated that they used the Internet to research how to do the activities of the project, for example, how to budget and how to do systems analysis. They also looked for technical information such as coding. They could surf the Internet to look at how to solve a specific technical problem. One team indicated that they used the Internet to find help on how to set-up the Apache, MySQL, PHP for Windows (WAMP) interface. The w3schools website is said to have provided much support to the teams. They also relied on books, senior students and professionals to complete their projects. Because this was an MIS group, most teams relied on senior students in computer science for technical support such as linking the database to the website and other coding activities. Surprisingly, they also sought help from other competing groups. One group stated that '... we sought help from other groups to do some of the activities'.

This leads to the conclusion that student teams seem to use readily available sources of information for knowledge-creation. These sources are slightly different from sources used by professional teams. Professional teams seem to use mostly in-house databases (experience repositories) containing knowledge from past projects (Basili, Caldiera & Rombach 1994; Spohrer *et al.* 2013). However, the sources that students used were also good enough because they enabled the teams to create new knowledge.

Channels of communication that facilitate knowledge-creation

Different communication channels were used by teams during knowledge-creation. Mobile devices such as mobile phones and BlackBerrys and the Internet were mostly used for information transfer that facilitated knowledge-creation. Teams used these channels of communication to share ideas. They used mostly emails, chat services such as Whats application (WhatsApp), BlackBerry Messenger (BBM), Mxit and social networking sites (Facebook and Twitter). They stated that they used some of these channels at their convenient time and places to look for information and that they shared it faster than other devices. These results are consistent with results found by Kyobe and Shongwe (2011) who concluded that students use devices such as mobile phones and social networks for learning purposes. Juárez-Ramírez and Ocegueda-Miramontes (2013) also found similar results. They concluded that social networks (Facebook in particular) are used widely by students in software-development to solve problems and share knowledge.

Challenges of knowledge-creation

There were a number of challenges facing the teams involved in knowledge-creation. The major challenge was financial resources. Before the start of the project, teams had to identify a client for whom they had to develop a system. The client had to be rurally based. This meant that the teams had to travel to rural areas to find the client and collect information about their business before developing the system. All the teams indicated that they did not have enough money for such an exercise. The average distance they had to travel was 50 km. They did not have enough money for travelling and subsistence. They also lacked financial resources for doing activities such as photocopying and printing documents. One team stated that '… we did not have money to go and interview the client the way we could have liked. We also did not have money for printing our documents'. Another group concurred that '…as a group, we did not have the funds to help us successfully achieve our goal'.

Another challenge that the teams faced was a lack of technical skills. This is not a surprise because these were amateur teams. One team stated that '… we had no skills and experience of web design'. The main technical problem that most teams faced was connecting the database to the website (the WAMP platform).

A lack of material resources was another challenge that the teams faced. The material resources that they lacked were computers, software and a dedicated computer laboratory for their project. Some teams had only one laptop computer to work with. The university's computer laboratory did not have the PHP software, which made it difficult for teams to complete the project. The teams also complained greatly about the ever-crowded school laboratories. One group indicated: 'We encountered the challenge of limited resources that would have helped with the organising, planning, and research about the project'.

Time pressure was another big challenge that student teams faced. Teams stated that there was not enough time to complete the project. They complained that each milestone was to be submitted earlier than they would have liked. They also complained that they had to do courses other than the project. One student lamented: 'I had to juggle between activities of the project and other courses'. Another one concurred: 'The challenge was to balance between the amount of work the project had and studying for other courses'.

Not all students were resident students. Some teams were made up of on-campus and off-campus students. Off-campus students frequently had to travel from off-campus to the campus for group meetings. At times, they had to leave meetings earlier in order for them to travel off-campus. This caused challenges because it delayed the completion of the project. Some group members could not turn up for meetings, which also affected the quality of ideas contributed to the team. One student stated that:

> … since I am staying off-campus, my difficulty was always travelling to university and going back in the late hours of the day when it is not safe out there.

Other teams complained of lazy team members who did not complete their given activities. Strode and Clark (2007) report similar challenges in their study of student projects. They report that student projects have the following constraints: time and commitment, experience level, scope and complexity, technology and the need to meet the assessment criteria. Issues of time, commitment and technology seemed to be serious challenges to students. Wang (2009) also found that a lack of time was a major challenge in students' software projects. Faculty should look at how this could be addressed. However, these challenges are also faced by professional teams (e.g. time and financial challenges) as reported by Rus and Lindvall (2002).

Successful completion of the project

The teams were then asked to indicate whether they have successfully completed the project. All the teams indicted that they did complete their projects successfully. They indicated that they have successfully built a working e-commerce interactive website. One group stated that, '… although it was hard, we successfully created an e-commerce site that will help our client expand their business'. Another group stated: 'We were able to create a website that is working'. The groups indicted that, although they successfully completed the project, it was a challenging task.

Knowledge gained from the project

All the teams indicated that they had learnt a lot from the project. They indicated that the project had improved their knowledge and experience in software-development ('I have learned how to create a complete website'). Some respondents indicated that they had learnt to work in a team, a skill that is essential in the job market: 'I believe I gained both knowledge and experience when it comes to programming and working in a team'. Others indicated that they had learnt to work under pressure and in a group to achieve a singular goal.

A summary of the research findings is presented in Table 1.

Recommendations and further research

I recommend, therefore, that university departments engaged in such projects should look at the challenges that student teams face because they affect learning. Departments are also encouraged to formally adopt technology devices such as smart phones for teaching because they play an important role in learning. Further research is recommended to investigate the quality of the knowledge that students create and also to investigate the impact that the challenges have on knowledge-creation.

TABLE 1: A summary of research findings.

Research questions	Findings
What knowledge-creation activities take place in student teams?	At the individual level: coding, documentation, preparing slides for presentations, designing the user interface, research and information gathering, sourcing finance.
	At team level: brainstorming which led to the refinement, consolidation and adoption of individual tasks.
What channels of communication facilitate knowledge-creation in student teams?	Emails, chat services such as Whats Application (WhatsApp), BlackBerry Messenger (BBM), Mxit and social networking sites (Facebook and Twitter).
What information sources do students use to create knowledge?	Class presentations, the lecturer, lecture notes, text books, the Internet and external sources (senior students and professional software developers).
What challenges do student teams face when they create knowledge?	Lack of material and financial resources, lack of technical skills, lack of time, students staying off-campus and ambivalent team members.

Limitations of the study

The major limitation of this study is that it was conducted in only one university and in only one department. This compromises the representativeness of the total population.

Conclusion

The article contributes to the literature by showing how knowledge is created in student software-development teams. The literature on knowledge-creation covers mostly knowledge-creation in professional teams in business organisations. The article presents a different perspective by focusing on knowledge-creation in amateur teams in an education institution. Several conclusions are drawn from the study: (1) Student software-development teams can create knowledge (a working system) just like professional software-development teams; (2) knowledge is created by the whole team, but the knowledge-creation process starts from individual team members; (3) class presentations, lectures, the Internet and senior students and professional developers are major sources of information that students consult to create knowledge; (4) a lack of technical skills, limited time and a lack of resources are major hindrances to knowledge-creation.

Acknowledgements

Competing interests

The author declares that there are no financial and personal relationship(s) that may have inappropriately influenced him when he wrote this article.

References

Alavi, M. & Leidner, D.E., 2001, 'Knowledge management systems: Issues, challenges and benefits', in S. Barnes (ed.), *Knowledge management systems: Theory and practice*, pp. 15–32, Thompson Learning, Oxford.

Arent, J. & Norbjerg, J., 2000, 'Software improvement as organisational knowledge creation: A multiple case analysis', Proceedings of the 33rd International Conference on System Sciences, Hawaii, USA, 4–7 January 2000, p. 105.

Argyris, C. & Schon, D., 1978, *Organisational learning: A theory of action perspective*, Addison-Wesley Publishing Company, Reading.

Bailin, S., 1997, 'Software development as knowledge creation', *International Journal of Applied Software Technology* 3(1), 75–89.

Basili, V.R., Caldiera, G. & Rombach, D.H., 1994, 'The experience factory', *Encyclopedia of Software Engineering* 2, 469–476.

Chaffey, D. & Wood, S., 2005, *Business information management: Improving performance using information systems*, Pearson Education Limited, London.

Dingsoyr, T., 2002, 'Knowledge management in medium-sized software consulting companies', *Empirical Computing* 7(4), 383–386.

Dorairaj, S., Noble, J. & Malik, P., 2012, 'Knowledge management in distributed agile software development', Paper presented at the Agile Conference, Dallas, Texas, United States of America, 13–17 August.

Elfving, S. & Funk, P., 2006, '*Enabling knowledge transfer in product development and production: Methods and techniques from artificial intelligence*', Paper presented at the 1st Nordic Conference on Product Lifecycle Management, Goteborg, Sweden, 25–26 January.

Gladstone, B., 2000, *From know-how to knowledge: The essential guide to understanding and implementing knowledge management*, Industrial Society, London.

Grant, R.M., 1996, 'Toward a knowledge-based theory of the firm', *Strategic Management Journal* 17, 109–122. http://dx.doi.org/10.1002/smj.4250171110

Hedlund, G., 1994, 'A model of knowledge management and the N-Form corporation' *Strategic Management Journal* 15, 73–90. http://dx.doi.org/10.1002/smj.4250151006

Heeks, R., 2002, 'Information systems and developing countries: Failure, success, and local improvisations', *The Information Society* 18(2), 101–112. http://dx.doi.org/10.1080/01972240290075039

Hey, J., 2004, 'The data, information, knowledge, wisdom chain', viewed 16 July 2008, from http://scholar.google.co.za/scholar?q=The+Data,+Information,+Knowledge,+Wisdom+Chain+%2Bhey+2004&hl=en&um=1&ie=UTF-8&oi=scholart

Holsapple, C.W. & Singh, M., 2001, 'The knowledge chain model: Activities for competitiveness', *Expert Systems with Applications* 20(1), 77–98. http://dx.doi.org/10.1016/S0957-4174(00)00050-6

Hsieh, H-F. & Shannon, S.E., 2005, 'Three approaches to qualitative content analysis', *Qualitative Health Research* 15(9), 1277–1288. http://dx.doi.org/10.1177/1049732305276687

Juárez-Ramírez, R. & Ocegueda- Miramontes, R.P-R.V., 2013, 'Supporting the software development process using social media: Experiences with student projects', Proceedings of the Institute of Electrical and Electronics Engineers 37th Annual Computer Software and Applications Conference Workshops, Kyoto, Japan, 22–26 July 2013.

Kess, P. & Haapasalo, H., 2002, 'Knowledge creation through a project review process in software projects', *International Journal of Production Economics* 80(1), 49–55. http://dx.doi.org/10.1016/S0925-5273(02)00242-6

Kimmerle, J. Cress, U. & Held, C., 2010, 'The interplay between individual and collective knowledge: Technologies for organisational learning and knowledge building', *Knowledge Management Research & Practice* 8(1), 33–44. http://dx.doi.org/10.1057/kmrp.2009.36

Klint, P. & Verhoef, C., 2002, 'Enabling the creation of knowledge about software assets', *Data & Knowledge Engineering* 41(2/3), 141–158. http://dx.doi.org/10.1016/S0169-023X(02)00038-1

Kyobe, M.E. & Shongwe, M.M., 2011, 'Investigating the extent to which mobile phones reduce knowledge transfer barriers in student project teams', *South African Journal of Information Management*, 13(1).

Lee, A.S., 1991, 'Integrating positivist and interpretive approaches to organisational research', *Organisational Science* 2(4), 242–365. http://dx.doi.org/10.1287/orsc.2.4.342

Lee, G.K. & Cole, R.E., 2003, 'From a firm-based to a community-based model of knowledge creation: The case of the Linux kernel development', *Organisation Science* 14(6), 633–694. http://dx.doi.org/10.1287/orsc.14.6.633.24866

Li, M. & Gao, F., 2003, 'Why Nonaka highlights tacit knowledge: A critical review', *Journal of Knowledge Management* 7(4), 6–14. http://dx.doi.org/10.1108/13673270310492903

Linden, T. & Cybulski, J., 2009, 'Knowledge creation in an application domain: A hermeneutic study in ICKM 2009', Proceedings of the 6th International Conference on Knowledge Management: Managing knowledge for global and collaborative innovations, Hong Kong, China, 3–4 December 2009, pp. 1–13.

Lindvall, M., Rus, I. & Sinha, S., 2002, 'Technology support for knowledge management', in S. Henninger & F. Maurer (eds.), *Advances in learning software organization: Lecture notes in computer science*, pp. 94–113, Springer Verlag, Berlin.

Lyytinen, K. & Robey, D., 1999, 'Learning failure in information systems development', *Information Systems Journal* 9(2), 85–101. http://dx.doi.org/10.1046/j.1365-2575.1999.00051.x

Mitchell, R. & Boyle, B., 2010, 'Knowledge creation measurement methods', *Journal of Knowledge Management* 14(1), 67–82. http://dx.doi.org/10.1108/13673271011015570

Mitchell, R. & Nicholas, S., 2006, 'Knowledge creation in groups: The value of cognitive diversity, transactive memory and open-mindedness norms', *Electronic Journal of Knowledge Management* 4(1), 67–74.

Morner, M. & Von Krogh, G., 2009, 'A note on knowledge creation in open-source software projects: What can we learn from Luhmann's theory of social systems',

Systems Practice and Action Research 22(6), 431–443. http://dx.doi.org/10.1007/s11213-009-9139-7

Myers, M.D., 1999, 'Investigating information systems with ethnographic research', *Communications for the Association of Information Systems* 2(23), 1–20.

Myers, M.D. & Young, L.W., 1997, 'Hidden agendas, power, and managerial assumptions in information systems development: An ethnographic study,' *Information Technology & People* (10)3, 224–240. http://dx.doi.org/10.1108/09593849710178225

Neves, F.T., Correia, A.M.R., Rosa, V.N. & Neto, M., 2011, 'Knowledge creation and sharing in software development teams using Agile methodologies: Key insights affecting their adoption', Proceedings of the 6th Information Systems and Technologies Iberian Conference (CISTI), Chaves, Portugal, 15–18 June 2011, pp. 1–6.

Nickols, F.W., 2000, 'The knowledge in knowledge management', in J.W. Cortada & J.A. Woods (eds.), *The knowledge management yearbook 2000–2001*, pp. 12–21, Butterworth-Heinemann, Boston.

Nonaka, I., 1994, 'A dynamic theory of organisational knowledge creation', *Organisation Science* 5(1), 14–37. http://dx.doi.org/10.1287/orsc.5.1.14

Nonaka, I. & Takeuchi, H., 1995, *The knowledge-creating company*, Oxford University Press, New York.

Nonaka, I., Toyama, R. & Konno, N., 1998, 'SECI, Ba and Leadership: A unified model of dynamic knowledge creation', *Long Range Planning* 33(1), 5–34. http://dx.doi.org/10.1016/S0024-6301(99)00115-6

Olikowski, W.J. & Baroudi, J.J., 1991, 'Studying information technology in organisations: Research approaches and assumptions', *Information Systems research* 2(1), 1–28. http://dx.doi.org/10.1287/isre.2.1.1

Parent, M., Gallupe, R.B., Salisbury, Wm.D. & Handelman, J.M., 2000, 'Knowledge creation in focus groups: Can group technologies help?', *Information & Management* 38(1), 47–58. http://dx.doi.org/10.1016/S0378-7206(00)00053-7

Phan, P.H. & Peridis, T., 2000, Knowledge creation in strategic alliances: Another look at organisational learning', *Asian Pacific Journal of Management* 17(2), 201–222. http://dx.doi.org/10.1023/A:1015857525048

Poh, L-G. & Erwee, R., 2004, Knowledge creation and integration in project teams: A study of international telecommunications companies in Singapore', *Journal of Management & World Business Research* 1(1), 23–44.

Polanyi, M., 1962, 'Tacit knowing: It's bearing on some problems of philosophy', *Reviews of Modern Physics* 34(4), 601–616. http://dx.doi.org/10.1103/RevModPhys.34.601

Rumizen, M.C., 2002, *The complete idiot's guide to knowledge management,* CWL Publishing Enterprise, Madison.

Rus, I. & Lindvall, M., 2002, 'Knowledge management in computing', *Institute of Electrical and Electronic Engineers Software* 19(3), 26–38.

Senge, P.M., Ross, R., Smith, B., Roberts, C. & Kleiner, A., 1994, *The fifth discipline fieldwork: Strategies and tools for building a learning organisation*, Doubleday Inc. Publishers, New York.

Spohrer, K., Kude, T., Schmidt, C.T. & Heinzl, A., 2013, 'Knowledge creation in information systems development teams: The role of pair programming and peer code review,' *Proceedings of the 21st European Conference on Information Systems*, Utrecht, Netherlands, 6–8 June 2013, pp. 1–12.

Strode, D.E. & Clark, J., 2007, 'Methodology in software development capstone projects', *Proceedings of the 20th Annual National Advisory Committee on Computing Qualifications*, Nelson, New Zealand, 8–11 July 2007, pp. 243–251.

Styhre, A., Roth, J. & Ingelgard, A., 2002, 'Care of the other: Knowledge creation through care in professional teams', *Scandinavian Journal of Management* 18(4), 503–520. http://dx.doi.org/10.1016/S0956-5221(01)00022-7

Suchman, L., 1995, 'Making work visible', *Communications of the Association for Computing Machinery* 38(9), 56–64. http://dx.doi.org/10.1145/223248.223263

Wang, A.I., 2009, 'Post-mortem analysis of student game projects in a software architecture course: Successes and challenges in student software architecture game projects,' Paper presented at the International Consumer Electronic Games Innovations Conference, London, England, United Kingdom, 25–28 August.

Wan, J., Zhang, H., Wan, D. & Huang, D., 2010, 'Research on knowledge creation in software requirement development', *Journal of Software Engineering & Applications* 3(5), 487–494. http://dx.doi.org/10.4236/jsea.2010.35055

Wasko, M. & Faraj, S., 2000, 'It is what one does: Why people participate and help others in electronic communities of practice', *The Journal of Strategic Information Systems* 9(2/3), 155–173. http://dx.doi.org/10.1016/S0963-8687(00)00045-7

Wenger, E., 1998, *Communities of practice: Learning, meaning, and identity*, Cambridge University Press, Cambridge. http://dx.doi.org/10.1017/CBO9780511803932

22

Comparative case study on website traffic generated by search engine optimisation and a pay-per-click campaign, versus marketing expenditure

Authors:
Wouter T. Kritzinger[1]
Melius Weideman[1]

Affiliations:
[1]Website Attributes Research Centre (WARC), Cape Peninsula University of Technology, South Africa

Correspondence to:
Melius Weideman

Email:
weidemanm@cput.ac.za

Postal address:
PO Box 652, Cape Town 8000, South Africa

Background: No empirical work was found on how marketing expenses compare when used solely for either the one or the other of the two main types of search engine marketing.

Objectives: This research set out to determine how the results of the implementation of a pay-per-click campaign compared to those of a search engine optimisation campaign, given the same website and environment. At the same time, the expenses incurred on both these marketing methods were recorded and compared.

Method: The active website of an existing, successful e-commerce concern was used as platform. The company had been using pay-per-click only for a period, whilst traffic was monitored. This system was decommissioned on a particular date and time, and an alternative search engine optimisation system was started at the same time. Again, both traffic and expenses were monitored.

Results: The results indicate that the pay-per-click system did produce favourable results, but on the condition that a monthly fee has to be set aside to guarantee consistent traffic. The implementation of search engine optimisation required a relatively large investment at the outset, but it was once-off. After a drop in traffic owing to crawler visitation delays, the website traffic bypassed the average figure achieved during the pay-per-click period after a little over three months, whilst the expenditure crossed over after just six months.

Conclusion: Whilst considering the specific parameters of this study, an investment in search engine optimisation rather than a pay-per-click campaign appears to produce better results at a lower cost, after a given period of time.

Introduction

The growth of the Internet has produced an important information resource during the last two decades that has advanced at a much faster rate than was previously envisaged. It took seven years to reach a 25% international market share – 70% faster than the development of the radio and 80% faster than the development of the telephone. This growth makes the Internet the fastest growing technology the world has ever encountered (Singh 2002). Boyes and Irani (2004:191) support this trend by claiming that the Internet had acquired 50 million global users in five years as opposed to the 38 years it took for radio and 13 years for television.

The implementation of the World Wide Web (WWW) has seen the world confronted with the concept of a website. Websites act as connection and communication points between the user and digital information. Therefore, most corporations (according to Akakandelwa 2011), organisations or institutions have been making efforts to launch themselves into the virtual world using this modern platform. The WWW is more than two decades old and, due to its complexity, its size is impossible to measure with regard to the number of websites or servers. It is claimed that, for January 2014, the nine most popular websites in the United States of America (USA) drew between 100 million and 370 million visitors each (Nielsen 2014). The WWW is a decentralised environment constructed and controlled by various people and access to it is less restricted than access to the common information media (Brunn & Dodge 2001).

The base of Internet users is massive; hence, there is much interest in leveraging this user base for commercial gain. This commercial gain could be realised by ensuring that many thousands of users view a given website daily, with some of them being converted from browsers to buyers. It is generally accepted that the two types of interventions which could be implemented to increase the traffic to a website are search engine optimisation (SEO) and a paid campaign. However, no research could be found which compares the expenditure in a controlled environment with the value received from that expenditure for these two approaches. It is against this background that this study has originated.

The research problem on which this project was based is the fact that the respective value of the two marketing methods has not been directly compared, leading to resources being wasted on marketing. The purpose of this study was to compare these two categories to see how they produce traffic over a period of time, and to offset them against the expenditure.

Literature review

Search engines

According to Green (2000), a search engine is a search service that uses retrieval software called crawlers that examine websites and then index them in a database of website listings according to their relevancy. Search engines use their own indexing software and strategies to continuously traverse the Web, searching for the most up-to-date content possible. The indexing software (also referred to as spiders or bots) is responsible for visiting webpages following links between pages. The pages found are then analysed, parts are copied back to the site running the indexing software and added to the database for the purpose of including them in the search engine results (Weideman 2009).

Even though search engines use different algorithms to rank a webpage, they operate on similar principles. All search engines, primarily, strive to retrieve and display relevant results (webpages) that contain words or terms that match the user's search query (Green 2000; Guenther 2004:47).

Oppenheim et al. (2000:191) are of the opinion that, although search engines search a vast amount of information at impressive speeds, they are criticised on issues such as the retrieval of duplicate and irrelevant records owing to spamming techniques. The sheer mass of these irrelevant results is one of the main user complaints against search engines.

Much research has been done recently on search engines, the way they operate, the way users generate queries, and the way they affect our lives. Moreno and Martinez (2013) indicated that webpages can be designed to be both SEO and human friendly. This was confirmed by another study on the effect of usability elements on the way search engine crawlers view websites (Visser & Weideman 2011).

In summary, the availability and use of search engines affect our lives on a regular basis through user interaction with results produced by them. It is now certain that the use of search engines, together with the power of advertising, plays a role in peoples' daily decisions on various aspects and is not limited to purchasing only.

Search engine marketing

Search engine marketing (SEM) is a strategy that makes use of the power of search engines to potentially attract millions of views per day to websites. Even academic universities need to consider how they should market themselves to prospective students as they are the paying clients (Weideman 2013). Crowley (2014) discusses some of these strategies, including SEO and tracking analytics, to determine user behaviour. Many systems are fighting for 'eyeballs'; these are users reading and responding to advertisements on websites. Social media has added to the frenzy through their advertisement offerings, although research has proven that it has not been all that successful. Barreto (2013) indicated that Facebook banner advertisements have less business value than recommendations from friends, possibly because of banner blindness. These ads (advertisements) were located outside the main viewing area first scanned by most users.

A recent study was done to determine the effectiveness of a search marketing campaign and the effect of print advertising on SEM (Olbrich & Schultz 2014). It was found that the budget and the degree of keyword matching had the largest effect on the yield in business gained, followed by the click-through rate and the bid amount. This result seems to indicate that SEM needs to be planned with care as a larger budget might reduce expenditure on other marketing efforts. This fact supports the current study. SEO and pay-per-click schemes (PPC) are generally considered to be the two main categories of SEM which are to be investigated.

Pay-per-click

PPC schemes, producing non-natural rankings, are systems which display advertisements on a search result screen, co-located with organic results but ranked separately. The location of these advertisements is normally to the right and above the organic search engine listings (Chen et al. 2011). This sharing of the prime real estate space on the user's screen has caused some problems for users. No longer can they simply evaluate the quality of answers based on which answer is listed the highest on the result screen as they have to also consider the ranking difference between organic and paid results. Even libraries have found this to be an obstacle for their users (Moxley, Blake & Maze 2004). However, many industries, particularly the tourism sector, have been making extensive use of this marketing opportunity. In some cases even small businesses went to extremes to do research to identify the better search engine PPC scheme to use (Kennedy & Kennedy 2008). At the same time, the 'newness' of this form of marketing initially scared off other smaller businesses for example some smaller hotels did not make use of PPC (Murphy & Kielgast 2008).

PPC, as the name suggests, charges the advertiser the bid amount every time an Internet user clicks on an advertisement. The keywords all have different competition ratings and the more popular a keyword, the higher the cost per click would be (Chen *et al.* 2011). A recent study on the value of the bid price per keyword for a new PPC campaign determined the best of a number of methods to determine this price (Nabout 2015). This study confirms the importance of financial expenditure, which could easily grow beyond what a company decided they could spend on a marketing campaign.

The PPC ranking system operates in stark contrast to the value associated with the quantity and quality of inlinks, in other words SEO (Thelwall 2001). In the past Google specifically used a simple formula to determine the ranking of PPC results: Rank = Bid price X Quality Score (Sagin 2013). The bid price is the amount the advertisement owner is prepared to pay per user click on the ad, and the quality score is Google's interpretation of the quality of the landing page. However, in October 2013 Google announced a third factor, namely ad extensions (Mancuso 2013). Where two competing advertisements achieve an equal score, the use of ad extensions is used to determine the highest ranker.

A recent study was done on the relationship between print and search engine advertising (Olbrich & Schultz 2014). The results proved that print advertising did not directly affect the number of advertisements impressions produced by the search engine. However, there was an indirect relationship between print advertising and the number of conversions indicating that e-commerce marketers cannot ignore the traditional advertising methods and focus only on SEM. Since exposure through PPC requires constant and accumulative expenditure, past research has also focused on maximising this expense. The performance of PPC advertisements is crucial in recapping the expense, hopefully bypassing it to provide a profit. Another recent study determined the role of ranking of these advertisements, branding, and the role of the device used to search (Gupta & Mateen 2014).

In summary, PPC has been a successful business model. In the case of Google, it has produced the bulk of its profits over the years, playing a major role in its financial success (Kumar & Kohli 2007). At the same time, an e-commerce business running PPC schemes on multiple keywords across many campaigns is advised to budget for specialised staff to manage these campaigns. Still, some authors actually prescribe that PPC is a better way to spend marketing dollars than SEO (Sen 2005).

Search engine optimisation

SEO is a method that uses data observation and marketing research to identify the most suitable keyword for a website (Malaga 2010). However, it requires a base of knowledge to implement, such as how to choose keywords and how to use keywords in order to enhance a website's ranking, etc.

There is a need for any e-commerce business to be ranked highly with search engines (Kent 2012). Another author states that to increase the volume of traffic to individual websites from search engines, SEO must be considered and invested in (Kisiel 2010). For successful SEO there are many concepts that need to be understood and applied; some of these are discussed later. The ultimate goal of SEO is to increase a website's ranking with search engines, thus increasing the traffic to the website, which should result in increased sales (Lee 2010; Lee, Chen & Wu 2010; Lee & Lin 2011).

Lately, much research has been done on the visibility of content to search engine crawlers. Onaifo and Rasmussen (2013) found that the principles of SEO can, and should, be applied to increase the visibility of library content to search engines. A number of elements affect SEO; it is not just a case of implementing a simple set of rules, thereby ensuring high visibility. Some of these elements are listed below.

Another recent study considered the value of using search query data to obtain business information. Search query data is much more recent than, for example, business reports published at the end of a financial year. A significant correlation was found between business performance and position and search query data (Vaughan 2014). This kind of timely information could be used to predict business performance, leading to financial gains.

It is clear that both SEO and PPC could play a role in marketing a website to the search engine crawlers. The purpose of this study was to determine how much traffic each of SEO and PPC produces and to measure and compare the expenditure in each case.

Some of the aspects of SEO are considered below. They are all discussed with regard to the components of a webpage over which the website owner has direct control.

Header tags

Metatags are elements of a webpage that are mostly optional, invisible to the casual browser, but which could affect the way a crawler views a webpage. One of these is the H (Heading) meta tag.

A Web designer can choose whether or not to highlight headings inside a block of text on a webpage. To this effect, there are six levels of heading tags. H1 is the most important (biggest text); H2 is slightly less important, down to H6 which is the least important. Some search engines recognise the use of header tags as a safe method to weight keywords, owing to its connection with a heading of a paragraph. Henzinger, Motwani and Silverstein (2002:9) state that the higher the importance of the headings, the more weight a search engine could assign to a given webpage. For example, text in an <H1> would appear prominently on a webpage and therefore some search engines could see it as safe to assign a high weight to the text in that heading.

Research by Craven (2003) to determine the relevant weight of meta tags indicates that the H1 (heading 1) and H2 (heading 2) tags are the second and third most highly weighted (after the TITLE tag) of all the meta tags. As with Microsoft Word, the hypertext mark-up language (HTML) has built-in styles for headings to differentiate between importance levels of text that are usually used to break up text into paragraphs. The different options allow the designer to develop large and bold text in an HTML document, marking the beginning of a new paragraph or section (Henzinger *et al.* 2002:9).

Image filenames

Search engine crawlers cannot interpret the content of an image, a video or an audio file. The designer has to provide text-based information to allow the crawler to make some association between this type of file and its contents (Weideman 2009). For still images, the name of the file is the most obvious way of establishing this association. A simple experiment can prove that the name of an image file does play a role in its visibility. When doing an image search on Google or Bing for the term 'rolls royce' for example, page after page of images of this car are produced. Upon closer inspection of the first result page, virtually every image has those two words as part of the file-name.

Image alternative tags

ALT (alternative) tags are used to display text in the place of an image on a webpage if graphics are turned off. The ALT text will also display if a user places his or her mouse pointer over an image for a few seconds. Currently, automated crawlers can read only text elements within a webpage and are unable to read multimedia elements, as discussed earlier. For this reason, it is of importance to apply ALT tags, where possible, that accurately describe the graphics on the webpage (Hubbard 2004).

By implementing ALT text within a webpage, the developer ultimately caters for users who turn graphics off to increase loading speed. Without the use of ALT tags a site could become impossible to navigate when graphics are turned off. The use of ALT tags also provides the ability to cater for users with a visual impairment. Voice-output screen readers (benefiting those users) will not 'read' a non-text element (Oppenheim *et al.* 2000:204), but will do so if an ALT element is provided. Ironically, the implementation of techniques to allow the visually impaired to better interpret website contents could also play a major role in improving the user experience of other users, as well as the way crawlers interpret webpages.

Metadata

Another meta tag which plays a role in visibility is the TITLE tag. It is also invisible as part of the body text of a webpage being displayed, but it is often displayed on a user screen as part of search engine results. Search engines often claim that the presence of a well-written TITLE tag can positively influence a webpage's visibility (Guenther 2014).

In summary, only a few of the many elements affecting the crawler visibility of a webpage have been discussed. There are many others (keyword usage, HTML file-names, links, etc.), as well as a long list of negative elements that should specifically not be implemented (Weideman 2009).

Methodology

Data were gathered from a real-life website where first the one (PPC) and then the other (SEO) of the marketing approaches were followed exclusively. Usage behaviour and statistics were recorded and analysed in an attempt to compare the expenditure with the gain from each approach.

A company in Cape Town, South Africa, manufactures PVC, polypropylene and leather promotional and stationery products. The company's name is not listed; for the purposes of recording they will be named XYZ. The company invested in PPC from May 2010 to May 2011 in an attempt to drive traffic to the website. During that time no SEO implementation was done on the website. Each month XYZ spent, on average, R3000 on PPC. However, after the PPC campaign was terminated, they paid a once-off fee of R19 000 for the SEO project.

The XYZ concern is a relatively small company. Considering that they have a typical monthly website traffic figure of hundreds as compared to millions for large companies, their business model must be sound to run a successful e-commerce concern. The most important requirement of the client was that their website remained optimised in such a way that it could lead to sales. The authors did a detailed investigation of the XYZ website, identifying elements that could be improved through SEO with the estimated short-term cost it may entail.

The following elements which needed improvement were identified:

- Header tags (were not being used).
- Image filenames (were inappropriate and non-descriptive).
- Metadata (was outdated).
- Alternative tags (were inappropriate and non-descriptive).
- Product descriptions (were too short or non-existent).
- The bounce rate (was too high).

Header tags

All the headings on the XYZ website were placed in strong tags. Best practice prescribed that all strong tags be replaced with H1 and H2 Tags. This would imply that the authors would have to inspect every one of the 55 webpages and either write new H1 tags, or rewrite the existing ones.

Image filenames

Some of the image filenames did not contain relevant keywords. An example of this was '_MG_2174.jpg'. Again, best practice was that these filenames be renamed with appropriate keywords that reflect the objects on each image. A total of 246 images were found and renamed in the 55 HTML pages.

Metadata

Throughout the year the website was updated with new products, whilst older products were removed. However, the metadata was not updated accordingly. It was recommended that the metadata of all 55 HTML pages be updated to reflect the new content. This was done, and it included updating the TITLE-, DESCRIPTION- and KEYWORD tags of all 55 HTML pages.

Image alternative tags

Some of the ALT tags of the images were too long. These ALT tags, in accordance with best practice, needed to be shortened and rewritten to contain relevant keywords that reflect the images that they are associated with. There were a total of 256 images whose ALT tags were reviewed and rewritten.

Product descriptions

Some of the products listed on the XYZ website were identified by only one short sentence. It was decided, based on best practice, that all product descriptions be rewritten to have at least two to three descriptive sentences each. Sixty four of the 128 products did not have sufficient descriptive text and were subsequently rewritten. The remaining 64 descriptions were also reviewed to ensure that they contained relevant keywords.

Bounce rate

The XYZ website had a bounce rate of 48%, where a lower figure is considered to be better (Plaza 2009). In industry, a bounce rate of 30% is considered to be a breakpoint; higher than 30% is 'bad' and lower is 'good'. It was necessary that the homepage text be reviewed with the aim to reduce the high bounce rate. However, the bounce rate is not an element that a Web developer can improve by doing coding updates or any other direct actions. It is a figure which will decrease (i.e. improve) as users spend more time on webpages as a result of other elements described here being put into place.

Project plan

The project was thus split into three stages:
* Throughout June 2011 the header tags were modified.
* Throughout July 2011 the image filenames and image ALT tags were modified.
* Throughout August 2011 the product descriptions, copy, and metadata were modified.

These timescales appear in the figures following, to indicate the effect of each alteration.

Results and interpretation
Header tags

The effect (if any) of the header tag improvement, as discussed earlier, was measured by viewing statistics on website usage as from when the header tags were redone. Refer to Figure 1.

The company stopped their PPC campaign on 31 May 2011. The immediate effect of this action was a drop in total traffic by 15.42% (1130 vs 1336) when comparing June 2011 with May 2011. The authors then proceeded to review and modify all headings on the website. This process involved modifying the CSS file and defining the Header Tags. There were 244 instances where strong tags were used, and all of them were replaced with H1 and H2 tags.

Also, the headings were modified to include appropriate keywords. The authors ensured that each page only had one instance of the H1 tag, which is considered the most important of the heading tags. The work was conducted throughout June 2011 and was completed in the final week of June 2011. It must be noted that all the work was completed on the live website. As the authors progressed a slight increase in traffic in the second week of June 2011 was noted.

It must also be noted that 01 May 2011 and 02 May 2011 were Worker's Day and a public holiday respectively in South Africa. These two calendar events would have had a negative impact on the statistics as the biggest part of the workforce would not be at work on those days. However, this pattern repeated the next month: 16 June 2011 and 17 June 2011 were Youth Day and a school holiday respectively. These two calendar events would have had a similar effect on the figures of June 2011. Also, during 25 June to 18 July 2011 the schools in South Africa were closed for recess which would also have had a negative impact on the June 2011 statistics.

By this time half of the 244 instances of strong tags were replaced by either H1 tags or H2 tags. The fact that the authors saw an increase in organic traffic was somewhat unexpected, since it can take search engines up to a month (Zuze & Weideman 2013) to re-index and rank webpages after significant changes have been implemented. From the author's point of view this highlights the importance search engines place on Header tags. For any website it is a simple matter to assign header tags to headings. The website, from a search engines perspective, was seen in a more favourable position because of the above action taken.

ALT tags

The effect of the updating of the ALT tags was also measured by viewing the relevant statistics – see Figure 2.

The modifications of the image ALT tags were completed in the final week of July 2011. Whilst performing this task

FIGURE 1: Effect of header tag improvement on website visitations.

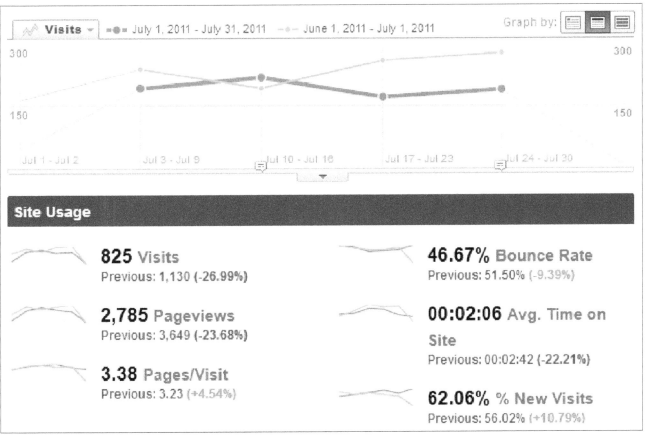

FIGURE 2: Effect of image file-name and image ALT improvement on website visitations.

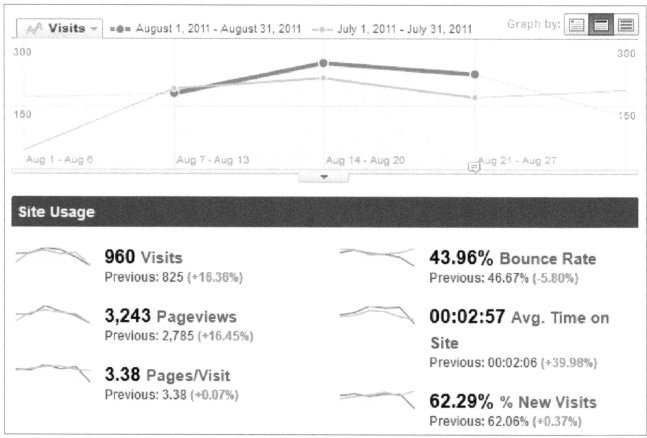

FIGURE 3: Effect of product descriptions, content and metadata improvement on website visitations.

the authors observed a slight decrease in traffic from the second week to the third week of July 2011. However, a slight increase in total traffic followed the initial decline as the month of July 2011 drew to a close. By this time, the total number of visitors dropped from 1336 (May 2011) to 825 (July 2011). As mentioned previously, during the month of June the holiday events would have impacted on these figures. Some users at that time would have gone on family holidays, reducing Internet activity to an extent.

It is expected to note decreases in traffic when extensive work is being performed on a website. Search engines take note of content changes after which they have to re-index and rank the individual webpages. This process can take anything from a few days to months. The increase by the end of July 2011 was also, in a sense, unexpected as the authors argued that the process of re-indexing and ranking would take longer than it did. This increase also indicates the value basic SEO elements can have on a website's ranking.

Body content

The role of body text and the use of keywords have been noted many times in previous research. As mentioned above, sections of this body text had to be rewritten and the graphs of Figure 3 indicate the effect of these changes.

A lack of regular updating of HTML metadata content was noted in the webpages of the company. Whilst descriptive text in the body was updated, the relevant metadata was simply left with the original content, leading to a severance of the connections between these two elements.

Care was taken to ensure that all three meta-elements were rewritten according to Google's guidelines. The new version contained relevant keywords and reflected the product that it related to. This work was completed in the last week of August 2011.

The August 2011 total traffic increased compared to July 2011 (16.36%). This indicated to the authors that Google was starting to re-index the text website with the modifications. It must also be noted that the schools in South Africa were closed for recess between the periods of 24 June 2011 and 18 July 2011, which would have negatively impacted the statistics for the month of July 2011. However, August 2011 did have two public holidays on 08 August 2011 (school holiday) and 09 August 2011 (Women's Day). These two calendar events would have had a similar negative effect on the August 2011 figures.

A relative simple update to the content, and ensuring that the metadata was reflective of the new content, produced a significant increase in website traffic. This was mostly because of the presence of relevant, unique, keyword rich and regularly updated content. This increase in traffic confirms

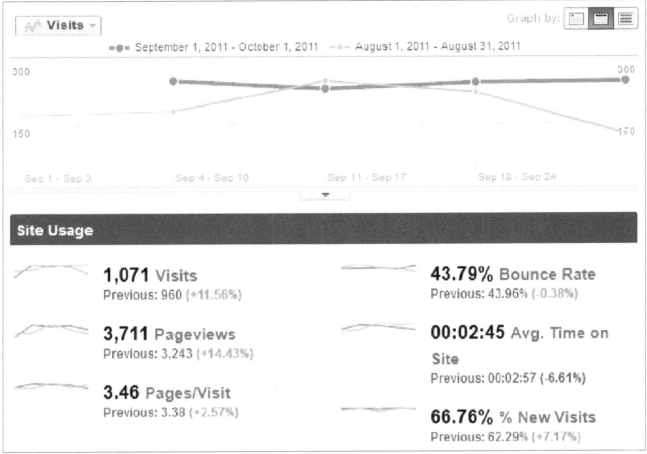

FIGURE 4: Total website traffic: September 2011 compared to August 2011.

this conclusion and website authors should seriously consider this crucial aspect of a website.

Overall traffic trends

Month 1

Next, two one-month periods are compared to determine whether a trend is evident. See Figure 4.

During the month of September 2011 no work was conducted on the test website. In this time, the total traffic increased further compared to August 2011; 11.56% in total. Although August 2011 had not quite reached the traffic levels of May 2011, which included the PPC traffic, the data looked promising. Also note that August 2011 had two calendar events that would have negatively impacted the results for August 2011, as noted earlier. Furthermore, September 2011 also had one event on 24 September 2011 when South Africans celebrated Heritage Day.

By this time it was safe to assume that Google had indexed all the on-site changes. It was evident that all the website's pages were being re-indexed and ranked. However, the continuing climb in traffic indicated that rankings were indeed improving and more and more users were finding the website via Google's search result pages. This has to be seen against the fact that no further investment in PPC was done after campaign shutdown in May 2011.

Month 2

In October 2011 the authors continued to monitor the results and noted another slight increase in total traffic (1.21%). This was an indication that Google had completed the re-indexing of the modified test website. By this time the website traffic had increased from 825 visits to 1084 (31.4% increase) in a period of four months. It should be noted that, in October 2011, the schools in South Africa closed for recess from 01 October 2011 to 10 October 2011. This would have had a negative impact on the October 2011 data. Also, as mentioned before, Heritage Day was celebrated on 24 September 2011.

Annual comparison

Finally, a year on year comparison is performed – see Figure 6.

In Figure 6 the authors compare the period 01 June 2011 to 31 October 2011 (no PPC included) to 01 June 2010 to 31 October 2010 (PPC traffic included). In June, the data regarding website traffic for the two years appear similar, however a sharp decrease in traffic can be observed when the PPC campaign was shut down and the modifications to the website started. By August 2011 the traffic already started increasing to just below the levels of the previous year after the header tags, image file names and image ALT tags were modified. Then, in August 2011 when the product descriptions, new homepage content, and

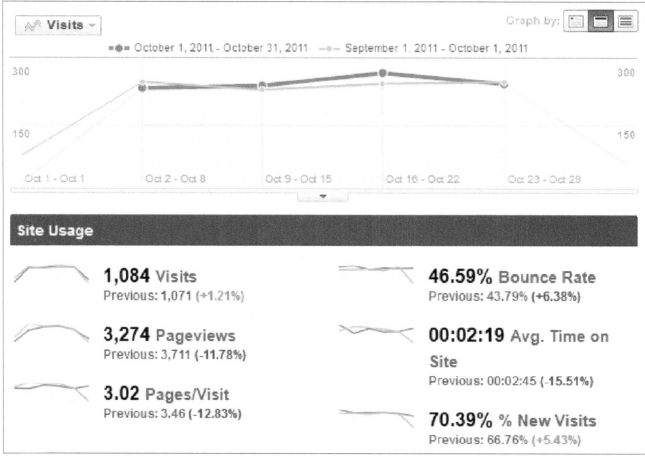

FIGURE 5: Total Traffic October 2011 compared to September 2011.

metadata were concluded the traffic increased further. By end of September 2011 the total traffic had increased to levels higher than the previous year, which included the PPC traffic.

Final traffic or expenditure summary

The results of this study are best described by summarising traffic to the XYZ website during the two test periods, whilst comparing it to the expenditure. Table 1 summarises the relevant figures.

The date column lists the date of measurement of both traffic values and the expenditure of company XYZ on SEM. 'Traffic PPC' lists the number of visitors for the period originating from all search traffic; direct, referral and PPC sources. However, the actual figures for November 2010 until May 2011 were not available, and these figures were taken to be the average of the preceding months (718).

The 'Traffic SEO' column contains the number of visitors for the relevant period, all of which is search traffic. However, by this time the PPC campaign had been terminated, so part of the source is SEO-generated traffic. The 'Expenses Original' column is a summary of the SEM expenditure of the XYZ Company, being R3000 per month spent on PPC for 11 consecutive months. In May 2011 there was no expenditure,

since the PPC campaign was terminated. Then, in June 2011, an amount of R19 000 was paid (once-off) to do the SEO as agreed.

Finally, the 'Expenses Adjusted' column is simply the 'Expenses Original' figure divided by 21. The figure of 21 was chosen as a scale-down factor to bring the Rand values in line with the other figures in the table. This would ensure that graphs of these values plotted on the same scale (see Figure 7) would be comparable in amplitude.

A graphical presentation of the relevant figures as noted above is done in Figure 7.

An analysis of the graphs in Figure 7 is required. The PPC graph indicates that the amount of search traffic had stabilised over the 12 month period from June 2010 to May 2011. Since this component consists of three parts and the split is unknown, it cannot be determined what the exact contribution of PPC was to the monthly figure. However, it is assumed that it must have been substantial considering the steep drop in traffic in the months (June and July 2011) directly following the termination of the PPC campaign.

The SEO graph of Figure 7 again lists all search traffic to the website, but this time with the PPC component having been

FIGURE 6: Year on year comparison: 01 June 2011 – 31 October 2011 compared to 01 June 2010 – 31 October 2010.

replaced by the newly introduced SEO component. The initial drop over the first two months is owing to the SEO campaign taking time to influence rankings and therefore traffic. However, as from the third month into the SEO section, the graph shows a continued rise indicating a growing trend in traffic volumes. This resulted from the fact that search engine crawlers had started visiting the site, indexing the new content, and their algorithms had started giving the

site an ever increasing rank in the result listings. The rising trend appears to flatten towards the last recorded month, but without more figures this trend cannot be confirmed past the last recorded month.

Finally, the expenses of XYZ to achieve this increase in traffic need to be put into perspective – refer to the 'R' line on Figure 7. At a fixed rate of R3000 per month, XYZ had spent

TABLE 1: Comparative traffic during two periods.

Date	Traffic PPC	Traffic SEO	Exp. Adj.	Exp. Orig.
Jun-10	650	-	142.8571	3000
Jul-10	706	-	142.8571	3000
Aug-10	723	-	142.8571	3000
Sep-10	721	-	142.8571	3000
Oct-10	788	-	142.8571	3000
Nov-10	718	-	142.8571	3000
Dec-10	718	-	142.8571	3000
Jan-11	718	-	142.8571	3000
Feb-11	718	-	142.8571	3000
Mar-11	718	-	142.8571	3000
Apr-11	718	-	142.8571	3000
May-11	718	-	0	0
Jun-11	-	639	904.7619	19000
Jul-11	-	536	0	0
Aug-11	-	696	0	0
Sep-11	-	792	0	0
Oct-11	-	822	0	0

PPC, pay-per-click; SEO, search engine optimisation; Exp. Adj.; Expenses Adjusted; Exp. Orig.; Expenses Original'.

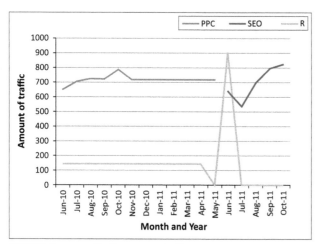

FIGURE 7: Summary of traffic versus expenditure.

R33 000 over the 11 month period in an attempt to maximise the number of visitors to their site. This expenditure played a large part in achieving the traffic volumes listed as the PPC line as noted above. During June 2011 there was a sharp increase to R19 000, but this was a once-off expenditure. After that time it dropped to zero for the rest of the recording period.

It should be noted that the traffic volume during the SEO period had bypassed the highest level achieved during the PPC period after only three months of running on SEO. This occurred whilst the average monthly PPC expense of R3000 compared well to the R3800 (R19 000/5) average per month spent on SEO for this short period. However, this R3800 average figure is for only five months as compared to the PPC figure of 11 months. The average cost for SEO, if calculated further, would decrease dramatically as follows:

- November 2011: R3167 per month
- December 2011: R2714 per month
- May 2012: R1727 per month

In both cases, after 11 months the PPC expense would still be R3000 per month with the SEO averaging out at R1727 per month. This trend of downward spiralling costs for SEO would continue. At the same time, if the SEO graph is extrapolated, it can be expected that the traffic volumes could increase past those achieved during the PPC period.

It should be noted that in a real-life SEO campaign there will be further expenses past the initial layout, but not necessarily of the monthly recurring type. In the time period of this case study there were none, bar the initial amount. However, a study over a much longer period of time is needed to do a long-term comparison. It is likely that the longer an SEO campaign is running, the lower the average monthly costs will become.

Limitations of this study include that the data were obtained from a relatively low-traffic site. Also, data across a longer period of time would provide a clearer trend. Finally, a comparison was done on the traffic generated from certain marketing expenses only, not the profit eventually generated by that traffic.

Conclusion

An existing commercial website (that of company XYZ) was considered as the central object of this research project. An experiment was done on the XYZ website to start implementing SEO immediately after the PPC was terminated. At the same time, monitoring was done of traffic to the website and of other relevant analytic measures. The SEO was done based on industry best practice supported by academic research.

The owners had been spending 'marketing dollars' on this website, using firstly, only one of the two main types of SEM for a period: PPC. The main disadvantage of PPC is that expenditure has to be consistent for results to appear; the moment a PPC budget is cut, the resultant traffic drops to zero immediately. Therefore, the overall PPC expenditure should be calculated from the monthly expenditure; in the case of XYZ, R3000.

After the PPC campaign was terminated, XYZ spent R19 000 once-off on SEO. This amount was for the implementation of the elements as listed under 'Methodology' above. As noted from the literature, where PPC produces immediate ranking improvements once payment has been arranged, SEO takes longer to affect rankings. This is mostly due to the waiting period for search engine crawlers to visit or refresh their copy of the website content.

When these expenditure figures are compared, it can thus be claimed that, after 6.33 months, the expenditure on the two systems for XYZ would have been the same. From this point in time onwards, SEO would continue to provide a growing return on investment over PPC, assuming that no further expenses would be required for SEO.

In conclusion, it can be claimed that, in this specific case, SEO provides a better investment than PPC. It is also predictable that this advantage will increase as time goes by. It should also be noted that traffic to a website on its own is not the only indicator of success. A high conversion rate, leading to more revenue generated, and eventually leading to increased profit would be the final indicator of the success of an e-commerce website. However, owing to the sensitivity of company financial information, this kind of evidence will be harder to come by and use as proof.

Acknowledgements

Competing interests

The authors declare that they have no financial or personal relationships which may have inappropriately influenced them in writing this article.

Authors' contributions

Both W.T.K. (Cape Peninsula University of Technology) and M.W. (Cape Peninsula University of Technology) worked together in conceptualising the research work, completing the literature survey and reference hunting, doing the write-up and checking results. W.T.K. gathered and summarised the data, checked accuracy and did the write-up of the skeleton of the whole article, specifically the results section. M.W. did the conclusion, abstract, proofreading, editing and overall checking.

References

Akakandelwa, A., 2011, 'An exploratory survey on the SADC e-government web sites', *Library Review* 60(5), 421–431. http://dx.doi.org/10.1108/00242531111135317

Barreto, A.M., 2013, 'Do users look at banner ads on Facebook?', *Journal of Research in Interactive Marketing* 7(2), 119–139. http://dx.doi.org/10.1108/JRIM-Mar-2012-0013

Boyes, J.A. & Irani, Z., 2004, 'An analysis of the barriers and problems to web infrastructure development experienced by small businesses', *International Journal of Information Technology and Management* 3(2/4), 189–207. http://dx.doi.org/10.1504/IJITM.2004.005032

Brunn, D.S. & Dodge, M., 2001, 'Mapping the "worlds" of the World Wide Web: (Re) structuring global commerce through hyperlinks', *American Behavior Scientists* 44(10), 1717–1739. http://dx.doi.org/10.1177/0002764201044010011

Chen, C.-Y., Shih, B.-Y., Chen, Z.-S. & Chen, T.-H., 2011, 'The exploration of internet marketing strategy by search engine optimization: A critical review and comparison', *African Journal of Business Management* 5(12), 4644–4649.

Craven, T.C., 2003, 'HTML tags as extraction cues for webpage description construction', *Information Science Journal* 6, 1–12.

Crowley, M., 2014, 'Take the guesswork out of your marketing strategy', *Journal of Financial Planning* 27(1), 16.

Green, D., 2000, 'The evolution of Web searching', *Online Information Review* 24(2), 124–137. http://dx.doi.org/10.1108/14684520010330283

Guenther, K., 2014, 'Getting your website recognized', *Online Magazine*, Issue May/June, 47–49. *Guidelines for optimising and making your site searchable*, 2014, viewed 01 March 2015, from http://www.ananzi.co.za/submit/guidelines

Gupta, A. & Mateen, A., 2014, 'Exploring the factors affecting sponsored search ad performance', *Marketing Intelligence & Planning* 32(5), 586–599. http://dx.doi.org/10.1108/MIP-05-2013-0083

Henzinger, M.R., Motwani, R. & Silverstein, C., 2002, 'Challenges in web search engines', viewed 30 April 2015, from http://www.acm.org/sigs/sigir/forum/F2002/henzinger.pdf

Hubbard, J., 2004, 'Indexing the Internet', in *Essay for Drexel University College of Information Science and Technology*, viewed 25 April 2015, from http://www.tk421.net/essays/babel.html

Kennedy, K. & Kennedy, B.B., 2008, 'A small company's dilemma: Using search engines effectively for corporate sales', *Management Research News* 31(10), 737–745. http://dx.doi.org/10.1108/01409170810908499

Kent, P., 2012, *Search engine optimization for dummies*, 5th edn., Wiley and Sons, Hoboken.

Kisiel, R., 2010, 'Dealers get on top of search engine results', *Automotive News* 84(6408), 24–25.

Kumar, E. & Kohli, S., 2007, 'A strategic analysis of search engine advertising in web based-commerce', *Journal of Internet Banking & Commerce* 12(2), 1–13.

Lee, W.I., 2010, 'The development of a qualitative dynamic attribute value model for healthcare institutes', *Iranian Journal of Public Health* 39(4), 15–25. PMID: 23113034.

Lee, W.I., Chen, C.W. & Wu, C.H., 2010, 'Relationship between quality of medical treatment and customer satisfaction - A case study in dental clinic association', *International Journal of Innovative Computing, Information and Control* 6, 1805–1822.

Lee, W.I. & Lin, C.H., 2011, 'Consumer hierarchical value map modeling in the healthcare service industry', *African Journal of Business Management* 5(3), 722–736.

Malaga, R.A., 2010, 'Search engine optimization - Black and white hat approaches', *Advances in Computers* 78, 1–39. http://dx.doi.org/10.1016/S0065-2458(10)78001-3

Mancuso, A., 2013, 'How Google AdWords' Ad Rank Algorithm Update Increased Brand CPC's by 600 Percent', viewed 12 May 2015, from http://www.seerinteractive.com/blog/how-google-adwords-ad-rank-algorithm-update-increased-brand-cpcs-by-600

Moreno, L. & Martinez, P., 2013, 'Overlapping factors in search engine optimization and web accessibility', *Online Information Review* 37(4), 564–580. http://dx.doi.org/10.1108/OIR-04-2012-0063

Moxley, D., Blake, J. & Maze, S., 2004, 'Web search engine advertising practices and their effect on library service', *The Bottom Line: Managing Library Finances* 17(2), 61–65. http://dx.doi.org/10.1108/08880450410536080

Murphy, H.C. & Kielgast, C.D., 2008, 'Do small and medium-sized hotels exploit search engine marketing?', *International Journal of Contemporary Hospitality Management* 20(1), 90–97. http://dx.doi.org/10.1108/09596110810848604

Nabout, N.A., 2015, 'A novel approach for bidding on keywords in newly set-up search advertising campaigns', *European Journal of Marketing* 49(5/6), 668–691. http://dx.doi.org/10.1108/EJM-08-2013-0424

Nielsen, J., 2014, 'Top ten global web parent companies', viewed 08 March 2015, from http://www.nielsen.com/us/en/top10s.html

Olbrich, R. & Schultz, C.D., 2014, 'Multichannel advertising: Does print advertising affect search engine advertising?', *European Journal of Marketing* 48(9/10), 1731–1756. http://dx.doi.org/10.1108/EJM-10-2012-0569

Onaifo, D. & Rasmussen, D., 2013, 'Increasing libraries' content findability on the web with search engine optimization', *Library Hi-Tech* 31(1), 87–108. http://dx.doi.org/10.1108/07378831311303958

Oppenheim, C., Morris, A. & McKnight, C., Lowley, S., 2000, 'The evaluation of WWW search engines', *Journal of Documentation* 56(2), 190–211. http://dx.doi.org/10.1108/00220410010803810

Plaza, B., 2009, 'Monitoring web traffic source effectiveness with Google Analytics: An experiment with time series', *Aslib Proceedings* 61(5), 474–482. http://dx.doi.org/10.1108/00012530910989625

Sagin, E., 2013, 'What the new AdWords ad rank algorithm really means', viewed 29 January 2015, from http://www.wordstream.com/blog/ws/2013/10/24/adwords-ad-rank-algorithm

Sen, R., 2005, 'Optimal search engine marketing strategy', *International Journal of Electronic Commerce* 10(1), 9–25.

Singh, A.M., 2002, 'The Internet – Strategies for optimal utilization in South Africa', *South African Journal of Information Management* 4(1). http://dx.doi.org/10.4102/sajim.v4i1.152

Thelwall, M., 2001, 'Commercial web site links', *Internet Research* 11(2), 114–124. http://dx.doi.org/10.1108/10662240110388224

Vaughan, L., 2014, 'Discovering business information from search engine query data', *Online Information Review* 38(4), 562–574. http://dx.doi.org/10.1108/OIR-08-2013-0190

Visser, E.B. & Weideman, M., 2011, 'An empirical study on website usability elements and how they affect search engine optimisation', *South African Journal of Information Management* 13(1). 9 pages. http://dx.doi.org/10.4102/sajim.v13i1.428

Weideman, M., 2013, 'Comparative analysis of homepage website visibility and academic rankings for UK universities', *Information Research* 18(4), viewed 30 April 2015, from http://InformationR.net/ir/18-4/paper599.html

Weideman, M., 2009, *Website visibility: The theory and practice of improving ranking*, Chandos Publishers, Oxford.

Zuze, H. & Weideman, M., 2013, 'Keyword stuffing and the big three search engines', *Online Information Review* 37(2), 268–286. http://dx.doi.org/10.1108/OIR-11-2011-0193

23

Measuring the success of business-intelligence systems in South Africa: An empirical investigation applying the DeLone and McLean Model

Authors:
Taurayi Mudzana[1]
Manoj Maharaj[1]

Affiliation:
[1]School of Management, IT and Governance, University of KwaZulu-Natal, South Africa

Correspondence to:
Taurayi Mudzana

Email:
mudzana@yahoo.com

Postal address:
Private Bag X54001, Durban 4000, South Africa

Background: Business intelligence systems (BIS) hold promise for improving organisational decision-making in South Africa. Yet, the use of BIS has been associated with a number of challenges.

Objectives: The aim of the study was to identify post implementation factors that contribute to the success of BIS in South African organisations.

Method: This study draws on the DeLone and McLean Model of Information Systems success and recent literature on business-intelligence (BI) to develop and test a BIS success model. A quantitative study was conducted in the form of a survey of 102 BI users to validate the BIS success model.

Results: Five interrelated factors of BIS success were confirmed. The study found that the quality of information has a strong influence on system use and user satisfaction. It was found that system quality is positively associated with user satisfaction. The results also indicated that service quality is negatively related to user satisfaction. The study also found that user satisfaction is positively associated with nett benefits of a BI system.

Conclusion: The study provides insights for both managers and practitioners on the factors to focus on when implementing BIS thereby minimising the adoption risks associated with BI failures.

Introduction

Business-intelligence systems (BIS) have a potential to provide many benefits to an organisation. Business intelligence (BI) has been identified as a significant growth area due to its valuable functionality and its ability to add value (Woodside 2011). Furthermore, Gartner (2011) reports that worldwide expenditure in BIS was more than USD 10 billion in 2010 and was expected to continue to grow at a rate of approximately 8.1% annually. However, implementing new BIS is often a challenge (Benard & Atir 1993; Clavier, Lotriet & Van Loggerenberg 2012; Olbrich, Poppelbuß & Niehaves 2012). Hence, understanding the drivers of and barriers to BIS success is very important. The success of BIS has not been fully investigated (Chaveesuk 2010; Yeoh & Koronios 2010). A search in the main electronic databases for journals, such as EbscoHost, Emerald, Google Scholar, Proquest and ScienceDirect, suggests that no academic research has validated the DeLone and McLean (2003) model of information-systems (IS) success in the context of BI in South Africa. This study seeks to address this gap. It is important to study the South African context because most reports on IS success are drawn from settings in industrialised countries and are focused on e-government and enterprise resource planning ERP system success (Heeks 2010). Furthermore, the results of these reports cannot easily be translated to the South-Africa context because South Africa is a developing economy. In most developing countries, a shortage of expertise, staff turnover and limitations in financial resources are cited as challenges to the implementation and utilisation of IS (Avgerou 2008).

This paper is organised as follows. The next section briefly reviews the existing literature on BI. Then the information-systems success model used in the study is highlighted. The model chosen for this study is the DeLone and McLean (2003) model. Next, the proposed BIS success model is presented, and the research methodology is discussed. The results of the study are then presented, followed by the discussion section. The conclusion is presented in the final section of the article.

Business intelligence

BI is defined as a collection of technology and applications used to enhance decision-making (Wixom & Watson 2010). Turban *et al.* (2011:12) classify a BI system into four main components: (1) a data-warehouse (DW) environment, (2) business analytics, (3) business performance management (BPM) and (4) a user interface such as a dashboard. BI offers many benefits to the adopting organisation, for example increasing sales, reducing costs and providing new products and services (Hwang & Xu 2007). BI enables organisations to make well-informed business decisions and can thus be a source of competitive advantage (Ranjan 2009). Similarly, Vitt, Luckevich and Misner (2010) argue that the primary goal of BI is to help people make better decisions that improve a company's performance and promote its competitive advantage in the marketplace. Ranjan (2009) asserts that BI reveals the following:

(1) the position of the firm in comparison to its competitors
(2) changes in customer behaviour and spending patterns
(3) the capabilities of the firm
(4) market conditions, future trends, demographic and economic information
(5) the social, regulatory, and political environment
(6) what the other firms in the market are doing. (p. 63)

Hwang and Xu (2007) further point out that return on investment in BI could be as high as 400%. However, international evidence suggests that BIS are expensive and have generally not been a success (Beal 2005; Legodi & Barry 2010). Some explanations for the low levels of success include the following: system quality; information quality; service quality; user satisfaction (Shin 2003), support for end users; accuracy, format and preciseness; fulfilment of end users' needs; reduced effort by developers to produce information; user ability to produce information and better decision-making (Wixom & Watson 2010). BI is clearly very important to an organisation, but it is evident that a number of issues may limit its use and adoption. It is important therefore that we improve our understanding of the key factors that influence the success of BIS in South Africa. The next section of this paper describes the DeLone and McLean (2003) model of IS success, which is the foundational model chosen for this study.

DeLone and McLean information-systems success model

The theoretical underpinning chosen for this study is the updated DeLone and McLean (2003) model of IS success. The DeLone and McLean (1992) model propose six major factors of IS success: (1) system quality, (2) information quality, (3) use, (4) user satisfaction, (5) individual impact and (6) organisational impact. Pitt, Watson and Kavan (1995) propose a modification of the DeLone and McLean (1992) model to include service quality. Seddon (1997) challenges the combination of a process and variance model. He (Seddon 1997:23) argues that the DeLone and McLean (1992) model is 'confusing and mis-specified'. The DeLone and McLean (2003) information-systems success model address

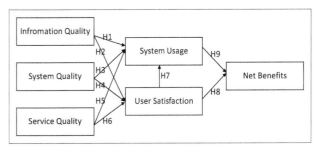

FIGURE 1: Research model.

the weaknesses of the original model. The model consists of the following six factors: system quality, information quality, service quality, use or intention to use, user satisfaction and nett benefit. For the purposes of this study, we have chosen to assess BIS success using the updated DeLone and McLean (2003) model. One of the reasons for this choice was because it was identified as the single most cited IS success model in IS literature (Lowry, Karunga & Richardson 2007). Furthermore, the DeLone and McLean (2003) model framework has been used extensively in various empirical works on IS success. Empirical work has drawn on the updated DeLone and McLean (2003) model to examine the success of a student information system using student users (Rai, Lang & Welker 2002), tourism websites (Stockdale & Borovicka 2006; Wang & Liao 2008), knowledge-management systems (Wu & Wang 2006), e-government systems (Hussein, Abdul Karim & Selamat 2007), online learning systems (Lin 2007) and e-commerce systems (Wang & Liao 2008). Prior studies confirm the model's usefulness in assessing different IS applications. However, in the South African BI context, the researchers found no study that has utilised the updated DeLone and McLean (2003) model to assess the success of local BI systems. The research model and the hypotheses are discussed next.

Research model and hypotheses

Figure 1 illustrates the research model developed for the study. The research model attempts to explain BIS success in a South African context. The research model posits that BIS success is represented by six factors, and each factor is in turn measured, using multiple variables adapted from current literature and input from BI experts.

Information quality

Information quality focuses on the characteristics of the information that is produced by the BIS (Petter, Delone & McLean 2008). This information is mainly in the form of reports. High-quality information is expected to lead to use and user satisfaction of the BIS. There is solid support for the association between information quality and system use and between information quality and user satisfaction (Halawi, McCarthy & Aronson 2007; Kositanurit, Ngwenyama & Osei-Bryson Kweku 2006; Livari 2005; Rai *et al.* 2002). Therefore, in this study, we propose the following hypotheses:

H_{1_0}: Information quality is not related to system use in a business-intelligence system.

H_{1_A}: Information quality is related to system use in a business-intelligence system.

H_{2_0}: Information quality is not related to user satisfaction in a business-intelligence system.

H_{2_A}: Information quality is related to user satisfaction in a business-intelligence system.

System quality

Petter *et al.* (2008) define system quality as follows:

> ... the desirable characteristics of an information system. For example: ease of use, system flexibility, system reliability, and ease of learning, as well as system features of intuitiveness, sophistication, flexibility, and response times. (p. 239)

Previous studies on the success of information systems have demonstrated the positive impact of system quality on user satisfaction and system use (DeLone & McLean 2003; Rai *et al.* 2002; Seddon 1997). Therefore, we propose the following hypotheses:

H_{3_0}: System quality is not related to system use in a business-intelligence system.

H_{3_A}: System quality is related to system use in a business-intelligence system.

H_{4_0}: System quality is not related to user satisfaction in a business-intelligence system.

H_{4_A}: System quality is related to user satisfaction in a business-intelligence system.

Service quality

Service quality focuses on the level of support that BI users receive. Service quality is measured, based on responsiveness, accuracy, reliability, technical competence and empathy of the personnel (Petter *et al.* 2008). Like most studies on IS success, quality service is expected to have a positive influence on user satisfaction and system use (DeLone & McLean 2003; Rai *et al.* 2002). Therefore, we propose the following hypotheses:

H_{5_0}: Service quality is not related to system use in a business-intelligence system.

H_{5_A}: Service quality is related to system use in a business-intelligence system.

H_{6_0}: Service quality is not related to user satisfaction in a business-intelligence system.

H_{6_A}: Service quality is related to user satisfaction in a business-intelligence system.

System use

System use focuses on the utilisation of the BIS by the users. System use is defined as follows:

> ... the degree and manner in which staff and customers utilise the capabilities of an information system. For example: amount of use, frequency of use, nature of use, appropriateness of use, extent of use, and purpose of use. (Petter *et al.* 2008:239)

Previous studies on the success of IS have demonstrated the positive impact of system use on user satisfaction and nett benefits (DeLone & McLean 2003; Rai *et al.* 2002). Therefore, we propose the following hypotheses:

H_{9_0}: System use is not related to nett benefits in a business-intelligence system.

H_{9_A}: System use is related to nett benefits in a business-intelligence system.

User satisfaction

Seddon (1997) defines user satisfaction as follows:

> ... the net feeling of pleasure or displeasure resulting from aggregating all the benefits that a person hopes to receive from interaction with the information system. Each user has a set of expected benefits or aspirations for the information system. To the extent that the system meets or fails to meet each of these aspirations, the user is more or less satisfied. (p. 246)

Previous studies on the success of IS have demonstrated the positive impact of user satisfaction on net benefits (DeLone & McLean 2003; Rai *et al.* 2002; Wang, Fan & Xu 2012). Therefore, we propose the following hypotheses:

H_{7_0}: User satisfaction is not related to system use in a business-intelligence system.

H_{7_A}: User satisfaction is related to system use in a business-intelligence system.

H_{8_0}: User satisfaction is not related to nett benefits in a business-intelligence system.

H_{8_A}: User satisfaction is related to nett benefits in a business-intelligence system.

Research methodology

In order to validate the research model, data were collected by means of an online questionnaire. The online questionnaire consisted of two main parts. The first part included demographic questions such as age, gender and industry. The second part consisted of 35 five-point Likert-scale questions aiming to assess the six factors of the proposed research model. The five-point Likert scale ranged from strongly agree to strongly disagree. The online questionnaire was developed from prior studies and adapted to suit the BI context. Table 1 below shows the items for each construct in the second section of the questionnaire.

Before the major study, the instrument was pilot tested by six professionals to ensure that the wording was understandable and that its length was appropriate. The final instrument was administered over a four-week period. Ethical clearance was obtained before conducting this study. The results of the data analysis used to test the hypotheses will be presented in the next section.

Results

A total of 102 conveniently selected professionals responded to the survey. Most of the responding professionals were

TABLE 1: Survey instrument constructs.

Construct	Description	Adapted from
System quality	Availability	DeLone and McLean (1992); Doll and Torkzadeh (1988); DeLone and McLean (2003)
	Ease of use	-
	Accessibility	-
	Usefulness	-
	Stability	-
Information quality	Content	Doll and Torkzadeh (1988)
	Availability	-
	Accuracy	-
	Timelines	-
	Conciseness	-
System use	I frequently use the system.	Seddon (1997)
	I depend upon the system.	-
	I only use the system when it is absolutely necessary for learning.	-
User satisfaction	Meets information needs.	Rai *et al.* (2002)
	I think the system is very helpful.	-
	Overall, I am satisfied with the system.	-
Nett benefits	The system has a positive impact on my work.	DeLone and Mclean (1992); DeLone and Mclean (2003)
	Overall, the performance of the system is good.	-
	Overall, the system is successful.	-
	The system is an important and valuable aid to me in the performance of my work.	-
Service quality	Assurance	DeLone and Mclean (2003)
	Empathy	-
	Responsiveness	-
	Knowledge	-

TABLE 2: Reliability tests.

Factor	Items	Cronbach alpha
System quality	8	0.77
Information quality	10	0.75
User satisfaction	3	0.86
System usage	3	0.79
Net benefits	6	0.74
Service quality	5	0.85

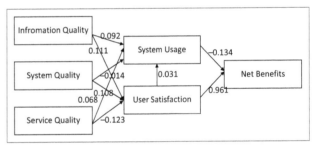

FIGURE 2: Structural model test results.

male (52%), roughly 60% of respondents were between 31 and 40 years of age, and 20% of respondents were between 41 and 50 years old. Over half of the respondents (55%) reported having more than five years of experience in their current role whilst 45% reported less than five years of experience. Approximately two thirds of the responding professionals reported that they use BIS for ad-hoc reporting. All participants participated voluntarily in this study.

Measurement model

The results of the reliability tests are shown in Table 2. The results show that the value of Cronbach's alpha for all constructs is higher than 0.7. This suggests that the questionnaire and its constructs are suited for the study (Hair *et al.* 2006).

Convergent validity was established by examining the average variance extracted (AVE) scores. These were all well above the recommended 0.50 (Fornell & Larcker 1981), confirming that constructs explained above 50% of the variance in their underlying items.

Structural model

After validating the measurement model, the hypotheses were tested by examining the structural model. Figure 2 shows the path coefficients, which indicate the strengths of the relationships between the independent and dependent variables.

The results indicate that information quality is positively related to both system use and user satisfaction. The null hypotheses (H_{10}, H_{20}) were thus rejected. Therefore, the alternative hypotheses (H_{1A}, H_{2A}) stand (0.092 and 0.011, respectively). The path coefficient between system quality and system use is –0.014 with a *p*-value of 0.624. The Kendall correlation coefficient between system use and system quality is 0.046 with a *p*-value of 0.568. System quality is thus not related to system use. Therefore, the null hypothesis cannot be rejected (H_{30}). Considering user satisfaction, however, the results indicate that system quality is positively related to user satisfaction. In this case, the null hypothesis was rejected. Therefore, the alternative hypothesis (H_{4A}) stands (0.108). The path coefficient between system use and service quality is 0.068 with a p-value of 0.188. The Kendall correlation coefficient between system use and service quality is 0.049 with a p-value of 0.574. Therefore, the null hypothesis cannot be rejected. Service quality, in turn, is not related to system use. For the sixth hypothesis, the path coefficient is −0.123 with a p-value of 0.051. The Kendall correlation coefficient between user satisfaction and service quality is −0.200 with a p-value of 0.019. Therefore, the null hypothesis can be rejected. User satisfaction is negatively related to service quality. The results indicate that, as service quality increases, user satisfaction decreases. The path coefficient between system use and nett benefits is −0.134 with a p-value of 0.495. The Kendall correlation coefficient between system usage and nett benefits is −0.028 with a p-value of 0.733. System use is not related to nett benefits. Therefore, the null hypothesis cannot be rejected. The results indicate that the path coefficient between user satisfaction and a nett benefit is 0.961 with a p-value of 0.000. The Kendall correlation coefficient between user satisfaction and nett benefits is 0.314 with a p- value of 0.000. Therefore, the null hypothesis can be rejected. User satisfaction is positively related to nett benefits. Overall, information quality exhibited a stronger effect than system quality and service quality in influencing system use and user satisfaction, respectively.

Discussion and implications

This study formulated and verified a BIS success model. Using the updated DeLone and McLean model as a theoretical framework, we constructed ten measures in information quality, eight measures in system quality, five measures in service quality, three measures in user satisfaction, three measures in system use and six measures in nett benefits. To our knowledge, this is the first study that extends the DeLone and McLean Model (2003) to a BI context in South Africa. Consistent with previous studies (DeLone & McLean 2003; Kositanurit et al. 2006; Halawi et al. 2007; Holsapple & Lee-Post 2006; Rai et al. 2002), our findings indicate that information quality is positively linked to system use and user satisfaction. The results are less clear with respect to the influence of system quality on system use and user satisfaction. System quality was not found to be related to system use. This finding is unexpected and inconsistent with previous studies where system quality is reported to have a significantly positive influence on system use (DeLone & McLean 2003; Fitzgerald & Russo 2005). The different types of applications investigated and the different contexts can explain differences amongst the findings of this study and the research in previous studies. Thus, whilst the present study examined BIS in South Africa, the DeLone and McLean (2003) study examined e-commerce in Western countries. Whilst the DeLone and McLean model is intended to be valid for all IS in general (DeLone & McLean 2003), they recommended that researchers should adapt the research model for specific domains to better address the characteristics of the latter (Dinter, Schieder & Gluchowski

2011). In this study, the success factors where adapted to suit the BI context. The results of the test of the effect of system quality on user satisfaction found that system quality is positively related to user satisfaction. As the quality of the system increases so does the user-satisfaction levels. The results of this study agree with the findings of previous studies (DeLone & McLean 2003; Halawi et al. 2007; Holsapple & Lee-Post 2006). The implication for management is that system quality plays an important role in the success of BI projects. Managers could make an effort to address system quality to increase the chances of success of the BIS as users are bound to be satisfied by a high-quality system. The empirical results of the study indicate that there is no significant relationship between service quality and system use. This finding suggests that the quality of service does not influence the use of the system. This is inconsistent with previous studies where service quality is reported to have a significant influence on system use (Caldeira & Ward 2002; Fitzgerald & Russo 2005).

A possible explanation for this is that service quality is outsourced to BI vendors who manage the service, and consequently, BI users do not view it as an integral part of the organisation and tend to take the availability of this service for granted. The results of this study indicate that service quality influences user satisfaction negatively, results which are inconsistent with the information-systems model of DeLone and McLean (2003). DeLone and McLean's work suggest that service quality is positively related to user satisfaction. The different types of systems investigated and their different needs for respective contexts can explain differences amongst the findings of this study and DeLone and McLean's. Hypothesis 7 investigated the relationship between user satisfaction and system use. The empirical results of the study indicate that user satisfaction does not influence system use. This is unexpected, given that one would have expected the levels of system use to increase as the levels of user satisfaction increase. A plausible explanation is that the model used in the present study did not include the intention-to-use factor, and it also did not include system-use and user-satisfaction association. However, this research is not alone in providing evidence of a non-significant relationship between user satisfaction and system use. Some previous studies (Ang & Soh 1997; Vlahos & Ferratt 1995) also found that user satisfaction did not directly influence system use. The influence of system use on the nett benefits of business-intelligence systems in South Africa was examined by hypotheses eight. The empirical results of the study indicate that there is no significant relationship between system use and nett benefits. These results were inconsistent with the theoretical arguments based on DeLone and McLean (2003). The results of this study also do not agree with the findings of other previous studies (Devaraj & Kohli 2003; Leclercq 2007; Zhu & Kraemer 2005). However, a study by Gelderman (1998) did not find a significant positive correlation between system and nett benefit. A plausible explanation for this difference is that the model for the present study focused only on system use and not on the intention to use a system. Furthermore, the model used in this study does not include the nett benefits to the system-use relationship but rather focuses on the relationship between system use and nett benefits. It was found that user satisfaction positively influences nett benefits, results that are consistent with the information-systems model of DeLone & McLean (2003) which suggested that user satisfaction is positively related to nett benefits. The results imply that, as levels of satisfaction increase, so do the nett benefits of the system. In this regard, the results of this study agree with the findings of other previous studies (Gelderman 1998; Law & Ngai 2007).

Implications

The study is one of only a few to formulate and test a BIS success model based on the DeLone and McLean's (2003) IS success model in a South African context. Therefore, this study contributes knowledge to information-systems literature in general and BI in particular. As a result, by using the DeLone and McLean's (2003) model as its basis, this study adds to the area of information-systems success by supporting the DeLone and McLean's (2003) model and by refining it to be more suited to BI success, specifically in the context of South Africa. Some of the factors identified through this study as important to BIS success corroborate previous literature. The different types of applications investigated and the different contexts can explain differences amongst the findings of this study and previous research. Thus, whilst the present study examined BIS in South Africa, the DeLone and McLean's (2003) IS success model examined e-commerce in Western countries. Whilst the DeLone and McLean's (2003) model is intended to be valid for all information systems in general, they recommend that researchers should adapt the research model for specific domains to better address the characteristics of the latter (Dinter *et al.* 2011). In this study, the success factors where adapted to suit the BI context. The model of BI-system success formulated and tested in this study will be of interest to organisations wishing to adopt BI systems. Two groups of people who could possibly be drawn from this study. Firstly, BI developers and BI Managers who will develop and implement a BIS would benefit. Secondly, the BI vendor industry would benefit from this study. The main practical implication of this study for BI developers and managers is that it would make them more aware of the factors that influence the success of the BIS they develop. With these factors in mind, they would then be able to incorporate into their development such factors as the ease of use, ease of learning, stability and security of their system. This research enables people in the BI vendor industry to understand the pitfalls of BI adoption and the reasons why adoption can be problematic. It could allow them to take a more proactive approach when new versions of solutions are been developed.

Limitations

There are some limitations to this study. The first limitation of the study is that context in which the study was set was limited to organisations operating in South Africa. Consequently, caution needs to be taken when generalising the results of this study. A second limitation was that we tested only part of the updated DeLone and McLean (2003) model. Further research could consider incorporating and validating the entire updated DeLone and McLean (2003) model.

Conclusion

The objective of this study was to identify key factors influencing BIS success in South Africa and to test those factors using data from BIS users. We developed a conceptual model for BIS success in South Africa, based on the updated DeLone and McLean (2003) model. Survey data from 102 BI users in South Africa were used to test the BIS success model. This study reached several conclusions based on the empirical findings. Firstly, the results of the empirical analysis indicate that the quality of information has a strong influence on system use and user satisfaction. Secondly, the results indicate that system quality is positively associated with user satisfaction. Thirdly, service quality is negatively related to user satisfaction. Fourthly, nett benefits are positively associated with user satisfaction. Overall, the empirical results of the study provide moderate support for the proposed research model. Of the nine relationships tested, five were significant. In summary, this research sheds light on the key factors to be considered by organisations that are considering implementing or which have already adopted a BI system. Therefore, this study has improved our understanding of the factors influencing the success of BIS in South Africa. The findings also contribute to the growing body of literature on the measurement of the success of information systems in general. Future research should aim to confirm the specific findings of this study and further to investigate the interdependency of the success factors.

Acknowledgements
Competing interests

The authors declare that they have no financial or personal relationships that may have inappropriately influenced them in writing this article.

Authors' contributions

T.M. (University of KwaZulu-Natal) and M.M. (University of KwaZulu-Natal) contributed equally to the writing of this article.

References

Ang, S. & Soh, C., 1997, 'User information satisfaction, job satisfaction, and computer background: An exploratory study', *Information & Management* 32(5), 255–266. http://dx.doi.org/10.1016/S0378-7206(97)00030-X

Avgerou, C., 2008, 'Information systems in developing countries: A critical research review', *Journal of Information Technology* 23(3), 133–146. http://dx.doi.org/10.1057/palgrave.jit.2000136

Beal, B., 2005, *Half of data warehouse projects to fail*, viewed 22 May 2014, from http://searchcrm.techtarget.com/news/1066086/Report-Half-of-data-warehouse-projects-to-fail

Benard, R. & Atir, A.S., 1993, 'User satisfaction with EISs: Meeting the needs of executive users', *Information Systems Management* 10(4), 21–29. http://dx.doi.org/10.1080/10580539308906953

Caldeira, M.M. & Ward, J.M., 2002, 'Understanding the successful adoption and use of IS/IT in SMEs: An explanation from Portuguese manufacturing industries', *Information Systems Journal* 12(2), 121–152. http://dx.doi.org/10.1046/j.1365-2575.2002.00119.x

Chaveesuk, S., 2010, 'The determinants of the adoption and application of business intelligence: An ERP perspective', PhD thesis, Victoria University.

Clavier, P.R., Lotriet, H.H. & Van Loggerenberg, J.J., 2012, 'Business intelligence challenges in the context of goods and service-dominant logic', *proceedings of the 45th Hawaii International Conference*, Hawaii, pp. 4138–4147. http://dx.doi.org/10.1109/hicss.2012.138

DeLone, W.H. & McLean, E.R., 1992, 'Information systems success: The quest for the dependent variable', *Information Systems Research* 3(1), 60–95. http://dx.doi.org/10.1287/isre.3.1.60

DeLone, W.H. & McLean, E.R., 2003, 'The DeLone and McLean model of information systems success: A ten-year update', *Journal of Management Information Systems* 19(4), 9–30.

Devaraj, S. & Kohli, R., 2003, 'Performance impacts of information technology: Is actual usage the missing link?', *Management Science* 49(3), 273–289. http://dx.doi.org/10.1287/mnsc.49.3.273.12736

Dinter, B., Schieder, C. & Gluchowski, P., 2011, 'Towards a life cycle oriented business intelligence success model', *proceedings of the Americas Conference of Information Systems* 361.

Fitzgerald, G. & Russo, N.L., 2005, 'The turnaround of the London ambulance service computer-aided dispatch system (LASCAD)', *European Journal of Information Systems* 14(3), 244–257. http://dx.doi.org/10.1057/palgrave.ejis.3000541

Fornell, C. & Larcker, D.F., 1981, 'Evaluating structural equation models with unobservable variables and measurement error', *Journal of of Marketing Research* 18(1), 39–50. http://dx.doi.org/10.2307/3151312

Gartner, 2011, 'Gartner says worldwide business intelligence, CPM and analytic applications/performance management software market grew seven percent in 2012', viewed 01 January 2013, from http://www.gartner.com/newsroom/id/2507915

Gelderman, M., 1998, 'The relation between user satisfaction, usage of information systems and performance', *Information & Management* 34(1), 11–18. http://dx.doi.org/10.1016/S0378-7206(98)00044-5

Heeks, R., 2010, 'Real money from virtual worlds', *Scientific American* 302, 68–73. http://dx.doi.org/10.1038/scientificamerican0110-68

Hair, J.F., Black, W.C., Babin, B.J., Anderson, R.E. & Tatham, R.L., 2006, *Multivariate data analysis*, 6th edn., Pearson Prentice Hall, New Jersey.

Halawi, L.A., McCarthy, R.V. & Aronson, J.E., 2007, 'An empirical investigation of knowledge management systems' success', *Journal of Computer Information Systems* 48(2), 121–135.

Holsapple, C.W. & Lee-Post, A., 2006, 'Defining, assessing, and promoting elearning success: An information systems perspective', *Decision Sciences Journal of Innovative Education* 4(1), 67–85. http://dx.doi.org/10.1111/j.1540-4609.2006.00102.x

Hussein, R., Abdul Karim, N. & Selamat, M., 2007, 'The impact of technological factors on information systems success in the electronic-government context', *Business Process Management Journal* 13(5), 613–627. http://dx.doi.org/10.1108/14637150710823110

Hwang, M.I. & Xu, H., 2007, 'The effect of implementation factors on data warehousing success: An exploratory study', *Journal of Information, Information Technology, and Organizations* 2(1), 1–16.

Kositanurit, B., Ngwenyama, O. & Osei-Bryson Kweku, K., 2006, 'An exploration of factors that impact individual performance in an ERP environment: An analysis using multiple analytical techniques', *European Journal of Information Systems* 15(6), 556–568. http://dx.doi.org/10.1057/palgrave.ejis.3000654

Law, C.C. & Ngai, E.W., 2007, 'ERP systems adoption: An exploratory study of the organizational factors and impacts of ERP success', *Information & Management* 44(4), 418–432. http://dx.doi.org/10.1016/j.im.2007.03.004

Leclercq, A., 2007, 'The perceptual evaluation of information systems using the construct of user satisfaction: Case study of a large French group', *The Database for Advances in Information Systems* 38(2), 27–60. http://dx.doi.org/10.1145/1240616.1240621

Legodi, I. & Barry, M.L., 2010, *The current challenges and status of risk management in enterprise data warehouse projects in South Africa*, PICMET, Phuket.

Lin, H.F., 2007, 'Measuring online learning systems success: Applying the updated DeLone and McLean mode', *CyberPsychology & Behavior* 10(6), 817–820. http://dx.doi.org/10.1089/cpb.2007.9948

Livari, J., 2005, 'An empirical test of the Delone-McLean model of information system success', *The Data Base for Advances in Information Systems* 36(2), 8–27. http://dx.doi.org/10.1145/1066149.1066152

Lowry, P.B., Karunga, G.G. & Richardson, V.J., 2007, 'Assessing leading institutions, faculty, and articles in premier information systems research journals', *Communications of the Associations of Information Systems* 20(16), 142–203.

Olbrich, S., Poppelbuß, J. & Niehaves, B., 2012, 'Critical contextual success factors for business intelligence: A Delphi study on their relevance, variability, and controllability', *proceedings of the 45th Hawaii International Conference*, Hawaii, pp. 4148–4157. http://dx.doi.org/10.1109/hicss.2012.187

Petter, S., DeLone, W. & McLean, E., 2008, 'Measuring information systems success: Models, dimensions, measures, and interrelationships', *European Journal of Information Systems* 17(3), 236–263. http://dx.doi.org/10.1057/ejis.2008.15

Pitt, L., Watson, R. & Kavan, C., 1995, 'Service quality: A measure of information systems effectiveness', *Management Information Systems Quarterly* 19(2), 173–185. http://dx.doi.org/10.2307/249687

Rai, A., Lang, S.S. & Welker, R.B., 2002, 'Assessing the validity of IS success models: An empirical test and theoretical analysis', *Information Systems Research* 13(1), 50–69. http://dx.doi.org/10.1287/isre.13.1.50.96

Ranjan, J., 2009, 'Business intelligence: Concepts, components, techniques and benefits', *Journal of Theoretical and Applied Information Technology* 9(1), 60–70.

Seddon, P.B., 1997, 'A respecification and extension of the DeLone and McLean model of IS success', *Information Systems Research* 8(3), 240–253. http://dx.doi.org/10.1287/isre.8.3.240

Shin, B., 2003, 'An exploratory investigation of system success factors in data warehousing', *Journal of the Association for Information Systems* 4(1), 141–170.

Stockdale, R. & Borovicka, M., 2006, 'Developing an online business community: A travel industry case study', *proceedings of the 39th Annual Hawaii International Conference*, Hawaii, 134. http://dx.doi.org/10.1109/hicss.2006.123

Turban, E., Sharda, R., Dursun, D. & King, D., 2011, *Business intelligence*, 9th edn., Prentice Hall, New York.

Vitt, E., Luckevich, M. & Misner, S., 2010, *Business intelligence*, O'Reilly Media.

Vlahos, G.E. & Ferratt, T.W., 1995, 'Information technology use by managers in Greece to support decision making: Amount, perceived value, and satisfaction', *Information and Management* 29(6), 305–315. http://dx.doi.org/10.1016/0378-7206(95)00037-1

Wang, J.-b., Fan, C.-j. & Xu, Q.-l., 2012, 'Empirical research on business intelligence system architecture', *International Journal of Applied Science and Technology* 2(7), 257–260. http://dx.doi.org/10.1016/j.giq.2007.06.002

Wang, Y.S. & Liao, Y.W., 2008, 'Assessing eGovernment systems success: A validation of the DeLone and McLean model of information systems success', *Government Information Quarterly* 25(4) 717–733.

Wixom, B. & Watson, H., 2010, 'The BI-based organization', *International Journal of Business Intelligence Research* 1(1), 13–28.

Woodside, J., 2011, Business intelligence best practices for success', *proceedings of the European Conference on Information Management*, Toronto.

Wu, J.H. & Wang, Y.M., 2006, 'Measuring KMS success: A respecification of the DeLone and McLean model', *Information and Management* 43(6), 728–739. http://dx.doi.org/10.1016/j.im.2006.05.002

Yeoh, W. & Koronios, A., 2010, 'Critical success factors for business intelligence systems', *Journal of Computer Information Systems* 50(3), 23–132.

Zhu, K. & Kraemer, K.L., 2005, 'Post-adoption variations in usage and value of e-business by organizations: Cross-country evidence from the retail industry', *Information Systems Research* 16(1), 61–84. http://dx.doi.org/10.1287/isre.1050.0045

24

Uncovering Web search tactics in South African higher education

Authors:
Surika Civilcharran[1]
Mitchell Hughes[2]
Manoj S. Maharaj[1]

Affiliations:
[1]School of Management, IT and Governance, University of KwaZulu-Natal, South Africa

[2]School of Economic and Business Sciences, University of the Witwatersrand, South Africa

Correspondence to:
Manoj Maharaj

Email:
maharajms@ukzn.ac.za

Postal address:
Private Bag X54001, Durban 4000, South Africa

Background: The potential of the World Wide Web ('the Web') as a tool for information retrieval in higher education is beyond question. Harnessing this potential, however, remains a challenge, particularly in the context of developing countries, where students are drawn from diverse socio-economic, educational and technological backgrounds.

Objectives: The purpose of this study is to identify the Web search tactics used by postgraduate students in order to address the weaknesses of undergraduate students with regard to their Web searching tactics. This article forms part of a wider study into postgraduate students' information retrieval strategies at the University of KwaZulu-Natal, Pietermaritzburg campus, South Africa.

Method: The study utilised the mixed methods approach, employing both questionnaires (Phase 1) and structured interviews (Phase 2), and was largely underpinned by Bates's model of information search tactics. This article reports and reflects on the findings of Phase 1, which focused on identifying the Web search tactics employed by postgraduate students.

Results: Findings indicated a preference for lower-level Web search tactics, despite respondents largely self-reporting as intermediate or expert users. Moreover, the majority of respondents gained their knowledge on Web searching through experience and only a quarter of respondents have been given formal training on Web searching.

Conclusion: In addition to contributing to theory, it is envisaged that this article will contribute to practice by informing the design of undergraduate training interventions to proactively address the information retrieval challenges faced by novice users. Subsequent papers will report on Phase 2 of the study.

Introduction and rationale

Owing to its obvious benefits of convenience and volume of material available, many higher education students naturally turn to the World Wide Web ('the Web') when searching for information, whether it is for academic or non-academic purposes (Ganaie & Khazer 2014; Shanahan 2008; Timmers & Glas 2010). Whilst the Web is considered a powerful tool for information retrieval (Nazim 2008), there are significant challenges associated with its use (Kriewel & Fuhr 2010), particularly in an academic context. The vast quantities of information available, as well as the independence of information suppliers, can cause the information retrieved to be obsolete, misguiding or imprecise (Flouris *et al.* 2012).

Students also tend to have a poor understanding of search engines and are therefore limited in their ability to use them effectively. In particular, they have difficulty in evaluating search results and sources (Timmers & Glas 2010). They often do not possess the ability to question the authenticity of the information retrieved (Asemi 2005; Nazim 2008; Zamani-Miandashti, Memarbashi & Khalighzadeh 2013) and the quality of their work and contribution to research inevitably suffer. South African postgraduate students are no exception, with the added complication of substantial socio-economic, educational and technological diversity. It is arguably inevitable that students across this spectrum will turn to the Web to address their information retrieval needs. The authors therefore call for South African higher education institutions to acknowledge this and proactively manage the challenges that information retrieval via the Web brings about. The first step in doing so is identifying the Web search tactics that postgraduate students currently employ.

Problem statement

Students are still faced with the difficulty of effectively retrieving information, even though the vast amount of information available on the Web is continuously increasing and the design of search engines is constantly evolving to enhance the search experience (Othman, Junurham &

Nilam 2014). Most undergraduate students are unaware of the advanced search features offered by a search engine, and those who are aware use them incorrectly (Alharbi, Smith & Mayhew 2013). Therefore students should be educated on how to use Web-based resources effectively and efficiently, and more so on how to evaluate information resources (Ganaie & Khazer 2014). Most Web users utilise search engines to find information and, as a result, it is imperative to understand and improve the interaction between end-users and search tools in order to promote successful information retrieval (Palanisamy & Sha 2014).

Theoretical underpinnings

The theoretical basis for this study was Bates's (1979) model of information search tactics, which, although developed before the rise of the Internet, has been shown to be applicable to both manual and online information retrieval (Carstens, Rittberger & Wissel 2009; Kriewel & Fuhr 2010; Smith 2012). Her model is comprised of search tactics (moves made to further a search) and search strategy (an overall plan for the entire search) (Bates 1979). Bates (1979) defines 29 tactics that are intended to assist in complex searching for both manual and online systems. Although search strategy plays an important role in the final result of a search, Bates's focus is on tactics. This article adopts a similar approach. A summary of the tactics from Bates's (1979) model of information search tactics are presented below; the detailed descriptions can be found in the original work (Bates 1979).

Bates's four types of information search tactics

The first type of information search tactic is monitoring: keeping track of the progress of the search and ensuring efficiency. Bates (1979) lists and summarises five monitoring tactics:

M1. CHECK – To compare the original request to the current search topic to determine if they are identical.

M2. WEIGH – To do a cost-benefit assessment of present and future actions at various points during the search.

M3. PATTERN – To identify a search pattern, assess it and improve on it if it is inefficient or obsolete.

M4. CORRECT – To guard against incorrect spelling and errors in the search topic.

M5. RECORD – To keep track of desired trails that are incomplete or not followed up.

The second type is file structure tactics: techniques for navigating through the file structure of a database to locate information. These are:

F1. BIBBLE – To locate a bibliography that has already been prepared before preparing one.

F2. SELECT – To break down complex queries in subqueries and work on one subquery at a time.

F3. SURVEY – To examine the available options at each decision point during the search, before making a selection.

F4. CUT – To choose a route that immediately eliminates a major portion of the search domain, when deciding the approach to take to search a query.

F5. STRETCH – To use an information resource for a purpose other than its anticipated reasons.

F6. SCAFFOLD – To plan an indirect, secondary route through the information resources to attain the required information.

F7. CLEAVE – To use binary searching when searching for a resource in an ordered file.

The third type is search formulation tactics, which aid in the formulation of search criteria. There are six search formulation tactics:

S1. SPECIFY – To use search terms that are as precise as the required information.

S2. EXHAUST – To include as many elements of the query in the original search; to add one or more query elements to formulated search criteria.

S3. REDUCE – To decrease the number of query elements in the original search formulation; to subtract one or more query elements from the formulated search criteria.

S4. PARALLEL – To broaden the search formulation by incorporating synonyms or conceptually parallel terms.

S5. PINPOINT – To narrow the search formulation to precise terms by reducing the amount of parallel terms, and in doing so keeping the more precise terms.

S6. BLOCK – To reject elements indexed by or containing certain terms, even if some sections of relevance gets lost.

The fourth type is term tactics, which aid in the selection and revision of specific terms within the search formulation. There are 11 term tactics:

T1. SUPER – To ascend to a broader (fundamental) term.

T2. SUB – To descend to a precise (subordinate) term.

T3. RELATE – To move to a synonym.

T4. NEIGHBOUR – To find supplementary search terms by evaluating neighbouring terms that may be similar in subject, proximate alphabetically or otherwise.

T5. TRACE – To assess acquired information so as to find more terms for additional searching.

T6. VARY – To alter the search terms in one of several ways.

T7. FIX – To try different prefixes, suffixes or infixes.

T8. REARRANGE – To rearrange the order of the search terms.

T9. CONTRARY – To search for an antonym.

T10. RESPELL – To search with a different spelling.

T11. RESPACE – To try spacing alternatives.

Several information search tactics, such as monitoring tactics (CHECK, WEIGH, PATTERN, CORRECT and RECORD) are directly relevant to the Internet, as they are largely technology independent (Smith 2012).

Web searching in higher education

Information retrieval tactics have been of interest to many disciplines, including education, information studies, psychology and information technology (Bates 2010). Information retrieval via the Web is an interdisciplinary topic, incorporating computer science, cognitive science, library and information science and sociology (Szucs *et al.* 2013). Bhavnani, Drabenstott & Radev (2001:2) argue that 'information retrieval is central to functioning as an informed society' and that effective information retrieval is therefore a critical skill. This is particularly true in developing contexts like South Africa, a country that is attempting to establish itself as an economic and research hub in Africa.

Students are required to develop information skills to assist them in identifying, evaluating and using information effectively (Ganaie & Khazer 2014). Furthermore, recent shifts toward a learning-centred approach in higher education and the focus on independent learning implies that information retrieval skills are vital to the survival and success of a student (Ganaie & Khazer 2014). Both basic and higher education students increasingly prefer the Web to traditional books and journals (Smith 2012). It is therefore essential to understand how students use the Web to retrieve information (Alharbi *et al.* 2013; Shanahan 2008; Thornton & Kaya 2013).

Web search tactics

Information retrieval is a complex task, requiring numerous combinations of moves and tactics (Smith 2012). For this study, it is important to distinguish between the two. A move is a single step in executing a search tactic (Bates 1979; Marchionini 1995; Wildemuth, Oh & Marchionini 2010; Xie 2007). Bates (1979:207) defines a tactic as 'a move made to further a search'. Marchionini (1995) defines a tactic as a group of behaviours, such as capturing a query using general terms and then later narrowing the search by using more specific search terms. Hung *et al.* (2008) define a tactic as a localised manoeuvre made to further a strategy, where tactics are typically utilised to reduce the number of results retrieved and/or improve the precision or recall of a search. Xie (2007) explains that tactics for information retrieval are signified by entities including attributes and methods. In addition, Wildemuth (2004:246) maintains that 'a set of moves that are temporally and semantically related can be a search tactic'. In this article, a tactic is viewed as a combination of moves.

The Web compels searchers to employ several information retrieval tactics, forcing them to shift from one search tactic to the next (Nordlie & Pharo 2013; Xie 2007). The Web, by its dynamic nature, induces change in both information retrieval systems and in information itself, which creates difficulties for searchers (Nordlie & Pharo 2013; Xie 2007). Searchers are therefore required to employ their cognitive skills, domain knowledge and general knowledge, in addition to their understanding and expertise of a system and proficiency and ability in information seeking (Alexopoulou, Morris & Hepworth 2014; Marchionini 1995; Xie 2007). Searchers are also required to be active when searching the Web in order for valuable information to be extracted and for the information to be used effectively (Hoeber 2008; Hoque *et al.* 2013). 'These tasks include crafting and refining queries, browsing, filtering, investigating and exploring search result sets' (Hoeber 2008:29). Additional tasks may include analysing, understanding, organising and saving retrieved documents (Hoeber 2008). Further factors to be considered include the nature of the search task, system capabilities, user behaviour and search outcomes (Alharbi *et al.* 2013).

Research suggests that experience in the use of Web search engines, in addition to users' prior knowledge, can influence their Web search strategy as well as their observed level of satisfaction (Kinley 2014). Furthermore, trial and error may not effectively improve the skills required to search the Web, as this method is time consuming and novice searchers typically end up frustrated (Cassidy *et al.* 2014; Nachmias & Gilad 2002). Therefore, appropriate training is arguably necessary. Nachmias and Gilad (2002) argue that the learning objectives of any educational institution should involve the acquisition of Web search skills. It is recommended that methodical training resources concentrating on Web search strategies is required and must be considered and applied (Asemi 2005; Foss *et al.* 2013; Nachmias & Gilad 2002). Smith (2012) points out that information literate individuals should truly be able to search the Internet effectively, rather than retrieve information that satisfies an information need, but may not be comprehensive or the best available. Understanding Web search tactics will arguably help in addressing this issue.

Novice versus expert users

Novice users, those without formal training, typically battle to generate search terms that encapsulate their information needs and that will yield appropriate results (Kriewel & Fuhr 2010). It may be argued that novices seldom employ sophisticated search tactics and actually use counter-productive methods (Carstens *et al.* 2009; Kriewel & Fuhr 2010). Novices rarely recognise when and how to use advanced search features (Kriewel & Fuhr 2010; Markey 2007a). Chu and Law (2007) found that novice users often conduct erroneous searches and search merely by traditional browsing. This could be ascribed to the fact that most were novices both in their subject areas and in information retrieval (Chu & Law 2007). Aitken (2007) reports a case in which first-year undergraduate students were actually discouraged from using online sources for research owing to students' inability to judge academically reliable sources. Novices tend to be steered toward unsuccessfully meeting their information needs because of insufficient search knowledge (Tyonum & Shidi 2014).

Markey (2007b) states that high precision is the main objective of expert users. Experts rely on the accuracy of their search strategies, and they therefore employ activities and look for clues that best describe their information needs (Markey 2007b). Experts possess effective information searching strategies that enable them to acquire result sets that genuinely meet their information needs (Kriewel & Fuhr 2010).

The authors therefore sought to establish the Web search tactics employed in the South African higher education context.

Research design

Phase 1 of the wider study was quantitative in nature, employing structured questionnaires for data collection. Similar studies have also followed this approach (Aula, Jhaveri & Käki 2005; Chu & Law 2007; Tseng & Wu 2008). Questionnaire items were drawn from three studies, namely those of Bates (1979), Nachmias and Gilad (2002) and Aula *et al.* (2005). The questionnaire used was adapted to include more recent developments in both Web technologies and search tactics. The questionnaire comprised both closed and open-ended questions.

The questionnaire was evaluated using factor analysis to validate the subscales and a reliability analysis was performed to assess the internal consistency of the subscale items (Creswell & Clark 2007). The content of the questionnaire was validated by research professionals in Information Systems and Information Science to ensure content validity, which is described as a function of how well the scope and aspects of a concept have been outlined (Sekaran & Bougie 2010). Validity was also addressed by drawing the majority of questionnaire items from established research instruments employed previously, and by pre-testing the questionnaire with experts in both Information Systems and Information Science research. The questionnaire was pilot tested by ten potential respondents from the target population, who were then excluded from the final sample.

The target population was postgraduate students at the University of KwaZulu-Natal (UKZN), Pietermaritzburg campus, South Africa. Postgraduate students were chosen as the research population because they have all been required to search for information as part of their core curriculum (UKZN 2010). They therefore represent students with several years of Web searching experience and may be viewed as being positioned to reflect on the strengths and weaknesses of the tactics that they have adopted. Proportionate stratified random sampling was selected in order for the sample to reflect the population (Robson 2002). The target population was divided into five mutually exclusive groups according to level of study (Table 1) that were meaningful in the context of this study (Sekaran & Bougie 2010).

A target sample size of 331 respondents from a population of 2344 was calculated (Krejcie & Morgan 1970). Questionnaires were administered both in person and via email. A total of 331 questionnaires were administered and 315 completed questionnaires were returned, yielding an

TABLE 1: Proportions of postgraduate students.

Level of study	Number of students in relation to total population (i.e. 2344)	Number of students in relation to sample population (i.e. 331)	Percentage in relation to sample population (%)
Postgraduate certificate	548	76	23
Postgraduate diploma	231	36	11
Honours degree	453	63	19
Master's degree	657	93	28
Doctorate	455	63	19
Total	2344	331	100

TABLE 2: Level of study * number of years respondents have been searching the Web cross-tabulation.

Level of study	How long have you been searching the Web? (in years)				Total (%)
	0–2 (%)	2–4 (%)	4–6 (%)	6+ (%)	
Postgraduate certificate	1.3	2.2	5.7	12.7	21.9
Postgraduate diploma	1.3	1.3	4.1	4.5	11.2
Honours degree	0.6	3.5	6.7	9.2	20
Master's degree	0.6	1.6	7.9	19.7	29.8
PhD	0.3	1.6	1.9	13.3	17.1
Total (N)	4.1	10.2	26.3	59.4	100

acceptable (Saunders, Lewis & Thornhill 2000) response rate of 95%. Data was then captured and cleaned using IBM's SPSS® software in preparation for quantitative analysis, both descriptive and inferential.

Findings and discussion
Web usage and expertise

Respondents were asked to indicate their level of study and specify how long they have been searching the Web (Table 2). Statistical tests revealed that a significant relationship exists between level of study and the number of years respondents have been searching the Web. Therefore, the higher the level of study, the greater the number of years respondents have been searching the Web. This is similar to the findings by Chu and Law (2007) and justifies the target population chosen for this study.

More than half (64.8%) of the respondents rated their expertise as intermediate, whilst 29.8% rated their expertise as expert and only 5.4% rated their expertise as novice (Figure 1). This finding indicates how respondents perceive their expertise and is not indicative of their actual expertise level.

Given that the research population constituted postgraduate students, it is not surprising that a large portion (59.4%) of the respondents have been searching the Web for more than 6 years. Respondents that have been searching for less than 4 years (12.4%) perceive themselves to be non-experts.

Most respondents (73.9%) gained their knowledge on Web searching through experience and only 26.1% have been given formal training on Web searching (Figure 2). This finding substantiates the argument that there is a lack of

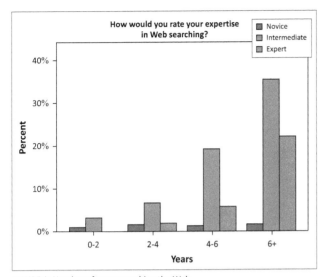

FIGURE 1: Number of years searching the Web.

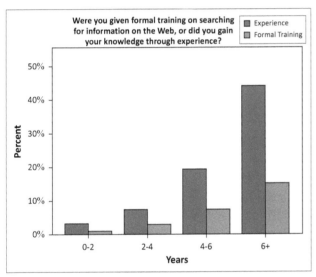

FIGURE 2: Experience vs formal training.

formal training (Bhatti 2014; Chu & Law 2007). Of those that gained their knowledge on Web searching from experience, 3.2% have been searching the Web for less than two years, 7.3% have been searching the Web for two to less than four years, 19.1% have been searching the Web for 4 to less than 6 years and 44.3% have been searching the Web for six years or longer. The training received was either library orientation, computer literacy courses, workshops or tutorials.

This research shows that most students gained their knowledge on Web searching through experience, which suggests that students in their first year of study should receive formal training in complex Web search services and tools, so that they may be more efficient in their searches early in their studies rather than learning through trial and error. This is supported by Asemi (2005), Bhatti (2014), and Nachmias and Gilad (2002).

Thatcher (2008:1325) suggests that 'respondents who have less experience with the Web would need to devote their cognitive resources to the search task at hand within a complex searching environment rather than spend extra cognitive resources switching between browser windows'. Therefore, if training in the use of Web searching tools is not acquired by students in their first year of study, then they will need to devote more cognitive resources in trying to figure out how to search the Web effectively rather than spending their cognitive resources on the sources retrieved.

Web search tactics

In trying to establish the respondents' search behaviour, the questionnaire required them to indicate the frequency of the Web search tactics used (Table 3 presents the most fundamental findings of Phase 1 of the study). Contrary to the findings shown in Figure 1, in which the majority of respondents self-reported as being intermediate or expert users, Table 3 illustrates that the most commonly used tactics are not those traditionally associated with expert users. This is not surprising given the lack of formal training (Figure 2).

The top three Web search tactics 'always' used by respondents were Web search engines (47.6%), the opening of multiple Web browser tabs (42.2%) and the opening of multiple Web browser windows (26%). The top three Web search tactics 'often' used by respondents were finding the relevant information in the first page of the search results (44.1%), using multiple keywords (42.5%) and searching the UKZN online library databases (41%). The top three Web search tactics 'sometimes' used were using single keywords (34.9%), browsing through a directory or catalogue (33%) and using advanced search features (32.1%). The top three Web search tactics 'rarely' used were searching for specific phrases using quotation marks (33.7%), using multiple search engines (27.9%) and browsing through a directory or catalogue (27.3%). The top three Web search tactics 'never' used were searching the 'invisible' Web (54.9%), the use of meta-search engines (49.8%) and the use of truncation or wildcards (46.7%).

Most respondents, for example, never use truncation or wildcards, the 'find' feature, proximity searching, meta-search engines – confirming the findings of Hochstotter and Koch (2009) and Othman *et al.* (2014) – or the 'invisible' Web during information retrieval. Chu and Law (2008:175) suggest that 'training provided to the students should comprise various search skills, such as truncation and proximity search'. Over half the respondents rarely or sometimes use multiple search engines, a tactic regarded as important by Asemi (2005). The majority of the respondents rarely or sometimes use advanced search features, which arguably contradicts their self-reporting as intermediate and expert users.

Only a small fraction (6%) always searches for specific phrases using quotation marks. O'Reilly (2007) explains that one should search in phrases or questions and those phrases are then highlighted in the results to make browsing easier. Most respondents rarely or sometimes use synonyms when searching the Web, whilst only a minority (8%) always do.

TABLE 3: Web search tactics distribution.

Web search tactics	Never (%)	Rarely (%)	Sometimes (%)	Often (%)	Always (%)	No response (%)
Open multiple Web browser windows	8.9	18.7	20	25.1	26	1.3
Open multiple tabs	2.5	10.2	16.5	27.3	42.2	1.3
Type in the Web address	4.8	21	28.3	25.4	18.7	1.9
Access a specific portal	10.8	24.4	29.8	21.9	8.6	4.4
Find required information in the first page of the results	3.2	9.2	29.5	44.1	12.1	1.9
Use advanced search features	9.8	26.7	32.1	21	8.3	2.2
Use single keywords	11.4	24.4	34.9	21.9	5.4	1.9
Use multiple keywords	2.9	7	19.4	42.5	25.1	3.2
Search for specific phrases	23.2	33.7	21.6	14.9	5.7	1
Use truncation or wildcards	46.7	27.3	15.2	7.3	2.2	1.3
Modify the query	4.4	7.6	27.9	38.7	19.4	1.9
Use synonyms	12.1	24.4	31.4	22.5	7.6	1.9
Use Boolean operators	21.3	27	27.3	20	3.8	0.6
Use the find feature	36.2	27	17.1	10.2	7	2.5
Use proximity searching	46.3	24.8	16.5	10.2	0.6	1.6
Use Web search engines	2.2	3.2	11.1	34	47.6	1.9
Use multiple search engines	21.3	27.9	24.8	18.7	6	1.3
Use meta-search engines	49.8	24.1	14.6	5.4	1.6	4.4
Search the 'invisible' Web	54.9	22.2	11.7	2.9	1.9	6.3
Search the UKZN online library OPAC system	7.9	12.4	25.1	37.8	16.8	0
Search the UKZN online library databases	6.3	9.2	22.2	41	21	0.3
Browse through a directory or a catalogue	12.4	27.3	33	18.4	5.4	3.5
Collaborate with colleagues	7.3	25.7	31.4	20.3	10.5	4.8

UKZN, University of KwaZulu-Natal; OPAC, online public access catalogue.

Bates (1979:211) refers to this tactic as 'PARALLEL', which is 'to make the search formulation broad (or broader) by including synonyms or otherwise conceptually parallel terms'.

The majority rarely or sometimes use Boolean operators, whilst only a minority (4%) always do. Nachmias and Gilad (2002) advise that the ability to apply Boolean logic rules (for example AND, OR, NOT) is a skill that is required for effective information retrieval. A large portion rarely or sometimes uses UKZN's electronic databases and catalogues. This is of major concern when one considers that these resources are subscription based and represent a substantial annual expense to the institution even though it is being under-utilised. Finally, the majority rarely or sometimes collaborate with colleagues. Lazonder (2005) found that students who collaborated produced better search results more efficiently than students who searched on their own.

Only 13.3% or respondents indicated that they understood how a search engine processes a query containing multiple terms. This is a similar finding to that of Aula *et al.* (2005) and provides insight into the respondents' limited understanding of how search engines work. Similarly, a minority (12.4%) indicated that they know how a search engine orders results. This finding is again similar to that of Aula *et al.* (2005). Once again, this finding demonstrates respondents' limited understanding of how a search engine works.

These findings reveal that the majority of respondents, whilst regarding themselves as either intermediate or expert users, do not employ Web search tactics associated with expert users. It may be argued that most respondents are self-taught and therefore tactics involving a deeper knowledge of information retrieval are understandably not being utilised. This illustrates an alarming knowledge gap that needs to be addressed if academics are going to demand high-quality information retrieval from their students.

Limitations

The major limitation of this study is that respondents are restricted to postgraduate students at UKZN, Pietermaritzburg campus. Restricting the research population to postgraduate students meant that experienced undergraduate students will not contribute their Web search strategies to this study. Other universities did not form part of this study. If they were included, the Web search strategies used by postgraduates from other institutions could have been compared to those of UKZN (Pietermaritzburg) students.

Conclusion

This article has presented the findings of Phase 1 of a wider study into the Web search strategies used by postgraduate students at UKZN, Pietermaritzburg campus, South Africa, focusing specifically on Web search tactics. The most commonly used Web search tactics used by postgraduate students have been identified and discussed. The key finding was that although the majority of respondents labelled themselves intermediate or expert users in terms of information retrieval, the most commonly used tactics were those requiring very little cognitive effort and were most likely self-taught after a process of trial and error. These are the Web search tactics most often associated with casual Internet usage rather than academic usage. A problem therefore exists as academics continue to demand information sources of high quality from their students.

The authors therefore support Nachmias and Gilad (2002), Asemi (2005), Smith (2012) and Bhatti (2014) in calling for a training intervention at undergraduate level, ensuring that students are exposed to more sophisticated methods of information retrieval at the beginning of their academic careers. The findings of Phase 1 of this study can potentially be used to identify gaps in postgraduate students' knowledge of Web searching, so that the potential of Boolean operators, meta-search engines, the 'invisible' Web and other tools can be unlocked. Such a strategy will provide students with more exposure to subscription-based electronic databases and catalogues. This strategy will address the problem of the under-utilisation of these costly electronic databases and catalogues that South African universities can ill afford unless they contribute to significant research output.

In future work, the authors will address a number of objectives. One objective will be to determine the broader Web search strategies (i.e. combinations of tactics) used by postgraduate students. Another objective will be to determine how postgraduate students judge whether Web searches have been successful or not. Establishing these best practices has the potential to further feed into the design of training interventions at undergraduate level.

Acknowledgements

Competing interests

The authors declare that they have no financial or personal relationship(s) that may have inappropriately influenced them in writing this article.

Authors' contributions

This article resulted from the Master's research of S.C. (University of KwaZulu-Natal) under the supervision of M.H. (University of the Witwatersrand). M.S.M. (University of KwaZulu-Natal) provided editorial oversight and final approval.

References

Aitken, W., 2007, 'Use of web in tertiary research and education', *Webology* 4(2), Article 42, viewed 13 September 2013, from http://www.webology.org/2007/v4n2/a42.html

Alexopoulou, P., Morris, A. & Hepworth, M., 2014, 'A new integrated model for multitasking during web searching', *Procedia – Social and Behavioral Sciences* 147(25), 16–25. http://dx.doi.org/10.1016/j.sbspro.2014.07.088

Alharbi, A., Smith, D. & Mayhew, P., 2013, 'Web searching behaviour for academic resources', paper presented at the Science and Information Conference, Thistle Hotel, London, 7–9 October.

Asemi, A., 2005, 'Information searching habits of internet users: A case study on the medical sciences University of Isfahan, Iran', *Webology* 2(1), Article 10, viewed 16 September 2013, from http://www.webology.org/2005/v2n1/a10.html

Aula, A., Jhaveri, N. & Käki, M., 2005, 'Information search and re-access strategies of experienced Web users', paper presented at the 14th International Conference on World Wide Web, Nippon Convention Centre, Chiba, Japan, 10–14 May. http://dx.doi.org/10.1145/1060745.1060831

Bates, M.J., 1979, 'Information search tactics', *Journal of the American Society for Information Science* 30(4), 205–214.

Bates, M.J., 2010, 'Information behavior', *Encyclopedia of Library and Information Sciences* 3, 2381–2391. http://dx.doi.org/10.1002/asi.4630300406

Bhatti, R., 2014, 'HEC Digital library and higher education: Trends and opportunities for faculty members at the Islamia University of Bahawalpur, South Punjab, Pakistan', *Library Philosophy and Practice*, Article 1059, viewed 10 October 2014, from http://digitalcommons.unl.edu/libphilprac/1059

Bhavnani, S., Drabenstott, K. & Radev, D., 2001, 'Towards a unified framework of IR tasks and strategies', paper presented at the American society for information science and technology annual meeting, J.W. Marriott Hotel, Washington, 3–8 November.

Carstens, C., Rittberger, M. & Wissel, V., 2009, 'How users search in the German education index - tactics and strategies', paper presented at the workshop on information retrieval at the LWA, TU Darmstadt, Germany, 21–23 September.

Cassidy, E.D., Jones, G., McMain, L., Shen, L. & Vieira, S., 2014, 'Student searching with EBSCO Discovery: A usability study', *Journal of Electronic Resources Librarianship* 26(1), 17–35. http://dx.doi.org/10.1080/1941126X.2014.877331

Chu, S.K.W. & Law, N., 2007, 'Development of information search expertise: Postgraduates' knowledge of searching skills', *Libraries and the Academy* 7(3), 295–316. http://dx.doi.org/10.1353/pla.2007.0028

Chu, S.K.W. & Law, N., 2008, 'The development of information search expertise of research students', *Journal of Librarianship and Information Science* 40(3), 165–177. http://dx.doi.org/10.1177/0961000608092552

Creswell, J.W. & Clark, V.L.P., 2007, *Designing and conducting mixed methods research*, Sage, Thousand Oaks.

Flouris, G., Roussakis, Y., Poveda-Villalón, M., Mendes, P.N. & Fundulaki, I., 2012, 'Using provenance for quality assessment and repair in linked open data', paper presented at the 2nd Joint workshop on knowledge evolution and ontology dynamics, Boston Park Plaza, Boston, 11–12 November.

Foss, E., Druin, A., Yip, J., Ford, W., Golub, E. & Hutchinson, H., 2013, 'Adolescent search roles', *Journal of the American Society for Information Science and Technology* 64(1), 173–189. http://dx.doi.org/10.1002/asi.22809

Ganaie, S.A. & Khazer, M.K., 2014, 'Information-seeking behavior among postgraduate students of University of Kashmir: An analytical study', *Journal of Advancements in Library Sciences* 1(1), 64–72.

Hochstotter, N. & Koch, M., 2009, 'Standard parameters for searching behaviour in search engines and their empirical evaluation', *Journal of Information Science* 35(1), 45–65. http://dx.doi.org/10.1177/0165551508091311

Hoeber, O., 2008, 'Web information retrieval support systems: The future of Web search', paper presented at the 2008 IEEE/WIC/ACM International Conference on web intelligence and intelligent agent technology, Citigate Central Hotel, Sydney, 9–12 December.

Hoque, E., Hoeber, O., Strong, G. & Gong, M., 2013, 'Combining conceptual query expansion and visual search results exploration for Web image retrieval', *Journal of Ambient Intelligence and Humanized Computing* 4(3), 389–400. http://dx.doi.org/10.1007/s12652-011-0094-7

Hung, P.W., Johnson, S.B., Kaufman, D.R. & Mendonça, E.A., 2008, 'A multi-level model of information seeking in the clinical domain', *Journal of Biomedical Informatics* 41(2), 357–370. http://dx.doi.org/10.1016/j.jbi.2007.09.005

Kinley, K., 2014, 'Users' perception of using web search engines and their impact on the perceived intention to reuse the systems', *Journal of Emerging Trends in Computing and Information Sciences* 5(7), 568–579.

Krejcie, R.V. & Morgan, D.W., 1970, 'Determining the sample size for research activities', *Educational and Psychological Measurement* 30(3), 607–610.

Kriewel, S. & Fuhr, N., 2010, 'Evaluation of an adaptive search suggestion system', paper presented at the 32nd European Conference on Information Retrieval, The Open University, Milton Keynes, 28–31 March. http://dx.doi.org/10.1007/978-3-642-12275-0_47

Lazonder, A.W., 2005, 'Do two heads search better than one? Effects of student collaboration on web search behaviour and search outcomes', *British Journal of Educational Technology* 36(3), 465–475. http://dx.doi.org/10.1111/j.1467-8535.2005.00478.x

Marchionini, G., 1995, *Information seeking in electronic environments*, Cambridge University Press, Cambridge. http://dx.doi.org/10.1017/CBO9780511626388

Markey, K., 2007a, 'Twenty-five years of end-user searching, Part 1: Research findings', *Journal of the American Society for Information Science and Technology* 58(8), 1071–1081. http://dx.doi.org/10.1002/asi.20601

Markey, K., 2007b, 'Twenty-five years of end-user searching, Part 2: Future research directions', *Journal of the American Society for Information Science and Technology* 58(8), 1123–1130. http://dx.doi.org/10.1002/asi.20601

Nachmias, R. & Gilad, A., 2002, 'Needle in a hyperstack: Searching information on the World Wide Web', *Journal of Research on Technology in Education* 34(4), 475–486. http://dx.doi.org/10.1080/15391523.2002.10782362

Nazim, M., 2008, 'Information searching behavior in the internet age: A users' study of Aligarh Muslim University', *The International Information & Library Review* 40, 73–81. http://dx.doi.org/10.1016/j.iilr.2007.11.001

Nordlie, R., & Pharo, N., 2013, 'Search transition as a measure of effort in information retrieval interaction', *Proceedings of the American Society for Information Science and Technology* 50(1), 1–7. http://dx.doi.org/10.1002/meet.14505001044

O'Reilly, D., 2007, 'Search evolution: New ways to get better results', *PCWorld*, viewed 26 January 2011, from http://www.pcworld.com/article/137633/article.html

Othman, R., Junurham, N.L.N.P. & Nilam, N.L., 2014, 'Search strategies formulation among Library and information science students in online database', *Middle-East Journal of Scientific Research* 19(3), 338–345.

Palanisamy, R. & Sha, W., 2014, 'An empirical analysis of user evaluation factors on attitude and intention of using a search engine', *International Journal of Business Information Systems* 15(3), 261–290. http://dx.doi.org/10.1504/IJBIS.2014.059751

Robson, C., 2002, *Real world research: A resource for social scientists and practitioner-researchers*, 2nd edn, Blackwell, Malden.

Shanahan, M.C., 2008, 'Transforming Information search and evaluation practices of undergraduate students', *International Journal of Medical Informatics* 77, 518–526. http://dx.doi.org/10.1016/j.ijmedinf.2007.10.004

Saunders, M., Lewis, P. & Thornhill, A., 2000, *Research methods for Business students*, 2nd edn, Pearson Education, Harlow.

Sekaran, U. & Bougie, R., 2010, *Research methods for business: A skill building approach*, 5th edn, John Wiley, Chichester.

Smith, A.G., 2012, 'Internet search tactics', *Online Information Review* 36(1), 7–20. http://dx.doi.org/10.1108/14684521211219481

Szucs, J.J., Warner, K.L., Paris, T.C. & Moye, C.D., 2013, *System, method and computer program product for automatic topic identification using a hypertext corpus*, US patent application 13/829,472.

Thatcher, A., 2008, 'Web search strategies: The influence of web experience and task type', *Information Processing and Management* 44, 1308–1329. http://dx.doi.org/10.1016/j.ipm.2007.09.004

Thornton, D.E. & Kaya, E., 2013, 'All the World Wide Web's a stage: Improving students' information skills with dramatic video tutorials', *Aslib Journal of Information Management* 65(1), 73–87. http://dx.doi.org/10.1108/00012531311297195

Timmers, C.F. & Glas, C.A.W., 2010, 'Developing scales for information-seeking behaviour', *Journal of Documentation* 66(1), 46–69. http://dx.doi.org/10.1108/00220411011016362

Tseng, Y.H. & Wu, Y.J., 2008, 'A study of search tactics for patentability search – A case study on patent engineers', paper presented at the 1st ACM Workshop on Patent Information Retrieval, Marriott Hotel & Spa, Napa Valley, 30 October. http://dx.doi.org/10.1145/1458572.1458581

Tyonum, N.M. & Shidi, H., 2014, 'Problems of Internet utilization by students in Benue State University, Makurdi, Benue State-Nigeria', *International Journal of Innovative Research and Development* 3(3), 200–205.

University of KwaZulu-Natal (UKZN), 2010, 'Postgraduate application guide 2011', viewed 20 September 2010, from http://applications.ukzn.ac.za/Libraries/2011-Postgraduate-Prospectus/2011_Postgraduate_Prospectus.sflb.ashx

Wildemuth, B.M., 2004, 'The effects of domain knowledge on search tactic formulation', *Journal of the American Society for Information Science and Technology* 55(3), 246–258. http://dx.doi.org/10.1002/asi.10367

Wildemuth, B.M., Oh, J.S. & Marchionini, G., 2010, 'Tactics used when searching for digital videos', paper presented at the Third Symposium on Information Interaction in Context, Rutgers University, New Brunswick, 18–21 August. http://dx.doi.org/10.1145/1840784.1840821

Xie, H., 2007, 'Shifts in information-seeking strategies in information retrieval in the digital age: Planned-situational model', *Information Research* 12(4).

Zamani-Miandashti, N., Memarbashi, P. & Khalighzadeh, P., 2013, 'The prediction of Internet utilization behavior of undergraduate agricultural students: An application of the theory of planned behavior', *The International Information & Library Review* 45(3/4), 114–126. http://dx.doi.org/10.1016/j.iilr.2013.10.003

25

The role of records management as a tool to identify risks in the public sector in South Africa

Author:
Mpho Ngoepe[1]

Affiliation:
[1]Department of Information Science, University of South Africa, South Africa

Correspondence to:
Mpho Ngoepe

Email:
ngoepms@unisa.ac.za

Postal address:
PO Box 392, University of South Africa 0003, South Africa

Background: Records management is a vital element in the identification of risks. However, there is a consensus amongst scholars that the relationship between records management and risk identification has not been clearly articulated. As a result, risks associated with records are often dealt with via internal audits, legal processes and information technology.

Objectives: The study utilised the King III report on corporate governance in South Africa as a framework to investigate the role of records management in identifying risks in the public sector, with a view to entrench the synergy between records management and risk management.

Method: Quantitative data were collected through questionnaires distributed to records managers, risk managers and auditors in governmental bodies in South Africa. Provisions of the King III report, guided the research objectives.

Results: Even though the study established that there is a reciprocal relationship between risk identification and records management, most governmental bodies in South Africa lack records management and risk-mitigating frameworks or strategy. Furthermore, records management did not feature in most governmental bodies' risk registers. It has been established that most governmental bodies have established risk committees that do not include records management practitioners. In most governmental bodies, risk management resides within internal audit functions.

Conclusion: The study concludes by arguing that a strong records management regime can be one of an organisation's primary tools in identifying risks and implementing proper risk management. Therefore, records management should be integrated with risk management processes for organisations to benefit from the synergy.

Introduction

Both public and private organisations face different kinds of risks that affect the reliability of records and effectiveness of internal controls daily, such as losses, negative cash flows and, ultimately, bankruptcy, which can lead to liquidation. According to Ebaid (2011:108), it is difficult for organisations to avoid risk. However, what matters most is the identification and management of risks that the organisation is exposed to. Records management is one of the functions that can play a vital role in identifying and assessing risks and leading to effective risk management. Effective risk management plays an integral part in the development of the control environment which, in turn, provides management with the necessary assurances that the organisation will achieve its objectives within an acceptable degree of residual risk.

Despite the role that records management can play in identifying risks within organisations, it is clear from the literature that the role has not been clearly articulated, particularly in the public sector in South Africa as compared to elsewhere in the world (Bhana 2008). Lemieux (2001; 2004:57) contends that risks associated with records are often dealt with on an ad-hoc basis via internal audits, legal processes, information technology and in few instances records management. Akotia (1996:6) has also observed that 'a major defect in financial administration arises from failure to integrate accounting and records management process, with the result that essential information is lost or becomes subject to inaccuracies'. Palmer (2000:63) points out that the chaotic and collapsed state of records management systems is one of the primary reasons why accounting standards will not easily be implemented in developing countries. Indeed, when accounting systems are weakened due to poor record-keeping, management is unable to access records for decision-making. In this light, it is essential that records are managed properly throughout their entire life cycle to enable identification of risk and management thereof.

Willis (2005:88) is of the view that a robust records management programme should form part of the organisation's risk management process, as records and the management of risk are considered inseparable. In this regard, proper records management can be used as a tool to identify risks in the organisation. Fraser and Henry (2007:393) identify two contexts in which the inseparability of and nexus between records and risks can be considered: records for identifying business risk and business risks associated with managing records. Furthermore, Lemieux (2010) provides a typology between records management and risk management:

- Using records to explore types of risk.
- Risk to records.
- Records as causes of other types of risk.
- Risks associated with the traditional archival function.
- Records management applying the risk management process (pp. 210–211).

In view of the above, this study utilised the King III report on corporate governance to develop a theoretical argument for the role of records management in identifying risk in the public sector of South Africa, with a view to entrench the synergy between records management and risk management. A study by Ngoepe and Ngulube (2013a) covered other chapters of the King III report, but excluded the governance of risk from the role of records management in corporate governance. Therefore, this study attempts to fill the gap by using chapter 4 and chapter 5 of the King III report as a framework to define the role of record-keeping as a tool to identify risks in governmental bodies. As Isa (2009:3–4) would attest, it is essential to explore the relationship between these two areas in order for organisations to benefit from the synergy of their integration.

The King III report was launched on 01 September 2009 by the Institute of Directors of Southern Africa (IoDSA), and came into effect on 01 March 2010. It heralded a new era in which risk management and recorded information were regarded as important. The King III report has nine chapters[1]. Chapter 4 and chapter 5 are relevant to this study as they deal with risk management and information management respectively. The chapters provide valuable guidance on how the various processes can be integrated. For example, in terms of the King report, people responsible for organisational governance must be able to rely on competent and trustworthy internal resources, capable of accurately assessing the effectiveness of the processes in place to manage and mitigate risks (IoDSA 2009:86). The King III report applies to all private and public entities in South Africa. Records are regarded as important assets of the organisation as they are evidence of business activities. The King III report recommends that management should ensure that there are systems in place for the management of information assets to ensure the availability of information in a timely manner, implement a suitable information security management, ensure that sensitive information is identified, classified and assigned appropriate handling criteria, implement the management of risks associated with information and establish a business continuity programme addressing the organisation's information and recovery requirements. In this regard,

according to the King III report, information management encompasses: protection of information (information security), the management of information and the protection of personal information processed by organisations (information privacy) (IoDSA 2009:86).

Problem statement

Despite the importance of records management to risk identification, as highlighted in the preceding section, it would seem that records management in the public sector in South Africa does not satisfy the threshold specified by the King III report. For example, the general reports on audit outcomes by the Auditor-General of South Africa express concerns on the lack of adequate records that automatically increase audit risks and fees (Bhana 2008; Ngoepe & Ngulube 2013b:52). This implies that records are not properly managed to mitigate information-related risks; hence, the public sector in South Africa is characterised by auditing findings relating to poor records management. Hence, Sarens and De Beelde (2006:64) and Fraser and Henry (2007:393) observe that the relationship between records management and risk identification has not been clearly explored and articulated by scholars, practitioners and organisations. According to the Institute of Internal Auditors (2009), many organisations are fearful that they do not really understand the link between risk management and records management. Erima and Wamukoya (2012:32) are of the view that as a tool for risk management, records management is important in strategic decision-making, helps cut down costs and reduces risks from litigation, amongst others. Isa (2009:4) ponders that the embedding of records management into the risk management function is a long-term exercise to ensure that records consideration is at the heart of all management processes. Organisations create an array of records relating to relevant internal and external activities. These records are needed at all levels of an organisation to identify, assess and respond to risks (Committee of Sponsoring Organizations of the Treadway Commission 2004:67). Failing to manage records throughout their life cycle is a growing risk facing every organisation across the globe. According to Isa (2009:75) organisations have neglected proper record-keeping, which results in exposure to risks from various angles. If records management is used as a risk identification tool, many of the risks associated with poor record-keeping, such as litigation, loss of information, reputation risks and others, can be mitigated.

Research purpose and objectives of the study

The general purpose of this study was to investigate the role of records management as a tool to identify risks in the public sector in South Africa, with a view to entrench the synergy between records management and risk management. The specific objectives were to:

- Investigate the availability of enterprise risk management strategies that embrace records management in governmental bodies.
- Identify risks emanating from poor or lack of records

1. The nine chapters of the King report can be accessed from http://www.iodsa.co.za/?kingIII

management in the public sector in South Africa.

- Investigate how records are managed to mitigate risks in the public sector in South Africa.
- Make recommendations on integrating records managements into risk management.

Literature review

Literature for this study is reviewed under two themes: the role of records management in identifying risks and risks emanating from poor or lack of records management in organisations.

The relationship between records management and risk management

Chernobai, Rachev and Fabozzi (2007:xv) contend that there is a historical relationship between risk management and records management, even though the risk management field has its origin in the insurance industry. From time immemorial, human beings have striven to understand risk affected by factors such as storm, fire or flood (Graham & Kaye 2006:1). In the 1980s, risk management in manufacturing industries took hold with the adoption of total quality management. Very few organisations took a wide-angle view of risk and controls beyond finance. Even in these cases, as postulated by Lemieux (2010:210), attention was generally focused on hazard-related or insurable risk. It was only in the 1990s that the field of risk management received greater recognition.

Risk commentators such as Fraser and Henry (2007:393), Hiles (2002), Lemieux (2010:211) and Sarens and De Beelde (2006:64) argue that the incident on 11 September 2001 in the United States of America changed the world with regard to risk management as many companies ceased to exist after the event. However, the roots of modern risk management are much older and were already deeply embedded in the management of many organisations long before that fateful day. Risk was rarely projected and it was only when records were kept that an opportunity presented itself to scrutinise these records to offer prediction of the future. Today, most organisations have, as part of their corporate executive staff, an individual with the title of chief risk officer. As a result, risk management to many is synonymous with good governance. This also manifests itself in governance tendrils such as the King III report on corporate governance in South Africa.

Whilst internal monitoring bodies within organisations such as internal audit functions and audit committees are becoming increasingly involved in risk management, records management is conspicuous by its absence. Fraser and Henry (2007:393) argue that historically no unit within organisations has been charged with risk management. As a result, internal audit departments and audit committees took the opportunity to fill the gap simply because many risks have an obvious financial dimension. According to Isa (2009:4), records management ensures the availability of records for risk assessment and as such should be involved in

or incorporated into the risk management process. Isa (2009) proposes some guidelines for how the integration could be done:

> Record-keeping practice and risk management elements must be nurtured and embedded in all business activities across the organisation. This can be realised by forming a working committee comprising the audit committee, archivist and records manager and risk management team to implement such an approach across the board. Therefore, records management professionals should embrace the opportunity to contribute to the achievement of corporate governance. (p. 258)

Effective records management ensures the availability of records for future assessment in order to determine whether the recommended risk mitigation has been followed by relevant business process owners. The success of risk management is partly dependent on the accuracy of records in organisations, as every judgement made must be based on reliable information. In an age in which transparency, accountability and compliance are of increasing concern, it is essential that organisations comply with regulations and, if they do not, are able to explain why not (Isa 2009:53; Lomas 2010:191).

Sampson (1992:134; 2002:169) asserts firmly that the main contribution of records management to risk management is through records retention schedules, which allocate a suitable retention period to various records, especially perceived threats of litigation. However, it should be noted that there are instances of public organisations in South Africa destroying records, for accountability purposes, as a way of managing political risks (Harris 2002; 2007). Harris and Merrett (2007:270) are of the view that, even in an era of more open government, it is inconceivable that compliant procedures can be applied uniformly as they simply cost too much. Reed (1997) suggests that not all processes generate records and that it is the role of records management working within a risk management framework to identify how far each process should be recorded. However, as Isa (2009:66) would attest, this role cannot be accomplished in the absence of commitment from managers of various departments across an organisation.

The strength and effectiveness of a record-keeping system mainly depend on the effectiveness of risk management that prioritises and identifies risks across an organisation. Allocating the identified risks into an organisational directory or a file plan structure enables the identification of contextual information, which in turn ensures that the authenticity and integrity of electronic records are controlled (Isa 2009:91). As risk is associated with avoiding or mitigating obstacles to achievement, from a liability standpoint, records are necessary to demonstrate that an organisation has conducted itself reasonably. If nothing is recorded, it difficult to prove that it happened. Relying on human memory is dangerous due to its elusiveness, frailty and the tendency of people to remember things that never happened (Jimerson 2003:90; Ngoepe 2012:44). This can lead to records and information management risks, which encompass any threat to the business arising from inadequate records management (Lemieux 2004:56).

Risks emanating from poor or lack of records management in organisations

In his keynote address to the South African Records Management Forum conference, Bhana (2008) questions whether it is fair to equate poor records management to high risk. Putting it differently, Sampson (1992:134) questions whether proper records management can help to identify and assess risk. To answer these questions, the Auditor-General of South Africa (2011) is on record noting the importance of keeping records as a key component of any entity's risk management process. Organisations operate in a world that grows more litigious, risky and highly regulated (KPMG 2011). Failing to manage records throughout their entire life cycle is a growing risk facing every organisation. In the past, records management was purely paper based and the challenge was less onerous. Traditionally, records management processes have been undertaken by records management staff. The digital world brings new complexities to records management. Now the work has been transferred to end-users which has proved to be unsuccessful (Henttonen & Kettunen 2011:87). In an electronic environment, the challenges include managing access, versioning, controlling and surrogates. Therefore, records management can no longer be a tactical solution to a departmental problem, but must be approached as an enterprise-wide strategy (KPMG 2011). The starting point is to identify key areas of records management that pose a risk to the organisation or have a significant cost impact.

Indeed, how well an organisation manages its records will impact on certain business and legal risks. Often, the cost of poor record-keeping is hidden; hence, few organisations especially in the public sector bother to establish a records management programme. There are several risks that come to mind, but four risks stemming from poor or lack of proper record-keeping identified by Bhana (2008) and Ngoepe (2011:75–76) that need to be considered are reputation, legal, financial and information loss. Bhana and Ngoepe posit that a governmental institution with lack of proper record-keeping is at risk of information loss when individuals resign or leave office. This is a common phenomenon and has almost become a cliché since organisations often refer to individuals that they hold in high regard because of their 'institutional memory'. The institutional memory should in fact be vested in the organisation's records management systems, which are further supported by appropriate knowledge management frameworks. Furthermore, governmental bodies need to comply with legislation regarding retention of records.

Several other scholars also identify risks associated with poor or lack of records management. For example, Fraser and Henry (2007:393) identify two types of process-level risk assessments for record-keeping. The first is a strategic approach to managing business information by undertaking a systematic, risk-based assessment of record-keeping needs

and designing appropriate record-keeping strategies. The second is an assessment, by individual work units, of the risks they face in achieving their objectives, including record-keeping. Furthermore, Egbuji (1999:94) classifies risks into reputation, litigation and environmental risks. The Institute of Charted Accountants in England and Wales classifies risks into five main categories: financial, business, compliance, operational and knowledge management (Fraser & Henry 2007:392–393). McKemmish and Acland (1999) suggest that failure of the record-keeping system may lead to organisational risks and societal risks. These risks include the following:

- Lack of evidence that an organisation did something under contract or according to regulation.
- Inability to find mission-critical information.
- Loss of proof of ownership, rights and obligations.
- Lack of documentation of who knew what and when.
- Inability to locate proper context information for records that may be incriminating in one context and innocent in another.
- Inability to demonstrate that policies and procedures were in place and consistently followed.
- Impairment of functioning of society and its institutions.
- Loss of evidence of the rights of people as citizens and clients.
- Inability of societal watchdogs to call to account governments, corporations and individuals.
- Loss of collective, corporate and personal identity.

From the discussions, it is no exaggeration to suggest that a solid records management programme can be an effective insurance policy for an organisation to identify risks. Ngoepe (2011:33) contends that organisations without proper records management run the risk of destroying records too soon and consequently of not being able to produce the records when legally required. Alternatively, organisations adopt the costly practice of keeping everything forever, a practice that can also backfire in legal proceedings. The organisation is then required to produce everything it has relating to the proceedings, not just what it is legally required to provide. At the very least, producing all related records is time-consuming and expensive (Ngoepe 2012:84). Therefore, it is appropriate to manage records to enable identification and assessment of risks within organisations.

Research methodology

This study relied on quantitative data collected via questionnaires distributed to governmental bodies in South Africa, which were listed on a government website as follows: 283 municipalities, 37 national government departments, 108 provincial government departments in all nine provinces and 30 public entities (South Africa Government Online n.d.). Data collected via questionnaires were supplemented through content analysis of documents such as risk strategies and registers of eight of the participating organisations who were willing to provide such documents. Since the population being studied was large and heterogeneous, a stratified random sampling technique was used. The assumption was that if other types of probability sampling were applied, chances are that national government departments and statutory bodies could have been under-represented as they were few, whilst municipalities and provincial government departments could be over-represented as they were many. The population was divided into strata of municipalities, national departments, provincial departments and public entities to ensure representativeness. Municipalities and provincial departments were further grouped into sub-strata according to their respective provinces. Participants from the chosen sample were selected purposively and were either a records management staff member, risk manager or internal audit staff member. In some instances, especially in municipalities, municipal managers were selected, as there were no records managers or auditors. A proportional sample size of 37% (171) was taken from the population based on a scientific calculator available online. Therefore, the sample consisted of 105 municipalities, 14 national departments, 40 provincial departments and 12 public entities.

Data analysis and research findings

This section analyses and presents the results of the data obtained via questionnaires and document review. Out of 171 questionnaires distributed, only 94 were returned, a 55% response rate. Data from questionnaires were analysed using survey software available online. Results are presented through written descriptions and numerical summaries. Of the 94 responses, 42.5% (40) were completed by records managers, 28.7% (27) by registry clerks, 15.9% (15) by other information professionals such as librarians, knowledge managers and information technology specialists, whilst 12.7% (12) were completed by different officials such as municipal managers, risk managers and internal auditors.

The availability of risk management strategies in governmental bodies

Principles 4.1 and 4.4 in chapter 4 of the King III report require organisations to develop risk management policy and plans that are aligned to the purpose of the organisation (IoDSA 2009:29). The policy should be widely distributed throughout the organisation. When asked if their organisations had developed a risk management strategy, 57.4% (54) of the respondents indicated that their organisations have developed an enterprise risk management strategy as compared to 42.6% (40) which did not have. The respondents indicated that the risk management policy and plan formed part of the strategy and were monitored by the risk committee. Of those who indicated that their organisations have developed a risk management strategy, only 36.1% (34) mentioned that the strategy included record-keeping as a risk. Another 21.2% (20) indicated that the strategy was not clear on records as it just mentioned security of information without specifying the type of information.

With regard to responsibility in risk management, 44.6% (42) indicated that the accounting officers have delegated the responsibility and designated the head of internal audit

as the chief risk officer. It was only in a few instances 23.4% (22), that respondents indicated that responsibility lay with compliance and legal service units. Only 31.9% (30) indicated that it was not clear who was responsible for risk management as there was no such unit in their organisation. However, no respondents indicated that the records management unit was involved in risk management in their organisation. Four (4.2%) respondents indicated that records management was represented by information technology managers in risk management meetings. With regard to the availability of risk committees, 77.6% (73) indicated that their organisation had established risk committees as compared to 22.3% (21) that did not. Again, no member of a records management team was part of the risk committees. When asked about the interval of risk assessment, 57.4% (54) indicated that the assessment is conducted once a year, as compared to 42.5% (40) which did not. Only 36.1% (34) of those who conducted risk assessments indicated that records management was included in the assessment.

Risks relating to records management in governmental bodies

Principle 5.7 in Chapter 5 of the King III report indicates that the risk committee should consider information as a crucial element of the effective oversight or risk management of the organisation. When asked about the availability of a risk register, 53.2% (50) indicated that there was a risk register in their organisations as compared to 46.8% (44) who did not have one. The respondents indicated that the risk register was reviewed once a year. The risks that kept recurring as identified by the respondents were loss of information, leakage of information, security of information and litigation due to unavailability of information. However, three respondents indicated that the top risk issues in their organisation were confidential and, therefore, could not divulge information to the researcher. Perusal of risk registers from eight participating organisations revealed that security of information was considered a high risk, especially in an electronic environment. Issues identified in the registers include: sufficient security measures to prevent unauthorised or untracked access to the computers, networks, devices or storage and the inclusion of user permissions, passwords control and firewalls in the systems. However, none of the eight risk registers mentioned the possible risks related to paper records and their storage.

The respondents were further asked to list five records management areas that pose a risk to or have a significant cost impact on their organisation. The top five issues were information security, data integrity, information loss, non-compliance and leaking of information. The internal audit unit was identified by respondents as responsible for providing assurance regarding risk management. However, 53.2% (50) of the respondents indicated that internal audit units and records management did not always work in unison on risk management issues.

How records management mitigate risks in the public sector

The King III report views information contained in records as the most important information assets as they are evidence of business activities. Therefore, it is essential for organisations to manage records for sustainability and to minimise risks associated with poor records management (Ngoepe & Ngulube 2013a). The availability and implementation of key records management documents such as strategy, policy, procedure, file plans, retention schedules, disposal authority, vital records schedules and disaster recovery plans goes a long way in helping organisations to mitigate risks. Respondents were asked to indicate or state the availability of key records management documents, as reflected in Table 1.

It is distressing to reveal that only a pitiable figure of 9.5% (9) of governmental bodies have implemented disaster recovery plans. With regard to disposal authorities, respondents cited lack of support from the National Archives of South Africa (NASA) as a contributing factor to unavailability of disposal authority and a retention schedule in their organisation. One respondent indicated that their organisation requested a disposal authority from NASA in 2010, but had not yet received a response in 2014. This according to the respondent was despite several follow-ups with NASA. The respondent indicated that NASA cited lack of capacity as a contributing factor.

When asked how records management mitigates risk in governmental bodies, respondents replied that with proper records management in place, the governmental bodies will comply with archival legislation, minimise loss of information and be able to present records as evidence in court and base decisions on records rather than thumb-sucking or mental memory. They also identified that records management allows for the availability of comprehensive documented information about all aspects of risks and risk sources, retention and disposal of records. The following were further identified by respondents as areas of records management that will create risks for organisations if not attended to:

- Absence or poor implementation of records management strategies, policies and procedures.
- Approved file plans not implemented in filing structures.
- Inability to distinguish historical records from those with ephemeral value; as a result, the 'keep everything syndrome' is applied.
- Low awareness of the importance of proper records management practices.
- An overwhelming volume of older stored records.
- Staff changes that leave the context of many records unknown.
- Vital records not identified and secured (lack of a disaster preparedness plan).
- Failure to implement an electronic document and records management system (EDRMS).
- Staff not adhering to a central filing strategy (keeping files at their desks), resulting in inability to locates files later.
- Documents not verified as being complete before being returning to the registry, filing room or archives.

Discussion of results

It is clear from the study that internal audit units have assumed the functions, systems and processes of risk management in most governmental bodies in South Africa. As a result, risk management in most governmental bodies resides within internal audit functions. However, in a few instances the risk management function resides within areas such as compliance and legal services. There was no single instance in which the records management unit was responsible for risk management. Therefore, records management practitioners have taken a backseat with regard to risk identification. Even though most governmental bodies have established risk committees, records management practitioners did not form part of such committees. Instead, in most cases, records management was represented by the information technology division. The study has further revealed that there was an absence of a records management risk-mitigating framework or strategy in most governmental bodies. As a result, governmental bodies are vulnerable to information loss and litigations. The study has established that records management was excluded from the risk register of many governmental bodies. In the case in which records management was identified as a risk issue, only security and loss of information were considered the top risks associated with records.

The study has established that key records management documents that have been developed in the majority of governmental bodies include policy, procedures and a file plan. However, these documents were not implemented in most governmental bodies. Documents such as disaster recovery plans, vital records schedules and retention schedules were non-existent in many governmental bodies. This implies that the government is sitting on an 'information ticking time bomb' that could have dire consequences, such

TABLE 1: Availability and implementation of key records management documents (N = 94).

Document	Available but not implemented	%	Implemented	%	Unavailable	%
Strategy	7	7.4	13	13.8	74	78.7
Policy	15	15.9	57	60.6	22	23.4
Procedures	17	18	58	61.7	19	20.2
File plan	21	22.3	60	63.8	13	13.8
Disposal authority	16	17	26	27.6	52	55.3
Retention schedule	15	15.9	16	17	63	67
Vital records schedule	3	3.1	10	10.6	81	86.1
Disaster recovery plan	2	2.1	9	9.5	83	88.3

as loss of vital national memory and legal actions against government. In the absence of rules and guidelines as to what should be kept and for how long, staff should be reluctant to authorise the destruction of records, which is what was happening in most governmental bodies in South Africa. By not implementing records management policies and carrying out disposal authorities, governmental bodies are vulnerable in that they may not be able to meet legislative or other obligations required of them. For example, governmental bodies might find it difficult to respond to requests in terms of freedom of information legislation, as they would struggle to sift through an ever-increasing mountain of records. As a result, the retrieval of a particular record will be akin to searching for the elusive needle in the haystack. Furthermore, in an environment of ever-decreasing budgets, the over-retention of records may force governmental bodies to spend more money in order to preserve records that could have been disposed of a long time ago.

In this study, it has been established that proper records management can mitigate risk through compliance with legislation, minimisation of information loss and provision of evidence of transactions. It is clear from the study that record-keeping is viewed in the context of a key enabler without which risk management becomes unsuccessful. Relevant records are required to support activities performed in the course of business, decision-making and accountability. Therefore, how well organisations manage records will impact on certain business and legal risks, including:

- Loss of revenue (financial risk).
- Loss of legal rights and failure to comply with legislation (legal risk).
- Exposure to penalties in litigations and investigations (legal and financial risk).
- Violation of the law (compliance risk).
- Waste of staff time in searching for lost or mislaid documents (knowledge management risk).
- Inability to prove what has been done or agreed upon (legal risk and reputation risk).
- Fruitless expenditure due to storage of records with no archival or business value (financial risk).
- Lack of continuity in the event of disaster or employees resigning or changing positions (knowledge management risk).
- Accidental access to organisational records by external people due to employees leaving records in their work stations unprotected (security and reputational risk).

Conclusion and recommendations

It is clear from the study that a strong records management regime can be one of an organisation's primary tools in identifying risks and can therefore lead to proper risk management. Therefore, records management should be integrated with risk management and record-keeping must be viewed by organisations as a risk management function, thereby leveraging its status in the public sector. The integration of risk and records management has a bright

future as its synergy enables the identification of not only risk but also business opportunities, maintains competitive advantage and facilitates the achievement of the strategic objectives of the organisation. Therefore, as Isa (2009:257) would attest, a risk-based approach to records management identifies and gives priority to risky records and in the process ensures that records are protected against destruction and damage, retrieved when needed and disposed of at the end of their life cycle.

An effective records management programme covering the full life cycle of a record will ensure that records are not merely kept, but are kept well, as a resource and an asset to increase the organisation's efficiency. As part of risk management, organisations should develop business continuity plans and contingency measures to ensure that records that are vital to the continued functioning of the organisation are identified as part of risk analysis, protected and recoverable when needed. As Isa (2009:91) would attest, to limit the risks associated with records, records need to be protected. Furthermore, organisations need to ask the following questions:

- What are the risks if the records are available, not available or fall into the wrong hands?
- Will there be sufficient evidence for a defence or to file a claim?

In view of all of the identified risks, record-keeping must be approached by governmental institutions as a risk management function. In this regard, the records management unit should be involved in the management of risks associated with records. Furthermore, records management practitioners should be included in risk committees. Effective risk management is the cornerstone of good governance and can lead to improved performance, resulting in better service delivery, more efficient use of resources, as well as helping to minimise waste and fraud. The risk assessments in governmental bodies should also review record-keeping, so that government entities' records management priorities do not pose any legislative or business risk to the organisation. Applying the principles and practices well is no guarantee for success, as other factors can influence and determine outcomes. Nevertheless, failure to do so would most likely lead to less than desired results and, probably, even failure.

Acknowledgements
Competing interests

The author declares that he has no financial or personal relationship(s) that may have inappropriately influenced him in writing this article.

References

Akotia, P., 1996, 'The management of public sector financial records: The implications for good government', University of Ghana, Legon, viewed 10 January 2013, from http://ww4.msu.ac.zw/elearning/material/1174370018Pino%20Akotia%20 1996%20on%20governance.pdf

Auditor-General of South Africa, 2011, *Simplifying audit opinions and findings to enable government leadership to exercise meaningful oversight towards clean administration*, AG online column, viewed 16 July 2013, from http://www.agsa. co.za/portals/0/AG/Simplifying_audit_opinions_and_findings_to_enable_ government_leadership_to_exercise_oversight.pdf

Bhana, P., 2008, 'The contribution of proper record-keeping towards auditing and risk mitigation: Auditor-General of South Africa's perspective', paper presented at the 3rd Annual General Meeting of the South African Records Management Forum, Midrand, South Africa, 10–11 November, viewed 15 June 2013, from http://www.khunkhwane.co.za/uploads/The Contribution of Proper Records Keeping towards auditing and risk mitigation Auditor General Perspective.pdf

Chernobai, A.S., Rachev, S.T. & Fabozzi, F.J., 2007, *Operational risk: A guide to Basel II capital requirements, models and analysis,* John Wiley & Sons, New Jersey.

Committee of Sponsoring Organizations of the Treadway Commission, 2004, *Enterprise risk management – Integrated framework,* viewed 16 May 2013, from http://www.coso.org/publications/erm/coso_erm_executivesummary.pdf

Ebaid, I.E., 2011, 'Internal audit function: An exploratory study from Egyptian listed firms', *International Journal of Law and Management* 53(2), 108–128. http://dx.doi.org/10.1108/17542431111119397

Egbuji, A., 1999, 'Risk management of organisational records', *Records Management Journal* 9(2), 93–116. http://dx.doi.org/10.1108/EUM0000000007245

Erima, J.A. & Wamukoya, J., 2012, 'Aligning records management and risk management with business processes: A case study of Moi University in Kenya', *Journal of the South African Society of Archivists* 45, 24–38.

Fraser, I. & Henry, W., 2007, 'Embedding risk management: Structures and approaches', *Managerial Auditing Journal* 22(4), 392–409. http://dx.doi.org/10.1108/02686900710741955

Graham, J. & Kaye, D., 2006, *A risk management approach to business continuity: Aligning business continuity with corporate governance,* Rothstein Associates, Brookfield.

Harris, V., 2002, 'The archival sliver: Power, memory, and archives in South Africa', *Archival Science* 2, 63–82, viewed 10 January 2014, from http://www.nyu.edu/classes/bkg/methods/harris.pdf

Harris, V., 2007, '"They should have destroyed more": The destruction of public records by the South African State in the final years of apartheid, 1990-1994', in V. Harris (ed.), *Archives and justice: A South African perspective,* pp. 305–336, The Society of American Archivists, Chicago.

Harris, V. & Merrett, C., 2007, 'Toward a culture of transparency: Public rights of access to official records in South Africa', in V. Harris (ed.), *Archives and justice: A South African perspective,* pp. 269–288, The Society of American Archivists, Chicago.

Henttonen, P. & Kettunen, K., 2011, 'Functional classification of records and organisational structure', *Records Management Journal* 21(2), 86–103. http://dx.doi.org/10.1108/09565691111152035

Hiles, A., 2002, *Enterprise risk assessment and business impact analysis: Best practices,* The Rothstein, Brookfield.

Institute of Directors in Southern Africa, 2009, *King report on corporate governance for South Africa,* Sandton, South Africa.

Institute of Internal Auditors, 2009, 'A new level of audit committee involvement', *Tone at the Top* 44, 1–3.

Isa, A.M., 2009, 'Records management and the accountability of governance', PhD thesis, Humanities Advanced Technology and Information Institute, University of Glasgow, Glasgow, Scotland, viewed 15 May 2013, from http://www.theses.gla.ac.uk/1421/

Jimerson, R.C., 2003, 'Archives and memory', *Archives and Manuscript* 19(3), 89–95.

KPMG, 2011, *Records risk management diagnose,* viewed 10 December 2013, from http://www.kpmg.com/US/en/IssuesAndInsights/ArticlesPublications/Documents/records-risk-management-diagnostic.pdf

Lemieux, V.L., 2001, 'Competitive viability, accountability and record keeping: A theoretical and empirical exploration using a case study of Jamaican Commercial Bank failures', PhD thesis, Dept. of Information Studies, University of London, London, viewed 10 December 2013, from http://discovery.ucl.ac.uk/1317703/1/272289.pdf

Lemieux, V.L., 2004, 'Two approaches to managing risks', *Information Management Journal,* Sep/Oct, 56–62, viewed 15 January 2014, from http://www.arma.org/bookstore/files/Lemieux.pdf

Lemieux, V.L., 2010, 'The records-risk nexus: Exploring the relationship between records and risk', *Records Management Journal* 20(2), 199–216. http://dx.doi.org/10.1108/09565981080001362

Lomas, E., 2010, 'Information governance: information security and access within a UK context', *Records Management Journal* 20(2), 182–198. http://dx.doi.org/10.1108/09565691011064322

McKemmish, S. & Acland, G., 1999, 'Archivists at risk: Accountability and the role of the professional society', paper read at the Annual Conference of the Australian Society of Archivists, Brisbane, Australia, 29–31 July.

Ngoepe, M., 2011. *Records management practices in the South African public sector: Challenges, trends and issues,* Lambert Academic Publishing, Saarbrücken.

Ngoepe, M., 2012. 'Fostering a framework to embed the records management function into the auditing process', PhD thesis, Dept. of Information Science, University of South Africa.

Ngoepe, M. & Ngulube, P., 2013a, 'An exploration of the role of records management in corporate governance in South Africa', *SA Journal of Information Management* 15(2), Art. #575, 8 pages. http://dx.doi.org/10.4102/sajim.v15i2.575

Ngoepe, M. & Ngulube, P., 2013b, 'Contribution of record-keeping to audit opinions: An informetrics analysis of the general reports on audit outcomes of the Auditor-General of South Africa', *ESARBICA Journal* 32, 46–54.

Palmer, M., 2000, 'Records management and accountability versus corruption, fraud and maladministration', *Records Management Journal* 10(2), 61–72. http://dx.doi.org/10.1108/EUM0000000007256

Reed, B., 1997, 'Electronic records management in Australia', *Records Management Journal* 7(3), 191–204. http://dx.doi.org/10.1108/eb027111

Sampson, K.L., 1992, *Value-added records management: protecting corporate assets and reducing business risks,* 1st edn., Quorum Books, New York.

Sampson, K.L., 2002. *Value added records management: protecting corporate assets, reducing business risks,* 2nd edn., Quorum Books, New York.

Sarens, G. & De Beelde, I., 2006, 'Internal auditors' perception about their role in risk management: A comparison between US and Belgian companies', *Managerial Auditing Journal* 21(1), 63–80. http://dx.doi.org/10.1108/02686900610634766

South Africa Government Online n.d., *Together we move South Africa forward,* viewed n.d., from http://www.gov.za

Willis, A., 2005, 'Corporate governance and management of information and records', *Records Management Journal* 15(2), 86–97. http://dx.doi.org/10.1108/09565690510614238

Permissions

List of Contributors

Everd J. Jacobs and Gert Roodt
Department of Industrial Psychology and People Management, University of Johannesburg, South Africa

Judith Mavodza
Zayed University Library, Zayed University, Abu Dhabi

Patrick Ngulube
Department of Interdisciplinary Research, College of Graduate Studies, University of South Africa, South Africa

Cornelius (Neels) Kruger and Roy D. Johnson
Department of Informatics, University of Pretoria, South Africa

Cleophas Ambira
Kenya Commercial Bank Ltd, Kenya
School of Information Sciences, Moi University, Kenya

Henry Kemoni
School of Information Sciences, Moi University, Kenya

Rene Pellissier
School of Business Leadership, University of South Africa, Pretoria, South Africa

Tshilidzi E. Nenzhelele
Department of Business Management, University of South Africa, Pretoria, South Africa

Rene Pellissier and Tshilidzi E. Nenzhelele
Department of Business Management, University of South Africa, South Africa

Stephen M. Mutula
Information Studies Programme, University of KwaZulu-Natal, South Africa

Christoffel J. Hendriks
Department of Public Administration and Management, University of the Free State, South Africa

Rene Pellissier
School of Business Leadership, University of South Africa, Pretoria, South Africa

Tshilidzi E. Nenzhelele
Department of Business Management, University of South Africa, Pretoria, South Africa

Jacky Bessick
Information Systems Department, University of the Western Cape, South Africa

Visvanathan Naicker
Information Systems Department, University of the Western Cape, South Africa
Graduate School of Business Leadership, University of South Africa, South Africa

Francois Lottering and Archie L. Dick
Department of Information Science, University of Pretoria, South Africa

Liezel Cilliers
Information Systems Department, University of Fort Hare, South Africa

Andy Bytheway and Isabella M. Venter
Department of Computer Science, University of the Western Cape, South Africa

Khutso Maahlo and Molefe Ratsoana
Centre for Information and Knowledge Management, University of Johannesburg, South Africa

Martie A. Mearns
Department of Information and Knowledge Management, University of Johannesburg, South Africa

Janet Adekannbi and Wole M. Olatokun
Africa Regional Centre for Information Science, University of Ibadan Nigeria

Isola Ajiferuke
Faculty of Information and Media Studies, University of Western Ontario, Canada

Eugene B. Visser and Melius Weideman
Faculty of Informatics and Design, Cape Peninsula University of Technology, South Africa

René Pellissier
Department of Business Management, University of South Africa, South Africa

Trywell Kalusopa
Department of Library and Information Studies, University of Botswana, Botswana

Patrick Ngulube
Department of Interdisciplinary Research of the College of Graduate Studies, University of South Africa, South Africa

Babasile D. Osunyomi and Sara (Saartjie) S. Grobbelaar
Department of Engineering and Technology Management, Graduate School of Technology Management, University of Pretoria, South Africa

Dina Adamovic, Andrea Potgieter and Martie Mearns
Department of Information and Knowledge Management, University of Johannesburg, South Africa

Mzwandile M. Shongwe
Department of Information Studies, University of Zululand, South Africa

Wouter T. Kritzinge and Melius Weideman
Website Attributes Research Centre (WARC), Cape Peninsula University of Technology, South Africa

Taurayi Mudzana and Manoj Maharaj
School of Management, IT and Governance, University of KwaZulu-Natal, South Africa

Surika Civilcharran and Manoj S. Maharaj
School of Management, IT and Governance, University of KwaZulu-Natal, South Africa

Mitchell Hughes
School of Economic and Business Sciences, University of the Witwatersrand, South Africa

Mpho Ngoepe
Department of Information Science, University of South Africa, South Africa

Index